THE BROADVIEW READER IN BOOK HISTORY

THE BROADVIEW READER IN BOOK HISTORY

EDITED BY

MICHELLE LEVY & TOM MOLE

broadview press

Library and Archives Canada Cataloguing in Publication

The Broadview reader in book history / edited by Michelle Levy & Tom Mole.

Includes bibliographical references and index.
ISBN 978-1-55481-088-8 (pbk.)

1. Books—History. I. Mole, Tom, 1976-, editor
II. Levy, Michelle Nancy, 1968-, editor

Z4.B76 2014 002.09 C2014-905645-1

Broadview Press is an independent, international publishing house, incorporated in 1985.

We welcome comments and suggestions regarding any aspect of our publications—please feel free to contact us at the addresses below or at broadview@broadviewpress.com.

North America
PO Box 1243, Peterborough
Ontario K9J 7H5, Canada

555 Riverwalk Parkway
Tonawanda, NY 14150, USA
Tel: (705) 743-8990
Fax: (705) 743-8353
email: customerservice@broadviewpress.com

UK, Europe, Central Asia, Middle East, Africa, India, and Southeast Asia
Eurospan Group
3 Henrietta St., London
WC2E 8LU, United Kingdom
Tel: 44 (0) 1767 604972
Fax: 44 (0) 1767 601640
email: eurospan@turpin-distribution.com

Australia and New Zealand
NewSouth Books
c/o TL Distribution
15-23 Helles Ave., Moorebank
NSW 2170, Australia
Tel: (02) 8778 9999
Fax: (02) 8778 9944
email: orders@tldistribution.com.au

www.broadviewpress.com

Broadview Press acknowledges the financial support of the Government of Canada through the Canada Book Fund for our publishing activities.

Copy-edited by Martin R. Boyne
Cover and interior design by Michel Vrana
Typesetting by Jennifer Blais
Typeset in Adobe Caslon Pro and ITC Legacy Sans

PRINTED IN CANADA

Contents

Acknowledgments vii
Introduction ix
The History of the Book: A Brief Chronology xxi
A Note on the Text xxvii

Chapter 1: Materiality 1

1. W.W. Greg, "What Is Bibliography?" (1914) 3
2. Lucien Febvre and Henri-Jean Martin, "The Book: Its Visual Appearance" (1976) 15
3. Michael Twyman, "What Is Printing?" (1998) 37
4. D.F. McKenzie, "The Dialectics of Bibliography Now" (1986) 45
5. Paul C. Gutjahr and Megan L. Benton, "Reading the Invisible" (2001) 63
6. Roger Chartier, "The Press and Fonts: Don Quixote in the Print Shop" (2007) 73
7. Robert Darnton, "Bibliography and Iconography" (2010) 93

Chapter 2: Textuality 111

8. Jerome J. McGann, "Shall These Bones Live?" (1985) 113
9. W.W. Greg, "The Rationale of Copy-Text" (1950–51) 125
10. G. Thomas Tanselle, "The Editorial Problem of Final Authorial Intention" (1976) 139
11. S.M. Parrish, "The Whig Interpretation of Literature" (1988) 157
12. Jack Stillinger, "A Practical Theory of Versions" (1994) 165
13. Brenda R. Silver, "Textual Criticism as Feminist Practice: Or, Who's Afraid of Virginia Woolf Part II" (1991) 181
14. Beth A. McCoy, "Race and the (Para)Textual Condition" (2006) 199

Chapter 3: Printing and Reading 213

15. Elizabeth L. Eisenstein, "The Unacknowledged Revolution" (1979) 215
16. Robert Darnton, "What Is the History of Books?" (1990) 231
17. Roger Chartier, "Communities of Readers" (1994) 251
18. Adrian Johns, "Introduction: The Book of Nature and the Nature of the Book" (1998) 267
19. James Raven, "Markets and Martyrs: Early Modern Commerce" (2007) 289
20. Jonathan Rose, "The Welsh Miners' Libraries" (2001) 313

Chapter 4: Intermediality 333

21. Pierre Bourdieu, "The Field of Cultural Production, or: The Economic World Reversed" (1993) 335
22. David Scott Kastan, "From Playhouse to Printing House; or, Making a Good Impression" (2001) 353
23. Margaret J.M. Ezell, "The Social Author: Manuscript Culture, Writers, and Readers" (1999) 375
24. Paula McDowell, "Towards a Genealogy of 'Print Culture' and 'Oral Tradition'" (2010) 395
25. Matt Cohen, "Native Audiences" (2010) 417
26. Meredith McGill, "Circulating Media: Charles Dickens, Reprinting, and Dislocation of American Culture" (2003) 439

Chapter 5: Remediating 457

27. Jerome J. McGann, "The Rationale of Hypertext" (2001) 459
28. Ray Siemens, Meagan Timney, Cara Leitch, Corina Koolen, and Alex Garnett, "Toward Modeling the Social Edition: An Approach to Understanding the Electronic Scholarly Edition in the Context of New and Emerging Social Media" (2012) 475
29. N. Katherine Hayles, "How We Read: Close, Hyper, Machine" (2010) 491
30. Andrew Piper, "Turning the Page (Roaming, Zooming, Streaming)" (2012) 511
31. Franco Moretti, "Style, Inc. Reflections on Seven Thousand Titles (British Novels, 1740–1850)" (2013) 525
32. Ted Striphas, "E-Books and the Digital Future" (2009) 541
33. Anthony Grafton, "Codex in Crisis: The Book Dematerializes" (2009) 555

Glossary 575
Further Reading 597
Permissions Acknowledgments 603
Index 607

Acknowledgments

As we hope the collection of essays in this book will suggest, the making of any book is a complex social endeavor, requiring a great deal of assistance and support at every stage of the process. This book is no different.

We have been fortunate to have worked with several gifted research assistants over the years that this project has been in development. Heath Wood, when he was an MA student at Simon Fraser University, provided invaluable assistance and feedback with editing and annotation in the early days of the project; Whitney Mallett, Hilary Sloan, and Danielle Barkley, students at McGill University, provided assistance with transcriptions, copy editing, and the glossary.

The students we have taught—as part of the SFU English Department's MA in Print Culture and the McGill English Department's course on Materiality and Sociology of Texts—have shaped this volume. *The Broadview Reader in Book History* is designed for students, and we relied on their input to ensure that it would satisfy (and even exceed) the expectations and needs of its readers.

We also wish to acknowledge the generous support of our home institutions and Canadian provincial and federal funding agencies: SFU awarded Michelle Levy an internal SSHRC grant in 2011; Tom Mole's work was supported by a grant from FQRSC to the Interacting with Print research group and by a SSHRC insight grant.

From Broadview Press, we wish to thank Leonard Conolly, Series Editor, and Marjorie Mather, Publisher and English Editor, both of whom were a delight to work with and provided substantive, constructive input from the outset; and we are indebted to Martin Boyne for the exceptional care and thoughtfulness he provided in the copy-editing phase.

We are also thankful to have had each other as co-editors. Working on any project that unfolds over a period of years on one's own can be a lonely and isolating task, and we are fortunate that we decided to work as a team, exchanging ideas, sharing work, and jointly developing our conceptualization of the field. Though divided by a continent and later by a continent and an ocean, we have taken advantage of collaborative real-time editing interfaces such as Google Docs, and of opportunities to meet and work together in person, in Vancouver, Montreal, and elsewhere. The result, from our perspective, has been a strong conviction not merely that working collaboratively can be far more enjoyable than solitary labor, but that the final product is also improved.

One of the most exciting aspects of this project was to compile a large selection of essays in the field, many of them relatively recent, to represent a range of voices that showcase its depth and variety, and to discover the compelling ways in which they speak to each other. This Reader would not have been possible without the authors whose work you see in the following pages agreeing to be included; and we are grateful to them and their publishers for their permission to appear in this volume.

The field of book history is at once dynamic and expanding, particularly given new computational and digital technologies. As a result, the task of selection was extremely difficult, and for every essay included in the volume there were dozens we wish we could have included. Our sincerest hope is that the essays in this volume will incite students to want to learn more about the book and its history at the very moment that this history is being rewritten. The study of the book—as an historical and material artifact, as a carrier of meaning between individuals and across time, as a product of sociable activity, and as a form in which intellectual, creative, political, and economic forces converge—has been a source of lasting fascination to us, and we have attempted to convey that enthusiasm for the field throughout the following pages.

Introduction

Over the last thirty years, book history has emerged as one of the fastest-growing and most exciting new interdisciplinary fields in the humanities. We use the term book history broadly, to encompass the existing scholarly endeavors of **analytical bibliography**,[1] publishing history, textual editing, and material text studies that have in recent years been united and revitalized, such that the field is now beginning to achieve a greater degree of theoretical sophistication and reflect on its own practice. As Leah Price wrote in a recent special issue of *Publications of the Modern Language Association of America* (*PMLA*) devoted to "The History of the Book and the Idea of Literature," book history is now "a player in theoretical debates rather than [...] a bolt-hole from which to wait them out."[2]

This Reader is designed to offer a map to help students navigate this new region of knowledge by introducing them to some of its landmarks and by providing some signposts pointing to areas that might be explored more fully in the future. The Reader divides the 33 essays it collects into five conceptual categories: Materiality (Chapter 1), Textuality (Chapter 2), Printing and Reading (Chapter 3), Intermediality (Chapter 4), and Remediating (Chapter 5). In this way, we aim to avoid some of the misconceptions that would arise with a more explicitly chronological organization. A chronological arrangement might imply a narrative of media change in which newer media seem to displace older media. This understanding of technological change has now been rejected by most scholars. The structure we have adopted instead provides a sense of traditional disciplinary practices (insofar as the five chapters focus on different ways in which bibliographers, textual scholars, book and media historians, and digital humanists have approached the study of the book). But we hope as well that the chapters transcend these boundaries and illustrate what Robert Darnton, writing nearly 25 years ago, described as the "interdisciplinarity run riot" that characterized the emergent field of book history.[3]

In addition to this introductory overview, each essay is prefaced with a substantial headnote that situates the essay in the context of its original publication, and the author in terms of his or her contributions to the field. These headnotes also attempt to offer a brief introduction to the essay and to relate the essays to others, in order to help readers trace conversations and developments within the larger field. Each essay has been annotated by the editors (editorial annotations appear as footnotes) to clarify historical and scholarly references. Finally, a detailed glossary containing all terms specific to the field is included at the end of the volume. We believe this contextualization and annotation will make the study of the theory and methods of book history accessible to a wide range of students at both the graduate and the undergraduate levels.

---

1 Terms in bold can be found in the Glossary.

2 Leah Price, "Introduction: Reading Matter," *PMLA* 121.1 (2006): 9–16, 16.

3 Robert Darnton, "What Is the History of Books?," *The Kiss of Lamourette* (New York: Norton, 1990), 111.

Much important research has been done on the history of the book before the era of print, and the field of book history is now global, with important work being done on the cultures of the book in almost every continent. This depth and breadth of work, however, cannot be covered in a single volume. Accordingly, we have limited our focus both temporally (from the Early Modern period to the present) and geographically (to Western Europe, with some attention to North America) to allow more depth of coverage. We have also attempted to provide a broad range of critical, methodological, and theoretical approaches to the field, as well as essays attentive to the issues of class, gender, and race, which have been important critical categories for literary and historical study for some time. Page limitations constrained even more diversity, but we believe that the essays included in this Reader provide a substantial foundation for studies in book history, and that these readings can easily be supplemented by instructors with additional materials relevant to courses focused on other historical periods and geographical regions, or on other more specific topics.

Chapter 1: Materiality

We often think of literary texts as made out of language, or even out of ideas. But we can only encounter those texts through material objects. These objects vary according to time and place, and the kind of text concerned. They may be **sheets** of **papyrus** or **rolls** of **parchment**, paper **codices** or computer screens, but, in every case, to encounter a text means to encounter a material object. Some people treat these material objects as simply the "vehicle" that conveys the text to the reader, and so they think that nothing important is lost if a text is reproduced in a different format—for example in an **anthology** or on a website. So long as the words are the same, they say, that is what matters. But book historians tend to think of the material object of the book as an essential part of the text's existence. For book historians, texts are not simply linguistic constructs; they are composites of linguistic and material elements. Considered like this, the material book is an integral part of the text, and something important *is* lost when the linguistic component of a text is detached from its material counterpart.

Unlike the linguistic codes of a text, its material dimension is not usually entirely under the author's control. In some cases, authors exercise quite a lot of control over the physical production of their work: Samuel Richardson was a **printer** as well as an author, William Blake printed his own works by hand, and the Canadian writer Robert Bringhurst is a **typographer** as well as a poet. In many cases, however, the physical aspects of the material text will be determined by forces only minimally within the author's control, and many other people will be involved in the production of the book: printers, typesetters, designers, **publishers**, and so on. For this reason, the meanings encoded in the physical book may work alongside the meanings encoded in the text's language, or they may work against each other. The key point is that the text's language and the book's physical properties are both involved in constructing meaning. Jerome McGann, a critic who has pioneered this approach to texts, puts it like this: "Every literary work that descends to us operates through the deployment of a double helix of perceptual codes: the linguistic codes, on the one hand, and the bibliographical codes on the other."[4]

The essays in Chapter 1 all focus attention on the material form of the book. They describe how books are produced and how their appearance has changed historically. We're so used to handling books and decoding the meanings of their physical forms that we tend to overlook the fact that something like a **title page** has its own history, as Lucien Febvre and Henri-Jean Martin explain (see pp. 15–36). The conventions that now govern the design of books did not appear ready-made with the invention of printing and the codex. Instead, they were established over time. In their essay, Febvre and Martin explain in historical detail how the book came to assume its modern form. Michael Twyman (pp. 37–44) explains how books were printed on the **handpress**, and W.W. Greg and D.F. McKenzie (pp. 3–14, 45–62) introduce **bibliography**, which (for our purposes here) simply means the study of the physical form of books. McKenzie uses examples from John Locke and James Joyce to show how the physical form of the printed book conveys information that we absorb alongside the meanings of the words the book contains. We are all, in fact, quite adept at deciphering the bibliographical codes of contemporary publishing. We take it for granted that a cheap thriller purchased from an airport bookstore will look and feel different from a textbook for use in classrooms, and that both will look and feel different from a volume of academic essays intended for purchase by university libraries. Book history can make us more self-conscious about how we decode the messages that books as physical objects are sending, and it can help us to begin to learn how they sent those messages in the past, in codes with which we're no longer familiar.

Typography—the shapes of the letters on the page—is an important part of the "bibliographical code," as Paul C. Gutjahr and Megan L. Benton argue (pp. 63–72). This is an interesting and challenging idea, because typography is often designed to be invisible—not to draw attention to itself, but to encourage the reader to look beyond the words on the page to the ideas they convey. Once we've learned to pay attention to the bibliographical codes, and to decipher what they're saying, we have an additional tool for reading at our disposal. Roger Chartier (pp. 73–92) and Robert Darnton (pp. 93–110) provide two case studies that illustrate some of the benefits of this kind of approach. Chartier explores how the production and **circulation** of books becomes part of the story in Cervantes' *Don Quixote*. Darnton investigates the importance of printed books, including both text and images, in the rapidly shifting political landscape of Revolutionary France.

Chapter 2: Textuality

If the typesetters, printers, designers, publishers, and **booksellers** involved in turning an author's **manuscript** into a printed book that circulates are one concern of book history, editors are another. **Editing**, roughly speaking, divides into pre- and post-publication editing.

4 Jerome J. McGann, "The Socialization of Texts," *The Textual Condition* (Princeton, NJ: Princeton UP, 1991), 77.

Pre-publication editing is done by publishers' editors, and may involve substantive engagement with the author's words and ideas (sometimes called "developmental editing"), or making specific changes to the text that make it conform to rules of grammar, conventions of usage, and the press's "house style" (this is usually called "copy editing"). Post-publication editing, on the other hand, is work done by scholarly editors producing new **editions** of **canonical** texts. These editions may be aimed at other scholars (as in the "**variorum**" editions, usually in many expensive volumes, that track the variant readings in all significant, extant versions of an author's works); or at students (as in anthologies used in university courses); or at general readers (as in affordable paperback editions of novels and poetry). The essays in Chapter 2 focus on post-publication editing, especially the kind undertaken for major scholarly editions.

Very few readers of this volume will become scholarly editors, so these essays are not designed to teach the craft of editing. But because all readers use the books that editors produce, it is worthwhile to understand how editors make changes to literary texts and why. Some of the decisions editors make are controversial, and even among themselves editors don't agree on when it is permissible to emend a text. The essays in Chapter 2 introduce these debates, which, as Jerome McGann argues (pp. 113–24), are not secondary to other theoretical debates in the humanities, but fundamentally engaged with them. Works often exist in several versions that differ from each other, sometimes in significant ways. An author's manuscript, when available, may differ from the first edition of the work, which may differ from later editions. For example, the versions of Shakespeare's plays printed in the First **Folio** differ from the versions printed in **quarto** volumes. Editors therefore say that there are several "texts" of the "work." Editors traditionally choose one of these as a "**copy-text**" to be the basis for a new edition; W.W. Greg, in his essay "The Rationale of Copy-Text" (pp. 125–38), was the first to formulate a set of guidelines for which text to choose as a copy-text and when to alter it. Editors traditionally choose an early text of the work as their copy-text, but emend it to reflect the author's later revisions. To do this, they have to distinguish between those variants in later texts that appear because the author changed something and those that appear because a typesetter made a mistake, or the publisher censored the text, or for some other reason that the author did not know about or would not have approved of. When dealing with a work that the author revised, editors look for the author's "final intentions," on the assumption that a mature author's revisions will usually be improvements. But working out what the author's final intentions are, exactly, can be complicated. Thomas Tanselle (pp. 139–56), develops a rigorous approach to final authorial intention by distinguishing three levels of intention and two kinds of revisions.

However, both the idea that an early text of the work makes the best copy-text and the idea that an editor should respect the author's final intentions have been controversial. Some people have argued that, where pre-publication manuscripts of the work are available, they should *not* be used as copy-texts, on the basis that the author expected and valued the interventions of publishers' editors. Others have argued that authors sometimes make their works worse by revising them, or revise them reluctantly, for example in response to the poor reception of earlier versions. Final intentions, then, are not always best intentions. Stephen Parrish (pp. 157–64), makes this argument about William Wordsworth's long autobiographical poem *The Prelude*. Wordsworth revised the poem over a period of almost 50 years, and Parrish argues that earlier versions have their own interest and integrity, and that Wordsworth's revisions were not always improvements. Still others have argued that works are best understood in the context of their first publication, and so they assert that the earliest published text of the work is the best one to re-print, even if it did not represent the author's final intentions. A possible solution to this problem, proposed by Jack Stillinger (pp. 165–80), is to treat the different texts as "versions" of the work, and to argue that there is no "best" text of a work, but that the work is the sum of all its versions. This "textual pluralism" seems to offer a way out of debates about what makes the "best" edition, but some editors argue that it abdicates the editor's responsibility to make choices about the work, and simply passes that responsibility on to the reader.

These debates are not simply technical disagreements of interest only to editors, because they influence the texts we get to read and because they reflect underlying assumptions about how authors write and what literary works are. Those who see writing as a kind of inspiration may prefer earlier texts of a work on the grounds that they are closer to the inspired origin. Those who see writing as a kind of craftsmanship, on the other hand, may prefer later texts of the work on the grounds that they are more polished. Those who see literary works as primarily the productions of an author may prefer editions that respect the author's intentions. Those who see literary works as primarily the products of their socio-political contexts, on the other hand, may prefer editions that re-print the texts that circulated in those contexts. And, finally, editorial decisions do not only reflect assumptions about literature; they can also be sites where assumptions about cultural categories such as race and gender are re-iterated or resisted. Essays in this chapter by Beth A. McCoy (pp. 199–211) and Brenda R. Silver (pp. 181–98) examine cases in which an editor's decisions about how to handle paratexts and authorial revisions can have racial or feminist implications.

Chapter 3: Printing and Reading

The first two chapters of this Reader consider the book as a material object and as a container for different kinds of textual and paratextual material. Chapter 3 is concerned with the activities of "printing and reading," and, not surprisingly, all of the essays are focused on the print era, that is, the period following the invention of the printing press in the mid-fifteenth century. These essays are book historical in a traditional (but by no means old-fashioned) sense. They seek to bring the book, as it were, into history, to investigate how books move through time and space. Printing and reading are separate phenomena, both of which have been subject to scrutiny by book historians, but they are also related processes, and many of these essays ask broad questions about the effect of printing on reading and vice versa. In asking, as Robert Darnton does in his essay of the same title, "What Is the History of Books?" (pp. 231–50), book historians inquire into human history in the most capacious sense, seeking to ascertain how individuals and groups interacted with books, and how the dissemination of books has shaped our knowledge, our social, religious, economic, and political institutions, and our local and national cultures.

The chapter opens (pp. 215–30) with an excerpt from Elizabeth Eisenstein's groundbreaking study, *The Printing Press as an Agent of Change* (1979). As her title implies, Eisenstein argues that the effect of the introduction of the printing press was immediate and widespread. The shift from a culture in which all texts had to be produced by hand to one in which multiple copies could be reproduced quickly and efficiently by machine meant that knowledge could be more easily disseminated, accumulated, and preserved. According to Eisenstein, printing "revolutionized all forms of learning" (p. 215) and, with them, human society as we know it. Indeed, her book as a whole makes the bold claim that print was a revolutionary "agent of change": specifically, that the press's functions of dissemination, standardization, and preservation enabled scientific experimentation, artistic experimentation, and religious debate, thereby ushering in the Scientific Revolution, the Renaissance, and the Protestant Reformation. More recent scholarship, particularly by Adrian Johns, has contested these claims. In his essay (pp. 267–88), Johns examines the early use of print by astronomers to dispute the assertion that print itself brought about greatly improved standardization, dissemination, and fixity. For Johns, the introduction of print did not in itself revolutionize scientific discourse. Rather, Johns claims that human actors had to agree on the use and meaning of print, which was not inherent to the technology itself. In his attempt "to portray print culture in the making" (p. 269), Johns offers a very different approach to media change than that offered by Eisenstein; both models, however, have great utility as we puzzle through our own moment of rapid media change (where this Reader concludes, in Chapter 5).

One distinguishing aspect of Eisenstein's work has been her demand that the history of the book be linked to the history of ideas. Roger Chartier's essay (pp. 251–66) likewise asks, "how did increased circulation of printed matter transform forms of sociability, permit new modes of thought, and change people's relationship with power?" (p. 253). Chartier introduces some of the difficulties and complexities of constructing such a history of reading (often a silent and solitary act that leaves no apparent trace); in his essay on the printing of *Don Quixote*, included in the first chapter of this Reader (pp. 73–92), Chartier argues that individuals do not read works but rather texts embodied in some specific material form that contributes to their meaning; furthermore, Chartier insists that "reading is always a practice embodied in gestures, spaces, and habits."[5] In other words, a history of reading must be attentive to the specifics of materiality and practice that are particular to different communities at different times. An exceptional realization of this method is found in Jonathan Rose's essay (pp. 313–31) on reading habits within Welsh mining communities in the early twentieth century. By investigating the **archives** of "The Welsh Miners' Libraries," Rose is able to re-construct a vivid account of these "underground universities," compellingly drawing together the history of the book with the social and intellectual history of the working classes.

Robert Darnton's influential model of the "communications circuit," first introduced in 1982, represents another watershed in the evolution of book history. His model emphasizes the connections between groups of actors (authors, publishers, printers, distributors, readers) engaged in the production and dissemination of printed books. Darnton has recently re-stated his key questions as follows:

5 Roger Chartier, "Laborers and Voyagers: From the Text to the Reader," *diacritics* 22.2 (1992): 49–61, 51.

> How do books come into being?
> How do they reach readers?
> What do readers make of them?[6]

His aim within the field of book history was for the concept of the communications circuit to avoid "fragmentation and specialization"[7] by imagining the complete cycle of the book. One of the most profound contributions of Darnton's model to literary scholarship has been to re-embed authors within the larger fields of activity in which books were made and sold, distributed, and read. The essay by James Raven (pp. 289–312) further enhances and complicates this model, by examining how political and legal regimes, as well as commercial practices, have enabled and constrained what can be published and hence read and debated. Raven examines the Early Modern book trades: the marketing innovations of booksellers, the demographic and economic shifts that expanded the demand for books, and the state controls and punishments used to regulate "undesirable" books. He provides a fascinating account of the "print martyrs" of the Early Modern period, those who were literally martyred at the stake for their involvement in the printing of works deemed dangerous by the government of the day. These individuals initiated a long march toward the freedom of the press, and the religious and political freedoms that follow.

Chapter 4: Intermediality

Chapter 4 introduces the concept of intermediality, one that is based on the understanding that no single medium (such as print) exists independently of a range of other media. Scholars of intermediality are interested in the interconnected and shifting relations between media. Even though print may have been a dominant medium during the period discussed in most of the essays in this Reader, as the essays in this chapter demonstrate, print interacted with other media throughout the post-**Gutenberg** period. This relatively new line of inquiry has been the product of an important shift in scholarly understandings of media change. According to Paul Duguid, the narrative of media change, up until recently, was that of the "rhetoric of supercession," whereby it was assumed that "each new technological type vanquishes or subsumes its predecessors."[8] However, there has been sufficient evidence gathered by Early Modern scholars "to argue that 'this'—the printing press—did not kill 'that'—the manuscript";[9] and we also see every day that print survives in an increasingly digital age. Older and newer media always co-exist and mutually influence one another, and attention to these interactions can provide important historical insights. Margaret Ezell's examination (pp. 375–94) of the survival, indeed flourishing,

6 Robert Darnton, "What Is the History of Books? Revisited," *Modern Intellectual History* 4.3 (2007): 495–508, 495.

7 Ibid.

8 Paul Duguid, "Material Matters: The Past and Futurology of the Book," *The Future of the Book*, ed. Geoffrey Nunberg (Berkeley and Los Angeles: U of California P, 1996), 63–102, 65.

9 Roger Chartier, "The Order of Books Revisited," *Modern Intellectual History* 4.3 (2007): 509–19, 511.

of manuscript culture in the seventeenth century bears importantly on women's literary history, insofar as she shows that manuscript publication (the dissemination of works in handwritten form) could be at once a preferable mode to print and a respectable and sociable one.

The first essay in this chapter (pp. 335–52), by Pierre Bourdieu, describes his theory of "the field of cultural production," encompassing all forms of cultural production from well-known literary genres such as poetry and the novel to vaudeville. Bourdieu's understanding of the French literary field in the second half of the nineteenth century is mapped for us spatially in a diagram, as he attempts to chart the differing amounts of audience appreciation (or commercial success) and "consecration" (or cultural respect) afforded to different types of literary productions across a range of media. Bourdieu claims that no one form of cultural production can be understood apart from others, and that cultural production itself is constrained by economic and political power. David Scott Kastan's essay (pp. 353–74) undertakes a similar dissection of Shakespeare's unrivaled cultural status. While today Shakespeare appears as an author of supreme achievement, Kastan shows how, in his own lifetime, he was a commercial playwright whose interest was in the production of his plays on stage; he took no interest whatsoever in the printing of his plays, and, indeed, those who printed his works rarely invoked his authorship of them. The notion of an entity "Shakespeare" that we ascribe to the printed plays (what Michel Foucault termed "the author function"[10]) is very much a construction that evolved after Shakespeare's death in 1616. Similarly, Paula McDowell examines (pp. 395–416) how the concept of **oral culture** that developed in the eighteenth century was itself a product of print culture. For McDowell, the rising dominance of a commercialized print marketplace prompts a formulation of "oral culture" (in print) that is valorized as being precisely what current print literature is not (uncommercial, natural, sociable). That is, though it is common to think of oral culture as preceding (and being superseded by) print culture, in fact, we only come to understand orality retrospectively. But the problem suggested is a somewhat intractable one: as McDowell shows, to formulate a conception of a supposedly "earlier" form of media (such as orality), later forms (such as print) are inevitably used.

Matt Cohen's essay (pp. 417–38) further disrupts this account by refusing to understand relations between early American settlers and Native Americans as a clash between written and oral cultures. For Cohen, both groups simultaneously used oral and written forms of communication (which are themselves interconnected). To comprehend their interactions, however, Cohen argues that we must expand our notions of what counts as communication beyond words and symbols: for Cohen, "traps, paths, wampum, monuments, medical rituals, and other messaging systems" [*The Networked Wilderness*, p. 4] uncover a deeper set of communication practices that allowed for meaningful exchanges between different cultural groups. Similarly, Meredith McGill's essay (pp. 439–55) is about transnational and transcultural exchange, based on her analysis of Charles Dickens's 1842 tour of the United States. She considers Dickens's fraught position in America, as an extremely popular author who was frustrated by his inability to profit from sales of his books abroad (given the absence of an international **copyright** agreement), and further examines the

10 Michel Foucault, "What Is an Author?," trans. Donald F. Bouchard and Sherry Simon, *Language, Counter-Memory, Practice* (Ithaca, NY: Cornell UP, 1977): 124–27.

complex intermingling of various media (the author's readings/performances of his works, the publicity tour, the periodical press, the **serialized** novel).

Chapter 5: Remediating

Chapter 5 offers a series of essays that continues to explore our multimedia world, but also incorporates the shift to digital media. A separate chapter is warranted, we believe, because even if the supersession narrative of media change no longer seems accurate, the introduction of digital media has nevertheless had profound consequences for print media. In 2011, for the first time, eBook sales were higher than sales of printed books,[11] and *Newsweek* magazine announced it would no longer be issuing a print edition after the end of the year; frequent announcements arrive about the closures of major publishing houses or bookstore chains.

Digital technologies have transformed both the way in which many people read and the ways in which critics and students study the texts of the past. This means that now is arguably an especially important time to study book history, because we are living through an historical shift in how books are published, circulated, read, and discussed. Sometimes it can be difficult to analyze a phenomenon so ubiquitous that it comes to seem natural or unquestionable. When the printed word was by far the dominant form for the circulation of information, it was difficult to understand it critically as a technology of communication. Now that the historical dominance of print may be coming to an end, it may be possible to develop new understandings of print's cultural significance as an historical phenomenon. At the same time, digital media are so new and shifting that attempts to understand their implications will necessarily be provisional and speculative.

Early accounts of the rise of screen reading, which suggested that it would lead to the demise of the printed book, are premature at best and are likely to continue to be untrue. Many of the new technologies do not simply replace print with digital media; they *remediate* print in a digital environment. Jay David Bolter and Richard Grusin use the term "remediation" to describe how one medium can incorporate aspects of another medium.[12] From the page images rendered in Google Books—some of them centuries old—to the news that Apple has patented the page-turning feature in e-reader applications, many recent developments should prompt us to think not only about whether digital media are displacing print from its position of cultural centrality but also about how print interacts with other media.[13] Such inter-medial concerns stretch back as far as **incunabula**—the earliest printed books, produced at the end of the fifteenth century—which often imitated the appearance of the manuscript volumes that circulated alongside them.

11 Claire Cain Miller and Julie Bosman, "E-Books Outsell Print Books at Amazon," *New York Times* 18 May 2011. Web. 25 May 2014.

12 Jay David Bolter and Richard Grusin, "Immediacy, Hypermediacy, and Remediation," *Remediation: Understanding New Media* (Cambridge, MA: MIT P, 1999), 44–50.

13 Nick Bilton, "Apple Now Owns the Page Turn," *Bits: The New York Times Technology Blog*, 16 November 2012. Accessed 3 May 2013. <http://bits.blogs.nytimes.com/2012/11/16/apple-now-owns-the-page-turn/>.

The development of new digital technologies is changing the work of critics and scholars in at least three ways: they must now practice screen reading, machine reading, and **hypertext** editing. Large-scale digitization projects, from Google Books to specialized commercial projects such as Early English Books Online (EEBO) and Eighteenth-Century Collections Online (ECCO), offer access to vast numbers of books, including many that were previously available in only a few of the world's largest libraries. These resources allow scholars—including those who live far from major libraries, or who lack funds to travel for their research, or who work outside the traditional academy—to read digital surrogates of printed books and manuscripts that would otherwise be inaccessible to them. Moreover, because these large databases provide page images of early editions of the books—and often include several editions of the same books—they may actually encourage scholars to pay attention to the physical form of the books they study. While some kinds of study will always require first-hand examination of books (looking at **watermarks** is difficult online, for example), reading on the screen may, in some cases, promote book history approaches.

All the same, as Katherine Hayles points out in her essay (pp. 491–510), early reports suggest that we do not read screens in the same way as we read pages, and that there are different cognitive outcomes of reading within different environments. In particular, it may be that deep, immersive reading (associated in the humanities with practices of close reading) is more difficult in hyperlinked online texts. Our own classroom experience with students seems anecdotally to support these findings, insofar as students reading a literary text often want to read a printed, rather than a digital, version of it. Nevertheless, Hayles suggests that it is not and indeed cannot be an either/or situation. Students and researchers will inevitably use multiple reading strategies: close reading (the intense attention to the details of a text advocated by New Critics[14]) for the examination of some kinds of material, and what Hayles calls hyperreading (involving scanning and skimming) for navigating other forms of digital material.

Large databases of books also promote different kinds of reading. Because the works in these databases are "machine readable," scholars can now undertake sophisticated searches and develop analytical "text-mining" applications. These kinds of approaches can reveal in seconds information that would have been prohibitively laborious to collect from the printed books themselves. As a result, Franco Moretti has argued that scholars should abandon close reading in favor of what he half-ironically calls "distant reading." Distant reading shifts attention from particular books to large corpora of books, in some cases thousands of volumes. His essay (pp. 525–40) provides one example of how we can use large collections of digital material to historicize the rise of the novel and to articulate its specific contours. Hayles also examines the different kinds of computer-assisted reading made possible by large collections of digital texts.

14 New Criticism was a formalist literary theory and practice that dominated American literary criticism in the middle of the twentieth century. The chief strategy of the new critics was close reading, carefully examining a literary text (especially poetry) as an aesthetic object that could be interpreted and understood apart from its social, economic, and historical context.

As more and more reading is done online, new possibilities emerge for creating online editions of texts that initially appeared in print or manuscript. (This is a separate area of concern from "born-digital" texts.) Online editions can do a number of things that printed and handwritten books cannot. They allow readers (or "users") to compare two versions of a work side-by-side by performing dynamic **collations** of them, revealing the variants between any two texts of a work. They also allow editions to include non-linguistic materials, such as extensive color illustration (which is often prohibitively expensive in printed books), audio recordings of songs, staged scenes from plays, and so on, not to mention a much larger collection of text simply because the commercial limitations on adding more pages, as well as the physical limits of the codex form, do not apply. Because the online edition or online archive does not attempt to use a book to study books—as Jerome McGann argues in his essay "The Rationale of Hypertext" (pp. 459–74)—it offers new possibilities for readers who concern themselves with the materiality of the book.

Digital editions also offer new ways to exploit the capacities not only of digital media but also of networked communication afforded by the Internet. In their essay "Toward Modeling the Social Edition," the authors, Ray Siemens, Meagan Timney, Cara Leitch, Corina Koolen, and Alex Garnett, posit a new kind of digital edition that would allow for user input, or crowd-sourcing, enabling the creation of a truly collaborative and process-based model of scholarship. It is an extremely enticing model of the book—one that is multi-authored and subject to constant re-thinking and enlargement. It seems certain that such a scholarly edition would be structurally and functionally unlike any other kind of book we have seen. *A Social Edition of the Devonshire MS (BL Add 17,492)*, developed by the authors of this essay in wikibooks, offers the first instantiation of such an edition.[15] But as this edition demonstrates, and as we hope this Reader will make clear, what comes next will necessarily be informed by the history of the book that has preceded it: by the practices of "social authorship" Ezell describes in Chapter 4, for example, and by the theory of textual instability put forward by Stillinger in Chapter 2. And this digital edition (as with others), will not be immediately accepted or valued; just as Adrian Johns has argued that "the very identity of print itself has had to be *made*" (p. 269; emphasis in original), so too will the identity of the digital media have to be made; and it is likely that this too will come about only "by virtue of hard work, exercised over generations and across nations" (p. 269).

Three other essays explore the current state of books and reading, using the history of the book to understand its future. Ted Striphas argues (pp. 541–54) that we are now in the "Late Age of Print," when a combination of technological shifts and changes in the book trade is altering the place of print in our culture. Striphas helps us to understand e-books not only as a technological innovation, but also as a change in the commercial circulation of texts. He points out that publishers have wanted for a long time to restrict the secondary circulation of books, from which they cannot profit. Because books are a commodity that is not destroyed in the process of "consumption," they can be borrowed, lent, shared, re-used, and re-sold. It is much harder to

15 See <http://en.wikibooks.org/wiki/The_Devonshire_Manuscript>.

do all these things with e-books and so, Striphas claims, they allow publishers to control our patterns of consumption more thoroughly and—for them—more profitably.

While Striphas concentrates on the social and commercial context of e-book publication, Andrew Piper (pp. 511–24) meditates on the differences between reading the codex and reading on the screen. Paying close attention to the page, and the imperfect ways in which it is imitated by e-readers, Piper turns our attention to the embodied nature of reading and to our long history of physical interaction with the codex. For Piper, our experience of holding and carrying books, of turning and marking their pages, is quickly being transformed by our turn to screen reading. This shift entails the loss of a range of practices associated with our use of the codex form, and, according to Piper, digital books have thus far failed to improve upon our original experience. One of their chief failures, Piper suggests, results from importing the concept of the physical page into a digital realm, where the very idea of the page should be contested and re-imagined.

Finally, Anthony Grafton (pp. 555–73) examines the Google Books project in the context of the longstanding dream of a universal **library** of all human knowledge. Grafton points to the great advantages of Google Books, but he also points out that it is never likely to live up to the millennial pronouncements of its most intoxicated enthusiasts. For the foreseeable future, at least, anyone seriously interested in the literature and culture of the past will need to cultivate two sets of approaches and follow two avenues of access to the knowledge they seek. Some kinds of reading and research will be carried out most effectively online or on e-readers, and some will continue to require physical libraries and archives and printed codices—such as the one you are holding now.

The History of the Book: A Brief Chronology

BCE

c. 3500	Sumerians use cuneiform alphabet, pressed in clay with a triangular stylus.
c. 2500	Animal skins are used for scrolls in Western Asia.
c. 2400	**Earliest surviving papyrus scrolls with writing.**
c. 650	Papyrus scroll introduced into Greece from Egypt.
c. 300	**Library of Alexandria, the largest library known to have existed, is founded.**
c. 250	Chinese shift from writing on bamboo to writing on silk.
c. 196	Rosetta Stone is cut; it contains same text in Egyptian hieroglyphic, Egyptian demotic, and Greek.
c. 150	**The first paper is made in China from hemp and water.**
c. 150 BCE–40 CE	Creation of the "Dead Sea Scrolls," Hebrew and Aramaic documents, biblical and non-biblical, found near the Dead Sea in 1957.

CE

39	First public library established in Rome at the Libertas Temple.
47	The Library of Alexandria is damaged by fire when the city is besieged by Julius Caesar.
c. 150–450	**Manuscript book gradually shifts from scroll to codex.**
c. 300–700	Shift in West from papyrus to parchment.
391	Library of Alexandria destroyed under the direction of Archbishop Theophilus of Antioch.
c. 400–600	In the West, many manuscripts are destroyed and the production of new manuscripts slows dramatically.
610	Papermaking introduced into Japan from China.
c. 750–800	Papermaking reaches Central Asia and Middle East.
868	**First dated book made by block-printing is the *Diamond Sutra* published in China; it also includes one of the oldest colophons.**
896	Oldest known manuscript colophon, in Books of the Prophets written by Moses ben Asher in Tibet.
1041	**First book printed in China from moveable type.**
1119	Printing in clay using stamped individual carved wooden Roman square capitals into clay on the Prüfening dedicatory inscription, possibly the first use of the typographic principle in Europe.
c. 13th	In Italy, the production of books moves from monastic scriptoria to civilian professional scribes in cities.

1276	Watermarked paper introduced in Tuscany at Fabriano Mills, also the first paper mill in Italy.
1338	Oldest known paper mill in France.
1373	Bibliothèque nationale founded in Lyons, France.
1377	*Jikji, Selected Teachings of Buddhist Sages and Seon Masters,* the world's earliest-known book printed with moveable metal type, is printed in Korea.
1403	Guild of Stationers founded in London.
1418	Earliest extant example of woodblock printing in Europe.
1454	**Gutenberg prints indulgences on lead-based moveable type in Mainz, the earliest known European book printed by moveable type.**
1456	Gutenberg prints 42-line Bible.
1457	Mainz Psalter published by Fust and Schoffer: first extant book printed with moveable type with colophon and color printing.
1465	Cicero's *De oratore,* believed to be the first book printed in Italy, published in Subiaco.
1465	First drypoint engravings made in Germany by the Master of the Housebook.
1470	Ulrich Gering establishes first printing press in Paris.
1477	First book with intaglio illustrations, *Il Monte Sancto di Dio,* published in Florence.
1486	Caxton prints his first book in Westminster, England.
1493	First books with etchings published in Germany and Switzerland.
1495	John Tate establishes first English paper mill in Hertfordshire.
1498	Ottaviano Petrucci of Venice develops types for printing music.
1534	Cambridge University Press founded; first book printed 1583.
1536–41	**Henry VIII disbands the monasteries and seizes the books and manuscripts, many of which are lost or destroyed.**
1539	First North American Press established in Mexico City; and first North American book, *La escala espiritual de San Juan Clímaco,* is published.
1557	London Stationers' Company granted royal charter.
1575	First North American paper mill, in Mexico City.
1605	German-language *Relation aller Fürnemmen und gedenckwürdigen Historien* recognized as the first newspaper; over the next few decades, newspapers quickly follow in other European and British cities.
1626	First facsimile edition by Plantin, sixteenth-century *Martyrologium Hieronymianum* (engraved on copper plates).
1640	First printed book in British North America, *Bay Psalm Book,* published in Cambridge, Massachusetts.
c. 1660	First known mezzotint, "The Grand Executioner," by Prince Rupert, c. 1660; process invented c. 1640 by Ludwig von Siegen.
1653	First North American public library founded in Boston.

1662	**Licensing Act establishes legal copyright and codifies practice of deposit library in England.**
1683–84	Joseph Moxon publishes *Mechanick Exercises on the Whole Art of Printing*, the earliest printing manual.
1690	First Paper mill in North America, near Germantown, Pennsylvania.
1694	Licensing Act of 1662 expires.
1702	*The Daily Courant*, **the first British daily newspaper, published in London.**
1705	*The Boston News-Letter*, **the first continuously published newspaper in British North America.**
1709	*The Statute of Anne*, **the first copyright law in England and the world, limits the terms of copyright protection in England to 14 years, with the possibility of extending another 14 years.**
1725	William Ged invents the stereotype in London.
1734	Aquatint process invented by Jean-Baptiste Le Prince.
c. 1740	James Whatman makes first-known woven paper in Maidstone, England.
1746–73	Johnson's *Dictionary of the English Language* published.
1752	Publication of the first Canadian newspaper, *Halifax Gazette*.
1753	British Library founded.
1774	*Donaldson v. Beckett*, a decision of the British House of Lords, denies the existence of perpetual copyright and holds it be a creation of statute.
1788	First press imported to Australia.
1790	The first US federal Copyright Act grants copyright for a term of 14 years with the possibility of another 14 years renewal.
1793	France sets copyright protection for ten years after author's death.
1798–99	Louis-Nicolas Robert patents the first paper-making machine.
1798	Alois Senefelder invents lithography.
1799	Rosetta Stone discovered near the mouth of the Nile and is used to decipher ancient Egyptian hieroglyphs.
1800	Library of Congress founded.
1800	**Charles Stanhope, third Earl Stanhope, builds the first cast-iron press; they quickly replace wood presses.**
1803	**Henry and Sealy Fourdrinier buy patent for Robert paper-making machine, the basis for the Fourdrinier machine.**
1802–18	Friedrich Koenig develops the first steam-powered cylinder press.
1814	*The Times* (of London) uses the Koenig cylindrical press for the first time; it is capable of printing 1,000 impressions per hour.
1822	William Church patents the first typesetting machine.
1829	William Austin Burt invents the typographer, a predecessor to the modern typewriter.
1833	**Daguerreotype, the earliest photographic process, invented by Louis Jacques-Mandé Daguerre.**

1837 Chromolithography, a process allowing multi-color printing, is developed by Godefroy Engelmann in France.

1838 Moritz von Jacobi develops an electrotype process, first used for reproducing illustrations and later for moveable type and illustrations.

1841 Tauchnitz Verlag publishes the first paperback editions in Germany.

1840s **The use of wood to make pulp for paper begins in Germany.**

1851 Microphotography first suggested as a means of document preservation.

1853 Mechanically processed wood pulp used for paper making in England.

1860s Pencils and erasers begin to be mass-produced.

1863 The rotary perfecting press, invented by William Bullock, is capable of printing 10,000 double-sided sheets per hour.

1867 **The first commercially successful typewriter is invented in Milwaukee.**

1874 Chemically produced wood pulp (using sulfite) is introduced for paper making in Sweden.

1878 Remington introduces typewriter featuring shift key for upper-case letters.

1886 Ottmar Mergenthaler invents Linotype hot metal composing machine, used by the *New York Tribune*.

1886 **Berne Convention establishes international reciprocity of copyright protection.**

1890 Edinburgh Bibliographical Society founded, followed by the Bibliographical Society of London (1892) and of America, founded in New York in 1904.

1935 **IBM markets Electromatic, first successful electric typewriter.**

1938 Chester F. Carlson invents xerography.

1940 **Laszlo Biro invents the ballpoint pen.**

1942 The first electronic digital computing device, Atanasoff-Berry Computer (ABC), used to solve linear equations.

1946 ENIAC (Electronic Numerical Integrator and Computer) was the first general-purpose electronic computer.

1951 First inkjet printers sold by Siemens.

1955 Universal Copyright Convention establishes another system of international copyright protection than the Berne for signatory nations.

1959 Xerox markets first xerographic photocopier.

1967 OCLC (Online Computer Library Center, Inc.) produces Worldcat, the largest public access catalogue (now online).

1969 MARC (Machine-Readable Cataloging), is the first known use of metadata.

1969 ARPANET, the precursor to the Internet, was developed in Southern California.

1972 Stephen Dorsey, of Automatic Electronic Systems (AES), introduces the world's first programmable word processor with a video screen.

1976 IBM introduces the first commercial laser printer, the IBM 3800.

1977 **First commercial sales of personal computers (Commodore PET and Apple II).**

1991 **The World Wide Web, invented and developed by Tim Berners-Lee, is publicly launched.**

1993 Adobe launches the PDF (portable document format), a file format that represents a document independent of hardware, software, and operating systems.

1994 Jeff Bezos founds Amazon.com.

1996 **XML (Extensible Markup Language) is developed.**

1998 **Google, now the world's most widely used web-based search engine, uses the PageRank algorithm.**

2001 Wikipedia, an online, open-source, crowd-sourced encyclopedia is launched; by 2014, it is estimated that if Wikipedia were printed, it would comprise over one million pages.

2003 3D printing machines, the process of making three-dimensional objects from a digital file, begin to be used and sold.

2003 *Deep Love*, the first cell-phone novel, is published by a Japanese man, writing under the pen-name "Yoshi."

2004 Google announces Google Print project, now known as Google Books.

2004 Sony Librie, the first modern e-reader, is released.

2005 More than 300,000,000 copies of J.K. Rowling's *Harry Potter* series are printed worldwide.

2007 Amazon's Kindle is released.

2009 According to Amazon.com, sales of Kindle e-books surpass print books for the first time during the Christmas season.

2009 Apple introduces ibookstore; one year later, they announce that over 100,000,000 ibooks (Apple's name for ebooks) have been downloaded in the previous year.

2010 Apple introduces the iPad.

2010 The University of Texas at San Antonio's Applied Engineering and Technology Library is possibly the first library to contain no physical books.

2010 Google Books has scanned more than 15 million books since its inception, six years earlier.

2012 After 80 years in print as one of the world's most recognizable magazines, *Newsweek* issues its last print edition.

A Note on the Text

Original publication details of the essays reprinted here are given in the headnote to each essay. All essays have been edited for length, and omitted passages are marked with ellipses in square brackets. Where it is necessary for comprehension of the essay, a summary of the omitted passage is included in square brackets. All essays have been standardized for conventions of spelling, punctuation, and citation. In some cases, this has meant re-formatting essays from their original, parenthetical citation style to an endnote citation style. In these cases Works Cited lists have been omitted, because the full citation information is now contained in endnotes. The author's notes are retained as endnotes, and editorial **glosses** are added as footnotes, allowing readers easy access to explanations of difficult or obscure terms or passages. A glossary of terms can be found at the back of the book, and terms that appear in the glossary have not been footnoted in the essays. Words that appear in the glossary are highlighted in bold on their first appearance in each essay. Illustrations and diagrams from the original essays have been reprinted where they contribute significantly to the reader's understanding, and they have thus been renumbered consecutively.

CHAPTER I

Materiality

1.

W.W. Greg, "What Is Bibliography?" [1914], *Collected Papers*. Edited by J.C. Maxwell. Oxford: Clarendon, 1966. 75–88

Sir Walter Wilson Greg (1875–1959) was a pioneer of modern bibliography, a scholar of Shakespeare and early modern drama, and an important textual critic. Greg had a private income from shares in *The Economist* magazine (which his grandfather had founded), which allowed him to devote his energies entirely to scholarship. In this essay, originally given as an address in 1912 to the Bibliographical Society—a scholarly society founded in London in 1892—Greg lays out his vision of bibliography's potential. Greg urges the need for a "scientific" bibliography that works according to set procedures and produces results that are as verifiable as those produced by scientific experiments.

Greg distinguishes between "descriptive" (or "systematic") bibliography and "critical" bibliography. Descriptive bibliography involves writing descriptions of particular books (not works, but individual copies of particular editions of a work), setting out the size of the book, the paper used, the way in which the book was produced, the number of pages, the binding, and other details. Bibliographical descriptions also pay special attention to printing errors, for example when a word is misprinted, a page is misnumbered, or a leaf is "cancelled" (that is, a leaf containing a misprint is removed from the book and a new one is substituted in its place).

Critical bibliography puts this information to use in solving textual problems. For example, where a text exists in two versions, it may be important to know which was printed first (especially if it's more likely that the author had greater control over the first printing). If a printer's error is corrected in one version but not the other, it is likely that the corrected version was printed after the uncorrected one. Because he understands bibliography's importance for editing, Greg argues that paying close attention to the material form of the book is not just for book collectors, but for all serious scholars.

What Is Bibliography?[i]

It is a commonplace among those who have written on the subject that **bibliography** has grown from being an art into being a science, and if we are content not to press the terms too closely, the remark may be accepted as indicating a certain truth. There was a time not so long ago when the typical occupation of bibliographers was the writing of elegant essays on individual points of archaeological or artistic interest, more or less closely, and more or less accidentally, connected with books. It is no reproach to a generation of book-lovers, many of whom are fortunately still active in our midst, that this should have been so. If bibliography is today a science by which we co-ordinate facts and trace the operation of constant causes, if we are gradually evolving a rigorous method for the investigation and interpretation of fresh evidence, if we are able, within the sphere of our work, in any way adequately to reconstruct the past out of the indications of the present, it is in a large measure due to the patient accumulation and recording of facts achieved by those bibliographical pioneers. As has happened over and over again in the history of science, these workers pursued the subject for its own interest and their individual amusement, and in doing so evolved a powerful instrument of investigation, of the practical applications of which they never dreamed. All this we have inherited, and our debt is great. Nevertheless the difference is not merely one of knowledge, but of outlook as well. Reading through that remarkable series of papers[1] in which our founders sought to determine the true position of bibliography in its various branches, I cannot help thinking that a sense of dissatisfaction with the artistic method, a perception, perhaps dim as yet, of the scientific developments of which the subject was capable, present in the minds of those pioneers, is among the chief causes of our being assembled here this evening.

[...]

But if bibliography is a science, it can hardly as yet be called a satisfactory science. I am inclined
4 to think that it suffers from its name, and I half regret that "bibliology" is past praying for.[2] When "bibliography" does not mean the writing of books, it must mean the description of books. This limitation of sense seems to me unfortunate, for though the description of books may form an important branch of bibliography it is certainly not synonymous with it. It will perhaps be contended that bibliography has been, probably that it must be, a descriptive science. In a sense this is true. In a sense every science is descriptive. But in so far as a science is merely descriptive it is sterile. You may dissect and you may describe, but until your anatomy becomes comparative you will never arrive at the principle of evolution. You may name and classify the colors of your sweet peas and produce nothing but a florist's catalogue; it is only when you begin grouping them according to their genetic origin that you will arrive at Mendel's formula.[3] It is the same everywhere. Facts are observed and catalogued by the systematizers, and then suddenly, as if by chance, an idea is born that introduces order and logic into what was chaos, and we are in possession of a guiding principle, of an instrument of thought and investigation, that may transform the whole of our relation to knowledge or alter the face of the physical globe. Perhaps no discoveries that we make in bibliography are likely to have such far-reaching results as these,

---

1 Published in the journal *Transactions of the Bibliographical Society* from 1892 onwards.

2 "Bibliography" is from the Greek *biblio*, book, and *graphy*, writing. Bibliology would be the study of books, rather than writing them or writing about them, but the term has not entered common use.

3 Alluding to Gregor Mendel (1822–84), who discovered genetics by observing differences between selectively bred sweet-pea plants.

but they are quite capable of revolutionizing the subject itself and the methods by which it is pursued. That is why any tendency to confine the scope of bibliography within descriptive limits seems to me deplorable. And its name encourages—I believe has encouraged—the belief that bibliography consists in the compilation of bibliographies.[4] You might as well say that geography means map-making, or bacteriology the breeding of disease. Moreover, the objections to restraining the scope of bibliography are not merely the theoretical ones I have mentioned. They are of serious practical importance as well. For the wider applications of bibliography, of critical bibliography, are no mere playthings. They are essential to the advance of knowledge. Therefore they will be made—they are being made. All that is done by restricting the official cognizance,[5] so to speak, of bibliographers, is to exclude from the field of these new developments the only men who by training are qualified to carry them to a successful issue.

Before I pass to a consideration of the meaning and methods of bibliography a word must be said regarding its scope. The view has been, and I believe still is, maintained by many able practitioners that bibliography is properly confined to the study of printed books. **Manuscripts**, they hold, belong to another department. Now, I do not wish to waste words over a matter of verbal definition. But when I read the accounts of bibliographical descriptions given by these same writers I observe that a large part of their method is just as applicable to manuscripts as to printed books. And as it happens to be in the methods of the science that I am at present interested, I regard the distinction between written and printed books as irrelevant. What I am concerned with is a system of investigation and a method of description, and if, with minor modifications, it can be made to apply to clay cylinders and **rolls** of **papyrus** as well as to **codices** of **vellum** or paper, so much the better.[6] It is the method itself, not the object to which that method is applied, that gives unity to a science. You may state the laws of motion in a form more suitable to the movements of the planets, as did Newton,[7] or in one more suitable to those of an electron, as is the modern tendency; but that does not affect the principles of rational dynamics. Thus it may be called bibliography, or it may be called by any other name you please, but what I want understood is that the characteristics of the science about which I am speaking cut far deeper than the distinction between writing and printing and apply to the transmission of all symbolic representation of speech or other ordered sound or even of logical thought. [...]

Now let us consider for a moment what bibliography really is. Before we can describe or classify any book we must be able to find out about it. Descriptive, or as I shall call it, systematic bibliography presupposes an acquaintance with the elements of the science. I call

4 "Bibliographies" here means lists of books, which might be early editions of a certain work, or books relating to a certain subject, or lists of books by a certain author.

5 Range of observation.

6 Clay cylinders and rolls of papyrus (paper made from rushes) were early materials for writing on; codices (the plural of codex) are books bound along a spine. They can be made from vellum (very fine leather, usually made from calf-skin) or paper (made from either linen rags or wood pulp).

7 Sir Isaac Newton (1643–1727), whose *Principia Mathematica* (1686) described the movement of the planets in mathematical detail for the first time.

them elements in Euclid's sense.[8] They are elementary not because they are easy but because they are fundamental: they are the prerequisites of all further study. But I do not think these elements have as a whole received the attention they deserve. Too often they are brought in incidentally in the course of instructions for describing books, and as though they had no significance in themselves and no application outside the pages of a **catalogue**.[9] Take a single instance. The elaborate and highly important rules for ascertaining the **format** of a book are commonly given as though their sole object was to guide the describer in his choice of what particular symbol to put at the end of a title. If that were so, I confess it would seem to me simpler to toss up. I believe that many people would be puzzled to say exactly wherein lies the importance of putting such symbols at all. It is regarded as part of the game, just as in arithmetic children are taught to play certain tricks with a row of figures and extract something called a square root, though as to how the result is obtained, or what it really means, nothing is said. In reality, of course, the rules of format have nothing to do with description. We require them to discover how a **sheet** of paper has been folded. And we require them to know how the sheet has been folded, not in order to put a particular symbol in a catalogue, but because it is an important bibliographical fact. Its importance, by the way, only partly arises from its being a salient factor in the history of the book. It is mainly due to considerations lying beyond the field of what is usually called bibliography. For it is only a knowledge of the format that enables us to say in the case of a printed book (for a manuscript has no true format) that if variants occur on such and such a **page** they may be expected also on such and such other
6 pages. Thus a matter which is really of very small importance to the cataloguer, becomes of great significance to the textual critic—though, indeed, he is only just beginning to wake up to the fact. So again with the much-debated question of U and V.[10] This is almost always discussed in the form of rules for transcription. Yet what rules a cataloguer follows is really a matter of mere academic interest. What is important is the practice of the old **printers** and the gradual advance of **philological** awareness that it reveals. My complaint is that, all through, bibliography is studied and taught—so far as it is taught—too much from the point of view of the cataloguer or descriptive bibliographer, not enough for the interest of the principles involved, and that as a consequence those wider applications of the subject that lie beyond the cataloguer's horizon suffer. The printed book or the manuscript itself is an object of intense interest, and the booklover must wish to find out everything he can about it, irrespective of any actual description. And it is the elements of bibliography that supply him with a method and a set of logical tools as it were for the prosecution of his search. Any description he may find it convenient to make is merely a means of communicating to others, or of recording for

---

8 Euclid was a Greek mathematician active around 300 BCE. His *Elements* is a foundational text of geometry.

9 That is, a library catalogue or the catalogue of a sale of books.

10 In books prior to about 1750, the letters represented by *u* and *v* in modern books were used interchangeably. When transcribing from such a book, therefore, it is necessary to decide whether to modernize these letters or to follow the original usage.

his own subsequent information, the results at which he has arrived, and, however useful, is of purely secondary concern.

Thus the elements of bibliography are what every bibliographer will have more or less to master. He will probably not cover the whole field, for it is a large one, but he will require an intimate knowledge of certain parts and some familiarity with the paths that lead from one part to another, if he is to do any good in his subject. The expert in **typography** is unlikely to be also a skilled **paleographer**, but he will require some knowledge of the handwritings upon which various types are based. Both alike will need some familiarity with the history of paper-making, though they will probably leave the closer investigation of **watermarks** to a specialist. What is important is that every serious bibliographer should have some general plan of the subject in his mind that will, so to speak, enable him to find his way about, and to understand the advances made in other fields and the possible light they may throw upon his own immediate studies.

Those who have followed me so far will not be surprised that I call the field a wide one. It includes the study of bookmaking and of the manufacture of the materials of which books are made, it includes a knowledge of the conditions of transcription and reproduction, of the methods of printing and **binding**, of the practices of publication and bookselling it includes the whole of typography and the whole of paleography. Naturally enough the subject tends to shade off into others that are not bibliographical. Bookbinding is certainly a province of bibliography, yet it almost merges into a fine art, as do even more clearly book-illustration and illumination.[11] Bibliography has to take cognizance of these subjects, but it can never make them altogether its own. Book-plates[12] have a purely superficial connexion with books: their study is but a bastard branch of the subject. Another useful limitation lies in this, that bibliography only concerns itself with processes that leave their mark on the character of the finished book. Printing it is very largely concerned with, but it does not study the mechanism of the modern steam press. Pens it is certainly interested in, but hardly in their growth or manufacture. It attends to the preparation of vellum, though indifferent to the breeding of calves.

That typography is a branch of bibliography will probably be allowed by all except the adherents of the narrowest "descriptive" school. It is, indeed, the most progressive branch of all, the one in which bibliographers have won their greatest successes of recent years, and if it shows any signs of severing itself from the parent stock, it is in the direction of becoming a graft upon biology. But it has not done so yet. It has only illustrated, like almost every other science, the value of the comparative method and the general significance of the evolutionary idea. Far less unanimity will attend the inclusion of paleography. Yet, obviously, this stands in exactly the same relation to manuscripts as typography does to printed books. If, therefore, bibliography is to take cognizance of manuscripts we must necessarily include paleography in its field. To my mind a bibliography which should exclude either manuscripts or printed books from its purview would be robbed of more than half its interest and significance.

11 "Illumination" is the addition of decorative initials or marginal decorations, usually to manuscripts.

12 Labels, sometimes elaborate or decorative ones, pasted into the front of books to indicate the identity of their owners.

Descriptive, or to use the wider term, systematic bibliography, the classification of individual books according to some guiding principle, seems to be regarded by most writers on the subject as bibliography *par excellence*. It is this part of my subject therefore that has been the most exposed to the onslaughts of previous writers, and I shall not say very much about it. A few remarks will, however, be relevant, and may conceivably be useful. It is sometimes said that a bibliographer should distinguish the relative merit and importance of the books enumerated, and that the ideal bibliographer will read and judge as well as record and describe. The ideal bibliographer will not waste his time over what is no concern of his. His subject is books, not universal knowledge; and the relevant sense of the word "book" is that in which the Ellesmere *Canterbury Tales* is a book, not that in which Chaucer's *Book of the Duchess* is a book.[13] To the bibliographer the literary contents of a book are irrelevant. This does not mean that special bibliographies should not be compiled, or that the merits of the works included, or somebody's opinion thereon, should not be recorded. It means that this is not the task of the bibliographer. [...] Thus the compilation of bibliographies is in truth but a mixed and subsidiary art. The mere bibliographer who criticizes the works he catalogues is guilty of impertinence: at best he is only the systematizer of the other men's knowledge.

If anyone thinks that I am unduly limiting the functions of the bibliographer in this direction and depriving him of a part of his hereditary domain, I will endeavor to make up for it by what I believe to be a logical and necessary extension of his activities elsewhere. For I have at length come to the real subject of this paper, namely, to what I shall call critical bibliography.

8 After what I have said it should I think be clear that I regard bibliography as an important subject. It is one which may quite legitimately be pursued for its own sake and it is by those who so pursue it that it is likely to be most advanced. Possibly every subject that is worth cultivating possesses some intrinsic value apart from practical applications. But I do not think that bibliography is one of the great sciences, of which pure mathematics is the type,[14] whose interest would hardly be diminished by entire dissociation from the actual world. At any rate I freely confess that my own interest in bibliography is by no means purely bibliographical. It is literary. I stumbled into bibliography by accident. Finding it impossible to obtain the information I required about a certain class of literature, I set to work to collect it. It was the results of bibliography that I wanted, but my search led me to the far greater discovery of the importance of the subject itself. Any value my literary work may have will be chiefly owing to that discovery. For, if I may be allowed a violent metaphor which is always coming to my mind, it is only by the application of a rigorous bibliographical method that the last drop of information can be squeezed out of a literary document. Thus in spite of my interest in bibliography it is as the handmaid of literature that I still regard it, and it is this side of my theme that I wish to develop tonight.

---

13 The Ellesmere Chaucer or Ellesmere Manuscript is an early-fifteenth-century illuminated manuscript of Geoffrey Chaucer's *Canterbury Tales*, held in the Huntington Library in San Marino, California. Here Greg distinguishes between two uses of "book": a particular physical object (like the particular copy of the book in your hands) and a written work that might exist in many copies.

14 Exemplary case.

There is a remark in Dr. Copinger's[15] inaugural address before this Society that recently caught my attention. "Bibliography," he said, "has been called the grammar of literary investigation." It is an extraordinarily penetrating remark, but one which seems to me to have been strangely misunderstood. Bibliography has hardly ever attempted to be the grammar of literary investigation; it has tried to be a dictionary. It has chronicled and described, sometimes it has even criticized, the books needed for the study of literature, and it has rendered valuable service in this line; but seldom if ever has it concerned itself with the methods of that study. By this, of course, I do not mean either the **canons** of criticism—if there are any—or the methods of literary history; I mean what is antecedent to both, namely the investigation of texts. Strictly bibliographical investigation forms three-quarters of textual criticism, and therefore of the work of the scientific editor. For editing should be none the less scientific because it must at the same time be literary. No editor, however sure his taste, ever did valuable work without technical skill in handling textual evidence: just as no editor, however scientific, is worth his salt without taste. And apart from taste he requires much knowledge that has nothing to do with bibliography. He requires a thorough knowledge of linguistics and a thorough knowledge of antiquities. But these are presupposed in the subject and differ with the accidents of the subject. What is constant as a requirement, what every editor, what every textual investigator needs, what may therefore be truly called the grammar of literary investigation, is critical bibliography. Critical bibliography is the science of the material transmission of literary texts, the investigation of the textual tradition as it is called, in so far as that investigation is possible without extraneous aids. It aims at the construction of a calculus for the determination of textual problems. 9

This, of course, is no new science: editors have been forced to solve the problems as they went along, and in doing so they have necessarily evolved a method of their own. It is strange, however, when one inquires into the subject, how little and often how unsatisfactory is the writing of a general nature in this connexion. I say this advisedly in spite of full knowledge of, and sincerest respect for, the profound observations for instance of Westcott and Hort in connexion with the manuscripts of the Greek Testament.[16] Everywhere the editor suffers from not being a bibliographer; he gives himself all sorts of unnecessary trouble and arrives at all sorts of impossible results. In the current number of one of the chief critical journals a writer goes hopelessly wrong over the order of two issues of a printed book, simply because he does not know how to distinguish an original **leaf** from a **cancel**.[ii] It is pathetic to find editors discussing the order of undated **editions** on a basis of vague probabilities, when often the erroneous retention of a **catchword** or some similar bibliographical trifle puts the matter beyond dispute. It is not that bibliographers ought to rush into the task of editing, but that editors ought to give themselves a thorough bibliographical training. For a large part of their work is bibliography,

---

15 Walter Arthur Copinger (1847–1910) was a lawyer, academic, and polymath. He was the first president of the Bibliographical Society (of London), which he helped to found.

16 Brooke Foss Westcott (1825–1901) and Fenton John Anthony Hort (1828–92) produced a critical edition of the New Testament in the original Greek in 1881, based on extensive examination of the earliest known manuscripts.

critical bibliography, and this can only be properly carried out when the elements of the subject have been mastered. For anyone without a competent knowledge of bibliography to endeavor to deal with textual evidence is mere impertinence. It is the task of bibliographers at present to systematize the knowledge acquired in this department and to perfect the method, in order that it may be acquired with the least possible trouble and applied with the greatest possible certainty.[iii] There is much to be done in this line. [...]

As I have said, no attempt has yet been made to systematize critical bibliography, and I confess that I am by no means clear in my own mind what we shall finally agree to include under the name, always supposing that we recognize such a subject at all. To begin with it will embrace all that an editor requires, in the way of knowledge and method, apart from linguistics and *realien*.[17] But how much more it may be expedient to include I will not venture to guess.

[...]

Bibliography is a wide subject and the field of critical bibliography is no less extensive. But it may not unreasonably be suggested that the more immediate concern of this Society is with the bibliography of English literature. And now, with your permission, I will spend what remains of my allotted hour in describing a dream of my own. It is of a course of lectures on English bibliography which may one day be delivered at one of our so-called seats of learning, neither this year nor next year, but perhaps someday. And I will tell you what, as I dream, the lecturer will tell his class. He will begin with the general principles of textual transmission, which are for the most part obvious enough, how a number of steps often intervene between the work as it formed itself in the author's mind and as it reaches modern readers. He will pass on to describe the conditions under which manuscripts were written and copied, the kinds of mistake that **scribes** habitually made, and the manner in which bibliographical investigation may reveal them, the extent of the **corruption** to be expected and the degree to which it is reasonable to rely on the textual tradition. He will consider the influences to which manuscripts have been subjected, the injury they have suffered, the degree to which this can be repaired, the reagents that may be used with safety, the way vellum should be treated, and the way it should not.[iv] He will then deal with the principles of textual criticism, the grouping of manuscripts according to their genetic relations,[18] the manner in which those relations are to be determined, and the way in which they affect the choice of readings: in what cases a reading in the archetype[19] can be postulated with certainty, in what cases it is only a matter of probability: what evidence forces us to suppose conflation, what latitude should be allowed for coincidence: when conflation is

17 German, literally meaning "realities," but here used to mean "modern language studies."

18 When several manuscript copies of a work exist, it is sometimes possible to reconstruct the sequence in which they were copied, and thus to arrange the manuscripts in a kind of "family tree" (known as a stemma). The relationships described on this "family tree" are what Greg refers to as "genetic relations."

19 The archetype is the manuscript that served as the source of a later copy or copies. Sometimes details of a lost archetype can be conjectured from careful examination of the copies.

due to the scribe, when to a reviser: how archetypal foliation[20] may be inferred and what is its importance. He will then proceed to take individual monuments of literature and describe the manuscripts in which they are preserved and the relation of those manuscripts. He will also consider the contents of various manuscripts and the light which they may throw upon the works contained. He will not neglect external evidence as regards the authors and their works, but will direct attention to the main contemporary authorities and records to be studied. Further, he will consider the appeal of the manuscripts; the learned English manuscripts of Anglo-Saxon times, the popular manuscripts of the centuries following the Conquest. *Pari passu*[21] he will investigate the changes in the methods of book-making and the gradual changes in handwriting. He will indicate the evolution from the half-uncial of the earliest charters to the final dissolution of Saxon writing about 1200, and from the adoption and adaptation of the Carolingian minuscule to the book and current hands[22] of the fifteenth century: he will also trace the elaboration and decay of the system of contractions borrowed from Latin writing.[23] Naturally he will not be able to deal fully with all the extant manuscripts of all surviving works, but he will consider all the more important monuments, and will in particular devote attention to those that present problems of a typical nature. He will discuss the so-called three texts of the *Vision of Piers Plowman*,[24] for if bibliography is not concerned with the question whether they are the work of one author or of three, it is concerned with the determination and differentiation of the three types, a question the investigation of which has been as yet only begun, but which when answered will go far towards answering the other. [...]

He will next pass to the introduction of printing, and indicate the differences which that event made in the transmission of texts. He will discuss the relation of editions and their grouping, and also the minor differences which copies of the same edition present, and he will indicate how the change from manuscripts to printed books affects the problems of textual criticism. He will call attention to the particular errors which are likely to happen in **composition** and imposition,[25] as he previously did to those peculiar to copying. He will describe the differences

20 Foliation concerns which words were on which sheets of paper in the manuscript, just as pagination concerns which words are on which pages in a codex.

21 Equally, on an equal footing.

22 Prior to the modern age, handwriting, especially among professional scribes, was far more standardized than it is today. Half-uncial, Carolingian minuscule, book hand, and current hand are all historical styles of handwriting.

23 Contractions, such as "Dr." for "Doctor," were commonly used to save space and effort in handwritten documents.

24 *Piers Plowman*, a medieval poem attributed to William Langland (c. 1332–c. 1386), exists in three distinct versions, known as the A-text (the shortest of the three) and the much longer B- and C-texts. It is generally accepted that the A-text is the earliest, though scholars continue to debate the relation between the three texts.

25 "Composition," here, means the process of setting up the type to be used in printing a book; "imposition" means arranging the set type so that it produces correctly printed pages.

of type and their value in dating books, and also the particular literal confusions[26] to which each is liable. He will consider methods of detecting false **imprints** and misleading dates. He will then proceed to deal with individual works, and beginning with the great compilation known as the *Morte Darthur*,[v] [27] will trace the fortunes of English literature as they depend on the printed page. He will call attention to the difference between various ages in the extent to which we may presume an author to have exercised control over the first edition of his work, or over the first and subsequent editions as well. He will enumerate the many small points, the corrections, the cancels, the withdrawals, that bear witness to editorial supervision, and will discuss the relations of the author, the **publisher**, and the printer, the control that one had over the other, and that those in authority had over them all. He will expound the conditions of **copyright** and estimate the effect they had on literary production. Following in the footsteps of our Honorary Secretary he will reconstruct the history of the first **folio** of Shakespeare's plays from the evidence of exceptional copies and other bibliographical peculiarities, and he will explain the variants in the different issues of *Paradise Lost*.[28] He will account for the duplicate setting of Erasmus's *Paraphrase*,[29] and estimate the force of trades-unionism in the sixteenth century. Nor will he forget the manuscripts of a later date. He will give help in the deciphering and dating of Tudor and Stuart hands, and will discuss the most satisfactory way of printing works written in them. This is an important matter, and he will devote considerable attention throughout to various styles of editing. For there is no one method which is correct to the exclusion of others; it is a question which is best adapted to peculiar needs. And it is largely the business of the bibliographer to see that, whatever method is adopted, it is carried out consistently and made to yield the very best results of which it is capable.

It is no light task that I have sketched, and we may well wonder how many men there are today who would be capable of undertaking it with any chance of success. But the way to success lies through failure, and until someone has been found bold enough to make the venture there is no knowing what may or may not be possible. Anyhow that is my dream, and it is to the preliminary task of asking the necessary questions, of defining the problems, and systematizing the method, that I invite the Bibliographical Society this evening.

26 Literal confusions occur when one letter is mistaken for another, so that the compositor uses a *b* in place of a *d*, for example.

27 Thomas Malory's *Morte D'Arthur* (or *Morte Darthur*) is a prose collection of tales about the legendary King Arthur and the Knights of the Round Table, first published in 1485.

28 John Milton's epic poem *Paradise Lost* was first published in 1667. An edition of a work has more than one issue if errors were noticed and corrected during its printing.

29 Erasmus produced Latin paraphrases of parts of the Bible between 1517 and 1524. Most of the paraphrases appeared almost simultaneously from two publishers, making their textual history rather complicated.

Notes

i. W.W. Greg, "What Is Bibliography?," Bibliographical Society, February 19, 1912. Printed in the *Transactions* of the Society xii (1914): 39–53. Guest Lecture.

ii. I have forgotten the particular instance I had in mind.

iii. R.B. McKerrow performed an invaluable service in his *Introduction to Bibliography for Literary Students*, but that epoch-making work did not appear till 1927, 15 years after the present paper was written.

iv. Malice reported that the authorities at the British Museum once boiled a Caxton indulgence on vellum by way of cleaning it, and were surprised to find that it had shrivelled to half its size.

v. The paper was of course written long before any manuscript of Malory's work came to light.

2.

Lucien Febvre and Henri-Jean Martin, "The Book: Its Visual Appearance," *The Coming of the Book: The Impact of Printing, 1450–1800.* Trans. David Gerard; ed. Geoffrey Nowell-Smith and David Wooton. London: Verso, 1976. 77–108

Lucien Febvre (1878–1956) was a highly influential French historian who co-founded the journal *Annales d'Histoire Economique et Sociale* in 1929, which emphasized an approach to history that was long-term, multinational, often grounded in quantitative data, and attentive to the experience of ordinary people. Toward the end of his career he turned his attention to the history of books and printing and began to write a book on the subject. In 1953 he invited Henri-Jean Martin (1924–2007), then a young librarian in the *Bibliothèque nationale* in Paris, to edit his work. Febvre died in 1956, leaving the work unfinished. Martin completed the book after Febvre's death and it was published in 1958.

Febvre and Martin led the way in studies of book history and print culture by drawing attention not to particular books, such as the First Folio of Shakespeare, which had already received detailed attention from W.W. Greg and others, but to the history of the production, circulation, and reception of books. Together with studies by D.F. McKenzie (see p. 45), Elizabeth Eisenstein (see p. 215), Roger Chartier (see p. 73), and others, they helped to redirect attention toward printing as a transformative communications technology, and the book as a privileged object, in which historical and cultural meaning came to inhere. The history of the book, for Febvre and Martin, was not simply another historical topic; it was about the new communications technology that ushered in modernity itself. In the process, books became such a natural part of daily life that few people stopped to consider them in any detail.

That process of naturalization, however, was neither smooth nor rapid. In this extract, Febvre and Martin show how the book slowly obtained its modern appearance. The cover, title page, and even the text of the book in fact took some time to evolve. The earliest printed books imitated manuscripts and used typefaces designed to look like the different styles of handwriting common in the fifteenth century. Only gradually did the book develop its own conventions, with the roman and italic types that are familiar today, and the page numbers, title pages, and bindings that now seem so essential to the printed book.

Febvre and Martin also remind us that the history of printing is not only the history of the transmission of texts. It is also about the reproduction of images. Different techniques for printing images drastically affect the relationship between image and text. While woodcuts can be printed at the same time as moveable type, copperplate engravings have to be printed separately. (For why this is, see Michael Twyman's essay, p. 37.)

The Book: Its Visual Appearance

Let us open the books and see how they changed their appearance in the course of time, and for what reasons.

The earliest **incunabula** looked exactly like **manuscripts**. The first **printers**, far from being innovators, took extreme care to produce exact imitations. The 42-line Bible[1] for example was printed in a letter-type which faithfully reproduced the handwriting of the Rhenish missals.[2] For a long time printers did not merely use the same individual characters but also groups of letters linked by the same ligatures as those used in manuscripts.[3] For an even longer time initials in printed books were rubricated[4] by the same calligraphers and **illuminated** by the same artists who worked on manuscripts. So much is this the case that the layman sometimes has to examine a book very carefully before deciding whether or not it is printed or handwritten. Many theories have been advanced to explain this. It has been suggested, for example, that it was to deceive the buyer who might distrust the new mechanical process or that it was intended to pass off printed books as manuscripts in order not to offend the susceptibilities, or even arouse the unwelcome attention, of copyists and their "Guilds," which were jealous of their monopolies.

Such theories do not stand up to examination. A desire to deceive the buyer? Any such deceit would be easily spotted because a fifteenth-century eye would be more acute in detecting such things than our eyes and would have quickly distinguished a manuscript from a printed book despite all the resemblances. Besides, people soon came to prefer printed texts which were more readable and accurate than the older manuscripts. Resistance from copyists and stationers? Certainly. But we must not forget that most of them were subject to strict university control and were not strictly speaking members of an autonomous corporate body. Consequently they were under university authority which was favorably disposed to printing in its early days,

---

1 Also known as the **Gutenberg** Bible, this is an edition of the Vulgate text of the Bible printed by Johannes Gutenberg in the 1450s. It was one of the most important works printed by Gutenberg using his newly invented moveable type, and played an important role in legitimating the new medium of print. Only 21 copies survive.

2 Prayer books containing instructions for celebrating the Mass, produced in the Rhine region of present-day Germany.

3 Ligatures are lines connecting adjacent letters, as in cursive handwriting. For example, where the letters "t" and "i" appear together, the cross-bar of the "t" may connect with the top of the "i." Some typefaces include ligatures, so that, in this example, they would include pieces of type for the letters "t" and "i," but also a single piece of type for the "ti" combination.

4 Decorated using red ink.

so that the **scribes'** complaints were in fact ineffectual. Besides, printers and stationers sometimes seem to have collaborated. If copyists undoubtedly complained about the rivalry of those newcomers, the printers, the **booksellers** who specialized in the sale and trade of manuscripts did not necessarily take the same view. In many cases, in Paris or Avignon for example, they were quite prepared to sell printed books and manuscripts alongside each other. Many of them, sensing the obvious importance of the new method of reproducing texts, went into printing themselves or helped finance the establishment of printing shops. Antoine Vérard,[5] for example, produced printed books which were often on **vellum** and illuminated, and were faithful copies of the deluxe manuscripts he had previously had written and painted when he directed a scribal workshop. That the earliest printers scrupulously copied, and often indeed slavishly reproduced, the manuscripts in front of them, should hardly be a matter of surprise. Nor does it require fanciful theories to account for it; it could not have been otherwise. How could they have imagined a printed book other than in the form of the manuscripts on which they were in fact modeled? And would not the identity of book and manuscript be the most obvious proof of their technical triumph, as well as the guarantee of their commercial success? The advent of the printing press did not mean a sudden change in the appearance of the book. It was the first phase in an evolution which we must now try to trace, so as to isolate the various stages by which the printed book moved by degrees away from its original model, the manuscript. We must also explain why and to what extent its appearance varied in the first hundred years of its existence, before it assumed, in the mid-sixteenth century, an appearance which is essentially the same as the one it has today.

I. Type Founts[6]

Around 1450, when printing was invented, texts were being written, according to their contents or their intended recipients, in very different hands. In fact four main styles of script were current, each with its own specific purpose. Firstly, the gothic of scholastic texts, the traditional "**blackletter**" beloved of theologians and university professors. Then the larger size gothic, less rounded, with straight uprights and fractured letters:[7] the missal letter used for ecclesiastical books. Next a script derived from that used in the Chancelleries[8] (each of which had its own tradition): the "bastard" gothic,[9] a hand current in luxury manuscripts in the **vernacular** and

5 Antoine Vérard (active 1485–1512), an important Parisian publisher who is especially remembered for his illustrated editions in the early days of print.

6 A fount of type is a full set of a particular size of one typeface, including multiple copies of each letter.

7 Fractured letters are ones formed with straight edges (as in the Germanic Fraktur), as opposed to the more rounded styles of Roman or italic letters.

8 The offices of the Chancellors of European states, which developed a set of distinct but related handwriting styles for official documents and diplomatic correspondence.

9 Bastard gothic, also called bastarda or *lettre bâtarde* in French, was a Gothic script used primarily in France and Germany during the fourteenth and fifteenth centuries. It was a simplified version of earlier gothic scripts (hence, metaphorically, their bastard or illegitimate descendent).

in some Latin texts, generally narratives. Finally, the last to emerge, but that with the greatest future which became the normal script for printed books: the "littera antiqua," the humanist, or roman script. Inspired by the Carolingian minuscule,[10] this script was made fashionable by Petrarch[11] and his disciples but in 1480 was used only by a few exclusive groups of humanists, or by aristocratic book collectors who wanted their classical texts to have a look of antiquity and authenticity about them (or at least of what was taken to represent antiquity and authenticity) to contrast them not only in content but also in appearance with the medieval texts. With this roman script there can be associated a cursive script, the *Cancelleresca*, based on the handwriting used by the Vatican Chancellery about the middle of the fifteenth century, and used afterwards in the Chancelleries of Florence, Ferrara, and Venice; this was the origin of italic.

This rapid summary of what was in reality a much more complex set of overlapping styles, defying rigid classification, must not mislead the reader. Intermediate styles of all kinds are extant between the four ideal types just enumerated; the gothic used by the scribes of Bologna, for example, was influenced by the humanist script; and there existed considerable regional variations within each type of script. The Parisian bastarda type, which was born in the Royal Chancellery and was used in vernacular manuscripts, and which was to inspire the type of Vérard and of Le Noir, differed from the bastarda used in the Low Countries to reproduce the texts of John of Bruges, which was in turn the model for the type produced by the Bruges printer, Colard Mansion.[12] In fact, regional characteristics were so marked a feature that the experienced eye can assign a manuscript to a particular locality with ease.

18 Such were the different models that were available to early printers; and this diversity explains the extraordinary variety of the letters used in the first incunabula and even in early sixteenth-century books.[13] There was a conventional type for each class of book and reader, just as there had been in the manuscript period: for the clerk or scholar, scholastic books or manuals of **canon** law printed in blackletter; for the layman, vernacular narratives printed in bastarda type; for the admirer of a polished style, **editions** of the Latin classics and of their humanist emulators, printed in roman. A typical instance is provided by Gering and his partners, who first brought printing to Paris.[14] They were summoned to the Sorbonne by humanist men of letters, and so naturally they used roman in the printing shop they set up under university **patronage**. But later, when they left the university and set up shop in

---

10 A style of handwriting common in The Holy Roman Empire between approximately 800 and 1200.

11 Francesco Petrarca (1304–74), known in English as Petrarch, an Italian humanist scholar and poet.

12 Colard Mansion was a Flemish scribe, printer, translator, and illustrator, active in the last quarter of the fifteenth century. In addition to being remembered for being the publisher of the first illustrated book with engravings and for printing texts in the vernacular, he also worked with William Caxton (1415 or 1424–92), who introduced printing to England.

13 For illustrations of early types, see the essay by Gutjahr and Benton (p. 63).

14 Ulrich Gering, Michael Friburger, and Martin Crantz set up a printing press within the Sorbonne in Paris and produced 22 works between 1470 and 1472.

the Rue St. Jacques, producing law texts and the Schoolmen[15] for a larger reading public of students and lawyers, they used gothic. Some printers went further in imitating manuscript handwriting, as did Le Talleur,[16] a printer of Rouen, who published two treatises on Anglo-Norman law for Richard Pynson, the English bookseller of Norman extraction.[17] To do this work he cast a type quite different from his normal model, and tried to copy the cursive script used peculiarly by English scribes for this class of work.

Gradually, printing became more uniform for quite material reasons. When the trade of letter founding had not yet started, printers had to make their own punches, and even a single fount cost a small fortune.[18] As each printer could afford to possess only a small number of founts it was difficult if not impossible to cut or acquire one identical with the script of a particular manuscript he wished to print. The sale of copies of the same edition in different towns and countries and, even more important, the nomadic careers of the first printers, inevitably led to the development of uniform types, especially as the scripts of the different regions often varied only slightly between each other. It is true that the first German printers who left the Rhineland to teach Europe the new art attempted at first to imitate the local scripts. In Italy they copied the humanist script, and, even more often, the round script of the scribes of Bologna. But many of them, particularly those with limited means, could not work like this. Having set out from home and with no capital other than a little equipment, a few matrices, and some punches, they used founts already cut although far from their own locality. Hence we can follow the journey of a blackletter from Basel, for example, to Lyons, to Toulouse, and on as far as Spain. Similarly, the letters in the first books printed at Lyons, which were printed by Le Roy, were cut in Germany. In England for quite a long time they used letters which came from Rouen and Paris.

Regional styles were the first to disappear. Then, more slowly, the major forms of script were standardized until eventually the new roman type triumphed in the greater part of Europe—in Italy, France, parts of Switzerland, Spain, and England.

[...]

Roman grew constantly in importance as humanism spread. It began to be used to print vernacular texts, until then traditionally printed in gothic bastarda. Thus in 1529 Galiot Du Pré "rejuvenated" the presentation of the *Roman de la Rose* and the works of Alain Chartier; he did the same for Villon's *Grant Testament* in 1532 because the public for these works had come

---

15 A schoolman is one learned in medieval scholasticism, usually teaching or studying in one of the earliest European universities. In this context, the word is used to refer to textbooks for university students.

16 Guillaume le Talleur, (d. c. 1491), punchcutter and printer in Rouen. (A punchcutter is someone who makes original "punches" used to create the matrices or moulds from which type is produced.)

17 Richard Pynson (1448–1529) was one of the first printers of English books. Born in Normandy, he became King's Printer to Henry VII and subsequently Henry VIII.

18 Letter founding is the process of making moveable type. Punches are the molds used to create the type.

to prefer roman which thenceforth was used each year in an increasing number of editions.[19] But the new letter did not enjoy complete acceptance. For some time, university professors continued to prefer the blackletter; it only disappeared in the following decades, first from law manuals and then from theology, and it continued even longer in liturgical works. In particular the huge numbers of bourgeois and townsmen, accustomed to decipher manuscript, remained attached to gothic bastarda which resembled it more than roman or italic. Rabelais' *Gargantua*, to be bought by a huge public at the Lyons fair and elsewhere, was printed in blackletter.[20] For a long time, therefore, gothic bastarda was used to print popular books, **almanacs** and "gothic booklets." The poorer printers ran off thousands of these, wearing out their founts in the process and buying cast-offs from their richer colleagues who no longer wanted them. Only later, in the second half of the sixteenth century, when obliged to restock with new types, did they acquire the roman which the public had grown to expect.

Thus the roman script was being used throughout Europe within a century after printing. This triumph of a design artificially made for the lovers of Latin classical texts is less surprising when we remember that Latin was the international language and that the Latin book trade was also international. The extraordinary variety in letter forms must frequently have been a hindrance to the sale of editions abroad, with the result that roman eventually took on the character of a sort of international alphabet. But if it was quickly adopted for the publication of vernacular texts in Italy, and then, after much resistance, in France and Spain, and eventually in England, it never completely won over readers in the Germanic countries. Certainly, Latin texts were printed in roman in Germany, Austria, and the Low Countries, but most vernacular texts continued to be printed in blackletter. In the sixteenth century two kinds of gothic made their appearances and have lasted to the present day: *Umlaut* and *Schwabach*. They were easier for most readers and were taken up in the trade. So Luther, whose first works were printed in roman, reverted to the national type face when he wanted to reach the mass of his compatriots.[21] Thus on the one side we have the Latin world and England, and on the other side the Germanic world where for a long time the majority of works were printed in a different script. At the same time in the Slav countries, printers adopted a different script entirely: Cyrillic, adapted from ancient Greek script.

---

19 Galiot Du Pré (active 1512–60) was a Parisian bookseller and publisher. The *Roman de la Rose* was a tremendously influential Old French vernacular love poem written by two different authors at different times during the thirteenth century. François Villon (1431–c. 1463?) and Alain Chartier (c. 1385–1430) were both important French poets of the Middle Ages.

20 François Rabelais (1494?–1553) was a French writer, physician, and polymath. His *Pantagruel* (1532) and the story of Pantagruel's father, *Gargantua* (1534), recount the comic and often grotesque adventures of their giant-protagonists.

21 Martin Luther (1483–1546) was a German priest and professor of theology, who became the central figure in the Protestant Reformation. Luther was one of the first people to use printed texts systematically to help sway public opinion.

II. Inside the Book: Title Page, Colophon and Printer's Mark

The reader today knows that when he opens a new book he will find on the **title page** the basic information necessary to decide whether to read the book or not: author, title, place of publication, **publisher**, and date. In theory the law insists on this, at least in France.

But in the fifteenth and even the sixteenth century this was not the case. There was no title page in the first books; men had to turn the pages to see what the book contained, and just what it was. As in manuscripts, the text began on the **recto** of the first **leaf**, immediately after a brief form of words giving the subject of the work and occasionally the author's name. At least until the beginning of the sixteenth century, the reader would find most of his information at the end of the book in the "**colophon**," a residue from the manuscript: it was there that he could expect to find the name of the printer, place of publication, perhaps the title, and the name of the author.

However, from the fifteenth century another element appeared, an identifying sign called the printer's mark made with a **woodcut** and included with either **incipit** or colophon. At first it was often simply an outline of the mark printers placed on consignments of books they were sending to customers, originally intended for the convenience of carters. Appearing on a blank **page** at the end of the last gathering or directly above the colophon, it became a species of pictorial publicity not only telling the book's origin but adorning it and affirming its quality. Booksellers and printers had their house sign reproduced as their device and, when the fashion for allegories and **emblems** inspired by antiquity developed with the triumph of humanism, a complicated symbolism grew up. Aldus used an anchor, Kerver a unicorn, Estienne an olive tree, Galiot Du Pré a ship (a galley, after his first name).[22] The mark once relegated to the last page commonly appears on the title page, which became general usage from the end of the fifteenth century.

The story of the title page—its purpose to indicate to the reader the "civil status" of a book—is a curious one and typical of the evolution of the book as a whole. It is instructive inasmuch as it shows us how new ideas emerged which led to new ways of making books easier to use. Since the recto of the first leaf always had a tendency to soil, printers conceived the idea of starting the text on the **verso**, leaving the recto blank. Then, from a quite natural desire to fill in the blank, they printed a short title on it and this helped to identify the book.

It was in this way that the title page made its debut between 1475 and 1480, and its utility soon became obvious. In France, publishers particularly concerned with the appearance of their

---

22 Aldus Manutius, the Elder (1449–1515) and his grandson, Aldus Manutius, the Younger (1547–97) were Italian Renaissance humanists who founded and directed the Aldine Press at Venice. Thielman Kerver (d. c. 1524) was a German-born printer who worked in Paris, mostly producing religious books. Henri Estienne was a printer and bookseller active in Paris from 1502 to 1520; he is sometimes credited with introducing errata slips.

books, Vérard, for example, began to decorate the page with large initials often adorned with grotesque figures. Others put their mark in the blank space beneath the title, or perhaps a woodcut like the one in Alexandre Villedieu's *Doctrinal*, a study book for beginners, showing a teacher and pupils.[23] In other popular booklets, a master key would be shown.

At the end of the fifteenth century nearly all books had title pages, but they were not quite like those of today. Beginning brief, they soon grew to inordinate length, and in the first third of the sixteenth century, in a desire to fill the entire page, publishers tended to embed the title in a long formula, often adding an indication of the principal parts of the book, and some verses of the author and his friends. Publishers also, in their desire for publicity, quickly adopted the habit of printing their name and address at the foot of the page. But it was still necessary to turn to the back of the book and look at the colophon to find more precise information—the name of the printer for example, and the precise date of printing. At the same time, more and more care was taken to decorate the title page. The fashion for **engraved** frames spread. Baldung-Grien[24] was using them in Strasbourg from 1510, for Knobloch, Schott, and then for Grüninger. A little later Holbein designed a large number of frames for Froben in Basel.[25] Then the new style spread to Nuremberg, Augsburg, and to Paris, where Joost Bade reproduced it in a decorative architectural style.[26]

In the German countries and England this fashion for frames persisted for a long time, with the title often drowned in a long formula and surrounded by multiple signs. But the Aldi in Italy, and humanist publishers in France, like Simon de Colines,[27] and the Estienne and de Tournes houses, attempted to clarify the presentation of the title page. From around 1530, the time of the triumph of humanism, more and more new books were to be found with short titles accompanied by only the name of the author and, at the bottom of the page, the publisher's address. Thus, at the same time as roman and italic script began to prevail, the title page gradually assumed its current form.

23 Alexandre Villedieu (or Alexander of Villedieu, c. 1175–c. 1240) was the author of several books, including a versified Latin grammar which became a standard educational text.

24 Hans Baldung Grien (c. 1484–1545) was a German artist and printmaker, who studied printmaking with Albrecht Dürer.

25 Johann Froben (c. 1460–1527) was the patriarch of a line of printers in Basel during the fifteenth and sixteenth centuries. Hans Holbein the Younger (1497 or 1498–1543) was a German printmaker and painter. Holbein was a central figure in the development of woodcuts and borders for title pages.

26 Joost Bade, printer from Lyons who moved to Paris and was active there by 1499.

27 Simon de Colines (1480–1546), was active in Paris between 1520 and 1546. He was known for producing high-quality small-format books.

The replacement of the woodcut by **copper engraving** brought new changes in the title page at the end of the sixteenth century. The title pages of most books looked the same, but it became noticeable, first of all in the large and carefully prepared **folio** editions, and subsequently in volumes of all kinds, that the technique of the framed title page was coming back into favor. Originally the title was often placed in the center of an engraved frame. But this method called for a delicate technique, that of double imposition. In contrast to woodcuts, typeset words of the title could not be printed at the same time as the copper engraving. Besides, the thick black look of the type did not harmonize happily with the elegant thin lines of the engraving. So a technique was soon devised whereby both title and decoration were engraved on the same plate. From then on, the title page became the concern of artists alone, and they were quite naturally inclined to develop the decorative aspect at the expense of the written text. Gradually illustration came to occupy the whole of the page's surface, and the address of the publisher and the date of publication were relegated to a single line at the bottom of the page, while the title was inscribed in the open pages of a book, or on a plinth or draped hangings placed in the center of the page. The engravings after Rubens which Moretus used in his books were like this, as were many others in the first half of the seventeenth century.[28] They seem excessive to our modern eyes, accustomed as we are to more simplicity, and certainly in no other area was the baroque style so excessive as in book decoration. In particular, the design of religious works too often became the pretext for an artist of as great a talent as Rubens to create compositions containing multiple figures, each with allegoric meaning so complicated as to impair the vitality of the ensemble. Simpler work was that of Thomas de Leu in France, or Léonard Gautier, who put the title within the center of an architectural portico. Michel Lasne, who had worked in Antwerp, imitated Rubens but avoided allegories and over-embellished compositions. Soon, in 1640, Poussin,[29] asked to design the publications of the Imprimerie Royale, brought a new approach which caught on immediately and revolutionized design. He went for clarity of outline with just a few figures clothed in antique drapery in a design of wholly classical simplicity. But, as a painter, like Rubens, his first concern was for the unity of his composition and he relegated the title far from the center of the page. In his work, the purely ornamental engraved title became the **frontispiece**, an illustration at the front of the book—which meant publishers had to concentrate bibliographic information on a purely **typographical** page following the frontispiece. From then on, the title page, whose utility was proving indispensable, more or less assumed the form it still has today.

28 Jan Moretus I (1543–1610) succeeded Christopher Plantin in 1589 as the head of the Plantin Press. Sir Peter Paul Rubens (1577–1640) was a Flemish painter and illustrator who designed a number of title pages and illustrations for the press.

29 Nicolas Poussin (1594–1665), French Classical painter who spent most of his life in Italy.

III. The Text and Format of the Book

The move toward a simpler, more uniform product was equally apparent in the appearance of the text. But evolution here, as in every other feature of book production, was a gradual process. To understand what happened, first consider the difficulties confronting scholars and students during the manuscript age. It was impossible to cite page references as we habitually do nowadays, because the leaf **signature** or the page on which the passage was to be found would vary with each manuscript; hence the chapter number or its heading had to be quoted and even the paragraph, and the text often had to be arranged by subparagraphs for ease of reference. Again, books were written in a crabbed hand, full of contractions[30] because of the need to economize with expensive vellum, so that as much as possible was crammed on to a page, with no space between paragraphs or chapters, no headings or page layout. It is easy to see therefore why manuscripts were difficult both to decipher and to consult.

The first printed books were, as we have seen, exactly like manuscripts, with the same general arrangement, the same abbreviations, and the same crabbed writing. Gradually, the lines became more spacious, the script became bigger and the abbreviations less numerous. But the presentation remained almost the same. There is hardly any difference between a manuscript of Aristotle or of *Lancelot* produced between 1480 and 1490 and the same works printed in, say, 1520. Only when public taste gave rise to a new form of literature and roman script came into general use, was the presentation of the text modified.

24 It is characteristic that signatures were first printed in books not for the convenience of readers but to guide the work of artisans in preparing a book, particularly in **binding**, which was a very delicate task in a period when each section to be bound might have an unequal number of leaves, and each **sheet** be inset in a different way. So, to help the **binder**, printers imitated scribes and added a table on which was listed the first word of each gathering or of each double leaf. This table was called the *register*. With the same aim in view they began designating each section with a letter of the alphabet usually printed at the bottom and to the right of the sheet. The letters were followed by a number, to show the sequence of the leaves (the "signature"). Probably for the same reason they began numbering the leaves (it is noteworthy that the earliest pagination has no signatures and vice versa). Be that as it may, the practice of showing the sequence of the leaves was slow to develop. Many books were not paginated as late as the beginning of the sixteenth century and what pagination there was was often faulty. It took even longer before books were no longer numbered by the leaf but, as today, by the page. Perhaps the first example of pagination is Aldus's edition of the *Cornucopia* of Perotti (1499); but it became common only in the second quarter of the sixteenth century, thanks mainly to humanist printers.

From then on, the book began to have a contemporary look. A triumphant humanism had imposed the use of roman type, which was usually larger and so more readable than gothic script. More and more texts were set across the page in one long line, not in double columns. At the same time, lines became more spacious, attempts were made to achieve greater clarity, and

30 Shortened forms of words, such as "wch" for "which" or "dr." for "doctor."

chapter headings were more clearly demarcated through use of white space. Gradually the book assumed its modern appearance.

As printed texts multiplied the book ceased to be a precious object consulted in a **library**. People wished to take a book with them and to be able to transport it easily, to read or consult at any time; hence the growing success of the "portable format" which also dates from the first half of the sixteenth century. In addition to the more traditional readers drawn from the clergy, students, and the upper classes, the bourgeoisie began to form their own libraries. **Quarto** and **octavo** books, though common enough in the fifteenth century, were only for short texts too slight to publish in **folio**. Books intended for the pulpit were of large **format**. In fact the main books which systematically used small formats in this period were devotional works, especially Books of Hours.[31] For these books, which were in constant use and already intended for a large market, had to be easily transportable. Another literature produced in small format and intended for an even larger market, was that of popular tales, known from their shape as "plaquettes gothiques."[32]

But from the end of the fifteenth century, anxious to ease the reading of classical authors, the Aldi launched their famous "portable" collection.[33] Taken up by the small humanist readership, this format was adopted increasingly at the beginning of the sixteenth century. In Paris, for example, Simon de Colines started a series like the Aldines, which found many imitators, particularly at Lyons where Venetian models were regularly copied. Soon new literary works were systematically published in small format, easy to handle and consult. If the old romances of chivalry continued to appear in folio and quarto, the Latin poems of the humanists, the works of Marot, of Rabelais, and of Marguerite of Navarre and the group of poets known as the Pléiade all came out in small format.[34] It was in this form that Erasmus' *Adages* spread through Europe, and this too was the form used for the innumerable **pamphlets** in which Luther and the reformers diffused their ideas. Books with illustrations were often like this as well. Holbein in 1540 drew little vignettes for a 4to [quarto] and 8vo [octavo] edition of *Images de la Bible* and *Simulacres de la Mort* which had an enormous success. De Tournes at Lyons and Denis Janot[35] in Paris and printers elsewhere published editions of *Figures de la Bible* and the *Emblems* of Alciat or Ovid's *Metamorphoses*.

31 Books of Hours were volumes containing prayers and devotions to be said at different times throughout the day.

32 I.e., small popular books, easily carried in a pocket, similar to English "chapbooks."

33 The Aldine Press published versions of classical texts in inexpensive small format books bound in vellum.

34 Clément Marot (1496–1544) was a French Protestant poet of the Renaissance. Marguerite de Navarre (1492–1549) was a humanist writer and patron of Reformers such as Marot. The Pléiade, led by Pierre de Ronsard (1524–85), was a group of seven poets who played a key role in preparing the basis for modern poetry in France.

35 Jean de Tournes (1504–64) was a printer and bookseller in Lyon; from 1559 he was printer to the French king. Denis (or Denys) Janot (fl. 1529–44) was a printer and bookseller from Paris known for producing books in the vernacular.

For students and scholars however the folio was still preferred, since although it was more difficult to handle, it was more legible and it was an easier form in which to trace references.

Thus the book trade in this period was, more than anything, characterized by the division between ponderous, learned tomes intended for use in libraries, and small size literary or polemical works for a larger public. Such a contrast continued to dominate the history of the book in the seventeenth century. The period 1600 to 1650, the age of the Counter-Reformation, was one in which France was covered with monasteries which were also libraries, in which Protestant theologians fought a battle of erudition with the Jesuits, and in which lawyers, imitating the ecclesiastics, collected great libraries of religious works. The bourgeois classes, apparently, lost the taste for reading they had possessed in the sixteenth century. Great editions of the sacred texts, and of the Church Fathers, official records of the Great Councils, and treatises on canon law enjoyed a revival and large editions in folio multiplied. But for short works in French, quarto was preferred because it was more readable, although less portable, than octavo editions. The trend was clear. When, for example, the Elzeviers, cut off from their main suppliers of paper by the Wars, adopted for their editions of classical authors a small format, the famous 12mos [**duodecimos**], of minute type to conserve stocks, their scholarly readership began to complain. In the second half of the seventeenth century by contrast, a public for imaginative literature was growing again. Novels and works of popularization multiplied and economic conditions did not favor the publication of costly works of reference. These were the reasons for the renewed success of the small format. Similarly, in the eighteenth century the folio was hardly used at all except for works of permanent value like dictionaries and encyclopedias. The types of book which were customarily published in quarto or octavo—novels, literary works, popular science and polemic, and editions of Latin and Greek authors—now represented the great bulk of book production.

IV. Illustration

Manuscripts were often decorated with miniatures;[36] they would be found for example in Books of Hours, missals,[37] devotional works, romances of chivalry, and treatises on hunting. But, even more than ordinary manuscripts, illuminated manuscripts, copied by the cleverest **calligraphers** and illuminated sometimes by famous painters, were only within the reach of the privileged—nobles, both lay and spiritual, and rich merchants. Here again, the invention of printing did not cause any immediate transformation. Illuminators and miniaturists continued to work after printing began—think, for example, of the *Hours* of Anne of Brittany, of Bourdichon, who died in 1521, or again of Columba. Editors who specialized in the luxury book trade, like Vérard, when they wished to sell a book capable of rivaling luxury manuscripts, had the text illustrated by the same painters who illuminated the manuscripts. But the method was too costly and time-consuming, except perhaps for a few dedicatory copies printed on vellum for important people. When the need came to supply illustrations for the hundreds of copies of the same book—when

36 A small picture painted in a manuscript.

37 A book containing the liturgy and other necessary texts for celebrating the mass.

books became "democratized" as it were—other means were essential. Mechanical reproduction of texts meant a corresponding method of reproducing pictures.

One method, xylography,[38] had been in common use and applied in standardized production before printed books had appeared. From the end of the fourteenth century block-prints began to multiply and the xylography industry was fully developed by the time that the printing industry began. A woodcut was easily inserted in a **forme** alongside the text, and simultaneous printing of picture and text presented no difficulties, so the convention was quickly adopted. In 1461 Albrecht Pfister[39] of Bamberg conceived the idea of illustrating several books in this way; one of them was a small collection of popular fables by Ulrich Boner, the *Edelstein* (precious stone). In this first illustrated book, the simple figures in line without shadow, afterwards quickly colored in wash, primitive though they might be, were not without charm, and would have seemed quite natural to a public used to seeing block-prints. Soon Günther Zainer[40] was turning out illustrated books at Augsburg, popular works and devotional books, while Pfister continued to print stories illustrated with cuts,[41] such as the so-called *Four Stories* (the tales of Daniel, Joseph, Judith, and Esther). The same process was used by Ulrich Zell at Ulm and many other printers in other German towns. As in block-printing itself, the purpose of the cuts was always to amplify the text and make it concretely real, not to produce a work of art.

[...]

Thus, in the great publishing centers, schools of illustrators began to grow up, often influenced by local styles of painting and illumination, and by the monumental architecture under their eyes. Each regional school acquired its own manner, its personal language, and began to specialize. In Florence, for example, printers above all illustrated popular books designed for a local clientele. In the big commercial cities like Venice and Lyons on the other hand, printing was largely for export, and printers concentrated on illustrated Bibles and Church books. [...]

While each school had a manner and language of its own, external influences continued to be felt. Every illustrated book, even the less important ones, was known throughout Europe and often imitated. Koberger's Nuremberg Chronicle was copied by Schönsperger[42] at Augsburg in 1496, 1497, and 1500. The blocks for the Basel edition of Sebastian Brandt's *Ship of Fools* (1494) served as a model for Parisian engravers (1497) and Lyonnese (1490s). The artists who copied them did try to bring off original versions. For instance one of the most famous Parisian illustrated books in the Renaissance, the *Hypnerotomachia Poliphili,* was only an adaptation

38 Printing pictures from carved blocks of wood.

39 Albrecht Pfister (c. 1420–c. 1466) was an early German printer. Little is known about his life, but he is usually thought to be the first printer to print woodcuts alongside letterpress text.

40 Günther Zainer (d. 1478) was active in Augsburg from 1468; he printed about 80 books, including two German editions of the Bible.

41 Woodcuts, made by incising the end of a block of wood, inking it, and printing it to produce an image.

42 Johann Schönsperger the Elder (c. 1455–1521) was a printer and publisher in Augsburg, Germany.

of an edition by Aldus which had appeared fifty years earlier at Venice. But the blocks for the Paris book were cut in a very different spirit from those of the Italian model: the adaptation to French taste comes out in a search for affectation. Often, however, in the hands of less skilled or practiced cutters, or perhaps simply under pressure, the copy became a simple **plagiarism.** If Venetian engravers of the fifteenth century could assimilate the twofold influence of France and Germany, this was no longer the case in the sixteenth century when they were busy with orders from printers for the export market and contented themselves with hackneyed copies of foreign models without any effort at originality.

In each center the styles of other, foreign, cities were evident and quite often the blocks used in one place came from another. Often publishers with shops in a number of different towns would proceed in this way. Conrad Resch, with branches in Basel and Paris, used blocks cut in Basel to illustrate books he published in Paris. Likewise some publishers would often ask their foreign colleagues to have the blocks they needed cut by a local artist of repute. Urs Graf, for example, the famous Basel artist working as an illustrator for Froben, occasionally worked for Matthias Schürer and Hupfuff of Strasbourg, and for Anshelm of Haguenau, Pierre Vidoue and Conrad Resch of Paris.

[...]

Originally we saw that the illustrated book, successor to the block book,[43] had the same aim and
28 the same clientele. It was intended to edify a huge public that could hardly read, to explain the text through the medium of pictures, to make real and comprehensible the different episodes in the life of Christ, the prophets, and the saints, and to give some reality to the demons and angels who disputed for the souls of sinners, and also to the mythical and legendary personalities familiar to the men in that age. Such was the aim of xylographs and such was the aim of the first illustrated books. It was not surprising therefore that the most popular illustrated books in the fifteenth century were works of devotion, pious and moralizing, usually in the vernacular. To judge by the **catalogues** of incunabula, the most frequently reprinted illustrated books of the fifteenth century in France and Germany were stories of the Passion and Life of Christ, stories of Satan like the *Bélial* of Jacques de Théramo,[44] the *Mirror of the Redemption*, and others like the *Speculum humanae vitae*,[45] the *Art de bien mourir et celui de bien vivre*,[46] the *Golden Legend* of Jacques de Voragine,[47] the *Story of the Bible*, the *Shepherds' Calendar*, and the innumerable

43 Block books are short books printed entirely from wood blocks. The minimal text and the images are both cut into the wood block, rather than the text being printed using moveable type.

44 Jacques (or Jacobus) de Théramo wrote a tract around 1382 that dramatized a lawsuit between Lucifer and Jesus: in part of the text the demon Belial represented Lucifer in court. The work was often reprinted (including under the title *Belial*), but was censured by the Catholic Church.

45 Mirror of Human Life (Latin).

46 The Art of Dying Well and that of Living Well (French).

47 Jacobus de Varagine or Voragine (c. 1230–98) was an Italian chronicler and archbishop of Genoa. His book *The Golden Legend* is a collection of legendary saints' lives.

popular and moralizing fables attributed to Aesop, Bidpay, and Cato. Book illustration answered a practical rather than an artistic need: to make graphic and visible what people of the time constantly heard evoked. There is no subtle variation of light and shade, or of tone; just a few simple figures cut with clear and obvious features.

[...]

Certainly, the first humanists, especially those of the late fifteenth and early sixteenth centuries, scholars before all else, showed as much disdain for illustrated books as the theologians of the Sorbonne. Wasn't an illustration merely a simple way to instruct those who were too ignorant to read the text? Thus scenes intended to illustrate the translations of Terence[48] and Ovid—intended, that is, for a public they scorned—could only cause them pain, especially as they were drawn by artists with little concern for archaeology, and for readers who knew nothing about Antiquity, who would be quite happy if the characters of Terence were depicted wearing fifteenth-century dress. Even when Aldus published his *Hypnerotomachia Poliphili,* which was more in line with classical feeling, the humanists seemed to have held aloof from this magnificent edition and it was not reprinted in Venice.

[...]

By 1550 the book trade was beginning to feel the effect of the rise in prices affecting the European economy: the crisis which was to characterize the second half of the sixteenth century was under way. From that time on the illustrated book made little advance. The work of the engravers seems careless and hurried, and they tend more and more just to turn out poor copies of earlier illustrations. Fewer pictures were published and when publishing revived at the end of the century wood was no longer the medium, but copper. This was a change in technique which represented a new intellectual climate and we must consider its implications. Copperplate engraving was already well known since the fifteenth century and had been perfected (like printing) by goldsmiths. It allowed a more faithful rendering of light and shade, lines of greater subtlety were possible, and it had always been preferred by painters. From the end of the fifteenth century Italians like d'Andrea and Germans like Schongauer[49] had brought the technique to perfection. Attempts had also sometimes been made to apply the technique to printed books; but they had not been too successful, because of a technical obstacle. In the case of woodcuts it was possible both to place the cut and the typographic composition in the forme, to ink them in the same way and to print both text and illustration at the same time, but engraving meant separate printing of the copper plate, a costly and delicate matter if it was to harmonize with type.

---

48 Terence (Publius Terentius Afer, 195/185–159 BCE) was a Roman dramatist. His comedies were performed for the first time around 170–160 BCE.

49 Martin Schongauer (c. 1440–91) was a German engraver and painter.

For a long time, as long as the public only wanted pictures which helped its efforts at imagination, woodcuts, however worn and lifeless, were preferred to copper engraving. But things were changing by about 1600. It must be remembered that the sixteenth century had been an age of painters. The taste for painting had spread across Europe. Rich merchants in Paris and Lyons, patrician families in Venice and Antwerp had their portraits done, and ordered from a growing number of painters canvasses no longer intended to decorate the walls of churches, but those of their own homes. At the same time, painters became engravers and less wealthy people kept copper engravings as their "poor man's picture gallery." Mantegna in Italy and Dürer in Germany[50] made plates that were an immediate success and have remained famous. In France, copper engravers were most often originally goldsmiths and worked in isolation until the Italians, Primaticcio and Il Rosso, came to decorate the chateau of Fontainebleau. A school of copper engravers formed around Fontainebleau and their aim was to spread the new Italian style of decoration in France. The traditional woodcut seemed coarse compared with these copper engravings. Copper already seemed perfect for rendering architecture, classical monuments, or an exact likeness of the face. Soon, despite the technical difficulties, copper was increasingly used in book illustration. At first it was used only in exceptional cases to illustrate technical works or volumes studded with portraits, but gradually it extended to books of all kinds.

[...]

30 From the end of the sixteenth century onwards the woodcut declined and almost disappeared as a form of book illustration, outside of hawkers' literature. In fact it practically disappeared altogether. Copper began its long reign of more than 200 years, and this was no merely technical change. The technique triumphed because of its powers of minutely accurate representation. As a means of communication conveying a realistic image and a permanent record it was unrivalled. The print became increasingly analogous in its diffusion of pictorial fact to the book in its diffusion of typographic fact. Thus the adoption of copper and the international trade in prints at the end of the sixteenth and beginning of the seventeenth centuries helped to widen men's horizons. We need only mention as an example the monumental collection of travels by Thomas de Bry in the early seventeenth century which imparted a sometimes erroneous but always precise idea of the world, from Lapland to Brazil, through the medium of copper engravings.[51] And we should not forget the enormous work accomplished in one particular domain—mapmaking—by the Dutch publishers of the seventeenth century.

Books of engravings became collectors' pieces, and, increasingly, merchants and even humbler people, too poor to possess paintings, adorned the walls of their houses with prints: no longer

---

50 Andrea Mantegna (c. 1431–1506) was an Italian painter and engraver. Although respected as an engraver he almost never signed his engravings. Albrecht Dürer (1471–1528) was a German painter, engraver, and printmaker, acknowledged as one of the masters of the engraver's art.

51 Theodorus de Bry (1528–98) published a number of illustrated travel books collecting and illustrating the observations of other explorers.

crude woodcuts, but copper engravings which depicted, faithfully and in detail—and therefore with a greater appearance of reality—religious or historical subjects or different aspects of everyday life.

If there was a call to commemorate an important event which had captured the imagination, a victorious battle for example, the coronation of a king, or fêtes, ballets and spectacles given by a prince; if one wished to know the likeness of a great man; if a man of letters or a rich merchant wished to circulate his portrait to friends or correspondents; if one wished to preserve the memory of a picturesque scene in the street—the engraver was there to do it. Much more so than the painter, since prints could be reproduced. He was the photographer of his day. [...]

The print also played its critical part in the diffusion of works of art. From the seventeenth century, thanks to the engraving, most people were acquainted with the masterpieces of art scattered throughout Europe. A host of engravers from every country devoted themselves to reproducing the paintings, monuments, and ruins of Italy. Engravers were often also commissioned to reproduce the paintings of the great masters of their native country in their own day. Nanteuil and Morin, for example, produced prints after the portraits of Philippe de Champaigne[52] and that portrait painter owed much of his contemporary fame to them. Rubens was well aware of the value of having his works made more widely known through this medium and established an atelier for engravers to turn out prints of his pictures. Henceforth, living in the neighborhood of the shops of the big printsellers like Mariette of Paris, engravers reproduced the works of the great Italian, Flemish, French, or German masters. Everyone could examine them and compare them at their leisure. From then on, it was engravers who made known and diffused ornamental styles.

The engraving was thus an essential medium of information in the seventeenth century. In the midst of these transformations, the illustrated book lost some of its interest. Forced as they were by economic difficulties to cut costs, publishers confined illustrations to a few plates which could be separated from the text, or to a frontispiece, to avoid the extra expense of double imposition necessary to secure an impression from a copper engraving and letterpress on the same page. [...] With them the divorce between text and image became so marked that by the end of the seventeenth century it was enough to call a book "illustrated" if a picture of the author was inside. In the classical period[53] there were very few real book illustrators.

In the eighteenth century circumstances were different again. Economic conditions evolved further, publishers were once more concerned about the quality of their products and vignettes reappeared in the midst of printed pages. Once more, there was a public keenly interested in illustrated books. But times had changed since the fifteenth and sixteenth centuries when illustrated books had been destined for a vast public. The new eighteenth century demand was in the luxury market and came from the aristocracy of wealth, bankers and financiers who,

52 Philippe de Champaigne (1602–74), French painter who produced mostly portraits and religious works. Robert Nanteuil (1623 or 1630–78) and Jean Morin (1590–1650) were both engravers based in Paris, and were at one time assistants to and students of Philippe de Champaigne.

53 French designation for the period extending roughly from the mid-sixteenth century to the late eighteenth.

proud of their recently acquired fortunes, wished to start a library of their own. Having no inclination for serious works which bored them, they turned bibliophiles with a taste for sumptuously decorated books. [...] But the illustrated book represented only an insignificant proportion of printed output and reached only a small part of the public, one comparable to the contemporary market for bibliophile productions and limited editions of art books. At this period, therefore, the illustrated book would be of small interest to this study had it not been for the great technical skill applied by engravers to the scientific and technical works of the period in providing illustrations essential to the comprehension of the text. In the age of the "philosophes"[54] these books were numerous and of particular importance. Buffon's work, and of course the huge enterprise of the *Encyclopédie*, could not have been conceived without the aid of detailed and precise copper engraving which brought to life the many technical articles.[55] Nor could the accounts of explorations, which became increasingly numerous in the time of Cook and La Perouse[56] and which were accompanied by prints, faithfully reproducing sketches made on the expeditions.

V. Clothing the Book: The Binding

When we examine the old bindings preserved, often in pristine condition, on manuscripts and books printed in any period up to the nineteenth century one thing strikes us right away: the bindings which cover even quite ordinary books are strong and infinitely better in quality than those which do service today. To take an actual example—the books in the old Bibliothèque Royale, now the Bibliothèque Nationale, were bound in the seventeenth century with red morocco[57] using gold tooling, and emblazoned with the royal arms. Today most books received by the Bibliothèque Nationale are only bound in cloth.

There is no reason to be surprised by this care for solidity, and the quality of materials used in binding, which arouses admiration in the trade today. At that time a manuscript or its successor, a printed book, was so comparatively rare and costly an item of merchandise that it merited care in its preservation and adornment. From the invention of printing right up to the eighteenth century, although the readership increased, the book was still the preserve of a small and favored elite. In days when paper was made by hand and books printed on **hand presses,** the book was still seen as a precious object, which it was important to preserve, and therefore had to be bound carefully.

54 French philosophers of the Enlightenment, active in the second half of the eighteenth century, immediately before the French Revolution.

55 The natural histories of Georges-Louis Leclerc de Buffon (1708–88) and the *Encyclopédie*—the great repository of knowledge spearheaded by *philosophes* Denis Diderot (1713–84) and Jean le Rond d'Alembert (1717–83)—included numerous highly detailed engravings. The *Encyclopédie* included 11 volumes of plates alone.

56 Captain James Cook (1728–79) and Jean-François de Galaup, Comte de la Perouse (1741–88?), naval explorers.

57 Tanned goat skin, dyed in different colors and used for binding high-quality books.

What were the distinctive features of bindings between the fifteenth and eighteenth centuries? That is, commercial bindings: it is not our intention to discuss luxury bindings, art objects destined for a small circle of princes and bibliophiles. How did binders, between the fifteenth and eighteenth centuries, adapt their technique to cope with growing numbers of books? What consequences did increased output have on the quality and the appearance of bindings? These are the main questions we want to answer here.

Again, the coming of printing produced no sudden revolutionary upheaval. The same craftsmen who bound manuscripts applied their skill in the same way to books. They continued to cover the back and the boards, made of solid wood, with precious fabrics like velvet, silk, cloth of gold, if binding luxury editions destined for important people. Otherwise they used leather—tanned calf, sheepskin, and in Germany also pigskin. Then with their finishing tools they impressed designs often in repeated patterns made with fillets or roulettes, sometimes "blind" (i.e., without gold leaf) and sometimes "tooled" (with gold leaf). Styles varied from area to area and subjects and motifs were of infinite variety: *fleurs de lys*, eagles with one or two heads, animals of all kinds, real or imaginary, lions and griffins, dragons and greyhounds, coats of arms, the four evangelists, streamers and inscriptions, sometimes just the simple monograph IHS, the pascal lamb, a picture of a saint, the cross, or the head of Christ.

There is no immediate change in appearance between the manuscript books of the early fifteenth century and the first incunabula up to about the year 1480. They continued to be bound in heavy, solid bindings with metal clasps, their covers studded with nails for protection (books were stored flat or kept on desks). Many were bound in monasteries, in binding workshops, situated in the proximity of the copyists. Others were the products of private workshops, whose binders worked in liaison with copyists serving the secular market, in particular the stationers near the universities.

From around 1480 the consequences of printing began to be felt. The printed book multiplied and its use became more common. Private individuals developed libraries of their own and books ceased to be a purely monastic possession. Monastic **binderies** diminished in importance while the private binders grew more affluent, especially in university towns where they were assured of finding a clientele. Most often they set up near stationers, or were stationers themselves as well as publishers. Big publishers like the Kobergers owned binderies equipped to carry out mass production. But it must be stressed that books were not bound as part of the normal publishing process as they are now. Only a few copies of a work could expect to be sold in any one town, and many printers had agents in all parts of Europe selling books for them. Since binding was heavy and expensive and transport costs were high, books were sent in unbound sheets from one town to the next in barrels. A few were bound as they were bought, but inventories show that only a small number of copies were bound in the shop, most of the edition being stored in sheets since the buyer preferred to buy it thus and have it bound to his taste later. Unaware of this situation, historians of binding have until recently tended to assume that books were generally bound in the towns where they had been printed.

When, however, the press began to turn out many more books, binders had to adapt their methods to respond to new demands. Work had to be done more rapidly, and **serial production** was necessary to make bindings of suitable but less ponderous quality to satisfy a larger and less wealthy clientele. Printing encouraged the growth of the paper trade and this increased the number of waste sheets; so began the habit of using "cardboard" for covers in place of wooden boards. It was cheaper and not as heavy, made by pasting several sheets together which toughened them. Paper of all kinds was used—old **proof** sheets, old books used as scrap, letters, business files, **archives.** The dismantling of old bindings often brings interesting finds to light.

The decoration of covers, too, had to be done more quickly and at less cost. By using ornamental plates instead of decorating the whole surface with tiny fillets[58] repeated over and over again, which was laborious and demanded great care, they achieved an impressive effect and saved time. A whole scene could be impressed at once on to the cover with the iron. In France, for example, these plates reproduced scenes from the Old and New Testament, preferably those which figured in the Book of Hours or the images of saints. Most of the subjects chosen had a pious intention, even if the content of the book was not religious. Otherwise, plates were used to impress personal devices of booksellers, or, lastly, for pure decoration. In Flanders, the plates showed a taste for animals and miniatures, and in the Germanic countries, somewhat later, allegorical and mythological subjects inspired by the Renaissance were often used.

In the first years of the sixteenth century, there was another change. Confronted by the incessant increase of books, binders, always on the lookout for a more rapid method which would economize labor and reduce the cost of their products, developed a different technique, that of the roulette. The roulette was a tiny metal wheel, on which was engraved a simple, repeatable motif. By this means it became possible to decorate bindings with a series of rapidly executed headbands. Sometimes the plate system and the roulette system were used simultaneously. This meant that the centerpiece of a cover could be decorated with a figure and the surrounds run off with the roulette.

Such was the appearance of commercial bindings in the first third of the sixteenth century. Meanwhile, new processes were introduced into the making of luxury bindings. Copies made for princes had traditionally been bound in cloth, because skins could not be prepared finely enough for the purpose so long as only the "cold" process of **stamping** was known. The situation changed, however, when morocco leather and the technique of gold tooling were introduced into Europe from the Islamic world. From the close of the fifteenth century morocco from Cordova was imported into Naples via the Balearics, and Levant morocco came to Venice via Constantinople. From about that time, Aldus used it in Venice but it was not used in France until the middle of the sixteenth century. Meanwhile, gold tooling, which had long been known in the East, was also adopted by the Italians. It was in use at Naples in 1475 to decorate bindings for King Ferdinand of Aragon, by applying heated irons to thin gold or silver leaf. By 1500 the Venetians were following this example. Aldus, who had just founded a workshop specializing in Greek typography, did more than anyone to promote the fashion for gold tooling in Eastern motifs which spread to Northern Italy, so that when the French invaded Italy they too developed a taste for gorgeous decoration. The Kings of France, and also the famous Grolier, who

---

58 "A plain line impressed upon the cover of a book. Also, a rolling tool used for impressing the line" (*OED*).

was treasurer of Milan, had work carried out for them in Italian binderies and brought the new technique to France. In the second third of the sixteenth century, French artists surpassed their Italian masters, using polychrome mosaics, interlacings, and fleurons painted with resins, or, for more somber bindings, pure geometric designs in Renaissance style. These bindings are unequalled in the perfection of their technique, but we shall not discuss them further since they were confined to Kings and to a small number of very rich bibliophiles.

At the same time, the semi-luxury binding appeared, the technique of hot-stamping being applied to commercial bindings. From 1520 it was used for plate work as in Geoffroy Tory's famous "pot cassé" or broken urn.[59] Plates decorated with filets[60] and interlacing were sometimes used to make more economical bindings in imitation of the roulette method. Sometimes a motif—the mark of a bookseller or the bust of a character—is placed in the center. Finally, until the end of the sixteenth century, particularly in religious books, an oval-shaped central motif was impressed with a die stamp. But all such methods were costly and time consuming and gradually simple calf bindings appear without decoration. When worsening economic conditions led to a demand for the lowest possible prices less valuable books began to be bound in vellum and even prelates like Cardinal Charles de Bourbon were satisfied with bindings of morocco decorated only with borders of gold fillets.

During the seventeenth and eighteenth centuries calf binding was the norm, with a plain gold-filleted border. Morocco was used for more elegant books. When books belonged to a great nobleman or private collector he would often have his arms struck on the center of the covers. Bibliophiles however continued to have gold decorated bindings "au petit fer"[61] made in the seventeenth century. Then, when bibliophile tastes developed in the eighteenth century, luxury binding in France received a new impulse: mosaic designs were made for Philippe d'Orléans the Regent and his court around 1720; decorated polychrome bindings inspired by Chinese art came into fashion, and especially popular were bindings "à la dentelle,"[62] the surrounds of the plates being gilded by the application of a hot iron frame decorated in a lacework motif. This was the age when Pasdeloup, Monnier, and Derôme[63] worked on illustrated luxury orders, vied for by the public. But, once again, these bindings, like the books they covered, were destined for a small and privileged market. The average mass-produced binding was a perfunctory product. From the end of the seventeenth century, simple marbled paper was sometimes used for small books and for the increasing number of journals.

So if we compare bindings on ordinary books from the fifteenth to the eighteenth centuries we find that when the clientele was small (in the fifteenth and early sixteenth centuries) binders

59 Geoffroy Tory (c. 1480–c. 1533), a Parisian printer, produced a fine Book of Hours in 1531, including his printer's mark of an urn pierced by a spear.

60 "A kind of net or lace having a square mesh" (*OED*).

61 I.e., using the hot-stamping process (literally "with the little fire" [French]).

62 French: in the lace style.

63 All bookbinders working on fine bindings for rich clients. A number of members of the Pasdeloup and Derôme families worked in bookbinding over several generations.

still decorated even "trade" books. But as in the course of the sixteenth century book production increased, editions proliferated and the book reached a larger public, binders sought techniques which would enable them to bind suitably decorated books more rapidly. Soon they had to stop decorating the covers of commercial bindings. While the art of luxury binding enjoyed a boom in the middle of the sixteenth century and then again in the eighteenth century, the average book, although durably bound, no longer had any cover decoration. Since books were now stored upright and pushed up closely against one another to save space, only the spine which was to be seen on the shelves of libraries bore any tooling: usually some decorative motifs and a stamped title. With the steam press and papermaking machinery of the nineteenth century, books were printed more cheaply and quickly in larger editions, and binding was often abandoned in favor of a simple stitched cover. In a word, with the growth in production of books and the increase in the reading public, the average binding gradually shed first its beauty and then its solidity.

3.
Michael Twyman, "What Is Printing?" *The British Library Guide to Printing.* London: British Library, 1998. 8–17

Michael Twyman (b. 1934) was one of the founders of the Department of Typography and Graphic Communications at the University of Reading, the first department of its kind in the world, and a founding member of the Printing Historical Society, and is now Professor Emeritus in the department. He has written extensively on typography and the history of printing, and is the leading historian of lithography. In this extract, from his illustrated *British Library Guide to Printing* (1998), he explains in layman's terms some of the processes of printing and how they have changed over time. Twyman particularly draws attention to the three kinds of printing process: relief, intaglio, and planographic. He outlines the differences between printing text and printing images and examines different stages of the printing process. As he shows, for much of printing's history, it has been difficult to combine printed text and printed images on the same page, because most methods for printing text use relief printing, and most methods for printing high-quality images use intaglio printing. Finally, he draws attention to the wide range of things that are printed, reminding us that over half of most printers' output did not consist of books, but of a very wide range of "job printing" and ephemera.

What Is Printing?

Printing can be described as a means of giving form to and multiplying graphic signs and messages. Before printing was invented such things would have been produced singly by drawing and writing; today, they may well be generated entirely by electronic means. The extraordinary social, artistic, and intellectual impact printing has had derives to a large degree from its technical appropriateness and adaptability. The ideas that lie at the heart of printing have simply been modified over the years in response to major technological shifts from hand to machine and then electronic production.

It may be helpful to define two distinct stages in what we call printing: origination and multiplication. These terms are not sacrosanct, and in electronic production may not be easily differentiated. Nevertheless, it is important to consider them separately when discussing the history of printing because, at certain points in time, major advances were made in the one and not in the other.

I. Origination

The word origination is used here to describe the organization and production of the marks to be printed; it applies to marks cut by hand, made photomechanically, and controlled by computers. The word commonly used for this stage of printing today is pre-press. Both terms cover the arrangement of words in linear strings (as in the text pages of books) and when displayed (as in most advertising); they also cover the use of pictorial, decorative, and other non-verbal material.

What is usually referred to as the invention of printing relates to a set of advances made at the origination stage. This was the contribution of Johann **Gutenberg** (1390s–1468) in Germany in the mid-fifteenth century, and it involved the replication of separate reusable letters and their arrangement in rows. This was a highly significant step in the advance of printing because it allowed for corrections to be made relatively easily and in a seamless way. It has also strongly influenced our interpretation of the word printing. All the same, there are artifacts that we rightly describe as printed which owe little if anything to Gutenberg's invention in terms of origination. They include numerous books and prints made in the Far East several hundred years earlier, in addition to present-day work as diverse as wrapping paper and reproductions of paintings.

At one end of the origination spectrum of printing lie images that can be made directly by hand: that is, they are cut or otherwise produced on a printing surface, such as wood or metal, by the person who designed them. At the other end lie drawn or written marks that are turned into printable form by someone else (for example, by a **compositor** using pre-manufactured pieces of metal type, or specialist engravers working manually on a physical surface from someone else's originals). In the nineteenth century certain kinds of work that started life as marks made by an artist or letterer on paper were later transferred, without alteration, to the printing surface; these methods can be seen as falling somewhere near the middle of the origination spectrum.

For centuries, all printing surfaces could be fitted into a binary classification: **relief** and **intaglio.** In relief printing the marks to be printed stand higher than the non-printing parts; in intaglio printing the opposite is the case and it is the hollow parts of the surface that produce the printed marks. Printing from metal type and wood blocks fall into the first category; printing from **engraved** or etched copper plates and the associated tonal processes of mezzotint and aquatint[1] into the second. This simple classification began to be challenged when **lithography** was invented in Bavaria by Alois Senefelder (1771–1834) in or around 1798. Unlike the two older branches of printing, which depend on physical differences in relief to determine the printing and non-printing areas, lithography rests on chemical principles. Lithographic printing surfaces are to all intents and purposes on the same level, which explains why this third category of printing has come to be described as **planographic.**

1 Mezzotint involves roughening the surface of the plate with a metal tool with small teeth, called a rocker. Aquatint involves using acid-resistant resins to cause the acid to eat into the plate at different rates. Both techniques produce shading effects not available in simple engraving.

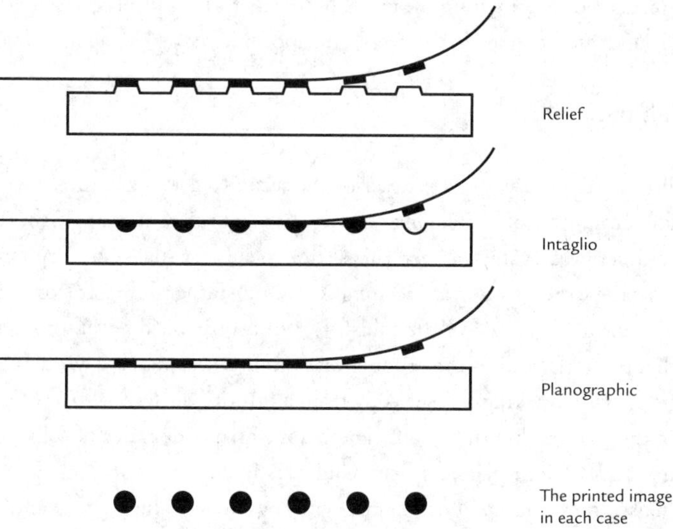

Fig. 1.1: Diagram showing the main categories of printing: relief, intaglio, and planographic. In each case a piece of paper is shown being removed from the inked-up printing surface. Nearly all printing surfaces were flat before the middle of the nineteenth century; thereafter they were frequently cylindrical. Reprinted with the permission of Michael Twyman.

By the beginning of the nineteenth century, therefore, the binary classification of printing had turned into a tripartite one: relief, intaglio, and planographic (Fig. 1.1). This remains the orthodox way of classifying printing processes generically, though by the middle of the nineteenth century so many different forms of printing had been tried that it was beginning to become a little shaky. For example, William Stannard, who compiled a compendium of printing processes called *The Art Exemplar*, which he published in just 10 copies around 1859, described and illustrated as many as 156 printing methods, some of which do not fit very neatly into the tripartite model. In recent years too the model has become a little frayed at the edges with the introduction of output devices used in conjunction with computers. Nevertheless, the tripartite model, which was first advanced by the inventor of lithography in the early nineteenth century, still provides a convenient one for considering the origination and multiplication stages of printing in relation to both hand and machine production.

Before the nineteenth century all printing involved the lateral reversal of images. This meant that words and other material designed for printing had to be made the wrong way round: the letters on metal type were produced back to front (Fig. 1.2), and so too were images on wood blocks, intaglio plates, and, later, lithographic stones. This was an inescapable problem until two nineteenth-century developments provided a solution to it at the origination stage: first transfer lithography, and then, from the middle of the century, the application of photography to printing processes. Later the problem was solved at the multiplication stage by offsetting the image on to an intermediate cylinder within the press. In this method of printing the image started life the right way round, was reversed in the press, and appeared the right way round when printed.

II. Multiplication

The word multiplication is used here to describe the second stage of printing, the production of more or less identical copies of an item in the form of a print **run.** Confusingly, the word printing is also used to describe this stage alone. This seems to suggest that—in common language at least—we accept the word printing as meaning something rather different from what we credit Gutenberg with having invented in the mid-fifteenth century. Moreover, though we have an expectation that printing involves the production of multiple copies, the word can also be used to describe the activity of taking a single copy from a printing surface.

Printing in the sense of multiplication can be done on a wide range of substrates and with different kinds of inks. Cloth, glass, leather, metal, plastic, and wood are among those materials that have been used for printing. But from its beginnings in both the Far East and Europe printing of all kinds found a natural ally in paper. Paper consists primarily of vegetable fiber and is

Fig. 1.2: A form of type that is type locked up in a metal frame (chase) and ready for printing. The letters are back to front and the lines read from right to left. The pages of type are separated by spacing material made of wood (furniture) and made secure by pairs of wedges (quoins), which apply pressure sideways. To the right are a mallet and planer for leveling the type and a shooting stick, which was used with the mallet to drive the quoins together. Reprinted with the permission of St. Bride Library, Bride Lane, Fleet Street, London.

well suited to printing because of its absorbency and flexibility. It was invented in the Far East long before printing was practiced and, when made by hand from good-quality material such as rags, has proved extremely durable. What is more, paper can be made in a wide variety of sizes, textures, colors, and finishes. It was originally made in **sheets**, but from the early nineteenth century, when paper began to be manufactured by machine, it was produced in a continuous length on a reel. Its greatest drawback is that it is hygroscopic, which means that it is sensitive to moisture and therefore dimensionally unstable. Nevertheless, for all its limitations, no better all-purpose alternative has yet been found for printing.

The inks used for printing have also remained remarkably consistent, given the enormous changes printing has undergone over the centuries. Though water-based inks have been used in Europe from time to time, and more generally in the Far East, most printing inks consist of pigments mixed in oil; in this respect they are not substantially different from printing ink used in the mid-fifteenth century.

The multiplication of prints can be done without any special apparatus if the printing surface is not too large and not very many copies are needed. Some of the earliest printing in the Far East and Europe would have been done by pressing an inked-up relief block against a sheet of paper or piece of cloth, or by placing paper on the inked surface and rubbing it from behind. The last of these methods is occasionally used by artist wood-engravers today. The special apparatus that was developed to make it easier to produce multiple copies of a document in large quantities was the press.

The first printing presses were those devised for relief printing in the mid-fifteenth century. From then on, presses came to be regarded as essential at the multiplication stage of printing. In addition to speeding up production, they made it easier to produce more or less uniform prints in a precise position on a sheet of paper. In the course of time, presses were tailor-made for each of the three major branches of printing in order to apply sufficient pressure in an appropriate way and without doing damage to the printing surface.

As more and more copies of items were needed in response to the growth of **literacy**, trade, and travel, emphasis shifted to speed of output. In the first quarter of the nineteenth century hand-operated printing presses began to be replaced by powered printing machines, and from the 1860s the fastest machines were fed with paper from the reel rather than in the form of sheets. The vastly increased quantities of materials needed as a result of the greater output of printing machines inevitably led to changes in the manufacture of paper, and especially in the materials used in its production.

III. Words and Pictures

Printing is, and always has been, concerned with both words and pictures, and this presents several problems. First, though letters and numbers lend themselves to being arranged in different permutations, the same idea is not easily applied to pictures. Types are commonly designed for a range of applications whereas pictures, though sometimes re-used, are normally made for a single or limited range of applications. Secondly, the technologies that have been found

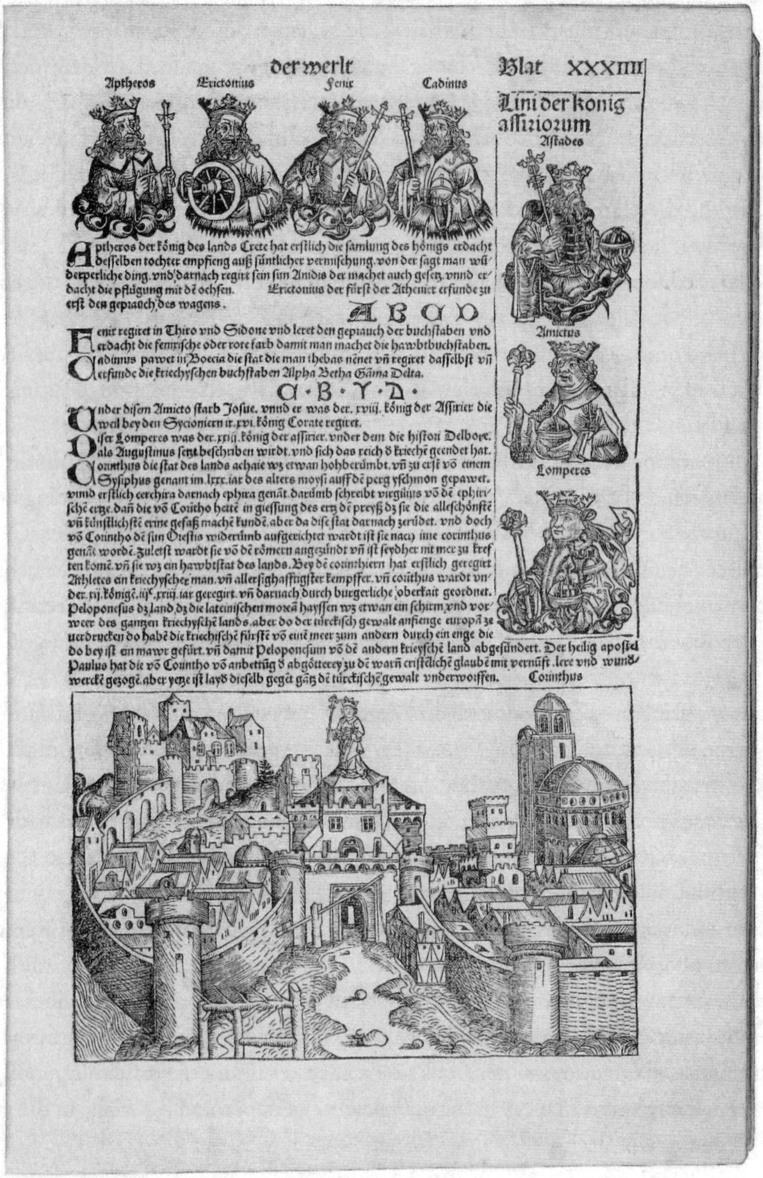

Fig. 1.3: Woodcuts were used in most of the earliest illustrated printed books, as here in Hartmann Schedel's *Weltchronik*, usually called the *Nuremberg Chronicle*, which was printed by Koberger in Nuremberg in 1493. It was very common for some copies of fifteenth-century books to be colored by hand in emulation of pictures in manuscripts. Woodcuts and later wood-engravings were made approximately the same height as type so that they could be combined and printed with it. For this reason wood blocks were commonly used for illustrated publications through to the nineteenth century. Page size 300 x 460 mm.

Fig. 1.4: Illustrations that were etched and engraved in copper had to be printed separately from typeset text and were therefore costly. The need for refined illustrations in luxury books, particularly of the eighteenth century, sometimes overrode considerations of cost, as here in C.-J. Dorat, *Lettres en vers et oeuvres mêlées* (Paris, 1767), with illustrations drawn by Eisen and engraved by De Longueil and others. Page size 176 x 113 mm.

appropriate for printing words have for centuries been very different from those suited to printing pictures; it is only in the digital age that we have returned to something like the production unity of the simplest documents made in the past with pen or brush and ink. Lastly, these and other factors have led to printed words and pictures being studied separately, and usually by people from different disciplines.

For the most part, those who made type (punchcutters and typefounders) and set text matter (compositors) worked in entirely different domains from those who drew pictures (artists and illustrators) or turned them into printing surfaces (trade engravers and lithographers). In addition, many **printers** specialized in categories of work that involved either pictures or words. Whereas **woodcuts** and wood-engravings were commonly printed along with text (Fig. 1.3), all intaglio prints on sheets bearing letterpress text involved a second working on a special press, and this often meant putting work out to another firm (Fig. 1.4).

It was presumably for these reasons that the first manuals devoted to printing divide clearly between those dealing mainly with words and those devoted to pictures. Joseph Moxon's *Mechanick exercises* (London, 1683–84) and Hornschuch's *Orthotypographia* (1608) dealt respectively with the printing and editing of text; Abraham Bosse's *Traicté des manières de graver en taille douce sur l'airin* (Paris, 1645) and Jean-Michel Papillon's *Traité historique et pratique de la gravure en bois* (Paris, 1766) were concerned exclusively with the making and printing of pictures.

It was not until the late eighteenth century that delicate and detailed pictures could be combined with text conveniently. This was first achieved by using wood engravings, but toward the end of the nineteenth century photographically produced relief blocks began to take their place. Lithography too helped to bridge the gap between picture-making and word-making technologies in the nineteenth century. Even so, the need to combine high-resolution pictures with lengthy passages of text imposed all sorts of constraints right up to the second half of the twentieth century. It could be argued that these difficulties served to reinforce a bias—seen first in the Renaissance—toward unillustrated books, or at the very least books with token illustrations only.

IV. Printed Artifacts

When we consider printing of the past, there is a good chance that books spring to mind. We have to remind ourselves therefore that printing has never been limited to books. Many other kinds of products, including newspapers, magazines, maps, sheet music, playing cards, religious prints, bookplates, notices, posters, security printing, forms, invitations, packaging, and even more ephemeral items than these, have had a long history in print. Some of them go back almost as far in time as printed books, some even further. The concentration on books in this account simply reflects the fact that **libraries** are primarily repositories of books and that, by definition, items of printed **ephemera** are unlikely to have been preserved to the same extent as books.

4.
D.F. McKenzie, "The Dialectics of Bibliography Now," The Panizzi Lectures, 1985: *Bibliography and the Sociology of Texts.* London: British Library, 1986. 55–76

Donald Francis McKenzie (1931–99) was Professor of English Language and Literature at Victoria University of Wellington, in New Zealand, from 1969 to 1987, a fellow of Pembroke College, Oxford University, from 1986, and Professor of Bibliography and Textual Criticism at Oxford University, from 1989 until his retirement in 1996. He was the author of the definitive history of Cambridge University Press in the early modern period, which revealed much previously unknown information about how printing houses actually functioned. He was also instrumental in expanding the scope of bibliography to include bibliographical approaches to non-book texts. A New Zealander, he put these ideas into practice by studying a controversial document of New Zealand history, the Treaty of Waitangi, "signed" in 1840 between non-literate indigenous peoples and the representatives of Queen Victoria.

McKenzie's book *Bibliography and the Sociology of Texts* emerged from the first Panizzi lectures at the British Library in 1985. Named for Sir Anthony Panizzi (1797–1879), Keeper of Printed Books and later Chief Librarian of the British Museum Library (later the British Library), these lectures in aspects of bibliography are given annually by invited speakers. McKenzie used his inaugural lectures to redefine the scope and the purposes of bibliography, pioneering an approach that—under various names (book history, material text studies)—has since become widespread. McKenzie also shows, using examples from John Locke and James Joyce, how the material form of the book can become part of its meaning.

He also moves away from W.W. Greg's austere focus on examination of the printed codex, in favor of a "sociology of texts" that pays attention to the human context in which books are produced, and the cultural meanings they acquire (see p. 3). While Greg's efforts to make bibliography "scientific" were an important phase in the development of the discipline, McKenzie now sees them as limiting its potential. Instead, he argues for an approach to the physical form of the text that situates it within its cultural, historical, and political surroundings. McKenzie advocates taking bibliographical approaches to a range of "texts," including film and television, and makes his case using the example of Orson Welles's *Citizen Kane.* He suggests that developing "bibliographical" approaches to film, television, and other media will promote and facilitate the preservation of these kinds of text.

The Dialectics of Bibliography Now

In the first two lectures I briefly contrasted two concepts of "text." One is the text as authorially sanctioned, contained, and historically definable. The other is the text as always incomplete, and therefore open, unstable, subject to a perpetual re-making by its readers, performers, or audience.

To stress the first is to confirm the usual assumptions of historical scholarship: it seeks, as objectively as possible, to recover, from the physical evidence of a text, its significance for all those who first made it. To do that, I have argued, we must have some concept of authorial meaning, consider carefully the expressive functions of the text's modes of transmission, and account for its reception by an audience or readership. As a locatable, describable, attributable, datable, and explicable object, the text as a recorded form is, pre-eminently, a *bibliographical* fact. Its relation to all other versions, and their relation, in turn, to all other recorded texts, is, again, pre-eminently, bibliographical fact. No other discipline—and certainly neither history nor criticism—commands the range of textual phenomena, or the technical scholarship, to deal fully with their production, distribution, and consumption. By commanding the one term common to all inquiry—the textual object itself—**bibliography** can be an essential means by which we recover the past.

As a way of further exemplifying one part of that argument—the relation of form to meaning in printed books—I should like to consider the cases of John Locke and James Joyce.[1] Locke was so troubled by the difficulty he had in making sense of St Paul's **epistles** that he decided to go right to the heart of the matter. In 1707 he published *An Essay for the Understanding of St Paul's Epistles. By Consulting St Paul himself.* In this essay he quite explicitly addresses the question of intention, and the role of **typographic** form in obscuring or revealing it. More than that, he implies that if we do not get these things right, they can have the most serious social and political effects. He ascribes his problems in reading the epistles to:

> The dividing of them into Chapters and Verses, ... whereby they are so chop'd and minc'd, and as they are now Printed, stand so broken and divided, that not only the Common People take the Verses usually for distinct Aphorisms, but even Men of more advanc'd Knowledge in reading them, lose very much of the strength and force of the Coherence, and the Light that depends on it.

---

1 John Locke (1632–1704), empiricist philosopher, was a major figure in the areas of epistemology and political theory. With his rationalist approach to scripture, Locke was a strong advocate for religious toleration in England. James Joyce (1882–1941) was a novelist of the modernist period. His great novel *Ulysses* (1922) adapts Homer's *Odyssey* to modern-day Dublin, following a single day in the life of the main protagonist, Leopold Bloom.

Locke objects to the eye being "constantly disturb'd with loose Sentences, that by their standing and separation, appear as so many distinct Fragments." As he develops it, his argument about editorial and typographic practice has far-reaching implications:

> ... if a Bible was printed as it should be, and as the several Parts of it were writ, in continued Discourses where the Argument is continued, I doubt not that the several Parties would complain of it, as an Innovation, and a dangerous Change in the publishing of those holy Books ... as the matter now stands, he that has a mind to it, may at a cheap rate be a notable Champion for the Truth, that is, for the Doctrine of the Sect that Chance or Interest has cast him into. He need but be furnished with Verses of Sacred Scriptures, containing Words and Expressions that are but flexible ... and his System that has appropriated them to the Orthodoxie of his Church, makes them immediately strong and irrefragable[2] Arguments for his Opinion. This is the Benefit of loose Sentences, and Scripture crumbled into Verses, which quickly turn into independent Aphorisms.

Those comments make it clear that Locke believed the form in which a text was printed not only radically affected the ways it might be read, but might even indeed generate religious and civil dissension. He then raises the whole question of authorial intention. As printed in verse, the epistles frustrated those sober, inquisitive readers who had a mind like his own "to see in St. Paul's Epistles just what he meant; whereas those others of a quicker and gayer Sight could see in them what they please." For Locke, an essential condition of following a true meaning was a proper disposition of the text, so that one might see "where the Sense of the Author goes visibly in its own Train." He then adds:

> And perhaps if it were well examin'd, it would be no extravagant Paradox to say, that there are fewer who bring their Opinions to the Sacred Scripture to be tried by that infallible Rule, than bring the Sacred Scripture to their Opinions, to bend it to them, to make it as they can, a Cover and a Guard for them. And to this Purpose its being divided into Verses, and being brought as much as may be into loose and general Aphorisms, makes it most useful and serviceable.

One finds these points repeatedly confirmed in all popular debates on moral issues. The most recent in my own experience is that about a Homosexual Law Reform Bill before the New Zealand Parliament, where, for nearly a year, members shot biblical verses from one side of the House to the other like paper darts in a schoolroom. Their substance was equally puerile;

2 Indisputable.

they made a mess, demeaned serious debate, and generated passions which led to serious civil disturbance. It was an exact replay in 1985 of Locke's argument of 1707.

Some less contentious illustrations of this relation between book forms and textual meaning may be drawn from the work of James Joyce. The 1984 "critical and synoptic" Garland **edition** of *Ulysses* has been welcomed as an impressive work of scholarship.[i] It offers in effect a parallel reading of the novel, to which it imputes a "many-layered and highly complex text that carries the dynamics of an extended textual development within it." On one page we have an editorial deconstruction of the documents into their successive moments of transmission and modification by typists, **printers**, and by Joyce himself as he corrected **proof**. This is imaged on the facing page by a new construction of the work, one presumed to be implicit in the bewildering, genetic[3] detail which opposes it, but with an explicit claim to an authority higher than that of any completed form known to Joyce. This, it is claimed, is "the emended continuous **manuscript** text at its ultimate level of **compositional** development."

Given the evidence which it chooses to present, what the new edition could not do was to represent the physical form of *Ulysses* as it was first published. I have therefore been intrigued to learn from Dr. John Kidd of ways in which the 1922 edition shows Joyce working to make textual meaning from book forms, re-writing in proof in a creative interplay with the fall of the text on the page, and nudging it into patterns of page-to-text, which offer markers, boundaries, and divisions directly related to its final "book" form. Being largely peculiar to that edition, these correspondent readings are automatically lost in any new setting which does not keep the identical form. They are therefore lost from the new edition, simply because its physical form is incompatible with them.[ii]

Some suspicion that Joyce, of all authors, would put the medium of the book to work might have been aroused by the consciousness he shows in *Pomes Penyeach*.[4] His superstition about the number 13 is well attested ("This year is to be incessant trouble to me," he wrote in 1921 to Harriet Beacher Weaver, adding in parentheses "1 + 9 + 2 + 1 = 13"). His mother died on 13 August 1903, and when he came to publish the poem which he wrote about her death in *Pomes Penyeach*, he placed it thirteenth in the book and called it "Tilly"—as in the phrase "Twelve and a Tilly," or a baker's dozen.[5] Its 12 lines of text and one of title repeat the idea of both acknowledging and denying the reality of the number 13 and its associations. The price of *Pomes Penyeach* was a shilling, or 12 pennies for 12 poems, with the thirteenth free.

For that example and those that follow, and for permission to use them here, I am indebted to Dr. Kidd. The first few are small, indicative ones. On reading a letter from his daughter Milly, who had just turned 15 on 15 June, Bloom says "Fifteen yesterday. Curious, fifteenth of the month too." More to the point, Joyce's revision in proof gives the letter 15 sentences. But every editorial attempt to "correct" Milly's adolescent syntax and punctuation, by reverting to earlier versions,

---

3 For "genetic" relations between texts, see p. 10, note 18.

4 A collection of 13 short poems by Joyce, written between 1904 and 1924 and published in 1927.

5 Bakers were traditionally imagined to give a thirteenth item free to people purchasing a dozen (i.e., twelve).

has of course changed the count and obscured the point. So too, the passage in which Bloom reflects on the rate at which an object falls to earth ("thirty-two feet per second") is heavily revised in print to make it the thirty-second sentence in the paragraph, where reversion to earlier readings, as in the 1984 edition, obscures that convergence of sign and sense. On page 88, Joyce added in proof a sentence of eight words to expand a newspaper death notice. It reads: "Aged 88, after a long and tedious illness." To page 77 he added in proof the phrase "seventh heaven"; and on page 360, Bloom meditates on cycles.

It is a commonplace that *Ulysses* retails the experience of one day and one night in a lifetime, as well as of a whole lifetime compressed into that single day and single night. But those general correspondences emerge more finely in the way Joyce develops them in proof. 1904 was a leap year. Since it is mentioned four times in the book, Joyce must have been highly conscious of it. The total number of days and nights in a leap year happens to be twice 366, or 732. The text of the 1922 edition of *Ulysses* falls on precisely 366 leaves or 732 pages. In a personal letter to me, Dr. Kidd writes:

> [It] also divides evenly into diurnal and nocturnal halves. The sun sets in the seaside "Nausicaa" chapter, not with a sudden plunge, but with a gradual waning, until daylight and Leopold Bloom's consciousness are extinguished on page 365. The remainder of the book is set in darkness.... Bloom, seated where shore and sea meet, attending the last glimmer of midsummer light, and remarking the semicircular profile of Dublin Bay, thinks there must be a divine order at work: "Done half by design."

That symmetry last appeared in the Odyssey Press edition of *Ulysses*, published in Hamburg in 1932. It was issued in two volumes. The final section of the first volume includes the phrase "Done half by design," signaling the reader to move on to volume two, the night volume, after a full day with Bloom.

Dr. Kidd's examples do, I think, illustrate the force of at least one half of my argument: that books *can* be expressive forms of some subtlety, and that an editorial policy which ignores that fact is likely to bring forth a text which, by its author's standards, is deficient, though I have no wish to criticize the Garland edition, which has its own distinct purpose. Joyce engineered the publication of the 1922 Shakespeare and Company edition to fall on his birthday. He received the first two copies that day, the second of the second, 1922. Some Joyce scholars may be ruefully reflecting that on this day of the year one also celebrates the feast of the purification.

I should like now to move back to that other, contrasting, concept of "text" and its nature as open, unstable, indeterminate. In this sense—a sense in which the recent editors of *Ulysses* have employed it—the "text" is in some degree independent of the documents which, at any particular moment, give it form. It is to recognize too that no text of any complexity yields a definitive meaning. The ostensible unity of any one "contained" text—be it in the shape of a manuscript, book, map, film, or computer-stored file—is an illusion. As a language, its forms and meaning derive from other texts; and as we listen to, look at, or read it, at the very same time we re-write it. The word "text-book," as first defined by Nathan Bailey in his *Dictionarium Britannicum* of 1730, reminds us of this truth: "*Text-book* (in Universities) is a Classick Author written very wide by the Students, to give Room for an Interpretation dictated by the Master, &c. to be inserted in the Interlines." Each student makes his or her own text.

That recognition brings us full circle. Whatever its metamorphoses, the different physical forms of any text, and the intentions they serve, are relative to a specific time, place, and person. This creates a problem only if we want meaning to be absolute and immutable. In fact, change and adaptation are a condition of survival, just as the creative application of texts is a condition of their being read at all. The 1984 critical and synoptic text of *Ulysses* has physically changed every previous version in the act of replicating it. It has become in its turn a new *bibliographical* fact; and it is these facts which constitute the primary evidence for any history of meanings. They alone make possible, in their sequence, any account of cultural change. Perceived from a bibliographical point of view, therefore, the ostensible contradiction between those two concepts of "text," the closed and the open, simply dissolves. But implicit in those comments are several points about the nature of bibliography which it might be helpful now to make quite explicit.

First, I imply that it is committed to the description of all recorded texts. In principle, it is comprehensive, and therefore indiscriminate. Any national collection formed largely by **copyright** deposit shows this non-elitist, non-**canonical**, non-generic, all-inclusive principle at work. International networking simply extends it. Ultimately, any discrete bibliography of subject, person, or collection merely contributes to an ideal of that universal bibliographical control.
50 It thereby enables the discovery of any possible relationship there might be between any one text and any other text—whenever, wherever, and in whatever form. In other words, bibliography is the means by which we establish the uniqueness of any single text as well as the means by which we are able to uncover all its inter-textual dimensions.

Second, because it is bibliography's job to record and explain the physical forms which mediate meaning, it has an interpretative function which complements and modifies any purely verbal analysis. In principle, it can fulfill this function in any of the modes in which texts are transmitted, not just printed books. It is therefore equally relevant, as a discipline, to any structure of meaning which is recordable and discernible.

Third, it impartially accepts the construction of new texts and their forms. The conflation of versions, or the writing of new books out of old ones, is the most obvious case. But the construction of systems, such as **archives**, **libraries**, and data-banks, is another. In every case, the elements from which they are constructed are bibliographical objects. A test case would be the sale and dispersal of, say, the library of a seventeenth-century scholar: we become acutely aware at such moments of a library's status as a text or a meta-text, and of its biographical and intellectual meaning.

Fourth, bibliography is of its nature, and not merely as a partial effect of some more essential function, concerned specifically with texts as social products. The human and institutional dynamics of their production and consumption, here and now, as well as in the past, have therefore led me to suggest that we might find in the phrase "a sociology of texts" a useful description of its actual scope.

I must now turn to some exemplary cases of non-book texts and at least try to set out my reasons for thinking that bibliography has a duty to these. In doing so, it is worth recalling, I think, Hobbes's comment in *The Leviathan* that:

> The Invention of *Printing*, though ingenious, compared with the invention of *Letters*, is no great matter ... But the most noble and profitable invention of all other, was that of SPEECH, consisting of *Names* or *Appellations*, and their Connexion.[iii]

He reminds us here of what we are now having to re-learn: that print is only a phase in the history of textual transmission, and that we may be at risk of over-stating its importance. The relatively recent introduction of printing into non-literate societies has seldom endorsed our traditional view of its efficacy as an agent of change. Even in our own society, **oral text** and visual image have not only enjoyed a continuity (albeit, enhanced by print), but they have now resumed their status as among the principal modes of discourse with an even greater power of projection. The origins of that revival are much older than we might care to recall: the telegraph and photograph, telephone and phonograph, and even the motion picture itself, are all nineteenth-century inventions. In retrospect, the failure to develop forms of bibliographic control,[6] adequate archiving, and proper public access on the model of the traditional library is understandable. But the cumulative force of those new media, together with even more recent ones like television, magnetic tape, optical disc, and computers, and the significance of the texts recorded in them, are now such that further neglect is inexcusable.

A future social historian, writing about the need for, and the political appeal of, say, "law and order" policies in the 1980s, would find the traditional texts of novels, plays, newspaper reports of football violence, official records of the parliamentary debates and legislation, relevant and accessible. But they would be quite incomplete without some account of television. I think in particular of a clip from a recent news item. A class of small children were being asked if they liked to watch programs which had lots of violent action in them. One small boy's eyes lit up as he told the reporter how exciting he found it, how it made him feel that he wanted to be strong like that, to run in and kick, and knock people down. "What do you want to be when you grow up?" asked the reporter. The instant reply was: "A policeman." I am not concerned here to pursue the interpretation of the text, but I am concerned to note that it *is* a text, and that future access to it might prove extremely instructive, not only about our present society, but about the nature of the one we may have become 20 years hence. But I cannot be sure how easy it might be to see a full range of films, or relevant television programs; and the chances of a particular news clip surviving in an easily accessible form are even more problematic.

In many ways, the film and video tape are the most complete summation of a tradition of oral, visual, and written and typographic communication. As the forms of text most immediately accessible to non-literate or a-literate societies, they perhaps make the most urgent demands

6 "Bibliographic control" is a term used in library and information science to indicate adequate cataloguing.

of traditional bibliography for its descriptive methods, and its skill in conserving and accessing textual records. Films are deliberated, composed works in their total organization; as completed texts, they are objects more amenable to complete study than, say, unrecorded speech or a theatrical event. They have a physical length, a temporal span, and repeatable presence. Their use of sound, image, color, and movement makes them an ideal starting point for the extension of bibliographical principle from book to text.

But I think it is only proper to select an undisputed classic in which to explore the analogies I should like to draw, and so I turn now in tribute to the work of Orson Welles, in particular of course, to *Citizen Kane*.[7] It is a film I think which might be familiar to most of us; certainly it is one of the few to be given high canonical status, and therefore to have an unusually rich supporting literature.

It opens and closes with a literal sign denying access, an image that is both verbal and visual. It is posted outside Kane's immense mansion of Xanadu, and reads "NO TRESPASSING." It is a playful image of enclosure, a detail of the film's tight textual construction, and of the intimate reciprocity of its verbal and visual text. Xanadu is no true pleasure dome. Reviewing the film in 1946, Borges[8] saw in it the familiar structure of the centerless labyrinth, a world of fragments without unity, a recurrent symbol of the archive, the library, the museum, posing the same challenge to order, creating the same fears of failure.[iv] With the prodigality of a Huntington or a Folger, or in this case even more pertinently a Pierpont Morgan,[9] Kane poured into Xanadu specimens of the world's treasures in the hope of modeling in them a system which eluded him in life.

Lying old and ill in their still *disordered* midst, Kane dies muttering the word "Rosebud." We hear it in his "old, old voice" at the start of the film, which then proceeds by flashback to recover the story of his life, the business of what Pauline Kael has called "raising Kane."[10]

In hopes of pinning down the meaning of the enigmatic "Rosebud," a reporter resurrects Kane's public life by running a nine-minute newsreel made up of clips of its main events, but this ostensibly factual source of evidence, the contemporary record of "News on the March," turns out to be as fragmentary and as full of false emphases as the printed newspapers which Kane himself published. As if to prove yet again that the truest poetry is the most feigning,[11] Welles's own film supplants the newsreel as the source of truth. In doing so, it re-presents the "news" in its true complexity with a clarity and a penetration which shows up the coarse conventions at work in the "factual" documentary record.

---

7 A 1941 American drama directed by and starring Orson Welles (1915–85). It tells the story of Charles Foster Kane, publishing mogul.

8 Jorge Luis Borges (1899–1986) was an Argentinian short-story writer, essayist, poet, librarian, and translator.

9 Henry E. Huntington (1850–1927), railroad magnate; Henry Clay Folger (1857–1930), owner of Standard Oil; and John Pierpont Morgan (1837–1913), banker; all collectors and founders of major libraries and art collections in the United States.

10 Pauline Kael, "Raising Kane," *The New Yorker*, 20 Feb. 1971 and 27 Feb. 1971.

11 "the truest poetry is the most / Feigning" (William Shakespeare, *As You Like It*, III.iii.16–17).

Welles can re-present and date those conventions all the more readily because flashback in films has always required a high consciousness of sign systems in order to establish a difference from the narrative present. It is a resource that Woody Allen exploits to hilarious effect in *Zelig* and *The Purple Rose of Cairo*. The first, if you are so inclined, may be read as a parody of all historical scholarship; the second, of all post-structuralist criticism. But my point of course is that films use, in a way more accessible than in books, formal systems of datable signs to recover the past. The conventions change with extreme rapidity, as we can tell from our own experience of re-viewing an old film we had thought quite natural when first we saw it. What once seemed to have the innocence of truth betrays—before long—an embarrassing artifice.

The press reporter's search for the explanation of "Rosebud" is frustrated. Oral witness fails too in its variant versions of the same events. The documentary "facts" are silent. Only as the film ends, and we see a workman toss an old sledge into a fire, do we catch a glimpse of the answer in the period lettering of the word "Rosebud" painted on the sledge. It is a trite, sentimental, novelettish note, but in it Kane's voice becomes visible. The verbal image takes on graphic form, and like the script itself becomes the necessary complement to the non-verbal, visual constructions, which would fail of meaning without it.

As a text, *Citizen Kane* generates a critical dialogue which has numerous affinities with literary criticism. In its counterpointing of an elusive past with a questing present, its contrasting of the sub-literary genres of newsreels and newsprint with the high-culture of the canonical art-film, in its posturing with hermeneutics[12] as the search for meaning within a closed structure, it is as fruitful a subject for critical inquiry as most printed texts. If that seems too solemn an account of its range of interests, then we can find in its cinematic poetry, as we can in *The Dunciad*,[13] a vulgar, rumbustious, and always entertaining satire on the muck-raking press as one aspect of the social history of printing and publishing. Indeed, in its own attack on William Randolph Hearst, it imitates its subject.[14] Those themes are not trivial, and they are recorded in a form which is so central now to the experience of our society, in particular that of the students who will be tomorrow's scholars, as to warrant an advanced scholarship to serve it.

Such a scholarship might note in Orson Welles himself the role, familiar in publishing, of the outsider as a significant source of innovation, the problems of funding, the threats of libel actions, the plot to buy up the film before its release and destroy the negative and all the prints; the formal features of the finished film, the semiotics of its textual detail; the constraints of **censorship**—indeed, the film's effectual suppression during the McCarthy era; the authorship and versions of the script, and subsequent re-releases; the manner of its distribution, the history of its reception; the annotational realm of Kane as a figure of Hearst, of the character Thatcher as J.P. Morgan junior, as well as the allusive plundering of the film by a generation of other directors.

---

12 Relating to issues of interpretation.

13 Mock-heroic satire by Alexander Pope (1688–1744), first published anonymously in 1728.

14 William Randolph Hearst (1863–1951), business magnate and newspaper publisher, who was the inspiration for the lead character in *Citizen Kane*.

The film is a total social fact and a total text. Filmmakers, spectators, and critics all think in terms of films as texts, because only some such word makes sense of the discrete parts of which a film is constructed. The concept of a text creates a context for meaning. In other words, we are back to the initial definition of text as a web,[15] a construction of warp and weft, and discover that, however we might wish to confine the word to books and manuscripts, those working in films find it indispensable. There is, I think, no profit to be gained by disputing the point: one accepts that the word now has a meaning which comprehends them all. Those who wish to contain it by confining it to books are like Milton's "gallant man who thought to pound up the crows by shutting his Parkgate."[16]

Film theory of the 1960s and 1970s was still strongly influenced by structuralism in one way which bears significantly on my own argument about "pure" bibliography (in the Greg-Bowers sense)[17] and historical bibliography or the sociology of texts. In discussing photography, for example, Roland Barthes drew a distinction between the finished artifact as a closed construction and its context:

> The emission and reception of [a photographic] message both lie within the field of sociology: it is a matter of studying human groups, of defining motives and attitudes, and of trying to link the behavior of these groups to the social totality of which they are part.[v]

The message itself, he claimed, had a structural autonomy in what it signified, and describing it was the business of semiotics. So too Christian Metz[18] drew a distinction between the film as a textual system (whether confined to a single film or extended to the infinite text of what we call genre) and the cinema, which is the whole social complex of a film's production and consumption. It is my contention of course that this distinction ultimately fails, since the definition of meaning—in reading the conventional details of a text—is logically dependent upon prior decisions and social effect. Like typography as a conscious, interpretative skill, every presentational feature of a film is calculated to express symbolic meaning. It is unceasingly deliberate in its selection, shaping, and pointing of significance.

Since it bears on the parallel I am suggesting between books and films as expressive forms, I should like to take up this last point with a comment from Gregg Toland, the director of photography for *Citizen Kane*. In "How I broke the Rules in *Citizen Kane*," he makes a distinction between "photographic commands and conventions in shooting the picture":

---

15 The word "text" comes from the Latin *texere*, to weave, also the root of "textiles."

16 John Milton, in *Areopagitica* (1644), his prose tract in defense of the freedom of the press, uses this comparison to suggest that censoring the press does not effectively restrict the circulation of ideas. "Pound up" here means to imprison, or impound.

17 See W.W. Greg's article "What Is Bibliography?" above (p. 3).

18 Christian Metz (1931–93), French film theorist, best known for his book *Film Language: A Semiotics of Cinema*, which adapts the linguistic theories of Ferdinand de Saussure to the study of films.

> Photographically speaking, I understand a commandment to be a rule, axiom, or principle, an incontrovertible fact of photographic procedure which is unchangeable for physical and chemical reasons. On the other hand, a convention, to me, is a usage which has become familiar through repetition. It is a tradition rather than a rule. With time, the convention becomes a commandment, through force of habit. I feel that the limiting effect is both obvious and unfortunate. With those definitions in mind, I'll admit that I defied a good many conventions in filming *Citizen Kane*.[vi]

[...] The analogy here with the technologies of print in relation to the finished book could be pushed further by a more technical discussion of how Welles altered our perception of reality by obtaining an unusual depth of field, of the experiments with high-speed film stock, the treating of the lens surface to eliminate refraction, the use of the twin-arc broadside lamp, the lap dissolves[19] and their relation to the foregrounding or backgrounding of images, or the composition of shots. All those technical details are of course peculiar to the construction of film texts, not books, but their function is still to create meanings by the skilled use of material forms. In that, and in the relation of technology to expression, I think the parallel holds. But it may be more readily granted in the area of description.

Pauline Kael has edited the final shooting script of *Citizen Kane* dated 16 July 1940, and the subsequent so-called cutting continuity. She explains the difference between them as that of before and after:

> The shooting script is written before the film is shot—it is the basis for the film; the cutting continuity is a stenographic record made from the finished film. Cutting continuities tend to be impersonal and rather boring to read, and if one examines only the cutting continuity it is difficult to perceive the writers' contribution. Shooting scripts are much more readable, since they usually indicate the moods and intentions.[vii]

Her use of the word "intentions" is only the most immediate note of a congruence with the traditional concerns of bibliography and textual criticism. The relationship of the shooting script to the finished script is much like that of a manuscript draft, not even perhaps a **fair copy**, to a printed text, whereas the more boring cutting continuity comes closer to the iconic record of a bibliographical description.

There are three versions of the shooting script as preserved in the Museum of Modern Art in New York. Another, described as the second, revised final script, dated 9 July 1940, and earlier than any of the other three, was submitted to the Production Code Office for clearance. It passed the test except for some four or five details. One of them recalls the effects on Shakespeare's

---

19 Lap dissolves, otherwise known as cross-fades, are a technique of film editing created when the fade-out of one shot is overlapped with the fade-in of another shot. This technique is used prominently in *Citizen Kane*.

text of the Act of Abuses of 1606:[20] "Please eliminate the word 'Lord' from Kane's speech '... the Lord only knows....'" Another puts one in mind of Polonius, concerned lest his son "enter such a house of sale, *Videlicet*, a brothel," because there was such a place nominated as a locale for set C. But the Production Code demanded that it be dropped. What it is important to know, as an aspect of Welles's intention, is that the scene had only been written in for trading purposes in the sure knowledge that it would have to be cut, but in the hope that other, less obtrusive, items would then slip through, as they did.

Pauline Kael reprints the shooting script as revised, although there is no table of variants. What we do have are brief notes on departures from the script as the film was made. Then there is the RKO[21] cutting continuity, dated 21 February 1941. Its apparatus consists of a brief note ("Slightly amended to correct errors in original transcription"), but for the rest, it represents a version of the full film text which, in default of being the film itself, is a bibliographer's dream of iconic accuracy. Like a description of ideal copy, it enables one to test all actual copies in the minutest details for sequence and completeness. For example, to correspond with the authentic version, a copy must run for one hour, 59 minutes, 16 seconds, though it will run shorter on television. There are seven reels, each divided into numbered scenes. The left-hand entries in the description are details of the length of each of these in feet; in the center are notes on the scene, the camera's and the actors' movements, and, under centered speech headings, the dialogue; on the right, is a description of the manner in which the scene is changed.

To anyone familiar with the making or teaching of films, these details are commonplace. Again, my concern is merely to establish the point that the older disciplinary structures of bibliography, in the description of books and the construction of texts from the extant versions, are closely comparable to those required for film, and that the common interest is at this stage served by acknowledging that the discipline comprehends them both. It is ironic that in an age when type for books is film-set, and when, for purposes of storing the information content of books, we would now turn them into photographic images on plastic, the film itself should still be laboring for bibliographical and textual attention. Those which get it, like *Citizen Kane*, are the rare exception.

Bibliographers—as "pure" bibliographers—may of course continue to insist on making a rigorous distinction between books as we commonly know them and non-book forms, and on the restriction of "pure" bibliography to description and analysis of the book as a physical object. But libraries—and especially national libraries, with a responsibility to the culture at large, past, present, and future—are under significant pressure to evolve systems which accommodate these new forms of text in a rational, coherent, stable, and yet socially accessible way.

The pattern is already pragmatically there in the transformation of our personal and city libraries. Some of us still buy books, of course; but we also borrow them, and we have left to the public conscience and public institutions the responsibility for preserving the newspapers and periodicals that we dispose of. Most of us have music, and could have videos, on disc or tapes, and

20 The Act to Restrain Abuses of Players, passed by the English Parliament in 1606, tightened censorship of public theater performances, especially in regard to players using oaths on stage.

21 RKO (Radio-Keith-Orpheum) Pictures is the American film production and distribution company that produced *Citizen Kane*.

the machines required to hear and see them. We are beginning to store information at home in our own computer files, or to buy access to other systems. That principle of buying access is simply an extension of the old idea of the lending library: we do not buy the book so much as the time in which to read it. With new forms of text, we buy, in bulk, the reading, viewing, or listening time in the form of an entrance fee to the cinema, a hiring fee for the disc or video, or a wireless and television license fee for all or any texts that might be made and transmitted in the year ahead, or we pay an access fee for the information in a data bank. By decision of the United States Supreme Court, it is no infringement of copyright there to record television programs in order to shift time. But in fact the technical capacity most consumers now command—as readers, listeners, or viewers—to **copy-texts** in that way, has also in part transformed the notion of purchase as a form of acquisition and the ways in which some of us at least form our personal libraries.

Such reflections form the terms of an all too familiar litany over the demise of the book. My concern is different. It is to find the continuity of these forms with past forms, of our new libraries with past libraries in their traditional function as collectors, conservators, classifiers, and communicators, as classically exemplified by Panizzi. Even the use of computer technology to supply information changes in only one respect that traditional function. Whereas libraries have held books and documents as physical objects, computer systems have been mainly concerned to retrieve content. Library conservation and inter-lending policies are already pushing certain classes of existing document into that mode; and the creation and supply of new texts in non-printed form for direct consultation on screen, or subsequent hard-copy print-out, is increasing. The principle of record and access, of **catalogue** and holdings, is not changed but only refined. It is too seldom remarked that library systems influenced computing in the development of its capacity to process basic catalogue functions by symbolic listing, selection, and arrangement. It should also be remembered that it was not the sophistication of computing in its early stages which biased its use toward science, but its limited memory and therefore its inability to handle the complexity and range of verbal language as distinct from combinations of the numbers 0 to 9. Only as its memory systems have grown has the computer changed its nature from blackboard to book. It has at long last become literate and qualified to join other textual systems. In time, I suppose, as it now learns to speak, it will constitute an oral archive as well.

But one consequence of the computer's retarded development for many years has been a much slower recognition of the essential consonance of its functions, like that of other non-book texts, with the traditional purposes of libraries. Large, long-established, institutional structures are not notable for their ability to adapt rapidly to changed conditions, but if a common principle can be perceived and acted upon, it does at least open up to us a politically important leadership role. Once that is acknowledged, it is not a question of creating a monolithic institution with the curatorial role of preserving all forms of text (the National Sound Archive is part of the British Library; the British Film Archive is not). What is important is the promotion of inter-institutional collaboration in the pursuit of a common aim, and the proper provision at last for the archiving and accessing, the bibliographical control, of the new kinds of text.[viii]

That reflection returns me to film as my chosen case. The concept of the archive has of course been recognized now in the use of the name in several countries. Where "film library" implies active lending and limited retention, the "film archive" implies the primacy of a custodial function and a principle of access restricted to conditional consultation. But despite much individual, dedicated work, it is rare to find resources available on a scale commensurate with the need. MARC (machine readable cataloging) standards have been set by the Library of Congress for the description of films, but books remain privileged over them, and in default of political imperatives with matching resources, the application of standards—as in my own country—is at best fitful or highly selective. Although films enjoy the benefits of copyright protection, in neither Britain nor New Zealand is there any provision for their legal deposit. What is done is again done by personal or commercial initiative, without legal sanction, and usually without adequate funding for archiving in the full range of its obligations. The problems of access can therefore be acute. They range from the philistinism which, in the name of commerce, has completely destroyed artifacts of outstanding merit, to mutilation by censorship, cutting, gross imping out with commercials, or the private retention or suppression of cultural documents of such quality and significance that they should be in the public domain.[ix] In the 1960s, British television drama, in quality of scripting, performance, and production, was of a standard it has rarely achieved since. But it might be difficult to prove the point because many of the programs have been destroyed. After the exact number of transmissions for which, by contract, the performers had been paid, Equity[22] rules required the master and all copies to be destroyed lest the contract be infringed by later, unauthorized transmissions.

I think those conditions force us to ask: "What principle, if it is *not* a bibliographical principle, determines questions of authority, transmission, and reception in all those cases? And in what measure must a *public* library as the traditional custodian of books, and bibliography as the relevant discipline, take up the cause for such texts?"

I stress "public" because commercial considerations rarely bear upon the past with much responsibility to historic depth. There are basically three points: copyright, storage, and access. Copyright deposit puts all specified works into the public domain and thereby ends all the uncertainties that informal and private arrangements are heir to. Storage will always be costly of space and labor, if the original artifacts are to be kept. Just as **vellum** manuscripts were scraped clean for re-use, so too are magnetic tapes vulnerable to re-use, with the destruction of the texts already in them. A principle of economy in the service of private interest renders all records vulnerable. Why keep them if the demand year by year diminishes to the point where they are seldom consulted and it becomes unprofitable to maintain the structures which house and service them? Even in the public realm, some texts are more equal than others, a principle of frequency of use is invoked, and policies of selective retention constantly advocated. But even given deposit and proper storage, access to original artifacts which are machine-specific will need batteries of historic equipment on which to re-play them. In fact, it is more likely to involve the frequent re-copying (and, by a well-known textual principle, their gradual degeneration?) to make them compatible with new technology.

Those considerations suggest that only a traditional, bibliographically informed concept of library service, dedicated to the public interest as a matter of principle and not of profit, will effect the preservation of such texts, guarantee their authenticity, and ensure access to them.

---

22 Equity is the union for actors in the United Kingdom.

I hope it is unnecessary for me to stress my personal interest in bibliography as the study of books and their history, but I hope there is no mistaking either the earnestness with which I have been concerned to argue the case for a comparable attention to other forms of recorded texts. I may be mistaken in my premises and in my logic, but I have tried to argue the case in terms of principles and continuities as I have come to experience them. The book as we know it will, of course, remain an important form of text—for many purposes, the most important. I want nothing to do with fashionable claims that—as Tom Stoppard[23] might have put it—the pages of the book are numbered. I am well aware that, when we are so committed to the force, indeed here to the encircling presence,[24] of their tradition, it seems impossible, this side of tragedy, to live without them. And yet there has always been that counter-mythology which has affirmed the demands of the world, against those of the book.

We find it at work even in such a bookish novel as Umberto Eco's *The Name of the Rose*.[25] You will remember that a bibliographical curiosity there flowers into life as Eco reconstructs from it an elaborate figure of the ingeniously ordered, but labyrinthine, Alexandrian archive, only to deconstruct it again in the old and fearful symbolism of the library as a furnace. Fire consumes the books. As it rages, the librarian as jealous conservator of knowledge, the reader (if you like) as bookworm, literally—letter by letter—eats the sole text of Aristotle's treatise on comedy in a desperate effort of enclosure. It is a last-ditch denial of the multiple life of the text as a communal property, the ultimate image of the library as a closed-book system. At the same time as it disappears from view into its only reader, the text itself, unique and therefore indistinguishable from the poisoned state of its physical form, consumes and destroys him as it becomes wholly his. The moral is deadly: we can become too absorbed by books.

Brilliant though it is, the factitious density of its inter-textual comedy has *The Name of the Rose*, like all accounts of texts and their readers, ending up as just another fiction about a non-existent text, yet another story (so to say) of Echo and Narcissus.

By contrast, Marlowe's *Faustus* gives us, perhaps, the most poignant statement we have of the tragedy which books can entail. When this scholar Faustus selects his texts and constructs from them his own version, his book of the self, he reads his way to hell.

> *Ieromes* Bible, *Faustus*, view it well.
> *Stipendium peccati mors est*: ha, *Stipendium, &c.*
> The reward of sinne is death: thats hard.
> *Si peccasse negamus, fallimur, & nulla est in nobis veritas.*
> If we say that we have no sinne,
> We deceiue our selues, and theres no truth in vs.

---

23 Tom Stoppard (b. 1937), British playwright of Czech origins, known for complex and playful dramatic structures, punning dialogue, and wordplay.

24 A reference to the book-lined room at the British Library where this lecture was delivered.

25 *The Name of the Rose* is the first novel by Italian novelist and cultural critic Umberto Eco (b. 1932). It was first published in Italian in 1980 (as *Il nome della rosa*) and appeared in English in 1983, translated by William Weaver.

Why then belike we must sinne,
And so consequently die.[26]

Faustus reads in Jerome only a single sense dictating a fixed fate. What he omits are the words that refer to mercy, the very foundation of which—if I may so put it—is the variant reading, an openness to interpretation, a deference to the spirit in preference to the letter. Trapped by the paradox that texts are both closed and open, fixed and flexible, defined by one context only to be redefined in others, Faustus despairs. Instead of using judgment, he suffers it; and with his agonized cry—"I'll burn my books"—he rejects the whole tradition of book-learning.

Of all the traditional enemies of books in this counter-mythology, none are so powerful as fire and water. These will devour sense, or drown it, with more dexterous celerity than a whole cortège of critics. If Faustus invokes the one, it is Prospero who invokes the other.

The Tempest towers above all other texts as an exposition of the instrumentality of the book, a key to open the mysteries of nature, a tool to oppress and confine the savage mind. Prospero makes plain how much they meant to him when he recalls Gonzalo who,

of his gentleness
Knowing I lou'd my books, ... furnish'd me
From mine owne Library, with volumes, that
I prize aboue my Dukedome.[27]

And yet one of the most remarkable perceptions in that spare but infinitely generative play is Prospero's even greater need to surrender his power, and with it the books which bestowed it:

And, deeper than did euer Plummet sound
Ile drowne my booke.[28]

Encased by his library, he had shut out the world.

Me (poore man) my Librarie
Was Dukedome large enough ...[29]

At the heart of the English Renaissance, a period unprecedented for its readerly-ness and writerly-ness, two voices warn us that books are not always enough.

---

26 Christopher Marlowe, *Dr. Faustus* (1592), I.i.37–44. Faustus reads the italicized phrases in Latin from the Vulgate translation of the bible by St. Jerome, and offers English versions of them immediately afterwards.

27 William Shakespeare, *The Tempest*, I.ii.192–95.

28 Ibid., V.i.61–62.

29 Ibid., I.ii.126–27.

It seems a simple point to end on, but the times again give it proof. As the British Library begins like Prospero to dismantle itself, and surrender its magic circle for the square,[30] its redefinition as a library of texts, verbal, numeric, and visual, and in many different media, is also imminent. Defining the ways our world might use them, the structure that orders them, and the future scholarship that they must serve, will demand of bibliographers more than I think we currently offer. It asks no less than a new concept of the text in history.

Notes

i. *Ulysses: A Critical and Synoptic Edition*, ed. Hans Walter Gabler, with Wolfhard Steppe and Claus Melchior (New York: Garland, 1984).

ii. The two principal papers from which Dr. Kidd has kindly allowed me to cite the examples given are: "'Thirteen. Death's Number' Structural Symbolism in *Ulysses*," delivered at the Second Provincetown Joyce Conference, June 1983; and "Errors of Execution in the 1984 *Ulysses*," delivered to The Society for Textual Scholarship, New York, April 1985. See also his contributions to *The Irish Literary Supplement: A Review of Irish Books* (Fall 1985): 41–42.

iii. Thomas Hobbes, *Leviathan Or the Matter, Forme, and Power of A Commonwealth Ecclesiasticall and Civil* (1651), Part I, Chapter 4.

iv. Jorge Luis Borges, *Focus on 'Citizen Kane,'* ed. R. Gottesman (Englewood Cliffs, NJ: Prentice-Hall, 1971), 127–28.

v. Roland Barthes, *Image, Music, Text: Essays Selected and Translated by Stephen Heath* (London: Fontana, 1984), 15.

vi. *Focus on 'Citizen Kane,'* 73. Robert L. Carringer, *The Making of 'Citizen Kane'* (London: John Murray, 1985), should also be consulted. There is a most useful bibliography at 165–71.

vii. In Herman J. Mankiewicz, Pauline Kael, and Orson Welles, *The Citizen Kane Book* (London: Methuen, 1985), 83. Comprising *The Shooting Script of Citizen Kane* by Herman J. Mankiewicz and Orson Welles; *The Cutting Continuity Transcript of the Completed Film*; preceded by *Raising Kane* by Pauline Kael.

viii. The British Library Act specifically empowers The British Library to extend its sphere of interest into films and other non-print materials. In a position statement prepared for The British Library in 1985 on non-book materials, Catherine F. Pinion wrote: "It is clear that [non-book materials] represent a major and increasing part of the nation's and the world's output and heritage of recorded knowledge. It is arguable, if not self-evident, that they should receive equivalent treatment to printed material, with regard to collecting, availability, preservation and 'bibliographic' control. In actual fact, the position is distinctly inferior in all those respects." The use of the word "bibliographic" is inevitable in such a context, but it is to be hoped that its still equivocal status, as signaled by the quotation marks, will be speedily resolved.

ix. The position is improving. While correcting proof for the first edition of this text, I purchased (Woolworth, £7.95) a video-cassette of *Citizen Kane*. The regular note in *TV Times*, however (paralleled in *The Radio Times*), makes an important textual point: "Feature films shown on television are not necessarily in the form seen in cinemas. Often several variations are made at the time of production for use according to the intended outlet. In some cases cinema versions may be used, with minor cuts for violence, explicit sex, and bad language."

---

30 McKenzie was speaking at a time when the British Library was in the process of moving from the British Museum, with its iconic round reading room, to new premises at its current location in St. Pancras.

5.

Paul C. Gutjahr and Megan L. Benton, "Reading the Invisible," *Illuminating Letters: Typography and Literary Interpretation.* Amherst: U of Massachusetts P, 2001. 1–11, 15

Paul C. Gutjahr is Professor of English, American Studies, and Religious Studies at Indiana University. He has written about the history of publishing religious texts in America, including the publication histories of the Bible and the Book of Mormon. Megan L. Benton is Associate Professor of English and director of the Publishing and Printing Arts Program at Pacific Lutheran University. She has written on luxury books and fine press books in early-twentieth-century America. Their combined interests in typography led them to edit a collection of essays by several scholars about the place of typography in literary interpretation, from which this extract is taken.

Every time you use a word processor, you can choose which font your text will appear in. Some of these fonts, or what we should technically call typefaces, have long histories in printing and publishing. One of the most commonly used, Times New Roman, was designed by Stanley Morison and Victor Lardent for *The Times* newspaper in 1931. It was largely based on another typeface called Plantin, designed in 1913, which in turn was based on Gros Cicero, a typeface from the sixteenth century. The practice of designing, choosing, and studying type is called typography.

Most readers pay very little attention to typography, unless it's either particularly striking, for example on a poster, or so badly used as the make the text difficult to read. But Gutjahr and Benton argue in this essay that, whether we attend to it or not, typography is one of the features of books (and other printed matter) that shapes how they are read and therefore has an impact on their meaning.

In some cases, writers maintained a great deal of influence over the typesetting of their works, and actively attempted to make the typography serve their purposes. Samuel Richardson (1689–1761), for example, was a printer as well as a novelist, and the decisions he made about which typefaces to use in his novels (especially *Clarissa*) form part of his authorial intention. Just as McKenzie (p. 45) showed James Joyce (1882–1941) making the pagination of his novel *Ulysses* significant, so Richardson—as another essay in Benton and Gutjahr's collection shows—made the typography of *Clarissa* significant for its meaning.

Benton and Gutjahr borrow from Johanna Drucker, a historian of the book and of graphic design at the University of California, Los Angeles, the distinction between "marked" and "unmarked" texts. Marked texts draw attention to their typography and visual layout, while unmarked texts do not. But Benton and Gutjahr assert that all printed matter is marked in some way by their typography, even when it aims to be a transparent window onto the text, so that you can look "through" the marks on the page to see the meaning they convey. Typefaces, they suggest, are another way in which the material forms of the book help to construct the meaning of the text it contains.

Reading the Invisible

Virtually from the beginning of his career in 1915, the eminent American **publisher** Alfred A. Knopf placed a **colophon** on the last page of each book bearing his **imprint**. This statement informed readers about key elements of the book's making: where it was printed, the paper used, the designer, and particularly the name, origin, and brief characteristics of the type used to print its text. To this day, readers of Knopf books encounter this perhaps mysterious message; most probably pay it little attention or are puzzled by its presence. To many it seems superfluous and self-indulgent. Why then is it there?

"Why, indeed?" wondered William A. Dwiggins, Knopf's leading book designer in those early decades. In 1939 he gently scoffed at his friend's colophonic habit. "It's all shop talk," Dwiggins remarked. "He [Knopf] likes 'em. He thinks it gives the books tone, I daresay. I think it doesn't matter a damn one way or the other. All that shop detail is zero. They don't care to know and they don't *need to* know. Just make your book so it will read handily and let it go at that."[i] Readers, Dwiggins insisted, neither cared about nor benefited from any behind-the-scenes technical details about type, paper, and the like. If handled properly, he implied, **typography**—the selection and arrangement of type and other visual elements on a **page**—and especially type itself should be invisible, deferential servants to the text they convey. When type does its job well, all the reader should "see" is the text's message.

The ethic of typographic invisibility has prevailed throughout much of modern Western bookmaking and publishing. The notion was immortalized in a stirring speech by Beatrice Warde[1] in 1932 when she likened good book typography to a crystal goblet. True connoisseurs of wine would prefer crystal to the finest gilded chalice, she declared, because "everything about it is calculated to *reveal* rather than to hide the beautiful thing which it was meant to *contain*." So too are text and reader best served by typography that strives to be unseen, she explained. "The mental eye focusses *through* type and not *upon* it. ... The type which, through any arbitrary warping of design or excess of 'color,' gets in the way of the mental picture to be conveyed, is a bad type."[ii] Type should be self-effacing and supremely humble; type that intrudes upon a reader's awareness, she warned, was bad: distracting, impudent, *visible*.

Much has changed since 1932. Although some may still prefer that those who serve others' needs retire into deferential transparency, we know that such "servants" are not invisible. We also know, although we may not have given it much thought, that types are not invisible either.

---

1 Beatrice Warde (1900–69) was the assistant librarian to the American Type Founders Company, a historian of typography, and a typeface designer.

They too have names, faces, personalities, jobs they are good at and others they are not, benefactors and detractors, ancestors and offspring. And thanks to computers, most of us now have at least rudimentary skills in manipulating type to suit our purposes: what sophomore writer has not discovered that an eight-page labor can be stretched to ten with a quick switch to fourteen-point type? With modern word processing and desktop publishing software we make a myriad of typographic decisions each time we produce a text, or we tacitly approve the decisions we allow the software to make for us. But both as writers and as readers, we often fail to notice, much less fully consider, the role of type and typography in making a text not only visible but meaningful.

In fact, too often our own experience at the keyboard leads us to conflate writing and typography, so that the latter seems to disappear as a discrete and independent function. It is an easy and natural confusion, since when we create personal documents—a term paper, a letter, instructions to the babysitter, and so on—writing and typography are virtually synonymous: the form given the text by its writer is the form that the reader receives. In the larger world of professionally published texts, however, the distinction is profound. There a book's content and its form are not created simultaneously by a single person. As a familiar truism in the publishing world reminds us, writers don't write books—they write texts. A book is created when a text is transformed by print, when it is literally shaped into a material object whose visual and tactile features render it perceptible and accessible to others.

For most readers this formal, intermediate presence of print is so familiar and conventional that it is indeed virtually transparent and so unseen and unpondered; we see only text on the page. But it is impossible to read the words on a page without also reading, albeit usually on a subconscious level, the visual text of the page itself. "Typography is to literature as musical performance is to composition," writes the poet-typographer Robert Bringhurst. Just as we can hear music only by listening to a particular performance of it, we can read a text only by reading a typographic presentation of it. Typography, then, is what Bringhurst calls "an essential act of interpretation, full of endless opportunities for insight or obtuseness."[iii]

This is a bold assertion. It interjects typography into an already crowded and contested arena: the complex thing that we call the "text." It also leads straight into the thorny question of who or what produces meaning in a text: The author's unique visions and expressions? Transcendent, universal truths? Language itself? Or a typographer's mediating perceptions of some combination of these elements, as Bringhurst asserts? Perhaps even the typography itself, an independent kind of visual language in its own right, employed but not finally controlled by a designer's intentions? The essays in this volume[2] contend that type and typography are indeed an intrinsic part of the text that a reader encounters when he or she reads a book.

Scholars have long recognized that a book is much more than simply text. In recent decades a great deal of fruitful thinking and research has revolved around closer scrutiny of "the book" as a constellation of social, cultural, economic, technological, aesthetic, and commercial as well as literary and linguistic forces. Beginning with the 1958 landmark work by Lucien Febvre and

---

2 The collection of essays that Gutjahr and Benton are introducing.

Henri-Jean Martin, *L'Apparition du livre* (translated into English as *The Coming of the Book*),[3] scholars in a wide range of fields have amply illustrated that there is a great deal to be learned from studying books. Delineating the relatively new interdisciplinary field broadly known as "history of the book" or history of "print culture," these scholars have demonstrated that the study of publishing, printing, authorship, bookselling, and reading constitutes an important dimension of social, intellectual, and cultural history.[iv]

Illuminating Letters focuses on one particular aspect of Book History, the relationship between a text's typography and its literary interpretation. It is thus grounded in the assertion that both the material form of a text and any interpretation of it are inflected by the historical contexts in which they are made. This general notion that the "materiality" of any cultural object necessarily affects its meaning has been thoroughly articulated in relation to books by D.F. McKenzie in *Bibliography and the Sociology of Texts* (1986), and others have explored and extended its ramifications.[4] The literary critic Jerome McGann, for example, contends that the material and typographic forms of a text, what he calls its "bibliographical codes," together with the commercial layers of its identity—prices, advertisements, distribution channels, and so forth—necessarily and essentially contribute to the meanings of the text, "*whether we are aware of such matters when we make our meanings or whether we are not.*" George Bornstein and Theresa Tinkle have edited *The Iconic Page in Manuscript, Print, and Digital Culture* (1998), an important volume whose essays illustrate the influence of material form on a text's reception and meanings. As Michele Moylan and Lane Stiles, editors of a volume of studies that showcase this theoretical approach to American literature, argue, there is "no such thing as a text unmediated by its materiality." Accordingly, "the material text [serves] as a nexus in the intersection of literature, culture, and history."[v]

As these scholars have shown, however, the relationship between how and why a book is produced and how and why it is read is often complex, even at times perverse. The meanings made from the text of a printed book derive not only from the many facets that shape how the author, designer, and publisher construct that book but also from the conditions—personal, political, social, and so on—in which the reader encounters it. Highly useful here is the distinction that Michel de Certeau[5] draws between *strategies* of cultural production and *tactics* of cultural consumption.[vi] Strategies describe the practices of those who create cultural products like texts or books—how they envision, compose, revise, edit, design, package, price, and distribute them. Tactics, on the other hand, describe how those who receive or "consume" these cultural goods in fact use them, understand them, derive meaning and value from them. Strategies of production usually attempt to influence tactics of consumption, and sometimes they succeed, but they certainly do not control them. Users' tactics often sidestep creators' intentions, and sometimes they subvert them. Readers may perceive meanings that neither author nor publisher intended, or they may fail or refuse to conform to expected understandings. This subversive slipperiness

3 See the essay by Febvre and Martin, from *The Coming of the Book*, in Chapter 1, p. 15.

4 See the essay by D.F. McKenzie, from *Bibliography and the Sociology of Texts*, in Chapter 1, p. 45.

5 Michel de Certeau (1925–86) was an important French cultural theorist.

is of course partly rooted in the nature of language, but it is also inherent in aspects of a text's materiality, including its typography.

An impressive array of important scholarship has begun to explore this complex network of agency and influence in the creation of textual meaning. The French cultural historian Roger Chartier has shown that the material aspects of inexpensive editions known as the **Bibliothèque bleue**—well-known texts peddled for more than two centuries throughout pre-Revolution France—yield important clues suggesting how and why they were both produced and read. By analyzing the typography as well as the content of texts in the margins of early modern English books, Evelyn Tribble "shows that the page can be seen as a territory of contestation upon which issues of political, religious, social, and literary authority are fought."[vii] And Claire Badaracco has chronicled the extraordinary care given by the R.R. Donnelley Company's Lakeside Press to the design, illustration, and printing of its heralded "Four American Books." In this project, which culminated in 1930, fine limited editions of Melville's *Moby Dick*, Thoreau's *Walden*, Dana's *Two Years Before the Mast*, and the *Tales of Edgar Allan Poe* were produced in bibliophilic[6] forms both to exalt American literature and to promote the printing firm's bookmaking prowess.[viii]

In her study *The Visible Word* (1994), the critic Johanna Drucker distinguishes between two fundamental kinds of typography, resulting in what she calls the marked and the unmarked text. A marked text bears highly noticeable typographic features that explicitly, even aggressively, manipulate how it is read. Varieties of type styles and sizes, selected uses of boldface and color, and so on function prominently to direct the reader's eye and mind, shepherding their understandings of the text. Such typography is typically commercial and bureaucratic; it overtly aims to "sell" a particular message and to provoke a particular behavior from the reader.

Drucker's study focuses on the highly marked typography of early twentieth-century experimental artists who sought to foreground typography itself. This volume, however, primarily looks at the typography of unmarked texts, so-called because it purports to efface its interpretive enterprise. Drucker describes "the even, gray page of prose and poetic convention" as an unmarked, "literary" text because, she contends, it bears no (obvious) marks of typographic manipulation by author, **printer**, or publisher. With its typography seemingly invisible, its text seems neutral and natural to the reader—and therefore true. The unmarked text ostensibly exudes an "authority which transcends the mere material presence of words on a page." Through its discreet typography the unmarked text is simply "there, and the unmarked author [is] indeed the Author of the Text as pure Word."[ix]

We assert, however, that literary texts are no less "marked" by their typography than more commercial or functional texts. Once given visual form, any text is implicitly coded by that form in ways that signal, however subtly, its nature and purpose and how its creators wish it to be approached and valued. A stage production of *Hamlet* in modern dress may seem more "marked" than another that adheres scrupulously to conventions of Shakespearean costume, staging, and so on, but it is not. Each feature of both productions represents an interpretive choice made by a director, actor, or stage manager, and is filtered through the physical and verbal skills and

6 Concerned with the love of books, and especially of fine printing and binding.

qualities of the actors. The words may be Hamlet's, but the uniquely inflected body and voice are Branagh's or Olivier's.[7] The body and the voice make a difference. Type and typography make a difference.

To better understand the role of type in literary interpretation one must examine both the apparent *strategies* behind its selection and arrangement and the *tactics* it may provoke or enable in readers' responses. Typography is an interpretive act, but one that must in turn be evaluated: Is it insightful, or obtuse? Consonant or dissonant with the linguistic text? "Transparent" or obtrusive? To answer that question, the wise reader must look at that which purports to not be there. To perceive typography's interpretive powers we must learn to see and read the invisible.

Can an ordinary reader, untrained in its forms and methods, develop an "eye" for typography as the music lover cultivates an "ear" for detecting a particular musician's performance of a score? Alfred Knopf certainly believed so. We also vigorously contend that yes, ordinary readers can readily learn to see what strives to be transparent. No matter how clear its glass, a window is perfectly visible when one simply alters one's gaze.

This collection[8] is devoted to exploring both the typographic strategies of those who produce books and the interpretive tactics of readers who make sense of a text's presentation. It is important to clarify, however, that none of the included essays focuses on typographic theory or analysis per se. Like Chartier, Tribble, and Badaracco (and many other scholars working in this rich new vein of textual studies), these authors are neither professional book designers nor typographic critics.[9] Rather, they are primarily concerned with literary and cultural meanings. Each author began as we hope our readers may begin, with a curiosity about the particular visual and physical printed forms of a specific text or genre. In each case that curiosity led to a closer inspection of aspects, implications, and consequences of those forms. In other words, each author has made the "invisible" not only visible but illuminating. We hope that these case studies will encourage readers to look in fresh ways at how texts are presented in print, and at how those presentations shape understandings of the texts' meanings and value. We believe these essays provide helpful models of that process of discovery and insight.

Because these essays are intended to introduce literary scholars, both experienced and beginning, to the interpretive layers of typography, they neither assume nor require that readers be well versed in typographic terminology, procedures, or theory. Only a very brief and simple introduction to the nature, structure, and evolution of type itself is needed here. Fig. 1.5 illustrates the basic vocabulary for understanding the nonprofessional discussions of type in these essays. References to *serifs*, for example, indicate the small strokes at the beginning or end of the main strokes of a letter. Type without serifs, which first began to appear in the nineteenth century, is described as *sans serif or sanserif*. Another important feature of type anatomy is the *x-height*, or

7 Kenneth Branagh (b. 1960) and Sir Laurence Olivier (1907–89), both actors who portrayed Hamlet on the British stage to great acclaim, and later played the same role in film adaptations.

8 I.e., the collection of essays that Gutjahr and Benton are introducing.

9 I.e., critics of the merits of particular typefaces.

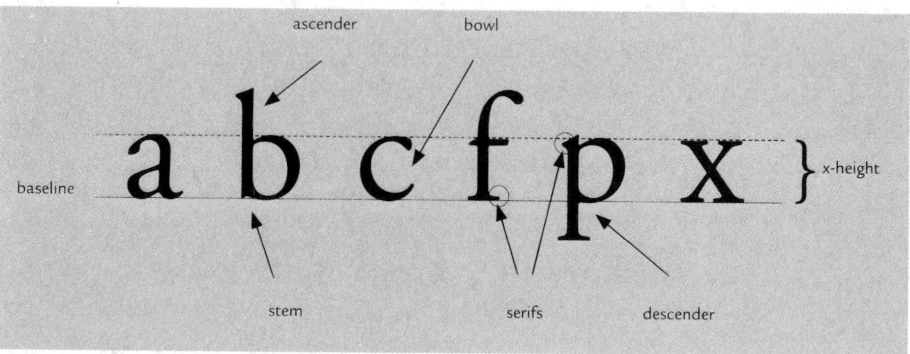

Fig. 1.5: Basic anatomy of the roman letterform. Reprinted with the permission of Paul C. Gutjahr and Megan L. Benton.

distance between the baseline on which the letters rest and the top of such lowercase letters as a, c, e, m, r, and x. The extensions of other lowercase letters (g, j, p, q, y) below the baseline are called *descenders,* while the parts of letters (b, d, f, h, k, l, t) that extend above the x-height are called *ascenders.* The distance from the baseline of one line of type to the baseline of the next is called the *leading,* because when composing metal type the typesetter adjusts vertical space by inserting thin strips of lead between the lines. Type is measured in *points;* there are approximately 72 points to the inch.

Although the full variety of **typefaces** has grown exponentially with the advent of digital design and desktop publishing, type used for reading matter—and particularly texts of books—remains a fairly small subset of that larger, dizzying spectrum of style. While there are many systems of classifying and characterizing type, a particularly intelligent and thorough one that focuses on type for text **composition** is offered by Robert Bringhurst in his highly regarded handbook, *The Elements of Typographic Style* (1992). Bringhurst relates shifts in fundamental elements of letterforms' shapes—the axis of letters with rounded strokes, or *bowls;* the presence or shape of serifs; the contrast between thick and thin strokes; and so on—to broader periods of cultural style: renaissance, baroque, neoclassical, romantic, realist, modernist, and the like (see Fig. 1.6).[x] This scheme emphasizes the intimate relationship between type and the cultural climates in which it is created and used, a relationship that we too contend is fundamental to any informed understanding of typography.

Written language is of course a vast subject, spanning many cultures and millennia. The parameters of this volume are more manageable: the essays address only printed productions of texts in the English language. They therefore do not directly deal with **manuscript** traditions that preceded the advent of Western mechanical printing in the mid-fifteenth century, or with recent electronic editions (although the visual dimensions of each are highly significant and worthy of precisely the kind of study we advocate here).

Although these momentous shifts in the technology of textual production make easy boundaries, it is important to note that letterforms and page layout conventions typically

Garamond roman & *italic*

Renaissance (fifteenth and sixteenth centuries)

Caslon roman & *italic*

Baroque (seventeenth century)

Baskerville roman & *italic*

Neoclassical (eigtheenth century)

Bodoni roman & *italic*

Romantic (eigtheenth and nineteenth centuries)

Helvetica roman & *italic*

Realist (nineteenth and early twentieth centuries)

Palatino roman & *italic*

Modernist (twentieth century)

Fig. 1.6: Evolving styles of text type, illustrating Robert Bringhurst's cultural classification system. Reprinted with the permission of Paul C. Gutjahr and Megan L. Benton.

blur those boundaries. The earliest types cast by Johann **Gutenberg**[10] and his associates in Mainz, Germany, in the 1430s and 1440s scrupulously mimicked contemporary medieval letterforms, for example, just as the earliest printed pages were virtually indistinguishable from their handwritten counterparts. The visual qualities of type and typography have steadily evolved to accommodate the limitations of changing bookmaking technologies and to exploit their strengths, but the process has been far more complex than such a formulaic equation suggests. Technology is an essential factor in the history of type and typography, but—as in the history of any cultural product—it is not the only important influence.[xi]

The variety of type styles that emerged soon after printing well illustrate this fact. While the technology of typecasting and printing was identical throughout Europe, significantly different types appeared, reflecting national or regional traditions and varying intellectual and political interests. In Germany and northern Europe, type resembled dominant **scribal** letterforms[11] there, those we know today as "gothic" or "**blackletter**." In Italy, however, types quickly followed the

---

10 Johannes Gutenberg (c. 1398–1468) was the inventor of moveable type and the modern printing press and the publisher of important early printed books, including the Gutenberg Bible.

11 I.e., the ways in which scribes, who wrote documents out by hand for a living, formed the shapes of letters.

humanist letterforms we now call "roman," letterforms associated with the great scholarly and linguistic discoveries of the Renaissance. By 1500 an alternative letterform developed by Italian Renaissance **calligraphy** masters was captured in a type style we call "italic." These three basic styles have remained foremost in Western book production for 500 years. They quickly came to register broad cultural and ideological as well as nationalist connotations; blackletter, for example, became associated with religious and especially Protestant texts, while roman and italic types prevailed for secular literary and scientific works.[xii]

[...]

In many ways, letterforms are the most immediate and visible link between writer and reader. But letters are neither as immediate—without mediation—nor as intellectually visible as one might think. These essays remind us all that type exerts a powerful role in the interpretive process whether or not that influence is apparent to us. We hope that by helping to make that "invisible" typographic presence visible to the reader's eye, the book will also help readers understand how a printed text's typographic meaning and literary meaning are essentially intertwined. They may confirm or subvert, clarify or complicate each other, but they cannot finally be disentangled. No one can fully read a text's literary content without also reading its typographic form.

Notes

i. William A. Dwiggins, "Twenty Years After," *Books and Printing: A Treasury for Typophiles*, ed. Paul A. Bennett, rev. ed. (1939; Cleveland: World, 1951), 147.

ii. Beatrice Warde, "Printing Should Be Invisible," *Books and Printing: A Treasury for Typophiles*, ed. Paul A. Bennett, rev. ed. (1932; Cleveland: World, 1951), 109, 113.

iii. Robert Bringhurst, *The Elements of Typographic Style*, 2nd ed. (Point Roberts, WA: Hartley & Marks, 1996), 19.

iv. Lucien Febvre and Henri-Jean Martin, *The Coming of the Book: The Impact of Printing, 1450–1800*, trans. David Gerard, ed. Geoffrey Nowell-Smith and David Wootton (1958; London: Verso, 1984). Subsequent seminal work establishing this field includes Elizabeth Eisenstein, *The Printing Press as an Agent of Change* (New York: Cambridge UP, 1979) and several multivolume national history projects, notably the *Cambridge History of the Book in Britain*, 7 vols., ed. D.F. McKenzie, David McKittrick, and Ian Willison (Cambridge: Cambridge UP, 2000) and *The History of the Book in America*, 5 vols., ed. David Hall (Cambridge: Cambridge UP, forthcoming [published in 2010]). For helpful assertions about the nature and direction of this emerging interdisciplinary field, see Robert Darnton's groundbreaking 1982 essay "What Is the History of Books?" reprinted in Cathy N. Davidson, ed., *Reading in America: Literature and Social History* (Baltimore: Johns Hopkins UP, 1989), 27–52; John B. Hench, "Toward a History of the Book in America," *Publishing Research Quarterly* 10 (Fall 1994): 9–21; and Thomas R. Adams and Nicholas Barker, "A New Model for the Study of the Book," *A Potencie of Life: Books in Society*, ed. Nicholas Barker (London: The British Library, 1993), 5–43.

v. D.F. McKenzie, *Bibliography and the Sociology of Texts* (London: The British Library, 1986); Jerome McGann, *The Textual Condition* (Princeton: Princeton UP, 1991), 12–13; George Bornstein and Theresa Tinkle, eds., *The Iconic Page in Manuscript, Print, and Digital Culture* (Ann Arbor: U of Michigan P, 1998); Michele Moylan and Lane Stiles, eds., *Reading Books: Essays on the Material Text and Literature in America*

(Amherst: U of Massachusetts P, 1996), 12. Another important theoretical work germane to these assertions is Gérard Genette, *Paratexts: Thresholds of Interpretation*, trans. Jane E. Lewin (1987; Cambridge: Cambridge UP, 1997).

vi. Michel de Certeau, *The Practices of Everyday Life*, trans. Steven Rendall (Berkeley: U of California P, 1984), xix-xxii. See especially the chapter titled "Reading as Poaching," 165–76.

vii. Roger Chartier, "The *Bibliothèque bleue* and Popular Reading," *The Cultural Uses of Print in Early Modern France*, trans. Lydia G. Cochrane (Princeton: Princeton UP, 1987); Evelyn Tribble, *Margins and Marginality: The Printed Page in Early Modern England* (Charlottesville: UP of Virginia, 1993), 2. For studies focusing on more modern texts and authors, see, for example, Jerome McGann, *Black Riders: The Visible Language of Modernism* (Princeton, NJ: Princeton UP, 1993).

viii. Claire Badaracco, *American Culture and the Marketplace: R.R. Donnelley's Four American Books Campaign, 1926–1930* (Washington, DC: Library of Congress, 1992). See also Badaracco's larger study, *Trading Words: Poetry, Typography, and Illustrated Books in the Modern Literary Economy* (Baltimore: Johns Hopkins UP, 1995), which examines the strategic roles of typography in serving modern commercial purposes.

ix. Johanna Drucker, *The Visible Word. Experimental Typography and Modern Art, 1909–1923* (Chicago: U of Chicago P, 1994), 46, 95. For a broader sense of modern theoretical approaches to Western book typography, see, for example, Jan Tschichold, *The New Typography*, trans. Ruari McLean (1928; Berkeley: U of California P, 1995); Jan Tschichold, *The Form of the Book*, ed. Robert Bringhurst (Point Roberts, WA: Hartley & Marks, 1991); Eric Gill, *An Essay on Typography* (1936; Boston: Godine, 1993); Harry Duncan, *Doors of Perception* (Austin, TX: W. Thomas Taylor, 1987); Herbert Spencer, *Pioneers of Modern Typography*, rev. ed. (Cambridge: MIT P, 1982); and various theoretical discussions in the quarterly journal *Visible Language* and the irregularly published serials *Serif* and *Matrix*.

x. See chapter 7, "Historical Interlude," and prefatory illustrations of these type categories in Robert Bringhurst, *Elements of Typographic Style*, 119–42, 12–15. For further reading on type itself, see Sebastian Carter, *Twentieth-Century Type Designers* (New York: Taplinger, 1987); Frederic W. Goudy, *Typologia: Studies in Type Design and Type Making* (Berkeley: U of California P, 1940); Ruari McLean, ed., *Typographers on Type: An Illustrated Anthology from William Morris to the Present Day* (New York: Norton, 1995); and Charles Bigelow, Paul Hayden Duensing, and Linnea Gentry, eds., *Fine Print on Type: The Best of Fine Print Magazine on Type and Typography* (San Francisco: Bedford Arts, 1988).

xi. For a comprehensive introduction to the technical processes of book production since Gutenberg, see Philip Gaskell, *A New Introduction to Bibliography* (New York: Oxford UP, 1972). See also D.C. Greetham, *Textual Scholarship: An Introduction* (New York: Garland, 1994), 77–151.

xii. Of the many excellent studies of the history of types and typography, among the best are Harry Carter, *A View of Early Typography* (Oxford: Oxford UP, 1969); Robin Kinross, *Modern Typography: An Essay in Critical History* (London: Hyphen Press, 1992); Alexander Lawson, *Anatomy of a Typeface* (Boston: Godine, 1990); S.H. Steinberg, *Five Hundred Years of Printing*, 4th ed., rev. John Trevitt (1974; New Castle, DE: Oak Knoll Books, 1996); and D.B. Updike, *Printing Types: Their History, Forms and Use*, 2nd ed. (1922; Cambridge, MA: Harvard UP, 1937).

6.
Roger Chartier,
"The Press and Fonts: Don Quixote in the Print Shop," *Inscription and Erasure: Literature and Written Culture from the Eleventh to the Eighteenth Century.* Philadelphia: U of Pennsylvania P, 2007. 28–45

Roger Chartier (b. 1945) is Directeur d'Études at the École des Hautes Études en Sciences Sociales in Paris, Professeur in the Collège de France, and Annenberg Professor of History at the University of Pennsylvania. He has been a pioneer in the French *histoire du livre* tradition of studies of book history and print culture, which tends to pay attention less to the details of particular books, and more to the circulation of books in society. His essay on "Communities of Readers" is reprinted below (p. 251). In this essay, he uses the example of *Don Quixote* to explore both how early modern books were printed and how they made the printing and circulation of books into one of their themes. In this way, he shows that the production, circulation, and reception of books are not "extrinsic" to the content of literature, but rather an integral part of it.

Don Quixote is an early novel written in Spanish by Miguel de Cervantes (1547–1616) and published in two volumes, a decade apart, in 1605 and 1615. It recounts the adventures of Quixote, a retired Spanish gentleman who is addicted to reading romances and works of chivalry. So absorbed is he in these stories that his reason is unseated and he sets out to become a knight-errant in search of adventure, having recruited his neighbor Sancho Panza as his squire. After many adventures, he regains his sanity on his deathbed.

In between publication of the two volumes of Quixote's adventures, a spurious second part was published, entitled *Second Volume of the Ingenious Gentleman Don Quixote of La Mancha*: by the Licenciado (doctor) Alonso Fernández de Avellaneda. When he published the authentic second volume, Cervantes included a number of references not only to the first volume, but also to this spurious continuation. Chartier traces some of these references in his essay, as well as examining an episode in which Don Quixote visits a printing shop and sees books being produced.

We often tend to think of literary works as the products of an author's imagination and skill, and of books as the vehicles that allow us to experience the author's vision. But in Chartier's view, literary works emerge from the labor of multiple agents, including the author, the publisher, the printer, the compositor, the proofreader, and others, who combine to produce books that are not incidentally material objects, but essentially so.

The Press and Fonts: Don Quixote in the Print Shop

In 1615, the Madrid print shop of Juan de la Cuesta printed for the **bookseller** Francisco de Robles the second part of *The Ingenious Knight Don Quixote de la Mancha* (*Segunda Parte del Ingenioso Cavallero Don Quixote de la Mancha*). Ten years after his first exploits, Don Quixote set out again on the routes of Spain. In chapters 61 to 65, Sancho and his master find themselves in Barcelona, where Don Quixote has decided to go instead of participating in the jousts at Saragossa. Roque Guinart, the highway robber they encounter on their way, has delivered them to the jests and mockery of Don Antonio Moreno and his friends. To avoid the laughter of the children who are following his ridiculous cortège,[1] Don Quixote decides to go on foot and without an escort:

> In the meantime, Don Quixote wished to go out for a quiet stroll, for he feared that if he went on horseback the small boys would follow him, and so, accompanied only by Sancho and a couple of servants that Don Antonio had furnished him, he set out with this object in view.[i]

> As he was going down a certain street he glanced up and saw a sign in large letters over a doorway, reading: "Books printed here." This pleased him very much, as he had never seen a printing shop up to that time and had a desire to find out what it was like.[ii]

This was not the first time that a fictional narrative was situated in a print shop, as the tales told around a print shop hearth in William Baldwin's *Beware the Cat* show.[iii] In Cervantes, however, the shop is more than just a backdrop. It introduces into the book itself the place and process that make its publication possible. If the work done in such shops is what allows the fiction to exist, the terms of this equation are reversed in chapter 62 of part two of *Don Quixote*, because the prosaic world of the print shop becomes one of those places where, as Borges[2] puts it, "Cervantes delights in fusing the objective and the subjective, the world of the reader and the world of the book."[iv]

I. Book, Body, and Soul

On entering the print shop, Don Quixote "saw them drawing **proofs** here, correcting them there, setting type in one place and making revisions in another—in short, he beheld everything that goes to make up a large establishment of this sort."[v] Cervantes immediately introduces his reader to the division of labor and multiple operations necessary to turn a text into a book: the

---

1 French: Entourage, train of attendants.

2 Jorge Luis Borges (1899–1986) was an Argentinian short-story writer, essayist, poet, librarian, and translator.

composition of **pages** by **compositors** (*componer*), the correction of the first printed pages, or proofs (*corregir, enmendar*), and, finally, the printing of **formes**, or pages secured in a chase, for printing on the same side of a large sheet of printing paper by the workers in charge of the press (*tirar*).

The accuracy of this description of the work process of a printing shop is corroborated by the first manual of the art of printing written in a vulgar tongue[3] (excepting the German translation, published in 1634, of Jerome Hornschuch's *Orthotypographia* [Leipzig, 1608]).[vi] This treatise in Castilian, set directly in **movable type** without a pre-existing **manuscript**, was composed around 1680 by the typesetter Alonso Victor de Paredes, who was a master **printer** in Seville and then Madrid; only a very few copies were printed.[vii] In the tenth chapter of the book, entitled "De la Correción," four types of correctors, copyeditors or proofreaders are identified: university graduates who know grammar, theology, and law but, not being printers, are unfamiliar with the techniques of the trade; master printers with a smattering of Latin; the more expert compositors, who may not know Latin themselves but can seek assistance from the author or some other educated person; and, finally, the ignorant, who barely know how to read and who are employed by the widows of printers or by booksellers who are not themselves printers.

All perform the same tasks (except the ignorant, who are not capable of them). First, the corrector must identify the compositors' errors by following the printed text while the original is read aloud (*escuchar por el original*). In addition, he also acts as censor, charged with rejecting any book in which he finds anything prohibited by the Inquisition or contrary to the faith, the king, or the republic (*algo prohibido por el Santo Tribunal, ò que sea, ò parezca mal sonāte contra la Fè, contra nuestro Rey, ò contra la Republica*), even if the work has been approved and authorized. Last but not least, the corrector is responsible for putting the finishing touches on the text by adding the necessary punctuation (*la apuntuacion légitima*) and fixing any authorial oversights (*descuidos*) or compositors' errors (*yerros*). These responsibilities require the corrector to understand not only the letter of the original text but also the author's intention (*entender el concepto del Autor*) so as to convey it comprehensibly to the reader.[viii]

Some years later, Joseph Moxon[4] assigned some of these same tasks to the compositor, others to the corrector. For him,

> A good Compositor is ambitious as well to make the meaning of his Author intelligent to the Reader, as to make his Work shew graceful to the Eye and pleasant in reading. Therefore, if his copy be written in a language he understands, he reads his Copy with Consideration; that so he may get himself into the meaning of the author, and consequently considers how to order his Work the better both in the title page, and in the matter of the Book: As how

3 That is, in a language currently in use, rather than in the scholarly languages of Latin or Greek.

4 Joseph Moxon (1627–91) was a printer of Puritan texts, globe maker, royal hydrographer (responsible for mapping bodies of water), and typefounder. The *Mechanick Exercises* on printing is his best-known work, but he also published *Exercises* on the trades of the smith, joiner, carpenter, and turner (lathe-worker).

> to make Indenting, Pointing,[5] Breaking, Italicking, etc. the better sympathize with the Authors Genius, and also with the capacity of the reader.[ix]

All decisions made by the compositor are nevertheless subject to modification by the proofreader, who plays a decisive role in the publishing process: "He examines the Proof and considers the Pointing, Italicking, Capittalling, or any error that may through mistake, or want of Judgement, be committed by the Compositor."[x]

In 1675, a lawyer, Melchor de Cabrera Nunez de Guzman, divided the responsibilities of compositor and corrector in an identical manner when he defended fiscal exemptions and immunities for printers on the grounds that the art of printing was a liberal and not a mechanical art, for in all its associated trades "the intellectual and speculative part is vastly greater than the manual activity."[xi] In his view, the compositor should "understand the meaning and argument." He should be an expert in the Castilian language and must know how to cast off[6] the copy, "because books are composed not in the order in which the text is written but by forms." He must be able to punctuate the text correctly, "so as to be clearly intelligible," to distinguish sentences, and to place accents, parentheses, question marks, and exclamation points where needed, "Because often the writer's expression becomes confused if these elements, which are necessary and important for the intelligibility and comprehension of what is written or printed, are missing; because if they are absent, the meaning is transformed, altered, and different."[xii]

Like Moxon, however, Cabrera believed that the corrector should be allowed to second-guess the decisions of the compositor because the former was better educated. He was obliged

> to know, at a minimum, grammar (there have been, and there are, some who are graduates in one discipline or another), spelling, etymology, punctuation, and where to place accents. He must have knowledge of the sciences, letters, Greek and Hebrew characters, and the rules of music; he must master eloquence, art, and elegance in order to recognize and correct barbarisms, solecisms, and other faults in Latin, Castilian, and other languages.[xiii]

For Paredes and Cabrera, Moxon, and Cervantes before them, textual production involved a variety of stages, techniques, and operations. Intervening between the author's genius and the reader's capacity for appreciation, to borrow Moxon's terms, the publication process did not divorce the materiality of the text from the textuality of the book.[xiv] Paredes stands a classic metaphor on its head to express the dual nature of the book, object as well as œuvre. Whereas countless texts describe the human body or the face as a book,[xv] Paredes treats the book as a human creature, because, like man, it has both a body and a soul: "I see a book as being made in the same way as a man, who has the rational soul with which Our Lord created it, with all the

---

5 I.e., punctuation.

6 Casting off is the process of estimating the number of pages required for a book, and so the amount of paper needed and the text that will fall on each page.

graces that His Divine Majesty has deigned to bestow on it; and with the same omnipotence He has given him an elegant body, handsome and harmonious."[xvi] It is possible to compare a book to a man because God created human beings in the same way as books are printed. Cabrera gives this analogy its most elaborate form when he says that man is the only printed book of the six that God wrote. The other five are the *Starry heavens*, which he compares to a vast **parchment** on which the stars figure as the letters of the alphabet; the *World*, which is the summa[7] and map of all Creation; *Life*, which is like a record book containing the names of all the elect; *Christ*, who is at once the *exemplum* and *exemplar*, that is, an example offered to all mankind and an authorial manuscript to be copied; and finally, the *Virgin*, the first of all, whose creation in the Spirit of God, the *Mente Divina*, pre-existed the creation of the world, of time, and of the earth. Among these various works of God, all of which are mentioned in Scripture or by the Church Fathers and all of which are related by Cabrera to some object in the written culture of his time, man is an exception, because he is the product of a print shop: "God placed his image and seal on the press and clamped it down, so that the copy would come out identical to the form it was supposed to have ... and it was also his wish to enjoy the numerous and varied copies of his mysterious original."[xvii]

Paredes used the image and stressed the idea that for him the soul of the book was not simply the text as composed, dictated, and imagined by its creator but the text as embodied in a form adequate to its intention: "A perfectly finished book consists in a good doctrine, presented as it should be by the printer and corrector: that is what I regard as the soul of the book. And it is a good impression on a clean and well-maintained press that makes for what I would compare to a gracious and elegant body."[xviii]

If the body of the book is the result of the pressmen's labor, its soul is not fashioned solely by the author but shaped by all who have a hand in its punctuation, spelling, and layout, including the master printer, the compositors, the copyeditors, and the proofreaders. Paredes thus rejects out of hand any separation of the essential substance of the work, taken to be the same regardless of the form in which it is presented, and the accidental variations of the text resulting from the printing process and alleged by some to be of no importance to the significance of the work.[xix]

II. Sancho's Ass

An episode from the editorial history of *Don Quixote*, which was printed in late 1604 in the shop of Juan de la Cuesta and published with the date 1605, illustrates the realities as well as the risks of collaboration inherent in any publishing process. In chapter 25 of the story, in the first **edition** of the book, Sancho mentions in passing the theft of his ass: "Good luck to him who has saved us the trouble now of stripping the ass." Four chapters later, Sancho follows on foot as his master rides on horseback: "The knight then mounted Rocinante and the barber his own beast, while Sancho came along on foot, which led him to think once more of the gray ass whose loss he now felt worse than ever." Without explanation, however, the ass reappears

7 I.e., the highest standard.

in chapter 42: "Sancho Panza alone was fretting over their delay in retiring, but he was the one that ended by making himself the most comfortable of all, for he simply threw himself down on the trappings of his ass."[xx]

Acknowledging the discrepancy, which was immediately noticed by his critics, Cervantes wrote two brief stories for the second edition of *Don Quixote*, which was also published in 1605 (a sign of the book's success). The first told of the theft of the ass by Ginés de Pasamonte, the galley slave who was inadvertently set free by Don Quixote; the second described Sancho's recovery of his mount after he recognizes the thief disguised as a Gipsy, chases him off, and reclaims his beloved gray ass.[xxi] In the second edition, the story of the theft was inserted in chapter 23, shortly after the two heroes enter the Sierra Morena, while the other story was included in chapter 30, when they leave the mountains along with Cardenio, Dorotea, the barber, and the curate, who have come to rescue Don Quixote from his sylvan folly. Everything seemed to have been set right, then, but unfortunately the first sentence of chapter 25 was not corrected. It read: "Taking his leave of the goatherd, Don Quixote once again mounted Rocinante and ordered Sancho, who was now in a very bad humor, to follow him, which the latter did *with his donkey*."[xxii] In other words, Sancho is still riding the ass, even though it has been stolen from him. In the edition that Roger Velpius published in Brussels in 1607, a more alert copy-editor eliminated the discrepancy, although we find it still intact in the third Madrid edition, which left the presses of Juan de la Cuesta in 1608.

The tribulations of the vanished but still present ass remind us first of all that texts, far from being fixed in their final form once and for all, are variable, unstable, and malleable. Variants are the result of a host of decisions and/or errors that may occur at any point in the publishing process. As the example of *Don Quixote* shows, the negligence of the author, the mistakes of the compositors, and the inattentiveness of the proofreaders all played a part in determining the work's successive states. How should editors and critics regard these inconsistencies and discrepancies? Francisco Rico thinks that one must try to recover the text that Cervantes wrote, imagined, and desired, which was subsequently distorted in the print shop.[xxiii] One should follow the classical **philologists**, who studied the whole manuscript tradition of a work in order to establish the most probable text,[xxiv] and compare all the printed states of a work to recover what the author wrote, or wanted to write, which in some instances does not appear in any edition.

Or consider another perspective: that of Shakespeare criticism, for which the forms in which a work was published, no matter how strange, must be regarded as different historical incarnations.[xxv] All states of the text, even the most inconsistent and bizarre, must be understood and eventually published, for, as the result of acts of writing and work practices, they constitute the work as it was conveyed to its readers. Every work exists only in its simultaneous and successive material forms. The search for a pure primary text that would somehow exist prior to or beyond its various material embodiments is therefore pointless. To edit a work is therefore not to recover an "ideal **copy-text**" but to make explicit the reasons for preferring one or another of its various states, along with the choices governing the presentation (divisions, layout, punctuation, spelling).[xxvi]

The decision is not always easy. Take a Shakespearean example: *Love's Labor's Lost*. In 1598, in the first edition of the comedy in **quarto** format, the couples are rearranged in the course of the play. The amorous dialogue initially links Berowne and Katherine (not Rosaline) and Dumaine and Rosaline (not Katherine). Only in the third act, following the divisions introduced into the text by eighteenth-century editors, does each of the young lords of Navarre fall in love with the woman who will occupy his thoughts to the end of the play. In 1623, the **Folio** edition, which for the first time brought together Shakespeare's "Comedies, Histories, & Tragedies," as the **title page** has it, "published according to the True Originall Copies," depicts a different situation: Berowne and Rosaline and Dumaine and Katherine are attracted to each other from their first encounter.

What are we to make of this difference? Did Shakespeare mix up the names of the characters in the original version? Did one of the compositors of the quarto edition make a mistake? Or was the original edition more faithful to the author's dramatic intention, since an abrupt shift of amorous passion is a theme that we find in other plays (most notably in the loves of Romeo), and the fickleness of the young "lords" of Navarre might explain why the young ladies of France are so hard on them in the play's final act? As Stephen Greenblatt[8] explains, the tension between aesthetic preference and textual tradition makes the choice difficult: "Although the version printed here is based on the near consensus among recent textual scholars, [the Quarto] may provide the most accurate rendition available of the romantic relations in *Love's Labor's Lost*."[xxvii] In other words, the editor is torn between respect for the more consistent version of the text, as sanctioned by a tradition dating back to 1623, and the nostalgic allure of a more exciting version.

The episode involving Sancho's ass has another lesson to offer. The textual inconsistencies that we find in *Don Quixote*, of which this is only one example, point up the similarities that exist between Cervantes' writing and certain practices of **orality**. As Francisco Rico notes, "Cervantes revolutionized fiction by conceiving it not in the artificial style of literature but in the ordinary prose of everyday life." In this sense, "*Don Quixote* is not so much *written* as *spoken*, written without submitting to the constraints of writing—neither the constraints of its time, with the baroque skills required by the styles then in fashion, nor, of course, the constraints of our own day."[xxviii]

For the first time, a novel was written in the rhythm and syntax of the spoken language, against the rules of grammar and aesthetic conventions. More than that, the narration, with its multiple digressions, parentheses, and free association of words, themes, and ideas, was composed not according to the principles of literary rhetoric but according to the codes that govern conversation and oral exchanges. Omissions, confusions, and discrepancies are of little importance to a style that constructs a narrative as though it were a manner of speaking.[xxix]

8 Stephen Greenblatt (b. 1943) is an important literary critic, and one of the founders of the New Historicist school of criticism. A specialist in Shakespeare, he is one of the editors of the edition of Shakespeare published by W.W. Norton.

III. Glory and Profit

The time has come to return to Don Quixote in the Barcelona print shop. There he encounters an "author" who has translated an Italian book entitled *Le Bagatele* into Castilian. In the dialogue that develops between them, Cervantes touches on three standard motifs of his day. First, there is an amusing reference to the success of Ariosto's poems: "'I,' said Don Quixote, 'am somewhat acquainted with Tuscan and pride myself on being able to recite certain stanzas of Ariosto.'"[xxx] [9] Then there is the comic effect that comes from Quixote's admiration for the most trivial translations: "I will lay you a good wager that you translate *piace* as *place, più* as *más, su* as *arriba,* and *giù* as *abajo.*"[xxxi] [10] Finally, there is the debate on the utility of translation. "It appears to me," says Don Quixote, "that translating from one language into another, unless it be from one of those two queenly tongues, Greek and Latin, is like gazing at a Flemish tapestry with the wrong side out: even though the figures are visible, they are full of threads that obscure the view and are not bright and smooth as when seen from the other side."[xxxii]

In addition to these references to shared knowledge, the dialogue is filled with allusions to the practices of printers and booksellers. In his discussion with the translator, Don Quixote mentions the two forms of book publishing that existed in Golden Age Spain and modern Europe:

> "But, your Grace, I should like to know, is this book being printed at your own expense or have you already disposed of the rights to some bookseller?"
>
> "I pay for the printing," said the author, "and I expect to clear at least a thousand ducats on this first edition of two thousand copies, which at two *reales* apiece ought to sell in no time at all."[xxxiii]

By printing *por su cuenta,* that is, paying to have the book printed "for his own account," the translator has retained the privilege that was granted to him and commissioned the Barcelona printer to produce two thousand copies to be sold either by booksellers or directly by the printer (which was not unusual, as Fernando Bouza has shown).[xxxiv]

In requesting the printing of two thousand copies for the first edition of his book, the translator of *Le Bagatele* was not altogether unpresumptuous. A press **run** of this magnitude was the highest contemplated by Paredes, who indicates that in one working day a press could print 1,500, 1,750, or 2,000 copies of two forms (that is, the pages corresponding to both sides of a printer's **sheet**).[xxxv] Cervantes may be using this detail to suggest that the translator is overconfident, or he may want to indicate that the public is enamored of translations, more so than of original stories. Recall that Juan de la Cuesta very likely printed only 1,750 copies of the second edition of *Don Quixote* in 1605, and that this was in any case a much larger than average print run,[xxxvi] and surely greater than that of the first edition.[xxxvii]

---

9 Ludovico Ariosto (1474–1533) was an Italian poet whose epic romance *Orlando Furioso* is laden with the themes of chivalry, romance, and heroism that Quixote admires and is meant to parody.

10 These examples are all correct translations of basic words from Italian to Spanish.

A remark by the translator contrasts two "economies of writing": "I do not have books printed to win fame in this world, for I am already well known through my works; it is money that I seek, for without it a fine reputation is not worth a cent."[xxxviii] The contrast between *fama* and *provecho*, reputation and profit, was a commonplace in Golden Age Spain. Here, however, it is linked to a sharp perception of the literary world. Translators were in fact the first "authors" to receive, in exchange for their manuscript, not only copies of the work to be given to their patrons but also monetary remuneration.[xxxix] This marked a first step toward the professionalization of writing, linked to an activity that was related to copying. In Castilian, the same word, *trasladar*, designated both activities, copying and translating, as Covarrubias's definition indicates.[xl] Concerned to earn money from his book, the translator had no intention of surrendering the privilege to a bookseller who would then reap all the profit from his eventual success.

In contrast to the classical model of writing, in which the writer was assumed to be a disinterested party by virtue either of his social status or the protection of a patron, the translator of *Le Bagatele* claims that it is possible to live on what he writes, and to live well. He hopes for what Cervantes, in his "Prologue to the Reader" in Part Two of *Don Quixote*, deemed impossible: "One of the greatest temptations [of the devil] ... consists in putting it into a man's head that he can write a book and have it printed and thereby achieve as much fame as he does money and acquire as much money as he does fame."[xli] This, for Cervantes, was an idle hope. Books could not bring both fame and fortune. For those without either status or wealth, like Cervantes himself, only the generosity of a patron—in his case the count of Lemos, viceroy of Naples, and the archbishop of Toledo, Bernardo de Sandoval y Rojas—could ensure the writer a decent life.

Don Quixote expressed skepticism regarding the expectations of the overconfident translator:

> "That," said Don Quixote, "is a fine bit of calculation on your Grace's part, but it is plain to be seen that you are not familiar with the ins and outs of the printers and the way in which they all work together. I can promise you that when you find yourself weighted down with two thousand copies, you will be astonished how your body will ache all over, especially if the book happens to be a little out of the ordinary and does not make spicy reading."[xlii]

Here the text plays with a commonplace of the Golden Age: the greed and dishonesty of printers, who were always quick to alter their account books and use accomplices to hide the true number of copies ordered, so that they could sell a certain number of copies more rapidly than the author and at a better price.[xliii]

Cervantes had used the theme earlier in one of the *Novelas ejemplares*, in the story of the "Licentiate of Glass." "Your trade would please me well if there were no fault in it," Tomás says to the bookseller in whose shop he is leaning against a wall (with a "thousand precautions," because, having bitten into a quince[11] on which a spurned lover has placed a curse, he believes that he is made of glass). To the bookseller, who asks him what that fault might be, the licentiate responds:

---

11 A type of fruit.

"The charlatans who pretend to be booksellers when they buy the privilege of a book, and the trick they play on the author, if by chance he has had the book printed for his own account, for instead of 1,500 copies, they print 3,000, and while the author thinks they are selling his books, it's actually their own that they are selling."[xliv]

The evil ways of booksellers were a favorite theme of writers critical of the printing trade: ignorant compositors left texts littered with errors, corrupting their integrity; booksellers fobbed books off on readers incapable of understanding them, thereby distorting their meaning; and the low standards of the book trade generally degraded literary intercourse.[xlv] "Well, good luck and God help you" are Don Quixote's last words to the translator, who is too presumptuous to recognize the perils that lie ahead.[xlvi]

IV. Don Quixote, Reader of Cide Hamete and Avellaneda

When Quixote visits the print shop in Barcelona, two books are being printed and proofread. The first is entitled *Light of the Soul* (*Luz del alma*). According to Francisco Rico, and contrary to classical commentary, this cannot be an allusion to the book of the same title that was printed by Felipe de Meneses in Salamanca in 1556 and reprinted as late as the 1590s. An allusion to such an old book, fraught with Christian humanism of Erasmian[12] inspiration, would scarcely have been compatible with Cervantes' vigorous commitment to the Counter-Reformation in the last years of his life: in 1609 he joined the Confraternity of Slaves of the Most Holy Sacrament, and in 1613 he took the habit of the Third Order of Saint Francis. *Light of the Soul* is therefore more likely a generic reference to the type of religious work that dominated Spanish publishing at the beginning of the seventeenth century, or else an allusion to a work that was one of the bestsellers of the time, the *Obras de Lodovico Blosio* (or Louis de Blois, abbot of the monastery of Liesse). As Francisco Rico observes, this book, which went through more than a dozen editions from 1596 to 1625, was printed several times by the same printer who did both parts of *Don Quixote*. Juan de la Cuesta printed it for Diego Guillen in 1604 at the same time and with the same font in which he set part one of *Quixote*. In 1608 and 1611 he reprinted this same work for Francisco Robles, who was the **publisher** of *Don Quixote*, and in 1613 of the *Novelas ejemplares*. Cervantes was therefore familiar with the work in the same way as Don Quixote, from having seen it in a print shop.[xlvii] Hence the following remark is no doubt to be taken seriously: "'These,' he said, 'are the books that ought to be printed, even though there are many of the sort, for many are the sinners these days, and an infinite number of lights are required for all those that are in darkness.'"[xlviii] The second work that Don Quixote encounters is even more interesting: "Going up to another case, he saw that here, too, they were correcting a book, and when he asked the title he was told that it was the *Second Part of the Ingenious Gentleman, Don Quixote de la Mancha*, composed by a certain native of Tordesillas. 'I have heard of this work,' he said."[xlix]

12 Influenced by the work of Desiderius Erasmus (1466–1536), Dutch humanist scholar who sought to reconcile Christian theology and classical learning.

He is not the only one to have heard of it, for the reader of Part Two knows, if he has read the Prologue, of the existence of this apocryphal[13] sequel to Cervantes' novel, which appeared in 1614 with a title page announcing the *Segundo tomo del Ingenioso hidalgo Don Quixote de la Mancha, que contiene su tercera salida; y es la quinta parte de sus aventuras* (*The Second Part of the Ingenious Knight Don Quixote of La Mancha, which contains his third sally; and constitutes the fifth part of his adventures*).[1] The "third sally" alludes to the final pages of Part One of *Quixote*, which indicate that

> The author of this history, although he has made a most thorough and diligent search, has been unable to come upon any account—at least none based on authentic sources—of the deeds performed by Don Quixote on his third sally. There is only the tradition, handed down in La Mancha, to the effect that in the course of this third expedition he went to Saragossa, where he was present at some famous tourneys that were held in the city.[li]

The "fifth part" refers to the four-part division of the book published in 1605, which at that time was not the first part of a diptych.[14] The book presented itself as the work of "el Licenciado Alonso Fernández de Avellaneda, natural de la villa de Tordesillas," and claimed to have been printed in Taragon by Felipe Roberto. Analysis of the fonts used in the book suggests that the **typographic** address on the title page concealed the actual location of the printing, which was allegedly the print shop of Sebastián de Cormellas in Barcelona. The print shop that Don Quixote visited was therefore not that of Pedro Malo, as has been claimed,[lii] but rather Cormellas',[liii] described by Cervantes on the basis of his own knowledge of the shop where *Don Quixote* was printed, that of Juan de la Cuesta in Madrid.[liv]

In the text of Part Two, the first mention of Avellaneda's work (the real identity of which has never been established for certain[lv]) occurs in chapter 59, when two of the guests in the inn where Don Quixote and Sancho are staying refer to both the novel of 1605 and the sequel of 1614. Don Juan says, "Upon your life, Señor Don Jerónimo, while they are bringing our supper, let us read another chapter of the *Second Part of Don Quixote de la Mancha*" and the other man replies, "Why would your Grace have as read such nonsense as that, Señor Don Juan, seeing that he who has read the First Part of the history of Don Quixote de la Mancha cannot possibly find any pleasure in the second one?"[lvi] The dialogue between the two noblemen reminds the reader of the passage in which the bachelor Carrasco, Don Quixote, and Sancho are discussing the reaction to the exploits of the knight-errant as recounted by the Arab historian Cide Hamete Benengeli (the supposed author of the narrative after chapter nine of Part One) and printed on the Madrid presses of Juan de la Cuesta.[lvii] Carrasco alludes not only to the great success of the book, of which more than 12,000 copies have already been printed,[lviii] but also to criticisms that have been leveled against it:

13 "Of doubtful authenticity" (*OED*).

14 A diptych is literally a pair of images, sometimes hinged together. The word is used here metaphorically to describe the two volumes of *Don Quixote*, published a decade apart.

> Some, to be sure, have complained of the author's forgetfulness, seeing that he neglected to make it plain who the thief was who stole Sancho's gray, for it is not stated there, but merely implied, that the ass was stolen; and a little further on, we find the squire mounted on the same beast, although it has not made its reappearance in the story.[lix]

The mistake made in the first edition and hastily patched up in subsequent ones was thus transformed into a theme of the narrative itself. Sancho comes back to it in the next chapter, where he tells the story of the theft and recovery of his ass, and when Carrasco, alluding to the inconsistency that still exists in the second edition, points out that the error resides "'in the fact that before the ass turns up again the author has Sancho riding on it,'" Sancho replies, "I don't know what answer to give you, except that the one who wrote the story must have made a mistake, or else it must be due to carelessness on the part of the printer."[lx] Well before Don Quixote visits the shop in which books are composed, printed, and corrected (sometimes quite carelessly), it thus makes its appearance in the story when Cervantes blames the Arab chronicle or the printers for his own negligence.

The fact that the characters in *Don Quixote* read and comment on the book that tells their story is one of the things that makes the novel "magical" for Borges, for whom this narrative device is one of the most effective ways to fuse the world of the book with that of the reader. The same is true in *Hamlet*, where the performance of the *The Murder of Gonzago* by the theater troupe from the city replays the murder of old Hamlet before the court of Elsinore. Borges asks "why does it disquiet us to know that Don Quixote is a reader of the *Quixote*, and Hamlet is a spectator of *Hamlet*? I believe I have found the answer: those inversions suggest that if the characters in a story can be readers or spectators, then we, their readers or spectators, can be fictitious."[lxi]

The protagonists of *Don Quixote* read of the *hidalgo's* early adventures but were also familiar with the sequel, published in 1614. Let us return to the inn to which Don Jerónimo and Don Juan have brought a copy of Avellaneda's book. On hearing Don Juan say that what he dislikes about the book is that it depicts Don Quixote as no longer in love (*desenamorado*) with Dulcinea, Quixote denies the insulting accusation and reveals his identity to the two *hidalgos*. Cervantes then plays a vertiginous game with the book that was published a year before his own Part Two appeared and in which the self-styled licentiate of Tordesillas described among other things Don Quixote's pitiful performance in the tilt for the ring in Saragossa.

Quixote refutes Avellaneda's false allegations: he is and will always be constant in his love for Dulcinea. And that is not all. He says that the events described in the sequel as having already occurred will in fact never take place. He had never been to Saragossa and would not go there now: "I will not set foot in Saragossa but will let the world see how this new historian lies, by showing people that I am not the Don Quixote of whom he is speaking."[lxii] Cervantes "falsifies" Avellaneda's account by describing what the sequel-writer had presented as an already completed past as a future that would never come to pass. And indeed, Quixote does not go to Saragossa but to Barcelona, where we found him in the print shop.

Before setting out, Quixote leafs through a copy of Avellaneda's book, which one of the gentleman has given him. In an ironic reversal, he accuses the author of carelessness and inconsistency:

> The third [thing for which the author deserves to be censured] is the mistake he makes, and the falsehood of which he is guilty in the essential part of the story, by stating that the wife of Sancho Panza, my squire, is named Mari Gutiérrez when the name should be Teresa Panza. And it is greatly to be feared that one who errs in so important a matter as this will be wrong in all the other particulars throughout the history.[lxiii]

This ridiculous criticism of the sequel writer is a way for Cervantes to knock not only his own detractors, such as Lope de Vega, who had made the theft of the ass "the most important point in the story," but also himself, since in Part One Sancho's wife appears under various names—Juana Gutiérrez, Mari Gutiérrez, and Juana Panca—while in the second she becomes Teresa Pança and ultimately Teresa Sancha.[lxiv]

V. The Plagiarist Plagiarized

From chapter 59 on, allusions to Avellaneda's sequel abound. In chapter 61, Don Quixote, before entering Barcelona, is welcomed by one of Roque Guinart's friends with these words:

> Welcome to our city ... O valiant Don Quixote de la Mancha—not the false, not the fictitious, not the apocryphal one that we read of in mendacious histories that have appeared of late, but the true and legitimate one, the real one that Cide Hamete Benengeli, flower of historians, has portrayed for us.

Which causes our hero to turn to Sancho and say, "These gentlemen plainly recognized us. I will wager you that they have read our history and that of the Aragonese as well, which was printed not so long ago."[lxv] In chapter 62, he leaves the print shop in irritation, saying in regard to this same book that "in all truth and upon my conscience, I think it ought to be burned to ashes as a piece of impertinence."[lxvi]

In chapter 70, in the vision of Altisidora, devils are playing a ballgame on the threshold of hell, but instead of playing with balls they play with books. One of them whacks a book so hard with the blazing shovels they use as rackets that the book falls apart, with pages flying in all directions:

> "Just see what book that is," said a devil to his companion, and the other devil replied,
>
> "This is the *Second Part of the History of Don Quixote de la Mancha*, written not by Cid Hamete, the original author, but by an Aragonese who, by his own account, is a native of Tordesillas."

> "Take it away," said the other. "Throw it into the bottomless pit so I shan't have to see it."
>
> "Is it as bad as all that?"
>
> "It is so bad," said the first devil, "that if I had deliberately set myself to write a worse one, I shouldn't have been able to achieve it."[lxvii]

The play with the apocryphal sequel culminates in chapter 72, where Don Quixote and Sancho, on their way back to their village, stop at an inn, where they run into Don Alvaro Tarfe, one of the characters invented by Avellaneda. Don Alvaro is obliged to say that the Don Quixote and Sancho Panza that he knew are not the ones he sees before him. The real Don Quixote never went to Saragossa and was never locked up in a madhouse in Toledo. Don Alvaro Tarfe swears to this before the mayor of the village and declares "with all the legal formalities" that "he was not personally acquainted with Don Quixote de la Mancha, also present, and it was to be further stated that this latter person was not the individual referred to in a history entitled *Second Part of Don Quixote de la Mancha*, composed by a certain Avellaneda, native of Tordesillas."[lxviii] Couched in the lexicon of legal documents (the deposition is a *petición* and begins with the legal formula "de que a su derecho convenia"), Don Alvaro Tarfe's statement is one of the many devices that Cervantes uses to transform Avellaneda's "**plagiarism**" into a theme of his own fiction. Perhaps he remembered Mateo Alemán, who, in part two of the *Life of Guzman d'Alfarache*, published in 1604, had transformed the author of a sequel that had appeared two years earlier into a character in his book. Written (essentially) by the Valencian Juan José Martí, this sequel was presented as having been composed by "Mateo Lujan de Sayavedra, natural vecino de Sevilla." In chapter nine of book two of part two of *Guzmán*, Mateo Alemán's Sayavedra "falls ill, lapses into a frenzy, thinks he is Guzman himself, and hurls himself into the sea, where he drowns."[lxix] Don Alvaro Tarfe does not meet with such a sad fate, but the game is the same: using the sequel published under a pseudonym as grist for the literary mill, providing characters and stories. In *Don Quixote*, the reality effect produced by the text stems not only from the fact that Cervantes, as Borges notes, set his story amid "the dusty roads and sordid inns of Castille" rather than the "vast and vague geography of the Amadis."[lxx] It comes, in the first place, from the constant interchange between the fiction and the technical and literary circumstances in which it was composed (in both senses of the word composed: aesthetic and typographical).

VI. Name, History, and Enchantment

The final allusion to Avellaneda's sequel comes in the will that Don Quixote dictates on his deathbed. The final clause is

> Item: I entreat the aforementioned gentlemen, my executors [i.e., the curate and the bachelor Samson Carrasco], if by good fortune they should come to know the author who is said to have composed a history now going the rounds under the title of *Second Part of the Exploits of Don Quixote de la*

> *Mancha*, to beg his forgiveness in my behalf, as earnestly as they can, since it was I who unthinkingly led him to set down so many and such great absurdities as are to be found in it; for I leave this life with a feeling of remorse at having provided him with the occasion for putting them in writing.[lxxi]

The ironic pardon granted to Avellaneda is intimately related to Don Quixote's return to reason, with which the final chapter of the novel begins: "My mind now is clear, unencumbered by those misty shadows of ignorance that were cast over it by my bitter and continual reading of those hateful books of chivalry."[lxxii] The first sign of the recovery of judgment is the recovery of identity: "'I have good news for you, kind sirs,' said Don Quixote the moment he saw them. 'I am no longer Don Quixote de la Mancha but Alonso Quijano, whose mode of life won for him the name of "Good."'"[lxxiii] By reclaiming his true name, Don Quixote marks the end of the fable, a few pages before his death. He thus cancels the opening act, when the *hidalgo* Quixana (or Quijana), as he was called in the second edition of 1605 (and not Quexana, as in the original edition),[lxxiv] begins calling himself Don Quixote.[lxxv]

At this point, the other major characters offer the reader an astonishing moment. They refuse to allow the *hidalgo* to resume his true identity, preferring to perpetuate the illusion. They want to become shepherds, as Don Quixote had decided to do after his defeat by the knight of the White Moon, when he promised to give up the life of knight-errant for a year. All the characters, and perhaps the reader as well, enticed by the prospect of reading a parody of yet another genre, dream of living in spirit in a pastoral world more pleasant than that of their everyday cares and travails. The bachelor Carrasco, Sancho, and the narrator himself persist in using the knightly appellation of the man who in his own mind is once again Alonso Quijano. Don Quixote is obliged to say a second time that he has reclaimed his authentic identity: "I was mad and now I am sane; I was Don Quixote de la Mancha, and now I am, as I have said, Alonso Quijano the Good. May my repentance and the truth I now speak restore to me the place I once held in your esteem."[lxxvi] Henceforth, "the ingenious knight of la Mancha" has a double identity. For his own time, he is "one of those gentlemen who always have a lance in the rack, an ancient buckler, a skinny nag, and a greyhound for the chase,"[lxxvii] but for posterity, thanks to his madness and Cide Hamete's pen, he will forever remain the madman to whom "it now appeared ... fitting and necessary, in order to win a greater amount of honor for himself and serve his country at the same time, to become a knight-errant and roam the world on horseback, in a suit of armor; he would go in quest of adventures, by way of putting into practice all that he had read in his books."[lxxviii]

Don Quixote is a man of many names: the name he gave himself (Don Quixote de la Mancha), his real name (Alonso Quijano the Good), and those attributed to him by scholars: "They will try to tell you that his surname was Quijada or Quesada—there is some difference of opinion among those who have written on the subject—but according to the most likely conjectures we are to understand that it was really Quijana."[lxxix] This amusing parody of learned debate allowed Cervantes to include in the story of the knight of La Mancha a common feature of contemporary literary texts: variability of names. This was true, as we have seen, of *Love's Labor's Lost*, and of *Lazarillo de Tormes*, in which, despite the title, the hero is named not Lazarillo but Lázaro (except in the play on words *lacerado/lazarillo*).[lxxx] These were but two of many examples of variability in naming, for which the reasons were many: carelessness on the part of authors, who forgot or mixed up the names of their characters; errors by compositors and proofreaders; and, underlying all this, a doubt as prevalent in life as it was in literature that individuals possess a single, stable, fixed identity.[lxxxi] Cervantes' genius was to use his hero's name changes to mark the beginning and end of the period of enchantment in his story.

In the time of *Quixote*, the print shop became the key place where texts in search of readers turned into books. The technology had its detractors, who denounced the dangers and uselessness of printing and continued to place their faith in manuscript copies.[lxxxii] Unlike printed texts, manuscripts allowed their authors to maintain control over the **circulation** of their works and to keep ignorant readers away from texts they would be unable to understand. Judgment was not unanimous, however, and even kings honored print shops with their visits, if we believe Melchor de Cabrera, who intended to demonstrate the honorable character of printing, the "art of arts." Cabrera reminds us that Louis XIII, who had a print shop in the Louvre, was reputed to be an excellent compositor, and then he describes the visit that Philip III and his daughter, the infanta Doña Ana, paid to the print shop of the duke of Lerma, his *váhdo*. The young infanta stopped in front of a case and, "wanting her name written in the palm of her hand, removed letters from the boxes that were pointed out to her and placed them in the compositor."[lxxxiii] Then "his Majesty entered the shop and asked the workers to stay where they were and, remaining seated, to go on with their work. When he came to a case, for as long as he stood there watching the work of composition, he allowed his hand to rest on the compositor's left shoulder."[lxxxiv] With this familiar and protective gesture, the king demonstrated better than any written text the ability and usefulness of the art of printing.

Like his sovereign, Don Quixote longed to visit a print shop. Like the king, he demonstrated respect and esteem for the work of those thanks to whom the great deeds of an illustrious prince as well as the amusing adventures of a poor knight could be conveyed to the world: "Going up to one of the cases, he inquired what was being done there, the workmen explained things for him, and, wondering at what he had observed, he passed on."[lxxxv]

Notes

i. Miguel de Cervantes, *Don Quijote de la Mancha*, Edición del Instituto Cervantes, dirigida por Francisco Rico (Barcelona: Instituto Cervantes/Critica, 1998), 1142. Miguel de Cervantes, *Don Quijote de la Mancha*, trans. Samuel Putnam (New York: Modern Library, 1949), 922.

ii. Ibid.

iii. William Baldwin, *A Marvelous Hystory intituled Beware the Cat* (London, 1570). For a modern edition, see *Beware the Cat: The First English Novel*, by William Baldwin, Introduction and Text by William A. Ringler and Michael Flachmann (San Marino, CA: Huntington Library, 1988). Thanks to Joshua Phillips for calling this text to my attention.

iv. Jorge Luis Borges, "Magias parciales del *Quijote*," *Otras inquisiciones* (1952; Madrid: Alianza Editorial, Biblioteca Borges, 1997), 74–79. English translation: "Partial Enchantments of the *Quixote*" *Other Inquisitions, 1937–1952*, trans. Ruth L.C. Simms (Austin: U of Texas P, 1964), 44.

v. *Don Quijote de la Mancha*, 1142–43. Putnam translation, 922.

vi. Hieronymus Hornschuch, *Orthotypographia, Hoc est Instructio operas typographicas correcturis, et Admonitio scripta sua in lucem edituris utilis et necessaria* (1608). English translation: *Hornschuch's Orthotypographia*, ed. and trans. Philip Gaskell and Patricia Bradford (Cambridge: University Library, 1972).

vii. Alonso Víctor de Paredes, *Institución y origen del arte de la imprenta y reglas generales para los componedores*, ed. Jaime Moll (Madrid: El Crotalón, 1984); reprinted with a "Nueva noticia editorial" by Víctor Infantes (Madrid: Calambur, Biblioteca Litterae, 2002).

viii. Ibid., fol. 42r-45r.

ix. Joseph Moxon, *Mechanick Exercises on the Whole Art of Printing* (1683–84), ed. Herbert Davis and Harry Carter (London: Oxford UP, 1958), 311–12.

x. Ibid., 247.

xi. Melchor de Cabrera Nuñez de Guzman, *Discurso legal, histórico y político en prueba del origen, progressos, utilidad, nobleza y excelencias del Arte de la Imprenta; y de que se le deben (y a sus Artífices) todas las Honras, Exempciones, Inmunidades, Franquezas y Privilegios de Arte Liberal, por ser, como es, Arte de las Artes* (Madrid, 1675), fol. 117V. Thanks to Fernando Bouza for pointing out the existence of this text, of which there exists a facsimile published by Amalia Sarria Rueda (Madrid: Singular, 1993). On Melchor de Cabrera's writings from 1636 on in defense of fiscal exemptions for printers, see Miguel María Rodríguez San Vincente, "Argumentos historico-jurídicos para la defensa de la inmunidad fiscal del libro español en el siglo XVII," *Cuadernos bibliográficos* 44 (1982): 5–31.

xii. Ibid., fol. 15, recto et verso.

xiii. Ibid., fol. 15, verso. A similar definition of tasks and skills can be found in a 1619 memoir by the proofreader Gonzalo de Ayala and the lawyer Juan de Valdes, who differentiated printers from booksellers on the grounds that printing was a liberal art, but not bookselling. See Victor Infantes, "La apologia de la imprenta de Gonzalo de Ayala: un texto desconocido en un pleito de impresores del Siglo de Oro," *Cuadernos bibliográficos* 44 (1982): 33–47.

xiv. Cf. Jeffrey Masten, "Pressing Subjects or, the Secret Lives of Shakespeare's Compositors," *Language Machines: Technologies of Literary and Cultural Production*, ed. Jeffrey Masten, Peter Stallybrass, and Nancy Vickers (New York and London: Routledge, 1997), 75–107.

xv. Cf. Ernst Robert Curtius, *Europaische Literatur und lateinisches Mittelalter* (1947), trans. Jean Bréjoux, *La Littérature européenne et le Moyen Age latin* (Paris: Presses Universitaires de France, 1957), 522–526. English translation: *European Literature and the Latin Middle Ages*, trans. Willard Trask (London: Routledge, 1953).

xvi. Paredes, *Institución y Origen del Arte de la Imprenta*, fol. 44V.

xvii. Ibid., fol. 3v-6r, citation fol. 4v.

xviii. Ibid., fol. 44V.

xix. On the rejection of the contrast between "substantive essence" and "accidentals" and an example of the effect of different typographic forms (including format, composition, and puncutation) on meaning, see the pioneering study by D.F. McKenzie, "Typography and Meaning: The Case of William Congreve," *Buch und Buchhandel in Europa im achtzehnten Jahrhundert*, ed. Giles Barber and Bernhard Fabian (Hamburg: Hauswedell, 1981), 81–125, reprinted in D.F. McKenzie, *Making Meaning: "Printers of the Mind" and Other Essays*, ed. Peter McDonald and Michael F. Suarez, S.J. (Amherst: U of Massachusetts P, 2002), 198–236.

xx. *Don Quijote de la Mancha*, 280, 339, 499. Putnam translation, 202, 252, 386.

xxi. *Don Quijote de la Mancha*, 1233–35.

xxii. *Don Quijote de la Mancha*, 270. Putnam translation, 195.

xxiii. Francisco Rico, "Historia del texto" and "La presente edición," *Don Quijote de la Mancha*, CXCII–CCXLII and CCLXXIII–CCLXXXVI.

xxiv. For a magisterial example, see Jean Bollack, *L'Œdipe roi de Sophocle: Le texte et ses interpretations* (Lille: Presses Universitaires de Lille, 1990), vol. 1, *Introduction, Texte, Traduction*, pp. XI–XXI, 1–178.

xxv. See, for example, Margreta De Grazia and Peter Stallybrass, "The Materiality of the Shakespearean Text," *Shakespeare Quarterly* 44, 3 (1993): 255–83; Leah S. Marcus, *Unediting the Renaissance: Shakespeare, Marlowe, Milton* (London: Routledge, 1996); and Stephen Orgel, "What Is a Text," in *Staging the Renaissance: Reinterpretations of Elizabethan and Jacobean Drama*, ed. David Scott Kastan and Peter Stallybrass (New York: Routledge, 1991), 83–87.

xxvi. D.F. McKenzie, *Bibliography and the Sociology of Texts*, Panizzi Lectures 1985 (London: British Library, 1986), 29–30.

xxvii. Stephen Greenblatt, "Textual Note," *The Norton Shakespeare Based on the Oxford Edition*, ed. Stephen Greenblatt (New York: W.W. Norton, 1997), 738–40.

xxviii. Francisco Rico, "Prólogo," Miguel de Cervantes Saavedra, *Don Quijote de la Mancha*, ed. Silvia Iriso y Gonzalo Pontón (Barcelona: Galaxia Gutenberg / Círculo de Lectores, 1998), 20, 22.

xxix. For other examples of this treatment of writing, especially in Milton, see D.F. McKenzie, "Speech-Manuscript-Print," *New Directions in Textual Studies*, ed. Dave Oliphant and Robin Bradford (Austin, TX: Harry Ransom Humanities Research Center, 1990), 86–109, reprinted in *Making Meaning*, 237–58.

xxx. *Don Quijote de la Mancha*, 1143. Putnam translation, 922. Cf. Maxime Chevalier, *L'Arioste en Espagne (1530–1650): Recherches sur l'influence du "Roland furieux"* (Bordeaux: Institut d'Études Ibériques et Ibéro-Américaines de l'Université de Bordeaux, 1966).

xxxi. *Don Quijote de la Mancha*, 1143–44. Putnam translation, 923.

xxxii. Ibid.

xxxiii. Ibid.

xxxiv. Fernando Bouza, "'Aun en lo material del papel y inpresión.' Sobre la cultura escrita en el Siglo de Gracián," in *Libros libres de Baltasar Gradan*, Exposición bibliográfica, siendo comisario Ángel San Vincente Pino (Saragossa: Gobierno de Aragón, 2001), 11–50.

xxxv. Paredes, *Institución y Origen del Arte de la Imprenta*, fol. 43V.

xxxvi. Francisco Rico, "Historia del texto," *Don Quijote de la Mancha*, CXCIV.

xxxvii. Ian Michael, "How *Don Quixote* came to Oxford: The Two Bodleian Copies of *Don Quixote*, Part I (Madrid: Juan de la Cuesta, 1605)," *Culture and Society in Habsburg Spain: Studies Presented to R.W. Truman by His Pupils and Colleagues on the Occasion of His Retirement*, ed. Nigel Griffin, Clive Griffin, Eric Southworth, and Colin Thompson (London: Tamesis, 2001), 95–120.

xxxviii. *Don Quijote de la Mancha*, 1145. Putnam translation, 924.

xxxix. See, for example, the contracts that Parisian booksellers signed with the translator Nicolas de Herberay for his translations of *Amadis de Gaule* in 1540 and 1542, and Palmerin in 1543, published in Annie Parent, *Les métiers du livre à Paris au XVIe siècle (1535–1560)* (Geneva: Droz, 1974), 300–04.

xl. Sebastián de Covarrubias Orozco, "Trasladar: Vale algunas veces interpretar alguna escritura de una lengua en otra; y también vale copier," *Tesoro de la lengua castellana o Española* (1611), ed. Felipe C.R. Maldonado, rev. Manuel Camarero (Madrid: Editorial Castalia, 1995), 933.

xli. *Don Quijote de la Mancha*, 619. Putnam translation, 506.

xlii. *Don Quijote de la Mancha*, 1145. Putnam translation, 923.

xliii. Deception by printers to conceal the true number of copies printed when books were published for the author's account was denounced in the first manual for confessors concerning the typographic art. This was written in Latin by Juan Caramuel Lobkowitz, abbot of the monastery of Emmaüs in Prague and later bishop of Satriano and Campagna. It can be found in the *Theologia moralis fundamentalis*, vol. 4, *Theologia praeterintentionalis* (Lyon, 1664), 185–200. For a recent edition of this text, which cites Cervantes in support of its condemnation, see Juan Caramuel, *Syntagma de Arte Typographica*, ed. Andrés Escapa (Salamanca: Instituto de Historia del Libro y de la Lectura, 2004), 134–43.

xliv. Miguel de Cervantes, "Novela del licenciado vidriera," *Novelas ejemplares*, Edición, prólogo y notas de Jorge García López (Barcelona: Crítica, 2001), 265–301. English translation: *Three Exemplary Novels*, trans. Samuel Putnam (Westport, CT: Greenwood P, 1982).

xlv. See Fernando Bouza, "Para qué imprimir: De autores, públicos, impresores y manuscritos en el Siglo de Oro," *Cuadernos de Historia Moderna* 18 (1997): 31–50.

xlvi. *Don Quijote de la Mancha*, 1145. Putnam translation, 924.

xlvii. Here I am following the brilliant argument of Francisco Rico, "Visita de imprentas: Páginas y noticias de Cervantes viejo" (Dissertation Defense, U of Valladolid, 1996).

xlviii. *Don Quijote de la Mancha*, 1145. Putnam translation, 924.

xlix. *Don Quijote de la Mancha*, 1145–46. Putnam translation, 924.

l. Alonso Fernández de Avellaneda, *El Ingenioso hidalgo Don Quijote de la Mancha*, ed. Fernando García Salinero (Madrid: Clásicos Castalia, 1971). Cf. Edward C. Riley, "Three Versions of *Don Quijote*," *Modern Language Review* 68 (1973): 807–19.

li. *Don Quijote de la Mancha*, 591. Putnam translation, 459.

lii. Pedro Malo, cf. Lluís C. Viada i Llluch, "L'estampa barcelonina d'En Pere i d'En Pau Malo davant de la rectoria del Pi: una conjectura cervàntica," *Bulletí de la Biblioteca de Catalunya* 4 (1925): 225–37. Thanks to Manuel Peña for pointing out this article.

liii. This hypothesis is endorsed by Rico in *Visitas de imprentas*, 48–49. Rico notes that in the same year, 1614, that the continuation of Avellaneda appeared, Sebastián de Cormellas also printed a new edition of the *Obras de Ludovico Blesio*.

liv. Cf. Ian Michael, "How *Don Quixote* Came to Oxford," 97.

lv. Cf. Luis Gómez Canseco, "Introdución," Fernández de Avellaneda, *El Ingenioso hidalgo Don Quijote de la Mancha* (Barcelona: Biblioteca Clásica Española, 1884), 29–59, "Pesquisa en torno a Avellaneda."

lvi. *Don Quijote de la Mancha*, 1110–11. Putnam translation, 895.

lvii. *Don Quijote de la Mancha*, 646–56.

lviii. The figure is entirely plausible, given the fact that between 1605 and 1615 the book went through three editions in Madrid (two in 1605, one in 1608), two editions in Lisbon in 1605, one edition in Valencia, two in Brussels (1607 and 1611), and one in Milan (1610). Cf. Michael, "How *Don Quixote* Came to Oxford," 116–17.

lix. *Don Quijote de la Mancha*, 655. Putnam translation, 532.

lx. *Don Quijote de la Mancha*, 657. Putnam translation, 534.

lxi. Jorge Luis Borges, "Magias parciales del *Quijote*," Borges, *Otras inquisiciones* (1952; Madrid: Alianza Editorial, Biblioteca Borges, 1997), 79. English translation: "Partial Enchantments of the *Quixote*," *Other Inquisitions, 1937–1952*, trans. Ruth L.C. Simms (Austin: U of Texas P, 1964), 46.

lxii. *Don Quijote de la Mancha*, 1115. Putnam translation, 898.

lxiii. *Don Quijote de la Mancha*, 1112. Putnam translation, 896.

lxiv. Cf. Edward C. Riley, "Who's Who in *Don Quijote?* Or, Approach to the Problem of Identity," *Modern Language Notes* 81 (1966): 113–30.

lxv. *Don Quijote de la Mancha*, 1131. Putnam translation, 912.

lxvi. Ibid.

lxvii. *Don Quijote de la Mancha*, 1195. Putnam translation, 965–66.

lxviii. *Don Quijote de la Mancha*, 1208. Putnam translation, 976.

lxix. Mateo Alemán, *Guzmán de Alfarache*, Edición, introducción y notas de Francisco Rico (Barcelona: Planeta, 1983), 708. English translation: *The Rogue, or the Life of Guzman de Alfarache*, trans. James Mabbe (New York: Knopf, 1924).

lxx. Jorge Luis Borges, "Magias parciales del *Quijote*," Borges, *Otras inquisiciones*, 74–79. English translation: "Partial Enchantments of the *Quixote*," *Other Inquisitions, 1937–1952*, 43.

lxxi. *Don Quijote de la Mancha*, 1220–21. Putnam translation, 987.

lxxii. *Don Quijote de la Mancha*, 1217. Putnam translation, 984.

lxxiii. Ibid.

lxxiv. Francisco Rico, "Quexana," *Euphrosyne: Revista de Filología Clásica* 22 (1994): 431–39.

lxxv. *Don Quijote de la Mancha*, 42.

lxxvi. *Don Quijote de la Mancha*, 1220. Putnam translation, 986.

lxxvii. *Don Quijote de la Mancha*, 35. Putnam translation, 25. On the historic identity indicated by this description, see the splendid essay by Pierre Vilar, "Le temps du 'Quichotte,'" *Europe* (January-February 1956): 3–16, reprinted in Vilar, *Une histoire en construction: Approche marxiste et problématiques conjoncturelles* (Paris: Gallimard, 1982), 233–46.

lxxviii. *Don Quijote de la Mancha*, 40. Putnam translation, 27.

lxxix. *Don Quijote de la Mancha*, 36–37. Putnam translation, 25–26.

lxxx. Francisco Rico, "La *princeps* del Lazarillo: Título, capitulación y epígrafes de un texto apócrifo," in Rico, *Problemas del Lazarillo* (Madrid: Cátedra, 1988), 113–51.

lxxxi. Peter Stallybrass, "Shakespeare, the Individual, and the Text," *Cultural Studies*, ed. Lawrence Grossberg, Cary Nelson, and Paula A. Treichler (New York: Routledge, 1992), 593–612; Random Cloud, "'The very names of the Persons': Editing and the Invention of Dramatick Character," in *Staging the Renaissance*, ed. David Scott Kastan and Peter Stallybrass (New York: Routledge, 1991), 88–96.

lxxxii. This was the case with novels of chivalry in the second half of the sixteenth century, when new works in a genre abandoned by the presses circulated as manuscript copies. José Manuel Lucía Megías, *De los libros de caballerías manuscritos al Quijote* (Madrid: SIAL Ediciones, Colección Trivium, 2004).

lxxxiii. Nuñez de Guzman, *Discurso legal, histórico y politic*, fol. 23r.

lxxxiv. Ibid., fol. 23r.

lxxxv. *Don Quijote de la Mancha*, 1143. Putnam translation, 922.

7.
Robert Darnton,
"Bibliography and Iconography,"
The Devil in the Holy Water or the Art of Slander from Louis XIV to Napoleon.
Philadelphia: U of Pennsylvania P, 2010. 60–79

Robert Darnton (b. 1939) is a cultural historian specializing in eighteenth-century France. He has been a pioneer in the field of book history and print culture, and has done more than perhaps any other figure in the United States to bridge the divide between the Anglo-American bibliographical tradition, which scrutinizes the production of individual books, and the Continental *histoire du livre* tradition, which investigates the circulation of books in society. His proposal that book historians should study the "Communications Circuit" of a book's production, circulation, and reception, is reprinted in Chapter 3 (p. 231). His painstaking original research in French and Swiss archives has resulted in a number of books that demonstrate the importance of print in Revolutionary and Pre-Revolutionary France; his eye for telling details and revealing anecdotes has brought his research to life; and his gift for storytelling—honed by a brief stint as a journalist at the *New York Times*—has ensured that his books appeal to a wide audience. Darnton contributes regularly to publications such as the *New York Review of Books*.

In this essay, from his book on "the Art of Slander" in Revolutionary France, Darnton scrutinizes one example in the genre of "Secret Lives" of politicians and public figures: the *Vie secrète de Pierre Manuel*. These "Secret Lives" were cheaply produced and widely circulated gossipy, short biographies that often claimed (usually groundlessly) to reveal hidden information about their subjects, to trade on personal knowledge of their private lives, and to reveal their hypocrisy or personal immorality. What sets Darnton's reading of this example of the genre apart from more conventional historical or literary-critical approaches is the way in which—like Roger Chartier in the preceding essay—he pays attention both to the words in the book and to its physical production. He shows that the meaning of the book is the product of the interplay between the text it contains and the physical object through which that text circulates.

In particular, Darnton shows how this book brings together a portrait of Manuel with a text about him. He reveals that "a public figure like Manuel left a trail of images behind him as he rose through the ranks of the Revolution's leaders" and, by following this trail, he reconstructs the role that print played in shaping Manuel's public life and political career. The publishers of the *Vie secrète*, working fast and with limited resources, chose an existing portrait of Manuel to illustrate his life—probably based on one he had commissioned himself. For practical reasons, they placed that portrait in the middle of the book, rather than in the conventional position at the front. In doing so, they invited readers to contrast the "official" visual depiction of Manuel with the purportedly more accurate verbal description the *Vie secrète* contained. As Darnton points out, "Thanks to the visual as well as the textual portraits, they could compare the outer with the inner man and enjoy the frisson of seeing villainy stripped bare" (p. 109). This effect was not necessarily consciously intended by any one individual—whether author, publisher, artist, or engraver. Rather, it appears when we consider the book as a printed artifact that combines word and image, rather than just a verbal construct.

Darnton's concern with the social and political implications of how books circulate in society extends from the eighteenth century to our modern, digital age. In 2007, after almost 40 years at Princeton University, he was appointed Carl H. Pforzheimer University Professor and director of the Harvard University Library. In this new role, he is campaigning for a National Digital Library, which would make available digital versions of out-of-copyright books. The National Digital Library would resemble commercial enterprises such as Google Books, but would be a publicly funded undertaking that would guarantee open access and aim for more rigorous production standards than Google has so far achieved. These issues are discussed in more detail in Anthony Grafton's essay "Codex in Crisis," below, p. 555.

Bibliography and Iconography

Although *Vie secrète de Pierre Manuel* drew on the techniques of slander developed in the genre of "private lives" or "secret lives" from the Ancien Régime,[1] it belonged to the political culture of the Revolution. It mixed words and images in ways that were designed to appeal to Jacobins[2] and that look foreign to modern readers. To sort them out it is necessary to reconsider the text from the viewpoint of **bibliography** and iconography.

A book's **frontispiece** naturally belongs at its front, no matter how primitive it may be. The misplaced frontispiece in the libel against Manuel therefore needs to be explained, and the best explanation involves a brief detour into bibliographical analysis. By way of a reminder to non-bibliographers, it should be said that early modern books were composed of **sheets**, and each sheet contained several pages of text arranged so that they could be folded into gatherings—one fold (with four pages) in books of the **folio format**, two folds (eight pages) for **quartos**, and three folds (sixteen pages) for **octavos**. The gatherings, identified by **signatures** such as

1 Literally the old or previous regime (French). The period of French history preceding the Revolution of 1789.

2 Supporters of the French Revolution, especially those associated with the far left Jacobin Club.

A, B, and so on through the **printer**'s alphabet of twenty-three letters,[3] were stitched together and cut so that the pages could be read in consecutive order. *Vie secrète de Pierre Manuel* is an octavo composed of half-sheets. (The vertical chain lines[4] in the paper indicate the octavo format, which was common for casual publications of this kind.) Each gathering therefore consists of four leaves or eight pages (instead of eight leaves or sixteen pages), and the signatures run without interruption from A to H, leaving no extra paper. The bibliographical description of the book—8°: A4-H4—corresponds to its extremely simple structure: eight half-sheets stitched together with no extraneous matter—except the print of Manuel.

Normally, books and pamphlets contained **preliminary** leaves, which were used for front matter such as the **title page, half-title**, dedication, and table of contents, and the main sequence of signatures usually began with the start of the text. This is not the case with *Vie secrète de Pierre Manuel*. It has no preliminaries. Its title page functions as its cover and is the first page in the first of the eight gatherings that make up the book. Because the book lacks a half-title or covering of any kind, the frontispiece could not be inserted in the customary position—following a preliminary leaf and facing the title page. Instead it was glued like a **cancel** between the last two leaves of the first gathering. In this way, the printer saved paper but sacrificed elegance. The slipshod character of the work suggests that he did not worry about **typographical** niceties. He turned out a hack job at high speed.

But why should such a book have a frontispiece or any illustrations at all? It may seem strange, since frontispieces usually occurred in more elegant publications. But cheap prints of all sorts—caricatures, **broadsides**, canards,[5] posters, and **engravings** of current events—flooded the streets of Paris during the Revolution. They were churned out by shops in the rue Saint Jacques, hung up for sale along the quays, displayed prominently in bookstores, hawked by peddlers, and plastered on walls everywhere in the city. Many of them were portraits of revolutionary leaders. The public, hungry for information about political events, wanted to know what the new race of politicians looked like and what sort of private lives they had led before they appeared on the public scene. A print went perfectly with a "private life," and a public figure like Manuel left a trail of images behind him as he rose through the ranks of the Revolution's leaders.

By following that trail, one can turn up a good deal of information about Manuel and the way he appeared in the public eye. Although he never achieved the fame of a Marat or a Danton[6] and is hardly remembered today except among a few specialists in the history of the

3 The "printers' alphabet" does not distinguish u and v, i and j, or f and s, since these letters look very alike in some typefaces, which might lead to confusion.

4 Chain lines are marks running parallel to the shorter side of the sheet of paper, left by the mold used when making paper by hand. Because of the way in which the sheet of paper is folded to make the book, the chain lines usually run vertically in the leaves of a folio, horizontally in a quarto, and vertically in an octavo.

5 A baseless story or rumor.

6 Jean-Paul Marat (1743–93) and Georges Danton (1759–94), leading political figures in the early stages of the French Revolution. Danton was guillotined, and Marat was assassinated.

French Revolution,[i] he counted among the best-known deputies when the National Convention[7] first met on September 21, 1792, and began to cope with a staggering agenda of problems: the fate of Louis XVI, the creation of a new republic, the defense of the country against the invading armies of Austria and Prussia, and the increasing hostility of the sans-culotte[8] movement in Paris, which had erupted in the horrific massacres of September 2–6.

Manuel owed his election to support from the Parisian militants. Although *Vie secrète de Pierre Manuel* gave a tendentious account of his biography, it got most of the facts right. After struggling without much success to make a living and a name for himself as a man of letters before 1789, he found a new career in the officialdom created by the Revolution in Paris—first as an outspoken champion of the Third Estate in his local electoral district, then as its representative in the Paris Commune, and by 1790 as an administrator in the office of the mayor responsible for the policing of the book trade. Thanks to support from the Jacobin Club, where he became known for his outspoken oratory, he was elected as public prosecutor (*procureur*) of the Commune on December 2, 1791. From that post, he gained notoriety by writing his open letter to the king, the one mentioned by Pierre Turbat that began "Sire, I do not like kings" and went on to recommend that Louis XVI entrust the education of the dauphin[9] to the popular, Rousseauistic[10] author Bernardin de Saint-Pierre. Manuel was suspended from his functions for complicity in the insurrection of June 20, 1792, when a hostile crowd invaded the Tuileries Palace and forced the king to drink to the health of the nation. But he was reinstated in time to participate in the overthrow of the monarchy on August 10. For the next six weeks he rode the wave of sans-culotte power that swept everything before it until it engulfed all Paris in the massacres of September. Although he intervened to save some lives, he stood by the most radical leaders of the Commune[11]—including Robespierre, Collot d'Herbois, and Billaud-Varennes—during the massacres and therefore stood out as a champion of the people during the elections to the Convention. When he took a seat with the radical Parisian delegation on September 21, his portrait was being hawked in the streets along with those of other prominent deputies.

The **provenance** of these prints cannot be traced, but the images of Manuel that circulated at street level probably were derived, by means of engravings and copies of copies, from a portrait that hangs today in the Musée historique of Versailles. It, too, has an uncertain past. Manuel may well have commissioned it himself, probably sometime in the spring or summer of 1792. By then he had emerged as one of the most popular politicians in Paris, and according to one particularly shrewd observer he had a touch of vanity.

---

7 The constitutional and legislative assembly of Revolutionary France, which sat from September 1792 until October 1795.

8 Radical laboring-class faction in the French Revolution.

9 The heir to the French throne.

10 Influenced by the educational theories of Jean-Jacques Rousseau (1712–78), as set out in *Émile* (1762).

11 The government of Paris during the French Revolution. Maximilien de Robespierre (1758–94), Jean-Marie Collot d'Herbois (1749–96), and Jacques Nicolas Billaud-Varenne (1756–1819) were all French Revolutionary politicians and important figures in the Reign of Terror that followed the earliest stages of the Revolution. Robespierre was executed in 1794, while the other two were exiled.

In her *Considérations sur les principaux événements de la Révolution française* (1818), Mme. de Staël[12] includes a sketch of Manuel in an account of how she survived the September Massacres. During the last days of August as rumors of the impending catastrophe began to circulate, she considered herself safe. Her husband, the baron de Staël-Holstein, who was the Swedish ambassador, had left Paris, but the Swedish embassy, where she remained, was not a likely target of the crowd. Two of her closest friends, however, had been imprisoned for suspected aristocratic sympathies, and by the beginning of September 1792 the sans-culottes were calling for a slaughter of the prisoners. Rumors had spread about a counter-revolutionary conspiracy that might erupt at any moment from the prisons and spread carnage on the home front while the enemy invaded from abroad. France had declared war on Austria on April 20, confident that its armies would sweep to victory. Instead, the French offensive became stalled; Lafayette, France's most famous general, deserted to the enemy; and the Austrians with their Prussian allies picked off the key fortresses on the French border. They swept past Verdun, and nothing seemed capable of stopping them before they fell on Paris and slaughtered everyone who resisted. The Brunswick Manifesto, issued by the commander of the Austro-Prussian armies on July 25, threatened the sans-culottes with this fate. They responded by calling for a counter-massacre, which would eliminate the danger in the prisons so that they then could face the invasion in an ultimate fight to the death. The streets filled with rioters, the air with wild talk. Treachery, slaughter, an uprising to purge the earth of counter-revolution—anything seemed possible.

The situation looked so desperate, as Mme. de Staël observed it, that nothing could save her friends except the last-minute intervention by someone with some hold on power. But who? She scoured a list of all the members of the Commune, hoping to find a rescuer. Her eye hit upon the name of Manuel. It called up a vague memory: Wasn't he one of those obscure writers who had struggled to break out of the lower ranks of the republic of letters on the eve of the Revolution? He had published the correspondence of Mirabeau[13] with a **preface** that had demonstrated a desire for recognition, if not much talent. Perhaps he could be moved by someone who had directed a salon at the summit of the literary world before 1789.

A request for an audience led to a meeting in Manuel's study at seven o'clock—"a rather democratic hour"—on the morning of September 1. While she waited for the public prosecutor to appear, the baroness studied her surroundings: "and I saw his portrait, made for him and placed on his own desk; that made me hope that he might at least be vulnerable to an appeal to his vanity."[ii] Not every sans-culotte leader defended the cause of the people from a desk with his own portrait perched in front of him. Once softened up by Mme. de Staël, Manuel did not let his plebeian connections prevent him from coming to the aid of some aristocrats. He behaved generously, even heroically, according to Mme. de Staël's reconstruction of events. He ordered her friends released, and on the following day he saved Mme. de Staël herself. While attempting to escape from Paris in a coach drawn by six horses and mounted by

12 Germaine de Staël (1766–1817), French-speaking Swiss writer who survived the Revolution. She fled France in 1792 and lived in exile in Switzerland, where she established a famous literary Salon at Coppet.

13 Honoré Gabriel Riqueti, comte de Mirabeau (1749–91) was a moderate French Revolutionary.

lackeys in livery—an attempt to awe the sans-culottes, which backfired—she was surrounded by a crowd and carried off for interrogation in the Hôtel de Ville. There she encountered Manuel once again. He was receiving reports from the scenes of the slaughter and dispatching emissaries to try to stem it, but he spared a minute from the bloody business to direct her to his office. There she sat for seven hours, watching from the window as the massacrers, covered with blood, reported to the Commune. That night Manuel accompanied her back to her residence in his own vehicle. When groups of sans-culottes stopped them, he called out "Public Prosecutor of the Commune" and they gave way. With the help of a new passport that he arranged to have delivered, she escaped the next day to the safety of Switzerland.

The portrait studied so anxiously by Mme. de Staël almost certainly is the one that now hangs in the Musée de Versailles, the only painting of Manuel known to exist (see Fig. 1.7). Seen in its current setting, it appears impressive: Manuel sits upright and looks out squarely at the viewer in a dignified pose. It is a highly finished pastel by one of the masters from the Ancien Régime who had rallied to the Revolution, Joseph Ducreux. Despite some important commissions before 1789 (the duc de Choiseul had sent him to Vienna to produce the first official portrait of Marie-Antoinette after her betrothal to the future Louis XVI), Ducreux had failed to be admitted to the Royal Academy of Painting and Sculpture. Like Jacques-Louis David,[14] a close friend of his, he became an ardent Jacobin. He welcomed the transformation of cultural institutions produced by the Revolution, and he painted its foremost leaders, including Mirabeau, Barnave, Saint-Just, and Robespierre.[15] His portrait put Manuel in good, Jacobin company.

The collections of prints in the Bibliothèque nationale de France contain eight portraits of Manuel, all of them **copperplate engravings** or aquatints.[iii] [16] Most have no clues as to their origin, but one (see Fig. 1.8) is inscribed "Ducreux pinxt P.M. Alix Sculptr," meaning Alix had engraved it after Ducreux's painting. Its caption reads:

> P. MANUEL
>
> Public Prosecutor of the Commune of Paris in 1792;
> Deputy to the Convention in the First Year of the French Republic;
> Author *of L'Année française* in 4 volumes;
> of the *Coup d'oeil philosophique sur Saint-Louis;*
> of *La Police dévoilée;*
> Editor of the *Lettres de Mirabeau*
> At the author's residence, rue Christine no. 2

---

14 David (1748–1825) was an important neo-classical painter whose scenes from antiquity forged a vivid link between contemporary France and ancient Rome. David strongly supported the Revolution and, eventually, Napoleon.

15 Honoré, comte de Mirabeau (1749–91), Antoine Barnave (1761–93), Louis Antoine Léon de Saint-Just (1767–94) and Maximilien de Robespierre (1758–94) were all important orators, politicians, or revolutionary leaders in the early stages of the French Revolution.

16 "A method of etching on copper, by the use of a resinous solution and nitric acid" (*OED*).

Fig. 1.7: Portrait of Manuel by Joseph Ducreux. *Source:* Etablissement du musée et du domaine de Versailles.

Fig. 1.8: Print of Manuel. *Source:* Bibliothèque nationale de France, Département des estampes, D203608.

As the caption indicates, the engraving provided favorable publicity for Manuel soon after his election to the Convention. It presents him as a man of letters turned public servant, listing his most reputable works as if they constituted a pedigree (it passed over his more dubious publications in silence). The engraving may also have been meant to bring in some money, because the caption specified that it could be bought from Manuel at his home address. And it has a family resemblance to the other prints, which could have been copied from it or adapted with minor changes from the Ducreux painting.

Despite their similarity, however, the other prints of Manuel belonged to different contexts and transmitted different messages. One was produced after his death; we know this because it gives the date of his execution. Another is the same as the frontispiece in *Vie secrète*, but it has no caption and has been trimmed in such a way that one cannot tell anything about its provenance: it could have been clipped out of the book, or, as seems more likely, it could have circulated independently like other popular prints. Two other portraits probably date from the early days of the Convention and were sold from bookshops and peddler's packs like all the **ephemera** of 1792–93. The first, a **lithograph** by Auguste Bry, simply said it was for sale in the bookshop of Rosselin, Quai Voltaire. The second carried a caption that identified Manuel in a neutral manner and gave its source as the print shop of Basset at the corner of the rue Saint Jacques and the rue des Mathurins (see Fig. 1.9).

A caricature from February 1790 shows that shop (see Fig. 1.10 and Fig. 1.11). The Basset hound on the sign above the door is a rebus[17] evoking Paul-André Basset, one of the most important producers and dealers of prints from the late eighteenth century.[iv] He made a fortune by adjusting his output of images to shifts in the political temperature. In the 1780s he produced panegyrics[18] to Louis XVI; in the 1790s he adhered to the Jacobin line; and after 1800 he celebrated Bonaparte. In this case, he depicted his own shop in the background of a scene that served as a bawdy commentary on the secularization of the monasteries: two monks are being shaved and outfitted for civilian life; the one in the foreground, a stereotypical, oversexed man of the cloth, is cavorting with his female barber.

Inside the shop, a saleswoman sits behind the counter with prints piled in front of her. Other prints are displayed outside the door, and a peddler is leaving the shop loaded down with prints to be hawked in the streets. The caricature that dangles from the peddler's pack is one of the best-known prints from 1789: it protests against the exploitation of the Third Estate[19] by showing a prelate and a nobleman riding on the back of a bent-over peasant. To make the message clear, its caption is written out in the form of a note pinned to the pack: "It must be hoped that this game will finish soon."

The images of Manuel circulated in this kind of a setting, and, like Basset's print, they conveyed ideological messages. One caricature, a royalist print from December 1792, casts Manuel in the company of the radical republicans who had led the attacks on Louis XVI (see Fig. 1.12).

17 A visual trick or puzzle that uses pictures to represent words or parts of words.

18 "A public speech or published text in praise of a person or thing" (*OED*).

19 In this context, the First Estate is the clergy, the Second Estate is the aristocracy, and the Third Estate is the common people.

Fig. 1.9: Print of Manuel. *Source:* Bibliothèque nationale de France, Département des estampes, D203610.

Fig. 1.10: A satirical print about the secularization of monastic orders. *Source:* Bibliothèque nationale de France, Collection Vinck 3362.

While a motley crew of agitators tries to save the nation—represented as an ice sculpture that is melting under rays projected by a Bourbon[20] sun—he flounders ignominiously on a manure pile at the center of the picture, accompanied by his notorious "Sire, I do not like kings." The journalists around him—Brissot, Carra, Gorsas, Fauchet, Destnoulins, and Audouin—belong to different factions of the left that dominated the Convention when it first met.

The left fell apart, however, in the great debate about the king's fate in January 1793. Manuel typified their wavering. Although he did not hesitate to declare the king guilty of treason, he could not bring himself to vote for Louis's immediate execution. He walked out of the Convention as soon as the death penalty was pronounced, then resigned and withdrew to his hometown of Montargis. By March he had acquired such a reputation as a moderate—that is, in Jacobin terms, a Girondist[21] and a counterrevolutionary—that he was nearly killed in a local riot. He went into hiding in the outskirts of Paris but was hunted down after the overthrow of the Girondists on May 31 and was executed on November 14 as one of their co-conspirators.

The dramatic swings in Manuel's revolutionary career provided the main theme of the last print, a large folio sheet that may have been peddled in the streets as a broadside but has survived

20 The King of France was part of the Bourbon dynasty.

21 The Girondistes were a moderate faction in the French Revolution, less radical than the Jacobins.

Fig. 1.11: Detail showing Basset's shop. *Source:* Bibliothèque nationale de France, Collection Vinck 3362.

Fig. 1.12: A royalist caricature of 1792, depicting Manuel at the center of a group of radicals. *Source*: Bibliothèque nationale de France, Département des estampes, Collection Vinck, 4364.

in book form as one "tableau" in the *Collection complète des tableaux historiques de la Révolution française* (Paris, 1798–1802). This magnificent, three-volume folio collection of engravings offered a view of the Revolution from the perspective of the Napoleonic Consulate—a view that affirmed the fundamental changes produced in 1789–92 while condemning the excesses of 1793–94. Volume II contained portraits of the sixty persons who, in the judgment of the anonymous editors, had played the most important roles in the Revolution. Each portrait occupied one page and was composed of three parts: a shoulder-length engraving of the individual, a picture of some event in which he was involved, and an engraved text or "historical discourse containing the private and political life of the individual being depicted." By combining the text with the pictures, each tableau provided a "portrait" in the fullest sense of the word, one that fleshed out the imagery with a biographical sketch of the kind that had flourished in French literature since Jean de La Bruyère and Madeleine de Scudéry.[22]

22 Jean de La Bruyère (1645–96), French essayist best known for his *Caractères* (1688), which included pen portraits of his contemporaries. Madeleine de Scudéry (1607–1701), French novelist and *salonière,* who included disguised versions of contemporaries in some of her novels.

Many of the mini-biographies, including Manuel's, also had some affinity with libels, as the introduction made clear by emphasizing their treatment of the subject's "private life." The engravings and word pictures went together, very much as they had done in underground classics from the Ancien Régime such as the *Vie privée de Louis XV*. The last and most elaborate portrait of Manuel therefore shows how several elements had coalesced in a retrospective view of the Revolution that was hardening into an orthodoxy at the time of Bonaparte's seizure of power.

The portrait in the circular frame resembles the other prints of Manuel and could have been derived from the Ducreux pastel. The picture below it shows Manuel being attacked by a crowd of hostile Jacobins during the riot in Montargis of March 1793. A tiny inscription under the picture identified it as the work of Jean Duplessi-Bertaux [1747–1819], painted and engraved by him in the Year VIII[23] (1799–1800). Like Ducreux, Duplessi-Bertaux had won some important commissions under the Ancien Régime but never made it into the Royal Academy of Painting and Sculpture. He, too, followed David's lead into revolutionary cultural politics. He became an ardent Jacobin and turned out paintings and engravings of revolutionary events right up to 1800. Many of the engravings were published in the 1802 **edition** of *Tableaux historiques de la Révolution francaise*, which celebrated him as "the CALLOT of our time." In depicting violence, they echo the **etchings** about the atrocities of war produced by Jacques Callot [c. 1592–1635] in the 1630s, but they also have a monumental quality and a classical coolness that evoke ancient bas-reliefs.[24] Their choice of subjects suggests sympathy for the basic gains of the Revolution combined with repugnance at the Terror,[25] or what they referred to as "Maratism." That position, a kind of moderate Jacobinism that suited the early years of the Consulate,[26] came through clearly in the texts engraved beneath Duplessi-Bertaux's tableaux.

The biographical sketch of Manuel portrayed him as inconsistent and insincere, an opportunist who threw himself into the radical movement of the Paris sections only to renounce it after it had swept him into eminence. Here is Manuel's "private and public life," in synopsis, as it was presented to the public for the last time.

> If anyone during the Revolution exhibited a capacity for coming up with revolutionary conceptions at one time and a vacillating conduct at another, it was certainly Manuel. It is hard to know what to make of such a strangely contradictory character, considering his public declaration of hatred for kings and the regrets he expressed for the condemnation of the last king of the French, his intimate connections with the partisans of Maratism and his

---

23 The French republic adopted a new calendar, consisting of twelve months each divided into three ten-day weeks. It was in use for about 12 years from late 1793 to 1805.

24 A type of sculpture in which the depth of the faces or figures depicted is less than it would be if reproduced to scale.

25 The Terror (also known as the Reign of Terror) is the period of intense violence in 1793–94 following the early phases of the French Revolution, in which many "enemies of the Revolution" were executed.

26 The government of France between 1799 and 1804; also used as a term for this period of France's history.

> brave opposition to the activities of that party, and his love of philosophy and humanity contrasted with the part he played in the execrable massacres of September 2 and 3. It is generally believed that he only declared himself to be a partisan of Marat in order to get elected to the Convention and that in the end he was ashamed of the excesses he had committed.
>
> From a humble birth, he became a schoolmaster. Then he made a name for himself by publishing his *De la police dévoilée*. By flattering the common people and proclaiming himself an enemy of kings, he managed to get himself named as public prosecutor of the Commune. He was still in office during the uprising of August 10 and claimed responsibility for the success of that day. He was present in the same capacity when the murdering took place in the prisons on September 2. He admitted this himself, because during his interrogation [before the Revolutionary Tribunal] he said that he had seen two corpses still palpitating there. It seems that he did little to stop those atrocities, because they continued to take place. After that he was selected as a deputy to the Convention. But from the very beginning he broke with all his colleagues from the Parisian deputation. He joined the party of the Gironde and became one of the most ardent enemies of the Jacobins.
>
> During the trial of the last king, Manuel, who was one of the Convention's secretaries responsible for tabulating the votes, was accused of having mishandled the roll and of being decidedly partial in his behavior. A few days later he resigned and withdrew to Montargis, his hometown. There he was soon hunted down by the agents of the Maratists and the Orléanists and was assaulted by a gang of madmen, who left him for dead. A while later he was arrested and brought before the Revolutionary Tribunal, which sent him to the scaffold.[v]

As the images reproduced in this chapter make clear, the frontispiece of *Vie secrète de Pierre Manuel* belonged to the genre of popular prints hawked in the streets of Paris during the revolutionary decade.[27] Such prints could not be sold openly under the Ancien Régime because the Parisian police generally managed to curb the satirical bent of the artists and printmakers of the rue Saint Jacques. Despite clandestine production and foreign imports, France never developed a visual political culture comparable to the caricaturing that flourished openly in the London of Hogarth, Gilray, and Rowlandson.[28] But after the fall of the Bastille, the rue Saint Jacques exploded with activity; peddlers did a roaring business in prints as well as **pamphlets** and supplied a public eager to see the faces of the men whose "private lives" were exposed in print. As their slipshod quality attests, these illustrated booklets were designed to

27 The frontispiece portrait of Manuel (not reproduced here) has a satirical caption accusing him of treacherously pursuing his own interests instead of those of the state.

28 William Hogarth (1697–1764), James Gillray (1756–1815), Thomas Rowlandson (1757–1827), all British caricaturists.

appeal to ordinary readers. Unlike fine engravings, which commonly sold for 10 livres, cheap prints often cost 10 sous (there were 20 sous to a livre), about the same as a medium-size pamphlet or half the price of a short book.[vi] A skilled worker like a locksmith or a printer made 40–50 sous a day; he could afford to part with 30 sous for a "private life" with a frontispiece, though not easily, and he might prefer to read it in a tavern or a political club.

Of course, images were sometimes attached to texts in the underground literature of the Ancien Régime. A few libels carried frontispieces that combined sober portraits with slanderous epigraphs exactly as in *Vie secrète de Pierre Manuel*. *Anecdotes sur Mme. la comtesse du Barry* (1775), the supreme bestseller in this genre, pictured the royal mistress opposite the title page as if it had captured the true image as well as the inside story of its anti-heroine. Underneath the quite attractive portrait, the caption read:

> Without wit, without talent, from the midst of infamy,
> She was elevated to the throne.
> Never against an enemy cabale
> Did she conspire;
> And unmindful of ambition's warning signals,
> A puppet of intriguers, she reigned by nothing other than her charms.

Vie secrète de Pierre Manuel conformed to this well-established model. The continuity in technique—a matter of contrasting words and pictures—linked the propaganda of the Terror to the pamphleteering against Louis XV.

But when the printers assembled the ingredients of *Vie secrète de Pierre Manuel*, they found it impossible to place the frontispiece opposite the title page without adding another half-sheet. Therefore, they inserted it at a convenient place in the first gathering. In the rush to cobble together an attack on a prominent Girondin, the master printer in the Imprimerie de Franklin, rue de Cléry no. 75, may not have had time to commission a new engraving. Instead of investing in an original work, he probably drew on the stock of prints that were available in the nearby shops of the rue Saint Jacques, shops like that of Paul-André Basset, who had produced the engraving of Manuel that had been hawked in the streets several months earlier. The engravers could have touched up an old plate and added the slanderous epitaph, which undercuts the image in the same manner as does the verse engraved under the frontispiece of Mme. du Barry.

One can only guess at the exact nature of the production process. But whatever procedure they followed, the printers combined the visual material with a biographical text in a way that would have been familiar to their clients. Many of the other slanderous attacks on revolutionary politicians did the same. I have identified thirty-eight such libels. Most of them carry titles that begin with "vie privée" or "vie secrète," and 14 contain portraits, usually in the form of frontispieces with derogatory captions. *Vie secrète de Pierre Manuel* was a typical example of a general genre: the revolutionary libel.

The iconographic dimension of this literature hardly seems surprising. Readers wanted to see what such persons looked like, to read their countenances for clues to their character.

Thanks to the visual as well as the textual portraits, they could compare the outer with the inner man and enjoy the frisson[29] of seeing villainy stripped bare. Or, if they sympathized with the victims, they could resist the textual argument and look for redeeming features in a slandered politician exposed to the public's scorn. Either way, the message was carried by visual and verbal metaphors of unveiling and unmasking. Manuel himself had done more than any other libeler to exploit this rhetorical register in *La Police de Paris dévoilée* and his other works. In *Vie secrète de Pierre Manuel* he fell victim to the devices that he had perfected.

Not a happy ending—and perhaps not a satisfactory conclusion either for the argument might be vulnerable to a fundamental objection. It seems reasonable to assume that the libels were designed in a way that was meant to elicit particular reactions on the part of their readers, but how can one know how the readers read them?

Notes

i. Despite his prominent role in the events of 1792–93, there is no biography of Manuel before the publication of Huguette Leloup-Audibert, *Pierre Louis Manuel (1753–1793): Du pouvoir à l'échafaud* (Gien, 2006), which has little information about his early life. The biographical notice in Auguste Kuscinski, *Dictionnaire des conventionnels* (Paris, 1916–19), 2: 427–28, summarizes most of the available information about his life. Some key documents concerning his pre-revolutionary career are in the dossier related to his imprisonment in the Bastille on February 3, 1786: Archives Nationales W295, no. 246; Bibliothèque de l'Arsenal ms. 12460; *La Bastille dévoilée, ou recueil de pièces authentiques pour servir à son histoire* (Paris, 1789–90), 3: 105–06; and Frantz Funck-Brentano, *Les Lettres de cachet à Paris, étude suivie d'une liste des prisonniers de la Bastille (1659–1/89)* (Paris, 1903), 415–16. There are also some perceptive remarks on Manuel's life as a hack writer before 1789 in Gudrun Gersmann, *Im Schatten der Bastille: Die Welt der Schriftsteller, Kolporteure und Buchhändler am Vorabend der Französischen Revolution* (Stuttgart, 1993), 146–52. Aside from his own writings, the best sources on Manuel's role in the Revolution are F.A. Aulard, ed., *La Société des Jacobins: Recueil de documents pour l'histoire du Club des Jacobins de Paris,* 6 vols. (Paris, 1889–97), and Paul Robiquet, *Le Personnel municipal de Paris pendant la Révolution, 2 vols.* (Paris, 1890).

ii. Anne Louise Germaine Necker, baronne de Staël-Holstein, *Considérations sur la Révolution française*, ed. Jacques Godechot (1818; Paris, 1983), 283.

iii. Bibliothèque nationale de France, Département des estampes, D203602—5, D203608—10, and *Collection complète des tableaux historiques de la Révolution française, en deux volumes* (Paris, 1798). See also *Images de la Révolution française: Catalogue du vidéodisque coproduit par la Bibliothèque nationale et Pergamon Press*, 3 vols. (Paris, 1990).

iv. Although there is no full-scale study of Basset, the character of his trade can be pieced together from references in Maxime Préaud, Pierre Casselle, Marianne Grivel, and Corinne Le Bitouzé, *Dictionnaire des éditeurs d'estampes à Paris sous l'Ancien Régime* (Paris, 1987), 45–46; Roger Portalis and Henri Béraldi, *Les Graveurs du dix-huitième siècle* (Paris, 1882), 3: 719; and Marcel Roux, *Bibliothèque nationale Département des Estampes: Inventaire du fonds français* (Paris, 1933), 2: 157–58. For general accounts of prints during the eighteenth century, see Pierre-Louis Duchartre and René Saulnier, *L'Imagerie parisienne (L'Imagerie de la rue Saint-Jacques)* (Paris, 1944); Antoine de Baecq, *La Caricature révolutionnaire* (Paris, 1988); Klaus Herding and Rolf Reichardt, *Die Bildpublizistik der Französischen Revolution* (Frankfurt am Main, 1989); Christoph Denelzik-Brüggemann and Rolf Reichardt, *Bildgedächtnis eines welthistorischen Ereignisses: Die*

29 Thrill.

Tableaux historiques de la Révolution française (Göttingen, 2001); and François-Louis Bruel, *Un Siècle d'histoire de France par l'estampe*, 1770–1871, 8 vols. (Paris, 1909).

v. *Collection complète des tableaux historiques de la Révolution française* (Paris, 1798–1802), 2: n.p. On the complex publishing history of this work, see Claudette Hould, "Neue Hypothesen zu den französischen Ausgaben der *Tableaux historiques de la Révolution française*," Denelzik-Brüggemann and Reichardt *Bildgedächtnis eines welthistorischen Ereignisses*, 35–84.

vi. De Baecq, *La Caricature révolutionnaire*, 27.

CHAPTER 2

Textuality

8. Jerome J. McGann, "Shall These Bones Live?" *The Beauty of Inflections: Literary Investigations in Historical Method and Theory*. Oxford: Clarendon, 1985. 90–111

Jerome McGann (b. 1937) is John Stewart Bryan University Professor at the University of Virginia, where he has taught since 1986. Over a long career, he has published over forty books dealing with Romanticism, literary criticism, and editing, among other topics. McGann has been a strong advocate for literary critical approaches that situate texts in their historical contexts, and pay attention to their material dimensions. He has also been an important theorist and practitioner of digital humanities, and one of his essays on this topic is included in Chapter 5 (p. 459).

In this essay, first delivered as a paper at the inaugural meeting of the Society for Textual Studies in 1981, he identifies two opposing ways of approaching literary texts: on the one hand, a method that concentrates on "intrinsic," structural, and linguistic aspects of the text (which could, broadly speaking, be called post-structuralist); on the other, a method that concentrates on the historical context in which the text was produced and disseminated, including the physical formats in which it appeared, and the minutiae of publication history and textual variants (which we could call historical materialist). The first approach he associates with Roland Barthes, the French literary theorist who, in his famous essay "The Death of the Author" (1967), valorized the role of the reader in the interpretation of literary texts. The second approach he traces from the classical philologists and biblical scholars of the nineteenth century, such as F.A. Wolf and Johann Gottfried Eichhorn, to contemporary textual scholars such as James Thorpe and G. Thomas Tanselle. Those who take the second kind of approach are often called "scholars," and their work is thought to be preliminary and subordinate to the work of "critics" who take the first kind of approach. But McGann argues that the two approaches are interdependent and equally important, even if they cannot always agree.

Here, as in much of his work, McGann argues that literary texts emerge from particular socio-historical circumstances, some of them out of the author's control, and that studying these circumstances is crucial for understanding the full range of ways in which the text creates meaning. In this respect, he anticipates D.F. McKenzie's call four years later, in 1985, for a "sociology of texts." Among the circumstances McGann considers are the processes of publication, whether in a book, newspaper, or elsewhere, and the physical format in which the work appeared. In this essay, McGann offers a poem by Lord Byron as an example of how meaning is created not only by the words of the poem, but also by the circumstances in which it enters the reader's consciousness. In McGann's view, then, the art of interpretation must be grounded in factual knowledge of the text's history.

Shall These Bones Live?[1]

I.

A professional society launches itself in 1981 under the aegis of "textual studies" and proposes to issue scholarly papers in a journal called *Text*. These are notable events, all the more so because their initial impression belies their actual significance. For such a society and such a journal, in an academic world currently dominated by structuralist and post-structuralist theory and practice, necessarily suggest an interest in the semiological and Derridan "text," and in the entire critical enterprise which goes under the heading of "textuality."

One has only to cast a glance at the editorial and advisory board of this society, however, to see that its interests must be very different indeed. Riffaterre, Said, Derrida, de Man: none of these famous men are part of this project.[2] Instead we find other names—equally famous, perhaps, but residents of another planet—like Orgel, Litz, Vieth, and Tanselle.[3] So an illumination begins. *Text*, and the Society for Textual Scholarship, is a revisionist action by **philologists**, scholars, and "textual critics" in the traditional sense. The creation of such a society and such a journal at this particular historical moment is, in other words, a bold—even an aggressive—move. It will bring not peace but a sword.[4] Yet when the inevitable conflict is engaged, what will be the issues at stake? Is *Text* to be a sort of Vendéean Uprising, a center of reaction where **editors**, bibliographers, and philologists can meet and agreeably deplore all that is new-fangled, French, and transitory?[5]

I raise these matters here partly because I want to explain my own purpose in associating with this new venture, and partly because I want to make a polemic for a revisionist policy which

1 The title refers to Ezekiel 37:1–14. In this biblical story, God transports the prophet Ezekiel to a valley filled with dry bones. God asks "shall these bones live?" He tells Ezekiel to prophesy to the bones, and they rise up, join themselves together, and come to life.

2 Michael or Michel Riffaterre (1924–2006), Edward Said (1935–2003), Jacques Derrida (1930–2004), and Paul de Man (1919–83), all still living when McGann wrote this essay, are cited here as examples of critics who share a broadly post-structuralist understanding of "text" as an interpretative field.

3 Stephen Orgel (b. 1933), A. Walton Litz (b. 1929), David Vieth (b. 1925), and G. Thomas Tanselle (b.1934); all eminent textual scholars and editors.

4 Alluding to Jesus' statement "I came not to send peace, but a sword" Matthew 10:34; see also Luke 12:51.

5 The Vendéean Uprising was a Catholic and Royalist revolt against the French Revolution that occurred in the Vendée region of France between 1793 and 1796. McGann cites it here as an example of a doomed, reactionary agitation.

will not be a reactionary one. In order to make my position clear, I shall have to rehearse some familiar matters relating to the present state of literary studies.

Textual criticism, in the traditional sense, is an analytic discipline separated into two provinces, the so-called Lower and Higher Criticism.[6] Its practitioners are those guardians of our dry bones, the editors, bibliographers, and philologists of various sorts who are best known to the ordinary student of literature for the work they do *not* do: that is, interpretation and literary criticism.

It is an historical irony of some magnitude that twentieth-century stylistics and hermeneutics,[7] or literary criticism and interpretation, emerged directly from the traditions of critical philology which developed over the course of the eighteenth and nineteenth centuries. From F.A. Wolf to Wilamowitz,[8] philological analysis was intimately connected not merely to the elucidation of the text, but to what James Thorpe once (and forever) denominated "the aesthetics of textual criticism."[i] The New Criticism's devotion to "the poem itself," as well as the more recent fascination with texts not as specific objects but as "methodological fields"[ii] (or *foci* for interpretive strategies), descend to us through the mediation of various form critics, linguists, and philologists, and most immediately through people like Saussure, Sapir, and Jakobson.[9] In this descent, however, a gap opened up between the work of the scholar and the work of the critic. This gap confronts us today as almost unbridgeable, a gulf we locate by that ultimate sign of contradiction, The Text.

The problem with this polarization in literary studies is not at all that differences should exist between the methods and interests of scholars on the one hand and critics on the other, or
between so-called extrinsic and intrinsic studies. One might well recall here those famous words of William Blake, for they seem especially pertinent: "These two classes of men are always upon earth, & they should be enemies: whoever tries to reconcile them seeks to destroy existence." Blake's view was that "Without Contraries is no progression,"[iii] and his proverb holds equally well on our tight little island of literary studies. The problem is that these two classes of men (and women) tend to carry on their work in entire isolation from each other, and not at all that they engage in those struggles and intellectual combats which Blake called "Mental Fight."

---

6 Historically, "Lower Criticism" is the effort to determine an accurate, final version of a biblical text, whereas "Higher Criticism," which only fully emerged in the nineteenth century, is concerned with the sources of biblical documents, as well as their historical context.

7 Relating to issues of interpretation.

8 Friedrich August Wolf (1759–1824), German classical scholar, philologist, and textual editor best known for his work on Homer. Ulrich von Wilamowitz-Moellendorff (1848–1931), German classical philologist and authority on the ancient world. Both men are cited here as pillars of the philological tradition of textual scholarship, whose quasi-scientific method makes use of detailed analytical attention to resolve textual problems.

9 Ferdinand de Saussure (1857–1913), Edward Sapir (1884–1939), and Roman Jakobson (1896–1982) all cited here as examples of scholars from the generation before McGann whose work on linguistics has influenced an approach to literary criticism based on the study of literary language.

These struggles must begin, and I propose to aid the event here by examining some of the positions and fault-lines which appear on either side.

The enemies of traditional philology, from its early antagonists like Leavis to its most recent critics like Barthes, recurrently charge it with various sorts of dehumanization.[10] Philologists murder to dissect,[11] and where are the pleasures of the text for the editor and the bibliographer? Over and over again the literary critic struggles to tear the poetic work from the hands of the Casaubons of the world and to deliver it over to the Dorotheas.[12]

One of the most eloquent, and influential, pleas for such a delivery was made in 1971 by Roland Barthes in his essay "From Work to Text."[iv] In this exemplary paper Barthes distinguished sharply between the "work" of traditional literary studies, both critical and scholarly, and the "text" of a new type of hermeneutics. The distinction means to separate "the work," which "is concrete, occupying a portion of book-space," from "the text," which, because "it exists only as discourse" and never as concrete object, is in reality "a methodological field," a locus for the continuous production of literary signification. Barthes spoke for a generation of new literary readers and interpreters when he said that "*the text is experienced only as an activity, a production.*" This famous dictum announces a renewed method for dealing with the polysemous[13] aspects of literary productions. They are not "works," which Barthes called "objects of consumption," but "texts," which "ask the reader for an active collaboration."[v] Those of us who have worked with the dead letters of our literary pasts, whether as editors, bibliographers, or whatever, understand all too well the force of Barthes's polemic. William Todd's essay "On the Use of Advertisements in Bibliographical Studies"[vi] is a model of its kind, even a brilliant work, but one does not value it—or consult it—because it generates textual pleasure, any more than Todd wrote it to collaborate in an intertextual activity. Todd's essay treats literary works as concrete objects and—worse still—seems uninterested in aesthetic pleasures altogether. The essay merely (merely?) shows us a peculiarly reliable method for establishing accurate dates of publication.

Todd's is a piece of Dryasdust[14] scholarship, then, sure enough, and those of us who—like myself—admire it, are faced with the need to justify that fine piece of work. Nor will it do merely to launch a tit-for-tat rejoinder, and ask how much pleasure gets generated through a Derridean text like *On Grammatology*, or through the turgid academese one repeatedly confronts in journals like *Glyph* and *Diacritics*. And indeed, such journals merely represent the tactical failures of an impressive general strategy; to locate these failures is, at the most, to uncover the symptoms of what ought to be our true objects of investigation.

---

10 F.R. Leavis (1895–1978), influential liberal humanist literary critic, and Roland Barthes (1915–80), post-structuralist critic and theorist. Their critical approaches were widely divergent, but they shared a sense of the importance of the sophisticated pleasure literature gives, which they felt was ignored or deadened by philological approaches to it.

11 An allusion to William Wordsworth's poem "The Tables Turned," line 28.

12 Casaubon and Dorothea are characters in George Eliot's novel *Middlemarch* (1874); the desiccated and bookish Casaubon is here contrasted with the humane and compassionate Dorothea.

13 I.e., having multiple meanings.

14 "Dryasdust" was a tedious antiquarian who featured as a character in several novels by Walter Scott.

In fact, these contemporary textual strategies have no more strength than their limits permit, and to use them well one must understand those limits. Barthes, for example, speaks for a large number of influential contemporary critics when he sets a premium upon literature as a process of production rather than consumption, and when he disvalues a critical method which tries to treat artistic works as objects. In each case he appeals to that powerful tradition of aesthetic criticism which emerges with Kant and Coleridge[15] and continues into our own day. Coleridge declared that objects as objects are fixed and dead, and he elevated the activities of the so-called "creative imagination." Reason and what the Enlightenment termed "the critical faculties" are suspect powers in this tradition, which has developed that ideology of process and production—"something evermore about to be"[16]—that is perpetuated in post-structuralist criticism.

The great strength of this tradition lies in the freedom it can give to the critic-as-reader. Authority for literary creativity emerges from a dead past to a living present. In such a situation the function of criticism becomes, avowedly, to sustain its own productivity, and its object becomes the process of that productivity. But such a procedure will succeed only when it accepts the limits of its own method. One of those fundamental limits commands that such a method can generate literary experience only, not literary knowledge. Such criticism should not mean but be,[17] and as it yearns to embrace its own aesthesis, it also tends to abandon knowledge and science.[vii]

We must not mistake the character of this limitation, however. It is not a weakness or a fault in the method, it is simply one of its defining conditions. It appears in the method's lack of concern for historical studies, for philological pursuits of all sorts, for the *physique* and for the memory of artistic creations. These repudiations remind us that textual strategies carried out in a Barthesian mode occupy a definite, and antithetical, position throughout the modern periods. The function of such criticism is not to examine the newspaper advertisements of published books, or to assemble a **bibliography** of early printings, or to resurrect those historical references in a literary work which the passage of time has erased from our memories, or altered circumstances have concealed from view. This is a methodology which does not aim to study the text of the critic but to generate the text of the reader.

The post-structuralist text and the philological text represent, then, that fundamental opposition in the field of literary studies which used to be called "criticism" v. "appreciation," but which we now term analysis v. reading. The one aspires toward a science, the other toward an art, one toward knowledge, the other toward experience. These two classes of men are always upon the earth of humane letters, and whoever seeks to reconcile them seeks to destroy the existence of their shared world.

---

15 Immanuel Kant (1724–1804), philosopher and one of the key figures of the Enlightenment. Samuel Taylor Coleridge (1772–1834), poet, critic, and philosopher, and one of the key figures in English Romanticism.

16 William Wordsworth, *The Prelude*, VI.542.

17 Alluding to Archibald MacLeish's poem "Ars Poetica" (1926), which concludes "A poem should not mean / But be."

Blake's proverb does not mean to sanction peaceful coexistence, however. The refusal to seek reconciliation ought to entail a tension and struggle between these opposing interests, rather than an agreement to let each go its own way. This last option has been the road most often taken, and it has generally led to the even-handed excesses of Dryasdust and Skimpole—between whom there is, I think, little to choose.[18]

Problems arise in each case when either method fails to take its own powers and methods into account. In the case of the critic-as-artist, this problem takes the form of an *anamnesis*,[19] sometimes even a deliberate attempt to obliterate that aspect of an immediate experience which has necessarily recuperated the past. For there can be no production process, no continuous act of generation, except within the limits of those specific means and relations of production which the present must accept as its continuing inheritance. This necessity exists because all literary products descend into immediate experience; that is, they come to the reader in determinate forms. The most elemental of these determinate forms is the physical object—normally, a bound and printed "text" (in the traditional sense) which establishes the conditions for every particular experience of the "text" (in the contemporary sense). Even the critical attempt to erase (or deconstruct) the traditional text depends upon an acknowledgment of its presence and relative authority. [...]

Human beings are not angels. Part of what it means to be human is to have a body, to occupy physical space, and to move in real time. In the same way the products of literature, which are in all cases human products, are not disembodied processes. When Barthes says that literature "exists only as discourse," we must forcefully remind ourselves that discourse always takes place in specific and concrete forms, and that those forms are by no means comprehended by the limits of language. The aesthetic field of literary productions is neither an unheard melody[20] nor a linguistic event, as one can (literally) *see* by merely glancing at Trollope's *The Way We Live Now* either in its first printing, or in some subsequent **edition**, like Robert Tracy's recent critical text.[viii] If such productions are events in language, as of course they are, their eventualities are experienced in concrete and observable forms, and under specific circumstances of time and place. Nor are these concrete particulars merely "accidental" aspects of literary productions. Just as the human body in its particular socio-historical environment establishes certain fundamental and defining human particulars, the concrete forms and specific moments in which literary works emerge and re-emerge are defining constituents of their modes of aesthetic existence.

Thus, if we are to understand how poems mean—if we are to gain knowledge of literary productions—we must pay attention to a variety of concrete historical particulars, and not merely to "the poem itself" or its linguistic determination. Many literary critics, and even many post-structuralist critics, would not disagree with such a view. But I would urge a further proposition and

18 "Harold Skimpole" is a character in Charles Dickens's *Bleak House*, whose naïve sentimentality masks a calculating nature.

19 "The recalling of things past; recollection, reminiscence" (*OED*).

20 "Heard melodies are sweet, but those unheard / Are sweeter," John Keats, "Ode on a Grecian Urn," lines 11–12.

say that an encounter with the concrete particulars of an aesthetic object—an experience of the objectivity of "the text" in all its rich and various determinations—is fundamental to the *experience* of literary texts (or works) as well. [...]

The "discourse" of literature, then, is not an undifferentiated linguistic stream, but a continuing set of finite relationships that develop in a Valley of Dry Bones[21] between an author, **printers**, **publishers**, readers of various sorts, reviewers, academicians, and—ultimately—society at all its levels, and perhaps even international society. Every time a work of literature is encountered the reader places himself in a position where he is able to experience, and join with, that complex human endeavor. Great literary works are valuable to us precisely because they exist to foster and reproduce such discourse. Critics like Barthes aim principally to put us into contact with the *idea* of this discourse. The philologist, on the other hand, aims—or should aim—to put us into contact with such a discourse in a more concrete and experiential way. [...]

Various forces are always at work thwarting or modifying the author's intentions. The process of preparing the work for dissemination to a public (whether that process leads to publication in printed form or production in the theater or preparation of **scribal** copies) puts the work in the hands of persons who are professionals in the execution of the process. Similarly, the effort to recover a work of the past puts it in the hands of professionals known as textual critics, or editors. In all of these cases, the process must be adapted to the work at hand, and the work to the process. Sometimes through misunderstanding and sometimes through an effort to improve the work, these professionals substitute their own intentions for those of the author, who is frequently ignorant of their craft. Sometimes the author objects and sometimes not, sometimes he is pleased, sometimes he acquiesces, and sometimes he does not notice what has happened. The work of art is thus always tending toward a collaborative status, and the task of the textual critic is always to recover and preserve its integrity at that point where the authorial intentions seem to have been fulfilled.[ix]

In the field of literary production and reproduction, differentials are established through the elaboration of critical knowledge: specific details of (traditional) literary texts and their interacting historical contexts. Such knowledge is furnished by the normal "methodological fields" of our discipline, that is, in philological investigations carried out through the Lower and Higher Criticisms.

It is not the possession of such knowledge—in Barthes's terms, its "consumption"—which the critic-as-scholar must have as his object, however. It is the discovery, the repossession, and the use of such knowledge which matters. For knowledge in literary studies must be developed as a function of the aesthetic experience. If it is not, the knowledge is not literary knowledge; it is historical, and only potentially literary. Bibliographers, philologists, literary historians, and traditional textual critics grow ridiculous figures in the eyes of many literate persons because of this passion they have for details that seem ancillary to the experience of literary works. This ridicule is understandable but it is also deeply misconceived; for the development and elucidation

21 McGann again refers to the biblical story of Ezekiel in the valley of dry bones (Ezekiel 37:1–14). See above, p. 114, note 1.

of a work's "minute particulars" are, finally, the *sine qua non* of any aesthetic experience. This is so because all art, by its very character as a symbolic mode, operates in a medium of uniqueness.

A sure grasp of this fact is a distinctive mark of all the great textual critics of the eighteenth and nineteenth centuries, and it equally explains why their legacy continues to dominate their polarized inheritors in the twentieth. Their acts of revival, performed on classical, biblical, and national scriptures alike, were primarily attempts to define and sharpen the special character of the literary works they examined. The method entailed a massive program of rigorous and creative antiquarianism: literary works were made distinctive in and for the present by an immediate act of alienation and distancing. Art, which Time seemed bent upon reducing to obscure ruins, or rendering invisible through familiarity, was led across the Red Sea of the past and the deserts of the present to the Promised Land of History. The Ruins of Time, past and present, were overcome by agreeing to co-operate with its passages. Time thereby became History, and Art seemed reborn out of its losses, its otherness, its very distance. [McGann finishes this section by quoting a passage from the work of the biblical scholar Johann Gottfried Eichhorn in an extension of his discussion of eighteenth and nineteenth century scholarly practices of "alienation and distancing."][x]

II.

So far this mild polemic has maintained itself at a rather cool and distanced level. It is time for

specifics, illustrations, a few hard instances.

I mentioned earlier a celebrated paper by William Todd on the use of newspaper advertisements for establishing dates of publication. That paper focuses one of the recurrent preoccupations of bibliographers: their attempts to define precise details of place, date, and circumstances of publication, and even more the attempt to establish dependable methods for developing the information. The paper's fame rests on its procedural and methodological innovativeness.

His essay is not, of course, an act of immediate criticism. Its purposes are larger and more general—as, for example, Barthes's purposes were in *his* paper, which is also not a piece of literary criticism as such. Nevertheless, what Todd does in his essay indicates the importance he attaches to precision in matters of publication facts. He makes no plea for the aesthetic importance of such facts—scholars rarely do any more—but he might and could have done so. For one can make that demonstration in the case of *all* literary works, whose bibliographical histories are always, and necessarily, crucial to their literary and artistic character.

It makes a great difference, for example, that Byron's noble lyric "On This Day I Complete My Thirty-Sixth Year" first appeared posthumously.[22] Moreover, the character of the poem is decisively marked by its early process of dissemination. The pathos of its heroism and its hopelessness is fixed and critically defined in the way he wrote it in his private journal on

22 Lord Byron (1788–1824) died in Greece on 19 April 1824 while active in the Greek War of Independence. The lyric "On This Day I Complete My Thirty-Sixth Year" was for a long time thought to be the final poem Byron wrote.

22 January 1824, and in the way he then gave a copy of it, as an afterthought, to Pietro Gamba[23] later that same day. "You were complaining, the other day, that I never write any poetry now: this is my birthday, and I have just finished something, which, I think, is better than what I usually write."[xi] The poem projects itself directly in the emotional conflict which these remarks also call attention to. For we must remember—as, in fact, the poem scarcely allows us to forget—that it was written shortly after Byron had arrived in Greece to support the latest Greek effort to throw off the Ottoman Empire. It is a peculiarly Byronic poem, fully conscious of its immediate circumstances and of its author's entire history in life and letters. Indeed, that history is the fundamental subject of the poem, which reflects upon its author's past under the clarifying pressure of Byron's special immediate circumstances. The poem fairly epitomizes how the emotional force of a literary work is a function of the most specific and precise matters of fact.

The artistic process which Byron had begun on 22 January only receives its complete definition in the early history of the poem's transmission and publication. Here are equally crucial matters of fact in the emotional nexus which the poem has called into being.

Byron wrote and forgot about his journal poem, and in a few months he was dead (19 April). When this news reached England in mid-May it fell like a thunderbolt. Byron's body and his effects were brought back to England, along with his journal, and arrived early in July. Throughout this period, and for many months afterwards, the periodical press remained hypnotically fixed upon Byron, his career, and his final, haunting days in Greece.[xii]

At the same time, some of those who were with Byron in Greece made copies of the poem given to Gamba, who also sent a **transcript** to Mary Shelley, at her request. One of these copies was used by the (unknown) author of "Lord Byron in Greece," a long essay which appeared in the July 1824 *Westminster Review* and which contained a narrative of Byron's last months. Four lines of the poem were first printed in this essay. The complete poem finally appeared in the *Morning Chronicle* of 29 October 1824, printed from one of the many **manuscript** copies which were now in **circulation.** The poem was then reprinted in various other newspapers.

That the poem should have been transmitted and finally published in this way is in perfect keeping with every other aspect of its text and context. A poem about noble causes and the ephemeral, if willing, agents of those causes, "On This Day" properly (we must say) makes its first public speech through the newspapers, and not through the devotion of those several intermediaries who were with him in Greece when he wrote the verses and met his immortal death. That the actual **copy-text** for the *Morning Chronicle* printing should have disappeared in the complex network of the poem's early transmission history seems especially appropriate, for Byron's entire audience was in some way complicit in the process which brought this poem to be.

---

23 Pietro Gamba (1801–27) was the brother of Byron's mistress Teresa Guiccioli, and he and Byron became friends. Gamba was involved with the revolutionary Carbonari movement in Italy and later traveled to Greece with Byron to take part in the Greek War of Independence. He published a memoir of Byron's time in Greece in 1825.

The more we pursue the poem's early bibliographical history, the more sharply do we experience the fragility of such a work, and the special human character of the circumstances which it defines and perpetuates. The scholarly reconstruction of that text and its context is no more than a correspondent effort to provide the work with a yet further range of response, and one that will eventually meet it on its own terms. [...] [A second example, from a work by Edgar Allen Poe, is omitted here.]

III.

Poets and the guardians of poetry have always insisted that the products of imagination transcend time and circumstances. Art may appear in time, but its being's heart and home is with infinitude. It is a product of history, but an inhabitant of eternity. Yet we must sometimes wonder what such claims could possibly mean to Dryasdust, or to any scholar who repeatedly draws his transcendent subject back to its mortal and circumstantial condition.

As the passage from Eichhorn, quoted earlier, suggests, such claims can and should mean a great deal, even to the pedant digging patiently in his Valley of Dry Bones. Nevertheless, when we reflect upon the transcendent character of art, we do not normally find an image of that transcendence in the dead letters of the past, or in the scholar's obsession with what is ancient and completed. Rather, we are generally inclined to consider how ancient works find a contemporary relevance, a continuing ("general") application. In the Battle of the Books, the philologist, like Eichhorn, cries out, "Make it old" whereas the Modernist cries out, after Ezra Pound, "Make it new."[24] It is time to remind ourselves that "Making it new" can involve not the rebirth of art but its assassination, and the "Making it old" may establish the essential conditions for the resurrection of past achievement. For the special privilege of past human products, especially artistic ones, is that they come to us in finished and completed forms which, by their very finishedness, are able to judge the incompleteness of our present lives and works. They speak to the present precisely because they speak in other tongues, saying what we cannot say, and criticizing what we can. Literary works transcend their historical alienation by virtue of their definitive otherness, by their sharp and peculiar differentials with their later audiences, including our own.

Because criticism must articulate a system of differentials, then, a special demand is placed upon it to elucidate literary works at their point of origin, where the initial and determining sets of differentials are permanently established. The concentration upon origins has been traditional in the field of criticism, and for good reason, but it should not be taken to mean that historical criticism fetishizes the archaic object. The purpose of an historical approach is to deal with the literary work as a dynamic event in human experience rather than as an object of analysis, linguistic or otherwise.[xiii] *Paradise Lost*[25] as read in the seventeenth and

---

24 Ezra Pound (1885–1972), modernist poet. *Make It New!* was the title of one of his books (1935).

25 *Paradise Lost*, epic poem based on the biblical story of Adam and Eve, written by John Milton (1608–74) and published in 1667.

eighteenth centuries succeeded to a very different event in the Romantic Age, especially with people like Blake, Shelley, and Byron. Our own experiences with that poem today have been indelibly marked by those earlier ones, and by our awareness of the differences between them. To remain ignorant of those human events which constitute literary works like *Paradise Lost* throughout their periodic and continuing lives is to immortalize the present. For all knowledge and experience is historical, including our present knowledge and experience of the literary works we inherit and pass on.

The analytic methodologies necessarily adopted by philologists have produced, even among historical critics, recurrent misconceptions about the aims and purposes of such a critical approach. Thus, in a lengthy, if sometimes naive, recent attack upon philology, John M. Ellis argues that historical criticism is destructive because it pretends to offer the reader privileged and prepared solutions to the literary works we read: "Since literary texts are inherently challenging and often even puzzling, the critic's pose of supplying essential information and the key to the text has proved as tempting to the reader as it has to the critic. It has given him the illusion of understanding complex works with minimum effort."[xiv] Of course, one has only to pick up any of the great critical works from Wolf, Herder,[26] and Eichhorn to our own day to see how far this characterization strays from the truth. Nevertheless, what Ellis argues seems to me an accurate picture of the work of the philologian who has failed to grasp the soul of his great method, the spirit of his life in letters. I have tried in this essay to call that spirit back, to rouse it from its slumbers. [...] We do not, we must not, seek merely to reconstitute literary works in archaic forms; rather we try, in the full consciousness of our present circumstances, to raise up the past life of literary works in order to clarify and reveal the nature of our own present experience, including its dynamic relations of continuity and antithesis with all that has brought it to be.

We read literary works in present, but we have no way of judging such experiences—of testing their limits, their promises, and their ignorance—without an objective standard, a measure of absolute difference which will not submit to the absorption and manipulation of immediacy. That measure always, and necessarily, comes to us from the past. To study literature in the contexts of its origins and its later historical development is to free the reader from the ignorance of his presentness, alienate him from himself and make him a pilgrim, if not of eternity, then at least *with* all "the noble living and the noble dead."

Shall these bones live? Surely if they do not—surely if we neglect the dynamic relation which exists between past and present—the dead will bury the dead. There can be no present or future, in life or in art, if the past is not a living reality *in its pastness*. Editors, bibliographers, textual critics, and pedants of all sorts hold the keys in their hands, the keys to the kingdom not merely of literature, but of all human culture.

---

26 Johann Gottfried von Herder (1744–1803), German writer, scholar, and critic, mentioned here in connection with his works on the history of language.

Notes

i. James Thorpe, "The Aesthetics of Textual Criticism," reprinted in *Bibliography and Textual Criticism*, ed. O.M. Brack, Jr. and Warner Barnes (Chicago: U of Chicago P, 1969), 102–38.

ii. The phrase is Roland Barthes's. See below, note iv.

iii. See Blake, William, *The Marriage of Heaven and Hell*, plates 16–17 and 3.

iv. Roland Barthes's "From Work to Text" is reprinted in an excellent survey-anthology of post-structuralist criticism, *Textual Strategies*, ed. with an introduction by Josué Harari (Ithaca, NY: Cornell UP, 1979), 73–81.

v. See Barthes, 74, 75, 79, 80.

vi. The essay is reprinted in Brack and Barnes, 154–72.

vii. Another limit has been explored in Jean Baudrillard, *The Mirror of Production*, trans. with an introduction by Mark Poster (St. Louis: Telos P, 1975), where Baudrillard shows the capitalist and bourgeois ideological formations which are imbedded in every production-based approach to the study of social forms.

viii. That is to say, the printed numbers of Trollope's novel—their size, their format, their schedule of appearance—are all relevant aesthetic matters, as are the physical characteristics of any edition. Books with decorated covers and bindings—like those we see in Hardy's *Wessex Poems* or in Rossetti's various early editions—forcibly remind us of this important aesthetic aspect of all literary works, even of those which are not "beautiful," even mass-produced books. For an excellent discussion of these and related matters see Morris Eaves, "What Is the 'History of Publishing'?," *Publishing History* 2 (1977): 57–77.

ix. Thorpe, 136–37.

x. Johann Gottfried Eichhorn, *Einleitung ins Alte Testament*, trans. by Emery Neff in *The Poetry of History* (New York: Columbia UP, 1947), 57.

xi. See *The Works of Lord Byron*, ed. E.H. Coleridge vii (London: Murray, 1904), 85–88 and nn.

xii. For a good survey of these matters see Samuel C. Chew, *Byron in England* (London: J. Murray, 1924), 194–219.

xiii. These remarks are made in the context of the recent scholarship which has emphasized literary reception and the theory of literary reception.

xiv. John M. Ellis, *The Theory of Literary Criticism* (Berkeley and Los Angeles: U of California P, 1974), 154.

9. W.W. Greg, "The Rationale of Copy-Text" [1950–51], *Collected Papers.* Edited by J.C. Maxwell. Oxford: Clarendon, 1966. 374–92

While Jerome McGann, in the previous essay, argues that knowledge of the history of a work's production and transmission should inform all acts of literary interpretation, W.W. Greg (1875–1959)—whose essay 'What Is Bibliography?' is included in Chapter 1 (p. 3)—considers how that knowledge should inform the decisions editors make in preparing a new edition of the work. Thomas Tanselle, in "The Editorial Problem of Final Authorial Intention" (below, p. 139), also addresses the arguments that editors make for emending the works they edit. The Greg and Tanselle essays are primarily concerned with debates among editors and textual scholars, but these debates should concern all readers who study texts closely, since modern editors have almost always emended the texts we study.

The copy-text is the text of a work that an editor adopts as the basis for a new edition. Greg suggests that it should be a manuscript or an early printed edition. The editor doesn't simply reprint the copy-text, however, but compares it with other texts of the same work. Where there are variants between texts, the editor can emend the copy-text in an attempt to produce a better text of the work than any currently in existence. In this essay, Greg tries to explain the circumstances in which editors are justified in emending the copy-text.

To do so, he introduces a distinction between "substantive" aspects of the text and "accidental" ones. Variants in "substantives" affect the meaning of the text; variants in "accidentals" do not. Greg argues that the copy-text will usually be more likely than later texts to preserve accidentals from the author's lost manuscript. Later texts, however, may include substantive variants as a result either of the printer making mistakes or of the author correcting earlier mistakes or revising the work. Therefore, Greg argues that editors should follow the copy-text's accidentals but should be allowed to depart from the copy-text and prefer a later text if it seems likely to reflect the author's revisions.

According to Greg, editors have to distinguish between changes made by the author and changes made (intentionally or unintentionally) by other people involved in the production of the book. In order to work out who made a particular change, in the absence of other evidence, he suggests that editors should ask two questions: Could the author have written the earlier version? If so, could the author have changed the earlier version into the later version? If the answer to the first question is no, we should prefer the later version. If the answer to the first is yes and the second no, we should prefer the earlier version. If the answer to both is yes, we should prefer the later version. In this way, Greg claims, editors have the best chance of preserving the words the author intended, in the absence of his or her manuscripts. Greg thinks that editors should preserve the author's later revisions whether or not the editor thinks they are improvements.

The Rationale of Copy-Text[i]

When in his **edition** of Nashe, McKerrow invented the term "**copy-text**," he was merely giving a name to a conception already familiar, and he used it in a general sense to indicate that early text of a work which an editor selected as the basis of his own.[1] Later, as we shall see, he gave it a somewhat different and more restricted meaning. It is this change in conception and its implications that I wish to consider.

The idea of treating some one text, usually of course a **manuscript**,[2] as possessing over-riding authority originated among classical scholars, though something similar may no doubt be traced in the work of biblical critics. So long as purely eclectic methods prevailed, any preference for one manuscript over another, if it showed itself, was of course arbitrary; but when, toward the middle of last century, Lachmann and others introduced the genealogical classification of manuscripts as a principle of textual criticism, this appeared to provide at least some scientific basis for the conception of the most authoritative text.[3] The genealogical method was the greatest advance ever made in this field, but its introduction was not unaccompanied by error. For lack of logical analysis, it led, at the hands of its less discriminating exponents, to an attempt to reduce textual criticism to a code of mechanical rules. There was just this much excuse, that the method did make it possible to sweep away mechanically a great deal of rubbish. What its more hasty devotees failed to understand, or at any rate sufficiently to bear in mind, was that authority is never absolute, but only relative. Thus a school arose, mainly in Germany, that taught that if a manuscript could be shown to be generally more correct than any other and to have descended from the archetype independently of other lines of transmission, it was "scientific"

1 Ronald Brunlees McKerrow (1872–1940) was, like Greg, a pioneer of bibliography and textual scholarship, who focused on the early modern period. His *An Introduction to Bibliography for Literary Students* (1927) remains an important guide. *The Works of Thomas Nashe*, ed. R.B. McKerrow, 5 vols. (London: A.H. Bullen, 1904, repr. Oxford: Blackwell, 1958). Thomas Nashe (c. 1567–c. 1601) was a comic author and pamphleteer. *The Unfortunate Traveller* (see below), recognized as a prototype of the English novel, was his most popular work.

2 Note that Greg assumes a manuscript, where available, will make the best copy-text. Later editors, especially those working on works from the eighteenth century and after, have questioned this view.

3 Karl Lachmann (1793–1851) was a German philologist and textual editor, working mostly on classical and biblical texts. The key to Lachmann's method was to work out how early texts of a work related to each other, and to arrange them in a kind of family tree (or "stemma") showing how later texts were based on earlier ones. This also allowed the textual scholar to postulate hypothetical lost texts of a work.

to follow its readings whenever they were not manifestly impossible. It was this fallacy that Housman exposed with devastating sarcasm. He had only to point out that "Chance and the common course of nature will not bring it to pass that the readings of a MS are right wherever they are possible and impossible wherever they are wrong."[ii] That if a **scribe** makes a mistake he will inevitably produce nonsense is the tacit and wholly unwarranted assumption of the school in question,[iii] and it is one that naturally commends itself to those who believe themselves capable of distinguishing between sense and nonsense, but who know themselves incapable of distinguishing between right and wrong. Unfortunately the attractions of a mechanical method misled many who were capable of better things.

There is one important respect in which the editing of classical texts differs from that of English. In the former it is the common practice, for fairly obvious reasons, to normalize the spelling, so that (apart from emendation) the function of an editor is limited to choosing between those manuscript readings that offer significant variants. In English it is now usual to preserve the spelling of the earliest or it may be some other selected text. Thus it will be seen that the conception of "copy-text" does not present itself to the classical and to the English editor in quite the same way; indeed, if I am right in the view I am about to put forward, the classical theory of the "best" or "most authoritative" manuscript, whether it be held in a reasonable or in an obviously fallacious form, has really nothing to do with the English theory of "copy-text" at all.

I do not wish to argue the case of "old spelling" versus "modern spelling"; I accept the view now prevalent among English scholars. But I cannot avoid some reference to the ground on which present practice is based, since it is intimately connected with my own views on copy-text. The former practice of modernizing the spelling of English works is no longer popular with editors, since spelling is now recognized as an essential characteristic of an author, or at least of his time and locality. So far as my knowledge goes, the alternative of normalization has not been seriously explored, but its **philological** difficulties are clearly considerable.[iv] Whether, with the advance of linguistic science, it will someday be possible to establish a standard spelling for a particular period or district or author, or whether the historical circumstances in which our language has developed must always forbid any attempt of the sort (at any rate before comparatively recent times) I am not competent to say; but I agree with what appears to be the general opinion that such an attempt would at present only result in confusion and misrepresentation. It is therefore the modern editorial practice to choose whatever extant text may be supposed to represent most nearly what the author wrote and to follow it with the least possible alteration. But here we need to draw a distinction between the significant, or as I shall call them "substantive," readings of the text, those namely that affect the author's meaning or the essence of his expression, and others, such in general as spelling, punctuation, word-division, and the like, affecting mainly its formal presentation, which may be regarded as the accidents, or as I shall call them "accidentals," of the text.[v] The distinction is not arbitrary or theoretical, but has an immediate bearing on textual criticism, for scribes (or **compositors**) may in general be expected to react, and experience shows that they generally do react, differently to the two categories. As regards substantive readings their aim may be assumed to be to reproduce exactly those of their copy, though they will doubtless sometimes depart from them accidentally and may even, for one reason or another, do so intentionally: as regards accidentals they will normally follow their own habits or inclination, though they may, for various reasons and to varying degrees, be influenced by their copy. Thus a contemporary manuscript will at least preserve the spelling of the period, and may even retain some of the author's own, while it may at the same time depart frequently from the wording of the original: on the other hand a later **transcript** of the same original may reproduce the wording with essential accuracy while completely modernizing the spelling. Since, then, it is only on grounds of expediency, and in consequence either of philological ignorance or of linguistic circumstances, that we select a particular original as our copy-text, I suggest that it is only in the matter of accidentals that we are bound (within reason) to follow it, and that in respect of substantive readings we have exactly the same liberty (and obligation) of choice as has a classical editor, or as we should have were it a modernized text that we were preparing.[vi]

But the distinction has not been generally recognized, and has never, so far as I am aware, been explicitly drawn. This is not surprising. The battle between "old spelling" and "modern spelling" was fought out over works written for the most part between 1550 and 1650, and for which the original authorities are therefore as a rule printed editions. Now printed editions usually form an ancestral series, in which each is derived from its immediate predecessor; whereas the extant manuscripts of any work have usually only a collateral relationship, each being derived from the original independently, or more or less independently, of the others. Thus in the case of printed books, and in the absence of revision in a later edition, it is normally the first edition alone that can claim authority, and this authority naturally extends to substantive readings and accidentals alike. There was, therefore, little to force the distinction upon the notice of editors of works of the sixteenth and seventeenth centuries, and it apparently never occurred to them that some fundamental difference of editorial method might be called for in the rare cases in which a later edition had been revised by the author or in which there existed more than one "substantive" edition of comparable authority.[vii] Had they been more familiar with works transmitted in manuscript, they might possibly have reconsidered their methods and been led to draw the distinction I am suggesting. For although the underlying principles of textual criticism are, of course, the same in the case of works transmitted in manuscripts and in print, particular circumstances differ, and certain aspects of the common principles may emerge more clearly in the one case than in the other. However, since the idea of copy-text originated and has generally been applied in connexion with the editing of printed books, it is such that I shall mainly consider, and in what follows reference may be understood as confined to them unless manuscripts are specifically mentioned.[4]

The distinction I am proposing between substantive readings and accidentals, or at any rate its relevance to the question of copy-text, was clearly not present to McKerrow's mind when in 1904 he published the second volume of his edition of the Works of Thomas Nashe, which included *The Unfortunate Traveller*. **Collation** of the early editions of this romance led him to the conclusion that the second, advertised on the title as "Newly corrected and augmented," had in fact been revised by the author, but at the same time that not all the alterations could with

---

4 Note that Greg refers to printed books from the Early Modern period, where the manuscripts are usually lost. From the eighteenth century onwards it is much more common for pre-publication manuscript material to be available, which may complicate the editor's task.

certainty be ascribed to him.[viii] He nevertheless proceeded to enunciate the rule that "if an editor has reason to suppose that a certain text embodies later corrections than any other, and at the same time has no ground for disbelieving that these corrections, *or some of them at least*, are the work of the author, he has no choice but to make that text the basis of his reprint."[ix] The italics are mine.[x] This is applying with a vengeance the principle that I once approvingly described as "maintaining the integrity of the copy-text." But it must be pointed out that there are in fact two quite distinct principles involved. One, put in more general form, is that if, for whatever reason, a particular authority be on the whole preferred, an editor is bound to accept all its substantive readings (if not manifestly impossible). This is the old fallacy of the "best text," and may be taken to be now generally rejected. The other principle, also put in general form, is that whatever particular authority be preferred, whether as being revised or as generally preserving the substantive readings more faithfully than any other, it must be taken as copy-text, that is to say that it must also be followed in the matter of accidentals. This is the principle that interests us at the moment, and it is one that McKerrow himself came, at least partly, to question.

In 1939 McKerrow published his *Prolegomena for the Oxford Shakespeare*, and he would not have been the critic he was if his views had not undergone some changes in the course of thirty-five years.[5] One was in respect of revision. He had come to the opinion that to take a reprint, even a revised reprint, as copy-text was indefensible. Whatever may be the relation of a particular substantive edition to the author's manuscript (provided that there is any transcriptional link at all) it stands to reason that the relation of a reprint of that edition must be more remote.[6] If, then, putting aside all question of revision, a particular substantive edition has an over-riding claim to be taken as copy-text, to displace it in favor of a reprint, whether revised or not, means receding at least one step further from the author's original in so far as the general form of the text is concerned. Some such considerations must have been in McKerrow's mind when he wrote: "Even if, however, we were to assure ourselves ... that certain corrections found in a later edition of a play were of Shakespearian authority, it would not by any means follow that that edition should be used as the copy-text of a reprint.[xi] It would undoubtedly be necessary to incorporate these corrections in our text, but ... it seems evident that ... this later edition will (except for the corrections) deviate more widely than the earliest print from the author's original manuscript.... [Thus] the nearest approach to our ideal ... will be produced by using the earliest 'good' print as copy-text and inserting into it, from the first edition which contains them, such corrections as appear to us to be derived from the author."[xii] This is a clear statement of the position, and in it he draws exactly the distinction between substantive readings (in the form of corrections) and accidentals (or general texture) on which I am insisting. He then, however,

5 R.B. McKerrow, *Prolegomena for the Oxford Shakespeare: A Study in Editorial Method* (Oxford: Clarendon P, 1939). In this book McKerrow outlined the editorial principles for a projected edition of Shakespeare, which was left unfinished at his death.

6 A "transcriptional link" exists when an edition is printed directly from the author's manuscript, or from a copy (or a copy of a copy). A reprint, which is based on an earlier printed edition, is therefore always further away from the author's original manuscript.

relapsed into heresy in the matter of the substantive readings. Having spoken, as above, of the need to introduce "such corrections as appear to us to be derived from the author," he seems to have feared conceding too much to eclecticism, and he proceeded: "We are not to regard the 'goodness' of a reading in and by itself, or to consider whether it appeals to our aesthetic sensibilities or not; we are to consider whether a particular edition taken *as a whole* contains variants from the edition from which it was otherwise printed which could not reasonably be attributed to an ordinary press-corrector, but by reason of their style, point, and what we call inner harmony with the spirit of the play as a whole, seem likely to be the work of the author: and once having decided this to our satisfaction we must accept *all* the alterations of that edition, saving any which seem obvious blunders or misprints." We can see clearly enough what he had in mind, namely that the evidence of correction (under which head he presumably intended to include revision) must be considered *as a whole*; but he failed to add the equally important proviso that the alterations must also be *of a piece* (and not, as in *The Unfortunate Traveller*, of apparently disparate origin) before we can be called upon to accept them *all*.[7] As he states it his canon[8] is open to exactly the same objections as the "most authoritative manuscript" theory in classical editing.

McKerrow was, therefore, in his later work quite conscious of the distinction between substantive readings and accidentals, in so far as the problem of revision is concerned. But he never applied the conception to cases in which we have more than one substantive text, as in *Hamlet* and perhaps in *Henry IV*, *Troilus and Cressida*, and *Othello*. Presumably he would have argued that since faithfulness to the wording of the author was one of the criteria he laid down for

determining the choice of the copy-text, it was an editor's duty to follow its substantive readings with a minimum of interference.

We may assume that neither McKerrow nor other editors of the conservative school imagined that such a procedure would always result in establishing the authentic text of the original; what they believed was that from it less harm would result than from opening the door to individual choice among variants, since it substituted an objective for a subjective method of determination. This is, I think, open to question. It is impossible to exclude individual judgment from editorial procedure: it operates of necessity in the all-important matter of the choice of copy-text and in the minor one of deciding what readings are possible and what are not; why, therefore, should the choice between possible readings be withdrawn from its competence? Uniformity of result at the hands of different editors is worth little if it means only uniformity in error; and it may not be too optimistic a belief that the judgment of an editor, fallible as it must necessarily be, is likely to bring us closer to what the author wrote than the enforcement of an arbitrary rule.

The true theory is, I contend, that the copy-text should govern (generally) in the matter of accidentals, but that the choice between substantive readings belongs to the general theory of textual criticism and lies altogether beyond the narrow principle of the copy-text. Thus it may happen that in a critical edition the text rightly chosen as copy may not by any means be the one that supplies most substantive readings in cases of variation. The failure to

7 In other words, McKerrow did not take into account the possibility that some emendations were made by the author and some by someone else, such as the compositor.

8 Greg uses "canon" in the sense of a rule, law, or decree.

make this distinction and to apply this principle has naturally led to too close and too general a reliance upon the text chosen as basis for an edition, and there has arisen what may be called the tyranny of the copy-text,[xiii] a tyranny that has, in my opinion, vitiated much of the best editorial work of the past generation.

I will give a couple of examples of the sort of thing I mean that I have lately come across in the course of my own work. They are all the more suitable as illustrations since they occur in texts edited by scholars of recognized authority, neither of whom is particularly subject to the tyranny in question. One is from the edition of Marlowe's *Doctor Faustus* by Professor F.S. Boas (1932).[9] The editor, rightly I think, took the so-called B-text (1616) as the basis of his own, correcting it where necessary by comparison with the A-text (1604). Now a famous line in Faustus's opening soliloquy runs in 1604,

> "Bid *Oncaymæon* farewell, *Galen* come."

and in 1616,

> "Bid *Oeconomy* farewell; and *Galen* come."

Here "*Oncaymæon*" is now recognized as standing for "*on cay mæ on*" or ὂν καὶ μὴ ὄν:[10] but this was not understood at the time, and "*Oeconomy*" *was* substituted in reprints of the A-text in 1609 and 1611, and thence taken over by the B-text. The change, however, produced a rather awkward line, and in 1616 the "and" was introduced as a metrical accommodation. In the first half of the line Boas rightly restored the reading implied in A; but in the second half he retained, out of deference to his copy-text, the "and" whose only object was to accommodate the reading he had rejected in the first.[11] One could hardly find a better example of the contradictions to which a mechanical following of the copy-text may lead. 131

My other instance is from *The Gipsies Metamorphosed* as edited by Dr. Percy Simpson among the masques of Ben Jonson in 1941.[12] He took as his copy-text the Huntington manuscript, and I entirely agree with his choice. In this, and in Simpson's edition, a line of the ribald Cock Lorel ballad runs (sir-reverence!),

> All wch he blewe away with a fart

---

9 Christopher Marlowe's play *Doctor Faustus* exists in two early versions: one from 1604 and one from 1616. Editors of Greg's generation commonly sought to produce a single version of the play by conflating the two, as in the edition Greg refers to here: *The Tragical History of Doctor Faustus*, ed. Frederick S. Boas (London: Methuen, 1932). Greg himself was one of the first editors to produce an edition of the play that printed the two versions on facing **pages** (in 1950), a practice followed by later editors.

10 Greek for "being and non-being."

11 Note that the editor thus produced a version of the line that did not exist in any previous text of the work.

12 Simpson's edition appeared as part of *Ben Jonson*, ed. C.H. Herford and Percy Simpson, 11 vols. (Oxford: Clarendon P, 1925–52).

whereas for *blewe* other authorities have *flirted*. Now, the meaning of *flirted* is not immediately apparent, for no appropriate sense of the word is recorded. There is, however, a rare use of the substantive *flirt* for a sudden gust of wind, and it is impossible to doubt that this is what Jonson had in mind, for no scribe or compositor could have invented the reading *flirted*. It follows that in the manuscript *blewe* is nothing but the conjecture of a scribe who did not understand his original: only the mesmeric influence of the copy-text could obscure so obvious a fact.[xiv]

I give these examples merely to illustrate the kind of error that, in modern editions of English works, often results from undue deference to the copy-text. This reliance on one particular authority results from the desire for an objective theory of text-construction and a distrust, often no doubt justified, of the operation of individual judgment. The attitude may be explained historically as a natural and largely salutary reaction against the methods of earlier editors. Dissatisfied with the results of eclectic freedom and reliance on personal taste, critics sought to establish some sort of mechanical apparatus for dealing with textual problems that should lead to uniform results independent of the operator. Their efforts were not altogether unattended by success. One result was the recognition of the general worthlessness of reprints. And even in the more difficult field of manuscript transmission it is true that formal rules will carry us part of the way: they can at least effect a preliminary clearing of the ground. This I sought to show in my essay on *The Calculus of Variants* (1927); but in the course of investigation it became clear that there is a definite limit to the field over which formal rules are applicable. Between readings of equal extrinsic authority no rules of the sort can decide, since by their very nature it is only to extrinsic relations that they are relevant. The choice is necessarily a matter for editorial judgment, and an editor who declines or is unable to exercise his judgment and falls back on some arbitrary canon, such as the authority of the copy-text, is in fact abdicating his editorial function. Yet this is what has been frequently commended as "scientific"—"streng wissenschaftlich"[13] in the prevalent idiom—and the result is that what many editors have done is to produce, not editions of their authors' works at all, but only editions of particular authorities for those works, a course that may be perfectly legitimate in itself, but was not the one they were professedly pursuing.[14]

This by way, more or less, of digression. At the risk of repetition I should like to recapitulate my view of the position of copy-text in editorial procedure. The thesis I am arguing is that the historical circumstances of the English language make it necessary to adopt in formal matters the guidance of some particular early text. If the several extant texts of a work form an ancestral series, the earliest will naturally be selected, and since this will not only come nearest to the author's original in accidentals, but also (revision apart) most faithfully preserve the correct readings where substantive variants are in question, everything is straightforward, and the conservative treatment of the copy-text is justified. But whenever there is more than one substantive text of comparable authority,[xv] then although it will still be necessary to choose one of them as copy-text, and to follow it in accidentals, this copy-text can be allowed no over-riding or even

13 German, literally "strictly scientific" or "strictly scholarly."

14 Greg here distinguishes between editions that take into account all the early texts of a work, and editions that offer "diplomatic transcriptions" of one early text.

preponderant authority so far as substantive readings are concerned. The choice between these, in cases of variation, will be determined partly by the opinion the editor may form respecting the nature of the copy from which each substantive edition was printed, which is a matter of external authority; partly by the intrinsic authority of the several texts as judged by the relative frequency of manifest errors therein; and partly by the editor's judgment of the intrinsic claims of individual readings to originality, in other words their intrinsic merit, so long as by "merit" we mean the likelihood of their being what the author wrote rather than their appeal to the individual taste of the editor.

Such, as I see it, is the general theory of copy-text. But there remain a number of subsidiary questions that it may be worthwhile to discuss. One is the degree of faithfulness with which the copy-text should be reproduced. Since the adoption of a copy-text is a matter of convenience rather than of principle—being imposed on us either by linguistic circumstances or our own philological ignorance—it follows that there is no reason for treating it as sacrosanct, even apart from the question of substantive variation. Every editor aiming at a critical edition will, of course, correct scribal or **typographical** errors. He will also correct readings in accordance with any **errata** included in the edition taken as copy-text. I see no reason why he should not alter misleading or eccentric spellings which he is satisfied emanate from the scribe or compositor and not from the author. If the punctuation is persistently erroneous or defective an editor may prefer to discard it altogether to make way for one of his own. He is, I think, at liberty to do so, provided that he gives due weight to the original in deciding on his own, and that he records the alteration whenever the sense is appreciably affected. Much the same applies to the use of capitals and italics. I should favor expanding contractions (except perhaps when dealing with an author's **holograph**) so long as ambiguities and abnormalities are recorded. A critical edition does not seem to me a suitable place in which to record the graphic peculiarities of particular texts,[xvi] and in this respect the copy-text is only one among others. These, however, are all matters within the discretion of an editor: I am only concerned to uphold his liberty of judgment.

[...]

Much more important, and difficult, are the problems that arise in connexion with revision. McKerrow seems only to mention correction, but I think he must have intended to include revision, so long as this falls short of complete rewriting: in any case the principle is the same. I have already considered the practice he advocated—namely that an editor should take the original edition as his copy-text and introduce into it all the substantive variants of the revised reprint, other than manifest errors—and have explained that I regard it as too sweeping and mechanical. The emendation that I proposed is, I think, theoretically sufficient, but from a practical point of view it lacks precision. In a case of revision or correction the normal procedure would be for the author to send the **printer** either a list of the alterations to be made or else a corrected copy of an earlier edition. In setting up the new edition we may suppose that the printer would incorporate the alterations thus indicated by the author; but it must be assumed that he would also introduce a normal amount of unauthorized variation of his own.[xvii] The problem that faces the editor is to distinguish between the two categories. I suggest the following frankly subjective procedure. Granting that the fact of revision (or correction) is established, an editor should in every case of variation ask himself (1) whether the original reading is one that can reasonably be attributed to the author, and (2) whether the later reading is one that the author can reasonably be supposed to have substituted for the former. If the answer to the first question is negative, then the later reading should be accepted as at least possibly an authoritative correction (unless, of course, it is itself incredible). If the answer to (1) is affirmative and the answer to (2) is negative the original reading should be retained. If the answers to both questions are affirmative, then the later reading should be presumed to be due to revision and admitted into the text whether the editor himself considers it an improvement or not. It will be observed that one implication of this procedure is that a later variant that is either completely indifferent or manifestly inferior, or for the substitution of which no motive can be suggested, should be treated as fortuitous and refused admission to the text—to the scandal of faithful followers of McKerrow. I do not, of course, pretend that my procedure will lead to consistently correct results, but I think that the results, if less uniform, will be on the whole preferable to those achieved through following any mechanical rule. I am, no doubt, presupposing an editor of reasonable competence; but if an editor is really incompetent, I doubt whether it much matters what procedure he adopts: he may indeed do less harm with some than with others, he will do little good with any. And in any case, I consider that it would be disastrous to curb the liberty of competent editors in the hope of preventing fools from behaving after their kind.

134 I will give one illustration of the procedure in operation, taken again from Jonson's *Masque of Gipsies*,[15] a work that is known to have been extensively revised for a later performance. At one point the text of the original version runs as follows,

> a wise Gypsie ... is as politicke a piece of Flesh, as most Iustices in the County where he maunds

whereas the texts of the revised version replace *maunds* by *stalkes*. Now, *maund* is a recognized canting[16] term meaning to beg, and there is not the least doubt that it is what Jonson originally wrote. Further, it might well be argued that it is less likely that he should have displaced it in revision by a comparatively commonplace alternative, than that a scribe should have altered a rather unusual word that he failed to understand—just as we know that, in a line already quoted, a scribe altered *flirted* to *blewe*. I should myself incline to this view were it not that at another point Jonson in revision added the lines,

> And then ye may stalke The *Gypsies* walke

15 *The Gypsies Metamorphosed*, also known as *The Masque of Gipsies*, is a Jacobean masque written by Ben Jonson (1572–1637), with music composed by Nicholas Lanier (1588–1666). It was first performed in 1621.
16 I.e., scolding.

where *stalke*, in the sense of going stealthily, is used almost as a technical term. In view of this I do not think it unreasonable to suppose that Jonson himself substituted *stalkes* for *maunds* from a desire to avoid the implication that his aristocratic Gipsies were beggars, and I conclude that it must be allowed to pass as (at least possibly) a correction, though no reasonable critic would *prefer* it to the original.

With McKerrow's view that in all normal cases of correction or revision the original edition should still be taken as the copy-text, I am in complete agreement. But not all cases are normal, as McKerrow himself recognized. While advocating, in the passage already quoted, that the earliest "good" edition should be taken as copy-text and corrections incorporated in it, he added the proviso, "unless we could show that the [revised] edition in question (or the copy from which it had been printed) had been gone over and corrected *throughout* by" the author (my italics). This proviso is not in fact very explicit, but it clearly assumes that there are (or at least may be) cases in which an editor would be justified in taking a revised reprint as his copy-text, and it may be worth inquiring what these supposed cases are. If a work has been entirely rewritten, and is printed from a new manuscript, the question does not arise, since the revised edition will be a substantive one, and as such will presumably be chosen by the editor as his copy-text. But short of this, an author, wishing to make corrections or alterations in his work, may not merely hand the printer a revised copy of an earlier edition, but himself supervise the printing of the new edition and correct the **proofs** as the **sheets** go through the press. In such a case it may be argued that even though the earlier edition, if printed from his own manuscript, will preserve the author's individual peculiarities more faithfully than the revised reprint, he must nevertheless be assumed to have taken responsibility for the latter in respect of accidentals no less than substantive readings, and that it is therefore the revised reprint that should be taken as copy-text.

[...]

The fact is that cases of revision differ so greatly in circumstances and character that it seems impossible to lay down any hard and fast rule as to when an editor should take the original edition as his copy-text and when the revised reprint. All that can be said is that if the original be selected, then the author's corrections must be incorporated; and that if the reprint be selected, then the original reading must be restored when that of the reprint is due to unauthorized variation. Thus the editor cannot escape the responsibility of distinguishing to the best of his ability between the two categories. No juggling with copy-text will relieve him of the duty and necessity of exercising his own judgment.

In conclusion, I should like to examine this problem of revision and copy-text a little closer. In the case of a work like *Sejanus* [by Ben Jonson], in which correction or revision has been slight, it would obviously be possible to take the [earlier] **quarto** as the copy-text and introduce into it whatever authoritative alterations the [later] **folio** may supply; and indeed, were one editing the play independently, this would be the natural course to pursue. But a text like that of *Every Man in His Humour*[17] presents an entirely different problem. In the folio, revision and reproduction are so blended that it would seem impossible to disentangle intentional from what may be fortuitous variation, and injudicious to make the attempt. An editor of the revised version has no choice but to take the folio as his copy-text. It would appear therefore that a reprint may in practice be forced upon an editor as copy-text by the nature of the revision itself, quite apart from the question whether or not the author exercised any supervision over its printing.

This has a bearing upon another class of texts, in which a reprint was revised, not by the author, but through comparison with some more authoritative manuscript. Instances are Shakespeare's *Richard III* and *King Lear*. Of both much the best text is supplied by the folio of 1623; but this is not a substantive text, but one set up from a copy of an earlier quarto that had been extensively corrected by collation with a manuscript preserved in the playhouse. So great and so detailed appears to have been the revision that it would be an almost impossible task to distinguish between variation due to the corrector and that due to the compositor,[xviii] and an editor has no choice but to take the folio as copy-text. Indeed, this would in any case be incumbent upon him for a different reason; for the folio texts are in some parts connected by transcriptional continuity with the author's manuscript, whereas the quartos contain, it is generally assumed, only reported texts, whose accidental characteristics can be of no authority whatever. At the same time, analogy with *Every Man in His Humour* suggests that even had the quartos of *Richard III* and *King Lear* possessed higher authority than in fact they do, the choice of copy-text must yet have been the same.

136 I began this discussion in the hope of clearing my own mind as well as others' on a rather obscure though not unimportant matter of editorial practice. I have done something to sort out my own ideas: others must judge for themselves. If they disagree, it is up to them to maintain some different point of view. My desire is rather to provoke discussion than to lay down the law.

Notes

i. [Originally published in] *Studies in Bibliography*, iii. (1950–51), 19–36. Read before the English Institute on 8 September 1949 by Dr. J.M. Osborn for W.W. Greg.

ii. Introduction to Manilius, 1903, p. xxxii. Marcus Manilius, *Astronomicon*, ed. A.E. Housman, 5 vols. (Cambridge: Academiae, 1903–37).

iii. The more naive the scribe, the more often will the assumption prove correct; the more sophisticated, the less often. This, no doubt, is why critics of this school tend to reject "the more correct but the less sincere" manuscript in favor of "the more corrupt but the less interpolated," as Housman elsewhere observes ("The Application of Thought to Textual Criticism," *Proceedings of the Classical Association*, 1921, xviii. 75). Still, any reasonable critic will prefer the work of a naive to that of a sophisticated scribe, though he may not regard it as necessarily "better."

---

17 *Every Man in His Humour* is a play by Ben Jonson (1572–1637) first published in 1598 and reprinted in the folio edition of Jonson's works in 1616.

iv. I believe that an attempt has been made in the case of certain Old and Middle English texts, but how consistently and with what success I cannot judge. In any case I am here concerned chiefly with works of the sixteenth and seventeenth centuries.

v. It will, no doubt, be objected that punctuation may very seriously "affect" an author's meaning; still it remains properly a matter of presentation, as spelling does in spite of its use in distinguishing homonyms. The distinction I am trying to draw is practical, not philosophic. It is also true that between substantive readings and spellings there is an intermediate class of word-forms about the assignment of which opinions may differ and which may have to be treated differently in dealing with the work of different scribes.

vi. For the sake of clearness in making the distinction I have above stressed the independence of scribes and compositors in the matter of accidentals: at the same time, when he selects his copy-text, an editor will naturally hope that it retains at least something of the character of the original. Experience, however, shows that while the distribution of substantive variants generally agrees with the genetic relation of the texts, that of accidental variants is comparatively arbitrary.

vii. A "substantive" edition is McKerrow's term for an edition that is not a reprint of any other. I shall use the term in this sense, since I do not think that there should be any danger of confusion between "substantive editions" and "substantive readings."

I have above ignored the practice of some eccentric editors who took as copy-text for a work the latest edition printed in the author's lifetime, on the assumption, presumably, that he revised each edition as it appeared. The textual results were naturally deplorable.

viii. He believed, or at least strongly suspected, that some were due to the printer's desire to save space, and that others were "the work of some person who had not thoroughly considered the sense of the passage which he was altering" (ii. 195).

ix. Nashe, ii. 197 [see note i for publication details]. The word "reprint" really begs the question. If all an "editor" aims at is an exact reprint, then obviously he will choose one early edition, on whatever grounds he considers relevant, and reproduce it as it stands. But McKerrow does emend his copy-text where necessary. It is symptomatic that he did not distinguish between a critical edition and a reprint.

x. Without the italicized phrase the statement would appear much more plausible (though I should still regard it as fallacious, and so would McKerrow himself have done later on) but it would not justify the procedure adopted.

xi. Again he speaks of a "reprint" where he evidently had in mind a critical edition on conservative lines.

xii. McKerrow, *Prolegomena*, 17–18.

xiii. I think the phrase "the tyranny of the copy-text" was first used by Paul Maas in connexion with the Prolegomena in my book *The Editorial Problem in Shakespeare*. But what he then had in mind was the decision to preserve "old spelling." (See *The Review of English Studies*, April 20 [1944]: 159.)

xiv. At another point two lines appear in an unnatural order in the manuscript. The genetic relation of the texts proves the inversion to be an error. But of this relation Simpson seems to have been ignorant. He was again content to rely on the copy-text.

xv. The proviso is inserted to meet the case of the so-called "bad quartos" of Shakespearian and other Elizabethan plays and of the whole class of "reported" texts, whose testimony can in general be neglected.

xvi. That is, certainly not in the text, and probably not in the general apparatus: they may appropriately form the subject of an appendix.

xvii. I mean substantive variation, such as occurs in all but the most faithful reprints.

xviii. Some variation is certainly due to error on the part of the folio printer, and this it is of course the business of an editor to detect and correct so far as he is able.

10.

G. Thomas Tanselle, "The Editorial Problem of Final Authorial Intention" [1976], *Textual Criticism and Scholarly Editing.* Charlottesville: U of Virginia P, 1990. 27–72

G. Thomas Tanselle (b. 1934) is Professor Emeritus of English at Columbia University in New York and former president of the Bibliographical Society of America. He has written extensively on textual criticism and bibliography and has edited works by Herman Melville.

Editors since Greg have traditionally tried to produce a text that they believe reflects the author's final intentions. Where authors have had second thoughts, editors have usually assumed that the second thoughts are the results of more mature reflection, and should be respected. In a variety of situations, however, the matter is not so simple, and a more sophisticated understanding of authorial intention is required. Tanselle lays the groundwork for such an understanding in this essay by distinguishing between three kinds of intention, two kinds of revision, and two kinds of attitude that authors can take toward changes introduced by others.

Tanselle borrows the three kinds of intention from the literary critic Michael Hancher: *programmatic* intention, which is the intention to produce a particular kind of text; *active* intention, which is the intention the author forms in the process of composition to write one word rather than another; and *final* intention, which is the intention to accomplish something by writing, for example to change readers' minds or to make money (note that this is different from how "final intention" is used in the title). In choosing between textual variants, the editor is only concerned, Tanselle says, with the *active* intention.

The two kinds of revision authors can undertake are *horizontal* revision, which aims at improving the text without drastically rethinking its aims, and *vertical* revision, which aims to recast it as a new kind of text, one intended for a different market or publication venue, for example. Horizontal revision involves changes in the active intention only; vertical revision involves changes in the programmatic intention as well. Horizontal revisions produce a new text of the work, which an editor can include in his edition; vertical revisions produce a new version of the work, which might need an entirely separate edition.

Where changes are made by someone else, authors can either *embrace* these changes, in which case they come to form part of the author's intention, or merely *acquiesce* in them (for example in order to get published or to secure a larger circulation), in which case they form no part of the author's intention. By making these distinctions, Tanselle aims to bring clarity to editors' thinking about intention so that they can better identify and respect the author's final intention. It remains for Stephen Parrish, Jack Stillinger, and Brenda Silver, in essays reprinted below, to attack the ideal of following the final authorial intention itself.

The Editorial Problem of Final Authorial Intention

Scholarly editors may disagree about many things, but they are in general agreement that their goal is to discover exactly what an author wrote and to determine what form of his work he wished the public to have. There may be some difference of opinion about the best way of achieving that goal; but if the **edition** is to be a work of scholarship—a historical reconstruction—the goal itself must involve the author's "intention." The centrality of that concept to scholarly editing can be illustrated by W.W. Greg's "The Rationale of Copy-Text," which, in the quarter century since it first appeared, has established itself as the most influential document in modern editorial theory. What Greg succeeded in accomplishing was to provide a rationale for selecting, and then emending, a basic text in those cases in which the choice was not made obvious by the historical, biographical, bibliographical, and linguistic evidence available. In such instances, an editor requires some guiding principle by means of which he can maximize the chances of adopting what the author wrote and minimize the chances of incorporating unauthorized readings into his text. Greg's now celebrated solution rests on the position that, if a finished **manuscript** of a text does not survive, the **copy-text** for a scholarly edition should normally be the text of the earliest extant printed edition based on the missing manuscript, for it can be expected to reproduce more of the characteristics of the manuscript than any edition further removed; variants from later editions which are convincingly shown to be revisions by the author can then be incorporated into this copy-text. Because authors who revise their work do not always give as much attention to what Greg calls "accidentals" (matters of spelling and punctuation) as to "substantives" (the words themselves)—and because such attention is in any event extremely difficult to determine—the copy-text usually remains the authority for accidentals; and if an editor adopts as authorial certain substantive variants in a later edition, he need not adopt all the other variants in that edition. Following this plan, the editor has a rational means for deciding among indifferent variants (he retains the copy-text readings); and the resulting critical text should be closer to the author's intention than any individual surviving form of the text.

Although Greg did not address himself to the question of a precise definition of "author's intention," it is clear from such a summary that he considered the goal of an edition—and he was speaking of an "old-spelling critical edition"—to be the reconstruction of a text representing the author's final wishes about the version of his work to be presented to the public. In Fredson Bowers's words, the task is "to approximate as nearly as possible an inferential authorial **fair copy**, or other ultimately authoritative document";[i] or, as he put it another time, following Greg's theory will produce "the nearest approximation in every respect of the author's final intentions."[ii] If an author can be shown to have gone over his work with scrupulous care for a revised edition, examining accidentals as well as substantives, the revised edition (as the closest edition to an "ultimately authoritative document") would become the copy-text. Such a situation does not arise in most instances, but Greg recognized its importance: "The fact is," he said, "that cases of revision differ so greatly in circumstances and character that it seems impossible to lay down any hard and fast rule as to when an editor should take the original edition as his copy-text and when the revised reprint." In other words, an editor cannot avoid making judgments about the author's intention on the basis of the available evidence; the strength of those judgments, in turn, will depend on his historical knowledge and his literary sensitivity.[iii] The job of a scholarly editor, therefore, can be stated as the exercise of critical thinking in an effort to determine the final intention of an author with respect to a particular text.

Just what is meant by "author's final intention," however, has not been made entirely clear, although at first glance the concept may seem so self-evident as not to require formal definition. Its use in connection with editing suggests that an editor's task is not to "improve" upon an author's decisions, even when he believes that the author made an unwise revision, and that an editor's judgment is directed toward the recovery of what the author wrote, not toward an evaluation of the effectiveness of the author's revisions.[iv] Furthermore, the concept, as a goal of editing, would seem clearly to imply that, when an editor has strong reason to attribute a revision to the author, he will accept that revision as "final" on the grounds that, coming second, it represents the author's considered and more mature judgment.[1] Greg suggests that this procedure is equally valid for dealing with wholesale revision when he writes, "If a work 141
has been entirely rewritten, and is printed from a new manuscript ... the revised edition will be a substantive one, and as such will presumably be chosen by the editor as his copy-text."

It is true that, in many instances, the simple interpretation of "final intention" to mean that intention reflected in the last alterations made or proposed by the author is workable enough and results in no ambiguity as to the aim of the editorial process. Nevertheless, such an interpretation does not answer certain theoretical questions which can assume practical importance in the remaining instances. Two basic kinds of situations particularly require further consideration: cases where the editor must distinguish authorial alterations from alterations made by someone else and must decide what constitutes "authorial intention" at such times; and cases where the editor faces alterations unquestionably made by the author but must still decide which readings represent the author's "final intention." In what follows I shall offer some preliminary comments on these two situations. But it is necessary to begin with at least a brief consideration of the meaning of "intention" for this purpose and with some recognition of the critical implications of attempting to discover "authorial intention."

[...]

---

1 The idea that "more mature judgments" should always be preferred to earlier ones is attacked by Parrish in "The Whig Interpretation of Literature," see below, p. 157.

I.

If the aim of the editor is to establish the text as the author wished to have it presented to the public (and we shall postpone any consideration of other possible editorial aims), he cannot divorce himself from the "meaning" of the text, for, however much documentary evidence he may have, he can never have enough to relieve himself of the necessity of reading critically. Suppose, for example, that the only extant text of a work is a fair-copy manuscript in the author's hand. The editor in such a case cannot simply reproduce the text mechanically, without thinking about its meaning: there is always the possibility that the author, through an oversight or slip of the pen, did not write down what he meant to write, and the editor who is reading critically may be able to detect and correct such errors, or at least some of them. It is an act of criticism, however elementary, for an editor to recognize that where the author wrote "the the" he actually meant "to the." In other instances it may be equally obvious that the author cannot have meant what he wrote, and yet it may be impossible to say with certainty which of several possible corrections conforms with what he had in mind. Yet the editor will probably find it necessary to make *some* correction, since the reading of the manuscript is plainly wrong. When two or more texts of a work exist and there are differences between them, there may be no conclusive evidence to show which differences are the result of the author's revisions and which are not. Yet the editor must decide which of the readings to accept at each point of variation. These decisions are based both on whatever external evidence is available and on the editor's judgment as to how the author was most likely to have expressed himself at any given point. This judgment in turn is based on the editor's familiarity with and sensitivity to the whole corpus of the author's work and on his understanding of the individual work involved. He may be specifically concerned only with the author's intended meaning in one sentence, or even one phrase, but the interpretation of that sentence or phrase may depend upon the author's intended meaning in the work as a whole.

It is clear, then, as soon as one starts to talk about "intention," that various kinds of intention need to be distinguished, and many of the recent discussions of intention in literature do attempt to subdivide the concept. [...] Of such classifications of intention, one of the clearest and most useful has been set forth by Michael Hancher.[v] In his view, "author's intentions" can be divided into three types: (1) "programmatic intention"—"the author's intention to make something or other"; (2) "active intention"—"the author's intention to be (understood as) acting in some way or other"; and (3) "final intention"—"the author's intention to cause something or other to happen." The first refers to the author's general plan to write a sonnet, say, or a realistic novel; the third refers to his hope that his work will change the reader's viewpoint, say, or bring wealth to himself. The second is the one which concerns the meanings embodied in the work: "Active intentions characterize the actions that the author, at the time he finishes his text, understands himself to be performing in that text."[vi] Hancher's argument is that the first and third kinds of intention—programmatic and final—are indeed irrelevant to the interpretation of a literary work but that the second—active intention—must be taken into account in the interpretation (and evaluation) of the work.

Before pursuing the implications of that argument, we should pause long enough to note that what editors in the tradition of Greg are likely to call "final intention" does not correspond to what Hancher here calls "final intention." Rather, the intention with which editors are concerned is Hancher's "active intention," the intention that the work "*mean* (and be taken to mean) something or other."[vii] The fact that an editor, as briefly suggested above, must examine both the author's intention to use a particular word and the author's intention to mean a particular thing in the work as a whole—indeed, must make decisions about the first in the light of the second—is adequately accommodated in Hancher's concept of "active intention." [...] Accordingly, whenever I speak of "intention," unless otherwise specified, I am referring to the kind of intention included in Hancher's concept of "active intention"; even when I use the term "final intention," in conformity with the common practice of editors, the word "intention" still refers to the same concept (and not to what Hancher calls "final intention")—though just what "final" may mean in the phrase remains to be examined later.

[...]

How, then, is the author's intended meaning to be discovered? In answering that question, one is inevitably drawn back to the work itself as the most reliable documentary evidence as to what the author intended. If he made no statement setting forth his intention, one has nowhere else to go for direct evidence (though of course one can take into account various historical and biographical circumstances); and if he did make a statement, it may, for a great variety of reasons, 143
not be accurate. As [...] William H. Capitan has noted, "what an artist gives us as his intention is subject to the artist's limitations in putting his intention into words."[viii] The position has been well stated by Quentin Skinner:

> To discount a writer's own statements is not to say that we have lost interest in gaining a correct statement about his intentions in our attempt to interpret his works. It is only to make the (perhaps rather dramatic, but certainly conceivable) claim that the writer himself may have been self-deceiving about recognizing his intentions, or incompetent at stating them. And this seems to be perennially possible in the case of any complex human action.[ix]

Hirsch,[2] who does not recognize as "meanings" any meanings other than the author's, decides what Wordsworth "probably" meant in "A slumber did my spirit seal" by turning to "everything we know of Wordsworth's typical attitudes during the period in which he composed the poem" (p. 239). Contemporary statements about these attitudes may of course be useful, but are not Wordsworth's poems the chief source of information about his attitudes? And if a given body of

2 E.D. Hirsch, author of *Validity in Interpretation* (1967) and *The Aims of Interpretation* (1976), which argue that the author's intention determines how a text can legitimately be read. Tanselle discusses his views in an earlier section of this article, which is excluded here for reasons of space.

writings can provide such evidence, is it not possible that a smaller body of writings—or even the single poem—could provide it? As Hirsch admits, "A poet's typical attitudes do not always apply to a particular poem" (p. 240); so one is inevitably thrown back on the poem itself. [...]

The bearing of these ideas on the task of the editor is worth making explicit. At the start, the editor has settled one important question through his definition of his goal: he is concerned with establishing the text as intended by the author, and thus he has no doubts about the relevance of the author's intention to his undertaking. But then he recognizes that the most reliable source of information about the author's intention in a given work is that work itself. He will take other information into account, but he must always measure it finally against the very text which is the subject of his inquiry. The editor may at first feel that his job is different from the critic's in that he is concerned with establishing intended *wording*, not with explicating intended *meaning*. That is, he may think (in Austin's terms) that he is dealing only with the author's locutionary act, not his illocutionary act.[3] But he soon realizes that his discovery of textual errors or his choice among textual variants involves his understanding of the intended meaning of the text. For if either of two alternative words makes sense at a given point, the determination of which the author intended clearly involves more than his locutionary act. Greg's rationale tells an editor what to do when he is at an impasse, but it does not eliminate the need for judgments; indeed, it relies on them. So the editor finds himself in the position of the critic after all.

[...]

These considerations suggest, first of all, that editing is a critical activity and that the scholarly editor cannot avoid coming to terms with the critical problem of authorial intention. Second, there is a specific and clearly defined aspect of the broad concept of "intention" which is the appropriate concern of the scholarly editor—the intention of the author to have particular words and marks of punctuation constitute his text and the intention that such a text carry a particular meaning or meanings. Finally, the scholarly editor will amass all the evidence he can find bearing on each textual decision; but, whenever the factual evidence is less than incontrovertible, his judgment about each element will ultimately rest on his interpretation of the author's intended meaning as he discovers it in the whole of the text itself. What controls the editor's freedom of interpretation is his self-imposed limitation: he is concerned only with that intention which his knowledge of the author and the period allows him to attribute to the author.

II.

An editor who has given some attention to such preliminary questions has at least begun to reach an understanding of "authorial intention." But there are a number of further questions which

3 J.L. Austin (1911–60), philosopher of language best known for his book *How to Do Things with Words* (1962), which distinguishes locutionary acts (the act of making an utterance) from illocutionary acts (the act of doing something in the process of uttering).

arise as he attempts to make judgments in the light of this conception of intention. Perhaps the most common editorial situation is that in which the editor must decide whether a given variant reading is a revision by the author or an alteration (conscious or inadvertent) by someone else. In these cases, at least one intermediate stage of documentary evidence is lacking, and the editor is trying to determine from the surviving material those changes which the author made in that now missing document. He must also face the question whether it is ever possible to think of changes not made by the author as nevertheless fulfilling, or contributing to, the author's intention.

The basic situation can be illustrated by Sherwood Anderson's *A Story Teller's Story* (1924). The only surviving prepublication text of this work is the **typescript printer's** copy, which bears revisions by three people: Anderson himself, Paul Rosenfeld,[4] and E.T. Booth, the **publisher's** editor. One has direct evidence, therefore, for assigning the responsibility for each of these alterations; but the first printing of the book (Huebsch, 1924) contains additional changes, not marked on the surviving typescript and presumably entered on the now lost **proofs**. Deciding which of these changes were made by Anderson is the central task in editing this book. What the editor has to do is to familiarize himself with all the available relevant evidence—bibliographical, historical, biographical. He may then find that some of it is convincing enough to dictate certain decisions. For example, on (or just before) 28 October 1924 Anderson wrote to Rosenfeld explaining why he had cut out some material about Waldo Frank.[x] [5] Since several paragraphs about Frank are present in the typescript but not present in the first impression, one can conclude that this is the deletion referred to and that it was made by Anderson on the proofs. But for most of the alterations in the first impression there is no such compelling evidence; most of the editor's decisions must finally be critical judgments, resulting from an evaluation of what evidence there is, from an understanding of Anderson's habits of revision, and from a familiarity with and sensitivity to his style and ideas. Even the deleted Waldo Frank passage leads the editor to a related judgment, for that deletion is only a part of a considerably longer deletion made in the first impression. Because the entire passage concerns Anderson's reactions to various writers, one may conclude that he probably eliminated all of it, and not merely the part about Frank which he happened to mention to Rosenfeld. But that conclusion is a judgment, supported by a critical argument, not by verifiable facts.

The same observations can be made about situations involving variants between printed editions. In these cases the missing documents are the author's marked copy of the earlier edition (or its proofs, or whatever served as printer's copy for the edition set later) and the marked proofs of the later edition. If no document survives which antedates the proofs of the earliest setting of the text, then of course one is dealing with texts which have already been subjected to the routine

4 Sherwood Anderson (1876–1941) was an American novelist and short-story writer, whose works include *Winesberg, Ohio* (1919). Paul Rosenfeld (1890–1946) was a journalist, editor, critic, and friend of Anderson.

5 Waldo Frank (1889–1967) was a novelist, editor, historian, and critic, and a friend and supporter of Anderson's.

of the printing- or publishing-house. Thus the essential difference between this situation and the one described above is that here the editor is working at a greater remove from the author's fair-copy manuscript or typescript; but his approach to the problem remains the same. [...] In the case of *Moby-Dick*,[6] [...] it is known that the publisher's reader for the English edition made numerous substantive alterations and that Melville also had the opportunity to make revisions for that edition; distinguishing the two categories can result only from critical judgments as to which kinds of changes are likely to have been made by a somewhat pedantic reader concerned with expurgation and which are more characteristic of Melville. [...]

Once the editor has made his judgments as to which variants are attributable to the author and which to someone else, he must consider the exact status of the latter group. Are all variants for which someone other than the author is responsible to be rejected outright, or is it conceivable that the author's intention may sometimes be fulfilled by other persons? It is not only conceivable but unquestionably true that others can and do sometimes correct an author's writing and in the process fulfill his intention. An author may write down one word but be thinking of a different one, or in reading proofs he may fail to notice a printer's error which creates a new word. When these erroneous words are plausible in their contexts, they may never be recognized by anyone as erroneous; but when one of them does not make sense, and when the correct word is obvious, anyone who makes the correction is carrying out the author's intention. Frequently an editor may believe that a particular word cannot have been intended but is not certain just what the intended word should be; only his critical assessment of the whole matter can determine whether it is preferable in that case to let the questionable word stand and call attention to the problem in a note or to substitute a word which catches the apparent intended sense (again, of course, with an explanation), even though that word may not be the exact one which the author had in mind. In the typescript of *A Story Teller's Story*, then, alterations in the hand of E.T. Booth cannot simply be dismissed; they must be inspected carefully, because Booth may have noticed places where the typescript reading certainly (or almost certainly) cannot have been Anderson's intended reading, and there is always the chance that an editor might otherwise fail to detect some of them.

An examination of Booth's revisions, however, leads to a more difficult question. Since Booth was the editor for the publisher, can one argue that, because Anderson expected his book to be gone over in the publisher's offices, the changes made by Booth become a part of Anderson's intended wording? Or, to put the question in more general terms: can one argue that changes made (or thought to have been made) by the publisher and passed (or presumably passed) by the author in proof constitute changes intended by the author? [...] One might argue, for instance, that Anderson—aware of some of the shortcomings, by conventional standards, of his spelling, punctuation, and sentence structure—did not "intend" for his writings to be published exactly as he wrote them but "intended" for them to be made to conform with conventional practice.

6 *Moby-Dick; or, The Whale* (1851) is a novel by Herman Melville (1819–91) that narrates Captain Ahab's obsessive pursuit of the whale he names Moby Dick. The novel has many textual issues, including inconsistency about whether or not Moby Dick should be hyphenated.

But one might also argue, on the other side, that Anderson's writing as it came from him reflects his intention more accurately than it does after being standardized, and that any intention he may have held regarding publishers' alterations amounted only to his realistic understanding of what had to be done in order to get published (and thus was not part of his active intention in the text).

[...]

What the editor must attempt to assess is whether the author genuinely preferred the changes made by the publisher's reader or whether he merely acquiesced in them. The idea that an author can actively intend in his work a revision made by someone else depends in effect on the extent to which the two can be regarded as voluntary collaborators. Since collaboration implies shared responsibility, the "author's intention" in a collaborative effort results from a merging of the separate intentions of the individual authors; the final result is thus intended by each of the authors. A work need not be signed with more than one name, of course, for it to be a collaboration. Nor is it necessary for the authors involved to perform equal shares of the work; indeed, two people may collaborate only on certain aspects of a work, and their joint intention would apply only to the words or elements involved. The **facsimile** edition of the revised manuscript-typescript of *The Waste Land* offers a rare opportunity to observe some of the collaboration which can underlie a great work.[7] In certain passages Pound's revisions (such as "demobbed" in line 139) or deletions (as in "Death by Water") actually constitute collaboration, though there are other places where Eliot rejects Pound's suggestions (as in the lines on Saint Mary Woolnoth, lines 67–68). That the work is to some extent collaborative is implied by Valerie Eliot's comment, in her description of "Editorial Policy," that "It has been difficult to decide who cancelled certain lines, especially when both Eliot and Pound have worked on them together."[xi] A study of this facsimile does not suggest that an editor should incorporate into the text of the poem the lines which Pound rejected and Eliot did not restore; one can argue that at those points Eliot's intention merged with Pound's intention, even though Pound's markings are what survive on paper. The fact that Pound went over the poem as a friend and not as a publisher's editor does not alter the essential point: in either case it is possible for someone other than the "author" to make alterations which are identical with the intention of the "author," when the relationship partakes of the spirit of collaboration.

The question, posed earlier, of whether it makes sense to believe that an author can ask someone else to carry out his intention in some respect may now be answered in the negative.

7 *The Waste Land* (1922) was written by T.S. Eliot (1888–1965) in a number of drafts composed at different times, sometimes by hand and sometimes using one of several different typewriters. Eliot entrusted the fragmentary drafts to his friend the poet Ezra Pound (1885–1972), who edited them, making very extensive cuts and suggestions to bring the poem into its final form. The publication in 1971 of a facsimile edition of the drafts, edited by Eliot's widow Valerie Eliot, made Pound's annotations available to a wide audience for the first time.

By definition, an author's active intention cannot include projected activity and cannot include activity of which he is not in control. The ultimate example of delegated intention in writing would be for a person to ask someone else to write an entire work for him; if he then announced that it represented his "intention," he could only mean his intention to write a certain kind of work (his programmatic intention), for his active intention would not be involved. The same is true regardless of what portion or aspect of a work is at issue, as long as the element contributed by someone other than the author must be described with such expressions as "It is what the author expected to have done" or "It is what the author would have done if he had found time." However, if an author accepts what someone else has done not in a spirit of acquiescence but of active collaboration, the result does represent his active intention. Since the scholarly editor, in establishing a text, is concerned with an author's active intention in that text, he can accept into the text what he knows (or strongly believes) to be initially the work of someone else only when it can be regarded as having been accepted by the primary author as a true collaboration. This approach does not alter the crucial role which the editor's judgment plays in evaluating evidence, but it may provide a useful framework into which that evidence can be placed. It also suggests the relative infrequency with which publishers' alterations can be taken to supersede an author's known practice in a prepublication stage of his work.

III.

148 After the editor has separated authorial from non-authorial alterations and has decided how to treat the non-authorial ones, he still faces the question of how to define "final" with respect to the authorial variants. Normally, of course, when there are two authorial readings at a given point and their sequence can be determined, the later one is taken to represent the author's "final intention." However, there are in general two kinds of situations in which this view of "final intention" will prove unsatisfactory: (1) when the nature or extent of the revisions is such that the result seems, in effect, a new work, rather than a "final version" of an old work;[xii] and (2) when the author allows several alternative readings to stand in his manuscript or vacillates among them in successive editions. In the first case, one may say that there is more than one "final" intention; in the second, that there is no final intention at all.

[...]

Turning to the first of the two categories—in which an author's revisions produce, in a manner of speaking, a new work—one can identify several patterns. The most clear-cut involves those situations in which the author's revisions reflect motives which make it impossible for an editor to accept the later version of a work as truly representing the author's intention, even though, in temporal terms, this version is "final." If, for instance, an author deletes passages for the purpose of producing a condensation or simplifies the language to make the work appropriate for younger readers, the special motives in each case prevent the resulting revisions from being definitive. The revised version, in such cases, does not represent a refinement of the work as previously "completed" but a new work conceived for different purposes; if the new version has merit, it is as an independent work to be edited separately. This is not to deny that the author might make in the process some revisions which an editor would adopt as emendations in his copy-text, but in order to qualify for adoption they would have to be revisions unconnected with the aim of condensation or simplification.[xiii] In other words, two types of revision must be distinguished: that which aims at altering the purpose, direction, or character of a work, thus attempting to make a different sort of work out of it; and that which aims at intensifying, refining, or improving the work as then conceived (whether or not it succeeds in doing so), thus altering the work in degree but not in kind. If one may think of a work in terms of a spatial metaphor, the first might be labeled "vertical revision," because it moves the work to a different plane, and the second "horizontal revision," because it involves alterations within the same plane. Both produce local changes in active intention; but revisions of the first type appear to be in fulfillment of an altered programmatic intention or to reflect an altered active intention in the work as a whole, whereas those of the second do not.

[...]

The most familiar situation in which more than one "final" intention can be said to exist occurs when an author, at a later stage in his career, extensively revises a work completed years before—not because he is compelled to, nor because he wants to condense it, expand it, or adjust it to a different audience, but because he feels he can improve it artistically. The classic case of such revision is the New York Edition (1907–09) of Henry James. It seems to be generally agreed that an attempt to record in textual notes the variant readings between the original and revised versions of the novels and stories included in that edition would be of questionable utility, since the revisions are so pervasive that they create substantially new works. Both versions of a given work deserve to be read in their own right, and an essay generalizing upon and categorizing the differences between them may be more useful than a list of variants appended to one of the texts. Many essays of this kind have appeared, and a fairly recent one, on "Pandora," sums up the situation: "the net result is neither striking improvement nor fatal tampering. The story is better in some ways, worse in others. But it is different—one cannot assert that the changes really add up to nothing."[xiv] The revised version, because it is essentially "different," manifests a "final intention" which does not supersede the "final intention" of the earlier version. Merely because the revision came at the end of a long career, when James's artistry and insight were presumably more mature, it cannot invalidate the intrinsic merits of the original version. The two are discrete works.

If this point of view has been readily accepted in extreme cases of revision, it has scarcely been considered at all in instances of slight revision. But why should the *quantity* of alterations affect one's theoretical position? If one treats a heavily revised text as an independent work simply because the difficulties of handling the variants in any other way are overwhelming and then edits a less heavily revised work as a single text with notes because it is possible to do so, the theoretical basis of the whole operation is questionable. The idea that a revised version can be considered a separate work is sometimes said to rest on the concept of organic form—the view that form and content in a work of art are so integrated that any alteration produces a new entity. Of course, it is not necessary to adduce this concept in order to make the point: changing a word in any utterance results technically in a different utterance. Although the change of one word in a novel makes less practical difference than the change of one word in a brief lyric poem, strictly speaking each version (both of the novel and of the poem) is a "separate work." Maintaining this position would not quite put an end to all scholarly editing, because editors would still have the task of detecting non-authorial readings (emendations of publishers' readers, **compositors'** errors, and the like) and purifying the text of them; but they could not choose among authorial variants, for they would have to consider each group of them, for each successive impression or edition, as resulting in a new work to be edited separately.[xv] Clearly such a situation would be intolerable from a practical point of view; in the majority of instances editorial choice among authorial variants does not deprive readers of the opportunity for reconstructing other forms of the text on the basis of the material presented in the apparatus, and a list of variants has the positive advantage of drawing together the evidence from various versions into a form where it is conveniently comparable.

If, in practice, editors are not going to regard each version as necessarily a separate work, then some rationale is required for distinguishing those instances of revision which are to be edited as separate works from those which are not. A quantitative dividing line is not logical: it would be impossible to set up a particular number of revisions, or words involved in revisions, as the test for deeming a separate work in this sense.[xvi] What is more meaningful than the extent of the revisions is their nature. One author might make 3000 changes in his selection of adjectives and adverbs, for instance—and perhaps improve his book stylistically—without altering his original conception of the work at all; another might make only ten revisions in key passages and change the whole direction of the book. Whether or not two versions of a book are treated by an editor as independent works should depend on a qualitative, not quantitative, distinction. If revisions do not spring from the same conception of an organic whole as the original version manifested (what I have called vertical revisions), then they produce a new work, even though the actual number of new readings is small; if revisions are attempts to develop and improve the original conception (what I have called horizontal revisions), then they do not produce a separate work for practical purposes, regardless of the number of changes involved. Generally, large numbers of alterations do follow from a changed conception or programmatic intention, but the point is that there is no necessary connection between the two.

In making decisions about authorial intention, an editor may be inclined to take into account a related factor, the timing of the changes. When an author, late in his life, makes revisions in an early work, one could argue that the result will almost surely constitute an effectively different work, since it is unlikely that the author will have the same conception of his work in mind as he had during the process of its original composition. [...] [But] just as a quantitative measure of revision will not serve to distinguish what versions are to be edited as separate works, so a time limit is similarly unrealistic: one cannot say that all revisions made within a week, or a month, or a year of the original composition are to be accepted as part of the same conception, while those made after that time either result in different works or represent random thoughts not consistent with any coherent plan. What is important, once again, is the nature of the changes, and no mechanical rule—about their extent or their timing—can produce meaningful distinctions among them with respect to underlying conceptions or motives.

[...]

With some authors the possibility of multiple "final" intentions is further intensified. Instead of making one systematic revision of a work at some point later in life, they revise their work continually throughout their careers. An extreme example of this method [...] is Whitman's *Leaves of Grass*, which was extensively revised eight times between 1855 and 1892.[8] When an author works in this way, successive editions constitute a printed record of a developing mind. The fact that Whitman said of his final "deathbed" edition (1891–92) that any future edition should be "a copy and facsimile, indeed, of the text of these ... pages" does not mean that critics and scholars must reject all earlier editions as works in their own right.[xvii] Even if Whitman came to think of the earlier editions as preliminary drafts for his final version, each of those editions was published and at the time of its publication represented a final version that he was willing to present to the public and thus his final intention as of that moment.[xviii] If one decides that the revisions at each stage are the kind which spring from an altered conception of the whole, one can argue that each edition of *Leaves* is a separate work with its own final intention. (The situation would differ from that of Henry James only in the greater number of separate works, resulting from the greater number of stages of revision.) In that case, Whitman's last text is not—as an intended work—any more "final" than his earlier texts; it merely comes later. To one taking this position, Whitman's own judgment should of course be no embarrassment; it is only a critical pronouncement about his work, not an element within the work. [...] To say that an author's last version of a work means the same thing as his earliest is to abandon all criticism; but to find that a late version fails to supersede an early one is not to deny the author's right to do with his work as he pleases. In the end, whenever there are authorial revisions, an editor is not fulfilling his responsibility to the work of literature if he does not assess the nature of those revisions, in order to determine whether he is really dealing with only a single work.

Before glancing at the argument that this approach to editing gives the editor too much freedom to be eclectic, let us turn to the second major category in which "final intention" is problematical—those instances in which there is literally no final intention, either because the author never prepared his manuscript for publication or because he wavered in his revisions for successive printings.[xix] [...] In these cases the rejected readings, false starts, and un**canceled** variants are of interest in showing the writer's manner of working and stylistic development, just as they are when found in the surviving manuscripts of a published work; but they do not reflect

8 Walt Whitman (1819–92) self-published the first edition of *Leaves of Grass* in 1855, when the collection consisted of 12 poems. He returned to the collection throughout his life, adding and revising his poems until the so-called "deathbed" edition of 1891–92, which contained over 400 poems and constitutes a self-consciously American epic.

the essential nature of the work itself, as they do in a letter or a journal. An editor who completes the author's job by preparing such works for conventional publication (correcting errors, choosing among uncanceled variants, and the like) is not obscuring the final effect or meaning of the work but rather clarifying it. When a poem, left in manuscript, is posthumously published in the form of an exact **transcript**, it is being treated like a historical document; when it is published in a clear reading text, it is being treated like a work of literary art. Both forms may have their uses, but only the second can represent (or attempt to represent) the author's intention.[xx]

The poems of Emily Dickinson[9] present a special situation: they are clearly poems (not journal entries or letters), but they were not intended for publication. They contain both eccentric punctuation (often impossible to reproduce in type) and uncanceled alternative readings.[10] If an editor decides to publish as exact transcriptions as possible of these poems (or even photographs of the manuscripts), he is doing what normally is most sensible for works not intended for publication. But in this case he would be doing less than full justice to the material, which belongs to a genre conventionally circulated in some kind of published form and with decisions among alternative readings already made. The fact that Emily Dickinson did not "intend" publication does not alter the basic nature of the material and automatically convert into notebook jottings what would have been called poetry if published. Her distrust of publication does not obligate an editor to leave her poems unpublished (or to edit them as if they were private papers) any more than an author's "deathbed" edition obligates an editor to regard previous editions as superseded. In either case the work has an existence distinct from the wishes (expressed or implied) of its creator, and "intention" regarding publication is different from the active intention embodied in the work. Whether or not Emily Dickinson's manuscripts were specifically "intended" for publication is really beside the point; the important matter is that they are manuscripts of poems not prepared for publication. Although an editor will rightly feel an obligation to present as fully as possible the evidence available in those manuscripts (as documents in the history of American literature), he should feel equally obliged to make decisions among the author's alternative readings and produce a clear text of the poems (as literature).[xxi] An editor who thus "completes" unfinished poems is not being presumptuous but is simply facing his responsibility. One editor's choice among alternatives may of course differ from another's, but the excellence of any critical edition—whether based on unprepared manuscripts or not—is directly related to the critical powers of its editor.

9 Emily Dickinson (1830–86) wrote almost 1800 short poems but hardly any of them were published during her largely reclusive life. She sewed some of her handwritten poems together to make little handmade books or fascicles. After her death some of the poems were published in versions that drastically altered her unconventional syntax, punctuation, and imagery. Her complete poems became available in the typeset edition by Thomas H. Johnson (1955) and the facsimile edition by Ralph W. Franklin (1981).

10 I.e., places where Dickinson has written down two possible words (or sets of words), without crossing one of them out or otherwise indicating which she preferred.

IV.

[...]

Two issues are involved in these considerations, and they are basic to all kinds of editing, whether the copy-text is an uncompleted manuscript or a printed edition: (1) What does "intention" signify, and when is it final? (2) Does it matter whether the *author's* wording is recovered, particularly when emendations by others are improvements? These questions ask for definitions of the three words "final authorial intention" and for justification of them as an expression of the goal of editing. [...]

The second of the questions is easier to answer than the first. No one presumably would deny that any alteration in a literary work could be regarded as producing a different work and that the new work could be made the subject of critical analysis. Neither would anyone deny that non-authorial revisions could produce a work superior to the original and more rewarding for study. Nevertheless, if an editor sets out to edit the works of a particular writer, he has undertaken a task of historical research, and his goal must necessarily be the recovery of the words which the author actually wrote. [...]

The other question—the meaning of "intention"—is too complicated a philosophical issue to be settled here; but we can at least agree that authorial intention in literature cannot simply be equated with an explicit statement by the author explaining his motives, purposes, aims, wishes, or meaning, for intention must surely exist even if no such statements were made or are extant, and any available statements may be inadequate or misleading. The only direct evidence one has for what was in the author's mind is not what he says was there but what one finds in his work. An editor, only through his analysis and understanding of the meaning of the work in the light of his knowledge of the author and the times, will be in a position to use authorial active intention as a basis for editorial choice. That is to say, of the meanings which the editor sees in the work, he will determine, through a weighing of all the information at his command, the one which he regards as most likely to have been the author's; and that determination will influence his decisions regarding variant readings. Recognizing "finality" of intention, in turn, depends on his ability to distinguish revisions which develop an intention in the same direction from those which push it in another direction: the former represent final intentions, the latter new intentions. Whether the editor rejects such "new" intentions or edits a separate text embodying them will vary with the particular situation. But so long as he is producing an edition of an author's writings, he must choose among the author's uncanceled variants or published revisions in the light of his total understanding of the work and its author.

If it is objected that this conception of the editorial process gives an editor excessive freedom and substitutes subjectivism for rigorous discipline, two answers may be made. In the first place, a scholarly editor (as opposed to a creative one) is still pledged to print only the author's words. He may select readings on the basis of his own literary judgment only when the alternatives are authorial variants; when he chooses an authorial reading previous to the author's last one (or what he judges to be the last one), his justification is that the reading is "final" in terms of his view of the work as an organic whole and that the later reading either creates a new work or is an isolated alteration at odds with the spirit of the work. Beyond that, one may observe that critical perception is necessarily crucial to any act of historical reconstruction, any evaluation of evidence, and thus any edition labeled "critical"; therefore, as Greg says, "it would be disastrous to curb the liberty of competent editors in the hope of preventing fools from behaving after their kind." Perhaps the principal source of difficulty lies in thinking of the editorial and the critical functions as essentially distinct. When one recognizes that justice can be done to an author only by doing justice to his text, one also understands that the editor and the critic must be inseparable.

Notes

i. "Textual Criticism," *The Aims and Methods of Scholarship in Modern Languages and Literatures*, rev. ed. James Thorpe (New York: Modern Language Association of America, 1970), 33. Cf. his *Textual and Literary Criticism* (Cambridge: Cambridge UP, 1959), 120: a critical edition attempts "to approach nearly as may be to the ideal of the authorial fair copy."

ii. "Some Principles for Scholarly Editions of Nineteenth-Century American Authors," *SB* [*Studies in Bibliography*] 17 (1964): 227.

iii. I have made further comments on the role of judgment in editing in "Textual Study and Literary Judgment," *PBSA* [*Publications of the Bibliographical Society of America*] 65 (1971): 109–22.

iv. Sometimes the literary effectiveness of a variant reading is used as an argument that the revision is authorial; but it is fallacious to assume that an author's revisions will always result in improvements (as judged by the editor or present-day scholars) and that no one else was capable of making such improvements.

v. Michael Hancher, "Three Kinds of Intention," *Modern Language Notes* 87 (1972): 827–51.

vi. Hancher, 830.

vii. Hancher, 831.

viii. "The Artist's Intention," *Revue internationale de philosophie* 18 (1964): 328.

ix. "Motives, Intentions, and the Interpretation of Texts," *New Literary History* 3 (1971–72): 405. Of course, authors' statements may be deliberately deceiving rather than "self-deceiving." Beardsley points out that artists "are often inclined to the most whimsical and bizarre statements [about their work], and seem to enjoy being deliberately misleading"; see p. 292 of his "On the Creation of Art," *JAAC* 23 (1964–65): 291–304.

x. See Walter B. Rideout's review of White's edition of *A Story Teller's Story* in *English Language Notes* 7 (1969–70), 70–73.

xi. *The Waste Land. A Facsimile and Transcript of the Original Drafts Including the Annotations of Ezra Pound*, ed. Valerie Eliot (London: Faber and Faber, 1971), xxxii.

xii. One must use such qualifiers as "in effect" when calling this kind of version a "new work," since obviously there must be something similar about the two versions or they would not be regarded as "versions of a work" in the first place. At the same time, there is the implication that not every difference produces, for the practical purposes of editing, a "new work."

xiii. Of course, a revision which does not actually implement the aim of, say, simplification may have been made by the author in the belief that it does. It may be impossible for an editor to distinguish between such revisions and those which genuinely were unconnected with the motive of simplification. All he can do is to judge, on the basis of the texts in front of him and his knowledge of the author, which revisions the author can reasonably be thought to have considered simplifications (whether or not they seem such to the editor himself).

xiv. Charles Vandersee, "James's 'Pandora': The Mixed Consequences of Revision," *SB* 21 (1968): 93–108 (see p. 107). [...]

xv. If they considered the variants singly rather than in groups, even a relatively small number of variants would result in an astronomical number of separate works; it is true, however, that any group of authorial revisions may contain some which seem to move in a different direction from the others and which thus demand separate consideration.

xvi. From here on I use "separate work"—as I trust the context indicates—in the practical sense of "a work to be edited separately."

xvii. Some of the earlier versions have been edited separately: see, for example, *Whitman's Manuscripts: Leaves of Grass (1860)*, ed. Fredson Bowers (1955), which prints as parallel texts the manuscript versions of certain poems and their first published versions (in 1860); and *Leaves of Grass: The First (1855) Edition*, ed. Malcolm Cowley (London: Secker & Warburg, 1959). Cf. Bowers, "The Walt Whitman Manuscripts of 'Leaves of Grass' (1860)," in his *Textual and Literary Criticism* (Cambridge: Cambridge UP, 1959), 35–65.

xviii. As John Kemp says, "a published work of art has been, as it were, detached from the artist, and he has sent it out into the world, with the result that later versions do not necessarily cancel earlier published ones as later cancel earlier in the working-out stage before publication" ("The Work of Art and the Artist's Intentions," *British Journal of Aesthetics* 4 (1964): 152).

xix. If finality is defined in terms of publication, one could say that the latter case involves multiple intentions. The whole pattern of revisions in such a case, however, separates it from the usual instances of continual revision and suggests that the author had not really come to a decision when he was forced to select one reading or the other for publication at a particular time.

xx. E.A.J. Honigmann, in *The Stability of Shakespeare's Text* (London: Arnold, 1965), argues that Shakespeare perhaps made revisions in the process of copying, so that some of the variants we now have may represent authorial "second thoughts." The editor, therefore, must "screw his courage to the sticking place and choose between each pair of variants"; what he is doing is "to attempt a feat left undone by Shakespeare, to finalise an unfinalised text" (p. 168).

xxi. Thomas H. Johnson's Harvard edition of Emily Dickinson's poems (1955) presents a clear text, with variant readings in notes; but the decisions as to which readings were to be included in the main text were not generally made on the basis of literary judgment. Cf. Johnson's "Establishing a Text: The Emily Dickinson Papers," *SB* 5 (1952–53): 21–32.

11.

S.M. Parrish, "The Whig Interpretation of Literature," *Text: Transactions of the Society for Textual Scholarship*, 4. Edited by D.C. Greetham and W. Speed Hill. New York: AMS P, 1988. 343–51

Stephen Parrish (1921–2012) was Professor Emeritus of English at Cornell University. He was the general editor of the Cornell Wordsworth, a multi-volume edition of William Wordsworth's poems, published by Cornell University Press, which aims to present the texts of his poems in their earliest completed state, with all textual variants in earlier (incomplete) and later states recorded in the textual apparatus. The edition prefers the earlier versions of the poems to the final versions on avowedly aesthetic grounds. It therefore departs both from the orthodox approach of "respecting" the author's "final intentions," and from Greg's and Bowers's position that editors should not make judgments on aesthetic grounds. In this essay, Parrish defends his editorial procedure, and criticizes the assumptions underlying the editorial focus on final intention.

Wordsworth compulsively revised his poems, often keeping them in manuscript for many years before publishing them. In particular, he revised his long autobiographical poem, posthumously entitled *The Prelude,* over a period of more than fifty years. During this time, the poem was provisionally "finished" on at least five occasions: in two books in 1798, in five books in 1804, in thirteen books in 1805, again around 1818 (the "C-Stage Prelude"), and in fourteen books by Wordsworth's death in 1850. The latest version of the poem was published posthumously, and was the only known version for many years. The other versions have now been reconstructed by editors from Wordsworth's manuscripts.

The historian Herbert Butterfield identifies an approach to writing history that tends to treat historical events as significant insofar as they can be included in a narrative of progress toward the present. Butterfield calls this approach the "Whig" interpretation of history and associates it with the Whig party, the left-leaning British party that contested power with the Tories from the 1680s to the 1850s. Parrish argues that many editors approach texts like Whig historians approach historical events: they treat poetry as though poems progressed steadily toward completion with every revision. Their underlying assumption is that poets improve as they mature, and that poetry is crafted and polished over time. Instead, Parrish claims, in some cases poets may produce their best work in early versions, and—for whatever reason—may not preserve its initial character in their later revisions. On this view, poetry is more inspiration than craft.

Many readers find the earlier versions of Wordsworth's poems to be aesthetically superior to the later versions. Greg and Bowers did not allow aesthetic preferences to influence an editor's consideration, maintaining that authors were entitled to their second thoughts and that their mature judgment should be respected. Parrish, in direct opposition, argues that readers should be able to read the earlier versions of Wordsworth's poems—even versions he never intended to be published—because, often, "we can confidently say that the early Wordsworth was a better poet than the late Wordsworth."

When Parrish attacks the focus on final intentions and embraces aesthetic judgments as part of the editor's role, he reveals that questions of editorial theory are not purely technical, but are deeply bound up with questions about the nature of poetic composition and the merits of the poems in question.

The Whig Interpretation of Literature

[...]

This title I take from a brilliant little book published by Herbert Butterfield in 1931: *The Whig Interpretation of History*. Butterfield, Professor of Modern History at Cambridge, opened his

essay by characterizing the historian in a popular view as "the avenger": "standing as a judge between the parties and rivalries and causes of bygone generations he can lift up the fallen and beat down the proud, and by his exposures and his verdicts, his satire and his moral indignation, can punish unrighteousness, avenge the injured or reward the innocent"—thus rendering in a God-like way the "verdict of history."

Now we can all call to mind historians and critics of literature who adopt the punishing, judgmental manner as they survey the landscape of the past, peopled with aspirants to literary fame; on one side of the ocean we might nominate Ivor Winters, on the other, F.R. Leavis.[1] But Butterfield meant something rather more important. He was talking about the readiness of historians to look back upon the course of historical events and find them to be moving in an ordered, coherent way by a process of "unfolding logic" toward completion of a great design. All events and ideologies and persons are judged by their contribution to that design, which turns out to be their relevance to the present. Dividing the world into friends and enemies of progress, the Whig historian refuses sympathetic understanding, for example, to a perplexingly narrow but brilliant religious zealot who seemed to obstruct the march of liberal thought which has culminated in the set of freedoms we now cherish, and he will give exaggerated importance to a third-rate minor figure who seems to anticipate trends that seem to culminate

---

1 Ivor (or Yvor) Winters (1900–69) was an American poet and literary critic who argued for a return to classical meters and aesthetic restraint in verse. (For information on Leavis, see McGann's essay, above, p. 116, note 10.)

in those freedoms. Movements that lead into by-alleys, or seem to form patterns that are later overridden, are dismissed, as the historian in the grip of the Whig fallacy takes short-cuts through the complicated "maze of interactions," the complex "process of mutation," that leads up to the present, reasoning, perhaps subconsciously, that "if we can exclude certain things on the ground that they have no direct bearing on the present, we have removed the most troublesome elements in the complexity, and the crooked is made straight."

Historians of this persuasion thus tend, ironically, to wipe away the past except as it may in one particular or another foreshadow the present.

Now without pressing too hard my playful analogy between the history of a culture and the history of a text, we ought to be able to identify the pattern of Whig scholarship and Whig interpretation of literature. Tracing the elements of a poem, say, back to their origins—partly by study of the drafts, variant versions, and revisions that lead up to the final text, and partly by analysis of the poet's "intentions," so far as they can be made out from the strategies he appears to employ—the Whig scholar and literary historian will follow the evolution of the poem as it grows steadily toward completion. Rejected drafts, discarded variants, abandoned versions, while sometimes dutifully catalogued, are looked upon as false starts, misjudgments, or lapses of taste on the part of the poet, all happily rectified as the work, by obedience to some inner logic, reaches final form. That form, after all, represents the poet's "final intention," and its authority naturally reduces our interest in any previous or partial, deviant, forms.

Thus the past is pretty much wiped away except as it may in one particular or another foreshadow the present.

The problem is complicated by one other fact. We all know that the poet's "intentions" at any stage of his work, let alone his "final intentions," are impossible to measure: they are revealed only in the language which presumably embodies them. If—as all teachers of writing know it is—language is prior to thought, rather than the other way around, intention becomes not only elusive and illusory, but irrelevant. The poet's "final intention" chronologically supersedes his earlier intentions, but for the historian not blinkered by Whig bias the earlier "intentions" will command independent interest, especially as they reveal the poet's persistent struggle to redefine, and perhaps even to understand, his purposes. That is, the language of early versions, especially when those versions are complete, will be valued not for what it contributed to the late versions, not as a step in an inevitably evolving design, but for its own sake, as an achievement separate from the later history of the text.

I offer these remarks, which carry ethical implications, by way of introduction to the problems of editing Wordsworth. The problems arise partly from the fact that Wordsworth lived longer than most other poets, and partly from his compulsive habit of mending and patching his poems. It cost him great suffering to compose; he once confessed that whenever he picked up a pen he was seized with "an uneasiness at my stomach and side, with a dull pain about my heart" (Coleridge unsympathetically diagnosed it as "a pain in the right hypochondrium").[1] This suffering reflected the poet's terrible insecurity; desperately needing approval, he kept his works by him long after he had finished them, in order to add, improve, modify, extend, reshape them over the years: *Peter Bell* lay unpublished for 20 years, *The Waggoner* for 14, *The Borderers* for 40; when Wordsworth died he left in **manuscript**, unpublished, *Home at Grasmere* (the heart of the great *Recluse* on which he had pinned his literary hopes) and *The Prelude*, which we now recognize as his highest achievement.[2]

As we surveyed the rich profusion of variant texts that resulted from Wordsworth's insecurity, his compulsive habits, and the long duration of his active career (1785 to 1850 comes to 65 years), we resolved, in designing The Cornell Wordsworth, to break the Whig tradition and bring into view what we call the "early Wordsworth." We even ventured, somewhat rashly, to pronounce this as "often" a better Wordsworth than the "late Wordsworth," and generally more interesting. By saying "often" we intend to equivocate—not always, not even usually, but "often" we can confidently say that the early Wordsworth was a better poet than the late Wordsworth, for the plain reason that he was closer to the sources of his inspiration and less inhibited by the various orthodoxies—political, social, religious, and poetical—that he succumbed to in his later years.

In any event, we carried out our resolve by drawing up what we call Reading Texts to show the way a poem stood at a given stage of work on it. These are not, I should emphasize, efforts to create poems out of fragments. Rather, they represent something like a vertical slice cut through the continuum of text for a given poem. The slice is cut where the poet reached a stopping-place in his work, and it is generally based on a **fair copy** drawn up at that point by the poet or his household of amanuenses[3]—first his sister, then his sister and his wife and his wife's sister, then by all of the above, his daughter, his daughter's husband, and the clerk-secretary-handyman at Rydal Mount.[4] These fair copies were commonly used by Wordsworth as a base on which to enter revisions, and some of them were turned into **palimpsests**, the original text buried under three or four layers of work, and even pasted over with scraps of blank paper to receive further revisions (we have found paste-overs over paste-overs—we call them P1, P2r, P2v, and so on).[5] Clearing away the layers of revision to reach the underlying fair copy is thus archeological work in a literal and figurative sense, but it is straightforward, and seems to me to raise no serious ethical questions, except for readers whose ethical standards are shaped or bent by Whiggery. Wordsworth's five-act tragedy, later called *The Borderers*, was finished in 1797, sent to Covent Garden,[6] rejected, then allowed to sit for 42 years before the poet picked it up, rewrote it, and published the rewritten version. We print that version facing the original version, drawn from the original fair copy.[ii] Similarly, the two-part *Prelude* was published in the Cornell series from duplicate fair copies written out at the end of 1799.[iii]

---

2 *The Recluse* was the great philosophical poem that Wordsworth projected but left uncompleted at his death. He described it as the chancel of a great cathedral, to which all his other works would appear as transepts and side-chapels. *The Prelude*, the long autobiographical poem that Wordsworth worked on over a period of more than fifty years and left unpublished in his lifetime, was given its title posthumously because he conceived it as a preliminary undertaking to *The Recluse*.

3 Amanuensis: someone who writes down a text from dictation or copies it from a rough copy on behalf of its author.

4 Wordsworth lived at Rydal Mount in Ambleside in the English Lake District from 1813 to his death in 1850.

5 "r" and "v" here refer to recto and verso—the front and back of the leaf of paper.

6 The Theatre Royal Covent Garden was one of two "patent" theaters in London licensed to perform spoken drama in Wordsworth's lifetime, the other being in Drury Lane.

[...]

But I want to move to a higher level of controversy—both textual and ethical—by taking up five editorial problems which we handled in different ways. Three we resolved by printing texts which Wordsworth at one time or another probably intended to finish, but left behind as he moved on with his open-ended process of revision. Each of them thus represents a slice through the continuum, but a slice that is partially incomplete by reason of gaps or fractures in the material being cut (the image of a sausage unaccountably comes to mind). The earliest of these texts is the 1794 version of *An Evening Walk*, copied out, with some lacunae,[7] in preparation for a second **edition**, then put aside. Anticipating reproach, our editor prudently hedged by describing his text as an effort to present this "lost" version of *An Evening Walk* "in a form as close as possible to that which Wordsworth would have published" had a second edition appeared.[iv] Readers troubled by the conjectural nature of this apology will not be reassured by the hedging that surrounds the *Tuft of Primroses*—a long piece of *Recluse* writing scattered in two notebooks and rescued first by de Selincourt and then by the Cornell series. Here, the editor is obliged to present his text as an "editorial reconstruction" of "what would have resulted if, before abandoning his poem, Wordsworth had asked for a fair copy incorporating his latest carefully written entries."[v] In other words, lacking a fair copy to base our text on, we assumed the rôle of amanuensis and made one up!

The third of these cases is even more complex, though our solution is neater and perhaps more ethical. Between the two great *Preludes* of 1805 and 1850, now commonly printed as parallel texts, stands a third *Prelude* which can be dated about 1818. Put together by the "late-middle" Wordsworth (or the "early-late" Wordsworth?) this *Prelude* has never been printed for the reason that it could not be found. *Prelude* manuscripts were in use over half the poet's lifetime, and they reveal "intentions" shifting year by year, even week by week, with the "final intention" embodied in a gigantic fragment created by the poet's death. The only sensible way to treat this so-called text is clearly to slice down through it where there were significant pauses in the process of **composition** and revision. One such pause began about 1818 and lasted until about 1832, and it is this pause that makes possible the creation of what we call the C-stage *Prelude*. Constructing this *Prelude* involves grafting into the fair-copy-text of what has long been designated MS. C the C-stage revisionary work scattered not only through that manuscript but indiscriminately as the top layer over the two other manuscripts which form the basis of the 1805 *Prelude*. To separate layers, the editor, Mark Reed, has ingeniously employed infra-red photography, painstaking analysis of inks, careful study of the slope and spacing of letters, and the like. No one who thinks the world already has enough *Preludes* will thank Reed, but his work clearly represents one of the great editorial achievements of our age.[vi] Is there, then, no limit, you may be wondering, to the reconstructive zeal of the Cornell syndicate? No end to the creation

7 Lacunae are gaps in the text. In this case the word refers to blank spaces left to be filled in later, although it can also refer to gaps caused by damage to the manuscript.

of new Wordsworth texts? Well, yes, there is. To prove that we are after all sensitive to some of the limits of editorial ethics, I will conclude by touching on two cases where we held back, cases that, tempting as they were, seemed to lie across the border that divides legitimate from illegitimate editorial construction. In both cases the poet's momentary "intention" seems clear, but the intention altered so swiftly that textual evidence for it got swallowed up or scattered.

One case is a familiar one: it would be simply splendid to be able to present the great missing version of the *Prelude* in five books, as it stood in the spring of 1804. Jonathan Wordsworth,[8] who worked out the shape of this poem, called it "the most carefully structured of the different *Prelude* versions: it began and ended with the early memories that were the source of Wordsworth's creative power, and attempted *en route* to define the nature of their restorative effect."[vii] The fifth, final, book would have been especially magnificent: it opened with the climbing of Snowdon[9] and closed with the celebrated "spots of time." But, alas, no continuous fair copy survives of that book, or of the fourth book: we have chosen to draw back where Jonathan himself had feared to tread, and we have to live with tormenting visions of the perfect *Prelude* dancing in our heads.[10]

The other case involves the very earliest version of *Home at Grasmere*, which was to have been the centerpiece of the *Recluse*. Again, to reconstruct the version would require editorial imagination of a highly creative sort, and we have resisted temptation. But what a superb poem it must have been! Analysis of manuscripts shows that it opened with a Miltonic invocation, the familiar lines later moved to the end of the poem, and still later separated off as a "Prospectus" to the entire *Recluse*:

On Man, on Nature, and on human life
Thinking in solitude, from time to time
I find sweet passions traversing my soul
Like music: unto these, where'er I may
I would give utterance in numerous verse
Of Truth, of Grandeur, Beauty, Love, and Hope;
Of joy in various commonalty spread;
Of th'individual mind that keeps its own
Inviolate retirement, and consists
With being limitless, the one great Life;
I sing; fit audience let me find though few.[viii]

8 Jonathan Wordsworth (1932–2006) was a descendant of the poet's brother Christopher Wordsworth and a distinguished scholar and editor of William Wordsworth's poetry. He was the first to propose that *The Prelude* existed in a distinct five-book version between the two-book version of 1798 and the thirteen-book version of 1805.

9 Wordsworth climbed Snowdon, the highest mountain in North Wales, in 1791; the episode is recounted at a climactic moment in later versions of *The Prelude*.

10 This version of the Prelude has since been reconstructed by Duncan Wu. See William Wordsworth, *The Five-Book Prelude*, ed. Duncan Wu (Oxford: Wiley Blackwell, 1997).

The way this version closed in 1800 can only be guessed at, as the earliest surviving text contains intrusions written in 1806, after the poet's buoyantly celebratory mood had darkened, but it would certainly have turned on the eloquent lines that announce the end of the long voyage home, arrival in the Vale of Grasmere, a little Eden, a Center, a Whole, "Perfect Contentment, Unity entire."[ix]

The margin I have tried to draw between two kinds of textual reconstruction, one, I submit, ethical, the other perhaps not, can never be clean and precise. Cases near the margin will always seem problematic. But like a good and true Wordsworthian I return to my beginning by reasserting my dissent from Whig interpretations of a literary text, with their notions of an inner logic of inexorable growth toward what could have been foreseen from the start as the author's final intention. Against these notions I would plead the autonomy and the validity of each steady state of the text as it changes in confused, unpredictable ways, through patterns which the author may never have foreseen, let alone "intended." I would plead, that is, that we learn to resist what the Whig likes to cite as "the claims of history." "History," remarked Butterfield at the close of his essay, can be "all things to all men. She is at the service of good causes and bad. In other words she is a harlot and a hireling ... and this is the goddess the Whig worships when he claims to make her the arbiter of controversy."[x] She does not sound like the sort of creature we ought to go on keeping company with!

Notes

i. Wordsworth made this complaint to Coleridge in December, 1798; Coleridge relayed it to Humphry Davy on July 16, 1800.

ii. *The Borderers*, ed. Robert Osborn (Ithaca, NY: Cornell UP, 1982).

iii. *The Prelude, 1798–1799*, ed. Stephen Parrish (Ithaca, NY: Cornell UP, 1977).

iv. *An Evening Walk*, ed. James Averill (Ithaca, NY: Cornell UP, 1983), 21.

v. *The Tuft of Primroses*, ed. Joseph Kishel (Ithaca, NY: Cornell UP, 1986), 37.

vi. Mark L. Reed, *The Thirteen-Book Prelude* (Ithaca, NY: Cornell UP, 1991).

vii. "The Five-Book *Prelude* of Early Spring 1804," *Journal of English and Germanic Philology* LXXVI (1977): 1–25.

viii. I quote the earliest surviving text, printed in William Wordsworth, *Home at Grasmere: Part First, Book First, of The Recluse*, ed. Beth Darlington (Ithaca, NY: Cornell UP, 1977), 257.

ix. *Home at Grasmere*, MS. B, 1. 170; Darlington, 48.

x. My citations from Butterfield are from Scribner's first American edition, New York, 1951.

12.

Jack Stillinger, "A Practical Theory of Versions," *Coleridge and Textual Instability: The Multiple Versions of the Major Poems.* Cary, NC: Oxford UP, 1994. 118–41

Jack Stillinger (b. 1931) is Professor Emeritus of English at the University of Illinois at Urbana-Champaign. He has published 26 books, including definitive editions of the poetry of John Keats for Harvard University Press. His work editing Keats's poetry has led him to challenge solitary conceptions of authorship and to offer new approaches to textual editing. In his book *Coleridge and Textual Instability*, from which this chapter is taken, Stillinger argues that, for each of Coleridge's major poems, there is not a single "best" authoritative text, but rather several variant versions of the work. In Chapter 2 of that book, Stillinger identifies eighteen versions of "The Ancient Mariner," as well as multiple versions of many of Coleridge's other major poems. In the chapter reprinted here, he reflects on the theoretical implications of his work. He usefully summarizes the approach advocated by Greg, Bowers, and Tanselle, who argue that later authorial revisions should be prioritized, and also the approach advocated by Parrish and others, who argue for the value of earlier states of a work. Stillinger then advocates his own approach, which understands each text of a work to be its own "version," with independent authority. This approach recognizes that an author's intentions may often not be singular, but that authors may have multiple intentions for the same work at different times, and may indeed not have a single "final" intention at all. It also rethinks exactly what a literary work *is*: rather than thinking of it as a single entity, Stillinger thinks of the literary work as an interpretative field that might include many versions:

> If *The Ancient Mariner* is one poem, then in theory at least it *has* to be all its versions taken together. On the other hand, or simultaneously, *The Ancient Mariner* might theoretically be recognized as the title of eighteen different poems. (p. 169)

Stillinger recognizes, however, that his theory cannot easily be put into practice in a conventional edition, published as a book, which cannot easily display more than two versions simultaneously (on facing pages). He suggests that hypertext editions may offer a potential way to present multiple versions of a work for readers to navigate among, a suggestion that Jerome McGann takes up in his essay "The Rationale of Hypertext," included in Chapter 5, p. 459.

A Practical Theory of Versions

In the preceding chapters [of Stillinger's book], I have here and there juxtaposed some of the more speculative and theoretical ways of critical thinking—the kinds of thinking that construct ideal texts and unified interpretations—with the actuality of Coleridge's multiple versions.[1] We do not *really* know, in any factual sense, what *The Eolian Harp* or *The Ancient Mariner* or any of the other poems "means," or what Coleridge intended (in any definition of "intended") in writing the poems, or why he changed his texts so often, or what he hoped to achieve by any specific revision that we happen to pause over. We simply make our guesses, hope that they are somewhere near the (admittedly unrecoverable and therefore unverifiable) mark, and, if we are writing or lecturing, try to persuade readers and audiences that the guesses are right, useful, or at least (for the moment) interesting.

Coleridge's multiple versions, though, as I have described them thus far in this book, are a matter of fact rather than speculation. We really do have Version 1, Version 2, Version 3, and so forth of the poems examined in Chapter 2, and, according to the way I have defined them, anybody can look at the materials and verify that these versions do in fact exist. Now in this chapter, I wish to construct a theory of my own on the basis of those existing facts. More than

a century and a half ago, in the same year in which Coleridge published the second **edition** of his *Poetical Works*, the American popular historian Eliza Robbins defined "theory" as "a belief of certain presumed facts, without examination and knowledge." The theory offered here claims to be based on both knowledge and examination.[i] It is intended to explain the constitution of Coleridge's works—as exemplified in the seven major poems of this study—in terms of the irrefutable presence of authoritative multiple versions.

I. A Three Bears Array of Textual Theories

Theories about the constitution of a literary work are pretty much the same as editorial theories about what constitutes the "best" text of a work, and thus I can get into my topic most efficiently by rehearsing the three commonest current ideas about editing: the long-established theory that the latest text is the best; a more recent theory that the earliest text is the best; and a still newer theory that the best can be the latest, the earliest, or any other authoritative version in between.

These theories are also related to ideas about authorial intention. The latest-text theory is based on the notion that the latest is best because it is the best representative of the author's

1 Samuel Taylor Coleridge (1772–1834), Romantic poet and author of "The Ancient Mariner," "Kubla Khan," "Christabel," "Frost at Midnight," and other poems. He revised his poems almost obsessively, both before and after publication.

intention; the earliest-text theory is based on the notion that the earliest text (rather than the latest) is where the author's "real" intention resides; and the newest theory, which I shall here call textual pluralism, is based on the idea that each version of a work embodies a separate authorial intention that is not necessarily the same as the authorial intention in any other version of the same work. The three theories are also relatable to the story of the Three Bears. If we could imagine a textual theorist named Goldilocks, the latest-text theory might be judged to be too old-fashioned, stuffy, and mechanical a way to treat a literary work; the earliest-text theory might be judged to be too radical, too leveling, and above all too impractical; and the third of the theories, allowing for textual pluralism, might be judged to be "just right." With writers like Coleridge who repeatedly revised their works, I shall argue that a theory of textual pluralism is the "just right" way to view the constitution of a literary work.

For the past two centuries, the most widely agreed-on concept in textual theory has been that there should be—somewhere, whether already existing, or yet to be constructed by scholars—a single "best" or "most authoritative" text for each of an author's works, and that it is the job of the textual scholar to determine what that single best or most authoritative text is (and, if the scholar is doing an edition of the work, to construct and print that text as the standard to which all earlier variant texts lead up and from which all later variant texts descend).

During much of these two centuries, the leading school of textual theory held that the best or most authoritative text of a work had to be some form of "final" version, usually the latest text written or printed during the author's lifetime—the last that the author *could* or *might* have had a hand in. All earlier versions of the work, whether in **manuscript** or printed form, were routinely assigned inferior status, as so many temporary stages on the way to the final version. When they were given any recognition at all, these earlier versions were usually reported fragmentarily by scholars, in textual apparatuses at the foot of the **page** or in the back of an edition. In the rare instances where an edition presented early and late versions on facing pages, it was usually understood that the version on the left-hand side was some kind of incomplete preliminary text that stood as a milepost on the way toward the perfection of the text on the right-hand side.

Thus in the case of *The Ancient Mariner*, the text in one or another of Coleridge's late *Poetical Works*—1828, 1829, or 1834 (this last in the year in which the poet died)—was considered *the* best, *the* most authoritative, version. All earlier versions were routinely viewed as texts preliminary to the one that Coleridge most wanted us to read ever after, the version of the late *Poetical Works*. This is the kind of traditional thinking that Stephen Parrish, making an analogy with "the Whig interpretation of history," has recently described as "textual Whiggery": just as, in the Whig view of history, events are seen as progressing to ever better states of existence, so textual Whiggery has a retrospective view of a succession of texts "moving in an ordered, coherent way by a process of 'unfolding logic' toward completion of a great design."[ii] In the overall view, it does not matter whether the examples of textual Whiggery are the late-nineteenth- and early-twentieth-century editors who took for their **copy-texts** the latest edition published during the author's lifetime, or the more recent followers of Sir Walter Greg and Fredson Bowers beginning in the 1950s, who argued that we should use an early version of a work for copy-text but then emend that early text's substantives to arrive at the author's latest *wording* in each passage where there were changes.[2] Both of these schools are philosophically alike in wishing to recover and present the author's finally intended wording, on the assumption that the last is the most mature, self-perceptive, and wise.

A more recent school of thought concerning textual authority—sometimes associated in Romantics studies with Jonathan Wordsworth, Stephen Parrish, and the principles that led to the establishment of the Cornell edition of Wordsworth's poems, and in the field of American literature vigorously argued by Hershel Parker—favors the opposite idea: that the most authoritative version of a work is the *earliest* rather than the latest, and usually (where manuscripts are available) a manuscript form of the work rather than an early printed text.[3] Thus Wordsworth's tale of poor Margaret is seen as "best" in the early text called *The Ruined Cottage*, and this form of the story is (aesthetically as well as theoretically) preferred over the more complicated versions in *The Pedlar* and Book I of *The Excursion*. In the much-discussed instance of *The Prelude*, a number of influential critics are on record as preferring one or another earlier version rather than the latest recoverable text in which Wordsworth himself had a hand—that is, the thirteen-book text of 1805 over the fourteen-book text of 1850, and then a hypothetical five-book version of 1804 over the thirteen books of 1805, and, to move even farther backward, a two-part version of 1798–99 over the hypothetical five books of 1804.[4] In a polemical essay published a few years ago in *Studies in Romanticism*, I called this tendency "textual primitivism" and worried about its having some unintended bad consequences in the standardizing of early texts of Wordsworth and the corresponding loss of later texts.[iii] But the tendency has its attractive side, and certainly has a degree of theoretical justification in the supposition that earlier texts are fresher, more authentic, more representative of the original genius that created them.

[...]

Both of these views—the preference for the author's final text and the countering preference for a first or early text—alike depend on the belief that there is, whether late or early, some *single* version that is best or most authoritative. This is a belief that nowadays is being challenged, and gradually replaced, by a pluralistic concept first proposed by James Thorpe in the 1960s and then developed and championed more recently in Germany by Hans Zeller, in the United States by

---

2 See W.W. Greg's essay "The Rationale of Copy-Text," above, p. 125.

3 Jonathan Wordsworth is a critic of Romantic poetry and Advisory Editor to the Cornell Wordsworth edition. Stephen Parrish is the General Editor of the Cornell Wordsworth (see his essay "The Whig Interpretation of Literature" above, p. 157). Hershel Parker is an editor and biographer of Herman Melville, and a scholar of American Literature more generally. He is co-editor with Harrison Hayford of the landmark Norton Critical Edition of *Moby Dick* (1967 and 2001) and Associate General Editor of *The Writings of Herman Melville*, as well as author of *Flawed Texts and Verbal Icons: Literary Authority in American Fiction* (Evanston, IL: Northwestern UP, 1984).

4 For a discussion of the different versions of *The Prelude*, see G. Thomas Tanselle's essay, "The Editorial Problem of Final Authorial Intention," above, p. 139.

Jerome McGann, Donald Reiman, Peter Shillingsburg, and me (among others), and in Britain by James McLaverty and the next serious editor of Coleridge's poems, J.C.C. Mays. This newest idea is that every individual version of a work is a distinct text in its own right, with unique aesthetic character and unique authorial intention.

The concept of textual pluralism has more practical relevance to some writers than to others. Keats, who died young and had no time to revise over a long lifetime the way Wordsworth and Coleridge did, is generally a single-version author. As I remarked near the beginning of Chapter 3 [of the book in which this essay appears], he does not seem to have been interested in revising even where he had plenty of time to make changes, and frequently when one is looking around for the best or most authoritative version of a Keats poem (say, *Ode on a Grecian Urn*) there is only a single substantive text to choose.[5] But with writers like Wordsworth and Coleridge, obsessive revisers who lived for three or four decades after first drafting their most admired poems, numerous versions compete for attention; and a theory of textual pluralism—allowing that every separate version has its separate legitimacy and that all authoritative versions are equally authoritative—seems a much more appropriate way to regard their writing than an approach that ignores its extended textual history.[iv]

When we have eighteen different Coleridge-authored versions of *The Ancient Mariner* (to return to my continuing example),[6] it simply does not make good sense to argue that the latest (only) or the earliest (only) or any other single version (only) is the "real" *Ancient Mariner*, or the most authoritative, or the one (above all others) that best embodies Coleridge's intentions in the work. If *The Ancient Mariner* is one poem, then in theory at least it *has* to be all its versions taken together. On the other hand, or simultaneously, *The Ancient Mariner* might theoretically be recognized as the title of eighteen different poems.

II. The Ubiquity of Versions

From the reader-response and reception-theory points of view, there are of course many more versions of Coleridge's major poems than just the 94 singled out in Chapter 2. If one considers such traditionally extra-textual matters as book and magazine design, format, **typography**, illustration, and numerous aspects of context (the particular space of a text, the particular occasion in a reader's life), the possibilities for variation are virtually endless, even when the actual words of a text—and, for that matter, even when the accidentals of punctuation, spelling, and capitalization as well—remain the same. There are versions everywhere one looks. Hence *ubiquity* in my section heading.

5 Stillinger himself edited Keats's poems, producing *The Texts of Keats's Poems* (Cambridge, MA: Harvard UP, 1974) and *The Poems of John Keats* (Cambridge, MA: Harvard UP, 1978).

6 In the first chapter of his book, Stillinger identifies eighteen versions of the *Ancient Mariner*, all of which Coleridge can be said to have "authorized." They vary from manuscripts and published editions of the poem, to annotations Coleridge made in printed copies of his poem and revisions he introduced for collected editions later in his life.

Consider, for one obvious set of examples, how many different ways the same words of the late texts of *The Ancient Mariner* have been presented to readers over the years. In nineteenth-century editions, when the lines of the poem were unnumbered and the prose **glosses** were routinely positioned in the outer margins beside the verse, a marginal gloss was printed at the left or right side of the poetic text according to whether the associated verse happened to fall on a **verso** or a **recto** page. Thus Western readers, normally scanning any writing (including glosses and lines of verse) from left to right, might actually read the glosses *before* reading the lines being glossed on the verso pages, and the glosses *after* the lines on the rectos.[v] [...]

In texts having line numbers, the glosses are regularly set in the opposite margin from the numbers. E.H. Coleridge's edition of 1912 and *The Norton Anthology of English Literature* number the lines in the right margins and so have *all* the glosses at left, in effect preceding the corresponding passages of verse. In the text given in the Appendix,[7] the lines are numbered at left, and so the glosses are always printed at the right, in a position following the passages of verse. [...]

Then there are the appurtenances of editorial apparatus and commentary. The *Complete Poetical Works* edition records variant readings from eight or ten sources in fine print at the bottom of the page, and the reader of the poem in this context cannot help being conscious of the fact that this is a work by one of the **canonized** English poets whose manuscripts and successive printings constitute important information of some sort or other. In *The Norton Anthology*, the foot-of-the-page apparatus provides additional glosses and occasional interpretive explanation (though subsequent versions of the **anthology** will reduce the latter, to give users more freedom to think for themselves, thereby registering a different intention from earlier *Nortons*). Once again, the canonized character of the poem and author is unavoidable—this is the *Norton Anthology* of *famous* English literature. The text, which is [...] essentially that of *1834*, is vastly removed in format and surroundings from the original 1834 printing, when Coleridge, though in his last year of life, was still a contemporary poet and *The Ancient Mariner* a contemporary poem—with no line numbers, no textual apparatus, and no scholarly and critical commentary in sight, apart from the glosses that Coleridge himself supplied.

The Ancient Mariner has been many times illustrated by artists (as well as recorded and filmed on videotape for use in the classroom). An *Ancient Mariner* with pictures—or rather, since Coleridge provided numerous pictorial effects from beginning to end, an *Ancient Mariner* with the addition of someone else's pictures—is quite different from a text consisting only of Coleridge's and his characters' words. [...] Such illustrations are influential in the same way that critical introductions and commentary are, but much more immediately and effectively: unlike introductions and commentary, they cannot be ignored. No reader of an illustrated text can read uninfluenced by the illustrations.

[...]

7 The appendix to Stillinger's book, where he presents reading texts of several of the versions he discusses.

To an extent, the branching out of textual versions of poems can be likened to performance versions in music (and the other performance arts). I "perform" *The Ancient Mariner* every time I teach it, and no doubt a little differently each time (and certainly differently from the way my colleagues perform it when they teach the same lines and words in their classes). Students similarly perform the poem in their readings and discussions, and the process of variation and differentiation goes on indefinitely. [...]

Obviously, these versions are not all, or at least not entirely, authoritative. Coleridge did not author the specific positions—verso margins as opposed to recto—of the *Ancient Mariner* glosses in *1828* and *1834*, or E.H. Coleridge's textual apparatus,[8] or the *Norton Anthology* explanatory commentary, or Doré's and Calder's illustrations,[9] or my and my colleagues' and our students' "performance" interpretations. But he did author the words, both verse and prose, that are at the heart of all these, and, as I have urged on an earlier occasion (in *Multiple Authorship and the Myth of Solitary Genius*), writers are only the principal, not the sole, authors of even the most authoritative of their texts.[10] In this section, I merely point out the relative *conservatism* of my distinguishing only 94 versions of the major poems. The list would have grown to many thousands if I had included every separate subsequent printing and other appearance for the past two centuries.

[...] [In two sections omitted here, Stillinger first considers and rejects arguments advanced by Thomas Tanselle and Peter Schillingsburg that literary works properly exist in the minds of authors or readers, not in the documents that imperfectly transmit them; he then considers and endorses arguments advanced by James Thorpe, Hans Zeller, Jerome McGann, and James McLaverty that documents containing variant texts of a work create new versions of that work.]

With these four critics [Thorpe, Zeller, McGann, and McLaverty] as background, and Shillingsburg hovering (or dancing) in the wings, here is a five-point scheme that I propose as an aid to describing and thinking about the multiple versions of Coleridge's major poems. In the abstract, the principles are as follows:

1. A *version* of a work is a physically embodied text of the work. For all practical purposes, "version" and "text" are synonymous, both being particular manifestations of a larger entity, the work.
2. A *work* is constituted by all known versions of the work. It too can be thought of as being physically embodied, but only in the documentary forms of particular versions, whether already existing or newly created.

---

8 E.H. Coleridge (1846–1920) based his 1912 edition of his grandfather's poems on the 1834 edition.

9 Gustave Doré (1832–83) illustrated Coleridge's *Ancient Mariner* in 1876, and Alexander Calder (1898–1976) illustrated the poem in 1946.

10 Jack Stillinger, *Multiple Authorship and the Myth of Solitary Genius* (New York: Oxford UP, 1991).

3. The degree of textual difference necessary to *distinguish one version of a work from another* is entirely arbitrary. The most objective criterion (in the sense of being verifiable and even quantifiable) is substantive difference.
4. The *authority* of any particular version lies not necessarily in the version itself but in someone's arbitrary definition of what constitutes authority—for example, documented or presumed authorial intention, agreement between author and **publisher**, the character and quality of a document at hand, the separate or collective responses, preferences, and dictates of contemporary or later readers, "interpretive communities,"[ii] editors, anthologists, and so on.
5. The *relative authoritativeness* among versions of a work depends on (a) the criteria used to define authority and (b) interpretation of the evidence in each case.

The first of these points advocates the equation of "text" and "version" as two words meaning the same thing. [...] "Version" is a more useful word than "text" right now, because the latter word conveys so many different and conflicting meanings in current textual theory—for example, a socially constructed event, the outcome of an event, an utterance, the record of an utterance, a performance, the way someone is dressed, a section of landscape, an entire culture.[vi] "Version" is also preferable to "text" because it opposes by definition the idea that a

work exists in just a single (best, most authoritative) form. "Text of the work" can carry implications of "*the* text of the work"; "version," because of its routine use in ordinary language (to distinguish one form of something from another form), necessarily implies plurality—no one could possibly say (or think) that there is only one *version* of something when it is also known that there are several.

My specification of "physically embodied text" recognizes the material reality of versions. Textual versions—the words of a work as written in particular manuscripts or printed in particular books and periodicals—are physically embodied in these documentary forms and inseparable from them. (Other forms are also possible—**printer's proofs**, manuscript changes in the margins of printed copies, letters containing instructions for the alteration of existing texts, tape recordings, computer disks—but these are analogous to ordinary manuscript and printed versions, and there is no reason to consider them in a separate category. [...]) One could copy out exactly the words of a Coleridge manuscript—say, the British Library **holograph** of *Kubla Khan*—and claim that the copy represents the same version or text as that in the holograph, but it does not really, because the paper, handwriting, occasion, and purpose are entirely different from those of the original. It would be both more logical and more useful (for purposes of classification) to call such a copy simply one more version.

ii Stillinger here refers to the idea developed in Stanley Fish's influential book *Is There a Text in this Class? The Authority of Interpretative Communities* (Cambridge, MA: Harvard UP, 1980) that the meaning of texts is produced neither by the author nor by the lone reader, but by communities of culturally competent readers.

The knottiest problem in textual theory, regardless of who is doing the theorizing, is the relationship of the words of a text to the physical document embodying them. When we describe a text, or enumerate the differences between one text of a work and another, we most often are talking [...] about the words of the texts, or the words plus the punctuation, capitalization, spelling, and other so-called accidental features; and yet these things [...] have no material reality unless they are embodied in a physical document. Theoretically, it may be possible to transfer these things—the words, punctuation, and so forth—from one physical embodiment to another, as when an editor in a new edition "takes" or "reproduces" a text from a source in another document. What I wish to stress here is that this sort of problem and the inconsistencies inherent in it are *merely* theoretical. In scholarly practice, including the describing and editing of texts, there has never been a serious conflict among the beliefs that texts are physically embodied, that the most important features of texts are the words, punctuation, and so forth, and also that it is possible to reproduce these features in other material embodiments (in quotations, **facsimiles**, diplomatic transcriptions, and many kinds of editions). We operate within this contradiction all the time, and I have cheerfully ignored it throughout my discussion of Coleridge's versions in the first three chapters of this book. I think it should be recognized for what it is: a theoretical problem with no practical consequences.

Along with the idea that versions (and texts) are inseparable from their physical embodiments, I should like to propose, purely for the sake of convenience, that each document be considered as representing only a single version. Both Zeller and Shillingsburg maintain that a single manuscript containing cancellations and revisions can represent two or more versions of text—the text as originally written plus the new text or successive texts created by the revisions.[vii] Frequently, however, it is not possible to isolate the author's original writing or to distinguish separate versions within a manuscript in this way. The author may have made alterations near the beginning of the manuscript before going on to write the rest of the manuscript, or may have revised at different times in sequences not now recoverable. One cannot, in such situations, say with certainty which readings in one part existed simultaneously with which readings in another and thus cannot identify separate versions within the manuscript. In the face of such difficulties, the more nearly certain procedure is to take each manuscript as a discrete version, and all its cancellations and revisions as being part of that single version.

Concerning the second of my five points, I have defined "work" in this way—as being constituted by all the known versions of it—in order to deny the possibility that any single version, existing or newly created, can be equated with the work to the exclusion of all other versions. There are no logical grounds for excluding versions as such—only arbitrary rules and critical (aesthetic, political, moral) preferences. Thus Coleridge's *Ancient Mariner* consists of all recoverable versions of the poem plus any new ones that publishers, scholars, anthologists, artists, filmmakers, and groups of elementary schoolchildren produce subsequently. As I suggested in the section on "ubiquity of versions," there is no limit to the number of possible versions. But in practice, it may be convenient to restrict the number (as I did in most of my account of the poem in Chapter 2) to versions that Coleridge is known to have had a direct hand in producing. It is important to keep in mind, however, that any such restriction is purely arbitrary. Versions that

Coleridge did *not* have a direct hand in—such as the text in E.H. Coleridge's *Complete Poetical Works* of 1912 and that (or those) in J.C.C. Mays's volumes [...] in the *Collected Coleridge*—are still, by anybody's criteria, "Coleridge's *Ancient Mariner*."[12]

The question of whether or not a work thus multiply constituted has actual physical existence is purely a matter of definition. While it is necessary both practically and theoretically that versions be considered to have material form, the larger concept, the "work," can perfectly well be an abstraction, as Tanselle argues, or a classification device, as Shillingsburg suggests it should be.[viii] A more interesting question is whether the work consists of all its versions viewed separately—a collection of individual texts—or of all of them (if this were possible) viewed simultaneously together. Sometimes the question is posed in terms of "product" versus "process," the "product" being some single version (whether final or from one or another specific stage earlier in the history of the work) and the "process" being some kind of genetic or "continuous production" record of the work's progress from earliest to latest recoverable versions. With Coleridge's poems, either view has its interest and usefulness. It all depends on what one wants a view of.

Concerning my third point, there is of course no agreed-on definition of the degree of difference necessary to distinguish one version of a work from another. The possibilities range all over the map, from Zeller's idea that a single variant of wording constitutes a separate version to Thorpe's requirement of "major revision" that produces "a changed aesthetic effect." Tanselle attempts a distinction between "vertical" and "horizontal" revisions (vertical revisions create a new version by "altering the purpose, direction, or character of a work," while horizontal revisions do not).[13] Sometimes a concept of time (or unity of time) is invoked—a version consists of all the parts of a text that were in place, together, at one time—and sometimes a concept of function. Currently, much of the discussion focuses not on when to consider two texts separate versions but on the question of when two versions differ sufficiently to be considered entirely separate works.[ix]

None of the proposed ways of distinguishing versions has any compelling merit as a general method. Some are too subjective to be used practically (Thorpe's "changed aesthetic effect," Tanselle's "vertical" revision); others are emptily mechanical (Zeller's single word-change). I have employed Zeller's concept in this book simply because in most cases it can be applied unambiguously. Obviously, some versions of Coleridge's poems are more interesting and "important" (in various senses) than others, as the individual descriptions in Chapter 2 have pointed out. The more pressing need is establishing the presence and legitimacy of separate versions in the first place.

[...]

Concerning my fourth point, the locus of authority of a version, the clear answer from the golden age of editing—the author's presumed (final) intention—is now clouded by increasing

12 Since Stillinger wrote, these volumes have now been published as Samuel Taylor Coleridge, *Poetical Works*, a four-volume set which forms Volume 16 of *The Collected Works of Samuel Taylor Coleridge* (Princeton, NJ: Princeton UP, 2001).

13 For Tanselle's distinction, see p. 149, above.

recognition that authors' intentions are in general unrecoverable apart from the texts that the authors produce, and also by recognition that the privileging of authorial intention (even were such intention available) is a matter of arbitrary choice, not something inherent in the nature of texts per se. We are also coming to see (especially with the help of Shillingsburg's *Scholarly Editing in the Computer Age*) that in many cases the privileging of authorial intention has really been an excuse for carrying out the critic's or editor's own intentions instead. Claiming to "fulfill" Wordsworth's intentions, we edit or cite as standard an early or late version of *The Prelude* according to our own notions of what Wordsworth *should* have intended or, more simply, according to what we ourselves prefer aesthetically, politically, philosophically, or theologically. There are so many different definitions of "intention" to work with, one or another will easily make possible the choice of the version that we wish to print or cite.

Since this is a book about "Coleridge and Textual Instability," and one of its principal emphases is the fact that Coleridge himself produced numerous different versions of his major poems, and seemingly did so on purpose, I have arbitrarily chosen authorial intention as the basis for authority in the versions I am studying here. At the same time, however, I must register agreement with Zeller that authorial intention can (in general) be recovered only in the authorization of documents produced by the author. Zeller lists the commonest forms of authorization as follows:

> We regard as *authorized* those manuscripts which the author worked on himself, or which were demonstrably commissioned by him. Published texts are considered to be authorized if the author desired or approved their production, and if he influenced the text by supplying the printer's copy or by personal revision, or by revision undertaken at his request during the printing process.[x]

This description (even including the now-archaic masculine pronouns for author) fits Coleridge perfectly, covering the holograph manuscripts, of course, but also the **transcripts** made by people close to Coleridge, virtually all the early printings, and the various other forms—letters, proofs, marked copies—by which we know about the poet's revisions.

Since I have just explained my criteria for authority, the last of my five points in effect raises more narrowly the question of relative authoritativeness among authorized versions: if all (or nearly all) of the 94 versions of the seven poems discussed in Chapter 2 carry Coleridge's authority, aren't some of them more authoritative than others? The short answer is sure, why not?—some of them are bound to be more authoritative (in spite of my suggestion, at the end of the first main section of this chapter, that in a pluralistic view of the constitution of a literary work each separate version has its own legitimacy and all authoritative versions are equally authoritative). But there can be no general rule for determining relative authoritativeness. The question has to be decided case by case, and many of the decisions will be the result of critical interpretation rather than biographical or historical fact.

[...]

Obviously, there are more and less authoritative texts among the versions I have singled out in Chapter 2, and even totally non-authoritative elements among the authoritative—uncorrected printer's errors in the published texts (for example, "fast think pants" in the *1828* printing of *Kubla Khan* [line]18)[14] and uncorrected copying errors in the transcripts (no doubt a great many in the Bodleian transcript of *Christabel*, Version 8)—but most of the individual decisions can only be based on critical judgment and speculation. In any given case, when the text of a Coleridge poem has been changed, and Coleridge himself appears to have been the agent responsible for the change, the new text not only immediately acquires Coleridgean authority but becomes, at that point, the "latest" authoritative text produced by the poet. How this version then relates to other versions that preceded or follow it and why Coleridge made the changes are largely matters of interpretation.

III. Practical Consequences of a Practical Theory

The most obvious advantage of recognizing the existence and legitimacy of multiple versions lies in the more realistic recovery that it makes possible of authors and their activity in the production of literary works. This has a bearing on biography and literary history, of course, but also on almost any kind of theorizing about literary creativity and on any kind of practical criticism and interpretation that is based on what an author did or what an author meant.

As I have repeatedly emphasized, critics dealing with Coleridge's poetry have tended to work with standard texts, one per poem, treating them as if they were the only versions that Coleridge wrote, and mistakenly—at least from any historical point of view—juxtaposing texts that existed together, if they ever did, only very late in Coleridge's life. For illustration, let us imagine that a critic wants to investigate Coleridge's best years of poetic creativity—roughly the seven years between 1795 and 1802, when the poet was in his middle and later twenties—in order to discover, and say something interesting about, the ideas and techniques common to the work. Typically, the critic goes to the principal poems for those years, using the texts of Campbell's *Poetical Works* or E.H. Coleridge's *Complete Poetical Works*, and reads them over and over, searching out recurrent themes, structures, images, words, and phrases. At some point in the process, the critic calls a halt, decides definitively (for the occasion) what the principal poems have most in common—and writes it up as a book, an essay, or a conference paper.

What the critic is actually doing here, in this purported attempt to discover something about the young Coleridge, is investigating and discovering unity, recurrences, thematic relationships, and the like in a highly artificial array of texts that to a certain extent is the creation of Coleridge scholars rather than of Coleridge himself—a collocation of works in forms that never actually existed in Coleridge's lifetime but instead date from 1893, when Campbell published his edition, or from 1912, when E.H. Coleridge's edition appeared, or perhaps from some even later date, when scholarly sophistication changed the texts further from what they were in Coleridge's own day. The critic may be intent on studying Coleridge's development as a poet or thinker, but the

14 An error for "fast thick pants."

critic who works only with the latest versions inevitably ignores historical evidence concerning the poet's changing focuses in subject matter and theme as he revised his poems from one version to another over a long lifetime. With an awareness of multiple versions, the critic can begin to grasp the biographical and historical reality of Coleridge's work—can do a kind of archaeological excavation, as it were, in which versions actually existing at the same time can be connected to form layers of Coleridgean textual history.[xi]

[...]

A theory of versions also helps in the preservation of important literary artifacts of the past. [...] *The Ancient Mariner* was a different work for readers in 1798 from what it was two years later, and again from what it was in subsequent printings of *Lyrical Ballads*, and, in still other ways, from what it became in *Sibylline Leaves* in 1817 and in Coleridge's *Poetical Works* of 1828 to 1834. It continued to be a different work for readers at different times later in the nineteenth century, and the process of alteration—whether the result is considered improvement or deterioration—continues to the present day. Each of these stages has its separate historical significance. It seems certain that a theory of versions will make some of this process of successive differences clearer than it was before.

The most obvious *problem* resulting from a theory of versions, as the textual theorists already mentioned are well aware (McGann, McLaverty, and Shillingsburg in particular), is how to choose a specific text when we are restricted—in our editions and anthologies, and thence in our critical thinking—to one text per title. When there exists 18 versions of *The Ancient Mariner*, which one do we put in the next Oxford edition or in the next Norton Anthology—or do we construct a new version altogether out of selected parts of those 18?

At the theoretical level, as I have already suggested in the preceding section, this is a canonical problem, and it can be solved theoretically by a variety of arbitrary definitions of "work" and the relationship of "work" to "text" and "version." At the practical level, however, the acceptance of versions makes editing considerably more difficult. Textual pluralism may ultimately prove to be the most rational way to view the constitution of a literary work, but it renders rational practice virtually impossible in routine editing situations.

Obviously, we cannot print 18 separate *Ancient Mariners* in an edition of Coleridge or in *The Norton Anthology*, and—as the concept of versions gains currency—editors will increasingly have tough choices to make in presenting single texts for reading. Double-text predicaments have sometimes been solved by printing two versions of a work on facing pages; we have long had facing-page editions of *The Prelude*, and there are more recent examples of the same procedure in most volumes of the Cornell Wordsworth.[xii] [...] But even doubling the texts, though it presents twice the material that we had with single texts, cannot completely represent the work when there are 10, or 12, or 18 different authoritative versions in existence.

Some scholars think we shall ultimately solve this problem with computers, using programs such as **hypertext** that will allow us to store and retrieve all the versions of a work at once, and that will give us, as readers, the ability to call up any particular version with the press of a button and also the means to create new versions by synthesizing existing ones.[xiii] (Employing such technology, we can again be thought of as *performers* of a work—and the musical analogies that come to mind run all the way from exact reproduction of a score, at one end of the range of possibilities, to jazz improvisation at the other.) Very likely, since we are human beings and not computer scanners, we shall never be able to comprehend all versions of a work simultaneously. We may, however, be able to arrange them in multi-dimensional images on the screen that will be a better representation of the complexity of a literary work in the process of taking shape than anything so far achieved linearly on a flat page.

But the need to have flat pages of text for actual readers will continue for the foreseeable future, and so, therefore, will the need to make choices. Editors will increasingly have to involve themselves in what Thorpe called "the aesthetics of textual criticism," or else choose versions on such grounds as historical importance or "representativeness." In my *Studies in Romanticism* essay on "Textual Primitivism," I took a stand against Jonathan Wordsworth's frequently expressed preference for earlier rather than later versions of *The Prelude*. But Jonathan Wordsworth makes no attempt to hide the basis of his preference; he thinks the earlier versions are better poetry. And in my essay, I countered (triumphantly!) by asserting my own preference for later versions. This is nothing more than a kind of rhetoric or politics of aesthetic choice, and it will not make anyone happy who wants to operate according to general principles.

But general principles no longer seem workable in such matters. We are going to have to make and defend our specific choices on an ad hoc basis, hoping that someone else likes them or is moved to accept them. In theory, everybody can be right in such matters, and the one who is rightest will be the one who musters the best rhetoric to argue in favor of an actual, particular version of a work—even if it turns out that it was chosen simply because it was the version that the editor or critic liked best. Ultimately, the instability inherent in multiplicity of versions should be viewed as a positive. Greater richness and complexity are among the results—a textuality of Keatsian process rather than of Shelleyan white radiance. And the new theory is at one with democracy: there is something in it for everybody.

Notes

i. Eliza Robbins, *Tales from American History; Containing the Principal Facts in the Life of Christopher Columbus. For the Use of Young Persons* (1829; New York: Harper and Brothers, 1833), 24.

ii. Stephen Maxfield Parrish, "The Whig Interpretation of Literature," *TEXT* 4 (1988): 344. [See also the previous selection in this volume.] Independently of Parrish, the same idea—"the Whig interpretation of literary variants"—is discussed by James McLaverty, "Issues of Identity and Utterance: An Intentionalist Response to 'Textual Instability,'" *Devils and Angels: Textual Editing and Literary Theory*, ed. Philip Cohen (Charlottesville: UP of Virginia, 1991), 146–48.

iii. Jack Stillinger, "Textual Primitivism and the Editing of Wordsworth," *Studies in Romanticism* 28 (1989): 3–28.

iv. Stephen Parrish and his colleagues in the Cornell Wordsworth have done more than any other group of scholars and any other project that I know of to make this newest kind of thinking acceptable, because they have produced so many editions emphasizing the legitimacy of versions that differ from what we formerly accepted as the standard. Indeed, Parrish is one of the most eloquent of recent defenders of textual pluralism, making a strong plea (in the final paragraph of "The Whig Interpretation of Literature") for "the autonomy and validity of each steady state of the text [of a work] as it changes in confused, unpredictable ways, through patterns which the author may never have foreseen, let alone 'intended.'"

v. I do not know of any empirical research on the way readers take in the verse and glosses of Coleridge's poem. My surmise that if one normally reads from left to right, one would then read gloss and verse, or verse and gloss, in that order, may be entirely wrong. But it seems a certainty that readers do not read both verse and a gloss simultaneously, and therefore some order, in one direction or another, must be involved. Of course, there are readers (like some of my undergraduate students) who read only the verse, ignoring the glosses entirely; and there are some others who, even though strictly enjoined to read both, actually read neither.

vi. I draw this sample of concepts from *Devils and Angels*, ed. Cohen, passim. See my review: "Devils and Angels: Textual Editing and Literary Theory by Philip Cohen," *Modern Philology* 91.4 (1994): 542–45.

vii. Hans Zeller, "A New Approach to the Critical Constitution of Literary Texts," *Studies in Bibliography* 28 (1975): 236; Peter L. Shillingsburg, *Scholarly Editing in the Computer Age: Theory and Practice* (Athens: U of Georgia P, 1986), 50.

viii. G. Thomas Tanselle, *A Rationale of Textual Criticism* (Philadelphia: U of Pennsylvania P, 1989), 15; Peter L. Shillingsburg, "Text as Matter, Concept, and Action," *Studies in Bibliography* 44 (1991): 31–82.

ix. Zeller, "New Approach to the Critical Constitution of Literary Texts," 236, 241; James Thorpe, *Principles of Textual Criticism* (San Marino: Huntington Library, 1972), 185; G. Thomas Tanselle, "The Editorial Problem of Final Authorial Intention," *Selected Studies in Bibliography* (Charlottesville: UP of Virginia, 1979), 334–36. On the criteria of time and function, see Shillingsburg, "Text as Matter," especially 65–72, and McLaverty, "Issues of Identity and Utterance," especially 136–41.

x. Zeller, "New Approach to the Critical Constitution of Literary Texts," 260. 179

xi. In the process of organizing my information, I constructed a large grid consisting of seven vertical columns (one for each of the seven works whose versions I was tracing) and a series of forty horizontal lines across the columns (one for each year of Coleridge's life from 1795 to 1834) and entered notes detailing the successive revisions of the poems in the seven vertical columns. I could then, for any year of Coleridge's poetic career, by reading horizontally across the grid, see at a glance which version of a poem existed at the same time as which versions of the others. This simple device—which might be used routinely by anyone engaged in critical work grounded in biography and history—seemed to arouse considerable interest when I explained it in a lecture on Coleridge's texts at the 1990 Wordsworth Summer Conference in Grasmere.

xii. For a gathering of examples, see Reiman, *Romantic Texts and Contexts*, chapter 10, "'Versioning': The Presentation of Multiple Texts," 167–80. The Library of America has published a volume of Walt Whitman—*Complete Poetry and Collected Prose* (New York, 1982)—that includes the first and last editions of *Leaves of Grass* as independent artifacts; but even this radical solution omits the numerous intervening versions of the work.

xiii. See D.C. Greetham, *Textual Scholarship: An Introduction* (New York: Garland, 1992), 338, 340, 357–61, and the references there, and Peter Shillingsburg, "Polymorphic, Polysemic, Protean, Reliable, Electronic Texts," *Palimpsest: Editorial Theory in the Humanities*, ed. George Bornstein and Ralph G. Williams (Ann Arbor: U of Michigan P, 1993), 29–43. As it is described in the essays in *Hypermedia and Literary Studies*, ed. Paul Delany and George P. Landow (Cambridge, MA: MIT Press, 1991), and in Landow's *Hypertext: The Convergence of Contemporary Critical Theory and Technology* (Baltimore: Johns Hopkins UP, 1992), hypertext is currently much too cumbersome to accommodate most situations of multiple versions. See also Richard Taylor, *Variorum Edition of "Three Cantos" by Ezra Pound: A Prototype* (Bayreuth, Germany: Boomerang P, 1991), especially p. 7, and the review of Taylor's work by Warwick Gould in *Times Literary Supplement*, 26 June 1992, 23.

13.

Brenda R. Silver, "Textual Criticism as Feminist Practice: Or, Who's Afraid of Virginia Woolf Part II," *Representing Modernist Texts: Editing as Interpretation.* Edited by George Bornstein. Ann Arbor: U of Michigan P, 1991. 193–223

Brenda Silver (b. 1942) is the Mary Brinsmead Wheelock Professor Emerita of English at Dartmouth College. She has written extensively on Virginia Woolf and has edited Woolf's notebooks. In this article, Silver shows how textual scholarship can, in itself, be a feminist project. She recounts how critics and scholars working on Virginia Woolf have recovered and published manuscript versions of some of her novels, including *The Years*, *The Waves*, *The Voyage Out*, and *Between the Acts*, as well as her polemic *Three Guineas*. By doing this, Silver argues, they have not simply been recovering texts of antiquarian interest, or providing materials for the study of Woolf's working methods, or straightforwardly enlarging the Woolf canon. Instead, she asserts, "[b]y insisting on the significance of the recovered versions, and by altering the 'texts' that critics used as the basis of their reading, feminist editors altered the nature of the critical enterprise" (p. 186).

Recovering new versions for critics to consider not only changes how critics read Woolf (or any other author), but also has the power to change how they think about what constitutes a work of literature. Like Stillinger (above, p. 165), Silver thinks of different versions of a work as having their own integrity, and she argues for treating the work as the sum of all its versions, and for reading "intertextually" among several versions. Rather than thinking of the work as developing toward a definitive state, as Greg or Tanselle does, or thinking of its later versions as deteriorations from an earlier state, as Parrish does in the case of Wordsworth, Silver argues for an approach to Woolf's novels that can read "backwards" as well as "forwards," considering manuscript and printed versions alongside each other.

Silver then draws on the work of Susan Stanford Friedman, a feminist literary critic and Professor of English at the University of Wisconsin, Madison, who uses ideas taken from Sigmund Freud's study of dreams and the unconscious to interpret Woolf's texts. "Read intertextually," Friedman claims, 'drafts' are potentially the 'textual unconscious' of the 'final' text."[1] This approach also works "backwards" as well as "forwards."

1 Susan Stanford Friedman, "The Return of the Repressed in Women's Narrative," *Journal of Narrative Technique* 19 (Winter 1989): 145.

Earlier versions might be seen as the most authentic expression of the author's ideas and emotions, which are then repressed and made to conform to social expectations in subsequent drafts and the published version. Or earlier texts might be seen, conversely, as the most repressed, and subsequent versions as the stripping away of that repression in pursuit of a more authentic expression.

If the author made changes between versions in order to tone down political views that would have seemed unacceptable, or expressions of anger that would have seemed unfeminine, or discussions of sexuality that would have seemed inappropriate for a woman, then restoring and reading the earlier versions can also be a feminist practice. In the final section of her essay, Silver discusses some of the motivations for Woolf's revisions, and argues that "versioning" serves a feminist approach to her works.

Textual Criticism as Feminist Practice: Or, Who's Afraid of Virginia Woolf Part II[2]

[...]

I.

[...] When critics in the late 1960s and early 1970s began to reclaim Woolf from the Leavisite[3] orthodoxy that depicted her as a novelist of sensibility and reduced her to a footnote in the great tradition of ethical realism in the English novel, they found one of their strongest arguments in one of the most traditional forms of literary scholarship: textual editing, including the publication of **manuscript** versions of her novels. [...] The conjunction of textual editing, "versioning,"[4] and feminist criticism that has occurred over the past 20 years has not only assured Woolf's status as "major author," but has contributed to the critical debates that redefined modernism as an ideological as well as aesthetic construct and located it as much in the critic/reader as in the text. To trace the circumstances and the language that surround and shape the "versioning" of Woolf's novels is to illustrate the centrality of the critical contexts and the historical moment that necessarily connect editing and interpretation.[5] For the words editors use to describe their

---

2 The title alludes to Edward Albee's play *Who's Afraid of Virginia Woolf* (1962), which was made into a film with Richard Burton and Elizabeth Taylor in 1966.

3 Named for F.R. Leavis (1895–1978), one of the most influential literary critics of the mid-twentieth century. His book *The Great Tradition* (1948) identified a tradition of the English novel that extended from Jane Austen, George Eliot, and Henry James to Joseph Conrad and D.H. Lawrence, and tended to marginalize writers, such as Virginia Woolf, who did not fit into this tradition.

4 "Versioning" here means the recovery of different versions of a work produced by the author. See Jack Stillinger, "A Practical Theory of Versions" above, p. 165.

5 Editors from Greg onwards (see above, p. 125) have traditionally viewed editing as prior to interpretation, and separate from it. Part of the argument of Silver's essay is that the two are in fact inseparable.

texts and their project simultaneously construct and deconstruct the structures and perspectives that critics call their own.

II.

The first indications that Woolf's early drafts were not only available but worth critical study came in the late 1960s, initially in Wallace Hildick's pedagogical text *Word for Word: A Study of Authors' Alterations with Exercises,* which included extracts from the manuscripts of *Mrs. Dalloway,* and then in four essays by Charles Hoffman that described manuscript versions of several of Woolf's novels and discussed their differences from the published versions.[i] Both projects assume an audience curious about Woolf's alterations and both locate this curiosity in terms of her narrative experiments, her concern for the relationship of "art" and "reality," internality and externality, her use of imagery, and her presentation of "character": that is, in her formalist credentials. [...]

Yet in his introduction to the volume as a whole, Hildick provides a rationale for looking beyond the formal values of a work when exploring the "intention" behind an author's alterations. His series of categories ranges from "tidying-up" and "roughening-up changes," through what he calls the "power-group" ("where the power to be increased is the power of penetration as well as of projection and persuasion"[ii]), to major structural changes and, finally, the changes made for "ideological reasons." "Some," he notes, "would regard this as an extra-literary group, though if one declines to recognize any boundary between art and living, of which ideology is so extremely important a part, this description will not be applied."[iii] Hildick's language not only grants this category of revision legitimacy by deconstructing the boundary between art and ideology (a surprising move in 1965), but also represents literature, as one strand of current textual criticism does, as an essentially social act performed within specific institutional contexts. Once this construct is in place, Hildick can identify its sources: changes made under a repressive political regime; changes made, usually several years after the publication of the work, to accommodate an author's change of views; changes made to reflect shifts in public taste, to avoid echoing a model, to defer to what the author "considers to be the taste of his public" or to the feelings of individuals who might recognize themselves.[iv] What is missing from this list is both the role of an external critic, such as an editor, and what will later come to dominate the attention of Woolf's textual critics and interpreters: the existence of a self-censorship that grows from an intertwining of personal and cultural factors and speaks to more than "public taste."

[...]

The formalist representation of Woolf, and of critical practice, also governs John Graham's contribution to the 1972 collection *Editing Twentieth-Century Texts,* "Editing a Manuscript: Virginia Woolf's *The Waves*" and the major project it describes: the transcription and presentation of the two **holograph** drafts of *The Waves.*[v] Graham was the first person to prepare

Woolf's early drafts for publication, and his rationale—his need to defend what he portrays as a still rare editorial undertaking—illustrates clearly ideological debates within the editing and critical community: "The draft material for a text is an historical document, like a letter or diary, and should take its place with these other documents in the **library** stacks." The reason it has not already, he speculates, reflects the "post-romantic feeling that the draft of a text is more sacredly private than are the sexual peccadilloes, financial disasters, or mystical experiences of the writer in question: the ashes left behind by the Promethean flame[6] should be exposed to public gaze only on brief ritual occasions, preferably in glass cases in the lobby of the British Museum; and they may occasionally be examined by one of [the] priests, who can then allude cryptically in his footnotes to their presumed significance."[vi] Graham's language here anticipates Jerome McGann's influential critique of "final authorial intention" on the grounds that it privileges a "Romantic conception of literary production" by emphasizing "the autonomy of the isolated author" and the unmediated text, thereby obscuring the fact that "the 'mode of existence of a literary work of art' is fundamentally social."[vii]

And yet it could be argued that Graham himself, while opening the way for the publication of the manuscript versions of Woolf's novels that followed his own, did not perceive the historicity or sociability of his own "document," including its critical assumptions. His strong prohibition in his anticipatory essay against editorial interpretation of the revisions—against presenting interpretation or speculation as fact[viii]—can be read as a manifestation of a discourse that believed there was such a thing as textual criticism or editorial practice divorced from critical and hence subjective perspectives. Even more striking, his presentation of Woolf's creative process in the light of a consistent vision and conception (a "fin in a waste of water"; "two realities in tension with each other"), and a "preoccupation with the total artistic effect"[ix]—his contention that the preparatory notes and the revisions move toward a pre-conceived end and were "never altered by a fundamental shift in artistic intention"[x]—echoes not only G. Thomas Tanselle's arguments for "authorial intent" and the primacy of the integral, organic work of art that represents it, but Tanselle's belief that the editor will (objectively) recognize that "work of art" amidst all the possible versions.[xi] Expectation and (re)presentation become one.

Another way to see the sociability of Graham's (and Tanselle's) assumptions is to say that his "interpretations" of Woolf's revisions reflect the critical ideology still dominant in North America at the time by pointing the reader toward the formal characteristics of the novel and the ways in which the revisions illustrate "the larger strategies followed by Virginia Woolf in her struggle to give a literary form to the original design."[xii] *The Waves*, he argues in the introduction to the manuscripts, is a representative work of modernism, whose fictional experiments have been underrated and misunderstood.[xiii] To support this contention, he focuses his introductory remarks on Woolf's experiments in form and perspective and reads all of Woolf's critical and personal writings during the novel's gestation through a strictly formalist lens. This perspective leads him, for example, to read "Women and Fiction," the precursor

6 Alluding to Prometheus, the mythical figure who stole fire from the gods for the benefit of humankind. He is conventionally associated with poetic composition.

to *A Room of One's Own*, solely in terms of Woolf's predictions for a new poetic novel, to be written by "liberated" women, that "will look beyond the personal and political relationships to the wider questions which the poet tries to solve—of our destiny and the meaning of life."[xiv] What this reading elides is not only Woolf's insistence that fiction is never divorced from the material circumstances in which it is produced, but her prediction that women in the future would also write impersonal novels that would "become more critical of society."[xv] While *The Waves* is clearly Woolf's most "poetic" novel, Graham's perspective and language effectively preclude "society" and social criticism from playing any role in the novel at all.

However unconscious Graham might have been of his critical assumptions, his contribution to the future of Woolf studies—and the role of "versioning" within it—was enormous. The availability of the two pre-publication versions of the novel, each page transcribed exactly as it appears in the manuscript, provided the impetus and basis for future interpretations.[xvi] In fact, one of his major points is how few manuscript versions of works have been published and, as a result, how little we know about what these texts can teach us—not only about the "specific text in question, but [about] the foundation and superstructure of criticism itself." "If enough people seriously engage in this kind of discipline, it may lead slowly to the re-alignment of fundamental critical presuppositions, to the formulation of new questions, to the re-phrasing of old questions, to a sharper appraisal of our old instruments of analysis and to the invention of new instruments more delicate and precise."[xvii] His prophecy, at least in the case of Woolf, has proved stunningly accurate in terms of the proliferation of **editions** and of critical approaches to them.

III.

Graham's edition of the manuscripts of *The Waves* appeared in 1976; in 1977 two special issues on Woolf in very different journals—*Bulletin of the New York Public Library* and *Women's Studies*—signaled the growing intersection of feminist practice and textual criticism. Both of these issues were inspired by and included papers presented at conferences that set out to provide "Another Version of Virginia Woolf," a version that took the earlier versions of her works as the grounds for "exploring the often-neglected social and political aspects of Woolf's novels."[xviii] Suddenly the terrain of Woolf criticism began to shift, and textual criticism was at the center of the resulting fray. As feminist editors, versed in critical perspectives that challenged the isolation of formalist approaches to texts, made more and more of Woolf's texts available—including manuscript versions of those novels usually considered to be marginal to an oeuvre and a career defined solely in terms of aesthetic modernism—the critical discourse about all of Woolf's novels changed. It was not only, as Grace Radin argued in her 1981 study of the evolution of *The Years*, one of the central novels in this process, that critics turned to the drafts of these works to "learn more about Woolf's social theories"[xix]—although this was crucial—but also that the presence of the early drafts of this and other works, which are often far more explicit in their social and political attitudes, led to a re-appraisal of the whole of Woolf's published and unpublished writings, including a re-appraisal of her artistry.

By insisting on the significance of the recovered versions, and by altering the "texts" that critics used as the basis of their reading, feminist editors altered the nature of the critical enterprise.

The 1977 issue of the *Bulletin of the New York Public Library*, which could be said to have initiated this particular critical moment, took as its starting point a celebration of "the present strong interest in Woolf documents in our Berg Collection" and the imminent publication of the manuscript of *The Pargiters*, "the essay-novel portion of the manuscript that became *The Years*."[xx] Conceived as a historical critique of the status of women, including their sexuality, from 1880 to the 1930s, *The Pargiters* began by interleaving chapters of a fictional work with analytic essays but soon split apart, evolving not only into *The Years* but also into its polemic counterpart, *Three Guineas*. [...] Until this time, most critics of Woolf praised and studied her writings either in terms of psychology and "sensibility," or in the context of a modernism defined through formal experimentation, authorial perspective, symbolic systems, poetry, and a self-conscious attention to art itself. Within this latter context, they focused on *Mrs. Dalloway*, *To the Lighthouse*, and *The Waves* as the pinnacle of her achievement and viewed her writings in the 1930s, including *The Years* and *Between the Acts*, as a distinct falling off of her artistic powers. The early novels, *The Voyage Out* and *Night and Day*, were seen as interesting but false starts in a more realist manner, while *Jacob's Room* was read as a transitional text. The feminist essays *A Room of One's Own* and, even more so, *Three Guineas* had virtually disappeared. In this light it is not surprising that *The Waves*, situated as an underrated modernist masterpiece, should have been the first work whose manuscripts were considered worth publishing.

But with the publication of *The Pargiters* (1977) and, shortly afterwards, *Melymbrosia* (1982) and *Pointz Hall* (1983)—manuscript versions of *The Voyage Out* and *Between the Acts*, respectively—the perception of Woolf's artistry and the perception of "modernism," defined now as an ideological and gendered as well as aesthetic phenomenon, were indelibly altered. Works that were once considered marginal to Woolf's greatest achievements, and hence to modernism, disrupted the center and critics of Woolf could no longer ignore or dismiss either their presence or their importance.[xxi] The editors themselves were explicit not only about the ideological, revisionary nature of their project, but also about the role of textual editing within critical controversies. Lucio Ruotolo, for example, describes the special issue of *Twentieth Century Literature* on Woolf as being devoted entirely to previously "unpublished documents whose content further expands the ideological as well as the 'literary' context of her work."[xxii]

Radin, in her book on *The Years*, provides one rationale for the intersection of feminist and textual critique. In the past, she notes, "scant attention has been paid to [Woolf's] social theories, perhaps because they cluster around feminism, a point of view that has only recently been restored to serious consideration. For this reason *The Years* and its documents are at the heart of the current reappraisal of Woolf, since it is in these uncut documents that her social and political theories are developed most fully."[xxiii] For DeSalvo, the editor of *Melymbrosia*, who painstakingly reconstructed the multiple versions and at least two more or less completed drafts of Woolf's first novel, the convergence is more detailed. The emergence of an earlier, submerged draft, she argues, provides a document on the order of Joyce's *Stephen Hero* and

Camus' *La mort heureuse*:[7] "a document that can provide the basis for inquiry, not only into the genesis of Woolf's first novel but also into the creative processes of one of this century's most important writers." But the formal innovations are for DeSalvo, as for the other feminist editors, inseparable from the political contexts in which they occurred: "It is impossible," she adds, to read *Melymbrosia* and think of Virginia Woolf as an effete dreamer spinning out her private fantasies in the solitude of her study between bouts of madness. The narrative forces upon us the sense of her involvement with the most important issues of her day, of her awareness that every encounter between women and men occurs within the context of shifting and conflicting societal forces.[xxiv]

But more than the image and understanding of Woolf and her artistry began to change during the period of intense editorial production in the late 1970s: the language used to talk about the manuscript versions and their relationship to the published text also began to shift, reflecting shifts in the idea of the "text" within the broader critical and theoretical environment, in particular the deconstruction of the concept of a stable, unitary text. While it was still common for the editors of Woolf's manuscript versions to talk about the "drafts" as "documents" that provided a "context" for reading the published novel, another discourse began to be heard. DeSalvo hints at this discourse when she calls *Melymbrosia* a "submerged" draft.[xxv] Later in her introduction, borrowing terminology as well as theoretical ideas from Sandra Gilbert and Susan Gubar's *The Madwoman in the Attic*,[8] she describes it as "**palimpsestic**":[xxvi] a work "whose surface designs conceal or obscure deeper, less accessible (and less socially acceptable) levels of meaning."[xxvii] As a result, in DeSalvo's words, "there are two stories operating simultaneously," a surface story and a more radical "submerged story" that works to subvert and unsettle it, and both are present at once.[xxviii] [...] Read as one work, the "novel" contains both dimensions simultaneously, but each version foregrounds one or the other.

In this reading, the manuscript versions of a novel cease to be documents that provide background; instead, they produce a new figure, the composite work itself. In the process of effecting this transformation, however, DeSalvo suggests two different, and potentially contradictory, constructions of the relationship of the parts to the whole. One construction evokes Hans Zeller's concept of a "work" as "a diachronic succession of discrete semiotic systems": "If one imagines the textual history [of a work] in the shape of a 3-dimensional cylinder standing upright, then the different versions are horizontal planes perpendicular to the axis of the cylinder."[xxix] [...]

---

7 James Joyce's *Stephen Hero* is an early, autobiographical fragment that Joyce wrote around 1905, parts of which were later introduced into his novel *Portrait of the Artist as a Young Man* (1916), whose protagonist is called Stephen Daedalus. *Stephen Hero* was published posthumously in 1944. Albert Camus' *La mort heureuse* (*The Happy Death*) is the author's first novel, written between 1936 and 1938 but left unpublished. Camus later reworked several parts of the manuscript in his novel *L'étranger* (*The Stranger*; 1942). *La mort heureuse* was published posthumously in 1971 (English translation, 1972).

8 Sandra Gilbert and Susan Gubar, *The Madwoman in the Attic: The Woman Writer and the Nineteenth-Century Literary Imagination* (New Haven: Yale UP, 1979) is a hugely influential work of feminist literary criticism. Its title refers to Charlotte Brontë's novel *Jane Eyre* (1847), in which Mr. Rochester's unstable first wife Bertha is kept locked in an attic room.

But a second construction of the work, one evoked by a contradictory metaphorical system embedded in the image of the palimpsestic text, leads to a different critical project. While DeSalvo, like Zeller, appeals to an architectural metaphor for creation, borrowed from Woolf, in making her argument for Woolf's first novel as a palimpsestic text—"the best novels are deposited, carefully, bit by bit; and in the end, perhaps they live in all their parts"[xxx]—for the most part she and other commentators on the relationship between *Melymbrosia* and *The Voyage Out* echo Woolf's recurrent imagery of depths and merging (tunneling, or digging out caves) rather than hard, discrete objects in describing their perception of Woolf's texts. The goal is to blur the boundaries between planes of existence (or versions), not to distinguish or emphasize them. [...]

Once the construct of the palimpsestic work is in place, critics can begin to read within its parameters without necessarily distinguishing between the different versions. What was once perceived as the single, integral work—the published novel—becomes multiple, intertextual. Radin illustrates the beginnings of this activity when she talks about "projecting" the episodes deleted from the galleys of *The Years* "back into the novel";[xxxi] in her own discussion she goes back even farther to the holograph drafts. The effect is to suggest an archaeological project. [...]

One of the most explicit arguments for the critical implications—and potential—of the "composite, palimpsestic text" occurs in the recent work of Susan Stanford Friedman, which brings together psychoanalysis (in particular Freud's writings on dream-work, narrative as disguise, and the role of the "censor"), tenets of textual criticism (including "versioning"), and feminist perspectives. While not at the center of her inquiry, Woolf's multi-versioned novels provide an exemplary

instance of the "intertextual" reading she proposes. Presenting "women's writing as an insistent record—a trace, a web, a palimpsest, a rune, a disguise—of what has not or cannot be spoken directly because of the external and internalized censors of patriarchal social order,"[xxxii] she turns to textual criticism, in particular the relationship among versions, to illustrate its possibilities for "deciphering the textual and political unconscious in clusters of texts by the same author":

> One kind of cluster is made up of what we conventionally consider the "final" text and its surviving "draft" or "drafts." Another kind is composed of serial texts on related subjects and characters. New Criticism would separate each text into a harmoniously constructed autonomous text. Most textual criticism would privilege the "final" text over the aesthetically inferior "drafts." And a Barthesian[9] post-structuralist approach would ignore authorial and historical (con)texts to read these texts as part of an infinite series of signifying chains empty of meaning. A psycho-political hermeneutic,[10] in contrast, would read these clusters intertextually, psychoanalytically, and politically—as sites of disguised repression and oppression produced by an author who reflects and

---

9 Referring to Roland Barthes (1915–80), who argued, in *S/Z*, "From Work to Text," and "The Death of the Author" for a kind of criticism that would be indifferent to the intentions of the author.

10 Relating to issues of interpretation.

> re-presents a specific moment and process in history.... Read intertextually, "drafts" are potentially the "textual unconscious" of the "final" text.[xxxiii]

But Friedman is not arguing for privileging the "draft" versions any more than she is arguing for a teleological focus on final versions or ends. If "drafts" can represent more directly "narrative elements that are repressed and transformed as the author revises the text by the linguistic [and ideological] mechanisms of the dream-work," they can also be read as "repetitions" in which the author is "working through" conflicts in an effort [...] to move from "repetition" to "remembering." Within this context, the earlier draft(s) might well be the most repressed, most subject to resistance and transference. "What she wants is for critics to read 'both ways.' ... Rather than searching for the 'authentic' version, this approach regards all versions as part of a larger composite, palimpsestic text whose parts or imperfectly erased layers interact according to a psycho-political dimension."[xxxiv]

For Friedman, the dynamic of "reading both ways," which suggests "a new form of intertextual analysis for textual criticism,"[xxxv] can be applied to drafts and serial texts by men as well as women; her own extended project is to examine "the processes of self-censorship and the forms of disguised expression in the production of literary modernism."[xxxvi] Within this larger work, Woolf will play a major role, in particular for the ways in which the "'drafts'" of novels such as *The Voyage Out* and *The Years* reveal the workings of suppression and repression in the writings of modernist women. For Woolf, along with H.D.,[11] illustrates the process of condensing, displacing, or erasing an anger that is culturally forbidden from the "final," public, published versions of their texts.

IV.

Friedman's identification of Woolf's revisions with repression, suppression, and anger brings to the fore one of the most contested aspects of the intersection of textual criticism and feminist practice: self-**censorship**. From the moment Woolf's editors began to present and explore the manuscript versions and the documentary history of her novels as a primary source for understanding the depth and commitment of her cultural critique, they also began to debate the role of self-censorship in her revisions. Each novel poses its own set of questions about self-censorship, including those pertinent to the specific historical and personal contexts that surrounded its production. But one recurring issue is the fine line between self-editing and self-censorship, a distinction that is often difficult if not impossible to make, as Donald Pizer has suggested,[xxxvii] particularly when there is no external editor/censor: when, as in Woolf's case, the power of censorship seems to come from within. For as Woolf herself once

11 H.D. (Hilda Doolittle; 1886–1961), an American modernist writer associated with imagist poetry; she was a friend and sometime patient of Sigmund Freud.

commented, apropos of the Hogarth Press,[12] she might well have been "the only woman in England free to write"—or publish—what she liked.[xxxviii] But that freedom was necessarily relative; and Woolf continually struggled with the question of what she could say out loud, and in what tone of voice, without alienating her readers. In this way, the specter of an external critic became one of the multitude of factors that inevitably play a role in the process of revision, including the writer's awareness of her audience.

Woolf's feminist editors and critics brought to her drafts a keen awareness of the social as well as aesthetic factors that make any published work, in Pizer's use of the term, a "palimpsest": a text that emerges out of and inscribes the tensions of the period in which it was written and revised.[xxxix] As a result the debates take as given not only Woolf's commitment to social analysis and critique but also the external and internal pressures inscribed in her expression of these views. This leads them to ask whether the early, private versions of the novels are more explicit and hence more powerful expressions of Woolf's social and political critique, including her anger, than the published versions, and if so, whether and why this critique was edited out as the novels moved into the public realm. Do the revisions constitute self-censorship and, if so, are they attributable to Woolf's belief that art and propaganda should not mix—that is, to aesthetic concerns—or to fear?

[...]

190 One of the major concerns framing and framed by the feminist contributions to "versioning" was anger. Whatever stance early feminist commentators took on the debate between self-editing and self-censorship, and whether they ultimately find the final work aesthetically better or worse, almost all of them agree that what was lost in the revisions was the explicitness of Woolf's cultural critique, including her expression of anger. It is not surprising that feminist editors in the 1970s, engaged in recuperating not only Woolf's submerged texts but their social and political implications, should have made anger a major site for assessing her self-censorship. As I have argued elsewhere, this moment in Woolf scholarship coincided with a re-evaluation of anger as a political tool that was occurring simultaneously in a number of arenas, academic and activist alike.[xl] What was being questioned was both the long history of political, critical, and psychological discourses that have condemned women's anger—along with that of other marginalized and subordinate groups—as destructive of "civilized" behavior and established authority, and the role these discourses have played in silencing personal and political expression. The effect was to deconstruct the supposedly universal rules governing critical discourse and reveal them as myths: rhetorical claims made "by the dominant about their legitimacy."[xli]

12 The Hogarth Press was run by Woolf with her husband Leonard Woolf, and published most of her work to appear in her lifetime. Virginia Woolf ceased to take an active role in the business of the press after 1938. Leonard Woolf made comments on his wife's work, but did not request revisions before publication, as another publisher would likely have done.

Nor is it surprising that Woolf became a central figure for feminist critics struggling to find a voice to speak within the public realm, including the academy. Adrienne Rich[13] both identified the struggle and located it in Woolf when she wrote how in re-reading *A Room of One's Own* she recognized a tone common to herself and other women: "the tone of a woman almost in touch with her anger, who is determined not to appear angry, who is *willing* herself to be calm, detached, and even charming in a roomful of men where things have been said which are attacks on her very integrity."[xlii] The "willing" is crucial here, and it found support in Woolf's own statements about anger, including the comment in *A Room of One's Own* that in *Jane Eyre* "it is clear that anger was tampering with the integrity of Charlotte Brontë the novelist," interfering with the art and producing a book that is "deformed and twisted."[xliii] This statement not only led feminist critics to look more closely at the anger in nineteenth-century women's novels—and helped support Gilbert and Gubar's contention that the submerged text in their novels, exemplified graphically in *Jane Eyre*, was often one of rage[xliv]—but also encouraged them to look beyond Woolf's explicitly polemical tracts to her own novels for their political messages—and their "willfully" suppressed anger. And to the extent that Woolf's novels, like Brontë's, were perceived to be palimpsestic, it made sense to look to the submerged manuscript versions for their expression of anger and cultural criticism and to explore the revisions through the lens of possible self-censorship.

Within this context, *The Years* was the logical first choice for feminist "versioning" and analysis. For one thing, so many of the documents, ranging from drafts of the originary "Speech before the London/National Society for Women's Service, January 31, 1931" to **galley** and **page proofs**, were available, and Woolf so clearly deleted or altered passages with explicit sexual, feminist, or antiwar statements as late as the galley stage.[xlv] The holograph and **typescript** versions of the "Speech" proved especially fruitful, for in them Woolf not only illustrates how strongly she can express her opinions about "the masculine point of view" and war ("a stupid and violent and hateful and idiotic and trifling and ignoble and mean display"), but makes what are perhaps her clearest statements about the difficulty women writers have in describing their sexuality ("women's bodies for instance—their passions"), attributing it to the "prudery of men," the strength of literary and social conventions, and the danger inherent in defying those conventions ("I should need the courage of a hero") of becoming "hard and shrill and positive," of "[ceasing] to be writer."[xlvi] In addition, the ample evidence of her early excitement and her subsequent struggle to finish the novel, provided by documents such as her letters and diaries, made it possible to argue that Woolf's original intention was to write a novel that would trace "the sexual life of women" and contain "millions of ideas but no preaching—history, politics, feminism, art, literature—in short a summing up of all I know, feel, laugh at, despise, like, admire, hate, and so on,"[xlvii] and to use this as the basis for asking, Why the change? As Radin illustrates, one recurring note in the diary was her "horror of the Aldous [Huxley] novel," "something that I won't call propaganda."[xlviii] Finally, the discovery that Woolf's name for her fictional family in the novel, the Pargiters, was rooted etymologically in the word "parget," defined in the

13 Adrienne Rich (1929–2012), American feminist poet and essayist.

English Dialect Dictionary edited by Joseph Wright (who appears by name in the novel-essay version) as "to plaster with cement or mortar," or "to whitewash," and that "pargeter" appears in the *Oxford English Dictionary* not only as "a plasterer; a whitewasher" but by figurative extension "one who glosses and smoothes over," aroused speculation about how much Woolf herself contributed to the process of cultural whitewashing she was illustrating in her text: how much, that is, did she "parget" in her revisions, including the change in the title of the novel from *The Pargiters* to *The Years*?[xlix]

The assumption was that she did "parget," not only in producing *The Years* but in other of her novels, and this assumption reflects another aspect of "versioning" implicit in feminist explorations of self-censorship: the debate among textual critics about "authorial intention" and whether one should read successive versions as if they are moving inexorably toward some better end (what Stephen Parrish calls the "Whig interpretation" of textual history).[14] Here, the two constructs of the composite "work"—Zeller's "diachronic succession of discrete semiotic systems" and the more intertextual palimpsest—come into play as well. Like Parrish, the advocates of both constructs appear to reject the belief, implicit in Graham's edition of *The Waves*, that there was a fixed intention, or even multiple intentions, that govern the outcome and establish the value of the final version. But their ways of reading the instability established by this rejection differ, as do their interpretations. To some extent, the timing of the versions is important here, as well as changes in critical and theoretical orientation; what emerges is a shift in the representation of the relationship of "original intention" to "final" work from a one-way street to a more complex network of impulses.

Based on the documentary material for *The Years*, both Leaska, who edited *The Pargiters*, and Radin, who traced the evolution of *The Years* as a whole, posit an original intention and a movement away from it. Both agree that Woolf deleted and smoothed over—"pargeted"—materials that were more explicitly sexual and angry in the earlier versions, and both agree that in part the revisions are grounded in formal, aesthetic concerns. Where they differ is in their assessment of what was gained and lost, and this in turn suggests different perspectives on the relationship between Woolf's artistic demands and less easily identifiable factors, including self-censorship. For Leaska, who asks "Is the author creating with one part of her mind and at the same time editing—perhaps censoring—with another part?,"[l] the pargeting did not necessarily constitute a loss, particularly in terms of its political explicitness ("some preaching does indeed cloud many of the novel's pages"[li]). The framework for answering the question of self-censorship, provided in his "interpretative" essay rather than his introduction to the text, takes the reader into the recesses of Woolf's psyche; tracing the changes in the portrayal of Abel Pargiter, the Victorian patriarch, and his daughters' reactions to him, he attributes them to Woolf's awareness "that her unconscious mind was exhuming material of a seriously confessional kind" that "had in some way to be smoothed over and glossed if [it] were to be made acceptable"—although to whom is left unclear.[lii] But the results, in his view, are clearly beneficial: in the process of transforming the novel-essay into fiction only, "Woolf as

---

14 See p. 157 above.

novelist was also forced into becoming a pargeter—and ultimately one of great artistic fluency and moral courage."[liii] Nevertheless, he defines his goal in his edition as providing "the reader with what might be looked upon as a slow-moving picture of Virginia Woolf—unobserved and uncensored—during those vibrant moments of creation."[liv]

In almost direct contrast, Radin, whose frameworks for assessing the revisions are more social and political than aesthetic and psychological, reads the revisions as a failure of courage and locates this failure in Woolf's "fear of becoming shrill and one-sided, of allowing her ideas to destroy her art."[lv] Radin also directs readers to the earlier versions of the novel, which she describes as "a spontaneous outburst, an expression of anger, irritation, and disdain for the 'masculine point of view.' As was her wont," Radin continues, "when Woolf rewrote she softened her remarks and placed them in a broader context, believing that this would make them more palatable and persuasive" to her readers.[lvi] "By the time the novel was published," she concludes, Woolf "had softened, deleted, or made vague many of her strongest attacks on English society and its treatment of women and had eliminated most of the overt statements of her own beliefs," including her belief in women's need to acknowledge all of their impulses. "Sadly, the differences between her first draft and the novel and essay [*Three Guineas*] she published reveal that there had come a moment when her courage failed."[lvii]

The identification and rhetoric of an original intention and a movement through sequential versions away from it also colors the early discussion of *The Voyage Out*. DeSalvo, for example, even as she represents *Melymbrosia* as a "submerged" draft of a palimpsestic work, shares with Radin the perception that Woolf concealed her anger by deleting the social and cultural criticism from the published version or making it more oblique; in terms of the novels' feminist and political content, both read the revisions as moving in one direction only and experience the changes as a loss. In *The Voyage Out*, the loss resides for the most part in the revisions that changed the heroine, Rachel, in Elizabeth Heine's formulation, from "an intelligent, outspoken, critical young feminist" to a "vague and innocently naive dreamer,"[lviii] and took the sting out of Rachel's aunt, Helen Ambrose's, ironic attitude toward men. Citing passages from a version that preceded even *Melymbrosia* and the response it evoked from Woolf's brother-in-law Clive Bell that her "prejudice against men makes [her] didactic 'not to say priggish,'" DeSalvo argues that Woolf began by writing "an angry novel" about the erosion of women's power and that she was "terrified by the force of her own prose, about the depth of the rage and anger which gave her prose its power—not an uncommon problem for women writers."[lix] By the time Woolf completed *Melymbrosia* and began the draft of what became *The Voyage Out*, DeSalvo writes, "'Melymbrosia' indeed was becoming 'The Voyage Out'—a voyage away from the bluntness, candor, and the openness with which she had dealt with the reasons why women like Rachel and Helen are incapable of forming emotional attachments to men."[lx] The change in title for DeSalvo, as for Zeller, signifies a change in Woolf's perspective, or intention, and hence a change of the relations within the work as a whole.

[...]

In contrast to the unidirectional view of the revisions as self-censorship and loss that I have been outlining, Friedman's practice of reading "both ways" and her construction of a composite, palimpsestic text produce a dual discourse and a dual interpretation. Writing about the revisions that changed the representation of the heroine and distinguish *Melymbrosia* from *The Voyage Out*, Friedman agrees with DeSalvo's interpretation that self-censorship was at work and extends it to other women as well: "For a number of women writers in the modernist period, revisions of [their] texts reflected a sometimes conscious, sometimes unconscious negotiation between the desire to speak and the need to repress what was forbidden in their narratives of modernity. Often revisions, in making their texts more artfully modernist, also disguised the inscribed desire through mechanisms of condensation, displacement, and representation akin to the grammar of the dream-work described by Freud in *The Interpretation of Dreams*." "However," she continues, "self-censorship does not fully explain the changes in Rachel...."[lxi] Reading backward as well as forward, and using Freud's theories about repetition and recollection, she argues that in her later versions "Woolf was able to confront what she had repressed in the earlier drafts—namely, that part of herself which she considered 'dangerous' to her health." In other words, for Friedman, the revisions did not just censor Woolf's anger; they also allowed her to assess her own strength in comparison to that of her fictional heroine and illustrate the dangers of repression and censorship themselves. In this reading, Woolf not only becomes an agent in the act of revision, but actively confronts her fears rather than letting them control her.

Friedman's shift in emphasis, it could be argued, attests as much to contemporary feminist theory as it does to textual theory. Nevertheless, Friedman's insistence that the composite, palimpsestic work reveals continually shifting scenes of repression, censorship, and confrontation and not a linear progression both acknowledges McGann's influence and helps to validate his concept of the unstable text. Her concept of the "work" and how one approaches it is much closer, for example, to McGann's formulation of the "text" as unstable and multiple than it is to either Tanselle's integrated work of art or even Zeller's versions. Her reading of *Melymbrosia/The Voyage Out*, like Gabler's[15] reading of Joyce's *Ulysses* in McGann's interpretation of it, "overhauls *the way we think about the text as a whole*," and "forces us to think of [*The Voyage Out* or] *Ulysses* as something other than a given object of interpretation on the one hand (which is the traditional and New Critical view), or as an invention of interpretation on the other (which is the common post-structural view)." In this construction, "a number of different [*Voyage Outs*] begin to occupy the space of critical possibility."[lxii] In addition, Friedman's "interpretation," rooted as it is in a specific construction of a specific "text"—a composite, palimpsestic text—underlines McGann's contention that "the interpretative act 'constitutes meaning' ... only in terms that are licensed by the received socio-history of the text. And that socio-history, for *texts*, is constituted at its most elementary level as a set of empirical

15 Hans Walter Gabler, editor of James Joyce's *Ulysses: A Critical, Synoptic Edition* (New York and London: Garland, 1984). Gabler's *Ulysses* was criticized by some for both its methods and its execution, but was championed by McGann as offering an alternative to the Greg/Bowers tradition of identifying a copy-text and following "final authorial intention."

documents whose meaning is intimately bound up with the socio-history of the documents."[lxiii] As a result, "textual meaning is not an 'idea' or an interpretive function—is not, that is to say, a textual supplement. Rather, textual meaning is always materially constituted *as* some particular text (in the documentary sense)."[lxiv 16]

Within this framework, the intersections of feminist practice and textual criticism outlined in this essay begin to reveal the inseparability of interpretations of Woolf's novels and the "author" from the socio-history of the manuscript versions and the way they alter both the "texts" we analyze and how we analyze them. In this light, the widely accepted view of Woolf today as a serious political and social commentator is inseparable from the publication of the manuscript versions by feminist critics for whom the existence of these "texts" necessarily destabilized the published versions of the novels and the versions of Woolf they had generated. To ignore the existence of the re-configured texts that resulted is to limit what Woolf potentially "means" to her audience, to be afraid of Virginia Woolf and what her gaze can teach us. The palimpsestic text created by the presence of the manuscript versions and its critical reception, as in Pizer's construction, provides "a record of our civilization in the different ways that other men [and women] at other times have read it."[lxv]

Unfortunately, since the explosion of energy and editions that recorded the creative intersection of textual criticism and feminist practice, no new manuscript versions of Woolf's novels have appeared. The pre-publication versions of many of her novels, as well as of her two polemical works, remain submerged.[lxvi] Given the powerful re-readings of those novels that have been "versioned," this constitutes a powerful loss. The new editions of Woolf's novels that will appear
in the next few years should alert readers to the presence of the manuscript versions, published or not, as well as necessarily altering, through their very presence, our perceptions of her work. The words on Woolf's manuscript pages, like the portrait of Woolf that hangs on the wall of my study, may not provide any definitive answers, but [...] Woolf's palimpsestic texts suggest to me [...] the ways in which Virginia Woolf, the "writer" as well as the "author," speaks directly to a postmodern audience and continues to empower its cultural critique.

Notes

i. Wallace Hildick, *Word for Word* (London: Faber and Faber, 1965). Charles G. Hoffman, "From Short Story to Novel: The Manuscript Revisions of Virginia Woolf's *Mrs. Dalloway*," *Modern Fiction Studies* 14 (Summer 1968): 171–86; "From Lunch to Dinner: Virginia Woolf's Apprenticeship," *Texas Studies in Literature and Language* 10 (Winter 1969): 609–27; "Fact and Fantasy in *Orlando*: Virginia Woolf's Manuscript Revisions," *Texas Studies in Literature and Language* 10 (Fall 1968): 435–44; "Virginia Woolf's Manuscript Revisions of *The Years*," *PMLA* 84 (1969): 79–89. The publication of Woolf's *A Writer's Diary*, edited by Leonard Woolf, in 1953, followed by the publication of Leonard's diaries in the 1960s, had already alerted critics to the extended process of revision underlying Woolf's novels and to the existence of the manuscript versions. On the lack of interest in these manuscripts in

---

16 McGann here repeats the distinction he made in "Shall These Bones Live?" (see above, p. 113) between two uses of the word "text": the post-structuralist sense of text as an interpretative field and the "documentary" sense in which the word is used by textual scholars to refer to a single version of a work.

England and Leonard's sale of them to American booksellers, see *Letters of Leonard Woolf*, ed. Frederic Spotts (San Diego: Harcourt Brace Jovanovich, 1989), 499–500.

ii. Hildick, *Word for Word*, 14–15.

iii. Ibid., 21–22.

iv. Ibid., 22–24.

v. John Graham, "Editing a Manuscript: Virginia Woolf's *The Waves*," in *Editing Twentieth Century Texts*, ed. Frances G. Halpenny (Toronto and Buffalo: U of Toronto P, 1972), 77–92. Graham's edition of *The Waves—The Two Holograph Drafts* was published by University of Toronto Press (1976).

vi. Graham, "Editing a Manuscript," 77–78.

vii. Jerome McGann, *A Critique of Modern Textual Criticism* (Chicago: U of Chicago P, 1983), 8 and passim.

viii. Graham, "Editing a Manuscript," 80, 91.

ix. Graham, *Holograph*, 22.

x. Ibid., 28.

xi. See, for example, G. Thomas Tanselle, "The Editorial Problem of Final Authorial Intention," [above, p. 139]. My argument is not intended to dismiss the role of aesthetic choices in Woolf's revisions or to deny her artistry, but to illustrate how critical assumptions at this time, as later, shape the presentation of her texts and the interpretations suggested by this presentation.

xii. Graham, *Holograph*, 40.

xiii. Ibid., 13–14.

xiv. Ibid., 24.

xv. Virginia Woolf, "Women and Fiction," in *Collected Essays*, vol. 2 (New York: Harcourt, Brace and World, 1967), 147–48.

xvi. Graham's literal transcription of the manuscripts, with the strike-outs, substitutions, marginalia, and interlinear insertions presented just as they are on Woolf's page—a practice made possible in 1972 by the "flexibility and economy of a modern sophisticated typewriter and offset lithography" (qtd in Halpenny [ed.], *Editing Twentieth Century Texts*, 4)—is, when feasible, the preferable method, introducing the least editorial inference. The role of technology in editorial practice deserves more attention; Reiman, for example, notes the potential of the photofacsimile in making "versioning" a reality (Donald Reiman, *Romantic Texts and Contexts* [Columbia: U of Missouri P, 1987], 172).

xvii. Graham, "Editing a Manuscript," 92.

xviii. Madeline Moore, "Another Version of Virginia Woolf," *Women's Studies* 4 (1977): 149. Moore's title echoes that of the Virginia Woolf Seminar at the Modern Language Association Meetings in December 1974; the first Virginia Woolf Symposium was held at the University of California, Santa Cruz, November 1974.

xix. Grace Radin, *Virginia Woolf's "The Years": The Evolution of a Novel* (Knoxville: U of Tennessee P, 1981), xviii.

xx. "Front Matter," *Bulletin of the New York Public Library* 80 (Winter 1977): 137.

xxi. The other manuscript version published during this period, Susan Dick's edition of the original holograph draft of *To the Lighthouse* (Toronto and Buffalo: U of Toronto P, 1982), follows Graham's edition of *The Waves* both in its format (literal transcriptions) and its formalist, biographical approach to the revisions, including the assumption of an intentional movement toward an aesthetic end.

xxii. Lucio Ruotolo, "Preface," *Twentieth Century Literature* 25 (1979): iii. The "documents" are "The Journal of Mistress Joan Martyn," edited by Susan M. Squier and Louise A. DeSalvo, a story about a woman social historian that includes the fictional diary of a young woman in the sixteenth century; "Friendships Gallery," edited by Ellen Hawkes, a "'spoof biography' of Woolf's friend and teacher Violet Dickinson" (iii); extracts from the manuscript of *Orlando* deleted by Woolf in the published version and edited by Madeline Moore; and "Anon" and "The Reader," edited by Brenda R. Silver, reconstructions of the first two essays written for the history of English literature left unfinished when Woolf died.

xxiii. Radin, "The Years," xxii-xxiii.

xxiv. *Melymbrosia: An Early Version of "The Voyage Out,"* ed. Louise A. DeSalvo (New York: New York Public Library, 1982), x, xxxvii.

xxv. Ibid., xiii.

xxvi. Ibid., xl.

xxvii. Sandra M. Gilbert and Susan Gubar, *The Madwoman in the Attic: The Woman Writer and the Nineteenth-Century Literary Imagination* (New Haven, CT: Yale UP, 1979), 73.

xxviii. *Melymbrosia*, xl.

xxix. Hans Zeller, "A New Approach to the Critical Constitution of Literary Texts," *Studies in Bibliography* 28 (1975): 244.

xxx. Woolf is quoted in Louise A. DeSalvo, "Sorting, Sequencing, and Dating the Drafts of Virginia Woolf's *The Voyage Out*," *Bulletin of the New York Public Library* 82 (Autumn 1979): 288.

xxxi. Grace Radin, "'Two Enormous Chunks': Episodes Excluded during the Final Revisions of *The Years*," *Bulletin of the New York Public Library* 80 (Winter 1977): 227.

xxxii. Susan Stanford Friedman, "The Return of the Repressed in Women's Narrative," *Journal of Narrative Technique* 19 (Winter 1989): 142.

xxxiii. Friedman, "The Return of the Repressed," 144–45.

xxxiv. Ibid., 145, 146.

xxxv. Ibid., 146.

xxxvi. Susan Stanford Friedman, *Return of the Repressed in Modernist Narratives*. Manuscript.

xxxvii. Donald Pizer, "Self-Censorship and Textual Editing," *Textual Criticism and Literary Interpretation*, ed. McGann (Chicago: U of Chicago P, 1985), 144–61.

xxxviii. *The Diary of Virginia Woolf*, ed. Anne Olivier Bell, vol. 3 (New York: Harcourt Brace Jovanovich, 1980), 43. After she died the situation was different, and critics have questioned whether Leonard Woolf and Quentin Bell, her literary executors, have attempted to censor the more feminist, political aspects of her writing. See, e.g., Jane Marcus, "'No More Horses': Virginia Woolf on Art and Propaganda," *Women's Studies* 4 (1977): 265–89. But for the most part, the debates about censorship have focused on Woolf's revisions.

xxxix. Pizer, "Self-Censorship," 155.

xl. See my essay "The Authority of Anger: The Case of *Three Guineas*," *Signs: Journal of Women in Culture and Society* 16 (Winter 1991): 340–70.

xli. The quotation comes from Peter Lyman, "The Politics of Anger: On Silence, Ressentiment, and Political Speech," *Socialist Review* 11.3 (1981): 67.

xlii. Adrienne Rich, "When We Dead Awaken: Writing as Re-Vision," reprinted in Rich, *On Lies, Secrets, and Silence* (New York: Norton, 1979), 37.

xliii. Virginia Woolf, *A Room of One's Own* (New York: Harcourt Brace Jovanovich, 1929), 76, 72.

xliv. Gilbert and Gubar, *Madwoman*, 338.

xlv. See Radin, "'Two Enormous Chunks'" and "*The Years*." See also Susan M. Squier, "A Track of Our Own: Typescript Drafts of *The Years*," in *Virginia Woolf: A Feminist Slant*, ed. Jane Marcus (Lincoln: U of Nebraska P, 1983), 198–211. Squier prints and discusses a typescript version of a debate among the Pargiter women about women's responsibility to patriarchal society and the possibility of a feminist society in the future—a debate considerably less combative, and less optimistic, in the published version.

xlvi. These excerpts appear in Radin, "*The Years*," 4, 6–7; and Virginia Woolf, *The Pargiters. The Novel-Essay Portion of "The Years*," ed. Mitchell A. Leaska (New York: New York Public Library and Readex

Books, 1977), xxxix. The full passage about war memoirs in the holograph reads, "If I were reviewing books now, I would say this [a participant's memoir of World War I] was a stupid and violent and hateful and idiotic and trifling and ignoble and mean display. I would say I am bored to death by war books. I detest the masculine point of view. I am bored by his heroics, virtue, and honour." The holograph also reads, "literature which is always pulling down the blinds is not literature. All that we have ought to be expressed—mind and body—a process of incredible difficulty and danger" (Radin, "*The Years*," 6).

xlvii. *The Diary of Virginia Woolf*, ed. Anne Olivier Bell, vol. 4 (New York: Harcourt Brace Jovanovich, 1982), 6, 152.

xlviii. *Diary* 4: 281; in Radin, "*The Years*," 61–62

xlix. Jane Marcus traced the connection; Mitchell Leaska quotes the definitions. See Marcus, "*The Years* as Greek Drama, Domestic Novel, and Götterdämmerung," and Mitchell A. Leaska, "Virginia Woolf, the Pargeter: A Reading of *The Years*," both in *Bulletin of the New York Public Library* 80 (Winter 1977): 280, 172–74. The novel also had a number of other possible titles between these two.

l. Woolf, *The Pargiters*, xxii.

li. Ibid., xvii.

lii. Leaska, "Virginia Wolf, the Pargeter," 180.

liii. Woolf, *The Pargiters*, xix.

liv. Ibid., xxii.

lv. Radin, "*The Years*," xvii.

lvi. Ibid., 4.

lvii. Ibid., 35.

lviii. Heine, "The Earlier *Voyage Out*," 294.

lix. *Melymbrosia*, xxiii, xxxii-xxxiii.

lx. DeSalvo, "Sorting," 284.

lxi. Susan Stanford Friedman, "Virginia Woolf's Pedagogical Scenes of Reading: *The Voyage Out*, *The Common Reader*, and Her 'Common Readers,'" *Modern Fiction Studies* 30 (Spring 1992): 101–25.

lxii. Jerome J. McGann, "*Ulysses* as a Postmodern Text: The Gabler Edition," *Criticism* 27 (Summer 1985): 291.

lxiii. McGann, "*Ulysses*," 295.

lxiv. Ibid., 297.

lxv. Pizer, "Self-Censorship," 155–56.

lxvi. One exciting addition, however, is presently in progress: S.P. Rosenbaum's edition of the manuscript version of *A Room of One's Own*, which will be published by Blackwell's with Woolf's original title for the work, *Women & Fiction*.

14.
Beth A. McCoy,
"Race and the (Para)Textual Condition."
PMLA 121.1 (January 2006): 156–69

Beth McCoy is Distinguished Teaching Professor of English at the State University of New York, Geneseo. She specializes in African-American literature and has written about typography, paratexts, and Book History. As in the first essay in this chapter, where Jerome McGann argued that critics should pay attention to the material forms and circumstances of a work's publication, in this essay Beth McCoy argues that attention to the early editions of American slave narratives can inform a sophisticated analysis of how race, class, gender, and sexuality operate within them.

In particular, she advocates combining close readings of slave narratives, in this case Frederick Douglass's *Narrative of the Life of Frederick Douglass, an American Slave* (1845), with attention to the paratexts that surround them. Paratexts are the dedications, prefaces, blurbs, introductions, footnotes, endnotes, appendices, afterwords, and other passages of writing that surround books and provide what the main theorist of paratexts, Gérard Genette (b. 1930), calls "thresholds of interpretation." Paratexts are usually thought of as subordinate or accessory to the book, but they also shape how it is read.

McCoy suggests that paratexts are a subtly important place for white domination to operate, even in the guise of sympathy for black people and support for abolition. In particular, she examines how paratexts for Douglass's *Narrative*, crafted by white prefacers and editors, were vehicles for "an indirect white supremacy." However, she suggests, paratexts can also be a site of resistance, in which the paratext is appropriated to oppose the domination it elsewhere helps to naturalize. McCoy's article thus helps to reveal the extent to which the ways in which works are framed in particular editions shape how they are read. Even such apparently extraneous elements as prefaces, blurbs, and dedications can become part of the meaning of the work. Later editions sometimes exclude these paratexts, and almost always change the format, layout, pagination, and so on. These changes can involve both losses and gains for interpretation.

Race and the (Para)Textual Condition

I.

The Western book is suffused with a matrix of spaces that is frequently unnoticed and even disdained: the epigraphs, dedications, **prefaces**, and other bookish elements federated by Gérard Genette under the term ***paratext***. As both "threshold" and "zone of transaction," the paratext performs for Genette an important spatial function, "enabling a text to become a book and to be offered as such to its readers, and more generally, to the public."[i] For all its importance, however, he discerns fundamental limits to that function. The paratext, he says, is naturally "heteronomous"; it is an "assistant," "accessory," and "auxiliary" that always serves and only ought to serve its text by getting the text read properly according to the author's designs.[ii] In other words, for Genette the paratext is a spatial servant, pure and simple. Despite its "interminable boundaries," he declares, it is a "distinctive" and, most important, an "*undisputed* territory."[iii]

Texts and paratexts emerging from the African American freedom struggle, however, suggest that the paratext is territory neither subordinate nor undisputed. Rather, tangled throughout books (and other printed texts) as well as around the images that are the stock in trade of an increasingly visual culture, the paratext is territory important, fraught, and contested. More specifically, its marginal spaces and places have functioned centrally as a zone transacting ever-changing modes of white domination and of resistance to that domination. It may seem difficult, of course, even to hazard such an argument. The American spatial imaginary, after all, still understands white domination almost solely as a series of public, bodily, and, indeed, *textualized* confrontations between white and black. Yet careful attention to texts by and about African Americans challenges this understanding and reveals the hidden, indirect, and *paratextualized* forces impelling and complicating those confrontations. Toward this end, I explore the issues of paratextuality informing Frederick Douglass's *Narrative of the Life of Frederick Douglass, an American Slave* and James Allen's exhibition of lynching photography titled *Without Sanctuary*.[1] Even as they are quite different (one is verbal, the other visual), both texts demonstrate how the paratext has been deployed to transact white power, and both texts demonstrate what is gained and lost when the paratext is deployed to resist that power. The time for such work—especially that which draws together disparate textual forms—is now. Indeed, in an age anxious about the proliferation of things counted as texts and about the diffusion of power, increased (if perverse) attention to the paratext can open new, important possibilities for reading African American cultural production, revaluing the venerable language of the book as object, and forging a crucial coalition between bibliographic scholars and those studying the intersections of race, power, and culture.

II.

Charles Olney observes that readers of the fugitive slave narrative will be struck by the repetitiveness of this eminently American genre, its "overwhelming *sameness*."[iv] Over and above the fugitive's affirmations that "I was born" and other such conventions that Olney lists as internal to the text, much of that sameness is transacted through the paratext, especially the white-written prefaces that so often introduced slaves' tales to their primary audience: white women. In the Western tradition, authors are seen as possessing a self-generating autonomy

1 The discussion of James Allen's exhibition *Without Sanctuary* is omitted here for reasons of space.

similar to that of the liberal subject. Most white authors presumed that autonomy in their act of writing, and readers presumed it of them. For the writer of African descent, however—especially the fugitive autobiographer—there was no such luxury. As William Andrews points out, "[N]o group of American autobiographers has been received with more skepticism and resistance than the ex-slave," a class that had to contend with the white beliefs—engrained in the North and the South, in the personal and the juridical—that fugitives were incapable of telling the truth.[v]

Heading that belief off at the pass, the radical white abolitionist William Lloyd Garrison prefaces the *Narrative of the Life of Frederick Douglass, an American Slave* by thundering that Douglass will present only "SLAVERY AS IT IS," with "nothing drawn from the imagination."[vi] In this way, Garrison's preface would appear to fulfill Genette's definition of the paratext's proper function: "to ensure for the text a destiny consistent with the author's purpose."[vii] After all, for fugitive authors devoted to ending the institution of slavery, reading "consistent with the author's purpose" could be construed simply as believing what the author wrote. Yet many fugitive authors—and Douglass most notably among them—wrote not merely to be believed as tellers of fact or even as fact themselves. The paratext crafted by white prefacers and editors, however, reduces fugitive author to fugitive reporter, a construction that accommodates Thomas Jefferson's distasteful declaration that "never yet could I find a black had uttered a thought above the level of plain narration."[viii] In this way, serving neither the text nor its author, the paratext serves something else: an indirect white supremacy, different from the brutality against which white abolitionists fought but one that interferes with the fugitive writer's authorial primacy nonetheless. Thus does the paratext help produce what Andrews posits as the genre's difficult reality: that "[t]he reception of the fugitive's story as truth depended on the degree to which his artfulness could hide his art."[ix]

Through this archetypal paratextual germ, a sort of diaspora might be said to have emerged, scattering diverse paratextual symptoms and transactions of white power—many bookish, but many not. In *The Souls of Black Folk,* for instance, W.E.B. DuBois rues the "gleeful" catalogs of black "bastards" and "prostitutes," catalogs producing harmful political change through academic footnotes and other forms of paratextual documentation.[x] In the 1920s, black citizens found themselves vexed both by the title of Carl Van Vechten's controversial novel *Nigger Heaven* and by its glossary purporting to translate "Negro words and phrases" for Harlem-bound whites. The 27 July 1994 issue of *Time* magazine confronted readers with a cover that darkened the complexion of the recently arrested O.J. Simpson. More recently, the education scholar Audrey Thompson has identified "defensive" citation as a way white scholars build their careers by paratextually appropriating and containing the knowledge of non-white scholars and artists.[xi] And the historian Nell Irvin Painter acknowledges the paratext as a space where absence also transacts white domination; black academics, she says, understand all too well the significance of the "absence of one's publications from [non-black] people's footnotes and bibliographies."[xii]

Even as such anecdotes suggest the existence of larger patterns meriting further scrutiny, it may be difficult to mount a search for those patterns. As D.F. McKenzie has noted, redirecting "hermetic" or "enumerative"[2] **bibliography** to respond meaningfully "to recent developments in critical theory and practice is certainly not easy."[xiii] Similarly, arguing for a practical and theoretical link between the bookish realm of paratextuality and the larger political realm of racialized power is not easy. Doing so, after all, requires attention to that which the culture at large determines is marginal, minor, and beyond the reach of interpretation, as suggested by the moral adage "Don't judge a book by its cover." It also demands more intense exploration of how white power might be transacted through such inconsequential spaces, a possibility that for many remains counter-intuitive: how could something so minor perform such a major function?

For many Americans (and whites not the least), the classic space of white domination remains that of the black body marked directly by physical violence: the brutality employed by the slaveholder and that meted out by white lynch mobs or perpetrated on black protesters by evil white southerners during the modern civil rights movement. Such representations ought never to be forgotten, especially since they helped outlaw and render socially unacceptable the actions depicted (not to say that these brutal acts have ceased altogether). Yet the stubbornness with which these representations remain the only form that white domination takes has contributed to a linguistic and indeed spatial vacuum in the place of ways to describe, analyze, and combat the forms and paths white power has taken, especially in the movement's wake. This vacuum can be found in the repeated popular assertions that racism has become harder to see, name, narrate, and prove—and easier for its perpetrators (when any are found) to disavow. Such tactics of white power are even called subtle, a word that belies their cold efficiency. This lack of language testifies to how much is at stake in tracing white power transacted through the margins.

More than bibliography is at stake, as demonstrated by Edward P. Jones's Pulitzer Prize-winning novel *The Known World* (2003), a book brought to an agonizing halt on the evening when the freedman Augustus Townsend steers his wagon homeward. Stopped by whites everywhere he goes, Townsend has got used to carrying his free papers close to his body. The papers, whose words Townsend has memorized but cannot read, function as his paratext: they are preface and footnotes documenting his accession to property in himself, a supposedly natural state that John Locke believed to be protected and regulated—but not produced—by civil government.[xiv] On this night, Townsend is stopped yet again, this time by a group of patrollers. Without a word, he hands over the precious papers. Yet this inspection will be different. The white patroller named Travis bridles at the thin pleasantries his peers offer the silent black man and snaps, "This ain't no damn church social. This is the law's business."[xv] With that, Travis methodically and with relish eats Townsend's free papers, each terrible bite easing the freedman back into a slavery from which he will not emerge alive.

The Known World thus imagines a scene where, like the text presented to the world as a book, the liberal subject exists largely as an effect of paratextuality. Jones imagines an earlier version of

---

2 The two terms taken from McKenzie here are not entirely parallel. "Hermetic" describes the common perception of bibliography as an isolated or inward-looking field of scholarship, whereas "enumerative" labels the sub-field of bibliography devoted to drawing up lists of books.

a familiar contemporary scene wherein those hailed as subjects go about their daily lives within a prefatory, citational haze of paratext to their selves: Social Security numbers, driver's licenses, green cards, and voter registration forms.[xvi] It is a scene whose implications many, like Travis, would rather disavow, for it threatens to expose the audacious sleight of hand on which depends the naturalness both of United States liberalism and of the white supremacy that might be said to have emerged alongside it. And it is a scene that, though commonly associated with the paranoid world of the post-structural and the post-modern, repeats itself throughout African American history and memory. As Kenneth Mostern observes dryly, "[W]hat is presently deemed as 'post-modern' by certain well-known theorists was anticipated by the peoples of the African diaspora, among others, in the period generally referred to as the 'modern.' Being ahead of the curve on this has, of course, not necessarily been to the benefit of black people."[xvii] Toni Morrison argues that for black people such post-modernity before its time has meant "[c]ertain kinds of dissolution, the loss of and the need to re-construct certain kinds of stability."[xviii] One might guess that among these kinds of dissolution would be included the extraordinarily unstable—if not outright fractured—relation that chattel slavery created among the terms *authorship*, *citizenship*, and *the book*. One might guess also that because of such instability, spaces dismissed by whites as marginal, minor, and inconsequential would take on great importance to African Americans, who frequently had no choice but to apprehend them as key to individual and collective survival.[xix] Thus, even as African Americans diagnosed paratextual space as one way through which white supremacy could be channeled, they also saw that same space as offering possibilities for resistance.

It is important to note that African American culture—including its relation to paratextual 203
space—cannot and should not be reduced to a set of responses to oppression or plight. As Ivan Van Sertima has pointed out, many African American cultural features (e.g., trickster tales) have deep yet flexible roots that, predating the first European encounters, enabled transitions from relatively collective African societies to largely individualistic ones of the New World.[xx] Such roots are evident in western African concepts of space scattered throughout the diaspora, concepts that invest paratext-friendly thresholds, crossroads, and margins with special significance. Robert Farris Thompson, for instance, outlines Kongo burial practices that construe tombs not as bodily repositories but as thresholds that "honor the spirit in the earth, guide it to the other world, and prevent it from wandering or returning to haunt survivors."[xxi] Henry Louis Gates, Jr., traces the transatlantic journey of Esu-Elegbara, the deity whose governance of crossroads Gates renders as quite accommodating to Western conceptualizations of reading. And Harryette Mullen attends to the marginal sites where western African-derived spirit writing takes place.

Thus, much in the way that Yoruba deities found fruitful corollaries in the Catholic pantheon of saints, diasporic approaches to space might be said to have found a fertile matrix in the paratext of the Western book, and not least because of the paratext's relation to repetition.[xxii] In his monumental "On Repetition in Black Culture," James Snead examines how European- and African-derived cultures respond to repetition, which he sees as the symptom of "nature's ineluctable circularity."[xxiii] For Snead, Enlightenment-driven European cultures shape repetition into "accumulation and growth," a futile (if capitalism-friendly) disavowal of both the circularity and its attendant "accident and rupture," which African-derived cultures acknowledge and make room for.[xxiv] Recognizing the dangers of sweeping cultural generalizations, Snead nevertheless argues that cultural attitudes toward repetition reveal the "willed grafting onto culture of an essentially philosophical insight about the shape of time and history."[xxv] I would extend this logic to argue that the paratext's role in racialized struggle reveals the "willed grafting" of philosophical insight onto space as well. After all, what are the paratext's bibliographies, **edition** notations, **indexes**, page numbers, and **copyright** signs if not spaces of repetition progressively shaped to accumulate and increase knowledge, property, and power?[xxvi] To borrow again Mostern's dry phrasing, such accumulation historically has "not necessarily been to the benefit of black people." Thus, it must be tempting indeed to overwrite paratextual space by investing it with the kind of "accident and rupture" that the West has been at such pains to disavow.

Herein lies the rub as well as the benefit in attempting to exploit the paratext to resist racialized domination. Black artists, editors, and intellectuals (and anti-racist activists from other groups) who might seek to appropriate the paratext as a strategy of resistance often want (or need) to benefit from the very "accumulation and growth" symbolized and transacted by so much of a book's paratext: they wish to own their work, see their books enter second and third editions, see themselves in others' footnotes. To explore how the paratext has been drafted in racialized trial by space is to raise an old, old scar of a question: can the master's tools dismantle the master's house?

III.

Unsurprisingly, the fugitive slave narrative and the *Narrative of the Life of Frederick Douglass* raise questions immediately about using the paratext to combat a white supremacy that itself is transacted through the paratext. Reacting strongly both to the paratextual boundaries created by Garrison and Wendell Phillips (author of another preface to the *Narrative*) and to the political and philosophical differences contained within them, Douglass penned two more autobiographies, *My Bondage and My Freedom* (1855) and *The Life and Times of Frederick Douglass* (1881). Though the retellings cover many of the same facts as the first autobiography, Douglass nevertheless becomes so much more overtly philosophical, romantic, figurative, and detailed that the retellings function almost as **glosses** to the original. As Lisa Brawley explains, even the *Narrative*'s famous first utterance, "I was born in Tuckahoe," is given thick description in *My Bondage*, changing from what seems a simple articulation of fact to an etymological "speculative anecdote" linking his birthplace's name with the original theft on which chattel slavery depended.[xxvii] Thus are Douglass's two subsequent autobiographies doubly fugitive, telling the tale of a slave who fled both the brute white supremacy of slavery and the equally effective (if more genteel) paratextual domination exercised by Garrison and Phillips.

Yet the *Narrative* remains the most read, taught, and reproduced of Douglass's autobiographies, and so its paratextual echoes sound across time. Garrison's and Phillips's essays preface Douglass in nearly every edition of the *Narrative*, including the Dover Thrift, the Modern Library, the Penguin, the Bedford, and various Nortons. Perhaps because they so often are repeated, these echoes remain unpalatable enough to cause the editors of *Call and Response:*

The Riverside Anthology of the African American Literary Tradition[3] (Hill et al.) to make a change rare in editions of the *Narrative*: otherwise reproducing the *Narrative* in its entirety, *Call and Response* excises Garrison's and Phillips's prefaces and introduces Douglass's words only with the editorial apparatus accorded to every other work in the **anthology**. It is conceivable that the editors (all noted African Americanist scholars) removed the prefaces to save pages and thus money in a volume that already ran to many hundreds of pages. It seems likely, however, that the decision was also made as a valuable gesture of resistance against Garrison and Phillips's paternalism, for it gives Douglass (para)textual independence. It brings the text in line with the anthology's governing cultural-nationalist aesthetic, which contrasts with the more formalist and belletristic aesthetic of *The Norton Anthology of African American Literature* (Gates and McKay).[xxviii] Allowing Douglass as author and subject to stand without white paratextual custodianship produces a vision of black masculinity more consonant with the needs of cultural nationalism. In short, there was much to be gained by emancipating the *Narrative* from the paratext that, since the book's first publication, continued to transact a form of white superiority.

But much could also be lost. For one thing, without the prefaces, the *Narrative* loses its appearance as the textual object it was in its time. Admittedly, with each edition the *Narrative* has appeared in a different paratextual form: different cover, different **typeface**, different scholarly introduction and apparatus of other kinds. Even an edition that reproduces photographically the *Narrative*'s first-edition form still repeats that primal loss. Yet excising Garrison and Phillips intensifies the loss, evacuating the material testament to Douglass's writerly adeptness, including his accomplishment of the very things that his white custodians and he himself claimed he would not do.

For instance, Douglass tells his readers that he will withhold the details of how he escaped from South to North, because providing such details would place others in "embarrassing difficulties" and "induce greater vigilance on the part of slaveholders."[xxix] This withholding is not without its effect, he says, acknowledging that he and his, "curious" readers must be deprived of the "pleasure" and "gratification" that the telling and reading of his escape would provide.[xxx] For good reason, Andrews calls this decision one of the *Narrative*'s most "unconventional features," breaking with the genre's "stock in trade" climaxes that allowed feverish readers to watch "the panting fugitive seize his freedom just ahead of snapping bloodhounds and clutching slavecatchers."[xxxi] If readers understand through Garrison and Phillips that Douglass is merely narrating straight-forwardly "SLAVERY AS IT IS," then they must accept that they will not learn the method of escape, and they must move on.

But things may not be narrated as they seem. Earlier in the story, for example, Douglass makes his famous apostrophe to the ships. Garrison and Phillips each draw special attention to it; in particular, Garrison lauds Douglass's envious, anguished invocation to the freely moving Chesapeake Bay sails as a "thrilling" moment of "pathos and sublimity."[xxxii] Yet the abolitionists' effulgent praise appears doubly ironic in the light of what Douglass writes immediately after the despairing apostrophe. He resolves:

---

3 *Call and Response: The Riverside Anthology of the African American Literary Tradition*, ed. Patricia Liggins Hill et al. (Boston: Houghton Mifflin, 1997).

> I will take to the water. This very bay shall yet bear me into freedom. The steamboats steered in a north-east course from North Point. I will do the same; and when I get to the head of the bay, I will turn my canoe adrift, and walk straight through Delaware into Pennsylvania. When I get there, I shall not be required to have a pass; I can travel without being disturbed.[xxxiii]

Bearing a striking emotional contrast to the apostrophe's anguish, this passage might be read merely as a rhetorical downstroke, a way to return the reader to emotional equilibrium before the upswing provided by Douglass's battle with Mr. Covey lurking just a few pages away. At the same time, the passage might be read as an example of the author's doing the very thing he vowed not to: tell how he escaped from Maryland's Eastern Shore. For his resolution looks very much like a verbal road map for a journey taking a fugitive across land and water. Whether he intended to craft such a map in an unexpected place and, if so, whether he did it to indulge his subject-writer self or to inform those who might later need such knowledge, we cannot know. But the possibilities are intriguing. Andrews identifies Douglass's earlier determination to read despite Hugh Auld's prohibition as an act of "radical misreading of the teachings of his master."[xxxiv] Reading Douglass's post-apostrophe statement as revealing the path and method of his escape suggests that Douglass is performing a "radical misreading" of Garrison's declaration that his fugitive charge would present only "SLAVERY AS IT IS." If, as Andrews asserts, "[t]he reception of the fugitive's story as truth depended on the degree to which his artfulness could hide his art," then for Douglass the reception of his narrative as truth might also be understood to depend on the degree to which his artfulness could hide his fact.

Without the abolitionists' distasteful paratextual presence, such possibilities are obscured; *Call and Response* readers likely run past the passage as a flat, sequential anti-climax to the thrilling apostrophe. Thus, it is difficult to disentangle that which *Call and Response* gains (e.g., textually independent black masculinity) and that which it loses (e.g., another clue to Douglass's virtuosity) in excising the white-written paratext from the *Narrative*. Perhaps the only thing to be safely said is that *Call and Response*'s decision suggests the paratext as a site of extraordinary ambivalence. To point to this ambivalence is not to recommend the sort of post-modern-post-structural stasis regarding political action that so unnerves scholars like Patricia Hill Collins. Rather, to borrow Theodore O. Mason's words on the politics of anthologies, it is to "set the stage for work that needs to be done in understanding the conflicts comprising our history," to balance how things have changed and how simultaneously they have remained much the same.[xxxv]

IV.

[In a section of the essay omitted here, McCoy analyses an exhibition of photographs of lynchings and the paratexts surrounding it, including gallery captions and commentary from journalists and scholars.]

[...]

D.F. McKenzie notes that for textual scholars there is "no evading the challenge" posed by the proliferation of things now understood as texts, including "verbal, visual, oral, and numeric data, in the form of maps, prints, and music, of **archives** of recorded sound, of films, videos, and any computer-stored information, everything in fact from epigraphy to the latest forms of discography."[xxxvi] Arguably, all these kinds of texts have paratexts, and thus there remains much work to be done in all arenas, especially when we consider the link between paratextuality and race. What, for instance, does it mean when Tavis Smiley names "the credits" as his favorite part of his television show because "there's a big logo that says 'The Smiley Group Inc. 2004 Copyright, All Rights Reserved' and that's what I like most about the show—that [I] own the show?"[xxxvii] [4] What does it mean that the PBS documentary *Africans in America*, which features more black historians than, sadly, most Americans will encounter in a lifetime, is prefaced by ads for Banker's Trust, FannieMae, and McDonald's ("It's not just African American history. It's *American* history")? What does it mean that, in Ishmael Reed's *Flight to Canada*, the fugitive slave Raven Quickskill's eponymous poem functions both as preface to the novel and the means by which slave catchers are able to pursue him? What does it mean that the dedication in Toni Morrison's *Beloved* ("Sixty millions and more") sparked as much controversy as the novel itself?[5] Or that the texts of songs and videos from hip-hop culture are nearly supplanted by their paratexts, including myriad shout-outs to friends, deities, consumer brands, and long lists of peers that the text is featuring? What does it mean when the visual artist Glenn Ligon's exhibition *To Disembark* parodies slave narrative **frontispieces** in order to contemplate the way various black "oppressions" remain spectacles for consumption?[xxxviii] And what does it mean that the bid of the Mississippi Freedom Democratic Party to be seated at the 1964 Democratic National Convention was foiled not by police beatings but by demands for credentials?[6] Such questions suggest just how many kinds of texts and paratexts remain ripe for critical investigation.

At the least, it seems clear that the intersection of race and paratextuality offers ample fodder for artists and critics interested in the increasingly complicated issues of identity, space, power, and authorship confronting all people in the twenty-first century.[xxxix] The very old language of the book—especially that of its margins—and the very old knowledge of

---

4 Tavis Smiley (b. 1964) is a prominent African-American talk-show host, author, and commentator. His talk show moved from BET to NPR in 2002, and currently appears on PBS.

5 Toni Morrison's novel *Beloved* (1987) is dedicated to "sixty millions and more," the number of lives estimated to have been lost to trans-Atlantic slavery. The dedication was controversial because the estimate was contested and because it seemed to invite comparison with the number killed in the Holocaust, usually estimated at 6 million.

6 The Mississippi Freedom Democratic Party was established as an inclusive alternative to the whites-only Democratic Party in the state. Having held parallel ballots and a state-wide convention, the MFDP sent 68 delegates (including four whites) to the Democratic National Convention, in Atlantic City, New Jersey, in 1964, where they asked to be seated at the Convention in place of the regular, segregationist delegates from Mississippi. The matter was referred to the Convention's Credentials Committee, and attracted considerable publicity. The Party offered the MFDP two seats at the Convention, which they declined. McCoy suggests here that credentials function as a kind of paratext.

bibliographers can be invaluable for understanding these issues. Some of this work has begun in the realms of bibliographic studies and literary-cultural studies. William Andrews, for instance, calls for contemplation of how editions of United States "minority" texts can "foreclose rather than open up further editing of a writer."[xl] The art historian and *New Yorker* writer Hilton Als uses "GWTW," an essay solicited as a preface to Allen's *Without Sanctuary*, to rail against his being asked to perform blackness in a perverse replaying of the fugitive slave narrative prefaces. And Paul Gilroy has analyzed covers of African American record albums that, for him, represent a valuable "fund of philosophical and folk knowledge" supplementing the albums' musical texts.[xli] Not only is there much more work to be done, but it is work that must be done across the uneasy disciplinary lines that, according to McKenzie, cause enumerative bibliographers, descriptive bibliographers, and interpretation-minded literary and cultural critics to look askance at one another.

Curiously, this work must be done in the face of objections by the father of paratextual studies himself. Even as Genette establishes the paratext as a formal object of study ("it is appropriate to define objects before one studies their evolution"[xlii]), he warns that the paratext could violate its ostensibly natural servant propriety, leap its bounds, and end up "playing its own game to the detriment of its text's game." This is Genette's worst-case scenario. Strikingly, he intimates that scholarly attention to the paratext (even as a result of his own magisterial volume) might produce such a dreaded and even "perverse" effect.[xliii] Decrying what he calls the "imperialist tendency to annex to [the paratext] everything that comes within its reach or seems possibly to pertain to it," Genette recommends instead "the Occamian principle of economy,[7] which deters us from multiplying 'theoretical objects' unless the reason for doing so is of the utmost importance."[xliv] Thus, almost as soon as he opens the paratext as a field or object of study, he wants to close it.

Though it is impossible to determine what impels Genette's anxious move, it is compelling to read it in the context of larger cultural anxieties suggesting that the paratext has become an undutiful servant, "assistant," "accessory," or "auxiliary," to borrow the theorist's words once again. These anxieties suggest that, these days, there is too much paratext. There are too many credits to movies, and too many advertisements and trailers before them. There is too much fine print to credit card and cell-phone agreements. There are too many footnotes to academic articles. In front of novels and short story collections, there are too many acknowledgments, which, as the fiction writer Beth Lordan laments, have "mushroomed" to take over what she calls the book's "pure product": the story itself. Diagnosing these anxieties is beyond this essay's scope, yet there is more at stake in the paratext's seeming insurgence than the occlusion of the book's "pure product." In closing, then, I recommend willful, thoughtful perversity as a scholarly drive, the very thing that Genette fears. More work exploring race and paratextuality needs to be done. To appropriate Genette's command, "No more dawdling on the threshold of the threshold."[xlv]

---

7 Genette's "Occamiam principle" refers to the philosophical maxim known as "Occam's Razor" after the fourteenth-century English logician William of Occam, who asserted that one should reject complex explanations that make new assumptions when simpler ones were available based on known facts.

Notes

i. Gérard Genette, *Paratexts: Thresholds of Interpretation*, trans. Jane E. Lewin (Cambridge: Cambridge UP, 1997), 1.

ii. Ibid., 12, 140.

iii. Ibid., 407. My emphasis.

iv. Charles Olney, "'I Was Born': Slave Narratives, Their Status as Autobiography and as Literature," *The Slave's Narrative*, ed. Charles T. Davis and Henry Louis Gates Jr. (Oxford: Oxford UP, 1985), 148–75, 148.

v. William L. Andrews, *To Tell a Free Story. The First Century of Afro-American Autobiography, 1760–1865* (Urbana: U of Illinois P, 1986), 3.

vi. William Lloyd Garrison, Preface, Frederick Douglass, *Narrative of the Life of Frederick Douglass, an American Slave, Written by Himself*, ed. and introduction by David W. Blight (New York: Bedford, 1993), 29–35, 32.

vii. Ibid., 407.

viii. See *Notes on the State of Virginia*, "Query IV," where Jefferson participates in the very amalgam of Enlightenment and Romantic thought that Douglass himself appropriates as an intellectual weapon against slavery's peculiar institution.

ix. William L. Andrews, *To Tell a Free Story*, 3.

x. W.E.B. DuBois, *The Souls of Black Folk*, 1903, ed. and introduction by David W. Blight and Robert Gooding Williams (New York: Bedford, 1993), 42.

xi. Audrey Thompson, "Tiffany, Friend of People of Color: White Investments in Antiracism," *Qualitative Studies in Education* 16.1 (2003): 7–29, 10.

xii. Nell Irvin Painter, "Black Studies, Black Professors, and the Struggles of Perception," *The Chronicle of Higher Education*, December 15, 2000, <http://chronicle.com/article/Black-Studies-Black/9522>.

xiii. D.F. McKenzie, *Bibliography and the Sociology of Texts* (Cambridge: Cambridge UP, 1999), 13, 2.

xiv. John Locke, *Second Treatise on Government*, 1689 (Indianapolis: Hackett, 1980), ch. 5.

xv. Edward P. Jones, *The Known World* (New York: Harper, 2003), 211.

xvi. In this way, attention to the paratext as such helps make concrete the meditations of post-structuralists such as Jacques Derrida ("Signature Event Context," *Limited Inc.*, ed. Gerald Graff, trans. Samuel Weber and Jeffrey Mehlman [Evanston, IL: Northwestern UP, 1988], 1–24) and Judith Butler, who use the concept of citationality as a way to interrogate the idea of the pre-existing humanist subject, the idea that there is a she or he, a "one," as Butler puts it, at the heart of human agency (Judith Butler, *Bodies That Matter: On the Discursive Limits of "Sex"* [New York: Routledge, 1993], 12).

xvii. Kenneth Mostern, "Review Essay: Social Marginality/Blackness: Subjects of Postmodernity," *MELUS* 23.4 (1998): 167–87, 167–68.

xviii. Quoted in Paul Gilroy, *Small Acts: Thoughts on the Politics of Black Cultures* (London: Serpent's Tail, 1993), 178.

xix. Harriet Jacobs's *Incidents in the Life of a Slave Girl* (ed. and introduction by Jean Fagan Yellin [Cambridge, MA: Harvard UP, 1987]) provides several examples of the importance of thresholds and other spaces and places. Her persona Linda Brent tells the story, for instance, of Luke, the fugitive slave who gets his dead master's money by placing that money in his master's trousers. When the master was buried, Luke says, "Dis nigger ask for dem ole trousers, an dey gub 'em to me.... You see I didn't steal it; dey gub it to me" (193). And as Linda spends her astounding seven years in the garret to escape Dr. Flint, her son, attending closely to the eaves and margins of the house, hears his mother cough, realizes where she is, and uses his young intelligence to ward white people and untrustworthy black people away from those margins (154–155).

xx. Ivan Van Sertima, "Trickster, the Revolutionary Hero," *Talk That Talk: An Anthology of African American Storytelling*, ed. Linda Goss and Marian E. Barnes (New York: Simon, 1989), 103–11, 104.
xxi. Robert Farris Thompson, *Flash of the Spirit: African and Afro-American Art and Philosophy* (New York: Vintage, 1983), 132.
xxii. Ron Eglash implies as much in his striking *African Fractals* (New Brunswick, NJ: Rutgers UP, 1999), which charts how fractal mathematics and geometry's recursions (repetitions) of seed shapes—symptoms of which are found in many African expressions of space, from housing to textiles—exist on the same spatial template that European-derived mathematics and geometry interpreted as Euclidean symmetry.
xxiii. James Snead, "On Repetition in Black Culture," *Black American Literature Forum* 15.4 (1981): 146–54. 146.
xxiv. Ibid., 149, 150.
xxv. Ibid., 146.
xxvi. The paratext's invocation of repetition, reproduction, and sequence demands more attention than can be given in this essay. Further work on the paratext would need to engage Walter Benjamin's "The Work of Art in the Age of Mechanical Reproduction" and Judith Roof's *Reproductions of Reproduction*.
xxvii. Lisa Brawley, "Frederick Douglass's *My Bondage and My Freedom* and the Fugitive Tourist Industry," *Novel* 30 (1996): 98–129, 106.
xxviii. *The Norton Anthology of African American Literature* and the editorial decisions producing it received substantial attention in the late 1990s. This attention, as Theodore O. Mason ("The African-American Anthology: Mapping the Territory, Taking the National Census, Building the Museum," *American Literary History* 10 [1998]: 185–98) and Kevin Meehan ("Spiking Canons," *Nation* [12 May 1997]: 42–46) each noted, belies a varied, long standing tradition of anthology making in African American literature. As Mason notes, the "difficult to ignore" *Norton* "will itself become part of the canon it attempts to create" (185). Meehan argues that part of the *Norton*'s canon contributing energy is derived from its "conservative, text-bound stance," one that renders palely on the page Grandmaster Flash and the Furious Five's "The Message" (42). Such text-boundness is conceivably something that *Call and Response* might seek to remedy through excising Garrison's and Phillips's prefaces to the *Narrative*.
xxix. Frederick Douglass, *Narrative of the Life of Frederick Douglass, an American Slave, Written by Himself*, ed. and introduction by David W. Blight (New York: Bedford, 1993), 94.
xxx. Ibid.
xxxi. William L. Andrews, *To Tell a Free Story*, 128. Douglass could be read as parodying such climaxes when he recounts planning for the ill-fated collective escape and imagines the fugitives would be "stung by scorpions" in Maryland (86).
xxxii. Garrison, 33.
xxxiii. Douglass, *Narrative*, 74–75.
xxxiv. William L. Andrews, *To Tell a Free Story*, 13.
xxxv. Theodore O. Mason, "The African-American Anthology: Mapping the Territory, Taking the National Census, Building the Museum," *American Literary History* 10 (1998): 185–98, 197.
xxxvi. D.F. McKenzie, *Bibliography and the Sociology of Texts*, 13.
xxxvii. Quoted in Yoji Cole, "Tavis Smiley Knows Where the Power Is," *Diversity Inc.* 9 February 2004, <http://www.diversityinc.com/members/6346.cfm>.
xxxviii. Located during the mid-1990s at the Hirschorn Museum, in Washington, *To Disembark* has since been reprinted as "Narratives" in the *Yale Journal of Criticism* 7.1 (1994): 31–40. Collapsing nineteenth-century paratextuality with more contemporary content, Ligon's frontispieces are simultaneously deadly serious and very funny. One is titled "Black like Me, or, The Authentic Narrative of Glenn Ligon" and features an authenticating epigraph by "A WHITE PERSON" recommending this "panorama" of "oppression": "I know

there are a great many impostors and cheats going about through the country deceiving and picking up the people's money, but *this* is of another class altogether" (36). Another piece bears the title "The Narrative of the Life and Uncommon Sufferings of Glenn Ligon, a Colored Man, Who at a Tender Age Discovered His Affection for the Bodies of Other Men, and Has Endured Scorn and Tribulations Ever Since" (37). In keeping with paratextual convention, many of the pieces bear the phrase "Written by Himself," including "To My Mother's Land, an Interesting Account of a Journey among the People of South Carolina in the Year 1976." The narrative's action, the frontispiece affirms, will "embrac[e] reminiscences of four days spent in a motel in Darlington, South Carolina with sixty of the Author's relatives and the various adventures that befell them" (34).

xxxix. For a look at how typography, for instance, is intertwined consciously with nation and culture, see John D. Berry (ed.), *Language Culture Type: International Type Design in the Age of Unicode* (New York: Association Typographique Internationale, 2002).

xl. William L. Andrews, "Editing 'Minority' Texts," *The Margins of the Text*, ed. D.C. Greetham (Ann Arbor: U of Michigan P, 1997), 45–55, 53.

xli. Gilroy, *Small Acts*, 256.

xlii. Genette, *Paratexts*, 13.

xliii. Ibid., 410.

xliv. Ibid., 407.

xlv. Ibid., 15.

CHAPTER 3

Printing and Reading

15.

Elizabeth L. Eisenstein, "The Unacknowledged Revolution," *The Printing Press as an Agent of Change.* Cambridge: Cambridge UP, 1979. 3–42

Elizabeth Eisenstein (b.1923), Professor Emerita at the University of Michigan, is an American historian of the French Revolution; however, within the field of book history her best-known work examines the shift from script to print following the invention of the press in the mid-fifteenth century. *The Printing Press as an Agent of Change* (1979), the book for which she is best known, is a two-volume, 750-page examination of the effect that the invention of the printing press had on Western culture. Focusing on what she identifies as the printing press's three main functions of standardizing, preserving, and disseminating knowledge, Eisenstein claims that the introduction of print was revolutionary, largely responsible for fomenting the Protestant Reformation, the Renaissance, and the Scientific Revolution. In the chapter from which the following excerpt is taken, Eisenstein claims that the historical significance of the printing revolution has been neglected (or "unacknowledged") by her fellow historians. Also in this chapter, Eisenstein emphasizes some of the problems with attempts to understand the shift from script to print. She observes that the effect of print, still the dominant media in which scholarship took place (in 1979), had become invisible over time insofar as we are ourselves the inheritors and products of the effects that print has on learning and language, mentalities, and human behavior. She also points out that the highly specialized sub-fields of history (social, economic, religious, scientific, literary, and technological) have fragmented our understanding of the global effects of print, thus rendering it difficult to obtain "a sense of its significance as a whole." Eisenstein concludes by rejecting "a gradual, evolutionary" model for the history of the book (such as had been advanced by Febvre and Martin; see their essay included earlier, pp. 15–36) in favor of a model that underscores the discontinuity with the past that the invention of print produced. Eisenstein's work on the history of print continues to be both generative and contentious, as will be seen in Adrian Johns's essay on the history of science, included below, pp. 267–88.

The Unacknowledged Revolution

In the late-fifteenth century, the reproduction of written materials began to move from the copyist's desk to the **printer's** workshop. This shift, which revolutionized all forms of learning, was particularly important for historical scholarship. Ever since then, historians have been indebted to **Gutenberg's** invention; print enters their work from start to finish, from consulting card-files to reading **page-proofs**. Because historians are usually eager to investigate major changes and this change transformed the conditions of their own craft, one would expect the shift to attract some attention from the profession as a whole. Yet any historiographical[1] survey will show the contrary to be true. It is symbolic that Clio[2] has retained her handwritten **scroll**. So little has been made of the move into new workshops, that after 500 years, the muse of history still remains outside. "History bears witness to the cataclysmic effect on society of inventions of new media for the transmission of information among persons. The development of writing and later the development of printing are examples...."[i] Insofar as flesh-and-blood historians who turn out articles and books actually bear witness to what happened in the past, the effect on society of the development of printing, far from appearing cataclysmic, is remarkably inconspicuous. Many studies of developments during the last five centuries say nothing about it at all.

Those who do touch on the topic usually agree that the use of the invention had far-reaching effects. Francis Bacon's[3] aphorism suggesting that it changed "the appearance and state of the whole world" is cited repeatedly and with approbation. But although many scholars concur with Bacon's opinion, very few have tried to follow his advice and "take note of the force, effect, and consequences" of Gutenberg's invention. Much attention is paid to developments that paved the way for this invention. Many efforts have been made to define just what Gutenberg did "invent,"

to describe how **movable type** was first utilized and how the use of the new presses spread. But almost no studies are devoted to the consequences that ensued once printers had begun to ply their new trades throughout Europe. Explicit theories as to what these consequences were have not yet been proposed, let alone tested or contested.

[...]

Since we are concerned with "far-reaching effects" that, by common consent, left no field of human enterprise untouched, one might well wonder why such effects still remain undetermined. "Neither political, constitutional, ecclesiastical, and economic events, nor sociological, philosophical, and literary movements can be fully understood without taking into account the influence the printing press has exerted upon them."[ii] All these events and movements have been subjected to close scrutiny by generations of scholars with the aim of understanding them more fully. If the printing press exerted some influence upon them, why is this influence so often unnoted, so rarely even hinted at, let alone discussed? The question is worth posing if only

---

1 Historiography is the study of history as a discipline.

2 According to Greek mythology, Clio is the muse of history; she is commonly represented holding a scroll.

3 Francis Bacon (1561–1626) was an English philosopher, lawyer, and scientist who developed the scientific method, a systematic method of observation, measurement, and experiment, along with the formulation, testing, and modification of hypotheses.

to suggest that the effects produced by printing are by no means self-evident. Insofar as they may be encountered by scholars exploring different fields, they are apt to pass unrecognized at present. To track them down and set them forth—in an outline or some other form—is much easier said than done.

When McMurtrie or Steinberg [scholars of print] refer to the impact of printing on every field of human enterprise—political, economic, philosophical, and so forth—it is by no means clear just what they have in mind. In part at least they seem to be pointing to indirect consequences which have to be inferred and which are associated with the consumption of printed products or with changed mental habits. Such consequences are, of course, of major historical significance and impinge on most forms of human enterprise. Nevertheless it is difficult to describe them precisely or even to determine exactly what they are. It is one thing to describe how methods of book production changed after the mid-fifteenth century or to estimate rates of increased output. It is another thing to decide how access to a greater abundance or variety of written records affected ways of learning, thinking, and perceiving among literate elites. Similarly, it is one thing to show that standardization was a consequence of printing. It is another to decide how laws, languages, or mental constructs were affected by more uniform texts. Even at present, despite all the data being obtained from living, responsive subjects; despite all the efforts being made by public opinion analysts, pollsters, or behavioral scientists; we still know very little about how access to printed materials affects human behavior.[iii] (A glance at recent controversies on the desirability of censoring pornography shows how ignorant we are.) Historians who have to reach out beyond the grave to reconstruct past forms of consciousness are especially disadvantaged in dealing with such issues. Theories about unevenly phased changes affecting **literacy** rates, learning processes, attitudes, and expectations, do not lend themselves, at all events, to simple, clear-cut formulations that can be easily tested or integrated into conventional historical narratives.

Problems posed by some of the more important effects produced by the shift from script to print, by indirect consequences that have to be inferred and by imponderables that defy accurate measurement, probably can never be overcome entirely. But such problems could be confronted more squarely if other impediments did not lie in the way. Among the far-reaching effects that need to be noted are many that still affect present observations and that operate with particularly great force upon every professional scholar. Thus constant access to printed materials is a prerequisite for the practice of the historian's own craft. It is difficult to observe processes that enter so intimately into our own observations. In order to assess changes ushered in by printing, for example, we need to survey the conditions that prevailed before its advent. Yet the conditions of **scribal culture** can only be observed through a veil of print.

Even a cursory acquaintance with the findings of anthropologists or casual observations of pre-school age children may help to remind us of the gulf that exists between **oral** and literate cultures. Several studies, accordingly, have illuminated the difference between mentalities shaped by reliance on the spoken as opposed to the written word.[iv] The gulf that separates our experience from that of literate elites who relied exclusively on hand-copied texts is much more difficult to fathom. There is nothing analogous in our experience or in that of any living creature within the Western world at present. The conditions of scribal culture thus have to be artificially reconstructed by recourse to history books and reference guides. Yet for the most part, these works are more likely to conceal than to reveal the object of such a search. Scribal themes are carried forward, post-print trends are traced backward in a manner that makes it difficult to envisage the existence of a distinctive literary culture based on hand-copying.[v] There is not even an agreed-upon term in common use which designates the system of written communications that prevailed before print.[vi]

Schoolchildren who are asked to trace early overseas voyages on identical outline maps are likely to become absent-minded about the fact that there were no uniform world maps in the era when the voyages were made. A similar absent-mindedness on a more sophisticated level is encouraged by increasingly refined techniques for **collating manuscripts** and producing authoritative **editions** of them. Each successive edition tells us more than was previously known about how a given manuscript was composed and copied. By the same token, each makes it more difficult to envisage how a given manuscript appeared to a scribal scholar who had only one hand-copied version to consult and no certain guidance as to its place or date of composition, its title or author. Historians are trained to discriminate between manuscript sources and printed texts; but they are not trained to think with equal care about how manuscripts appeared when this sort of discrimination was inconceivable[vii]—when everything was off the record, so to speak, save that which was read to those who were within earshot. Similarly, the more thoroughly we are trained to master the events and dates contained in modern history books, the less likely we are to appreciate the difficulties confronting scribal scholars who had access to assorted written records, but lacked uniform chronologies, maps, and all the other reference guides which are now in common use.

Efforts to reconstruct the circumstances that preceded printing thus lead to a scholarly predicament. Reconstruction requires recourse to printed materials, thereby blurring clear perception of the conditions that prevailed before these materials were available. Even when the predicament is partly resolved by sensitive scholars who manage to develop a genuine "feel" for the times after handling countless documents,[viii] efforts at reconstruction are still bound to be frustratingly incomplete.

For the very texture of scribal culture was so fluctuating, uneven, and multiform that few long-range trends can be traced. Conditions that prevailed near the bookshops of ancient Rome, in the Alexandrian **library**,[4] or in certain medieval monasteries and university towns, made it possible for literate elites to develop a relatively sophisticated "bookish" culture.[ix] Yet all library collections were subject to contraction, and all texts in manuscript were liable to get **corrupted** after being copied over the course of time. Outside certain transitory special centers, moreover, the texture of scribal culture was so thin that heavy reliance was placed on oral transmission even by literate elites. Insofar as dictation governed copying in **scriptoria** and literary compositions were "published" by being read aloud, even "book" learning was governed by reliance on the

---

4 An ancient library in Egypt built in the third century BCE that was a major learning center until it was destroyed in the third century CE.

spoken word—producing a hybrid half-oral, half-literate culture that has no precise counterpart today. Just what publication meant before printing or just how messages got transmitted in the age of scribes are questions that cannot be answered in general.[x] Findings are bound to vary enormously depending on date and place. Contradictory verdicts are especially likely to proliferate with regard to the last century before printing—an interval when paper had become available and the literate man was more likely to become his own scribe.[5]

Specialists in the field of **incunabula**, who are confronted by ragged evidence, are likely to insist that a similar lack of uniformity characterizes procedures used by early printers. To generalize about early printing is undoubtedly hazardous and one should be on guard against projecting the output of modern standard editions too far back into the past.[xi] Yet one must also be on guard against blurring a major difference between the last century of scribal culture and the first century after Gutenberg. Early print culture is sufficiently uniform to permit us to measure its diversity. We can estimate output, arrive at averages, trace trends. For example, we have rough estimates of the total output of all printed materials during the age of incunabula. Similarly, we can say that the "average" early edition ranged between 200 and 1000 copies. There are no comparable figures for the last 50 years of scribal culture. Indeed we have no figures at all. What is the "average edition" turned out between 1400 and 1450? The question verges on nonsense. The term "edition" comes close to being an anachronism when applied to copies of a manuscript book.[xii]

[...]

As these comments may suggest, it is easier to generalize about the new system of book production than about the old, especially when considering the interval 1350–1450. Uniformity and synchronization have become so common since the advent of printing that we have to remind ourselves repeatedly that they were usually absent in the age of scribes. When one has been trained to view phenomena at a distance, however, one is prone to myopia about those that occur, so to speak, directly under one's eyes. The apparent blindness of most scholars to effects exerted by the medium they look at every day has been most emphatically stressed and elaborately treated by Marshall McLuhan.[xiii] [6] According to his thesis, subliminal effects are engendered by repeatedly scanning lines of print presented in a standardized format. Habitual book readers are so subjectively conditioned by these effects that they are incapable of recognizing them. The bizarre **typographical** format of *The Gutenberg Galaxy* is presumably designed to counteract this conditioning and to jolt the reader out of accustomed mental ruts. McLuhan attributes his

---

5 Paper is made from pulp usually derived from rags or wood. It was known in China from the second century CE, and spread to Southern Europe along trade routes by the tenth century; however, it was not widely produced in Northern Europe until around 1400. Prior to this, writing could be recorded on vellum, parchment (both made from animal skins), or papyrus (made from reeds).

6 Marshall McLuhan (1911–80) was a Canadian scholar whose most famous work, *The Gutenberg Galaxy* (1962), helped establish the importance of the study of print culture.

own awareness of and ability to withstand the quasi-hypnotic power of print to the advent of new audio-visual and electronic media. By affecting our senses and conditioning our perception differently, he holds, the new media have begun to break the bookish spell that held literate members of Western society in thrall during the past five centuries.

[...]

Elaborate media-analysis does not seem to be required to explain current myopia about the impact of print. Since Gutenberg's day, printed materials have become exceedingly common. They ceased to be newsworthy more than a century ago and have attracted ever less attention the more ubiquitous they have become. But although calendars, maps, time-tables, dictionaries, catalogues, textbooks, and newspapers are taken for granted at present (or even dismissed as old-fashioned by purveyors of novelties) they continue to exert as great an influence on daily life as ever they did before.[xiv] Indeed the more abundant they have become, the more frequently they are used, the more profound and widespread their impact. Typography is thus still indispensable to the transmission of the most sophisticated technological skills. It underlies the present knowledge explosion and much of modern art. In my view, at least, it accounts for much that is singled out as peculiarly characteristic of mid-twentieth-century culture.[xv] But, I repeat, the more printed materials accumulate, the more we are inclined to overlook them in favor of more recent, less familiar media. Articles speculating about the effects of television will thus find a larger market than conjectures about the impact of print. Because the latter has become increasingly less visible, repercussions that are actually being augmented and amplified at present are paradoxically believed to be diminishing instead.

The prolonged ubiquity of printed materials, however, does not completely explain current myopia. The era of incunabula had ended well before Bacon, Campanella, Galileo, or Kepler[7] were born. But none of them was inclined to take typography for granted; on the contrary, each commented on its great significance. To be sure, by present standards, printed materials were relatively scarce in the early-seventeenth century. Nevertheless, by contemporary standards they were remarkably abundant and were already being described as a glut on the market; "begotten only to distract and abuse the weaker judgments of scholars and to maintain the Trade and Mystery of Typographers" according to Sir Thomas Browne.[xvi] Since the scanning of printed **pages** had become a familiar daily routine in seventeenth-century scholarly circles and yet letterpress was still being discussed as a conspicuous innovation, our present tendency to overlook it needs further explanation.

Some additional points are worth considering. In the seventeenth century, many scholars and intellectuals were on much closer terms with print shops and typographers than they have been

7 Tommaso Campanella (1568–1639) was an Italian philosopher, astrologer, and political writer; Galileo Galilei (1564–1642) was a hugely influential Italian astronomer and mathematician who was instrumental in the acceptance of a sun-centered solar system among other scientific advancements; Johannes Kepler (1571–1630) was a German astronomer who developed a ground-breaking set of laws of planetary motion.

since the industrialization of printing led to new divisions of labor. Down through the Age of Enlightenment,[8] genteel **publishers** and mechanic printers had not yet come to a parting of the ways. An early seventeenth-century virtuoso, such as Kepler, who spent hours in print shops himself, closely supervising scientific **presswork**, was likely to be more alert to print technology than are contemporary astronomers, who send off their findings to the editors of journals and assume publication will be forthcoming, after receiving a favorable verdict from referees.[9] How this growing distance from printing plants has affected the attitudes of men of knowledge remains to be assessed. Has it helped, perhaps, to reinforce a disdain for technology and applied science on the part of those who are engaged in "pure" research?

In addition to the industrialization of printing trades and new divisions of intellectual labor, problems of **censorship** and ideology also need to be brought into the picture. In the early modern era, gaining access to publication outlets often entailed circumventing censors and engaging in illicit activities. A man of letters who had to smuggle out a manuscript for publication by a foreign press or locate a clandestine press in his native land was less likely to take the services of printers for granted than are most men of letters (in Western Europe, at least) today. This was especially true of Campanella, Galileo, and Kepler, as it was of the later *philosophes*[10] who lived under Catholic rule. Tributes to the power of the press were more compatible with patriotic themes in Protestant realms; emphasis on the epoch-making functions performed by printing had anti-papist[11] and anti-Roman overtones. The theme was thus developed by anti-Italian German humanists, amplified by Lutherans and other Protestants, carried on by Huguenots, Puritans, freethinkers, and Enlightenment *philosophes*, reaching a final climax in the writings of Whig historians, such as Macaulay, and anti-clerical ones, such as Michelet.[xvii] [12] Thereafter, however, the apostles of progress were diverted from gunpowder and printing, first to the steam engine and then to the dynamo. By the late-nineteenth century, the **hand press** itself was becoming something of a museum piece—a point that also helps to explain why it seems less conspicuous to us than to Francis Bacon or Condorcet.[13]

The cumulative impact of recent technological advance thus has also helped to relegate the fifteenth-century invention to the position of an antique; of more interest to rare book dealers

8 The intellectual movement that spread through Europe and North America in the eighteenth century, which emphasized secular, rational, and scientific approaches to understanding.

9 Other scholars with expertise in the field who are asked by the editors to assess the quality of new work submitted to scholarly journals.

10 Enlightenment philosophers in Continental Europe whose secular and rationalist approaches put them in conflict with Catholic authorities.

11 I.e., against the Catholic Church and the authority of the Vatican in Rome.

12 Thomas Babington Macaulay (1800–58), a British historian and Whig politician, who is known as one of the progenitors of the "Whig interpretation of history," which interprets the past as inevitably progressing toward greater liberty and enlightenment; Jules Michelet (1798–1874), a French historian of the Renaissance (a term he was the first to use) and the French Revolution.

13 Marie-Jean-Antoine-Nicolas de Caritat, marquis de Condorcet (1743–94), was a French philosopher and political thinker whose ideas are representative of the Enlightenment.

than to observers of the modern scene. It is symptomatic that incunabula have joined hand-produced books as highly valued scarce objects to be placed in glass cases and cherished as vestiges of a distant, lost past.[xviii] Given the recent rapid pace of innovation, moreover, the Renaissance convention of coupling printing with other post-classical inventions has also helped to diminish the attention focused upon it. The more rapidly new inventions proliferate, the less conspicuous earlier ones tend to become. The expansion of the so-called modern knowledge industry has produced similar results, with modern scholars uncovering old inventions almost as rapidly as modern technology has brought forth new ones.[xix] As just one more item in an increasingly cluttered inventory, the printing press has also become less distinctive.

[...]

Does it belong where we are most accustomed to finding it, in the context of late-medieval technology? In many ways it does seem appropriate to couple letterpress printing with other instruments of power and precision, and to place it in a sequence which includes developments in metallurgy[14] and textiles and experiments in oil-based pigments and ink.[xx] But if one is in the company of librarians and bibliophiles it will seem equally appropriate to place it in quite a different sequence associated with the history of the book. There it will be viewed as just one more stage of a long process which goes back at least to the slave labor of antiquity and to the shift from **roll** to **codex.**[xxi] Not late-medieval metallurgy but the twelfth-century book revolution will be taken as the most significant point of departure. As we have seen, this context favors a gradual, evolutionary view. Once manuscript book-publishing has been organized on a new basis and paper production developed to handle an expanding trade, little room is left for innovation by the printer and his new machines.

Yet another different context is supplied by the economic historian. The latter is much more likely than the librarian to place the **stationer's** successor in an innovative role. Accordingly, the early printer is viewed as an urban entrepreneur who substituted machine-made products for hand-produced ones, who had to recoup large investments and secure financial aid; who pioneered in early mass production and extended trade networks beyond the limits of late medieval guilds and towns; who experienced labor problems, including early strikes, and who confronted constant competition from profit-driving rival firms. For the economic historian, then, the first printers belong in the company of other early capitalists rather than with the manuscript book-dealers of an earlier age.[xxii]

To portray early printers as early capitalists enables one to regard them as innovators. But it also places them uncomfortably close to the company of philistines and invites other misleading inferences associated with the behavior of economic man. It means losing sight of many other roles that were performed—in connection with the arts and sciences or with the learning and letters of the day. "Printing was a mechanical art" writes Edgar Zilsel, "and the publishers, though themselves classical scholars, were not literary dispensers of glory

14 The scientific study of metals.

but business men."[xxiii] It seems more accurate to describe many publishers as being *both* businessmen *and* literary dispensers of glory. They served men of letters not only by providing traditional forms of **patronage** but also by acting as press agents and as cultural impresarios of a new kind. "To make illustrious this author's name and to benefit the world"—Tartaglia's Venetian publisher thus described his motives in printing a posthumous translation of Euclid by the self-made artisan-engineer. Doubtless, he hoped to make money as well as win for Tartaglia a measure of fame. The point is that the profit motive was combined with other motives that were self-serving *and* altruistic, and even evangelistic, at times. The printer could take satisfaction in serving humanity at large even while enhancing the reputation of authors and making money for himself. This distinctive mixture of motives entered into the rapid expansion of early printing industries. A variety of interests were served and not merely those represented by economic man.

As pioneers in new manufacturing and marketing techniques, early printers shared something in common with other urban entrepreneurs; but as pioneers in advertising and publicity, in agitation and propaganda, in **lexicography** and **bibliography** they must be placed in a class by themselves. Their shops were different from those run by earlier manuscript book-dealers and lay stationers, because they contained new machines and mechanics trained to operate them. At the same time, the new workshops also differed from those run by other contemporary manufacturers because they served as gathering places for scholars, artists, and literati; as sanctuaries for foreign translators, émigrés, and refugees; as institutions of advanced learning, and as focal points for every kind of cultural and intellectual interchange.

As these remarks may suggest, the establishment of print shops in urban centers throughout Europe rather resembles another topic described by Frances Yates as being everybody's business and thus nobody's business.[xxiv] Diverse aspects of the multi-faceted topic are handled by diverse specialists engaged in tracing different sequences and sharing few common concerns. Although problems relating to book production and distribution come under the aegis of economic and social historians; those relating to consumption are more likely to be handled by literary scholars or media analysts. Although the history of the book is normally allocated to courses in library studies, the topic of printing itself is assigned to historians of technology, while **type** design, layout, and lettering are treated as part of a sub-specialty taught in schools of design. Given a topic that is segmented, subdivided, and parceled out in this fashion, it is little wonder that one rarely gets a sense of its significance as a whole. Even the wide-ranging studies produced by social historians have failed to provide a full-length, well-rounded study of the new occupational culture represented by the early printer or a full assessment of his many roles.[xxv]

Thus a steady division of intellectual labor (perhaps an inevitable concomitant of the expanding knowledge industry) has also diminished the number of those who might be interested in following Bacon's advice. If printing often receives a somewhat cursory treatment in large volumes devoted to the history of the book, of Western technology or of early capitalism, it gets even shorter shrift elsewhere. Countless standard histories of Western philosophy, religion, and science, of political and economic theory, of historiography, literature, or the fine arts pass over the topic entirely. Not only modern specialization, but also the persistence of a venerable philosophical tradition of proud ignorance concerning material and mechanical phenomena, may help to account for neglect by intellectual and cultural historians. Because of this neglect the history of ideas is weakened as a discipline. When ideas are detached from the media used to transmit them, they are also cut off from the historical circumstances that shape them, and it becomes difficult to perceive the changing context within which they must be viewed. This point is not only pertinent to most histories of Western philosophy or literature; it also applies to most treatments of the history of science and of historiography.[xxvi]

The shift from script to print affected methods of record-keeping and the flow of information. We cannot, each of us, study all aspects of the past, and intellectual historians may be well advised to leave many inventions, such as stirrup or grist mill, to other specialists. To treat Gutenberg's invention in this way, however, is to miss the chance of understanding the main forces that have shaped the modern mind. The problem of relating intellectual history to the rest of history could also be handled more effectively if greater attention were paid to the impact of print. Attempts to relate ideas to social action, to link the Marxist "superstructure"[15] to actual modes of production, or to develop a "sociology of knowledge" are likely to produce strained and awkward solutions when the communications revolution is not taken into account. Most speculation about mind and society or mentalities and material conditions seems premature and excessively abstract. Before theorizing in general about these issues, should we not consider more concretely how specific forms of book learning may be related to specific techniques for producing and distributing books?

[...]

Separate marginal plots within the large, somewhat amorphous, field of social history are cultivated by authors of **monographs** devoted to the book-trade, to patronage and censorship, to *belles lettres*, journalism, and education, to public opinion and propaganda analysis, or to the internal organization of printing industries in diverse regions. Save for occasional references to the "rise" of the "reading public" and the emergence of "professional" authors in the eighteenth century, to the role of the "press" and of "public opinion" in the nineteenth century, one might conclude from the vast bulk of current history books, that the social and intellectual transformations introduced by printing had petered out with the last Reformation **broadside**. That the new presses disseminated Protestant views is, probably, the only aspect of the impact of printing which is familiar to most historians of modern Europe. In accounts of the Reformation as in accounts of other movements, the effects produced by printing tend to be drastically curtailed and restricted to the single function of "spreading" ideas. That new issues were posed for churchmen when the scriptural tradition "went to press," and that print contributed to dividing Christendom before spreading Protestantism are possibilities that

15 In Marxist theory, the base is the economic systems of a given society, whereas superstructure is all the social, political, legal, religious, and cultural institutions that rest upon (and for Marx are deeply related to) the base.

have gone unexplored. At all events, once chapters devoted to the Reformation are closed and the spread of Protestantism has been achieved, the activities of printers and publishers seem to become less newsworthy. The spotlight of history is focused on later, seemingly more significant developments.

Among historians dealing with the post-Reformation era, the invisibility of the cumulative impact exerted by the new communications system is particularly marked. The intellectual and political revolutions of the seventeenth and eighteenth centuries are placed in the context not of a post-print but of a pre-industrialized society. In setting the stage for the rise of modern science, for example, the state of communications in seventeenth-century Europe is often discussed. One is told about the rise of postal systems, the building of canals, and other improvements in transport. But the previous replacement of hand-copied tables, charts, and maps by printed ones is likely to be left out of account. The significance of a growing handwritten correspondence among virtuosi[16] is frequently underlined; the more novel appearance of "open letters" addressed to scattered observers tends to be ignored. The distribution of scientific talent is often examined; the distribution of scientific publication outlets is seldom explored.[xxvii]

The same point may be made about efforts to set the stage for Enlightenment thought or for the political revolutions of early modern times.[xxviii] In attempting to explain these revolutions, shifts associated with trade routes and prices, land use and crops, status groups and classes, are discussed at length. Changes which affected duplication of maps, charts, and tables, of law books and reference works, calendars and treaties, bills and petitions are noted infrequently, if at all. The rise of the middle class and the role of the bourgeoisie is always related to the growth of a money economy; yet the rise of men of letters and the role of the intelligentsia[17] is rarely related to the expanding powers of the press. We hear much about the effects of the commercial revolution but nothing about those of the communications revolution.[xxix]

[...]

... It is difficult to deal with the advent of typography without skewing perspectives by resorting simultaneously to two incompatible models of change: one gradual and evolutionary; the other, abrupt and revolutionary. There are cogent arguments for regarding Gutenberg's invention as part of a continuously unfolding process; for presenting it (as Febvre and Martin[18] do) as one element in a larger "ensemble" of transformations. Thus, the invention and utilization of movable type may be viewed as one by-product of previous developments, such as the spread of lay literacy, and as a factor, which, in turn, helped to pave the way for later developments,

16 A group of people who are naturally extremely talented in some area, often artistic.

17 A group of well-educated, well-cultured, and influential people.

18 Lucien Febvre (1878–1956) was a French historian most famous for establishing the *Annales* school, which developed historiography as a method; Henri-Jean Martin (1924–2007) was a French historian who was influential in the development of book history as a discipline and who co-wrote *The Coming of the Book: The Impact of Printing 1450–1800* with Febvre. See their essay above, p. 15.

such as modern mass literacy. Printers and scribes copied each other's products for several decades and duplicated the same texts for the same markets during the age of incunabula. In the mind of the Italian humanists "there was no distinct line of demarcation between the manuscript book and that printed by movable type."[xxx] For at least 50 years after the shift there is no striking evidence of cultural change; one must wait until a full century after Gutenberg before the outlines of new world pictures begin to emerge into view.

It seems plausible, in the light of such considerations, to favor a gradualist, evolutionary approach. But there are also compelling reasons for regarding the shift from script to print as a large "ensemble" of changes in itself and for contrasting the talents that were mobilized and the functions that were performed by copyists and cartolai[19] on the one hand and by early printers on the other. As various studies show, historical imagination is required to bridge the gap between the age of scribes and that of the printer.[xxxi] But before it can be bridged, the gap must be acknowledged, and this acknowledgement, in turn, implies acceptance of discontinuity. A persuasive case, then, can also be made out for regarding the age of incunabula as a major historical great divide and for viewing the advent of printing as inaugurating a new cultural era in the history of Western man.

[...]

Perhaps historians are too often discouraged in advance by being reminded repeatedly of the magnitude of the task:

> The cumulative effect of the continuing revolution wrought in every aspect of human thought and activity by the invention associated with the city of Mainz is too immense ever to be fully describable. Its consequences to religion, politics, and industry are far too vast for assessment by available historians and bibliographers or by any assemblage of scholars to be foreseen at present.[xxxii]

The prospect of tackling a subject that is "far too vast" to be assessed by any present or future assemblage is apt to daunt even the most audacious individual. If it is too vast to be handled by any single scholar, however, it is, by the same token, also too vast to be avoided by any single scholar. Given its almost limitless dimensions, the cumulative effect of the "continuing revolution" is bound to impinge, one way or another, on all fields of inquiry, even highly specialized ones. Hence individual specialists, who are careful and cautious about their work, must, sooner or later, come to terms with it. Consequences entailed by a major transformation have to be reckoned with, whether we acknowledge them or not. In one guise or another, they will enter into our accounts and can best be dealt with when they do not slip in unobserved. Enough warnings have already been issued. Historians scarcely need to be alerted again to

---

19 Italian word for bookseller and stationer.

the difficulties of following Bacon's advice. But the importance of trying to surmount these difficulties does need to be stressed. Although the task may never be completed, it should, at least, be begun.

Notes

i. N. St John, book review, *The American Journal of Sociology* 73 (1967): 255.

ii. S.H. Steinberg, *Five Hundred Years of Printing* (rev. ed., Bristol: 1961), 11.

iii. Bernard Berelson and Morris Janowitz, *Reader in Public Opinion and Communication* (Glencoe, IL: Free P, 1953) contains several relevant articles.

iv. For suggestive imaginative use of the distinction between oral and literate cultures to illuminate diverse phases of Greek thought, see Eric Havelock, *Preface to Plato* (Cambridge, MA: Harvard UP, 1963). The same distinction is discussed from the viewpoint of anthropologists by Jack Goody and Ian Watt, "The Consequences of Literacy," *Comparative Studies in Society and History* V (1963): 304–45. See also collection of essays, ed. Jack Goody, *Literacy in Traditional Societies* (Cambridge: Cambridge UP, 1968) for pertinent discussion and references. Despite passing reference to the work of McLuhan and Ong in Goody's introduction, the difference between scribal culture and print culture tends to be blurred by arguments which contrast alphabetic with ideographic writing and oral with written transmission but not script with print. For an earlier, somewhat neglected essay, comparing oral with written transmission, see Solomon Gandz, "The Dawn of Literature: Prolegomena to a History of Unwritten Literature," *Osiris* VII (1939): 261–515. As noted in my preface, recent interest in African studies has stimulated a new, large, and mushrooming literature on this question. See bibliography given by Jan Vansina, *Oral Tradition: A Study in Historical Methodology*, trans. H.M. Wright (1st French version, 1961; London: Penguin Books, 1973).

v. For elaboration on this point, see my essay, "Clio and Chronos," *History and Theory*, Beiheft 6 (1966): 36–65.

vi. I have found the term "scribal culture" useful as a shorthand way of referring to such activities as producing and duplicating books, transmitting messages, reporting news, and storing data after the invention of writing and before that of movable type. "Chirographic" is more correctly opposed to "Typographic" by Father Ong but seems somewhat too recondite for my purposes. As noted in my preface, the term "print culture" is used to refer only to post-Gutenberg developments in the West. How printing affected pre-Gutenberg Asia must be left to others to investigate.

vii. The need to distinguish between the pre-Gutenberg manuscript and the post-print one has been recognized by specialists in the history of the book. For general discussion of the "archeology" of the manuscript book, see Pierre Josserand, "Les Bibliothèques," *L'Histoire et ses Méthodes*, ed. C. Samaran (*Encyclopédie de la Pléiade* XI) (Paris: Gallimard, 1961): 1087–89. One scholar has suggested reserving the term "codicology" for the study of the pre-print manuscript book and using the term "manuscriptology" for the study of mss. after Gutenberg. See the important article by Albert Gruijs, "Codicology or Archeology of the Book? False Dilemma," *Quaerendo* II (1972): 87–108, where pertinent remarks of W. Hellinga at a Dutch Philological Congress in 1952 are cited (p. 107, note 4). The absent-mindedness of most modern book users about the nature of manuscript books handled by scholars before print is brought out by E.P. Goldschmidt, *Medieval Texts and Their First Appearance in Print* (London, 1943), 9.

viii. A remarkable imaginative reconstruction of the European mentality before print is offered by Lucien Febvre, *Le Problème de l'incroyance au XVIe siècle: la Religion de Rabelais* (*Evolution de L'Humanité LIII*) (Paris: A. Michel, 1942). See especially the sections devoted to the printing press and hearsay, pp. 418–87. For another example of sensitivity to the conditions of scribal culture, see Beryl Smalley, *The English Friars and Antiquity in the Early Fourteenth Century* (Oxford: B. Blackwell, 1960), 9–10. A pioneering effort to describe how medieval literature was shaped by scribal procedures is H.J. Chaytor, *From Script to Print* (Cambridge: Cambridge UP, 1945).

ix. I have not mentioned Moslem or Byzantine centers simply because they are off limits for this book. It is a truism that scribal culture flourished more vigorously in certain centers outside Latin Christendom than within it during much of the medieval millennium.

x. Although very old, the article by Robert K. Root, "Publication before Printing," *Publications of the Modern Language Association* XXVII (1913): 417–31, still provides the best introduction to this topic. See also H.S. Bennett, "The Production and Dissemination of Vernacular Manuscripts," *The Library*, 5th ser. I (1947): 167–78.

xi. How operations performed by actual early printers differed from those imagined by bibliographers is vividly described by D.F. McKenzie, "Printers of the Mind: Some Notes on Bibliographical Theories and Printing House Practices," *Studies in Bibliography* XXII (1969): 1–75. A warning against attributing Modern standardization to early editions is offered by M.H. Black, "The Printed Bible," *Cambridge History of the Bible*, Vol. 3, *The West from the Reformation to the Present Day*, ed. S.L. Greenslade (Cambridge: Cambridge UP, 1963): 408–75. [...]

xii. Here, as elsewhere, opinions vary. For references to an "edition" of a thirteenth-century Paris Bible, see Robert Branner, "Manuscript Makers in the Mid-thirteenth Century Paris," *The Art Bulletin* XLVII (March 1966): 65–67, and Branner, "The Soissons Bible Paintshop in Thirteenth-Century Paris," *Speculum* XLIV (January 1969): 13–43.

xiii. Marshall McLuhan, *The Gutenberg Galaxy: The Making of Typographic Man* (Toronto: U of Toronto P, 1962). The same theme is elaborated in McLuhan, *Understanding Media: The Extensions of Man* (New York: McGraw-Hill, 1965). [...]

xiv. The extent to which "ours is a typographical culture" and the accompanying tendency to take the functions wrought by printing too much for granted is brought out clearly by Pierce Butler, *The Origin of Printing in Europe* (Chicago: U of Chicago P, 1940), 2–4.

xv. As noted in Eisenstein, "Clio and Chronos," p. 63, present nihilistic and chaotic aesthetic trends owe more to the preservative powers of print than is often realized. [...]

xvi. *Religio Medici* (1643), sect. 24 in Sir Thomas Browne, *The Prose of Sir Thomas Browne*, ed. Norman Endicott (New York: New York UP, 1967), 32. See also citation from Lope de Vega in Preserved Smith, *A History of Modern Culture II: The Enlightenment, 1687–1776* (New York: Henry Holt, 1974), 276. Although Smith implies that it was only in the seventeenth century that the multiplication of books began to be felt as an oppression, Erasmus had already complained about the swarms of new books. See "Festina Lente," translated from the 1508 edition of *The "Adages" of Erasmus*, by Margaret Mann Philips (ed.) (Cambridge: Cambridge UP, 1964), 182–83. This complaint probably owed something to ancient scribal literary conventions. Both Petrarch and Juvenal had, after all, complained about the number of scribblers at work in their day.

xvii. [...] The recently published Louis Philippe, *Mémoires de Louis Philippe*, 2 vols. (Paris: Plon, 1973), 1, 4 start with describing the invention of printing as perhaps "the most decisive event in the history of man" and assign it a prime role in destroying feudalism.

xviii. The present "museum-culture" veneration of manuscripts and incunabula is in marked contrast to the careless approach of earlier eras. The fact that sixteenth-century men often discarded manuscripts "like old newspapers" once a printed edition had been made (see Jean Destrez, *La 'Pecia' dans les Manuscrits Universitaires du XIIIe et du XIVe Siècle* [Paris: Éd. Vautrain, 1935], 18) or that seventeenth-century Oxford librarians sold off Shakespeare's first folio as superfluous after the third had appeared (Curt Bühler, *Fifteenth Century Book, the Scribes, the Printers, the Decorators* [Philadelphia: U of Pennsylvania P, 1960], 101, note 44) is sometimes taken to indicate a benighted contempt for manuscripts that came with printing.

See e.g. P.S. Allen, *The Age of Erasmus* (Oxford: Clarendon, 1914), 159–60. But even before Gutenberg, some humanist book-hunters showed singularly little interest in preserving the manuscript from which they copied a given text. See L.D. Reynolds and N.G. Wilson, *Scribes and Scholars* (London: Oxford UP, 1968), 116. On the other hand, as an editor working for Sweynheim and Pannartz, de Bussi complained of niggardly collectors withholding their loan of manuscripts to the firm he served because "they esteemed the art of printing to be a depreciation of their property." Beriah Botfield, *Præfationes et Epistolae Editionibus Principus Auctorum Beterum* (Cantabrigiae: E Prelo Academico, 1861), vi-vii. Ralph Franklin, "Conjectures on Rarity," *The Library Quarterly* 44 (1974): 309–31, suggests that the ethos of the "rare book room" first appears in the seventeenth century.

xix. Publications by the Society of the History of Technology during the past decade suggest the problem of squeezing Gutenberg's invention onto crowded inventories. References to printing are infrequent in the articles, reviews, and cumulative bibliographies published in *Technology and Culture*.

xx. See Michael Clapham, "Printing." *A History of Technology III From the Renaissance to the Industrial Revolution*, ed. Charles Singer, E.J. Holmyard, A.R. Hall and Trevor Williams, 4 vols. (Oxford: Clarendon, 1957), 377–411.

xxi. For English language studies of classical book production, libraries and book-trade, see Frederick G. Kenyon, *Books and Readers in Ancient Greece and Rome* (Oxford: Clarendon, 1951); Felix Reichmann, "The Book Trade at the Time of the Roman Empire," *The Library Quarterly* VIII (1938): 40–76; Rudolf Pfeiffer, *History of Classical Scholarship from the Beginnings to the End of the Hellenistic Age* (Oxford: Clarendon Press, 1968). By comparison, G.H. Putnam's *Authors and Their Public in Ancient Times* (New York: G.H. Putnam's Sons, 1894) is not worth consulting. Putnam's survey of medieval *Books and Their Makers in the Middle Ages*, 2 vols. (New York: Putnam, 1896) is old-fashioned, anecdotal, and rambling but contains some useful data (albeit in a disorganized state). Reynolds and Wilson, *Scribes and Scholars* (Oxford: Clarendon Press, 1968) is intended to explain problems of transmission to "beginners in the field of classical studies" but also serves as a most useful succinct introduction to medieval scribal culture. In addition to McMurtrie, two books by David Diringer: *The Hand Produced Book* (London: Hutchinson, 1953) and *The Illuminated Book* (London: Faber and Faber, 1953) also offer a useful general introduction. Book provisions in medieval English monasteries are covered by Knowles, *The Religious Orders in England*, 3 vols. (Cambridge: Cambridge UP, 1948–1959), II, 331–51. For examples of the smooth transition from the late medieval manuscript book-trade to the early printed book-trade, see Hellmut Lehmann-Haupt, "Heritage of the Manuscript," *A History of the Printed Book*, ed. Lawrence C. Wroth (The Dolphin no. 3) (New York: Ltd. Editions Club, 1938) and J.H. Harrington, "The Production and Distribution of Books in Western Europe to the Year 1500" (Unpublished Dissertation, Columbia U, 1956).

xxii. For discussion of far-flung markets and pioneering publicity developed by expanding firms during the first half century of printing, see Albert Ehrman, "The Fifteenth Century," in Ehrman and Pollard, *The Distribution of Books by Catalogue* (Cambridge: Roxburghe Club, 1965). The use of printers' account books to illustrate facets of early capitalism is exemplified by Edler de Roover's articles, "Cost Accounting in the Sixteenth Century," *Accounting Review* 12 (1937): 226–37; "New Facets on the Financing and Marketing of Early Printed Books," *Bulletin of the Business Historical* Society 27.4 (Dec. 1953): 222–30; and by F. Geldner, "Das Rechnungsbuch des Speyrer ... Grossbuchhandlers Peter Drach," *Archiv fur Geschichte des Buchwesens* V (Frankfurt, 1962), 1–195.

xxiii. Edgar Zilsel, "The Origins of Gilbert's Scientific Method," *Journal of the History of Ideas* II (1941): 24.

xxiv. Frances Yates, *The Art of Memory* (London: Routledge and Paul, 1966), 374.

xxv. Of his *or her* many roles. That daughters and widows of printers often took over the family enterprise is noted by Lenkey and others. [...]

xxvi. See part 3, volume II [of Eisenstein's book] below for attempts to suggest how the so-called "external" advent of printing may be related to the so-called "internal" history of science. Issues pertaining to historiography are touched on at various points in chap. 3 and in my essay, "Clio and Chronos" [*Clio and Chronos: An Essay on the Making and Breaking of the History-book Time* (Middletown, CT: Wesleyan UP, 1966)], but full coverage would require another book.
xxvii. See sections on "improvements in communication" in G.N. Clark, *The Seventeenth Century* (rev. ed., Oxford: Clarendon P, 1947), 47–60, 330–33. See also treatment of slide rules and logarithms (p. 235), education (chap. 18) and literature (chap. 20) in the same work. Clark's approach has been carried over into the influential work of Robert K. Merton on the sociology of science and hence is still noteworthy despite its age. [...]
xxviii. Since this was written there have appeared many volumes sponsored by two sections of the *École Pratique des Hautes Études* (the IVe Section publications by H.-J. Martin and his colleagues and those of the VIe Section by Robert Mandrou, François Furet and their colleagues), which suggest that the history of the book is being broadened to encompass cultural and political trends. See essays in *Livre et Société au XVIIIe Siècle* and review articles by Alphonse Dupront, "Livre et Culture dans la Société Français au XVIIIe Siècle—Réflexions sur une Enquête," *Annales: Economies Sociétiés Civilisations* (1965): 867–98, Louis Trénard, "L'Histoire des Mentalités Collectives: Les Livres: Bilan et Perspective," *Revue d'Histoire Moderne et Contemporaine* 15 (1968): 691–703, Robert Mandrou, "Le Livre: Ce Ferment," *Revue Française d'Histoire du Livre* I (1971), 1–9. But in my view even these new studies muffle the impact of print in a manner suggested by Dupront's comment: "Le Livre retarde," 895. More explosive implications emerge from Robert Darnton's many pioneering articles [...]. For updated review of literature to 1976 see Raymond Birn, "Livre et Société after ten years: Formation of a discipline," *Studies on Voltaire and the Eighteenth Century* XXIX, ed. T. Besterman (Geneva: Institut et Musée Voltaire, 1964).

xxix. This statement, made in 1970, now must make room for a welcome exception. Joseph Klaits's *Printed Propaganda under Louis XIV* (Princeton, NJ: Princeton UP, 1976) contains a section on "The Sun King and the Communications Revolution." This entire monograph is devoted to the implications of new developments which came after print. In applying the term "communications revolution" to specifically seventeenth-century phenomena, such as the new periodical press, however, Klaits still uses the term more narrowly than I do in this book.
xxx. Hugh H. Davis, book review, *Renaissance Quarterly* XXVIII (Autumn 1973), 353. The Italian book under review shows that the same word "codex" was used for both.
xxxi. See e.g. works by H.J. Chaytor, E.P. Goldschmidt, and Lucien Febvre cited above.
xxxii. Stanley Morison, "The Learned Press as an Institution," *Bibliotheca Docet: Festgabe für Carl Wehmer*, ed. S. Joose (Amsterdam: Verlag der Erasmus-Buchhandlung, 1963), 153.

16.

Robert Darnton, "What Is the History of Books?" *The Kiss of Lamourette: Reflections in Cultural History.* New York: W.W. Norton, 1990. 107–35

Robert Darnton (b. 1939) was Professor of European History at Princeton University before becoming Carl H. Pforzheimer University Professor and the Director of Harvard University Library. He is widely regarded as one of the world's leading experts on revolutionary France and as a pioneer in the field of book history. He has written extensively on radical and popular literature in pre-revolutionary France; on slander and censorship in eighteenth-century France; and, more recently, on electronic publishing and the legal controversy surrounding Google Books. In the following essay, Darnton introduces the concept of the "communications circuit," offering his model for the study of book history as a circuit that runs from author to publisher to printer, distributor, bookseller, and reader. The essay was first published in 1982 and was based on the "biography of a book" he presented in *The Business of Enlightenment: A Publishing History of the Encyclopédie* (1979). Now over thirty years old, the framework Darnton establishes in the essay continues to be as influential today as when it was first introduced, although a new model has been put forward by scholars Thomas R. Adams and Nicolas Barker.[1]

Darnton's essay, part of a larger collection of essays that examine media history, treats book history as a newly established field of scholarly inquiry with "a distinct scholarly identity." Like Eisenstein (see above, pp. 215–230), he notes that attempts to understand the history of the book have often suffered from fragmentation. One of his aims in proposing a generalizable model that can encompass the life cycle of most printed books is "to show how [book history's] disparate segments can be brought together within a single conceptual scheme" (p. 241). He famously characterizes the new field of book history as "interdisciplinarity run riot," and emphasizes its capaciousness; book history, "[b]y its very nature," he says, "must be international in scale and interdisciplinary in method" (p. 247).

---

1 In this new model, Adams and Barker shift attention from the human actors involved in the "communication circuit" to the book itself, arguing that there are five key events in the life cycle of a book (publishing, manufacture, distribution, reception, and survival). See "A New Model for the Study of the Book," *A Potencie of Life: Books in Society*, ed. Nicolas Barker (London: British Library, 1993), 5–43.

What Is the History of Books?

"*Histoire du livre*" in France, "*Geschichte des Buchwesens*" in Germany, "history of books" or "of the book" in English-speaking countries—its name varies from place to place, but everywhere it is being recognized as an important new discipline. It might even be called the social and cultural history of communication by print, if that were not such a mouthful, because its purpose is to understand how ideas were transmitted through print and how exposure to the printed word affected the thought and behavior of mankind during the last 500 years. Some Book Historians pursue their subject deep into the period before the invention of **movable type**. Some students of printing concentrate on newspapers, **broadsides**, and other forms besides the book. The field can be extended and expanded in many ways; but for the most part, it concerns books since the time of **Gutenberg**, an area of research that has developed so rapidly during the last few years that it seems likely to win a place alongside fields like the history of science and the history of art in the **canon** of scholarly disciplines.

Whatever the history of books may become in the future, its past shows how a field of knowledge can take on a distinct scholarly identity. It arose from the convergence of several disciplines on a common set of problems, all of them having to do with the process of communication. Initially, the problems took the form of concrete questions in unrelated branches of scholarship: What were Shakespeare's original texts? What caused the French Revolution? What is the connection between culture and social stratification? In pursuing those questions, scholars found themselves crossing paths in a no-man's land located at the intersection of a half-dozen fields of study. They decided to constitute a field of their own and to invite in historians, literary scholars, sociologists, librarians, and anyone else who wanted to understand the book as a force in history. The history of books began to acquire its own journals, research centers, conferences, and lecture circuits. It accumulated tribal elders as well as Young Turks.[2] And although it has not yet developed passwords or secret handshakes or its own population of PhDs, its adherents can recognize one another by the glint in their eyes. They belong to a common cause, one of the few sectors in the human sciences where there is a mood of expansion and a flurry of fresh ideas.

To be sure, the history of the history of books did not begin yesterday. It stretches back to the scholarship of the Renaissance, if not beyond; and it began in earnest during the nineteenth century when the study of books as material objects led to the rise of **analytical bibliography** in England. But the current work represents a departure from the established strains of scholarship, which may be traced to their nineteenth-century origins through back issues of *The Library*[i] and *Börsenblatt für den Deutschen Buchhandel*[ii] or theses in the Ecole des Chartes.[3] The new strain developed during the 1960s in France, where it took root in

2 Specifically, members of the Turkish nationalist reform party in the early twentieth century who promoted the reform of the Turkish monarchy; but also used more generally (as Darnton does here) to suggest any group eager for progressive change.

3 Part of the University of Paris, a French institution providing education and training for archivists and librarians.

institutions like the Ecole Pratique des Hautes Etudes[4] and spread through publications like *L'Apparition du livre* (1958), by Lucien Febvre and Henri-Jean Martin, and *Livre et société dans la France du XVIIIe siècle* (two volumes 1965 and 1970) by a group connected with the VIe section of the Ecole Pratique des Hautes Etudes.

The new Book Historians brought the subject within the range of themes studied by the "*Annales* school"[5] of socio-economic history. Instead of dwelling on fine points of **bibliography**, they tried to uncover the general pattern of book production and consumption over long stretches of time. They compiled statistics from requests for *privilèges* (a kind of **copyright**), analyzed the contents of private **libraries**, and traced ideological currents through neglected genres like the *bibliothèque bleue* (primitive paperbacks). Rare books and fine **editions** had no interest for them; they concentrated instead on the most ordinary sort of books because they wanted to discover the literary experience of ordinary readers. They put familiar phenomena like the Counter Reformation[6] and the Enlightenment[7] in an unfamiliar light by showing how much traditional culture outweighed the avant-garde in the literary fare of the entire society. Although they did not come up with a firm set of conclusions, they demonstrated the importance of asking new questions, using new methods, and tapping new sources.[iii]

[...]

To get some distance from interdisciplinarity run riot, and to see the subject as a whole, it might be useful to propose a general model for analyzing the way books come into being and spread through society. To be sure, conditions have varied so much from place to place and from time to time since the invention of movable type that it would be vain to expect the biography of every book to conform to the same pattern. But printed books generally pass through roughly the same life cycle. It could be described as a communications circuit that runs from the author to the **publisher** (if the bookseller does not assume that role), the **printer**, the shipper, the **bookseller**, and the reader. The reader completes the circuit because he influences the author both before and after the act of composition. Authors are readers themselves. By reading and associating with other readers and writers, they form notions of genre and style and a general sense of the literary enterprise, which affects their texts, whether they are composing Shakespearean sonnets or directions for assembling radio kits. A writer may respond in his writing to criticisms of his previous work or anticipate reactions that his text will elicit. He addresses

4 Like the Ecole des Chartes, an elite higher education institution in France with a department devoted to historical and philological studies.

5 A school of historians in France that began in the late nineteenth century and continues to be influential to this day, it established a historiography (a method of studying history) that integrates the use of social scientific methods and that emphasizes social rather than political themes.

6 The Catholic revival, beginning in the mid-sixteenth century, which sought to strengthen the Catholic Church in the wake of the Protestant Reformation, which began in 1517.

7 Referring to the intellectual movement of the late seventeenth and eighteenth centuries amongst European elites, who sought to use rational thought to advance society and knowledge.

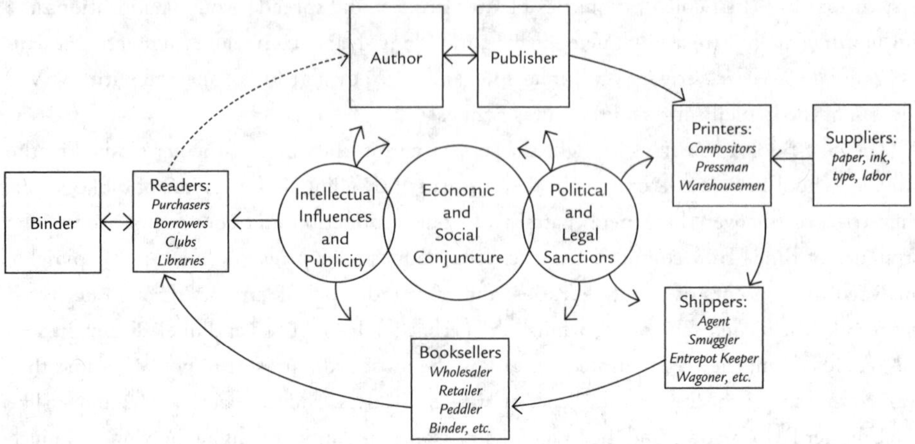

Fig. 3.1: The communications circuit. Reprinted by permission of W.W. Norton & Company, Inc. and Faber & Faber, UK.

implicit readers and hears from explicit reviewers. So the circuit runs full cycle. It transmits messages, transforming them en route, as they pass from thought to writing to printed characters and back to thought again. Book History concerns each phase of this process and the process as a whole, in all its variations over space and time and in all its relations with other systems, economic, social, political, and cultural, in the surrounding environment.

That is a large undertaking. To keep their task within manageable proportions, Book Historians generally cut into one segment of the communications circuit and analyze it according to the procedures of a single discipline—printing, for example, which they study by means of analytical bibliography. But the parts do not take on their full significance unless they are related to the whole, and some holistic view of the book as a means of communication seems necessary if Book History is to avoid being fragmented into esoteric[8] specializations cut off from each other by arcane techniques and mutual misunderstanding. The model shown in Fig. 3.1 provides a way of envisaging the entire communication process. With minor adjustments, it should apply to all periods in the history of the book (**manuscript** books and book illustrations will have to be considered elsewhere), but I would like to discuss it in connection with the period I know best, the eighteenth century, and to take it up phase by phase, showing how each phase is related to (1) other activities that a given person has underway at a given point in the circuit, (2) other persons at the time point in other circuits, (3) other persons at other points in the same circuit, and (4) other elements in society. The first three considerations bear directly on the transmission of a text, while the last concerns outside influences, which could vary endlessly. For the sake of simplicity, I have reduced the latter to the three general categories in the center of the diagram.

Models have a way of freezing human beings out of history. To put some flesh and blood on this one, and to show how it can make sense of an actual case, I will apply it to the publishing

8 Any doctrine or theory "designed for, or appropriate to, an inner circle of advanced or privileged disciplines" (*OED*).

history of Voltaire's *Questions sur l'Encyclopédie*,[9] an important work of the Enlightenment, and one that touched the lives of a great many eighteenth-century bookmen. One could study the circuit of its transmission at any point—at the stage of its composition, for example, when Voltaire shaped its text and orchestrated its diffusion in order to promote his campaign against religious intolerance, as his biographers have shown; or at its printing, a stage in which bibliographical analysis helps to establish the multiplication of editions; or at the point of its assimilation in libraries, where, according to statistical studies by literary historians, Voltaire's works occupied an impressive share of shelf space.[iv] But I would like to consider the least familiar link in the diffusion process, the role of the bookseller, taking Isaac-Pierre Rigaud of Montpellier as an example, and working through the four considerations mentioned above.[v]

I.

On August 16, 1770, Rigaud ordered 30 copies of the nine-volume **octavo** edition of the *Questions*, which the Société typographique de Neuchâtel (STN) had recently begun to print in the Prussian principality of Neuchâtel on the Swiss side of the French-Swiss border. Rigaud generally preferred to read at least a few pages of a new book before stocking it, but he considered the *Questions* such a good bet that he risked making a fairly large order for it, sight unseen. He did not have any personal sympathy for Voltaire. On the contrary, he deplored the philosophe's tendency to tinker with his books, adding and amending passages while cooperating with **pirated** editions behind the backs of the original publishers. Such practices produced complaints from customers, who objected to receiving inferior (or insufficiently audacious) texts. "It is astonishing that at the end of his career M. de Voltaire cannot refrain from duping booksellers," Rigaud complained to the STN. "It would not matter if all these little ruses, frauds, and deceits were blamed on the author. But unfortunately the printers and still more the retail booksellers are usually held responsible."[vi] Voltaire made life hard for booksellers, but he sold well.

There was nothing Voltairean about most of the other books in Rigaud's shop. His sales **catalogues** show that he specialized somewhat in medical books, which were always in demand in Montpellier, thanks to the university's famous faculty of medicine. Rigaud also kept a discreet line of Protestant works, because Montpellier lay in Huguenot[10] territory. And when the authorities looked the other way, he brought in a few shipments of forbidden books.[vii] But he generally supplied his customers with books of all kinds, which he drew from an inventory worth at least 45,000 livres, the largest in Montpellier and probably in all Languedoc, according to a report from the intendant's *subdélégué*.[viii]

Rigaud's way of ordering from the STN illustrates the character of his business. Unlike other large provincial dealers, who speculated on a hundred or more copies of a book when they smelled a bestseller, he rarely ordered more than a half dozen copies of a single work. He read

9 Written between 1770 and 1774, Voltaire's longest work (the modern Oxford edition is in seven volumes) provides a series of essays on topics including religion, history, art, and literature, in response to Diderot and D'Alembert's *Encyclopédie* (1751–72), a dictionary famous for its representation of Enlightenment views.

10 Members of the Protestant Reformed Church of France during the sixteenth and seventeenth centuries.

widely, consulted his customers, took soundings by means of his commercial correspondence, and studied the catalogues that the STN and his other suppliers sent to him (by 1785 the STN's catalogue included 750 titles). Then he chose about 10 titles and ordered just enough copies of them to make up a crate of 50 pounds, the minimum weight for shipment at the cheaper rate charged by the wagoners.[11] If the books sold well, he re-ordered them; but he usually kept his orders rather small, and made four or five of them a year. In this way, he conserved capital, minimized risks, and built up such a large and varied stock that his shop became a clearinghouse for literary demand of every kind in the region.

The pattern of Rigaud's orders, which stands out clearly from the STN's account books, shows that he offered his customers a little of everything—travel books, histories, novels, religious works, and the occasional scientific or philosophical treatise. Instead of following his own preferences, he seemed to transmit demand fairly accurately and to live according to the accepted wisdom of the book trade, which one of the STN's other customers summarized as follows: "The best book for a bookseller is a book that sells."[ix] Given his cautious style of business, Rigaud's decision to place an advance order for thirty 9-volume sets of the *Questions sur l'Encyclopédie* seems especially significant. He would not have put so much money on a single work if he had not felt certain of the demand—and his later orders show that he had calculated correctly. On June 19, 1772, soon after receiving the last shipment of the last volume, Rigaud ordered another dozen sets; and he ordered two more two years later, although by then the STN had exhausted its stock. It had printed a huge edition, 2500 copies, approximately twice its usual press **run**, and the booksellers had fallen all over themselves in the rush to purchase it. So Rigaud's purchase was no aberration. It expressed a current of Voltaireanism that had spread far and wide among the reading public of the Old Regime.[12]

II.

How does the purchase of the *Questions* look when examined from the perspective of Rigaud's relations with the other booksellers of Montpellier? A book-trade **almanac** listed nine of them in 1777:[x]

Printer-Booksellers:	Aug. Franç. Rochard
	Jean Martel
Booksellers:	Isaac-Pierre Rigaud
	J.B. Faure
	Albert Pons
	Tournel
	Bascon
	Cézary
	Fontanel

11 A person who transports goods (here books) by wagon.

12 Referring to the political regime in place before the French Revolution, which began in 1789.

But according to a report from a traveling salesman of the STN, there were only seven.[xi] Rigaud and Pons had merged and completely dominated the local trade; Cézary and Faure scraped along in the middle ranks; and the rest teetered on the brink of bankruptcy in precarious boutiques. The occasional **binder** and under-the-cloak peddler also provided a few books, most of them illegal, to the more adventuresome readers of the city. For example, the demoiselle[13] Bringand, known as "the students' mother," stocked some forbidden fruit "under the bed on the room to the right on the second floor," according to the report of a raid that was engineered by the established booksellers.[xii] The trade in most provincial cities fell into the same pattern, which can be envisaged as a series of concentric circles: at the center, one or two firms tried to monopolize the market; around the margin, a few small dealers survived by specializing in **chapbooks** and old volumes, by setting up reading clubs (*cabinets littéraires*) and **binderies**, or by peddling their wares in the back country; and beyond the fringe of legality, adventurers moved in and out of the market, selling forbidden literature.

When he ordered his shipment of the *Questions*, Rigaud was consolidating his position at the center of the local trade. His merger with Pons in 1770 provided him with enough capital and assets to ride out the mishaps—delayed shipments, defaulting debtors, liquidity crises—that often upset smaller businesses. Also, he played rough. When Cézary, one of the middling dealers, failed to meet some of his payments in 1781, Rigaud drove him out of business by organizing a cabal of his creditors. They refused to let him re-schedule the payments, had him thrown in prison for debt, and forced him to sell off his stock at an auction, where they kept down the prices and gobbled up the books. By dispensing **patronage**, Rigaud controlled most of Montpellier's binderies; and by exerting pressure on the binders, he produced delays and snags in the affairs of the other booksellers. In 1789 only one of them remained, Abraham Fontanel, and he stayed solvent only by maintaining a *cabinet littéraire*, "which provokes terrible fits of jealousy by the sieur Rigaud, who wants to be the only one left and who shows his hatred of me every day,"[xiii] as Fontanel confided to the STN.

Rigaud did not eliminate his competitors simply by outdoing them in the dog-eat-dog style of commercial capitalism of early modern France. His letters, theirs, and the correspondence of many other booksellers show that the book trade contracted during the late 1770s and 1780s. In hard times, the big booksellers squeezed out the small, and the tough outlasted the tender. Rigaud had been a tough customer from the very beginning of his relations with the STN. He had ordered his copies of the *Questions* from Neuchâtel, where the STN was printing a pirated edition, rather than from Geneva, where Voltaire's regular printer, Gabriel Cramer, was producing the original, because he had extracted better terms. He also demanded better service, especially when the other booksellers in Montpellier, who had dealt with Cramer, received their copies first. The delay produced a volley of letters from Rigaud to the STN. Why couldn't the STN work faster? Didn't it know that it was making him lose customers to his competitors? He would have to order from Cramer in the future if it could not provide quicker shipments at a lower price. When volumes one through three finally arrived from Neuchâtel, volumes four

13 A young woman.

through six from Geneva were already on sale in the other shops. Rigaud compared the texts, word for word, and found that the STN's edition contained none of the additional material that it had claimed to receive on the sly from Voltaire. So how could he push the theme of "additions and corrections" in his sales talk? The recriminations flew thick and fast in the mail between Montpellier and Neuchâtel, and they showed that Rigaud meant to exploit every inch of every advantage that he could gain on his competitors. More important, they also revealed that the *Questions* were being sold all over Montpellier, even though in principle they could not circulate legally in France. Far from being confined to the under-the-cloak trade of marginal characters like "the students' mother," Voltaire's work turned out to be a prize item in the scramble for profits at the very heart of the established book trade. When dealers like Rigaud scratched and clawed for their shipments of it, Voltaire could be sure that he was succeeding in his attempt to propel his ideas through the main lines of France's communications system.

III.

The role of Voltaire and Cramer in the diffusion process raises the problem of how Rigaud's operation fit into the other stages in the life cycle of the *Questions*. Rigaud knew that he was not getting a first edition; the STN had sent a circular letter to him and its other main customers explaining that it would reproduce Cramer's text, but with corrections and additions provided by the author himself, so that its version would be superior to the original. One of the STN's directors had visited Voltaire at Ferney[14] in April 1770 and had returned with a promise that Voltaire would touch up the printed **sheets** he was to receive from Cramer and then would forward them to Neuchâtel for a pirated edition.[xiv] Voltaire often played such tricks. They provided a way to improve the quality and increase the quantity of his books, and therefore served his main purpose—which was not to make money, for he did not sell his prose to the printers, but to spread Enlightenment. The profit motive kept the rest of the system going, however. So when Cramer got wind of the STN's attempt to raid his market, he protested to Voltaire, Voltaire retracted his promise to the STN, and the STN had to settle for a delayed version of the text, which it received from Ferney, but with only minimal additions and corrections.[xv] In fact, this setback did not hurt its sales, because the market had plenty of room to absorb editions, not only the STN's but also one that Marc Michel Rey produced in Amsterdam, and probably others as well. The booksellers had their choice of suppliers, and they chose according to whatever marginal advantage they could obtain on matters of price, quality, speed, and reliability in delivery. Rigaud dealt regularly with publishers in Paris, Lyon, Rouen, Avignon, and Geneva. He played them off against each other and sometimes ordered the same book from two or three of them so as to be certain of getting it before his competitors did. By working several circuits at the same time, he increased his room for maneuver. But in the case of the *Questions*, he was out-maneuvered and had to receive his goods from the circuitous Voltaire-Cramer-Voltaire-STN route.

14 Voltaire built his château in Ferney, France, closer to Geneva, Switzerland; he could easily move between the two countries when in trouble with the authorities of one.

That route merely took the copy from the author to the printer. For the printed sheets to reach Rigaud in Montpellier from the STN's shop in Neuchâtel, they had to wind their way through one of the most complex stages in the book's circuit. They could follow two main routes. One led from Neuchâtel to Geneva, Turin, Nice (which was not yet French), and Marseilles. It had the advantage of skirting French territory—and therefore the danger of confiscation—but it involved huge detours and expenses. The books had to be lugged over the Alps and pass through a whole army of middlemen—shipping agents, bargemen, wagoners, entrepôt[15] keepers, ship captains, and dockers—before they arrived in Rigaud's storeroom. The best Swiss shippers claimed they could get a crate to Nice in a month for thirteen livres, eight sous per hundredweight;[16] but their estimates proved to be far too low. The direct route from Neuchâtel to Lyon and down the Rhône was fast, cheap, and easy—but dangerous. The crates had to be sealed at their point of entry into France and inspected by the booksellers' guild and the royal book inspector in Lyon, then re-shipped and inspected once more in Montpellier.[xvi]

Always cautious, Rigaud asked the STN to ship the first volumes of the *Questions* by the roundabout route, because he knew he could rely on his agent in Marseilles, Joseph Coulomb, to get the books into France without mishap. They left on December 9, 1771, but did not arrive until after March, when the first three volumes of Cramer's edition were already being sold by Rigaud's competitors. The second and third volumes arrived in July, but loaded down with shipping charges and damaged by rough handling. "It seems that we are five or six thousand leagues apart," Rigaud complained, adding that he regretted he had not given his business to Cramer, whose shipments had already reached volume six.[xvii] By this time, the STN was wor- 239
ried enough about losing customers throughout southern France to set up a smuggling operation in Lyon. Their man, a marginal book-dealer named Joseph-Louis Berthoud, got volumes four and five past the guild inspectors, but then his business collapsed in bankruptcy; and to make matters worse, the French government imposed a tax of 60 livres per hundredweight on all book imports. The STN fell back on the Alpine route, offering to get its shipments as far as Nice for 15 livres per hundredweight if Rigaud would pay the rest of the expenses, including the import duty. But Rigaud considered the duty such a heavy blow to the international trade that he suspended all his orders with foreign suppliers. The new tariff policy had made it prohibitively expensive to disguise illegal books as legal ones and to pass them through normal commercial channels.

In December, the STN's agent in Nice, Jacques Deandreis, somehow got a shipment of volume six of the *Questions* to Rigaud through the port of Sète, which was supposed to be closed to book imports. Then the French government, realizing that it had nearly destroyed the foreign book trade, lowered the tariff to 26 livres per hundredweight. Rigaud proposed sharing the cost with his suppliers: he would pay one third if they would pay two thirds. This proposal suited the STN, but in the spring of 1772 Rigaud decided that the Nice route was too expensive to

15 A trading post where merchandise can be imported and exported without paying import duties.

16 "An avoirdupois weight equal to 112 pounds." An "avoirdupois weight" is the "standard system of weights used, in Great Britain, for all goods except the precious metals, precious stones, and medicines" (*OED*).

be used under any conditions. Having heard enough complaints from its other customers to reach the same conclusion, the STN dispatched one of its directors to Lyon, and he persuaded a more dependable Lyonnais dealer, J.-M. Barret, to clear its shipments through the local guild and forward them to its provincial clients. Thanks to this arrangement, the last three volumes of Rigaud's *Questions* arrived safely in the summer.

It had required continuous effort and considerable expense to get the entire order to Montpellier, and Rigaud and the STN did not stop realigning their supply routes once they had completed this transaction. Because economic and political pressures kept shifting, they had constantly to readjust their arrangements within the complex world of middlemen, who linked printing houses with bookshops and often determined, in the last analysis, what literature reached French readers.

How the readers assimilated their books cannot be determined. Bibliographical analysis of all the copies that can be located would show what varieties of the text were available. A study of notarial **archives** in Montpellier might indicate how many copies turned up in inheritances, and statistics drawn from auction catalogues might make it possible to estimate the number in substantial private libraries. But given the present state of documentation, one cannot know who Voltaire's readers were or how they responded to his text. Reading remains the most difficult stage to study in the circuit that books follow.

IV.

All stages were affected by the social, economic, political, and intellectual conditions of the time; but for Rigaud, these general influences made themselves felt within a local context. He sold books in a city of 31,000 inhabitants. Despite an important textile industry, Montpellier was essentially an old-fashioned administrative and religious center, richly endowed with cultural institutions, including a university, an academy of sciences, twelve Masonic lodges, and 16 monastic communities. And because it was a seat of the provincial estates of Languedoc and an intendancy, and had as well an array of courts, the city had a large population of lawyers and royal officials. If they resembled their counterparts in other provincial centers,[xviii] they probably provided Rigaud with a good many of his customers and probably had a taste for Enlightenment literature. He did not discuss their social background in his correspondence, but he noted that they clamored for the works of Voltaire, Rousseau, and Raynal.[17] They subscribed heavily to the *Encyclopédie*, and even asked for atheistic treatises like *Système de la nature*[18]

17 Jean-Jacques Rousseau (1712–78) was an Enlightenment philosopher born in Geneva, perhaps most famous for his concept of the social contract; Guillaume-Thomas Raynal (1713–96) was a French political and historical writer.

18 Published anonymously in 1770 by Paul Henri Thiry, Baron d'Holbach (1723–89), the book explicitly denies the existence of God; a work of philosophical materialism, it argues that there is no soul and that the universe operates according to deterministic laws of nature.

and *Philosophie de la nature*.[19] Montpellier was no intellectual backwater, and it was good book territory. "The book trade is quite extensive in this town," an observer remarked in 1768. "The booksellers have kept their shops well stocked ever since the inhabitants developed a taste for having libraries."[xix]

These favorable conditions prevailed when Rigaud ordered his *Questions*. But hard times set in during the early 1770s; and in the 1780s Rigaud, like most booksellers, complained of a severe decline in his trade. The whole French economy contracted during those years, according to the standard account of C.E. Labrousse.[xx] Certainly, the state's finances went into a tailspin: hence the disastrous book tariff of 1771, which belonged to Terray's unsuccessful attempt to reduce the deficit accumulated during the Seven Years' War.[20] The government also tried to stamp out pirated and forbidden books, first by more severe police work in 1771–74, then by a general reform of the book trade in 1777. These measures eventually ruined Rigaud's commerce with the STN and with the other publishing houses that had grown up around France's borders during the prosperous mid-century years. Foreign publishers produced both original editions of books that could not pass the censorship in Paris and pirated editions of books put out by the Parisian publishers. Because the Parisians had acquired a virtual monopoly over the legal publishing industry, their rivals in the provinces formed alliances with the foreign houses and looked the other way when shipments from abroad arrived for inspection in the provincial guild halls (*chambres syndicales*). Under Louis XIV [r. 1643–1715], the government had used the Parisian guild as an instrument to suppress the illegal trade: but under Louis XV [r. 1715–74] it became increasingly lax, until a new era of severity began with the fall of Choiseul's ministry (December 1770). Thus Rigaud's relations with the STN fit perfectly into an economic and political pattern that had prevailed in the book trade since the early eighteenth century and that began to fall apart just as the first crates of the *Questions* were making their way between Neuchâtel and Montpellier.

Other patterns might show up in other research, for the model need not be applied in this manner, nor need it be applied at all. I am not arguing that Book History should be written according to a standard formula but trying to show how its disparate segments can be brought together within a single conceptual scheme. Different Book Historians might prefer different schemata. They might concentrate on the book trade of all Languedoc, as Madeleine Ventre has done; or on the general bibliography of Voltaire, as Giles Barber, Jeroom Vercruysse, and others are doing; or on the overall pattern of book production in eighteenth-century France, in the manner of François Furet and Robert Estivals.[xxi] But however they define their subject, they will not draw out its full significance unless they relate it to all the elements that worked together as a circuit for transmitting texts. To make the point clearer, I will go over the model

19 First published by Jean-Baptiste-Claude Delisle de Sales (1714–1812) in 1770. Sales challenged the biblical dating of the earth as 6,000 years old. He was a good friend of Voltaire's.

20 The war fought between European powers between 1756 and 1763, which included colonial conflict in the New World, India, and the Philippines.

circuit once more, noting questions that have been investigated successfully or that seem ripe for further research.

i. Authors

Despite the proliferation of biographies of great writers, the basic conditions of authorship remain obscure for most periods of history. At what point did writers free themselves from the patronage of wealthy noblemen and the state in order to live by their pens? What was the nature of a literary career, and how was it pursued? How did writers deal with publishers, printers, booksellers, reviewers, and one another? Until those questions are answered, we will not have a full understanding of the transmission of texts. Voltaire was able to manipulate secret alliances with pirate publishers because he did not depend on writing for a living. A century later, Zola proclaimed that a writer's independence came from selling his prose to the highest bidder.[xxii] How did this transformation take place?

[...]

ii. Publishers

The key role of publishers is now becoming clearer, thanks to articles appearing in the *Journal of Publishing History* and **monographs** like Martin Lowry's *The World of Aldus Manutius*, Robert Patten's *Charles Dickens and His Publishers*, and Gary Stark's *Entrepreneurs of Ideology: Neoconservative Publishers in Germany, 1890–1933*. But the evolution of the publisher as a distinct figure in contrast to the master bookseller and the printer still needs systematic study. Historians have barely begun to tap the papers of publishers, although they are the richest of all sources for the history of books. The archives of the Cotta Verlag[21] in Marbach, for example, contain at least 150,000 documents, yet they have only been skimmed for references to Goethe, Schiller, and other famous writers.[22] Further investigation almost certainly would turn up a great deal of information about the book as a force in nineteenth-century Germany. How did publishers draw up contracts with authors, build alliances with booksellers, negotiate with political authorities, and handle finances, supplies, shipments, and publicity? The answers to those questions would carry the history of books deep into the territory of social, economic, and political history, to their mutual benefit.

The Project for Historical Biobibliography at Newcastle upon Tyne and the Institut de Littérature et de Techniques Artistiques de Masse at Bordeaux illustrate the directions that such interdisciplinary work has already taken. The Bordeaux group has tried to trace books

---

21 A German publishing house, in operation from 1659 and associated with Goethe and Schiller (see note below).

22 Johann Wolfgang von Goethe (1749–1832) was a German writer heavily associated with Romanticism; Friedrich Schiller (1759–1805) was a German writer interested in aesthetics.

through different distribution systems in order to uncover the literary experience of different groups in contemporary France.[xxiii] The researchers in Newcastle have studied the diffusion process through quantitative analysis of **subscription** lists, which were widely used in the sales campaigns of British publishers from the early seventeenth to the early nineteenth centuries.[xxiv] Similar work could be done on publishers' catalogues and prospectuses, which have been collected in research centers like the Newberry Library. The whole subject of book advertising needs investigation. One could learn a great deal about attitudes toward books and the context of their use by studying the way they were presented—the strategy of the appeal, the values invoked by the phrasing—in all kinds of publicity, from journal notices to wall posters. American historians have used newspaper advertisements to map the spread of the printed word into the back reaches of colonial society.[xxv] By consulting the papers of publishers, they could make deeper inroads in the nineteenth and twentieth centuries.[xxvi] Unfortunately, however, publishers usually treat their archives as garbage. Although they save the occasional letter from a famous author, they throw away account books and commercial correspondence, which usually are the most important sources of information for the Book Historian. The Center for the Book in the Library of Congress is now compiling a guide to publishers' archives. If they can be preserved and studied, they might provide a different perspective on the whole course of American history.

iii. Printers

The printing shop is far better known than the other stages in the production and diffusion of 243
books because it has been a favorite subject of study in the field of analytical bibliography, whose purpose, as defined by R.B. McKerrow and Philip Gaskell, is "to elucidate the transmission of texts by explaining the processes of book production."[xxvii] Bibliographers have made important contributions to textual criticism, especially in Shakespearean scholarship, by building inferences backward from the structure of a book to the process of its printing and hence to an original text, such as the missing Shakespeare manuscripts. That line of reasoning has been undercut recently by D.F. McKenzie.[xxviii] But even if they can never reconstruct an Ur-Shakespeare,[23] bibliographers can demonstrate the existence of different editions of a text and of different states of an edition, a necessary skill in diffusion studies. Their techniques also make it possible to decipher the records of printers and so have opened up a new, archival phase in the history of printing. Thanks to the work of McKenzie, Leon Voet, Raymond de Roover, and Jacques Rychner, we now have a clear picture of how printing shops operated throughout the **handpress** period (roughly 1500–1800).[xxix] More work needs to be done on later periods, and new questions could be asked: How did printers calculate costs and organize production, especially after the spread of job printing and journalism? How did book budgets change after the introduction of machine-made paper in the first decade of the nineteenth century and **Linotype** in the 1880s? How did the technological changes affect the management of labor? And what part did journeymen[24]

---

23 "Ur" refers to the earliest, original form of something.

24 Someone who has completed his apprenticeship but is not yet considered a master of his trade.

printers, an unusually articulate and militant sector of the working class, play in labor history? Analytical bibliography may seem arcane to the outsider, but it could make a great contribution to social as well as literary history, especially if it were seasoned with a reading of printers' manuals and autobiographies, beginning with those of Thomas Platter, Thomas Gent, N.E. Restif de la Bretonne, Benjamin Franklin, and Charles Manby Smith.[25]

iv. Shippers

Little is known about the way books reached bookstores from printing shops. The wagon, the canal barge, the merchant vessel, the post office, and the railroad may have influenced the history of literature more than one would suspect. Although transport facilities probably had little effect on the trade in great publishing centers like London and Paris, they sometimes determined the ebb and flow of business in remote areas. Before the nineteenth century, books were usually sent in sheets, so that the customer could have them bound according to his taste and his ability to pay. They traveled in large bales wrapped in heavy paper and were easily damaged by rain and the friction of ropes. Compared with commodities like textiles, their intrinsic value was slight, yet their shipping costs were high, owing to the size and weight of the sheets. So shipping often took up a large proportion of a book's total cost and a large place in the marketing strategy of publishers. In many parts of Europe, printers could not count on getting shipments to booksellers in August and September because wagoners abandoned their routes to work the harvest. The Baltic trade frequently ground to a halt after October, because ice closed the ports. Routes opened and shut everywhere in response to the pressures of war, politics, and even insurance rates. Unorthodox literature has traveled underground in huge quantities from the sixteenth century to the present, so its influence has varied according to the effectiveness of the smuggling industry. And other genres, like chapbooks and penny dreadfuls,[26] circulated through special distribution systems, which need much more study, although Book Historians are now beginning to clear some of the ground.[xxx]

v. Booksellers

Thanks to some classic studies—H.S. Bennett on early modern England, L.C. Wroth on colonial America, H.-J. Martin on seventeenth-century France, and Johann Goldfriedrich on Germany—it is possible to piece together a general picture of the evolution of the book trade.[xxxi] But more work needs to be done on the bookseller as a cultural agent, the middleman who mediated between supply and demand at their key point of contact. We still do not know enough about the social and intellectual world of men like Rigaud, about their values and tastes and the way they fit into their communities. They also operated within commercial networks, which

25 All printers, the best-known of whom is Benjamin Franklin (1706–90), who was also an author, inventor, scientist, diplomat, politician, and Founding Father of the United States of America.

26 Inexpensive, serialized, sensational fiction.

expanded and collapsed like alliances in the diplomatic world. What laws governed the rise and fall of trade empires in publishing? A comparison of national histories could reveal some general tendencies, such as the centripetal force of great centers like London, Paris, Frankfurt, and Leipzig, which drew provincial houses into their orbits, and the countervailing trend toward alignments between provincial dealers and suppliers in independent enclaves like Liège, Bouillon, Neuchâtel, Geneva, and Avignon. But comparisons are difficult because the trade operated through different institutions in different countries, which generated different kinds of archives. The records of the London **Stationers' company**, the Communauté des Libraires et Imprimeurs de Paris, and the Leipzig and Frankfurt book fairs have had a great deal to do with the different courses that Book History has taken in England, France, and Germany.[xxxii]

Nevertheless, books were sold as commodities everywhere. A more unabashedly economic study of them would provide a new perspective to the history of literature. James Barnes, John Tebbel, and Frédéric Barbier have demonstrated the importance of the economic element in the book trades of nineteenth-century England, America, and France.[xxxiii] But more work could be done—on credit mechanisms, for example, and the techniques of negotiating bills of exchange, of defense against suspensions of payment, and of exchanging printed sheets in lieu of payment *in specie*. The book trade, like other businesses during the Renaissance and early modern periods, was largely a confidence game, but we still do not know how it was played.

vi. Readers

245

Despite a considerable literature on its psychology, phenomenology,[27] textology, and sociology, reading remains mysterious. How do readers make sense of the signs on the printed page? What are the social effects of that experience? And how has it varied? Literary scholars like Wayne Booth, Stanley Fish, Wolfgang Iser, Walter Ong, and Jonathan Culler have made reading a central concern of textual criticism because they understand literature as an activity, the construal of meaning within a system of communication, rather than a canon of texts.[xxxiv] The Book Historian could make use of their notions of fictitious audiences, implicit readers, and interpretive communities. But he may find their observations somewhat time-bound. Although the critics know their way around literary history (they are especially strong on seventeenth-century England), they seem to assume that texts have always worked on the sensibilities of readers in the same way. But a seventeenth-century London burgher[28] inhabited a different mental universe from that of a twentieth-century American professor. Reading itself has changed over time. It was often done aloud and in groups, or in secret and with an intensity we may not be able to imagine today.

[...]

---

27 The study of the quality or nature of experience.

28 Generally speaking, a citizen of a town or village who was a member of the middle class.

But texts shape the response of readers, however active they may be. As Walter Ong has observed, the opening pages of *The Canterbury Tales* and *A Farewell to Arms* create a frame and cast the reader in a role, which he cannot avoid no matter what he thinks of pilgrimages and civil wars.[xxxv] In fact, **typography** as well as style and syntax determine the ways in which texts convey meanings. McKenzie has shown that the bawdy, unruly Congreve[29] of the early **quarto** editions settled down into the decorous neo-classicist of the *Works* of [Congreve in] 1709 as a consequence of book design rather than bowdlerization.[xxxvi] [30] The history of reading will have to take account of the ways that texts constrain readers as well as the ways that readers take liberties with texts.

[...]

If it is possible to re-capture the great re-readings of the past, the inner experience of ordinary readers may always elude us. But we should at least be able to reconstruct a good deal of the social context of reading. The debate about silent reading during the Middle Ages has produced some impressive evidence about reading habits,[xxxvii] and studies of reading societies in Germany, where they proliferated to an extraordinary degree in the eighteenth and nineteenth centuries, have shown the importance of reading in the development of a distinct bourgeois cultural style.[xxxviii] German scholars have also done a great deal in the history of libraries and in reception studies of all kinds.[xxxix] Following a notion of Rolf Engelsing, they often maintain that reading habits became transformed at the end of the eighteenth century. Before this

"*Leserevolution*,"[31] readers tended to work laboriously through a small number of texts, especially the Bible, over and over again. Afterwards, they raced through all kinds of material, seeking amusement rather than edification. The shift from **intensive** to **extensive reading** coincided with a desacralization[32] of the printed word. The world began to be cluttered with reading matter, and texts began to be treated as commodities that could be discarded as casually as yesterday's newspaper.

[...]

Questions about who reads what, in what conditions, at what time, and with what effect, link reading studies with sociology. The Book Historian could learn how to pursue such questions from the work of Douglas Waples, Bernard Berelson, Paul Lazarsfeld, and Pierre Bourdieu.

---

29 William Congreve (1670–1729), English playwright best known for his comedies.

30 Bowdlerization is the editing of works to remove material considered offensive or improper; named after Thomas Bowdler (1754–1825), a nineteenth-century editor who published an expurgated edition of Shakespeare.

31 German word for the reading revolution of the eighteenth century.

32 Divested of religious or sacred significance, referring to how early printing was closely associated with religious works.

He could draw on the reading research that flourished in the Graduate Library School of the University of Chicago from 1930 to 1950, and that still turns up in the occasional Gallup report.[xl] And as an example of the sociological strain in historical writing, he could consult the studies of reading (and non-reading) in the English working class during the last two centuries by Richard Altick, Robert Webb, and Richard Hoggart.[xli] All this work opens onto the larger problem of how exposure to the printed word affects the way men think. Did the invention of movable type transform man's mental universe? There may be no single satisfactory answer to that question because it bears on so many different aspects of life in early modern Europe, as Elizabeth Eisenstein has shown.[xlii] But it should be possible to arrive at a firmer understanding of what books meant to people. Their use in the taking of oaths, the exchanging of gifts, the awarding of prizes, and the bestowing of legacies would provide clues to their significance within different societies. The iconography of books could indicate the weight of their authority, even for illiterate laborers who sat in church before pictures of the tablets of Moses. The place of books in folklore, and of folk motifs in books, shows that influences ran both ways when **oral traditions** came into contact with printed texts, and that books need to be studied in relation to other media.[xliii] The lines of research could lead in many directions, but they all should issue ultimately in a larger understanding of how printing has shaped man's attempts to make sense of the human condition.

One can easily lose sight of the larger dimensions of the enterprise because Book Historians often stray into esoteric byways and unconnected specializations. Their work can be so fragmented, even within the limits of the literature on a single country, that it may seem hopeless to conceive of Book History as a single subject, to be studied from a comparative perspective across the whole range of historical disciplines. But books themselves do not respect limits either linguistic or national. They have often been written by authors who belonged to an international republic of letters, composed by printers who did not work in their native tongue, sold by booksellers who operated across national boundaries, and read in one language by readers who spoke another. Books also refuse to be contained within the confines of a single discipline when treated as objects of study. Neither history nor literature nor economics nor sociology nor bibliography can do justice to all the aspects of the life of a book. By its very nature, therefore, the history of books must be international in scale and interdisciplinary in method. But it need not lack conceptual coherence, because books belong to circuits of communication that operate in consistent patterns, however complex they may be. By unearthing those circuits, historians can show that books do not merely recount history; they make it.

Notes

This essay first appeared in *Daedalus* (Summer 1982): 65–83. Since then I have attempted to develop its themes further in an essay on the history of reading (Chapter 9) and in "Histoire du livre-Geschichte des Buchwesens: An Agenda for Comparative History," *Publishing History*, 22 (1987): 33–41.

i. Scholarly journal for the study of bibliography and of the role of the book in history.

ii. Weekly magazine of the German book trade.

iii. For examples of this work, see, in addition to the books named in the essay, Henri-Jean Martin, *Livre, pouvoirs et société à Paris au XVIIe siècle (1598–1701)*, 2 vols. (Geneva: Droz, 1969); Jean Quéniart, *L'Imprimerie et la librairie à Rouen au XVIIIe siècle* (Paris: C. Klincksieck, 1969); René Moulinas, *L'Imprimerie, la librairie et la presse à Avignon au XVIIIe siècle* (Grenoble: Presses Univ., 1974); and Frédéric Barbier, *Trois cents ans de librairie et d'imprimerie: Berger-Levrault, 1676–1830* (Geneva: Droz, 1979), in the series "Histoire et civilisation du livre," which includes several monographs written along similar lines. Much of the French work has appeared as articles in the *Revue française d'histoire du livre*. For a survey of the field by two of the most important contributors to it, see Roger Chartier and Daniel Roche, "Le livre, un changement de perspective," *Faire de l'histoire* 3 (1974): 115–36, and Chartier and Roche, "L'Histoire quantitative du livre," *Revue française d'histoire du livre* 16 (1977): 3–27. For sympathetic assessments by two American fellow travelers, see Robert Darnton, "Reading, Writing, and Publishing in Eighteenth-Century France: A Case Study in the Sociology of Literature," *Daedalus* (Winter 1971): 214–56, and Raymond Birn, "Livre et Société After Ten Years: Formation of a Discipline," *Studies on Voltaire and the Eighteenth Century* 151 (1976): 287–312.

iv. As examples of these approaches, see Theodore Besterman, *Voltaire* (New York: Harcourt, 1969), 433–34; Daniel Mornet, "Les Enseignements des bibliothèques privées (1750–1780)," *Revue d'histoire littéraire de la France* 17 (1910): 449–92; and the bibliographical studies now being prepared under the direction of the Voltaire Foundation, which will replace the outdated bibliography by Georges Bengesco.

v. The following account is based on the ninety-nine letters in Rigaud's dossier in the papers of the Société typographique de Neuchâtel, Bibliothèque de la ville de Neuchâtel, Switzerland (henceforth referred to as STN), supplemented by other relevant material from the vast archives of the STN.

vi. Rigaud to STN, July 27, 1771.

vii. The pattern of Rigaud's orders is evident from his letters to the STN and the STN's "Livres de Commission," where it tabulated its orders. Rigaud included catalogues of his major holdings in his letters of June 29, 1774, and May 23, 1777.

viii. Madeleine Ventre, *L'Imprimerie et la librairie en Languedoc au dernier siècle de l'Ancien Régime* (Paris and The Hague: La Haye, 1958), 227. [A *subdélégué* is an authorized agent.]

ix. B. André to STN, August 22, 1784.

x. *Manuel de l'auteur et du libraire* (Paris, 1777), 67.

xi. Jean-François Favarger to STN, August 29, 1778.

xii. The *procès-verbal* of the raids is in the Bibliothèque Nationale, Ms. français 22075, fo. 355.

xiii. Fontanel to STN, March 6, 1781.

xiv. STN to Gosse and Pinet, booksellers of The Hague, April 19, 1770.

xv. STN to Voltaire, September 15, 1770.

xvi. This account is based on the STN's correspondence with intermediaries all along its routes, notably the shipping agents Nicole and Galliard of Nyon and Secrétan and De la Serve of Ouchy.

xvii. Rigaud to STN, August 28, 1771.

xviii. Robert Darnton, *The Business of Enlightenment: A Publishing History of the Encyclopédie 1775–1800* (Cambridge, MA: Harvard UP, 1979), 273–99.

xix. Anonymous, "Etat et description de la ville de Montpellier, fait en 1768," in *Montpellier en 1768 et en 1836 d'après deux manuscrits inédits*, ed. J. Berthelé (Montpellier, 1909), 55. This rich contemporary description of Montpellier is the main source of the above account.

xx. C.E. Labrousse, *La Crise de l'économie française à la fin de l'Ancien Régime et au début de la Révolution* (Paris: Presses Universitaires de France, 1944).

xxi. Ventre, *L'Imprimerie et la librairie en Languedoc*; François Furet, "La 'librairie' du royaume de France au 18e siècle," *Livre et société dans la France du XVIIIème siècle*, I, (Paris and The Hague, 1965), 3–32; and Robert Estivals, *La Statistique bibliographique de la France sous la monarchie au XVIIIe siècle* (Paris and The Hague: Mouton, 1965). The bibliographical work will be published under the auspices of the Voltaire Foundation.

xxii. John Lough, *Writer and Public in France from the Middle Ages to the Present Day* (Oxford: Clarendon, 1978), 303.

xxiii. Robert Escarpit, *Le littéraire et le social. Eléments pour une sociologie de la littérature* (Paris: Flammarion, 1970).

xxiv. Peter John Wallis, *The Social Index: A New Technique for Measuring Social Trends* (Newcastle upon Tyne: Project for Historical Biobibliography at the University of Newcastle upon Tyne School of Education, 1978).

xxv. William Gilmore is now completing an extensive research project on the diffusion of books in colonial New England. On the political and economic aspects of the colonial press, see Stephen Botein, "'Meer Mechanics' and an Open Press: The Business and Political Strategies of Colonial American Printers," *Perspectives in American History* 9 (1975): 127–225; and *The Press and the American Revolution*, ed. Bernard Bailyn and John B. Hench (Worcester, MA: American Antiquarian Society, 1980), which contain ample references to work on the early history of the book in America.

xxvi. For a general survey of work on the later history of books in this country, see Hellmut Lehmann-Haupt, *The Book in America*, rev. ed. (New York: R.R. Bowker, 1952).

xxvii. Philip Gaskell, *A New Introduction to Bibliography* (New York and Oxford: Clarendon P, 1972), preface. Gaskell's work provides an excellent general survey of the subject.

xxviii. D.F. McKenzie, "Printers of the Mind: Some Notes on Bibliographical Theories and Printing House Practices," *Studies in Bibliography* 22 (1969): 1–75.

xxix. D.F. McKenzie, *The Cambridge University Press 1696–1712*, 2 vols. (Cambridge: Cambridge UP, 1966); Leon Voet, *The Golden Compasses*, 2 vols. (Amsterdam: Vangendt, 1969); Raymond de Roover, "The Business Organization of the Plantin Press in the Setting of Sixteenth-Century Antwerp," *De gulden passer* 24 (1956): 104–20; and Jacques Rychner, "A L'Ombre des Lumières: coup d'oeil sur la main-d'oeuvre de quelques imprimeries du XVIIIe siècle," *Studies on Voltaire and the Eighteenth Century* 155 (1976): 1925–55, and "Running a Printing House in Eighteenth-Century Switzerland: the Workshop of the Société typographique de Neuchâtel," *The Library*, sixth series, 1 (1979): 1–24.

xxx. For example, see J.-P. Belin, *Le Commerce des livres prohibés à Paris de 1750 à 1789* (Paris, 1913); Jean-Jacques Darmon, *Le Colportage de librairie en France sous le second empire* (Paris: Plon, 1972); and Reinhart Siegert, *Aufklärung und Volkslektüre exemplarisch dargestellt an Rudolph Zacharias Becker und seinem 'Noth-und Hulfsbuchlein' mit einer Bibliographie zum Gesamtthema* (Frankfurt am Main: Buchhändler-Vereinigung, 1978).

xxxi. H.S. Bennett, *English Books and Readers 1475 to 1557* (Cambridge: Cambridge UP, 1952) and *English Books and Readers 1558–1603* (Cambridge: Cambridge UP, 1965); L.C. Wroth, *The Colonial Printer* (Portland, ME: Southworth-Anthoensen Press, 1938); Martin, *Livre, pouvoirs et société*; and Johann Goldfriedrich and Friedrich Kapp, *Geschichte des Deutschen Buchhandels*, 4 vols. (Leipzig, 1886–1913).

xxxii. Compare Cyprian Blagden, *The Stationers' Company, A History, 1403–1959* (Cambridge, MA: Harvard UP, 1960); Martin, *Livre, pouvoirs et société*; and Rudolf Jentzsch, *Der deutsch-lateinische Büchermarkt nach den Leipziger Ostermesskatalogen von 1740, 1770 und 1800 in seiner Gliederung und Wandlung* (Leipzig: R. Voigtländer, 1912).

xxxiii. James Barnes, *Free Trade in Books: A Study of the London Book Trade Since 1800* (Oxford: Clarendon P, 1964); John Tebbel, *A History of Book Publishing in the United States*, 3 vols. (New York: R.R. Bowker, 1972–1978); and Barbier, *Trois cents ans de librairie et d'imprimerie*.

xxxiv. See, for example, Wolfgang Iser, *The Implied Reader: Patterns of Communication in Prose Fiction from Bunyan to Beckett* (Baltimore: Johns Hopkins UP, 1974); Stanley Fish, *Self-Consuming Artifacts: The Experience of Seventeenth-Century Literature* (Berkeley and Los Angeles: U of California P, 1972) and *Is There a Text in This Class? The Authority of Interpretive Communities* (Cambridge, MA: Harvard UP, 1980); Walter Ong, "The Writer's Audience Is Always a Fiction," *PMLA (Publication of the Modern Language Association of America)* 90 (1975): 9–21; and for a sampling of other variations on these themes, Susan R. Suleiman and Inge Crosman, *The Reader in the Text: Essays on Audience and Interpretation* (Princeton, NJ: Princeton UP, 1980).

xxxv. Ong, "The Writer's Audience Is Always a Fiction."

xxxvi. D.F. McKenzie, "Typography and Meaning: The Case of William Congreve," *Wolfenbütteler Schriften zur Geschichte des Buchwesens*, IV (1981), 81–125.

xxxvii. See Paul Saenger, "Silent Reading: Its Impact on Late Medieval Script and Society," *Viator* 13 (1982): 367–414.

xxxviii. See *Lesegesellschaften und bürgerliche Emanzipation. Ein Europäischer Vergleich*, ed. Otto Dann (Munich: C.H. Beck, 1981), which has a thorough bibliography.

xxxix. For examples of recent work, see *Offentliche und Private Bibliotheken im 17. und 18.Jahrhundert: Raritatenkammern, Forschungsinstrumente oder Bildungsstätten?* ed. Paul Raabe (Bremen and Wolfenbuttel: Jacobi, 1977). Much of the stimulus for recent reception studies has come from the theoretical work of Hans Robert Jauss, notably *Literaturgeschichte als Provokation* (Frankfurt am Main: Suhrkamp, 1970).

xl. Douglas Waples, Bernard Berelson, and Franklyn Bradshaw, *What Reading Does to People* (Chicago: U of Chicago P, 1940); Bernard Berelson, *The Library's Public* (New York: Columbia UP, 1949); Elihu Katz, "Communication Research and the Image of Society: The Convergence of Two Traditions," *American Journal of Sociology* 65 (1960): 435–40; and John Y. Cole and Carol S. Gold, eds., *Reading in America 1978* (Washington, DC: Library of Congress, 1979). For the Gallup report, see the volume published by the American Library Association, *Book Reading and Library Usage: A Study of Habits and Perceptions* (Princeton, NJ: Gallup Organization Chicago, 1978). Much in this older variety of sociology still seems valid, and it can be studied in conjunction with the current work of Pierre Bourdieu; see especially his *La distinction: Critique sociale du jugement* (Paris: Éditions de Minuit, 1979).

xli. Richard D. Altick, *The English Common Reader: A Social History of the Mass Reading Public 1800–1900* (Chicago: U of Chicago P, 1957); Robert K. Webb, *The British Working Class Reader* (London: Allen and Unwin, 1955); and Richard Hoggart, *The Uses of Literacy* (Harmondsworth: Penguin, 1960; 1st ed., 1957).

xlii. Elisabeth L. Eisenstein, *The Printing Press as an Agent of Change*, 2 vols. (Cambridge: Cambridge UP, 1979). [See also Eisenstein's essay above, pp. 215–30.] For a discussion of Eisenstein's thesis, see Anthony T. Grafton, "The Importance of Being Printed," *Journal of Interdisciplinary History* 11 (1980): 265–86; Michael Hunter, "The Impact of Print," *The Book Collector* 28 (1979), 335–52; and Roger Chartier, "L'Ancien Régime typographique: Réflexions sur quelques travaux récents," *Annales: Economies, sociétés, civilisations* 36 (1981): 191–209.

xliii. Some of these general themes are taken up in Eric Havelock, *Origins of Western Literacy* (Toronto: Ontario Institute for Studies in Education, 1976); Jack Goody, ed., *Literacy in Traditional Societies* (Cambridge: Cambridge UP, 1968); Jack Goody, *The Domestication of the Savage Mind* (Cambridge: Cambridge UP, 1977); Walter Ong, *The Presence of the Word* (New York: Simon and Schuster, 1970); and Natalie Z. Davis, *Society and Culture in Early Modern France* (Stanford, CA: Stanford UP, 1975).

17.

Roger Chartier, "Communities of Readers," *The Order of Books: Readers, Authors, and Libraries in Europe between the Fourteenth and Eighteenth Centuries.* Trans. Lydia G. Cochrane. Stanford, CA: Stanford UP, 1994. 1–23

Roger Chartier's (b. 1945) work in Early Modern European history is rooted in the tradition of the "Annales School," an influential branch of French social history founded by Lucien Febvre and others. His own contribution to this School has been in the social history of cultural practices, where he has worked extensively in the history of education, the history of the book, and the history of reading. Drawing on both English-speaking bibliographical traditions and French cultural theory, he is the author of several influential books, including penetrating accounts of the origins of the French Revolution, of private life, and of books. One of his most important contributions to the field of book history, *The Order of Books*, was first published in France in 1992 and translated into English in 1994. The book examines how the written word was classified, organized, and perceived by those involved in the production and dissemination of texts between the fourteenth and eighteenth centuries. This short but extremely generative book examines, in its three chapters, different historiographies available for studying readers, authors, and libraries.

The chapter excerpted below focuses on one aspect of Darnton's "communication circuit," the reader, beginning with Michel de Certeau's provocative analogy, expressed in *The Practice of Everyday Life* (1984), of reading as a form of "poaching." Although Chartier, like de Certeau, contrasts the fixity of writing with the freedom of reading, he also attempts to historicize the act of reading, which for him "is always a practice embodied in acts, spaces, and habits." Focusing on France between the sixteenth and the eighteenth centuries (the ancien régime), Chartier takes as his object of study "the relationship set up among the text, the book, and the reader."

Communities of Readers

> Far from being writers—founders of their own place, heirs of the peasants of earlier ages now working on the soil of language, diggers of wells and builders of houses—readers are travellers; they move across lands belonging to someone else, like nomads poaching their way across fields they did

> not write, despoiling the wealth of Egypt to enjoy it themselves. Writing accumulates, stocks up, resists time by the establishment of a place and multiplies its production through the expansionism of reproduction. Reading takes no measures against the erosion of time (one forgets oneself and also forgets), it does not keep what it acquires, or it does so poorly, and each of the places through which it passes is a repetition of the lost paradise.[i]

This magnificent passage from Michel de Certeau[1] which contrasts writing—conservative, fixed, durable—and reading—always of the order of the ephemeral—constitutes both an obligatory base and a disquieting challenge for any history that hopes to inventory and make sense out of a practice (reading) that only rarely leaves traces, that is scattered in an infinity of singular acts, and that easily shakes off all constraints. Such a proposal is based on a dual presupposition: that reading is not already inscribed in the text with no conceivable gap between the meaning assigned to it (by its author, by custom, by criticism, and so forth) and the interpretation that its readers might make of it and, as a corollary, that a text exists only because there is a reader to give it meaning. To return to Michel de Certeau:

> Whether it is a question of newspapers or Proust, the text has a meaning only through its readers; it changes along with them; it is ordered in accord with codes of perception that it does not control. It becomes a text only in its relation to the exteriority of the reader, by an interplay of implications and ruses between two sorts of "expectation" in combination: the expectation that organizes a readable space (a literality), and one that organizes a procedure necessary for the actualization of the work (a reading).[ii]

The historian's task is thus to reconstruct the variations that differentiate the *espaces lisibles*[2]—that is, the texts in their discursive and material forms—and those that govern the circumstances of their effectuation—that is, the readings, understood as concrete practices and as procedures of interpretation.

Michel de Certeau's suggestions provide a basis for suggesting some of what is at stake and the problems and conditions of possibility of this sort of history. Its space is usually defined by three poles that the academic tradition usually keeps separate: first, the analysis of texts, be they **canonical** or ordinary, to discern their structures, their themes, and their aims; second, the history of books and, beyond that, the history of all objects and all forms that bear texts; third, the study of practices that seize on these objects and these forms in a variety of ways and produce differentiated uses and meanings. For me, a fundamental question underlies this approach that combines textual criticism, **bibliography**, and cultural history: in the societies of the ancien

1 Michel de Certeau (1925–86) was an important French cultural theorist.

2 French: legible or readable spaces.

régime, how did increased **circulation** of printed matter transform forms of sociability, permit new modes of thought, and change people's relationship with power?

Hence the need to stress the way in which the encounter between "the world of the text" and "the world of the reader"—to use Paul Ricoeur's terms—operates.[iii] To reconstruct this process of the "actualization" of texts in its historical dimensions first requires that we accept the notion that their meanings are dependent upon the forms through which they are received and appropriated by their readers (or hearers). Readers and hearers, in point of fact, are never confronted with abstract or ideal texts detached from all materiality; they manipulate or perceive objects and forms whose structures and modalities[3] govern their reading (or their hearing), thus the possible comprehension of the text read (or heard). Against a purely semantic definition of the text (which inhabits not only structuralist criticism[4] in all its variants but also the literary theories most attuned to a reconstruction of the reception of works), one must state that forms produce meaning and that a text, stable in its letter, is invested with a new meaning and status when the mechanisms that make it available to interpretation change.

We must also keep in mind that reading is always a practice embodied in acts, spaces, and habits. Far from being a phenomenology[5] that wipes out all concrete modalities of the act of reading and characterizes that act by its effects, which are postulated to be universal (as with the operation of response to the text that makes the subject better understand himself or herself thanks to the mediation of interpretation), a history of reading must identify the specific mechanisms that distinguish the various communities of readers and traditions of reading. This move supposes the recognition of several sets of contrasts, the first of which is in the realm of reading ability. The essential but over-simplified separation of the **literate** from the illiterate does not exhaust the full range of differences in the reader's relation to writing. All who can read texts do not read them in the same fashion, and there is an enormous gap between the virtuosi[6] among readers and the least skilled at reading, who have to **oralize** what they are reading in order to comprehend it and who are at ease only with a limited range of textual or **typographical** forms. There are equally great differences between the norms and conventions of reading that define, for each community of readers, legitimate uses of the book, ways to read, and the instruments and methods of interpretations. Finally, there are differences between the expectations and interests that various groups of readers invest in the practice of reading. Such expectations and interests, which govern practices, determine the way in which texts can be read and read differently by readers who do not have the same intellectual baggage or the same relationship with the written word.

Michel de Certeau gives an illustration of this sort of approach when he discusses the characteristics of mystical reading: "By 'mystical readings' I mean the set of reading procedures advised or practiced in the field of experience of the solitaries or the collectives designated in

3 The mode of an object's being rather than its substance.

4 A branch of criticism that studies its subjects as a structure of interrelated objects rather than as a group of individual ones.

5 "The metaphysical study or theory of phenomena in general (as distinct from that of being)" (*OED*).

6 See p. 225, note 16.

the sixteenth and seventeenth centuries as 'illuminated,' 'mystic,' or 'spiritual.'"[iv] In this minor, marginal, and dispersed community that was the mystical milieu, reading was regulated by norms and habits that invested the book with original functions: it replaced the institution of the church, held to be insufficient; it made discourse possible (the discourse of prayer, of communication with God, of the *conversar*); it indicated the practices by which spiritual experience could be constructed. The mystical relationship with the book can also be understood as a trajectory in which several "moments" of reading succeed one another: the installation of an alterity[7] that provides a basis for the subjective quest, the unfolding of a sense of joy, a physical reaction to the "manducation"[8] of the text that leaves its mark on the body, and, at the end of the process, cessation of reading, abandonment of the book, and absolute detachment. One of the first tasks of a history of reading that hopes to understand the varieties of the paradigmatic figure of the reader as poacher is thus to ascertain the networks of reading practices and the rules for reading proper to the various communities of readers—spiritual, intellectual, professional, and so forth.[v]

But to read is always to read something. Naturally, if it is to exist the history of reading must be radically distinguished from a history of what is read: "The reader emerges from the history of the book, in which he has long been merged, indistinct.... The reader was taken to be the effect of the book. Today he becomes detached from those books whose mere shadow he was supposed to be. And now that shadow is unshackled, it takes on relief and acquires an independence."[vi] That founding independence is not an arbitrary liberty. It is limited by the codes and the conventions that regulate the practices of a membership community. It is also limited by the discursive and material forms of the texts read.

"New readers make new texts and their new meanings are a function of their new forms."[vii] D.F. McKenzie perspicaciously notes here the dual set of variations—variations in the readers' resources and in textual and formal mechanisms—that any history that takes on the task of restoring the fluid and plural signification of texts must take into account. One can profit from McKenzie's dictum in several ways: by noting the major oppositions that distinguish the various modes of reading from one another; by specifying the practices most popular among readers; by focusing attention on the publishing formulas that offer old texts to new readers of a humbler sort and in greater number.

This perspective reflects a dual dissatisfaction with the history of the book in France in the last 20 or 30 years, where the historians' chief concern has been to measure the unequal presence of the book in the various groups that made up the society of the ancien régime. This led to the construction (incidentally, quite necessarily so) of indicators to reveal cultural gaps at a given place and time: among such indicators are the percentage of probate[9] inventories mentioning ownership of books, the classification of book collections according to the number of works they included, and thematic description of private **libraries** according to the place that the various bibliographical categories occupy in them. In this perspective, giving an account of the reading matter of the French

7 "The fact or state of being other or different; diversity, difference, otherness, an instance of this" (*OED*).

8 Eating, chewing.

9 Relating to an officially recorded will.

between the sixteenth and the eighteenth century was above all a question of constructing data sets, establishing quantitative thresholds, and noting the cultural equivalents of social differences.

These procedures were adopted collectively (by the author of the present work among others), and they permitted the accumulation of a body of knowledge without which further investigation would have been inconceivable. They raise problems, however. First, such procedures rest on a narrowly sociographic[10] conception implicitly postulating that cultural cleavages are necessarily organized according to pre-existent social divisions. I think we need to reject this dependence that relates gaps in cultural practices to a priori social oppositions, whether on the macroscopic scale[11] of contrasts between dominant and dominated or between the elites and the people or on the scale of smaller differentiations, as for example among social groups in a hierarchy of conditions, professions, or levels of wealth.

Cultural divisions are not obligatorily organized in accordance with the one grid of social divisions that supposedly commands the unequal presence of objects or differences in behavior patterns. We must turn the perspective around and begin by designating the social areas in which each corpus of texts and each genre of printed matter circulates. Beginning with objects, in this fashion, rather than with classes or groups leads to considering that the French style of socio-cultural history has too long continued to exist on the basis of a mutilated conception of the social. By privileging only socio-professional classification it has forgotten that other and equally social principles of differentiation might explain cultural divisions even more pertinently. The same is true of gender-based and generationally based distinctions, of religious affiliations, of communitarian solidarities, of educative or corporative traditions, and more.

Furthermore, the history of the book in its social and quantitative definition attempted to characterize cultural configurations on the basis of the categories of texts that were supposed to be specific to those configurations. This operation was doubly reductive. First, it equated the identification of differences with mere inequalities in distribution; second, it ignored the process by which a text takes on meaning for those who read it. Several shifts of emphasis could be proposed to correct these postulates. The first situates the recognition of the differences most deeply rooted in society in differing uses of shared materials. In the societies of the ancien régime the *same* texts were appropriated by "popular" readers and other readers more than has been thought. Either readers of more humble social condition were put in possession of books that were not specifically designed for them (as was the case of Menocchio, the Friuli miller, Jamerey Duval, the shepherd from Lorraine, or Ménétra, the Paris glazier),[viii] or else inventive and canny **bookseller**-printers made available to a very large clientele texts that formerly had circulated only in the narrow world of wealth and letters (which was the case with the *pliegos sueltos* of Castile[12] and the Catalan *plecs*,[13] English **chapbooks** or the publishing formula known in France under

10 Influenced by sociology.

11 A view that widens out to a large scale rather than one that narrows in to a small one.

12 A Spanish chapbook.

13 A Catalan chapbook.

the generic title of the *bibliothèque bleue*). What is essential is thus to understand how the same texts can be differently apprehended, manipulated, and comprehended.

A second shift of emphasis re-constructs the networks of practices that organized historically and socially differentiated modes of access of texts. Reading is not uniquely an abstract operation of the intellect: it brings the body into play, it is inscribed in a space and a relationship with oneself or with others. This is why special attention should be paid to ways of reading that have disappeared in our contemporary world. One of these is reading aloud in its dual function of communicating the written word to those who are unable to decipher it themselves but also of cementing the interlocking forms of sociability that are emblematic of private life in the intimacy of the family circle, in worldly conviviality, and in literary circles and spheres of scholarly sociability. A history of reading must not limit itself to the genealogy of our own contemporary manner of reading, in silence and using only our eyes; it must also (and perhaps above all) take on the task of retracing forgotten gestures and habits that have not existed for some time. The challenge matters because it reveals not only the distant foreignness of practices that were common long ago but also the specific structure of texts composed for uses that are not the uses of today's readers of those same texts. In the sixteenth and seventeenth centuries the reading style implicit in a text, literary or not, was still often an oralization of the text, and the "reader" was an implicit auditor of a read discourse. The work, which was addressed to the ear as much as to the eye, plays with forms and procedures that subject writing to demands more appropriate to oral "performance." Many examples of this

sort of continuing link between the text and the human voice can be found, from the motifs in *Don Quixote* to the structure of texts adapted for the *bibliothèque bleue*.[ix]

"Whatever they may do, authors do not write books. Books are not written at all. They are manufactured by **scribes** and other artisans, by mechanics and other engineers, and by printing presses and other machines."[x] This remark can serve to introduce the third shift in emphasis that I would like to suggest. Contrary to representation elaborated by literature itself and taken up by the most quantitative form of history of the book, which state that the text exists in and of itself, separate from anything material, we need to remember that there is no text apart from the physical support that offers it for reading (or hearing), hence there is no comprehension of any written piece that does not at least in part depend upon the forms in which it reaches its reader. This means that we need to make a distinction between two sets of mechanisms, the ones that are part of the strategies of writing and the author's intentions, and the ones that result from publishing decisions or the constraints of the print shop.

True, authors do not write books: they write texts that become written objects, which may be hand-written, **engraved**, or printed (and, today, electronically reproduced and transmitted). The space between text and object, which is precisely the space in which meaning is constructed, has too often been forgotten, not only by the traditional sort of literary history that thinks of the work as an abstract text whose typographic forms are without importance, but also by the "aesthetic of reception" that, in spite of its desire to historicize the readers' experience, postulates a pure and unmediated relationship between the "signals" emitted by the text (which play with accepted literary conventions) and the "horizon of expectation" of the public to which those signals are addressed. In this perspective the "effect produced" in no way depends upon the material forms that operate as a vehicle for the text.[xi] Still, those forms also fully contribute to fashioning the reader's expectations and to calling for a new public or novel uses.

Thus we have been brought back to the triangle that was our point of departure, the relationship set up among the text, the book, and the reader. The variations in that relationship describe several simple figures for the connection between "readable space" (*espace lisible*) and "effectuation," to use Michel de Certeau's terms. The first variation considers a stable, literal text that is available for reading in printed forms that change. In his study of the innovations introduced into **editions** of William Congreve's[14] plays at the beginning of the eighteenth century, D.F. McKenzie has shown how apparently insignificant formal changes (moving from a **quarto** to an **octavo** edition, numbering scenes, the presence or absence of a decorative element printed between one scene and the next, recalling the names of characters present at the beginning of each scene, marginal indications of the name of the character speaking, mention of exits and entrances) had an important effect on the status of the works. A new readability was created by a format that was easier to manipulate and by a **page** layout that reproduced within the book something of the movement of the staging, thus breaking with time-honored conventions that required plays to be printed with no restitution of their theatrical character. This was thus a new manner of reading the same text, but it also provided a new horizon of reception because the mechanisms used in the octavo edition of 1710, borrowed from devices used for printed editions of French plays, gave a new legitimacy to Congreve's plays, henceforth "classics" and part of the literary canon, and induced their author to make changes here and there to refine the style of his works and make them conform better to their new "typographic" dignity.[xii] Variations in the most purely formal aspects of a text's presentation can thus modify both its register of reference and its mode of interpretation.

The same is true, on a greater scale, of the greatest change in the way texts were cast into print between the sixteenth and the eighteenth centuries, "the definitive triumph of white over black"[xiii]—that is, the introduction of breathing space on to the page by the use of more paragraphs to break up an uninterrupted continuous text and by paragraph indentations that make the order of discourse immediately visible. The new **publishers** suggested a new reading of the same texts or the same genres, a reading that fragmented the text into separate units and echoed the intellectual or discursive articulation of the argument in the visual articulation of the page.

Chopping up the text in this manner could have far-reaching implications where Scripture was concerned. John Locke[15] was troubled by the new custom of dividing the text of the Bible into chapter and verse. For him it risked obliterating the powerful coherence of the Word of God. Locke says, speaking of the **Epistles** of Paul, "Not only the Common People take the Verses usually for distinct Aphorisms,[16] but even Men of more advanc'd Knowledge in reading them, lose very much of the strength and force of the Coherence and the Light that depends on it."

---

14 See p. 246, note 29, above.

15 John Locke (1632–1704), English Enlightenment philosopher perhaps best known for his idea of the social contract.

16 A pithy statement of belief or truth.

The effects of breaking up Scripture in this manner were disastrous: it authorized every religious sect or party to found its legitimacy on the scriptural passages that seemed to support its views:

> If a Bible was printed as it should be, and as the several Parts of it were writ, in continued Discourses where the Argument is continued, I doubt not that the several Parties would complain of it, as an Innovation, and a dangerous Change in the publishing of those holy Books ... He [the member of a particular church] need but be furnished with Verses of Sacred Scriptures, containing Words and Expressions that are but flexible ... and his System that has appropriated them to the Orthodoxie of his Church, makes them immediately strong and irrefragable Arguments for his Opinion. This is the Benefit of loose Sentences, and Scripture crumbled into Verses, which quickly turn into independent Aphorisms.[xiv]

A second figure pertains when a text is transferred from one form of publishing to another, dictating both a transformation of the text and the constitution of a new public. This is quite obviously the case with the corpus[17] of titles that made up the **catalogue** of the *bibliothèque bleue*. If that series has long claimed the attention of French historians it is because it has seemed to furnish direct access to the "popular culture" of the ancien régime, which has been supposed to have been expressed and nourished by works such as these and distributed en masse among the humbler sort of readers.[xv] This was not really the case, and for three main reasons. First, it is clear that the works that made up the French stock of the peddler's book trade had never been written for that purpose. The *bibliothèque bleue* was a publishing formula that dipped into the repertory of already published texts and picked out the ones that seemed most likely to meet the expectations of the broad public it sought to reach. Thus we need to take two precautions: not to take texts in the familiar blue format as "popular" in and of themselves because they belonged to all the genres of learned literature; to keep in mind that such texts usually had an earlier publishing existence and often a long publishing history before they entered the repertory of books for a wide audience.

A study of the works in the "popular" catalogue has shown that techniques of the most formal and material kind can by themselves inscribe indications of cultural differentiation in published works. In fact, the basic specificity of the *bibliothèque bleue* resided in editorial changes made in the texts in order to make them readable by the wide clientele that the publishers were aiming at. The vast labor of adaptation—shortening texts, simplifying them, cutting them up, providing illustrations—was commanded by how the bookseller-publishers who specialized in that market envisioned their customers' abilities and expectations. Thus the very structure of their books was governed by the way that book publishers thought that their target clientele read.

That reading style was always thought to demand such visible signals as anticipatory headings, recapitulative summaries, or **woodcuts** that functioned as reading protocols much like the mansions in the system of the arts of memory—a style of reading at ease only with brief

17 A collected body.

and self-enclosed sequences set off from one another and readers content with a minimal level of coherence. It was certainly not the manner of reading typical of the lettered elites of the age, even if certain notables deigned to buy the blue-covered books. Works printed for a broad public counted on their readers' previous knowledge. By the recurrence of extremely coded forms, by the repetition of motifs that return from one work to another, and by re-use of the same illustrations, an acquaintance with texts that the reader had already encountered was mobilized into serving for the comprehension of unfamiliar reading matter. In this way the "blue" catalogue organized a manner of reading that was more recognition than true discovery. It is thus specific formal aspects of the "blue" editions and the modifications that they imposed on the works they made use of that reveal their "popular" character.

In proposing this re-evaluation of the *bibliothèque bleue* my intention has not been uniquely to reach a better understanding of the most powerful of the instruments of acculturation to the written culture in ancien régime France.[xvi] It has also been to say that the identification of sociocultural differentiations and a study of formal and material mechanisms, far from being mutually exclusive, are necessarily connected. This is so not only because forms are modeled on the expectations and abilities attributed to the public at which they are aimed, but above all because works and objects produce their social area of reception much more than they are produced by crystallized and previously existent divisions. Lawrence W. Levine has proposed a fine demonstration of this.[xvii] Analyzing the way in which Shakespeare's plays were produced in America (mixed in with other genres such as melodrama, farce, circus turns, dance, and so forth), Levine shows how this type of representation created a numerous public that was "popular" in that it was not limited to the lettered elite and that it participated actively in the performance by its emotions and reactions. In the late-nineteenth century the strict division that was established among genres, styles, and places split up this "general" public, reserving Shakespeare to the "legitimate" theater and a smaller audience and sending off the rest of the audience to more "popular" entertainments. Changes in the actual form in which Shakespeare's plays were presented (but the same was true of symphonic music, the opera, and works of art) played a large part in the constitution of a "cultural bifurcation," and a time of mixed and shared offerings was succeeded by a time in which a process of cultural distinction produced a social separation. The traditional mechanisms for representing the Shakespearian repertory in America were thus of the same order as the "typographic" transformations that the publishers of the *bibliothèque bleue* performed on the works they chose: in both cases, the intent was to inscribe the text into a cultural matrix that was not the one that its original creators had in mind, and by that means to permit "readings," comprehensions, and uses that might have been disqualified by other intellectual habits.

These two examples lead us to consider cultural gaps as the effect of dynamic processes rather than as an expression of static and fixed divisions. On the one hand, a transformation in the forms and the mechanisms through which a text is proposed authorized new appropriations, thus it created new publics and new uses. On the other hand, the fact that an entire society shared the same objects invited a search for new differences to mark distances that had been maintained. The trajectory of print works in ancien régime France stands as witness to this. It was as if the distinctions among ways to read were progressively reinforced as printed matter became less rare, less often confiscated, and a more ordinary commodity. Whereas the mere possession of a book had long signified cultural difference, with the conquests of printing, reading postures, and typographical objects were gradually invested with that function. Henceforth readers of distinction and handsome books stood opposed to hastily printed works and their awkward decipherers.

As we have seen, however, both groups often read the same texts, whose plural and contradictory significations were invented along with their varying uses. This means that the question becomes one of selection: why did certain texts lend themselves better than others to durable and multiple re-use?[xviii] Or at least why did book publishers consider them capable of reaching very different publics? The response lies in the subtle relationships that were set up between the structure of the works, which were not all open to re-appropriation in the same degree, and the multiple determinations, both institutional and formal, that regulated their possible "application" (in the hermeneutic[18] sense of the term) to very different historical situations.

There is a third figure of the relationship among text, print, and reading when a text that is stable in its letter and fixed in its form is apprehended by new readers who read it in other ways than did previous readers. "A book changes by the fact that it does not change when the world changes"[xix] or, to change the statement to fit the scope of the present work, "... when its mode of reading changes." This remark is enough to justify a projected history of reading practices that would seek to identify the major oppositions that can give different meanings to a *same* text. It is perhaps time to question three of these fundamental cleavages, which are held to be certain. First, the opposition between a reading in which comprehension depends upon oralization, either out loud or mumbled, and another, possibly visual, reading.[xx] Even though his chronology is open to question, let me recall Michel de Certeau's remark about the reader's freedom and silent reading:

> Reading has become, over the past three centuries, a visual poem. It is no longer accompanied, as it used to be, by the murmur of a vocal articulation or by the movement of a muscular manducation. To read without uttering the words aloud or at least mumbling them is a "modern" experience, unknown for millennia. In earlier times, the reader interiorized the text; he made his voice the body of the other; he was its actor. Today, the text no longer imposes its own rhythm on the subject, it no longer manifests itself through the reader's voice. This withdrawal of the body, which is the condition of autonomy, is a distancing of the text. It is the reader's habeas corpus.[xxi] [19]

---

18 Relating to issues of interpretation.

19 Latin for "Let you have the body." A writ of habeas corpus may be used to compel an imprisoned individual to be brought before a court, and either charged with a crime or released. Habeas corpus is thus a key legal provision against arbitrary detention. Certeau uses the term here as a metaphor suggesting that the body of a reader who vocalizes the text is in a sense imprisoned by the text, while the body of a reader who reads silently is not.

The second accepted cleavage falls between an "**intensive**," reverential, and respectful reading of a small number of books that relies on hearing and memory and an "**extensive**" **reading** that consumes many texts, passes nonchalantly from one text to the next, and holds less sacred what is read.[xxii] The third cleavage is between a private, cloistered, solitary reading, considered to be one of the essential elements for constituting a sphere of private life, and the collective reading—both disciplined and rebellious—of communitarian spaces.[xxiii]

These widely accepted oppositions suggest a chronology that sees as major mutations the gradual advances in silent reading in the Middle Ages and the entry into the world of extensive reading in the late-eighteenth century. They prompt several reflections, however: some of these would reduce the simplicity of the dichotomies present in these contrasts by shifting attention to gradations within each opposed entity, by introducing nuances into the criteria that too abruptly differentiate styles of reading, and by reversing the automatic association of the collective with the popular and the elite with the private.[xxiv] Others suggest a connection among three sets of transformations whose effects have often been imperfectly untangled: "revolutions" that have taken place in techniques for the reproduction of texts (first among them, a shift from "**scribal culture**" to "print culture"); changes in the very forms of the book (the change from the **roll** or *volumen* to the book in **signatures** or *codex* during the early centuries of the Christian era was the most fundamental of these but other and less sweeping changes modified the visual aspect of the printed page between the sixteenth and eighteenth century);[xxv] wide-scale change in reading skills and in modes of reading. These different evolutions did not develop at the same pace and were not punctuated by the same breaking-points. The most interesting question posed to and by the history of reading today is certainly that of the ways in which these three sets of mutations—technological, formal, and cultural—related to one another.

The response to that question obviously depends upon a re-evaluation of the trajectories and divisions characteristic of the society of the ancien régime. More than is admitted, they were organized on the basis of the presence of written matter. That presence has long been gauged uniquely in one of two ways: either by signature counts aimed at establishing literacy rates, hence at evaluating variations in the ability to read according to ages, sites, sexes, and conditions; or by scrutiny of library inventories drawn up by notaries or booksellers in an attempt to measure the circulation of books and reading traditions.

In societies of the ancien régime as in our own, however, access to print cannot be reduced to book ownership alone: every book that is read is not necessarily a book that is personally owned, and all printed matter kept in the home is not obligatorily a book. Moreover, written materials lay at the very heart of the culture of the illiterate and were present in rituals, public spaces, and the work place.[xxvi] Thanks to speech, which deciphered writing, and to the image, which mirrored it, written matter was made accessible even to those who were incapable of reading it or who, left to their own devices, would have had only a rudimentary comprehension of it. Literacy rates do not give an accurate measure of familiarity with the written word—all the more so since in older societies, where learning to read and learning to write were two separate and successive operations, there were many individuals (women in particular) who left school knowing how to read at least a little but not how to write.[xxvii] Similarly, individual possession of a book is an inadequate indication of how often those who were too poor to have any sort of "library" in their homes might have handled a printed text.

Even if it is totally impossible to establish the number of readers who were not even able to sign their names or the number of readers who owned no books (or at least no books worthy of being appraised by the notary who drew up the inventory) but who could read signs and posters, news-sheets and chapbooks, we none the less have to postulate that they were many in order to comprehend the impact of printed written matter on the older forms of a culture that was still largely oral, action-based, and iconographic. The two modes of expression and communication dovetailed in many ways. To take first the ways in which writing and gesture mixed: not only was the written word at the center of urban festivities such as religious ceremonies, but a number of texts were intended to cancel themselves out as discourse and to produce practical results in behavior recognized as being in conformity with social or religious norms. This was the case with the civility books, which aimed at teaching the rules of polite social intercourse or Christian propriety.[xxviii]

There was also a dovetailing of speech and writing, which operated in two ways: first, the texts destined by their author and (more often) by their publisher to the most popular public often contained formulas or themes that came directly from the culture of the tale and oral recitation. The writing style of certain *occasionnels* (news-sheets) that imitate the speech patterns of tale-tellers and the variants introduced in the "blue" editions of fairy tales (which all originally came from literary collections) are good examples of an orality coming to the surface in printed

matter.[xxix] Second, as we have seen, a number of "readers" apprehended texts only thanks to the mediation of a voice reading them. Comprehending the specificity of this relationship with the written word thus supposes that not all reading must necessarily be individual, solitary, and silent, but, quite to the contrary, that one must acknowledge the importance and the diversity of reading aloud, a practice that has largely been lost.

This acknowledgement, which points to the strength of the penetration of print culture in ancien régime societies, leads to several others. First, it can account for the importance given to written matter and to the objects that bore writing by all the authorities who intended to regulate behavior and fashion minds. Hence the pedagogical, acculturating, and disciplining role attributed to the texts put into circulation for a wide readership; hence also the controls exercised over printed matter, which was subjected to censorship to eliminate anything that might threaten religious or moral order. Michel de Certeau invited us to recognize both the efficacy of these constraints, which were more and more binding as the individual was more strongly connected with the institution that decreed them ("The creativity of the reader grows as the institution that controlled it declines"),[xxx] and the various modalities for bridling the reader's interpretation, which ranged from exterior censorship—administrative, judiciary, inquisitorial, scholastic, and so forth—to constraining mechanisms within the book itself.

Texts from bygone years construct representations of the possible uses of the written word and the various ways of handling printed matter in which we can recognize the cleavages that those who produced books held to be decisive. Such perceptions are essential to the extent that they underlie strategies for writing and for publishing that were governed by the supposed skills and expectations of the various target publics. Hence those perceptions acquire an efficacy traces of which can be found in explicit protocols for reading, in the forms given to typographical objects, or in the transformations that changed a text when it was given to new readers in a new publishing formula. It is thus on the basis of the various representations of reading and of the dichotomies constructed in the early modern age (between the reading of a text and the reading of an image; between literate reading and hesitant reading; between intimate reading and communitarian reading) that we must attempt to understand the uses of and adjustments made in these print pieces humbler than the book but just as omnipresent and which ranged from *images volantes* (illustrated **broadsheets**) and *placards* (topical illustrations and commentary) to the *occasionnels* and the little blue books (which often had illustrations).

Representations of older forms of reading and of the differences among them, as they are revealed on the practical level by the process of casting a text into printed form, or representations of their normative purposes in literary, pictorial, and autobiographical works constitute the basic data for an archaeology of reading practices. None the less, although they express the contrasts that were uppermost in the minds of their contemporaries, they mask other and less clearly perceived cleavages. For example, it is certain that many practices reversed the very terms of the opposition that has so often been depicted between solitary reading in the privacy of a bourgeois or aristocratic setting and reading in common among popular listeners. In reality, reading aloud while others listened long remained one of the practices that cemented elite sociability; conversely, printed matter penetrated to the very heart of the humble home, where it imbued modest objects that were by no means always books with traces of an important moment in private life, a memory of an emotion, or a sign of identity. Contrary to the classical image of "the people," a product of the early modern age, "the people" is not always to be sought in the plural, but rather in the secret solitude of the humble practices of individuals who cut out the images of the *occasionnels*, who colored printed engravings, and who read the chapbooks for simple enjoyment.

The approach proposed in the present work (and put into effect in a few others) is tied to a particular terrain (France between the sixteenth and the eighteenth century) and to a specific problem (the effects of the penetration of printed written matter on the culture of the greater number). It attempts to put into operation two propositions of Michel de Certeau. The first recalls, against all reductive attempts to deny the creative and inventive force of practice, that reading is never totally constraint and that it cannot be deduced from the texts it makes use of. The second stresses that readers' tactics, insinuated in the *lieu propre* (place of their own) produced by the strategies of writing, obey rules, follow logical systems, and imitate models. This reflects the paradox underlying any history of reading, which is that it must postulate the liberty of a practice that it can only grasp, massively, in its determinations. Constructing communities of readers as "interpretive communities" (Stanley Fish's expression), discerning how material forms affect meaning, localizing social difference in practices more than in statistical distributions—these are the routes laid out for anyone who wishes to understand as a historian the "silent production" that is "the activity of reading."[xxxi]

Notes

i. Michel de Certeau, *L'invention du quotidien, vol. 1, Arts de faire* (1980), rev. ed. Luce Giard (Paris: Gallimard, 1990), 251, quoted from Certeau, *The Practice of Everyday Life*, trans. Steven F. Rendall (Berkeley, Los Angeles, and London: U of California P, 1984), 174.

ii. Certeau, *L'invention du quotidien*, 247, quoted from *The Practice of Everyday Life*, 170–71. On the coupling of reading and writing in Certeau, see Anne-Marie Chartier and Jean Hebrard, "L'invention du quotidien, une lecture, des usages," *Le debat* 49 (March-April 1988): 97–108.

iii. Paul Ricoeur, *Temps et récit*, 3 vols., vol. 3, *Le temps raconte* (Paris: Editions du Seuil, 1985), 228–63, available in English as Ricoeur, *Time and Narrative*, trans. Kathleen McLaughlin and David Pellauer, 3 vols. (Chicago: U of Chicago P, 1984–88).

iv. Michel de Certeau, "La lecture absolue (Théorie et pratique des mystiques chrétiens: XVIe-XVIIe siècles)," in *Problèmes Actuels de la Lecture*, ed. Lucien. Dallenbach and Jean Ricardou (Paris: Editions Clancier Guenaud, 1982), 65–79, quotation p. 67. The suggestions in this essay also appear in Michel de Certeau, *La Fable Mystique: XVIe-XVIIe siècles* (Paris: Gallimard, 1982, 1987), esp. in pt 3, "La scène de renonciation," 209–73, available in English as Certeau, *The Mystic Fable: The Sixteenth and Seventeenth Centuries*, trans. Michael B. Smith (Chicago: U of Chicago P, 1992).

v. For one example of such an approach, see Lisa Jardine and Anthony Grafton, "Studied for Action: How Gabriel Harvey Read His Livy," *Past and Present* 129 (November 1990): 30–78.

vi. Certeau, "La lecture absolue," 66–67.

vii. D.F. McKenzie, *Bibliography and the Sociology of Texts*, The Panizzi Lectures, 1985 (London: The British Library, 1986), 20. [See also McKenzie's essay above, pp. 45–62.]

viii. Carlo Ginzburg, *Il formaggio e i vermi: Il cosmo di 14/1 mugnaio del '500* (Turin: Einaudi, 1976), available in English as *The Cheese and the Worms: The Cosmos of a Sixteenth-Century Miller*, trans. John and Anne Tedeschi (Baltimore: Johns Hopkins UP, 1980); Jean Hebrard, "Comment Valentin Jamerey-Duval apprit-il a lire? L'autodidaxie exemplaire," *Pratiques de la lecture*, ed. Roger Chartier (Marseilles: Rivages, 1985), 24–60; *Journal de ma vie, Jacques-Louis Menetra, compagnon vitrier au XVIIIe siècle*, presented by Daniel Roche (Paris: Montalba, 1982), available in English as Jacques-Louis Menetra, *Journal of my Life*, with an introduction and commentary by Daniel Roche, trans. Arthur Goldharnmer, foreword by Robert Darnton (New York: Columbia UP, 1986). [Domenico Scandella (Menocchio) (1532–1600), Italian peasant religious leader who was burned at the stake for heresy; Valentin Jamerey-Duval (b. 1695), French scholar who ascended from the lower classes to become the Librarian for the Duke of Lorraine; Jacques-Louis Ménétra (b. 1738), French working-class diarist whose journal has become influential in the study of the working class in eighteenth-century France.]

ix. Roger Chartier, "Loisir et sociabilité: Lire à haute voix dans l'Europe moderne," *Littératures classiques* 12 (1990): 127–47, available in English as "Leisure and Sociability: Reading Aloud in Early Modern Europe," *Urban Life in the Renaissance*, ed. Susan Zimmerman and Ronald F.E. Weissman (Newark: U of Delaware P, and London and Toronto: Associated UP, 1989), 105–20.

x. Roger E. Stoddard, "Morphology and the Book from an American Perspective," *Printing History* 17 (1990): 2–14.

xi. For a programmatic definition of *Rezeptionstheorie*, see Hans Robert Jauss, *Literaturgeschichte als Provokation* (Frankfurt: Suhrkamp Verlag, 1974), in French translation as *Pour une esthétique de la réception*, trans. Claude Maillard (Paris: Gallimard, 1978) and available in English as *Toward an Aesthetic of Reception*, trans. Timothy Bahti, introduction by Paul de Man (Minneapolis: U of Minnesota P, 1982).

xii. D.F. McKenzie, "Typography and Meaning: The Case of William Congreve," in *Buch and Buchhandel in Europa in achtzehnten Jahrhundert: The Book and the Book Trade in Eighteenth-Century Europe*,

Proceedings of the Fifth Wolfenbilttler Symposium, November 1–3, 1977, ed. Giles Barber and Bernhard Fabian (Hamburg: Dr Ernst Hauswedell, 1981), 81–126.

xiii. Henri-Jean Martin with Bruno Delmas, *Histoire et pouvoirs de l'écrit* (Paris: Librairie Académique Perrin, 1988), 295–99, English translation: *The History and Power of Writing* (Chicago: U of Chicago P, 1994).

xiv. Quoted in McKenzie, *Bibliography and the Sociology of Texts*, 46–47.

xv. The essential but debatable work on this topic is Robert Mandrou, *De la culture populaire aux XVIIe et XVIIIe siècles: La Bibliothèque bleue de Troyes* (Paris: Stock, 1964: new ed., Paris: Imago, 1975). For a critique of that work, see Michel de Certeau, Dominique Julia and Jacques Revel, "La beauté du mort: Le concept de 'culture populaire,'" *Politique aujourd'hui* (December 1970): 3–23, reprinted in Michel de Certeau, *La culture au pluriel* (1972), 2nd ed. (Paris: Christian Bourgeois, 1980), 49–80.

xvi. Roger Chartier, "Les livres bleus" and "Figures littéraires et expériences sociales: La littérature de la gueuserie dans la Bibliothèque bleue," *Lectures et lecteurs dans la France d'Ancien régime* (Paris: Editions du Seuil, 1987), 247–70, 271–351, respectively, available in English as "The *Bibliothèque bleue* and Popular Reading" and "The Literature of Roguery in the *Bibliothèque bleue*," *The Cultural Uses of Print in Early Modern France*, trans. Lydia G. Cochrane (Princeton, NJ: Princeton UP, 1987), 240–64; 265–342.

xvii. Lawrence W. Levine, "William Shakespeare and the American People: A Study in Cultural Transformation," *American Historical Review* 89 (February 1984), 34–66; Levine, *Highbrow/Lowbrow: The Emergence of Cultural Hierarchy in America*, The William E. Massey, Sr. Lectures in the History of American Civilization, 1986 (Cambridge, MA and London: Harvard UP, 1988).

xviii. For a recent reformulation of this question, see David Harlan, "Intellectual History and the Return of Literature," *American Historical Review* 94 (June 1989): 581–609.

xix. Pierre Bourdieu and Roger Chartier, "La lecture: Une pratique culturelle," in *Pratiques de la lecture*, ed. Chartier, 217–39.

xx. Paul Saenger, "Silent Reading: Its Impact on Late Medieval Script and Society," *Viator, Medieval and Renaissance Studies* 13 (1982): 367–414; Saenger, "Physiologic de la lecture et séparation des mots," *Annales E.S.C.* (1989): 939–52.

xxi. Certeau, *L'invention du quotidien*, 253–54, quoted from Certeau, *The Practice of Everyday Life*, 175–76.

xxii. Rolf Engelsing, "Die Perioden der Lesergeschichte in der Neuzeit: Das statistische Ausmass und die soziokulturelle Bedeutung der Lekture," *Archiv für Geschichte des Buchwesens*, 10 (1970), 945–1002; Erich Schön, *Der Verlust der Sinnlichkeit, oder, Die Verwandlungen des Lesers: Mentalitatswandel um 1800* (Stuttgart: Klett-Cotta, 1987).

xxiii. Philippe Aries, "Pour une histoire de la vie privée," and Roger Chartier, "Les pratiques de l'écrit," *Histoire de la vie privée*, ed. Philippe Aries and Georges Duhy, 5 vols. (Paris: Editions du Seuil, 1985–87), vol. 3, *De la Renaissance aux Lumières*, ed. Roger Chartier, 7–19 and 112–61, respectively, available in English as Aries, "Introduction" and Chartier, "The Practical Impact of Writing," *A History of Private Life*, trans. Arthur Goldhammer, 5 vols. (Cambridge, MA, and London: Belknap P of Harvard UP, 1987–1991), vol. 3, *Passions of the Renaissance*, 1–11 and 111–59.

xxiv. See Robert Darnton, "First Steps Toward a History of Reading," *Australian Journal of French Studies* 23.1 (1986): 5–30.

xxv. Roger Laufer, "L'espace visuel du livre ancien," in *Histoire de l'édition française*, ed. Henri-Jean Martin and Roger Chartier, 4 vols. (Paris: Prornodis, 1982–86), vol. 1, *Le livre conquérant: Du Moyen Age au milieu du XVIIe siècle* (1982), 579–601, reprint ed. (Paris: Fayard/Cercle de la Librairie, 1989), 579–601; Laufer, "Les espaces du livre," ibid., vol. 2, *Le livre triomphant: 1660–1830* (1984), 128–39, reprint ed. (Paris: Fayard/Cercle de la Librairie, 1990), 156–72.

xxvi. See the studies gathered in *Les usages de l'imprimé (XVe-XIXe siècle)*, ed. Roger Chartier (Paris: Fayard, 1987), available in English as Chartier, *The Culture of Print: Power and the Uses of Print in Early Modern Europe*, trans. Lydia G. Cochrane (Princeton, NJ: Princeton UP, 1989).
xxvii. Margaret Spufford, "First Steps in Literacy: The Reading and Writing Experiences of the Humblest Seventeenth-Century Autobiographers," *Social History* 4.3 (1979): 407–35.
xxviii. Giorgio Patrizi, "*Il libro del Cortegiano* e la trattatistica sul comportamento," *Letteratura italiana*, ed. Alberto Asor Rosa, 8 vols. (Turin: Einaudi, 1984), vol. 3, *Le forme del testa*, pt. 2, *La prosa*, 855–890; Roger Chartier, "Distinction et divulgation: La civilité et ses livres," in Chartier, *Lectures et lecteurs dans la France d'Ancien régime*, 45–86, available in English as "From Texts to Manners: A Concept and Its Books: *Civilité* between Aristocratic Distinction and Popular Appropriation," in Chartier, *The Cultural Uses of Print in Early Modern France*, 71–109.
xxix. For examples of this, see Roger Chartier, "La pendue miraculeusement sauvée: Etude d'un occasionnel," and Catherine Velay-Vallantin, "Le miroir des contes: Perrault dans les Bibliothèques bleues," *Les usages de l'imprimé*, ed. Chartier, 83–127 and 129–55, respectively, available in English as "The Hanged Woman Miraculously Saved: An *occasionnel*" and "Tales as a Mirror: Perrault in the *Bibliothèque bleue*," in *The Culture of Print*, ed. Chartier, 59–91 and 92–136, respectively.
xxx. Certeau, *L'invention du quotidien*, p. 249, quoted from *The Practice of Everyday Life*, p. 172.
xxxi. Stanley Fish, *Is There a Text in This Class? The Authority of Interpretive Communities* (Cambridge, MA, and London: Harvard UP, 1980).

18.

Adrian Johns, "Introduction: The Book of Nature and the Nature of the Book," *The Nature of the Book: Print Knowledge in the Making.* Chicago: U of Chicago P, 1998. 1–57

Adrian Johns (b. 1965) is the Allan Grant Maclear Professor of History at the University of Chicago, where he specializes in the history of the sciences, the history of the book and media, and, more recently, intellectual piracy and property from the Renaissance to the present. In *The Nature of the Book* (1998), Johns directly challenges Eisenstein's conception of a print revolution and attempts to disentangle her claim that the introduction of print resulted in the scientific revolution (see above, pp. 215–30). Eisenstein contends that the ability to mass produce the same text and to disseminate it meant that scholars were "freed from spending their lives eradicating scribal mistakes" and "thus made possible the progressive improvement of knowledge" (272). Johns specifically targets Eisenstein's assertion that the characteristics she (and now most of us) associate with print—namely, greatly improved standardization, dissemination, and fixity—were not simply the result of a new technology; in fact, he points out that in the early days of print, texts were not inherently more uniform, accurate, and reliable than their manuscript predecessors. Disparities between copies along with widespread practices of piracy meant that printing did not immediately usher in the revolution Eisenstein claims. According to Johns, because printing was not uniform, the claims Eisenstein makes for it are seriously undermined. (It should be noted that Eisenstein has recently defended her work from Johns,[1] re-asserting her argument that the shift in writing and reproductive technologies from script to print did usher in momentous change and forcefully advocating for the importance of attending to the momentous effects of shifts in communication technology.)

Instead, Johns argued that readers did not automatically confer credit on early print; and they accepted print as a reliable vehicle for communication only because of the efforts of those involved in printing. Johns's most important claim is that "the very identity of print itself has had to be made" and that this process came about only "by virtue of hard work, exercised over generations and across nations" (p. 269). Johns advances many of these important claims in the first chapter of his book, excerpted below. In this chapter, he takes up the specific examples of several early astronomers, including the

1 Elizabeth L. Eisenstein, "An Unacknowledged Revolution Revisited," *The American Historical Review* 107.1 (2002): 47 pars. 26 Oct. 2011. <http://www.historycooperative.org/journals/ahr/107.1/ah0102000087.html>.

Danish astronomer Tycho Brahe and the Italian astronomer Galileo Galilei, in order to support his argument that the arrival of print did not instantaneously usher in a new era and that the same problems that were pervasive with manuscript circulation continued in the early years of print.

Introduction: The Book of Nature and the Nature of the Book

Pick up a modern book. This one will do: the one you are looking at right now.[2] What sort of object is this? There are certain features about it of which you can be reasonably confident. Its professed author does indeed exist and did indeed write it. It contains information believed to be accurate, and it professes to impart knowledge to readers like you. It is produced with its author's consent, and it is indeed the **edition** it claims to be. If the dust jacket announces that it is the product of a given organization—in this case the University of Chicago Press—then this too may be believed. Perhaps you may even say to yourself that that fact vouches for the quality of its content. You may safely assume that the book you now hold will have been printed in many copies, and a copy of the same book bought in Australia, say, will be identical in all relevant respects to one bought in the United States or in Great Britain.

Begin to use this object. It should immediately become clear that there are things about its proper utilization of which a reader like you can be equally confident. This book has not been produced with a specific, individual reader in mind. To some extent, at least, it is a commercial product, designed to appeal to purchasers. Its cost may have limited its readership somewhat, but its distribution will still have been fairly widespread, and it may be available for consultation in a number of libraries. Readers will not have to endure any formal vetting or approval process before being permitted to read this book. You yourself are free to carry it around and to lend it to others. You are not free, however—beyond certain legal limits—to reproduce its contents in your own right for commercial gain. Nor may you now proceed to issue translations, epitomes,[3] or abridgments of those contents. It is improbable (but not impossible) that you will choose to declaim the text of this book aloud in a public place, and it is even more unlikely that you will make it the focus of a collective act of commemoration, worship, or similar ritual. Some books are indeed used in these ways, incidentally, but this is probably not going to be one of them. In short, while in some respects this book's usage is up to you, in others it appears to be quite closely constrained.

That we can assume all these things of such an object—that such an object actually exists—derives from our living in what many people call "print culture." Such phenomena, we say, are due to printing. Or rather, we would say this, but so infallibly reliable are they that we rarely even have to articulate the relation. It is obvious, self-evident, even necessary. The practical consequence is that we do not have to agonize over the reliability of a published book before we can put it to use. We do not need to undertake investigatory work to confirm that its author does exist

2 I.e., the book in which Johns's essay originally appeared.

3 A summary of a longer work's major points.

and that its text is authorized. No literary spy need be hired to ascertain that it was indeed made by its stated **publisher** and that its contents will be the same as those of another copy of the same book found in any other place. In our world, all these characteristics are inherent in virtually any published book (and the duties of a "literary agent" are comparatively mundane). We take them for granted, every day of our lives. We depend on them, and our reliance is, by and large, justified.

It is this very self-evidence that encourages us to ascribe all these characteristics to a technological order of reality. If called upon, we may assert that printed texts are identical and reliable because that is simply what printing *is*. The identification is as momentous as it is straightforward. It has become the point of departure for all current interpretations of print and its cultural consequences, and is the root from which the very concept of "print culture" has grown.[i] It is thereby also the foundation of a conviction that that culture has rendered possible the establishment of veracious knowledge in modern society. Yet this book argues that it is substantially false. Not only that: *The Nature of the Book* maintains that it is probably the most powerful force resisting the acceptance of a truly historical understanding of print and any cultural consequences it may foster.

This book contends that what we often regard as essential elements and necessary concomitants of print are in fact rather more contingent than generally acknowledged. Veracity in particular is, it argues, extrinsic to the press itself, and has had to be grafted onto it. The same may be said of other cognate attributes associated with printing. In short, *The Nature of the Book* claims that the very identity of print itself has had to be *made*. It came to be as we now experience it only by virtue of hard work, exercised over generations and across nations. That labor has long 269
been overlooked, and is not now evident. But its very obscurity is revealing. It was dedicated to effacing its own traces, and necessarily so: only if such efforts disappeared could printing gain the air of intrinsic reliability on which its cultural and commercial success could be built. Recovering it is therefore a difficult task, but one well worth attempting. This book tries accordingly to excavate the complex issues involved in the historical shaping of print—issues that our conventional notion of print culture obscures with all the authority of a categorical definition, *The Nature of the Book* is the first real attempt to portray print culture in the making.

Yet how could print conceivably be anything else? If it were really the result of a significant process of historical construction, then surely we could not now find it so obvious, universal, and undeniable. If it could have developed differently, then surely it would now differ noticeably from place to place, and in any one place it would still bear the traces of its development. We would *see* the wreckage of failed alternatives all about us. In practical terms, we would indeed have to worry about the specific status of a given printed book in order to use it. Questions of where it had come from, who had made it, and whether or not its putative author acknowledged its content would all need to be posed and answered before we could safely trust any printed book. That they do not constitutes a powerful reason to accept the obvious.

Even a little reflection suggests that there is greater complexity to the subject than this. Any printed book is, as a matter of fact, both the product of one complex set of social and technological processes and also the starting point for another. In the first place, a large number of people, machines, and materials must converge and act together for it to come into existence at all.

How exactly they do so will inevitably affect its finished character in a number of ways. In that sense a book is the material embodiment of, if not a consensus, then at least a collective consent. Its identity can be understood accordingly, in terms of these intricate processes. But the story of a book evidently does not end with its creation. How it is then put to use, by whom, in what circumstances, and to what effect are all equally complex issues. Each is worthy of attention in its own right. So a printed book can be seen as a nexus conjoining a wide range of worlds of work. Look closely and you are likely to find simplicity and inevitability in neither the manufacture of an object like this nor its subsequent construal. The processes leading to the deployment of a book and those consequent upon its use both depend on too many contingencies. That in turn means that print cannot be as straightforward as it seems.

[...]

If an early modern reader picked up a printed book—*De Natura Libri,*[4] perhaps—then he or she could not be immediately certain that it was what it claimed to be, and its proper use might not be so self-evident. **Piracy** was again one reason: illicit uses of the press threatened the credibility of all printed products. More broadly, ideas about the correct ways to make and use books varied markedly from place to place and time to time. But whatever the cause, it is not easy for us to imagine such a realm, in which printed records were not necessarily authorized or faithful. What could one know in such a realm, and how could one know it? We ourselves routinely rely on stable communications in our making and maintenance of knowledge, whether of the people around us or of the world in which we live. That stability helps to underpin the confidence we feel in our impressions and beliefs. Even the brisk skepticism we may express about certain printed materials—tabloid newspapers, say—rests on it, inasmuch as we feel confident that we can readily and consistently identify what it is that we are scorning. Instability in records would equally rapidly translate into uncertainty of judgment. The most immediate implication, then, would be epistemic.[5]

In a sense, the point is a well-entrenched one. It has been made at least since the sixteenth century, when **printers** and others took to lauding their craft for its power to preserve. The contrast they drew was with previous **scribal** forms of reproduction, which they delineated as intrinsically corruptive. It now seems almost indisputable. We should recognize, however, that the first identification of that contrast was partly a product of interest. Printers stood to gain from what was originally a contentious argument, not a straightforward observation. If, on the other hand, it is not printing per se that possesses preservative power, but printing put to use in particular ways, then we ourselves may usefully draw some rather different distinctions. We may look not just for differences between print and **manuscript** reproduction, but for different ways in which the press itself and its products have been (and continue to be) employed. The roots of textual stability may be sought as much in these practices as in the press itself. And knowledge, such

4 This is the title of Johns's book translated into Latin.

5 Relating to the study of knowledge.

Fig. 3.2: Changing representations of Uraniborg. Elevation, as shown in Tycho's own publication. Tycho Brahe, *Astronomiae Instauratae Mechanica* (1598). (The British Library, C.45.h.3.)

as it is, has come to depend on that stability. Here, then, is one way in which a social history of print can prove not just interesting, but consequential. A reappraisal of print in the making can contribute to our historical understanding of the conditions of knowledge itself.

I. Tycho Brahe, Galileo Galilei, and the Problems of "Print Culture"

[...]

In 1576 the king of Denmark granted Tycho [Brahe][6] feudal powers over a small island named Hven, lying in the sound just north of Copenhagen. Here Tycho erected a remarkable castle-observatory, in which he lived and worked for the next two decades. His work at this palatial observatory, which he called Uraniborg (Fig. 3.2), resulted in an unequaled series of observations and interpretations of the heavens. They secured for him a reputation as the greatest of all astronomers. Almost immediately, Tycho himself became an icon of the very enterprise of astronomy. Mathematical practitioners in succeeding generations came to see in him an unimpugnable[7] model of the harmony of nobility and "mechanic" skill. In the hands of mod-

6 Tycho Brahe (1546–1601), Danish nobleman and astronomer.

7 Beyond criticism.

ern historians, moreover, Tycho has again proved a powerful emblem, in two important and revealingly paradoxical respects. First, Uraniborg has become the outstanding Renaissance exemplar of the importance of locale in the making of knowledge.[ii] This is an important issue, to be addressed later in this chapter. At the same time, however, Tycho has come to personify the role of print in transcending place and rendering natural knowledge universal. He has thus become emblematic of the transformation of local craft into global science. This latter apotheosis has been due above all to Elizabeth Eisenstein's *The Printing Press as an Agent of Change*. Published in 1979, this is still probably the most influential anglophonic interpretation of the cultural effects of printing. Yet *The Nature of the Book* pursues for the most part a quite different approach from hers. A consideration of Tycho Brahe provides the ideal opportunity to specify how and why it does so.[iii]

The unifying concept of Eisenstein's argument is that of "print culture." This "culture" is characterized primarily in terms of certain traits that print is taken to endow on texts. Specifically, those produced in such an environment are subject to conditions of *standardization, dissemination*, and *fixity*. The last of these is perhaps the most important. According to Eisenstein, printing meant the mass reproduction of precisely the same text, repeatable on subsequent occasions and in different locations. No longer need any work suffer the increasing **corruption** that Eisenstein assumes to be endemic to any "script culture." She focuses on this attribute of fixity as the most important corollary of the press, seeing it as central to most of the effects of print culture.[iv] For example, in conditions of fixity the simple practice of juxtaposing texts became immensely significant. Newly available printed representations of opposing astronomical, anatomical, or other knowledge could be placed side by side, and their viewer could now be confident that conclusions drawn from comparing such reliable texts would be worthwhile. Correspondents on the other side of Europe could do the same, with representations that could be supposed identical.[v] Such scholars no longer needed to concern themselves primarily with the fidelity of their representations, and were freed from spending their lives eradicating scribal mistakes. It was fixity that liberated them from such labor and thus made possible the progressive improvement of knowledge. This is the basis on which Eisenstein can claim that the Renaissance and Reformation were rendered permanent by the very permanence of their **canonical** texts, that nationalism developed thanks to the stabilization of laws and languages, and that science itself became possible on the basis of phenomena and theories reliably recorded.[vi] With this new foundation of certainty at their disposal, "scientists" (as Eisenstein insists on calling them) could begin to develop new doubts about their previous authority, namely antiquity. The "Scientific Revolution" was thus inconceivable without a preceding printing revolution.[vii] And for Eisenstein Tycho Brahe personifies both.

[...]

... Maybe the Tycho so far portrayed will change somewhat if we investigate more closely how his "mediators" actually came into being and were put to use. For Tycho does indeed represent perhaps the purest example of a particular kind of printing, and a particular way of using the

Fig. 3.3: The presentation of an astronomical volume to an absolute monarch: Hevelius offering his *Cometographia* to Louis XIV of France. The vignette portrays Hevelius's dedication of the book to Louis; it does not represent a real scene. Hevelius, *Cosmographica*. (The Syndics of Cambridge University Library.)

products of the press. Like Regiomontanus[8] before him, and Hevelius[9] after, he controlled his
own printing operation. His was a singular printing house, however. It was as geographically
isolated on the island of Hven as it was socially isolated from the companies of the European
book trade. It was even physically embedded in the five-meter high, five-meter thick wall that 273
enclosed his entire estate. Such isolation meant, at least in principle, that Tycho could produce
books when, for whom, and in whatever form he liked.[viii] Works like his *Astronomiae Instauratae
Mechanica*, which described Uraniborg in all its glory, were scarcely intended to be published at
all, but were to be distributed as gifts to patrons at courts and universities (Fig. 3.3). The more
prestigious were not just printed books, but hybrids—hand-colored, individualized tributes,
presented to their intended recipients on specific dates.[ix] Tycho meant to bypass the structures
of the international book trade altogether.

The recipient of a book like Tycho's *Astronomiae Instauratae Mechanica* was thus likely to be found in a distinctive place: a royal court or a university. Here a book took its place and gained its meaning only amid a vast arsenal of other objects directed to similar ends. It would be encountered alongside natural curiosities, thaumaturgical[10] wonders, mathematical devices, paintings, musical compositions, alchemical[11] medallions, magical machines, and other books (Fig. 3.4). In such surroundings, every aspect of appearance and handling mattered for creating an impact. The reader of such a work, in such a place, would be consciously engaging in a dis-

---

8 Johannes Müller von Königsberg, Latin name Regiomontanus (1436–76), German mathematician and astronomer.

9 Johannes Hevelius (1611–87), Polish astronomer.

10 Relating to miracles.

11 Alchemy is the branch of science that attempts to turn metals into gold and to achieve eternal life.

tinctive system of practices and ideas—in Tycho's case, feudal ones. The giving and receiving of such gifts was an important part of court culture, enmeshed in conventions of status recognition, reciprocation, and reward. This could not fail to affect the way in which that reader regarded the book. It was invested with enhanced credit, being untainted by "mechanick" influence, and it was accorded the privileged reception due to such a noble gesture.[x] The veracity of its contents warranted respect. They could not be dismissed without cost. Yet at the same time such a gesture all but commanded creative responses—including challenges—from suitably prestigious interlocutors. Tycho's book would now fall subject to the conventions surrounding philosophical and mathematical disputes in these settings. The variables that determined both whether a "scientific" debate would even take place, and, once battle had been joined, how it would proceed, were local ones: to whom one presented the book, through which channels it was distributed, with which patron it was identified. Disputes like this were affairs of honor, conducted through appropriate intermediaries and champions. Printed books were their vehicles. That was what they were *for*.[xi]

When, therefore, Tycho found himself attacked by Nicolai Reymers Baer (or Ursus), a recognized mathematician but a man of low birth whom he himself had accused of **plagiarism**, a scientific debate was not the principal outcome. Rather unusually, Tycho did in fact deign to reply himself. But he did so with a series of elaborately indignant letters to his fellows across Europe, which he had printed on his press at Uraniborg and circulated in 1596. In this correspondence he recited the tale of Ursus's alleged theft and argued that, whatever the date of Ursus's publication, Tycho had *printed* the cosmology first. Ever willing to recall his opponent's low birth, he even seems to have suggested that Ursus be executed for his presumption. But the more philosophical side of the dispute he delegated to a second, the relatively humble Kepler.[12] The result was Kepler's "Defense of Tycho against Ursus," a remarkably sophisticated historical argument for the status of astronomical hypotheses and their creators. It was never printed.[xii]

Much even of this story could be taken as reinforcing Eisenstein's image. However, two elements make it less confirmatory. The first is that Tycho was extremely atypical in his successful use of print. Other writers regarded him not as representative of their own situation, but as a model that they sought, with widely varying degrees of success, to emulate. Like most icons, he stood for an ideal that was unrealizable. The second is that, as his argument against Ursus implies, even Tycho himself found the ideal impossible to achieve. That was why he built his own printing house and paper mill: he discovered that he could not otherwise obtain acceptable materials and workmanship.[xiii] Even with these in place, moreover, most of his work remained unprinted until after his death.[xiv] Latour's pre-printed forms,[13] for example, seem to be mythical;

12 Johannes Kepler (1571–1630), German astronomer who developed a ground-breaking set of laws of planetary motion.

13 A reference to Bruno Latour's (b. 1947) discussion of Tycho's preprinted forms for recording astronomical observations, which he supposedly distributed across Europe so that other astronomers could record their observations and return them to him, thus, as Johns summarizes, allowing him "effectively to turn every observatory in Europe into an extension of Uraniborg" (13). Latour argues that these forms were central to the development of modern science.

Fig. 3.4: The place of books in the cabinet of curiosities. In places like this—a museum of curiosities in Naples—books, along with crocodiles, fossils, and a panoply of natural and artificial marvels, served to facilitate conversation. Imperato, *Historia Naturale*. (The Syndics of Cambridge University Library.)

Tycho did correspond extensively, but left no trace of having used such objects.[xv] And while he began producing the images and descriptions for the *Astronomiae Instauratae Mechanica* as early as 1585, soon after building his printing house, the volume was not completed until thirteen years later. By that time he was in exile in Hamburg—the only place he could find with printers capable of finishing the book, even though he had brought his own press with him from Hven. Taken by his son to the Holy Roman Emperor, the book now became an instrument in Tycho's attempt to secure imperial **patronage.**[xvi] This proved successful, and he removed to Prague. But he soon discovered that even here, in the center of the empire, no printer able to undertake his prized star catalogue could be found. He was reduced to circulating hand-copied versions, and the catalogue remained unprinted on his death (Fig. 3.5).[xvii]

At that point his works began to fall out of court circles altogether. They descended into the hands of the book trade. Even the *Astronomiae Instauratae Mechanica* was reprinted commercially. Such books were likely to be produced to different standards. They stood at risk of piracy and imitation, despite Rudolf II's stern commands forbidding such "printers' frauds." They were also likely to be read in different ways, by different people, in different places and for different reasons.

Their accreditation became far more insecure. So, for example, the English astronomer royal, John Flamsteed—who, as we shall see, identified himself profoundly with Tycho—dismissed the posthumous printing of his star tables as, quite simply, a "fraud."[xviii] Tycho's inscriptions appear to have become distinctly mutable once they fell out of his control and left the courtly matrix.

If even Tycho Brahe found it so difficult to maintain his printed materials as mobile and immutable, what hope is there of explaining the achievements of less powerful figures in Eisenstein's terms? Attempting to do so would mean attributing to printed books themselves attributes of credibility and persuasion that actually took much work to maintain. It would thereby draw our attention away from important problems that any individual, even Tycho, had to overcome.[xix] Talk of "print culture" is strangely ethereal when compared to Tycho's struggles. It stands oddly disconnected from the professed experiences of real historical figures. For example, who actually printed (and reprinted) Tycho's pages? It is a question worth asking, since Tycho himself spent many frustrating years seeking suitable printers—and the astronomer Christoph Rothmann, at least, believed that Ursus had been able to plagiarize his world system because he had been employed in Tycho's printing house.[xx] And how were those pages employed by their recipients? Of what use were they *to them*? How did Tycho ensure that such distant readers took them as authoritative, especially when, as was often the case in early modern testimony about celestial observations, they conflicted with figures produced locally? Eisenstein and Latour begin by decreeing such issues peripheral. The *Nature of the Book* does the opposite. If we are to understand how and why printed texts became trustworthy, it argues, we need to appreciate

all of them, in something approaching their full "woof."

The disconnected air exhibited by Eisenstein's account is not accidental. In her work, printing itself stands outside history. The press is something "*sui generis*,"[14] we are told, lying beyond the reach of conventional historical analysis. Its "culture" is correspondingly placeless and timeless. It is deemed to exist inasmuch as printed texts *possess* some key characteristic, fixity being the best candidate, and carry it with them as they are transported from place to place. The origins of this property are not analyzed. In fact, the accusations of **technological determinism** sometimes leveled against Eisenstein may even be wide of the mark, since she consistently declines to specify *any* position on the question of how print culture might emerge from print.[xxi] But the example of Tycho does suggest that the focus of her approach is *in practice* highly selective. The portrait it generates identifies as significant only the clearest instances of fixity. It regards instances when fixity was not manifested as exceptional failures, and even in the successful cases it neglects the labors through which success was achieved. It identifies the results of those labors instead as powers intrinsic to texts. Readers consequently suffer the fate of obliteration: their intelligence and skill is re-attributed to the printed page. Tycho's labors deserve better. To put it brutally, what those labors really tell us is that Eisenstein's print culture does not exist.

There is an alternative. We may consider fixity not as an *inherent* quality, but as a *transitive* one. That is, it may be more useful to reverse our commonsense assumption. We may adopt the principle that fixity exists only inasmuch as it is recognized and acted upon by people—and

14 Existing in a class of its own.

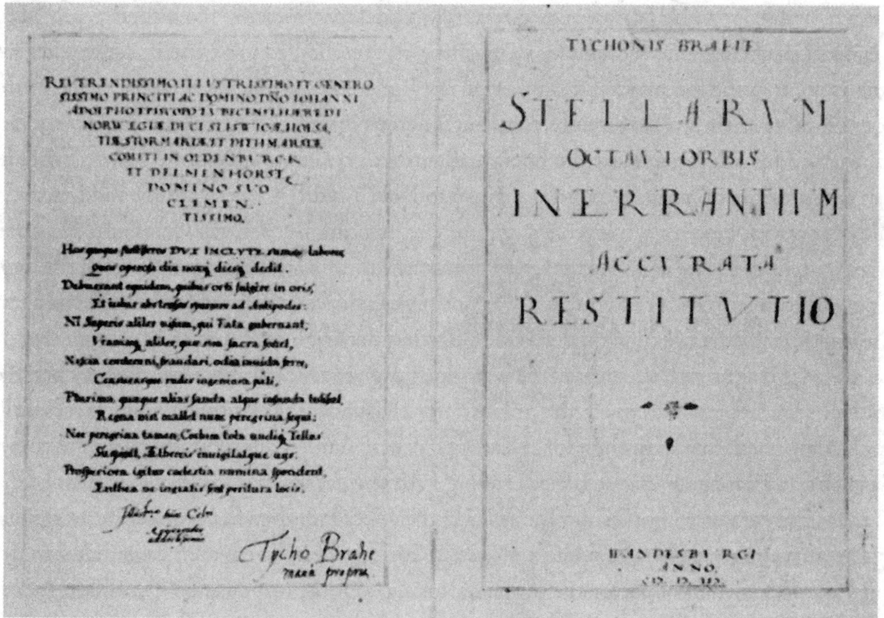

TYCHONIS BRAHE

STELLARVM OCTAVI ORBIS INERRANTIVM ACCVRATA RESTITVTIO

Tycho Brahe manu propria

Fig. 3.5: Tycho Brahe's star catalogue, distributed in manuscript to princes and patrons. Note the careful imitation of a printed page. Reproduced by Norlind, *Tycho Brahe*, 297. (The Syndics of Cambridge University Library.) 277

not otherwise. The consequence of this change in perspective is that print culture itself is immediately laid open to analysis. It becomes a *result* of manifold representations, practices and conflicts, rather than just the monolithic *cause* with which we are often presented.[xxii] In contrast to talk of a "print logic" imposed on humanity,[xxiii] this approach allows us to recover the construction of different print cultures in particular historical circumstances. It recognizes that texts, printed or not, cannot compel readers to react in specific ways, but that they must be interpreted in cultural spaces the character of which helps to decide what counts as a proper reading. In short, this re-casting has the advantage of positioning the cultural and the social where they should be: at the center of our attention.

If Tycho Brahe has hitherto been made the personification of print culture, then the experiences of his near-contemporary, Galileo Galilei,[15] may in turn stand for this new approach. In 1610, Galileo produced the first of a series of dramatically successful books, called the *Sidereus Nuncius*. In vivid illustrations, he showed mountains and valleys on the surface of the Moon, and the discovery of new stars in Orion and the Pleiades. These and other "nebulous" regions—the Milky Way in particular—could now be resolved into stars. Above all,

15 Galileo Galilei (1564–1642), often simply known as Galileo, was an Italian physicist, mathematician, engineer, astronomer, and philosopher.

however, Galileo revealed four previously unknown satellites revolving about Jupiter, providing a vivid model of Copernican cosmology. This discovery, embodied in a small book, would soon establish him as the foremost philosopher on the Italian peninsula. Yet it was not just for the intrinsic value of these observations that the Sidereus Nuncius had such an impact. In fact, Galileo and his allies deployed the book brilliantly to make its success.[xxiv] He was angling to enter the court of an absolute prince, Cosimo II de' Medici,[16] whose family had long been linked iconographically to Jupiter. Paying for the printing himself, Galileo named his new Jovian[17] satellites accordingly. As the "Medicean stars" they formed the centerpiece of the book he now presented to the grand duke. It was not easy. Galileo actually had to change the name in mid-printing, after Medici officials told him that his original choice of "Cosmian" would not meet with approval; the new name was glued over the old on the pages already printed. He then went in person to make the presentation, ensuring that Cosimo would successfully see the new phenomena through his telescope. When Galileo distributed additional copies to princes and cardinals across Europe, along with spyglasses to support his claims, he did so under the carapace[18] of Cosimo himself via the Medici diplomatic service. In promulgating the announcement, Galileo had presented Cosimo with heroic and noble homage, for which the conventions of patronage suggested an appropriate response. When that response came, Galileo declared that his whole "being" had been transformed. Perhaps for the first time, a mathematical practitioner underwent the transfiguration into court philosopher.[xxv]

Galileo was trying to create a new kind of authority on, and for, natural knowledge. The construction of this persona and the elaboration of his work in cosmology and mechanics thus took place together, and both rested on the skillful exploitation of patronage dynamics at an absolutist court. The point is a rather subtle one. Patronage was not simply something that could be used as a tool to achieve aims defined by other, perhaps scientific, criteria. It helped constitute at once what were reasonable aims to adopt, what were good claims to make in pursuit of those aims, how they could best be made, and to which audiences. Evidence came into being and was accredited by means of the civil culture of the court. There was no "Galileo, scientist" standing outside this cultural realm and manipulating its mechanisms in order to achieve objective ends. It is important to appreciate this, since at each crucial moment of transition—from Venetian patronage to Florentine, and thence to papal—books were central to Galileo's advance. From the *Sidereus Nuncius*, so effective in raising him to Cosimo's court, to the *Dialogo*, which triggered his downfall at the hands of Pope Urban VIII's Inquisition,[19] books were key elements in any strategy to take advantage of patronage opportunities.[xxvi]

16 Cosimo II de' Medici (1590–1621), Italian ruler who was Grand Duke of Tuscany from 1609–20; an absolute ruler is one that has unlimited power over his governed territory.

17 Of the planet Jupiter.

18 "The upper body-shell of tortoises, and of crustaceans" (*OED*), used figuratively here to mean a protective covering.

19 Pope Urban VIII (1568–1644) was pope from 1623–44; this was during the time of the Roman Inquisition, occurring from the mid-sixteenth century to the mid-seventeenth century, which sought to prosecute possible heretics against Catholicism.

At court, what appear to modern eyes to be scientific disputes were seen by participant and spectator alike in these different terms. They would be triggered and structured by Galileo's patron for purposes of diversion and the expression of status. He was expected to produce entertaining and involving debates, and to challenge other court philosophers of sufficient rank.[xxvii] While it was important not to lose such a dispute, it was also important to conduct it properly; and, as Tycho Brahe had known, regular challenges by qualified individuals were imperative to show that one's status was being recognized. So, for example, when the Medici ambassador presented a copy of the *Sidereus Nuncius* to imperial mathematician Johannes Kepler, he responded correctly with a printed reply dedicated not to Galileo, but to the ambassador. In a sense, Galileo was engaging with Kepler; but Cosimo was also communicating with the Holy Roman Emperor.[xxviii] Unlike Tycho, however, Galileo had no private press. His book fell immediately into the hands of commercial printers. By late 1610 an unauthorized impression had appeared in Frankfurt, his fine illustrations marred by hasty reproduction. For the rest of the century these adulterated images would be reproduced repeatedly. Countless readers saw them—far more, in all likelihood, than ever came upon the authorized originals of what are probably the most momentous astronomical images of their era.[xxix]

Even exempting such piratical enterprises, the social dynamics of challenges were modified by the unavoidable involvement of new personnel and places. The case of Galileo's 1623 work, *Il Saggiatore*, is instructive in this respect. It was printed in April and May in a few hundred copies. In October the work was ritually presented to the pope and important cardinals. This
was the courtly aspect of its production. But Galileo's allies also used the book in what looks 279
much more like a process of publication. They did so in order to expose the tactics of a Jesuit antagonist lurking behind the pseudonym of "Lotario Sarsi." They ensured that one of the licenser's copies was delivered early to the Sun bookshop. This was a well-known center for libertine[20] literature, which the Jesuit would surely be monitoring for such works. Its proprietor had agreed to co-operate in the plan. Sure enough, "Sarsi" arrived and seized upon that very copy. He "changed color" on the spot, attacked the **bookseller** himself as personally responsible for the text, and left declaring loudly that he would take up the challenge and produce a rebuttal within three months. In so doing, he revealed himself as Orazio Grassi, lecturer in mathematics at the Collegio Romano and the Jesuits' most prestigious architect. The bookseller immediately told Galileo's allies of his outburst. Two of them wrote excitedly to their friend to tell him the news, whereupon Galileo came to Rome and successfully preempted Grassi's rebuttal.[xxx] Access to the bookshop, and the character of both the premises and its proprietor, had transformed the dispute.

Here was something quite alien to Tycho's Uraniborg. For Galileo too, however, despite this success, it was ultimately to prove an inauspicious development. In the events of his notorious fall not only the printers and booksellers, but the entire licensing and publication mechanism, would be implicated. The *Saggiatore* incident led directly to this far more significant affair. It began in 1623 with the election of Galileo's ally, Maffeo Barberini, as Pope Urban VIII.

---

20 Sexually promiscuous and generally immoral.

This was the spur for Galileo, becalmed[21] in Florence, to seek a position of favor in Rome itself. He did so by using two tools: *Il Saggiatore* itself, which he re-directed at the last moment and presented to Urban, and his long-projected Copernican work on the tides. The first of these was a great success. After the incident at the Sun bookshop, Urban had it read to him at table, and seems to have relished its wit and rhetorical dexterity. He began to accord Galileo audiences, in which his favor seemed clear. So clear, in fact, that Galileo probably understood himself released from a private instruction issued some years earlier not to engage in public support for Copernicanism.[22] He returned to Florence and began writing his greater work, which became the momentous *Dialogo ... sopra i due Massimi Sistemi del Mondo.*

The *Dialogo* was not immediately or obviously scandalous. In fact, it successfully underwent an extensive licensing procedure, such that the printed edition could boast as many as five imprimaturs.[xxxi] [23] Initially planned to appear in Rome in 1630, it was finally published only in 1632, in Florence. The book was in the event duly licensed in both cities, but nonetheless it caused a stir. Another of Galileo's Jesuit opponents, Christoph Scheiner, immediately repeated Grassi's error by revealing his outrage in front of the bookseller, who dutifully reported it back to his friends.[xxxii] Murmurs soon spread that Galileo had violated Bellarmine's[24] confidential instruction, which was rumored to ban him from even discussing the issue of Copernicanism, let alone supporting it. Events then moved very quickly. In April, Galileo's ally and patronage broker in Rome, Ciampoli, fell from grace, just as Urban came under stringent attack from Spanish interests for insufficient zeal in pursuing the Thirty Years' War[25] and the struggle against heresy. This was a crucial development. Ciampoli was just the kind of intermediary needed by such a book to smooth its progress in courtly circles; he it was who had read *Il Saggiatore* to Urban at table. Without such mediation the *Dialogo* would soon prove vulnerable, especially as the pope now associated its publication with Ciampoli's newly established impropriety. In these circumstances, what might otherwise have been appreciated as witty dialogic sallies came to be read very differently. Papal sensibilities took its barbs as personal affronts. That summer Urban called in the book, appointing a commission to investigate the circumstances of its appearance. In the autumn he transferred the case to the Inquisition. In February Galileo was summoned to Rome. From April until June negotiations continued in secret. The pope urged the Inquisition on, however, and Galileo was finally resolved to be "vehemently suspected of heresy"—one of the most serious offenses in the Inquisition's ambit. He was forced to abjure,[26] and sentenced to permanent house arrest.[xxxiii]

---

21 Stranded or unable to move.

22 Copernicanism refers to the theories of Nicolaus Copernicus (1473–1543), who discovered that the sun—not the Earth—is at the center of the universe.

23 Latin for "let it be printed"; the formal signature by an official authorizing the publication of a book.

24 Roberto Francesco Romolo Bellarmino (1542–1621), Catholic Italian cardinal who was canonized in 1930.

25 Thirty Years' War (1618–48), a major European War, a component of which was the conflict between Catholicism and Protestantism.

26 To formally retract.

Sudden and irrevocable, Galileo's fall has remained one of the most resonant incidents in history, let alone in the history of science. Here, as throughout Galileo's life, the uses of a book had proved crucial to the transformation. This was no Tychonic success story. It would be difficult to identify fixity or immutability as important to the role of the *Dialogo* at any stage of its story. Galileo's fate was decided by different criteria. His fortunes, and in Mario Biagioli's terms perhaps even his identity, rested on the way in which his book would be read. As scholars working in the last two decades have revealed, Galileo was a fine mathematician, a profound philosopher, a superb rhetorician, a devious antagonist, and an agile courtier; but even he could not control such readers.[xxxiv]

II. From Fixity to Credit

A new historical understanding of print is needed. What will it look like? One immediately evident feature will be its regard for the labors of those actually involved in printing, publishing, and reading. Another will be its respect for their own representations of printing, embracing both its prospects and its dangers. The dangers in particular will loom larger and more substantial than they have hitherto. Historians tend to disregard such perils as accidental; early modern readers and writers knew otherwise. They had good cause to fear that in the realm of print seemingly in prospect, authorial control over such efforts as Galileo's would be undermined. More than that, some of them thought that it was *already* undermined. Increasingly they articulated responses by
which the culture of the learned gentleman could be saved from this "mechanick art." Perhaps we 281
should remind ourselves of the extent to which those responses appeared to fail—of the extent to which the print culture of the eighteenth century could be perceived by contemporaries, not as a realization of the rationalizing effects now so often ascribed to the press, but as destabilizing and threatening to civility. Such a stance, artificial though it would be, might help us to distance ourselves from the apparent stability of our own print culture, with its uniform editions, mass reproduction, and **typographical** fixity. Early modern fears would then begin to appear not as incidental lapses, defined a priori as marginal, but as credible statements of experience. They would finally be recognized as no less substantial than the phenomenon of fixity itself.

[...]

As the opening pages of this chapter implied, there was one concern in particular that possessed early modern readers, and that may be used as a key to the rest. Could a printed book be trusted to be what it claimed? Perhaps a reader would be prudent to reserve judgment. On the most obvious level, whether a *Sidereus Nuncius* printed in Frankfurt was really Galileo's text, or an *Astronomiae Instauratae Mechanica* produced in Nuremburg was really Tycho's, could justifiably be doubted. More broadly, the very apprehension that printed books might not be self-evidently creditable was enough to rule out any possibility of their bearing the power attributed to them by most modern historians. And that apprehension was widespread. Piracy and plagiarism occupied readers' minds just as prominently as fixity and enlightenment. Unauthorized translations, epitomes, imitations, and other varieties of "impropriety" were, they believed, routine hazards. Very few noteworthy publications seemed to escape altogether from such practices, and none at all could safely be regarded as immune a priori. It was regarded as extremely unusual for a book professing knowledge—from lowly **almanacs** to costly **folios**—to be published in the relatively unproblematic manner we now assume. Contemporaries had good reason to be wary. Their editions of Shakespeare, Donne, and Sir Thomas Browne[27] were liable to be dubious. So were those of Robert Boyle,[28] not to mention the first "scientific" journal, the *Philosophical Transactions*. Even Isaac Newton's[29] *Principia* suffered from unauthorized reprinting. From Galileo and Tycho to Newton and John Flamsteed,[xxxv] no significant learned author seemed to escape the kinds of practices soon colloquially subsumed under the label of piracy. This meant that even when a book was not so treated, the possibility that it might be still permeated the negotiations, practices, and conventions by which it was made, distributed, exchanged, and used. If piracy was as widespread as commonly feared, then trusting any printed report without knowledge of those processes could be rash. Profound problems of credit thus attended printed materials of all kinds. Without solutions there could be few meaningful uses for books—and perhaps no durable reasoning from them.

It should not be surprising, then, that contemporaries did not always identify fixity as a central characteristic of print. Surveying the books available to aid ocean navigators, Edmond Halley,[30] for one, noted that "the first Editions have generally been the best; frequent Copying most commonly vitiating[31] the Originals."[xxxvi] Even when people did refer to enhanced reliability, it was often in the face of direct evidence to the contrary. Textual corruption of even such closely monitored texts as the Bible actually increased with the advent of print, due to various combinations of piracy and careless printing.[xxxvii] The first book reputed to have been printed without any errors appeared only in 1760. Before then, variety was the rule, even within single editions. Martin Luther's[32] German translation of Scripture was actually beaten into print by its first piracy, and in succeeding years the proportion of unauthorized to authorized texts was roughly ninety to one; these included Luther's own translation, newly ascribed to others (including Catholics), and others' work re-attributed to him. A century later, the first folio of Shakespeare boasted some six hundred different **typefaces**, along with non-uniform spelling and punctuation, erratic divisions and arrangement, mispaging, and irregular **proofing**. No two copies were identical. It is impossible to decide even that any one is "typical."[xxxviii] In such a world, questions of credit took the place of assumptions of fixity.

---

27 John Donne (1572–1631), English metaphysical poet; Sir Thomas Browne (1605–82), English nonfiction writer and doctor.

28 Robert Boyle (1627–91), British natural philosopher and writer best known for his work in chemistry.

29 Isaac Newton (1642–1727), English physicist best known for his work on gravity and motion.

30 Edmond Halley (1656–1742), English astronomer after whom Halley's Comet is named.

31 Reducing the quality of.

32 Martin Luther (1483–1546), German theologian whose beliefs were the foundation of the Protestant Reformation.

In attending to this issue, *The Nature of the Book* builds on Steven Shapin's identification of trust as a key element in the making of knowledge.[xxxix] Where Shapin concentrates particularly on inter-subjective trust, asking fundamental questions about *whom* one should believe, why, and in what circumstances, *The Nature of the Book* identifies a similar issue in the trust accorded to printed materials. It asks how readers decided *what* to believe. A central element in the reading of a printed work was likely to be a critical appraisal of its identity and its credit. Readers were not without resources for such an assessment. When they approached a given book, with them came knowledge about the purposes, status, and reliability of printed materials in general—knowledge they used to determine the appropriate kind and degree of faith to vest in this unfamiliar object. Yet here too they also brought to bear knowledge about kinds of people. Their worries about literary credit were often resolved, as a matter of everyday practice, into assessments of the people involved in the making, distribution, and reception of books. Readers worried about who decided what got into print, and about who controlled it once it was there. The twin problems of whom and what to credit were in practice often combined into one.

When early modern readers determined a book not to be worthy of credit, they could do so on a number of grounds. It was in the attribution of "piracy," however, that the issues of credibility and print particularly converged. The term seems to have been coined by John Fell, bishop of Oxford, to describe the rapacious practices of London printers and booksellers. It had a technical meaning: a pirate was someone who indulged in the unauthorized reprinting of a title recognized to belong to someone else by the formal conventions of the printing and bookselling 283
community. But it soon came to stand for a wide range of perceived transgressions of civility emanating from print's practitioners. As such, almost any book could, in principle, find itself accounted a piracy, whatever its actual circumstances of production and distribution. Historians of printing have therefore misconstrued instances of alleged piracy in at least two senses. First, they have seen piracy, like fixity, as inherent in the object, and not as a contestable attribution. Second, furthermore, they have assumed cases of piracy to be exceptions, accidental (in the philosophical sense of the word) to the essentially stabilizing character of print. Contemporaries were not so sure of this. Incidents that have been retrospectively dismissed as isolated and exceptional often seemed to them commonplace and representative. They might even be seen as attempts to undermine, and thereby to reform, the whole structure of the book trade. Even when conducted in more humdrum circumstances, moreover, and with less ambitious ends in sight, piracy still had powerful implications. Its apparent prevalence affected the economic and cultural conditions of all printed and written communication. It conditioned the accreditation of printed materials of all sorts, from the humblest ABC to the most elaborate encyclopedia.[xl]

For the learned, and for natural philosophers in particular, this had peculiarly important consequences. In the agonistic[33] field of early modern natural knowledge, allegations of piracy readily shaded into charges of plagiarism. Such allegations therefore extended to the reputation of authors. That is, unauthorized printing threatened to "unauthorize" authors themselves.

33 Contentious.

Even more important, it threatened the credibility to be attributed to their ideas. Like print itself, piracy therefore had *epistemic* as well as *economic* implications: it affected the structure and content of knowledge. For an enterprise like experimental philosophy, in particular, which depended implicitly on the trust accorded to the printed reports issued by its protagonists, the consequences threatened to be nothing short of devastating.

[...]

The sources of print culture are therefore to be sought in civility as much as in technology, and in historical labors as much as in immediate cause and effect. The "printing revolution," if there was one, consisted of changes in the conventions of handling and investing credit in textual materials, as much as in transformations in their manufacture. The point deserves to be stressed explicitly. I do not question that print enabled the stabilization of texts, to some extent; although fixity was far rarer and harder to discern in early modern Europe than most modern historians assume. I do, however, question the character of the link between the two. Printed texts were not intrinsically trustworthy. When they were in fact trusted, it was only as a result of hard work. Fixity was in the eye of the beholder, and its recognition could not be maintained without continuing effort. At no point could it be counted on to reside irremissibly in the object itself, and it was always liable to contradiction. Those faced with using the press to create and sustain knowledge thus found themselves confronting a culture characterized by nothing so much as indeterminacy. If printing held no necessary bond to truth, neither did it show a necessary bond to falsity or corruption. Each link remained vulnerable to dispute. It is this epistemic indeterminacy that lends the history of the book its powerful impact on cultural history. Understanding how it could be overcome to make knowledge and hence cultural change is what the history of the book is for.

[...]

Notes

i. For this term, see E.L. Eisenstein, *The Printing Press as an Agent of Change: Communications and Cultural Transformations in Early Modern Europe*, I (Cambridge: Cambridge UP, 1979), 43–159. I am not sure of its genesis; Eisenstein, its prime recent exponent, seems to take it from M. McLuhan (e.g., *The Gutenberg Galaxy* [London: Routledge and Kegan Paul, 1962], 146–49).

ii. O. Hannaway, "Laboratory Design and the Aim of Science: Andreas Libavius versus Tycho Brahe," *Isis* 77 (1986): 585–610. Shackelford has responded to Hannaway, with more heat than really necessary, in J. Shackelford, "Tycho Brahe, Laboratory Design, and the Aim of Science," *Isis* 84 (1993): 211–30.

iii. Eisenstein, *Printing Press*, abridged as E.L. Eisenstein, *The Printing Revolution in Early Modern Europe* (Cambridge: Cambridge UP, 1983). For examples of Eisenstein's influence in a range of fields, see E.B. Tribble, *Margins and Marginality: The Printed Page in Early Modern England* (Charlottesville: UP of Virginia, 1993), 3–4; K.B. Neuschel, *Word of Honor: Interpreting Noble Culture in Sixteenth-Century France* (Ithaca, NY: Cornell UP, 1989), chap. 6; D.R. Olson, *The World on Paper: The Conceptual and Cognitive Implications of Writing and Reading* (Cambridge: Cambridge UP, 1994), 37 and passim; M. Rose, *Authors and Owners: The Invention of Copyright* (Cambridge, MA: Harvard UP, 1993), 3–4; C.J. Sommerville,

The Secularization of Early Modern England: From Religious Culture to Religious Faith (New York: Oxford UP, 1992), 48, 70, 79, 178, 180, 219 n. 1; B. Anderson, *Imagined Communities: Reflections on the Origin and Spread of Nationalism*, rev. ed. (London: Verso, 1983), 30–49; W. Eamon, *Science and the Secrets of Nature: Books of Secrets in Medieval and Early Modern Culture* (Princeton, NJ: Princeton UP, 1994), 6–9, 94–96; H.E. Lowood and R.E. Rider, "Literary Technology and Typographic Culture: The Instrument of Print in Early Modern Science," *Perspectives in Science* 2 (1994): 1–37 (where "typographic culture" and "print culture" are indistinguishable). Many more could be cited. It is difficult to be sure, but I would estimate that Tycho Brahe is referred to at least as frequently in *Printing Press* as any other Renaissance figure.

iv. Eisenstein, *Printing Press*, 71–88, 113–26.

v. Eisenstein, *Printing Press*, 74–75, 597; *Printing Revolution*, 42–88. It is worth pointing out that these phenomena are similar to those attributed by anthropologists to the invention of writing, e.g., in J. Goody, *The Logic of Writing and the Organization of Society* (Cambridge: Cambridge UP, 1986), 134–38, 174.

vi. Eisenstein, *Printing Press*, 80, 117, 180–82, 200–210, 212, 646. The argument about nationalism has since been developed more thoroughly by Anderson in *Imagined Communities*, esp. 41–49.

vii. Eisenstein, *Printing Press*, 107, 186, 193–94, 197, 640; M. Hunter, "The Impact of Print," *The Book Collector* 28 (1979): 335–52; E.J. Leed, "Elizabeth Eisenstein's *The Printing Press as an Agent of Change* and the Structure of Communications Revolutions," *American Journal of Sociology* 88 (1982): 413–29.

viii. V.E. Thoren, *Lord of Uraniborg: A Biography of Tycho Brahe* (Cambridge: Cambridge UP, 1990), 144.

ix. Tycho Brahe, *Astronomiae Instauratae Mechanica* (Wandesbek: n.p., 1598); Tycho Brahe, *Opera Omnia*, V, ed. J.L.E. Dreyer (Copenhagen: Gylendal), 317–18. A list of known copies with their recipients is in W. Norlind, *Tycho Brahe: En levnadsteckning med nya bidrag belysande hans liv och verk* (Lund, Sweden: C.W.K. Gleerup, 1970), 286–93.

x. R.S. Westman, "The Astronomer's Role in the Sixteenth Century: A Preliminary Study," *History of Science* 18 (1980): 105–47. See also Hannaway, "Laboratory Design"; and compare Eamon, "Court, Academy and Printing House: Patronage and Scientific Careers in Late Renaissance Italy," *Patronage and Institutions: Science, Technology and Medicine at the European Court 1500–1700*, ed. B.T. Moran (Woodbridge: Boydell, 1991), 41.

xi. In addition to the works of Biagioli and Hannaway cited here, see P. Findlen, "The Economy of Exchange in Early Modern Italy," in *Patronage and Institutions*, ed. B.T. Moran (Woodbridge: Boydell, 1991), 5–24; P. Findlen, "Courting Nature," in *Cultures of Natural History*, ed. N. Jardine, J.A. Secord, and E.C. Spary (Cambridge: Cambridge UP, 1996), esp. 61; B.T. Moran, *The Alchemical World of the German Court: Occult Philosophy and Chemical Medicine in the Circle of Moritz of Hessen (1572–1632)* (Stuttgart: F. Steiner, 1991), esp. 9, 93–94, 97, 110–12; P.H. Smith, *The Business of Alchemy: Science and Culture in the Holy Roman Empire* (Princeton, NJ: Princeton UP, 1994), 49–50; Daston, "The Factual Sensibility," *Isis* 79 (1988): 452–70; and N.Z. Davis, "Beyond the Market: Books as Gifts in Sixteenth-Century France," *Transactions of the Royal Historical Society*, 5th ser., 33 (1983): 69–88. Compare also the difficulties experienced by Becher in translating commercial documents for courtly readers: Smith, *Business of Alchemy*, 139.

xii. Tycho Brahe, *Epistolarum Astronomicarum Libri*, Vol. 1 (Uraniborg: from the author's printing house, 1596), 33–34, 148–51; Brahe, *Opera Omnia*, VI, 61–62, 179; N. Jardine, *The Birth of History and Philosophy of Science: Kepler's "A Defence of Tycho Against Ursus" with Essays on Its Provenance and Significance* (Cambridge: Cambridge UP, 1984), 9–28 and passim (15 for Ursus's peasant background); J.L.E. Dreyer, *Tycho Brahe: A Picture of Scientific Life and Work in the Sixteenth Century* (Edinburgh: A. and C. Black, 1890), 183; E. Rosen, *Three Imperial Mathematicians: Kepler Trapped between Tycho Brahe and Ursus* (New York: Abaris, 1986). Tycho's decision to strike at Ursus personally (which Kepler, for one, found surprising) may well be related to the fact that, as Hannaway points out, his status was feudal in origin; Tycho was not a courtier. See Hannaway, "Laboratory Design," 589 n. 11. For Tycho's conflicts see also O. Gingrich and R.S. Westman, *The Wittich Connection: Conflict and Priority in Late Sixteenth-Century Cosmology* (Philadelphia: American Philosophical Society, 1988, Vol. 78, no. 7 of *Transactions of the American Philosophical Society*), (which contrasts Tycho's treatment of Ursus to his response to the relatively well-born Wittich), and Thoren, *Lord of Uraniborg*. I am grateful to Robert Westman for conversations about this affair, which remains one of the more controversial among scholars of early modern astronomy.

xiii. Brahe, *Opera*, VI, 224, 365 n; VII, 214, 274; IX, 175; X, 302. Even with the mill in working order, he remained reliant on the cooperation of nearby parishioners to provide raw materials, as they were exhorted to do in regular "rag sermons."

xiv. In particular, the star catalogue (circulated only in manuscript until years after Tycho's death, and then inaccurately printed) and the *Astronomiae Instauratae Progymnasmata* (begun at Uraniborg, but completed only under the aegis of his heirs in 1602).

xv. I have found no trace of these preprinted forms in Tycho's *Opera Omnia*, nor in any relevant secondary authority. I am also unable to find Latour's source for this central claim; it may well derive from an imaginative reading of certain passages in Eisenstein's *Printing Press*, e.g., 626–27.

xvi. Brahe, *Opera*, V, 317–18; VIII, 166, 177, 388.

xvii. Thoren, *Lord of Uraniborg*, 150, 185–87, 367, 381–97, 414–15, 421, 478. Tycho had planned to present the catalogue to Rudolf II on New Year's Day, apparently a customary occasion for gift-giving: T.D. Kaufmann, *The Mastery of Nature: Aspects of Art, Science, and Humanism in the Renaissance* (Princeton, NJ: Princeton UP, 1993), 106. For Rudolf II's undertaking to provide a "new Uraniborg," see Brahe, *Opera*, VIII, 178, 188. It is also likely, of course, that Tycho's circulation of the catalogue in manuscript was intended to enhance its status as a collectible object.

xviii. Brahe, *Astronomiae Instauratae Mechanica* (Nuremburg: Levinus Hulsius, 1602); A. Curtius (Lucius Barettus, pseud.), *Historia Cælestis* (Augsburg: S. Utzschneider, 1666; reissue Ratisbon: J.C. Emmrich, 1672); J. Flamsteed, *The Preface to John Flamsteed's "Historia Cælistis Britannica"* (1725), trans. and ed. A.D. Johnson and A. Chapman (London: National Maritime Museum, 1982), 99–100. For Rudolf's condemnation of "Typographorum fraudem," see Brahe, *Opera*, II, 9.

xix. Compare S.J. Schaffer, "The Eighteenth Brumaire of Bruno Latour," *Studies in History and Philosophy of Science* 22 (1991): 178–92, on the concept of the "ideal reader."

xx. Dreyer, *Tycho Brahe*, 184 note 1.

xxi. Eisenstein, *Printing Press*, e.g., 159, 166–68, 609 n, 89–90, 702–03. See also A. Grafton, "The Importance of Being Printed," *Journal of Interdisciplinary History* 11 (1980): 265–86. The fact that Eisenstein is simultaneously too provincial (thus missing the contingent elements of print culture by her lack of a comparative perspective) and not local enough (thus missing the work needed to make print culture at all) may be inferred from Cohen's discussion in H.F. Cohen, *The Scientific Revolution: A Historiographical Inquiry* (Chicago: U of Chicago P, 1994), 357–67.

xxii. Compare the discussions of power in B. Latour, "On the Powers of Association," in *Power, Action and Belief: A New Sociology of Knowledge?*, ed. J. Law (London: Routledge and Kegan Paul, 1986), 264–80, and B. Latour, "Technology Is Society Made Durable," in *A Sociology of Monsters: Essays on Power, Technology and Domination*, ed. J. Law (London: Routledge, 1991), 103–31. This suggestion has obvious resonances with certain works in critical theory, such as S. Fish, *Is There a Text in This Class? The Authority of Interpretive Communities* (Cambridge, MA: Harvard UP, 1980). Since my aim is primarily historical I shall not be making many explicit links with such material, though the parallel deserves to be noted. Compare also D.F. McKenzie, *Bibliography and the Sociology of Texts* (London: British Library, 1985).

xxiii. E.g., A. Kernan, *Printing Technology, Letters and Samuel Johnson* (Princeton, NJ: Princeton UP, 1987), 48 ff.

xxiv. Galileo Galilei, *Sidereus Nuncius: or, The Sidereal Messenger*, trans. and ed. A. Van Helden (Chicago: U of Chicago P, 1989), 1–24, 87–113; M. Biagioli, "Galileo's System of Patronage," *History of Science* 28 (1990): 1–62; Westfall, "Science and Patronage: Galileo and the Telescope," *Isis* 76 (1985): 11–30.

xxv. Galilei, *Sidereus Nuncius*, 19, 90–91; Galileo Galilei, *Le Opere di Galileo Galilei*, X, (Firenze: G. Barbèra, 1964–68), 353; M. Biagioli, *Galileo, Courtier: The Practice of Science in the Culture of Absolutism* (Chicago: U of Chicago P, 1993), chap. 2. John Dee did request the title of Philosopher and Mathematician to Emperor Rudolf II before Galileo achieved his own elevation in Florence, but without success: N.H. Clulee, *John Dee's Natural Philosophy: Between Science and Religion* (London: Routledge, 1988), 224. Westman, "Astronomer's Role," is essential for understanding the significance of this transfiguration.

xxvi. For this portrayal I am indebted to Biagioli, *Galileo, Courtier*, esp. chaps. 1, 2, 6. See also Eamon, "Court, Academy, and Printing House"; Biagioli, "Galileo's System of Patronage." Some aspects of Biagioli's work—particularly his claim regarding the association between Cosimo and Jupiter—have been strenuously challenged by Shank, with results that remain inconclusive at the time of writing. The particular thrust of Shank's attack means that it does not directly impinge on my own argument. See especially M. Biagioli, "Playing with the Evidence," *Early Science and Medicine* I (1996): 70–105, and M.H. Shank, "How Shall We Practice History? The Case of Mario Biagioli's *Galileo, Courtier*," *Early Science and Medicine* I (1996): 106–50.

xxvii. Biagioli, *Galileo, Courtier*, 163; Biagioli, "Galileo's System of Patronage," 30; B. Castiglione, *The Book of the Courtier*, trans. T. Hoby (1561, Reprint, London: Everyman, 1928), esp. 68 ff.

xxviii. S. Drake, *Galileo Studies: Personality, Tradition, and Revolution* (Ann Arbor: U of Michigan P, 1970), 131–38.

xxix. Galileo Galilei, *Sidereus Nuncius* (Venice: T. Baglionus, 1610); Galileo Galilei, *Sidereus, Nuncius* [sic] (Frankfurt: printed at the Palthenius printing house, 1610). It is perhaps worth adding the rider that the latter edition was unauthorized as far as anyone then or now has known; Galileo (like Isaac Newton later in the century) was quite capable of perpetrating his own "unauthorized" publications. The point remains that he was unable to oversee the production of the work, and in particular that of its illustrations.

xxx. Galilei, *Opere*, XIII, 145–48; Galilei, *Sidereus Nuncius*, 94, 102; P. Redondi, *Galileo: Heretic*, trans. R. Rosenthal (Harmondsworth: Penguin, 1987), 28–67, 179–83; Drake, *Galileo at Work*, 268–77, 279, 284–85, 287–88. It is perhaps worth stressing that those involved in this plan probably knew "Sarsi's" actual identity throughout; the objective was to get an open declaration from Grassi of the fact, and of his future intentions.

xxxi. Its five licenses are reproduced in Galileo Galilei, *Dialogue Concerning the Two Chief World Systems*, trans. S. Drake, Foreword A. Einstein, 2nd ed. (Berkeley and Los Angeles: U of California P, 1967), [2]. For problems over printing and licensing, see S. Drake, *Galileo at Work: His Scientific Biography* (Chicago: U of Chicago P, 1978), 311–14, 319–20, 332–44, and Westfall, "Patronage and the Publication of Galileo's Dialogue," *History and Technology* 4 (1987), esp. 386–87, 393.

xxxii. Galilei, *Opere*, XIV, 359–60.

xxxiii. M.A. Finocchiaro, *The Galileo Affair: A Documentary History* (Berkeley and Los Angeles: U of California P, 1989), 32–39; Drake, *Galileo at Work*, 344–52. After this chapter was written, Paula Findlen and Tara Nummedal kindly showed me their "Words of Nature: Scientific Books in the Seventeenth Century," in Andrew Hunter (ed.), *Thornton and Tully's Scientific Books, Libraries and Collectors: A Study of Bibliography and the Book Trade in Relation to the History of Science*, fourth edition (Aldershot: Ashgate, 2000), 164–215, which includes an excellent discussion of Tycho, Galileo, and Kepler.

xxxiv. Biagioli, *Galileo, Courtier*, 2–3, 87. For the different aspects of Galileo cited here, see also Drake, *Galileo at Work*; P.K. Feyerabend, *Against Method: Outline of an Anarchistic Theory of Knowledge* (1975, Reprint, London: Verso, 1978); J.D. Moss, *Novelties in the Heavens: Rhetoric and Science in the Copernical Controversy* (Chicago: U of Chicago P, 1993); W. Wallace, *Galileo's Logic of Discovery and Proof: The Background, Content, and Use of His Appropriated Treatises on Aristotle's Posterior Analytics* (Dordrecht: Kluwer, 1992).

xxxv. John Flamsteed (1646–1719), English astronomer.

xxxvi. *Atlas Maritimus & Commercialis; Or, a General View of the World, so far as relates to Trade and Navigation* (London: printed for J. and J. Knapton, W. and J. Innys, J. Darby, A. Bettesworth, J. Osborn, T. Longman, J. Senex, E. Symon, A. Johnston, and the executors of W. Taylor, 1728), i-iii.

xxxvii. M.H. Black, "The Printed Bible," in *The Cambridge History of the Bible*, vol. 3, ed. S.L. Greenslade (Cambridge: Cambridge UP, 1963), 408–75. Eisenstein dismisses Black's argument out of hand: *Printing Press*, 80.

xxxviii. J.O. Newman, "The Word Made Print: Luther's 1522 *New Testament* in an Age of Mechanical Reproduction," *Representations* 11 (1985): 106–07 and passim; M. de Grazia, *Shakespeare Verbatim: The Reproduction of Authenticity and the 1790 Apparatus* (Oxford: Oxford UP, 1991), 15–19, 42; Kernan, *Printing Technology*, 48.

xxxix. S. Shapin, *A Social History of Truth: Civility and Science in Seventeenth-Century England* (Chicago: U of Chicago P, 1994); Schaffer, "A Social History of Plausibility: Country, City and Calculation in Augustan Britain," in *Rethinking Social History: English Society 1570–1920 and Its Interpretation*, ed. A. Wilson (Manchester: Manchester UP, 1993), 129.

xl. An inspiration for this treatment, as for other aspects of this book, has come from medieval history. Medievalists have devoted much attention to activities of "forgery" and "plagiarism." They have constructed a sophisticated historiography addressing the diversity of acts since subsumed under such labels, immersing the subject in a detailed and authoritative treatment of the cultural uses of writing and reading in general. Medieval "forgery" is appropriately seen as a form of truth-creation, justified (and perhaps even determined) by contemporary ideas about the nature and purposes of writing. It was also extraordinarily common. Perhaps half the documents known from Merovingian times are by our lights fake, and two-thirds of the documents known to have been issued to ecclesiastics before 1100 would now be reckoned forgeries. See A. Grafton, *Forgers and Critics: Creativity and Duplicity in Western Scholarship* (London: Collins and Brown, 1990), 24–25, 30–32; M.T. Clanchy, *From Memory to Written Record: England 1066–1307* (London: Edward Arnold, 1979), 118–20, 231–57; B. Stock, *Implications of Literacy: Written Language and Models of Interpretation in the Eleventh and Twelfth Centuries* (Princeton: Princeton University Press, 1983), 59–87; G. Constable, "Forgery and Plagiarism in the Middle Ages," *Archiv für Diplomatik* 29 (1983): 1–41. For a robust contrasting view, see E.A.R. Brown, "*Falsitas pia sive Reprehensibilis*: Medieval Forgers and Their Intentions," in *Fälschungen in Mittelalter: Internationaler Kongress der Monumenta Germaniae Historica München, 16–19 September 1986. Teil I: Kingressdaten und Festvorträge Literatur und Fälschung* (Hanover: Hahnsche Buchhandlung, 1998), 101–19. For these medievalists' perspectives on print—which deserve more attention than they have received—see M.T. Clanchy, "Looking Back from the Invention of Printing," in *Literacy in Historical Perspective*, ed. D.P. Resnick (Washington: Library of Congress, 1983), 7–22, and M.A. Rouse and R.H. Rouse, *Authentic Witnesses: Approaches to Medieval Texts and Manuscripts* (Notre Dame: U of Notre Dame P, 1991), 449–66.

19.

James Raven, "Markets and Martyrs: Early Modern Commerce," *The Business of Books: Booksellers and the English Book Trade 1450–1850.* London and New Haven, CT: Yale UP, 2007. 46–82

James Raven (b. 1959) is professor of Modern History at the University of Essex. Raven has worked on several topics within book history: from bibliographical surveys of the novel to the history of reading, from the history of book collecting to non-commercial print. He is a leader in the economic history of books, and *The Business of Books: Booksellers and the English Book Trade 1450–1850* (2007) is now regarded as the definitive account of the first four centuries of the English book trades. In this book, Raven presents a sweeping historical study of the risks and opportunities faced by those who published (that is, financed the publication of) books. A commercial history of the first four centuries of print, it begins with the introduction of the new technology in England in the mid-fifteenth century and ends with the rise of a mass print market in the mid-nineteenth century. The study is at once meticulously detailed in its reliance on archival and bibliographical sources and empirically driven in the attempt to quantify changes in the book trades over time. In its coverage of 400 years of English history, Raven traces broad patterns of change and continuity over time.

Though Raven specializes in the eighteenth century and his most detailed analysis focuses on that period, the chapter from which this selection is taken examines the Early Modern period. Here, he traces the close ties between the political and religious upheavals of the period and the fates of the book trade and the individuals involved in it. The following excerpt examines how publishers exploited the commercial opportunities of the new technology of print even as governmental controls (in the form of economic and licensing regulations and criminal prosecutions where sentences could include corporal and capital punishment) acted as grave checks on the robust circulation of books.

Markets and Martyrs: Early Modern Commerce

The late Tudor and early Stuart English book trade was distinguished by the vigorous industry of its **stationers**, **printers**, and **booksellers**, and by the resolve of Church and State to be rid of turbulent presses and pressmen. Religious but also commercial zeal animated the stationers and printers. Together, they fueled a publishing maelstrom of bibles, prayerbooks, homilies, and secular literature that included both luxury and cheap print (as well as vast quantities of **jobbing work**—institutional and commercial forms and the like—whose survival rates are pitiful). Print broadcast the fame of Foxe, Spenser, Marprelate, Hakluyt, Shakespeare, Jonson, and Prynne.[1] Print encouraged their rivals, imitators, and detractors. For many publishing booksellers, the search for the most printable texts meant avoiding the seizable and investing in the lowly, the bland, and the voguish. The changing market brought both opportunities and frustrations. The essential conservatism of the **Stationers' Company**, protective and guarded, contrasted with the spirited, expansive provincial business upon which so much of the book trade turned.

As Mark Bland has remarked, "for contemporaries, the copiousness of the press was one of its most defining characteristics."[i] The abundant commerce in books and **pamphlets** exacerbated religious and political conflict. The book propelled confrontation between mainstream and minorities, and between licensed and exiled. Evident also, however, is a diverse populism generated by the unstable but dynamic relationships between writers, book manufacturers, policing authorities, and consumers. Early seventeenth-century booksellers and printers took on more employees and raised **composition** rates. The counterpoint to this expansion is that government regulation ensured that (at least according to official estimates) between the 1580s and 1630s the number of London printing houses remained at just over 20 (accounting for a total of some 50 printing presses). The total of printing houses rose to about 40 by 1649, and 59 at the Restoration.[2] Numbers declined again thereafter, and still officially comprised only 55 by the late 1680s (see Table 3.6). In addition, calculations of output suggest a business concentration that resulted in some 44 per cent of the estimated total printed **sheets** in London from 1614 to 1618 published by just four establishments, including the King's Printing House and the Stationers'.[ii]

1 John Foxe (1516/17–87), English historian best known for his *Book of Martyrs*, emphasizing the suffering of Protestants at the hands of Catholics; Edmund Spenser (c. 1552–99), English poet and author of *The Faerie Queene* (1590, 1596); Martin Marprelate (1558–89), pseudonym for the anonymous writer of satirical pamphlets attacking the English church; Richard Hakluyt (1552?–1616), English geographer and author, best known for his work in promoting the settlement of North America; William Shakespeare (1564–1616), English playwright and poet; Ben Jonson (1572–1637), English playwright and poet; William Prynne (1600–69), English lawyer who also wrote Puritan pamphlets attacking the Church of England.

2 The Restoration of the English monarchy under Charles II, following the English Civil Wars and Interregnum.

Year	Printing Houses	Presses
1547	15	
1582	22	
1583	23	53
1586	25	53
1604	20? [14 proposed]	
1615	19 [+ King's Printer]	33 + ?6
1628	19 + 1	38 + ?6
1633	23 + 4	
1637	23 [20 proposed]	46–51
1649	40?	
1661–63	59	
1665	48	
1666	40?	
1668	26 [actually 33?]	65 [actually 82?]
1686	44 [actually 55?]	113 [actually 145?]
1705	70?	150 +
1723	80? London 40? provinces	

Table 3.6: Number of known printing houses and presses, 1547–1723.[iii] Reprinted with the permission of James Raven.

Very material publishing considerations rested on assessments of market profiles, but also on the form of protection offered to the owner of the right to publish the title, be it a state-protected patent, a Company monopoly, or, more generally, the Company's protection of registered titles.[iv] The import trade also continued to be critical to English book supply, as government and Company enforcement officers well knew. By 1600, the English State, by commission, authorization, and regulation, had effectively transformed the market for English printing, but traditional, as well as fresh, demand continued to sustain the importation of European books.

The reign of Edward[3] proved a watershed. Booksellers benefited from the state sponsorship of official publications and from a lucrative multitude of Protestant catechisms and evangelizing literature. Fortunes beckoned for those securing official patents[4] and orders, even if these were mortgaged on the regime's survival, but other entrepreneurs like the Dutch printer, Walter Lynn, profited from an independent understanding of the nature of advanced Protestant demand. From his Billingsgate shop, he adroitly used Continental contacts to secure new and appropriate devotional publications.[v] Rewarded for his Reform publishing by a 1549 license to import lucrative quantities of wine and woad[5] from France, Lynn appears to have retired from printing in about 1550,[vi] an early example of a bookseller whose demonstration of success in business was his

3 King Edward VI (1537–53), son of Henry VIII and King of England from 1547–53.

4 A patent refers to the official and usually exclusive rights to publish certain materials.

5 A blue dye made from the plant species *Isatis tinctoria*.

ability to leave it. Under Mary,[6] the hemorrhaging by hasty exile of recently established printing expertise was followed by desperate attempts to import more liturgical and Catholic publications from abroad. The trade reversed again under the cautious and then moderately Protestant regime that followed. The early commercial development of the printing trade was thus very largely state-sponsored and state-policed, but also, especially for continued importation and non-official cheap print, fundamentally reliant upon the capacity of the domestic economy.

The increased demand that supported the opening of shops more permanent than stall-board and shed lock-ups promoted new strains of literature. Under Elizabeth and James, most disputes over booksellers' stock in the cathedral precinct concerned religion; and several shops in St Paul's Cross Yard were certainly identified with advanced belief. Many booksellers profited from exploitable *causes célèbres*,[7] such as the 1547 Paul's Cross recantation by Richard Smith, Regius Professor of Divinity at Oxford, of his defense of traditional doctrine (his *Brief treatyse settynge divers truthes*).[vii] Toby Cooke, at the Tiger's Head in the Churchyard between 1577 and 1599, served as one of many conduits for new theological works, and his widow and sons continued the business.[viii] By the early seventeenth century, secular publishing, ranging from plays to books of mathematics, navigation, and domestic and practical guidance, claimed an increased share of the market. The career of Gervase Markham (c. 1568–1637) prospered from widening tastes. His books of husbandry and household advice comprised an increasingly rich commercial property fought over by jealous stationer-booksellers.[ix]

The balance between different traders and craftsmen shifted as the range of publication—if not printing productivity—expanded during the seventeenth century. The early importance of stationers dealing in the supply of paper resulted from its necessarily heavy importation. Printing hugely increased the demand for paper. During the first century of print, importing paper stationers and wholesalers, who also imported foreign book stock, were much more heavily capitalized and more strategically powerful than other members of the book trades. In the second half of the sixteenth century, however, many London printers also profited from the advancing market. The same strengthening demand ensured that publishing booksellers consolidated their position in the early seventeenth century, largely by investment in printing rights.[x]

Nevertheless, professional demarcations remained fluid. Certainly, we should not simply assume that book professions or even individual workshops acted as discrete entities (nor indeed that the wording of **imprints** and **colophons** imply that all those involved in publishing, printing, and selling a book are there listed). The ways in which leading practitioners combined their skills, however, are now obscured because the identities of so many involved in book manufacture are lost or problematic. Compared to the physical survivals of their work, for example, we know little about those engaged in **bookbinding**. We can only speculate that many worked as journeymen bookbinders before (if ever) dealing in books or stationery.[xi] Similarly, printers were supported by increasing amounts of jobbing work, including institutional orders from the ecclesiastical

6 Queen Mary (1516–58) reigned from 1553–58.

7 A famous case (or cases), which can more generally refer to any controversial issue or event that gives rise to considerable public attention.

visitation articles onwards. The great majority of this material and its record of production is, however, entirely lost from historical sight.

Many printers were evidently not selling to the public directly but to their paying clients, publishing booksellers, and authors. Alongside them, stationers and booksellers maintained a range of sales methods and schedules. Almost no bookseller was an exclusive retailer of books, stationery, and print, but usually sold other goods besides. From what we can tell from seventeenth-century ledgers and correspondence, credit terms offered to customers and to the trade appear normally to have been about six months, but longer allowances (or reluctant and unavoidable acceptances) were common. This was very much a face-to-face society, in which commerce turned upon personal trust. How much credit was allowed, and for how long, frequently depended upon the customers, their repute, and their influence.[xii]

[...]

I. Prices and Custom

Domestic publication costs included the capital start-up expenses and job-specific costs of paper, the press and type, the labor involved in all stages of printing, and, very rarely, what had been paid to the author or begetter of the text. Paper could claim up to two-thirds of total production costs, and in a few cases three-quarters of costs.[xiii] Judging by paper costs for the printers for Cambridge University, after a sharp hike between the mid-1580s and the mid-1590s, paper prices rose by no more than 7 per cent until 1642 (when duties imposed in France under Richelieu contributed to the end of this period of stability).[xiv] Labor costs, of **presswork** and of composition, also seem to have been relatively constant in late Tudor and early Stuart England, with the ratio between composition and presswork costs naturally varying with the length of the press **run** or (in other words) the size of the **edition**. Production cost factors alone, however, cannot explain the management of prices. The pricing of books indirectly responded to general economic conditions (including importing costs), but pricing was principally determined by decisions made by the individuals financing publication. In many cases, calculations about profit margins took advantage of legal protection against competitor products.

[...]

Whatever the exact methods used to determine the price of new books, it was increased custom from the propertied classes in both London and the country that was responsible for sustaining publication rates and re-fashioning the retailing of books. Books and print responded to the development of a consumer society from the late-sixteenth century, and for the majority of metropolitan booksellers, the sales of open market publications became the basis for survival. Much direct retailing centered on the sale of small productions, notably the thousands of **almanacs**, pamphlets, and **chapbooks** peddled by chapmen and general traders, but also (in a slightly higher-status market) by the extraordinary, if not always money-spinning, increase in the publishing and pirating of plays in the early seventeenth century.[xv] London booksellers extended provincial sales and launched new titles of religious and "entertaining and instructive" literature with none of the guaranteed bespoke[8] custom of old.

The active second-hand trade for printed books similarly advanced in the early seventeenth century, borne by the rising incomes of the propertied. Robert Wilson, trading in Holborn and later in Fleet Street[9] from about 1610 to 1639, featured among those second-hand dealers in books required to submit **catalogues** of their books to the Archbishop of Canterbury in 1628. Other booksellers, in a list of 39 "as dealt in old libraries, mart books, or any other" drawn up by the Warden of the Stationers' Company, included Richard Redmer, trading at St Paul's from 1610 to 1632, George Hodges and John Hopkinson, both of Little Britain, the similarly named Jonathan Hopkinson of Aldgate, and Benjamin Fisher (also a great owner of **copyrights**) of Aldersgate Street.[xvi]

Demographic and economic changes underpinned the basic demand that enabled such risk-taking by the booksellers. The population of England and Wales nearly doubled between 1450 and 1650 from under three million (after a century and a half of stagnation and probable decline at the end of the middle ages) to some five million. England's population increased by an annual rate of about seven per thousand in the second half of the sixteenth century and five per thousand in the first half of the seventeenth century. But the location of this population was also crucial. London eclipsed all other urban development. Beyond London, the market profile was essentially rural, with custom scattered between all the other settlements. By 1680, only four towns outside London had populations in excess of 10,000.[xvii]

Our problem is to assess exactly how much spending power was provided by what was an early modern, virtually subsistence economy, and how this changed with increased economic activity and modestly increasing population totals and concentrations. An expanding population is not inevitably good economic news. If agriculture resources do not increase or even respond commensurately, then non-essential spending is squeezed and consumer spending contracts. The early modern economic regime left very little disposable income for expenditure on inessential goods after the purchase of necessary items of food, shelter, and clothing. It certainly left very little to be spent on books and print. Optimization of assets remained an unfamiliar concept.

[...]

Nevertheless, by the early seventeenth century, and despite the cautions already suggested, England boasted an increasingly prosperous and modestly redistributive economy, in which the aggregate incomes of a rising propertied group contributed to the development of a luxury market. In the first two centuries of print, with the doubling of the population set against the six-fold increase in the price of grain, the gentry and some yeomanry[10] were the real gainers.

---

8 Customized, or tailored to the consumer's demands.

9 Important sites of bookselling in London in the period.

10 Landowning farmers who were not members of the gentry class.

They notably benefited from their improvement of land gained from the Church, the monasteries, and then the Crown in the reign of Elizabeth. The new book market existed in a landscape of expanding corn markets, sturdy farmhouses, and up-and-coming parish gentry. The proliferation of bookplates tracked the increase in armigerous[11] gentry, the furnishing and refurbishment of their houses, and the unprecedented building of funerary monuments in churches. Print also described and exposed bogus upstart gentlemen, from city and country.[xviii] Surviving inventories reveal the increased possession of books and other print, as well as the gradual private accumulation of **libraries** and print collections. Norfolk, by far the best-studied county in terms of country library history, boasted at least two dozen gentlemen's and noblemen's libraries by 1650.[xix]

The London market rivaled even the burgeoning demand in the country. Although not in the first rank of European cities, London dominated the national economy and, more importantly, grew disproportionately faster during these centuries, its population fed by immigration from the regions. London generated its own market, adjacent to the sources of production and importation, with relatively few distribution problems and an affluent leading-edge, especially in the Parliamentary season. The structural concentration of the trade in London encouraged entrepreneurs to stimulate demand and confound perceptions (not confined to the book trades) that market limitations must always curtail profit margins.

II. Marketing

The fragility of this economy, whatever the signs of expansion, ensured that manufacturers and retailers worked hard to build a market; all those selling goods that were not among the necessaries of life had to tempt and cajole their customers. In the case of the book industry, encouragement of demand was largely dependent upon good printed advertising. Publishing booksellers and printers used **title-pages** and personal **emblematic** devices to good promotional effect. Caxton and his successors, and especially de Worde and Pynson,[xx] soon recognized the marketing potential and **patronage** associations of the heraldic or pictorial device.[xxi] The advertising potential of the title-page became just as obvious.[xxii] The printed book retained many features of the structure of the **manuscript codex**, but the title-page was a new, if perhaps unanticipated, product of the new technology. The manuscript **incipit** and the simple text opening with the author's words were replaced by a printed title-page that, as Margaret Smith has pointed out, became a commercial vehicle.[xxiii]

Although a few printing houses continued use of colophons, their significance receded with the exploitation of the title-page from the mid-sixteenth century.[xxiv] Almost all printers retaining colophons, including de Worde, with his often sententious[12] final monikers, used them in addition, not in substitution, to title-pages. Like their Continental rivals, early sixteenth-century

11 Those "entitled to bear (heraldic) arms" (*OED*).

12 "Given to the utterance of maxims or pointed sayings. Now often in bad sense, addicted to pompous moralizing" (*OED*).

London printers repeatedly (and often extravagantly) experimented in book design, transferred incipits and colophons to title-pages, and, over the next few generations, adopted novel **frontispieces** and factotums (ornamental initials). **Woodcuts** added further allure to title-pages, appearing with increasing boldness and where the imprint soon became a practical commercial instrument. The various editions of the *Synonyma* issued by de Worde and Pynson over several decades paraded a succession of distinctive title-pages, together with splendid woodcut frontispieces depicting pupils studying the book in front of a birch-wielding master.[xxv]

Increasingly, stationers and booksellers recorded and advertised their role in printing and selecting (or modifying) a title, explicitly detailing the names of those publishing, printing, and retailing (often with several of these and without mention of the author's name). As part, moreover, of the government's policing activity (but not without business implications for the trade), a 1542 proclamation required for the first time "any English book, ballad, or play" to display the name of the printer, author, and the date of printing. In effect, the originating bookseller directed the resultant commercial packaging of the book toward retail needs. The colophon and the title-page imprint helped to inform retailing booksellers of where copies might be had (and the imprint was only this; for the prospective customer, imprint addresses might be the most obvious, but not the only possible, places to buy the books). Where authorial anonymity had been unremarkable in the past, the title-page introduced by print fixed the absence of the author in obvious contrast to the other named participants in publication. The distinction sharpened when, from the early seventeenth century, fuller addresses began to appear in order to guide potential customers more precisely to the originating shop. As Margaret Smith notes of the title-page, "the producer's name there clearly establishes the book as an object of commerce."[xxvi]

From an early date, booksellers pursued other marketing stratagems. **Bindings** decorated with blind panels[13] and **stamps** identified particular producers (with centerpiece binding decoration the most popular between about 1560 and 1640),[xxvii] while front and back **pages** (and sometimes both) broadcast trade badges and symbols of booksellers. Many such devices derived from or replicated ornate signs suspended above the shop front. E. Gordon Duff records 37 different signs in the Churchyard alone before 1558 and a further four in Paternoster Row,[14] including the Row Greyhound of Joseph (or John) Harrison and the Black Boy of Henry Sutton. A more recent listing enumerates 203 different signs, some of which (the Fleur-de-lis, Bible, Sun, and Star included) adorned more than a dozen establishments each.[xxviii]

The range of signs in the sixteenth century reveals wonderful whimsy. The Churchyard housed an Angel, Golden Ball, Bible, Bishop's Head, Blazing Star, Brazen Serpent, Cock, Crane, Greyhound, Flower de Luce, Grasshopper, Helmet, Holy Lamb, Marigold, Mermaid, Parrot, Red Bowl, Rose, Ship, Sun, Swan, Tiger's Head, White Horse, White Lion, and White Swan (among many others). Plomer lists more than 250 signs at different locations in London before 1641. These included fourteen different bibles, seven Crowns, six White Horses, five Angels,

---

13 Blind panels were created by the use of a panel stamp, used in a press to make a complete cover design from a single impression on a leather binding.

14 St. Paul's Churchyard, or the area immediately surrounding St. Paul's Cathedral in London which included Paternoster Row, was the center of book publishing during the period under discussion.

five White Bears, four Guns, four Mermaids, four Suns, four Talbots,[15] and four Unicorns. When booksellers changed premises, they could also take their signs with them, without great damage to shop recognition for customers (and readers of imprints). The much-moved sign of John Rastell[16] is an early case in point, first appearing in the Churchyard, and then in Cheapside and Lombard Street.[xxix]

By the close of the sixteenth century, publishing booksellers had developed further design novelties and continued to experiment with direct and witty marketing devices.[xxx] In an elaborate woodcut, Grafton amused customers with his visual pun of a grafted fruit tree flourishing from a ciphered barrel or "tun" (Fig. 3.7). William Camden, noting the widespread passion for the rebus[17] and "witcraft," described the teasing device of Churchyard bookseller Garrat Dewes (two men "casting Dews [deuce] at dice" in a garret) as "most memorable."[xxxi] More typically, Pynson and Rastell (among others) developed identifying marks from elaborate signs based on their initials.[xxxii] John Day's trade sign showed a rising sun above the motto "Arise, for it is Day."

In the popular market, some five-sixths of all ballads published between 1600 and 1640 incorporated woodcut illustration. As posted on tavern walls, the ballads, like additional promotional title-pages, served as natural advertisers and inducements to purchase more print.[xxxiii] A study of replicated images of St. George and the dragon has suggested certain evidence for its "brand" use by early modern London book producers, as well as by foreign printers directing their wares to the English market.[xxxiv] The development of metal engraving from the mid-sixteenth century ensured much finer illustrations, particularly for books of anatomy and cartography. In contrast to woodcuts (see Fig. 3.7) and wood **engraving** where ink was applied to the uppermost surfaces, metal engraving and **etching** (or "**intaglio**") involved printing from the ink left in the incisions after the plate was wiped clean. Copper intaglio work, in particular, required separate printing techniques and most originating booksellers bound engravings between letterpress sheets or even pasted them onto blank or part-printed pages.[xxxv]

[...]

III. Policing and Punishment

Assessments of the commercial development of the book trade in the first two centuries of print are therefore mixed: energetic importing, printing, and bookselling and a certain innovation in financing and the protection of publishing rights, but limited productivity, co-ordination, and distribution. There, was, however, one further check to the progress of business: book trade success impelled control and suppression. A nervous Church and State imposed sanctions that brought both benefits and handicaps for booksellers. The ecclesiastical courts intervened to

15 A term in heraldry to describe a well-mannered hunting dog. The Talbot was a breed of white hunting dog, originating in France and imported to England, that is believed to have become extinct by the end of the eighteenth century.

16 John Rastell (1475–1536), English lawyer, printer, and writer.

17 An allusional device that uses pictures to represent words, parts of words, or letters.

Fig. 3.7: Device of Richard Grafton (a graft and tun), taken from *Certayne Sermons and Homilies* (1547).

prevent "misorder and abusion" as soon as printing boosted the range and volume of books. Church courts ordered the public burning of certain Lutheran books in London in the 1520s, and brutal proclamations of 1529–30 forbade the printing of Lollard[18] texts. Ecclesiastical courts also arraigned individual booksellers. In 1526, two years after preliminary warnings, de Worde, John Gough, and Thomas Berthelet (or Bartlett, who was to be King's Printer from 1530 to 1547) all appeared before the vicar-general charged with selling heretical works.[xxxvi]

The earliest print martyrdom in England can be claimed by the lawyer James Bainham, son of a Gloucestershire gentleman, and who became free of the City as a Stationer in 1531. In the same year, he married the widow of Simon Fish, notorious author of the 1529 anti-clerical *The Supplicacyon for the Beggars*. Although not a printer or **publisher**, Bainham was a determined circulator of banned books by Luther and Tyndale. Within months of his marriage, Bainham was arrested on the orders of Thomas More and taken to his house in Chelsea. Bainham's treatment there and his later agonies on the rack in the Tower, in More's presence, earned him admission to Foxe's *Book of Martyrs*. Bainham's recantation of his beliefs in early 1532 temporarily saved his life, at the cost of a fine and public penance at St Paul's Cross, a nucleus not just of the City's religious life but of its book trade also (Fig. 3.8). Conviction, however, proved inexorable, and the authorities soon put to use the penitential faggots[19] that Bainham carried (as depicted) to St Paul's. A month later, Bainham wrote publicly to the Bishop of London renouncing his retractions and appeared in church clutching two of Tyndale's banned books. Bainham burned at Smithfield in April 1532, shouting out, according to Foxe, that in the flames "I fele no more payne, if I were in a bed of down; but it is to me as swete as a bed of roses."[xxxvii] The *Book of Martyrs* used a generic woodcut to commemorate his fate (Fig. 3.9).

Royal and government policing of the trade advanced sharply in 1538, with a proclamation charging the Privy Council,[20] or a delegated committee, with the pre-publication approval of all books. In 1542 (the year that the Stationers first applied to the King for incorporation) came the proclamation requiring the imprint of publication details, but the general requirements instituted four years earlier were also maintained, more or less intact, during the turmoil of the reigns of Edward and Mary.

It was the Council that effectively determined prosecutions in this period and ensured that many successful printers and publishers passed through the portals of judicial chambers and prisons. In 1541, Grafton was gaoled[21] for printing ballads relating to the death of Cromwell, and in April 1543 the Privy Council despatched Grafton, Whitchurch, and six other printers (and printing financiers) to the Fleet prison for "printing off suche bokes as wer thowght to be unlawfull."[xxxviii] Whitchurch was a fellow merchant (a Haberdasher,[22] like Marler) and the occupant, with his printing presses, of de Worde's old premises in Fleet Street.[xxxix] Whitchurch and Grafton were by then exclusive seven-year patentees for printing all church

18 Refers to an anti-Catholic religious sect.

19 A bundle of sticks.

20 A body that advises the head of state, usually the reigning monarch.

21 Jailed.

22 "A dealer in small articles appertaining to dress" (*OED*).

Fig. 3.8: James Bainham at Paul's Cross, February 1532, from John Foxe, *The Ecclesiastical History Containing the Actes and Monumentes* (1570) 2: 300.

service books.[xl] In the same month, the Privy Council bound over 25 more booksellers on fines of £100, and released five of those in the Fleet on condition of drawing up lists of "bookes and ballettes" they had bought and sold in the previous three years. The Council further ordered the booksellers to reveal "what marchantes they know to have browght in to the Realme any Englisshe bokes off ill matter."[xli] Grafton and Whitchurch were left languishing in the Fleet until early May.[xlii] Commercial and religious enthusiasms proved irresistible despite the risks. Even John Day, an establishment favorite by the 1570s, was sent to the Tower in 1546 "for pryntyng of noythy bokes."[xliii]

The accession of Mary brought fresh disorder to the print trade.[xliv] The Queen hastily deprived printers holding Protestant privileges under the former regime, and most alien printers fled abroad before they were banished. Grafton, who was replaced after six years as "regius impressor," did stay, even though he had incautiously printed Jane Grey's accession proclamation. Whitchurch and Grafton were again imprisoned but neither suffered at length. Whitchurch, released after a year, prospered in trade and married Cranmer's widow. Grafton entered the Commons as Member of Parliament for London and later for Coventry. From 1562 (and before an apparently impoverished old age), Grafton issued the popular *Abridgement of the Chronicles of England* with the assistance of Tottel.[xlv] Less fortunate was prebendary[23] John Rogers, publisher of the bible brought out in 1537 under the name of "Thomas Matthew," printed in Antwerp and bought by Grafton in sheets. In 1555, Rogers became the first of those burned at the stake under Mary. An Act of the same year decreed the loss of a right hand in punishment for the **circulation** of any slander against the Crown.

A commercial history of the Marian[24] press nevertheless rests uneasily in any simple equation of the banishing and burning of Protestants with the subjugation of booksellers. If, as has been claimed,[xlvi] the reign of Mary set back English printing, it was only certain types of printing. John Cawood, now Queen's Printer, and various others were encouraged to produce the required Catholic primers, books of hours and manuals of prayer, while the trade in imported Continental books necessarily advanced (even if the new regime might have trusted too naively to market forces).[xlvii] The departure of alien printers also eased the incorporation of the Stationers. There was money to be made from printing in England after the death of Edward. The history of bookselling under Mary supports revisionist rejection both of uncomplicated confessional division and of Catholic distrust of the printing press,[xlviii] albeit that the burgeoning commerce ensured further policing of publication. By 1557, the Council under Mary attempted to re-structure pre-publication approvals. The strategy followed the preamble to the Stationers' Company Charter of the same year prohibiting printing by non-members and granting the Company rights to seize "scandalous, malicious, schismatical,[25] and heretical" publications.[xlix] A Bill to license individual printers had passed its third reading in the House of Lords when Mary died in 1558.

---

23 A post associated with the administration of a cathedral.

24 During the reign of Mary I.

25 Schismatical texts are those that promote divisions within the Church.

Fig. 3.9: A martyr in flames, a woodcut used to illustrate the burning of James Bainham, stationer, April 1532, from John Foxe, *The Ecclesiastical History Containing the Actes and Monumentes* (1570) 2: 301.

While the confrontation between individual printer-booksellers and the State created celebrated cases and martyrs, another, more obviously commercial, battle played out between the Company and those holding privileges from the Crown. The removal under Mary of certain of the lucrative privileges exempt from the Stationers' control had actually enhanced remaining monopoly rights. To take one example, Edward VI's grant to Grafton's son-in-law, Tottel, of the sole right to print "almaner bokes of oure temporall lawe called the Common Lawe,"[l] had been buttressed by the explicit prohibition of competition. The patent, renewed under Mary, was directed to a whole class of books and extended to all future, as yet unwritten, texts of this sort. From the Hand and Star within Temple Bar in Fleet Street, Tottel issued not only his law books, but, from 1557, a hugely successful and lucrative **anthology**, *Songes and Sonnettes*, generally known as *Tottel's Miscellany*. In the same way, in 1553 the Crown granted William Seres (d. c. 1578) the right to print all primers and psalters,[26] a privilege revoked under Mary, but re-established at the accession of Elizabeth for English and Latin and extended again in 1571. The Crown similarly reinstated John Day with rights to the Catechism and ABCs. In all of this, William Cecil was the prime mover, and it was Cecil again who ensured that Richard Watkins (d. c. 1599) and James Roberts (c. 1540–1618) acquired the immensely valuable rights to almanacs and prognostications in 1571 (renewed in 1578 for 10 years and in 1588 for 21 years). Even when James I ceded part of the almanac monopoly to the Stationers in 1603, Roberts still received £50 per annum in respect of his former patent.[li]

Printers and booksellers were as disappointed as advanced Protestants by the failure of Elizabeth to reverse Marian directives. The new government upheld constraints to untrammeled book production. Legislation of 1559 required all new books to be submitted, before publication, for scrutiny to the Queen, six members of the Privy Council, the Chancellor of one of the universities, or an ecclesiastical judge, above the rank of archdeacon, in whose jurisdiction the book was to be printed. Licensing and publication details were to appear on every book, although the failure to conform exactly to this in imprints might be explained by the provision of the information on the original manuscript.[lii] The Council noted that commerce was the begetter of sedition and irreligion: it was "a great abuse in the printers of bokes, which for couetousnes cheifly regard not what they print, so thei may haue gaine, whereby arriseth great dysorder by publicatyon of vnfrutefull, vayne and infamous bokes and papers."[liii] The 1559 edict became the foundation text for all subsequent pre-Civil War regulation of the book trade. Three ecclesiastical commissioners for London were to sanction pamphlets, plays, and ballads under the even more stringent regulations of 1566, violators were to surrender illegal publications for destruction or damasking (the obliteration by ink of the text of printed paper for its re-use). Miscreants were liable to three months' imprisonment and a fine of 20 shillings for each unlawful title.[liv]

A succession of proclamations chronicle Elizabethan state intervention and the assistance given to increasingly restrictive business practices within the trade.[lv] Elizabeth confirmed the Stationers' charter in November 1559 and three months later the city authorities granted the Company the right to bear livery.[lvi] A series of ordinances, injunctions, and decrees safeguarded against laxness by the Company in prosecuting unwelcome literature by establishing

26 A volume containing the Book of Psalms, and sometimes other devotional material.

further ecclesiastical licensing. Such licensing, starting with an injunction of February 1560, was not—and could never be—fully carried out. It was certainly not in the Company's economic interests to prohibit everything that worried State and Church, but the threat to the Company remained. Proclamations of 1569, 1570, and 1573 (much repeated subsequently) offered rewards to informers against "the sowers and stirrers of sedition."[lvii] A proclamation of July 1583 "against certaine seditious and scismatical Bookes and Libelles" required the surrender of pernicious books,[lviii] and a further proclamation later the next year prohibited books "defacing true religion" and declared that

> all Marchantes, masters of shippes, officers of ports, or any other that shalbe bringer into this Realme of any the sayde seditious bookes or libelles, or a dispenser of the same ... shal be committed to prison there to remayne without bayle or mainepnse ... until he be proceded on according to Justice.[lix]

Five years later, a proclamation re-affirmed that any Catholic book must be yielded to authorities "with [notably imprecise] convenient speede."[lx]

Such injunctions increased the Crown's reliance on the policing services of the Stationers' Company, whose wardens were now further authorized to inspect ships' cargoes.[lxi] From 1576 the Crown charged the Company with gathering weekly reports of what every printer was printing, the number of presses operating and the number of apprentices employed.[lxii] In 1586 a Star Chamber edict detailed regulations about the rights to print and limited printing to London, Oxford, and Cambridge. The decree required all printers to report current presses to the Company within 10 days (re-affirming the authority of the Company against rivals),[lxiii] and gave the Archbishop of Canterbury and the Bishop of London the power to determine the number of presses and to authorize licensing of all publications. Searches in printing houses and at docksides accompanied the repeated (if sometimes modest) burning of books in Stationers' Hall. This was government-inspired containment far beyond that encountered by **scribal** copyists in earlier and more limited markets. Nevertheless, foreign-printed books conveyed by passengers and in cargoes continued to arrive in their thousands. At his trial in 1585, Thomas Alfield alone admitted to importing "ffyve or syx hundred" of Cardinal Allen's *True Sincere and Modest Defence of English Catholiques*. Alfield and Thomas Webley, also accused of circulating the books, were hanged at Tyburn.[lxiv]

The prosecution and resistance of booksellers generated glorious legends, but at the time, the risks to business, liberty, limb, and life were real and constricting. In 1579, most notoriously, the Lincoln's Inn bencher John Stubbe, or Stubbs (c. 1541–90), and his publishing bookseller William Page lost their right hands beneath a butcher's cleaver in the market-place at Westminster. The amputations followed Stubbe's printed attack on the Queen's possible marriage with the Duke of Anjou, and were graphically replicated in numerous later prints, together with brave and loyal words attributed to Stubbe before he was carried back to the Tower.[lxv] The tightening of control by the Crown in 1584 resulted in the condemnation of the Catholic printer

William Carter (c. 1549–84) for publishing Gregory Martin's *Treatise of Schisme*. Carter, "bokebinder de civitate London," had already been imprisoned in 1578 and 1579 for the "printinge of Lewd pampheletes" and "nawghtye papystycall Bookes." He nearly died on the rack in 1581, and was incarcerated in the Tower for the following year.[lxvi] In January 1584 Carter was "hanged, bowelled and quartered"[lxvii] at Tyburn (and beatified[27] by Pope John Paul II in 1987). Agnes Carter's appeal for mercy noted that her husband's printing house had been stripped of its contents and "certen roomes shutt vp," a plea repeated a year later when she requested the return of "goodes and books."[lxviii]

IV. Legacies

The resistance to Church and State, and sometimes to the policing by the Stationers' Company, contributed to the celebration of the book trade in numerous histories, a development sustained by more formal custom. The Stationers' Company also continued to hold its annual election feast on 6 May, St John the Evangelist's day. The feast originated in the 1560s, funded (together with a sermon at St Faith's earlier in the morning) by an annuity by the Clothworker, William Lambe.[lxix] It marked the opening of the guild year and the incoming elections to office. As good Protestants, the Stationers apparently failed to acknowledge the feast day as that of St John. The Stationers' livery dinner on the Sunday after St Peter's day, 29 June, further reflected the Company's original occupancy of St Peter's College.[lxx]

In similar fashion, many booksellers' signs continued to partner different religious and secular traditions and, in some cases, political convictions.[lxxi] This is not to attribute intrinsic significance to *all* the Bible and Crowns or Fleur-de-lis suspended above printing houses and bookshops in London and elsewhere (as they gain familiarity, many symbols lose their original meaning), but many renowned booksellers did develop the profile of signs and "heads" as they farmed their own heritage from the late seventeenth century. By word and image, print itself memorialized famous deeds soon after the event. An early legend recounted the escape in 1535 of Coverdale and Grafton from the Inquisitor General for France and their rescue from Paris of the newly printed sheets of the bible. Printing had conjured immense fascination; its practitioners proudly promoted its capabilities.

In exploiting the press, printers and booksellers continued to confront brutality in pursuit of religious and political conviction (allied, in notable cases, to commercial advantage). D.F. McKenzie concluded that "mild fines, remission of penalties, merciful release, pardon granted for kneeling at the bar of the House—and sheer recidivism"[28] all suggest that "licensing laws were not normally harshly punished,"[lxxii] but that "normally" is an important caution: safety nets were sometimes removed abruptly and the fall proved catastrophic.

The savagery of Tyburn and the bravery of Page and Stubbe found infamous repetition in the years leading to Civil War. At the end of 1637 John Lilburne, former printer's apprentice, was

27 To be made into a saint.

28 Repeated breaking of the law.

imprisoned for financing the printing and distribution of Henry Burton's *A Letany* and then, in April 1638, whipped and pilloried[29] for importing "scandalous" and "factious" books. Released from gaol in 1640, he was incarcerated many times subsequently. Michael Sparke, the publisher of the Puritan pamphleteer William Prynne, saved his ears from being chopped, but he endured the pillory and a crippling fine. Richard Royston (d. 1683), a bookseller of Ivy Lane, who was interned by Parliament in 1645, later thrived, and became Master of the Stationers' Company, in Restoration London. Yet the Lords had denounced Royston as "the constant factor for all other scandalous books and papers against the proceedings of Parliament,"[lxxiii] and Royston suffered alongside many others who attempted to exploit the market for royalist publication at mid-century.[lxxiv] The Council of State bound over no fewer than 43 printers, booksellers, and stationers, from London, Cambridge, Oxford, and York, between June and November 1645, most for a surety of £300 and the promise of destroying their "virulent" or "scandalous" or "seditious" unlicensed books and pamphlets.[lxxv] During this decade and the next, the army also sometimes joined in the regulation of the press, together with a range of officials from the Stationers' Company, justices of the peace and some others at municipal level. They exercised powers, however, that were as effective as the experience, motive, and luck of those individuals allowed.[lxxvi]

Not that aggression was restricted to State authorities or to the Wardens and other searchers of the Company. One Asplyn, a deranged religious apprentice, had attacked John Day and his wife in their bookshop in 1573. Mid-seventeenth-century controversialists and radical pamphleteers, including Thomas Simmons, Henry Overton, and the seller of Quaker books, Giles Calvert (d. 1664), courted the wrath of civil authorities and heightened both the profile of print and the tensions and hostilities between print producers.[lxxvii] Some troublemakers, like the bookseller William Larner (d. c. 1672), trading at the Golden Anchor in the Churchyard and then at the Bible in Eastcheap, frequented gaol by order of those for whom he once served. A Parliamentarian soldier in the mid-1640s, Larner's "Martin Marpriest" publications brought arrest on the order of no less a figure than Prynne.

Manuscript circulation remained a potent underground force, but the fast and prodigious replication and distribution of the printed text was swiftly appreciated by Quaker ministers and other radicals (and in a way which belies any projections of unworldliness or appearance as callow figures in the market-place).[lxxviii] Of printed news pamphlets alone, some 350 separate titles appeared between 1641 and 1659.[lxxix] At his death in 1666, George Thomason's collection of news publications numbered 7,216. Print offered spiritual redemption and political justice, not simply material satisfaction. Even so, the careers of some of the most hot-headed propagandists were not lacking commercial concern. Jason Peacey has chronicled the unprecedented exploitation of the mid-seventeenth-century press "in order to mobilise public opinion, and to justify political actions,"[lxxx] but this was good (as well as sometimes bad) for business.

29 A pillory was "a device for punishment, usually consisting of a wooden framework mounted on a post, with holes or rings for trapping the head and hands, in which an offender was confined so as to be subjected to public ridicule, abuse, assault, etc." (*OED*).

In 1645, in *England's Birth-Right Justified*, Lilburne condemned from his prison cell "that insufferable, unjust and tyrannical Monopoly of Printing."[lxxxi] Lilburne's use of "monopoly" here echoes the Levellers' attack on monopolies and was intended certainly to recall Parliamentary attacks in 1640–41 on Caroline patents and also, possibly, to remind the public that printing privileges were excluded from Stuart anti-monopoly legislation.[lxxxii] Yet it has also been suggested of the operations that led to his first imprisonment (and where the Stationers were defied as much as the State) that "he entered the enterprise with profit in mind."[lxxxiii] As Peter Lake has observed:

> the English reformations enabled a number of different groups, of ideological factions and fractions (Catholic as well as Protestant), as well as an almost entirely commercially motivated pamphlet press and popular drama, to make pitches for the attention, allegiance and money of a number of overlapping, socially and culturally heterogeneous (i.e., popular) audiences.[lxxxiv]

Booksellers like the popular royalist Humphrey Moseley (d. 1661) proved as innovative in publishing pocket books and **serial playbooks** as other eagle-eyed traders such as John Playford with his music book business (and invention of "new ty'd notes") and Peter Stent with his cheap prints, maps, and burgeoning trade in cheap **vernacular** medical books.[lxxxv] The religious political turmoil that made some booksellers martyrs also made many of them commercially shrewd and a few of them extremely rich.

Notes

i. Mark Bland, "Jonson, Stansby, and English Typography, 1579–1623," 2 vols. (unpublished PhD Thesis, U of Oxford, 1995), 1: 4.

ii. David L. Gants, "A Quantitative Analysis of the London Book Trade," *Studies in Bibliography* 55 (2002 [2005]): 202.

iii. Sources for Table 3.6: Edward Arber, *Transcript of the Registers of the Company of Stationers of London 1554–1640 AD*, Vol. 1 (London, 1875–1894): 108b, 246; 3: 327–327b [699–700]; 5: 52, 54; 1637 Star Chamber Lists, in Arber, *Transcript of the Registers of the Company of Stationers*, Vol. 4: addendum 528, 532–33; 1662 list, Lambeth Palace Library, MS 94 1/62; 1668 list PRO SP 29/243/126 (also, as annotated by D.F. McKenzie, appendix 2 of Barnard and McKenzie (eds.), *Cambridge History of the Book in Britain. Vol. IV: 1557–1695* [Cambridge: Cambridge UP, 2002]); 1675 list PRO SP 29/369/97; 1685/6 list Stationers' Company Archives (hereafter SCA), Supplementary Documents, ser. 1 box A; Michael Treadwell, "Lists of Master Printers: The Size of the London Printing Trade, 1637–1723," *Aspects of Printing from 1600*, ed. Robin Myers and Michael Harris (Oxford: Oxford Polytechnic P, 1987), 141–70.

iv. For the workings of the Stationers' Register, see in particular Peter W. M. Blayney, "The Publication of Playbooks," *A New History of Early English Drama*, ed. John D. Cox and David Scott Kastan (New York: Columbia UP, 1997), 383–422 (394–404).

v. Andrew Pettegree, *Foreign Protestant Communities in Sixteenth-Century London* (Oxford: Clarendon P, 1986), 86.

vi. Pettegree, *Foreign Protestant Communities*, 88.

vii. John N. King, "The Book-Trade under Edward VI and Mary I," *Cambridge History of the Book in Britain, Vol. III: 1400–1557*, ed. Hellinga and Trapp (Cambridge: Cambridge UP, 1999), 164–78 (166).

viii. GL MS 25626/31, Peculiar Court of the Dean and Chapter of St Paul's Cathedral, Book C (register of wills 1594–1608), f. 239 (will of Margerie Cooke, widow of Toby Cooke).

ix. F.N.L. Poynter, *A Bibliography of Gervase Markham 1568?–1637* (Oxford: Oxford Bibliographical Society, 1962); Lynette Hunter, "Books for Daily Life: Household, Husbandry, Behaviour," in Barnard and McKenzie (eds.), *Cambridge History of the Book in Britain*, 4: 514–32 (517–19).

x. For more on early modern distinctions between printers and publishers, see Blayney, "Publication of Playbooks," 389–92.

xi. David Pearson, "English Centre-Piece Bookbindings 1560–1640," *Eloquent Witnesses: Bookbindings and their History*, ed. Mirjam M. Foot (London and New Castle, DE: Oak Knoll P, 2004): 106–26 (122–23).

xii. Ian Maclean, "Market for Scholarly Books and Conceptions of Genre in Northern Europe, 1570–1630," *Die Renaissance im Blick der Nationen Europas*, ed. Georg Kaufmann (Wiesbaden: Harrassowitz, 1991), 20–21; Ian Maclean, "Melanchthon at the Book Fairs, 1560–61: Editors, Markets and Religious Strife," *Melanchthon und Europa*, ed. Günter Frank and Kees Meerhoff, 2 vols. (Stuttgart: Thorbecke Verlag, 2002); and cf. Craig Muldrew, *The Economy of Obligation: The Culture of Credit and Social Relations in Early Modern England* (Basingstoke: Macmillan, 1998).

xiii. Paper costs, though variable, seem always to have been by far the greatest production costs, David McKitterick, A *History of Cambridge University Press: Volume 1: Printing and the Book Trade in Cambridge 1534–1698* (Cambridge: Cambridge UP, 1992), 284–85.

xiv. John Bidwell, "French Paper in English Books," *Cambridge History of the Book in Britain*, ed. Barnard and McKenzie, 4: 583–601 (590–91); McKitterick, *History of Cambridge University Press*, 1: 285.

xv. On assumptions about profits from play publication see Blayney, "Publication of Playbooks," esp. 416.

xvi. *CSPDom*. CXVII, 9 (13 Sept. 1628); of the 39, 8 lived in Chancery Lane and 10 in Little Britain.

xvii. E.A. Wrigley and R.S. Schofield, *The Population History of England and Wales 1541–1871: A Reconstruction* (London: Edward Arnold, 1981); E.A. Wrigley, "Urban Growth and Agricultural Change: England and the Continent in the Early Modern Period," *Journal of Interdisciplinary History* 15 (1985): 683–728; and Peter Clark ed., *The Cambridge Urban History of Britain Vol. II 1540–1840* (Cambridge: Cambridge UP, 2000).

xviii. See Brian North Lee, "Gentlemen and Their Book-Plates," *Property of a Gentleman: The Formation, Organisation and Dispersal of the Private Library, 1620–1920*, ed. Robin Myers and Michael Harris (Winchester: St. Paul's Bibliographies, 1991): 43–76.

xix. Susie West, "The Development of Libraries in Norfolk Country Houses, 1660–1830" (unpublished PhD Diss., U of East Anglia, 2000); see also Nicolas Barker and Simon Jervis, *Treasures from the Libraries of National Trust Country Houses* (New York: The Royal Oak Foundation & The Grolier Club, 1999), 1–44.

xx. William Caxton (1415/24–1492), English printer who brought the printing press to England; Wynkyn de Worde (d. 1534/35), apprentice to and successor of Caxton; Richard Pynson (1449–1529/30), Norman printer working in England.

xxi. For the use of devices to make clear or suggest patronage association, see A.S.G. Edwards and Carol M. Meale, "The Marketing of Printed Books in Late Medieval England," *The Library* 6th Ser., 15 (1993): 95–124.

xxii. Elizabeth Eisenstein suggests that most scholars of printing have isolated the title-page as the most significant new feature of the printed book format, *The Printing Press as an Agent of Change: Communications and Cultural Transformations in Early-Modern Europe*, 2 vols. (Cambridge: Cambridge UP, 1979), 1: 106.

xxiii. Margaret M. Smith, *The Title-Page: Its Early Development 1460–1510* (London: The British Library, 2000), 124–25.

xxiv. The 32 per cent of editions carrying a title-page 1480–84 had already increased to 75 per cent by 1495–1500, digest of Smith's figures by Richard Sharpe, *Titulus: Identifying Medieval Latin Texts, An Evidence-Based Approach* (Turnhout: Brepols, 2003), note 3, 26–27.

xxv. Including *STC* 11612 (1502), 11613 (1502), 11614 (1505), 11615 (1509), 11616 (1514), all reproduced in *EEBO* and *STC* 11610 (1500).

xxvi. Smith, *Title-Page*, 143.

xxvii. J. Basil Oldham, *Blind Panels of English Binders* (Cambridge: Cambridge UP, 1958); Pearson, "English Centre-Piece Bookbindings."

xxviii. Katherine F. Pantzer, *A Printers' and Publishers' Index Vol. 3 of STC 1475–1640* (London: Bibliographical Society, 1991), index 3D (232–340), by "establishments." Here, I include different booksellers at the same premises.

xxix. E.J. Devereux, *A Bibliography of John Rastell* (Montreal and Kingston: McGill-Queen's UP, 1999), 6–13.

xxx. A great variety can be viewed in the final pages (and some title-pages) of sixteenth-century books reproduced in *EEBO* (and cf. *The Illustrated Incunabula Short-Title Catalogue*, 2nd ed. [1998]also online).

xxxi. William Camden, *Remains Concerning Britain*, ed. R.D. Dunn (Toronto, Buffalo, NY and London: U of Toronto P, 1984 [1605]), 139–41 (141).

xxxii. Devereux, *Bibliography of John Rastell*, 49–57; for modifications to Pynson's sign and those of others, see Ronald B. McKerrow, *Printers' and Publishers' Devices in England and Scotland 1485–1640* (London: Bibliographical Society, 1913).

xxxiii. Adam Fox, *Oral and Literate Culture in England 1500–1700* (Oxford: Oxford UP, 2000), 5–6, 335–405; Teresa Watt, "Publisher, Pedlar, Pot-Poet: The Changing Character of the Broadside Trade, 1550–1640," *Spreading the Word: The Distribution Networks of Print 1550–1850*, ed. Robin Myers and Michael Harris (Winchester and Detroit: St. Paul's Bibliographies, 1990), 66–67.

xxxiv. Yu-Chiao Wang,"The Image of St George and the Dragon: Promoting Books and Book Producers in Pre-Reformation England," *The Library*, 7th ser., 5.4 (December 2004): 370–401.

xxxv. Antony Griffiths, *Prints and Printmaking: An Introduction to the History and Techniques* 2nd ed. (London: British Museum, 1996), 29–39.

xxxvi. Foxford volume, probate records cited by Henry R. Plomer, *Wynkyn de Worde and His Contemporaries from the Death of Caxton to 1535* (London: Grafton, 1925), 93–95; Colin Clair, "Thomas Berthelet, Royal Printer," *Gutenberg Jahrbuch* (1966), 177–81 (179).

xxxvii. John Foxe, *Acts and Monuments of the Churche [...] The Variorum Edition* [1563 ed.] online (hriOnline, Sheffield, 2004), book 12, 1746.

xxxviii. *Acts of the Privy Council of England*, n.s. 1 (1542–1547) (London, 1890), 107 (8 April 1543). It is unclear whether this was treated as a seditious act or as the unwanted promulgation of domestic political news.

xxxix. Peter W.M. Blayney, "The Site of the Sign of the Sun," *The London Book Trade: Topographies of Print in the Metropolis from the Sixteenth Century*, ed. Robin Myers, Michael Harris, and Giles Mandelbrote (New Castle, DE, and London: British Library, 2003), 13.

xl. J.S. Brewer et al. (eds.), *Letters and Papers, Foreign and Domestic, of the Reign of Henry VIII*, 22 vols. 18: l (London: H.M. Stationery Office, 1864–1932), 68 (no. 100: 31).

xli. *Acts of the Privy Council*, n.s. 1, (21 April), 117, (25 April 1543), 120.

xlii. *Acts of the Privy Council*, n.s. 1, (2 May, incorrectly given as April), 125.

xliii. Cited in Gordon E. Duff, *A Century of the English Book Trade: Short Notices of All Printers, Stationers, Book-Binders, and Others Connected with It from the Issue of the First Dated Book in 1497 to the Incorporation of the Company of Stationers in 1557* (London: Bibliographical Society, 1905 repr. 1948), 38.

xliv. See Elizabeth Evenden, ed., *The Crucible of English Confessional Conflict: Censorship, Persecution and Resistance in Marian England* (Houndmills, forthcoming [published in 2008]).

xlv. For the war between Grafton and Stow over this, see Janet Ing Freeman, "'Lyes' and 'Hyghe Treason' in 1570: John Stow Annotates Grafton's *Abridgement of the Chronicles*," *The Library* 7th ser., 6 (2005): 251–73.

xlvi. Andrew Pettegree, "Printing and the Reformation: The English Exception," *The Beginnings of English Protestantism*, ed. Peter Marshall and Alec Ryrie (Cambridge: Cambridge UP, 2002), 178–79; David Loades, *The Reign of Mary Tudor* (London: Ernest Benn, 1979), 342–43; and David Loades, *Politics, Censorship and the English Reformation* (London and New York: Pinter Publishers, 1991), 138.

xlvii. Jennifer Loach, "The Marian Establishment and the Printing Press," *English Historical Review*, 101 (1986): 135–48; J.N. King, "The Account Book of a Marian Bookseller 1553–4," *British Library Journal*, 13.1 (1987), 33–38; P.M. Took, "Government and the Printing Trade, 1540–1560," (unpublished PhD Thesis, King's College, U of London, 1979), 255.

xlviii. Alison Shell, "Catholic Texts and Anti-Catholic Prejudice in the Seventeenth-Century Book Trade," in Robin Myers and Michael Harris, *Censorship and the Control of Print in England and France 1600–1900* (Winchester: St. Paul's Bibliographies, 1992): 33–58 (esp. 39–42); Alexandra Walsham, *Providence in Early Modern England* (Oxford: Oxford UP, 1999); Alexandra Walsham, "'Domme Preachers'? Post-Reformation English Catholicism and the Culture of Print," *Past and Present* 168 (August 2000): 72–123.

xlix. PRO C 82/1027 [30] Privy Seal warrant from which the original charter (now perished) was copied.

l. *Calendar of Patent Rolls, Edward VI*, vol. 5 (London: H.M. Stationery Office, 1926), 47 (7 Edward VI Part in 12 April 1553, listed as Tathill).

li. Cyprian Blagden, *The Stationers' Company: A History 1403–1959* (London: Allen and Unwin, 1960), 101.

lii. Frederick Seaton Siebert, *Freedom of the Press in England 1476–1776: The Rise and Decline of Government Controls* (Urbana: U of Illinois P, 1952), 57.

liii. *Injunctions given by Her Maiestie*, 1559 (*STC* 10095) reproduced in Arber, *Transcript of the Registers of the Company of Stationers*, 1: xxxviii-xxxix, and H.S. Bennett, *English Books and Readers 1558 to 1603* (Cambridge: Cambridge UP, 1965), 57.

liv. Thought to be an Order-in-Council signed by Archbishop Parker and six other members of High Commission, reproduced in J.R. Tanner, *Tudor Constitutional Documents AD 1485–1603 with an Historical Commentary* (Cambridge: Cambridge UP, 1922), 245–47; see also Siebert, *Freedom of the Press*, 56–57, 59.

lv. Of the 382 proclamations issued in Elizabeth's reign, twelve (3 per cent) directly concerned books (others affected publication indirectly), Frederic A. Youngs, Jr, *The Proclamations of the Tudor Queens* (Cambridge: Cambridge UP, 1976), 13, table 2, and 201–27.

lvi. An incorporation followed by livery is not exceptional; there were cases of unincorporated companies granted livery and incorporated companies without liveries. I am grateful for the guidance of Ian Gadd, Ian Archer, and others.

lvii. Proclamation 1 March 1569 prohibiting seditious books, given in Hughes and Larkin (eds.), *Tudor Royal Proclamations*, 2, 312–13; *By the Queene. A Proclamation Agaynst Seditious and Trayterous Bookes, Billes and Writinges*, 1570 (*STC* 2nd ed. 8032); *By the Queene. A Proclamation Agaynst Maynteyness of Seditious Persons, and of Trayterous Bookes and Writinges*, 1570 (*STC* 2nd ed. 8035); Proclamations of 1 July 1570 and 28 September 1573 given in Hughes and Larkin (eds.), *Tudor Royal Proclamations*, 2, 341–43, 376–79.

lviii. Proclamation 29 July 1583 is reproduced in Arber, *Transcript of the Registers of the Company of Stationers*, 1: 235.

lix. *By the Queene. A Proclamation for the Suppressing of Seditious Bookes and Libelles* 12 October 1584 (*STC* 2nd ed. 8146), given also in Hughes and Larkin (eds.), *Tudor Royal Proclamations*, 2, 506–08.

lx. Proclamation ordering the destruction of the Marprelate tracts, 13 February 1589 given in Hughes and Larkin (eds.), *Tudor Royal Proclamations*, 3, 34–35.

lxi. Leona Rostenberg, *The Minority Press and the English Crown: A Study in Repression 1558–1625* (Nieuwkoop: de Graaf, 1971), 19, 44.

lxii. Arber, *Transcript of the Registers of the Company of Stationers*, 2, 41; Siebert, *Freedom of the Press*, 84. Almost all reports are lost (53 presses were reported in 1583, Arber, *Transcript of the Registers of the Company of Stationers*, 1:108b) and no complete weekly report survives (and thus the Company's fidelity to this order also cannot be measured).
lxiii. For the struggle with the Drapers' Company, see Gerald D. Johnson, "The Stationers Versus the Drapers," *The Library*, 6th ser., 10 (1986): 1–17.
lxiv. Rostenberg, *Minority Press*, 38–39.
lxv. The printer, Hugh Singleton, was exonerated; an extensive proclamation (27 Sept. 1579) was devoted to denouncing Stubbe, reprinted in Hughes and Larkin (eds.), *Tudor Royal Proclamations*, 2: 445–49.
lxvi. BL Landsdowne MS 28 no. 81, report of John Aylmer, Bishop of London, to Burghley, 30 December 1579.
lxvii. John Stow, *The Annales, or, Generall Chronicle of England* (London: Impensis Thomae Adams, 1615).
lxviii. PRO SP 12/206/92 fol 184r, appeals of Agnes Carter, Rostenberg, *Minority Press*, 21, 22.
lxix. William Lambe (d. 1580), noted English philanthropist.
lxx. Ian Gadd, private communication, the two feasts are confused in W.W. Greg and E. Boswell (eds.), *Records of the Court of the Stationers' Company 1576–1602* (London: Bibliographical Society, 1930).
lxxi. Pantzer, *Printers' and Publishers' Index*, index 3D (232–40).
lxxii. D.F. McKenzie, "The London Book Trade in 1644," in Peter D. McDonald and Michael F. Suarez (eds.), *Making Meaning: 'Printers of the Mind' and Other Essays* (Amherst: U of Massachusetts P, 2002): 126–43 (139). McKenzie argued that punishments under Star Chamber decrees of 1586 and 1637 were less severe than those prescribed at "times of greatest danger (1588, 1601, the 1630s, 1649, immediately after the Restoration, and in the 1680s)" when government proceeded with death and mutilation sentences, but Lilburne's experiences were not the only ones that blurred these uninviting distinctions.
lxxiii. *Journal of the House of Lords VII*: 518 (31 July 1645), following a petition against Royston by John Wright, printer to the House, in *Sixth Report of the Royal Commission on Historical Manuscripts* (London: H.M. Stationery Office, 1879), 72.

lxxiv. John Barnard, "London Publishing, 1640–1660: Crisis, Continuity, and Innovation," *Book History* 14 (2001): 1–16.
lxxv. "List of Recognizances of the Council of State," *CSP Dom.* (1649–1650), 522–24.
lxxvi. For the inefficiencies of enforcement, see Jason McElligott, "'A Couple of Hundred Squabbling Small Tradesmen'? Censorship, the Stationers' Company, and the State in Early Modern England," *Media History*, 11, no. 1–2 (2005), esp. 96, 98.
lxxvii. D.F. McKenzie, "The London Book Trade in the Later Seventeenth Century," Sandars Lecture 1976, CUL mimeographed copy.
lxxviii. Notable exchanges survive in correspondence in the FHL, including SW MS. 3, 30, 38, 39; I.M. Green, *Print and Protestantism in Early Modern England* (Oxford: Oxford UP, 2000), 185–86, 230–31.
lxxix. Fox, *Oral and Literate Culture*, 394.
lxxx. Jason Peacey, *Politicians and Pamphleteers: Propaganda During the English Civil Wars and Interregnum* (Aldershot: Ashgate, 2004), 303.
lxxxi. Cited in Raymond, *Pamphlets and Pamphleteering*, 260.
lxxxii. See Raymond, *Pamphlets and Pamphleteering*, ch. 6.
lxxxiii. Andrew Sharp, "John Lilburne," *ODNB*.
lxxxiv. Peter Lake with Michael Questier, *The Antichrist's Lewd Hat: Protestants, Papists and Players in Post-Reformation England* (New Haven, CT and London: Yale UP, 2002), 713; Ian Maclean's account of Melanchthon's posthumous publications, in his own words, features "crude mercantile profiteering, religious polemic, and legal retribution," Maclean, "Melanchthon at the Book Fairs," 211.

lxxxv. John Curtis Reed, "Humphrey Moseley, Publisher," *PPOBS* 2 (1927–30): 57–142; Paulina Kewes, "Give me the Sociable Pocket-Books ...": Humphrey Moseley's Serial Publication of Octavo Play Collections *PH* 38 (1995): 5–21, John Barnard, "London Publishing, 1640–1660: Crisis, Continuity, and Innovation," *BH* 4 (2001): 8–11.

20.

Jonathan Rose, "The Welsh Miners' Libraries," *The Intellectual Life of the British Working Classes.* London and New Haven, CT: Yale UP, 2001. 237–55

Jonathan Rose (b. 1952) is William R. Kenan, Jr. Professor of History at Drew University and the Founding President of SHARP (Society for the History of Authorship, Reading, and Publishing). He is a leading innovator in the field of the history of reading and has co-edited both the journal *Book History* and the important reference work *A Companion to the History of the Book* (Blackwell, 2007). The book from which the following chapter is excerpted was the recipient of numerous awards due to its groundbreaking methodology, as it answered questions about what and how working-class men and women read that were previously thought unanswerable.

The Intellectual Life of the British Working Classes provides an "audience history," one that recovers the responses of readers, students, theatergoers, filmgoers, and radio listeners and thus provides a unique combination of social, economic, and literary history. The sources Rose draws on—workers' memoirs, oral history, social surveys, opinion polls, school records, library registers, and newspapers—opened up new possibilities for cultural history. The following chapter demonstrates the rich potential for historical research that resides within previously unexplored archives such as the Welsh miners' library registers that Rose examines here.

Rose demonstrates how a history of reading can change our understanding of literary history. In this chapter, Rose uses archival evidence to establish one of his larger arguments: that although the working-class communities he studied did not read the canon of what we might call high literary modernism (such as the novels of Virginia Woolf), they nevertheless read widely in a separate contemporaneous, and equally important, intellectual tradition.

The Welsh Miners' Libraries

At a street corner in Tonypandy I heard two young miners discussing Einstein's Theory of Relativity. I know this was exceptional, but it is significant; and it is true.
—H.V. Morton, *In Search of Wales* (1932)

The miners' institutes of South Wales were one of the greatest networks of cultural institutions created by working people anywhere in the world. One would have to look to the Social Democratic **libraries** of Wilhelmine Germany or the Jewish workers' libraries of inter-war Poland to find anything comparable.[i] Many of the Welsh miners' libraries began in the nineteenth century as mechanics' institutes, temperance halls,[1] or literary societies, at first under middle-class **patronage**. Victorian colliers[2] commonly authorized deductions from their wages to pay for their children's education, but when school fees were abolished in 1891, this flow of money (usually 1d. or 2d. per pound) was re-directed toward the miners' institutes. They also received contributions from coal companies and other benefactors, but as the miners themselves usually covered the ongoing expenses, they controlled acquisitions. In 1920 Parliament set up the Miners' Welfare Fund, which taxed coal production and royalties and directed the revenue to fund pit baths, welfare halls, scholarships, and libraries. By 1934 there were more than a hundred miners' libraries in the Welsh coalfields, with an average stock of about 3,000 volumes. In smaller villages the collection might consist of only a few hundred books, and the librarian was usually a miner who volunteered to mind the shop one evening a week.[ii] The larger institutes were well-equipped cultural centers offering evening classes, lecture series, gymnasia, wireless rooms and photography labs for amateurs, and theaters as well as libraries.[iii] They hosted concerts, amateur drama, traveling theatrical troupes, opera, dances, trade union political meetings, choirs, debating societies, and eisteddfodau (Welsh cultural festivals), and about 30 of the Welsh workmen's halls were equipped with cinemas.[iv] The pride of the movement was the Tredegar Workmen's Institute: by the Second World War its library was circulating 100,000 volumes a year. It boasted an 800-seat cinema, a film society, and a popular series of celebrity concerts, where the highest-priced tickets went for 3s.[v]

I. An Underground University

There were similar institutions in all the coal regions, many of them established by mine owners with the frank intention of making their workers sober, pious, and productive. Around 1850, 19 out of 54 collieries in Northumberland and Durham had some kind of library or reading room.[vi] Yet there was a special ferment in the South Wales coalfields, rooted in the peculiar cultural environment of the region. Wales had a tradition of weaver-poets, artisan balladeers, and autodidact[3] shepherds going back to the seventeenth century.[vii] Welsh Nonconformity,[4] Sunday schools, choral societies, temperance movements, and eisteddfodau all championed

---

1 A temperance hall was a community entertainment venue that did not serve alcohol.

2 Coal miners.

3 Self-educated.

4 Nonconformity is the refusal to "conform" to, or follow, the teachings and practices of the Church of England, the official Protestant church of Great Britain. Baptists, Methodists, and Presbyterians are some examples of nonconforming religious denominations popular in Britain.

education and especially self-education. Penny readings[5] had been especially popular in Wales, sponsored by chapels of all denominations, with a high level of participation by working-class members.[viii] In 1907, 13 out of 53 residential students at Ruskin College[6] were South Wales miners.[ix] Wales could also boast high concentrations of WEA[7] students in 1938–39: 2.90 per 1,000 population in South Wales, and 6.25 (highest in the nation) in North Wales.[x] But in 1914 public libraries served only 46 per cent of the Welsh population (compared with 62 per cent in England), and most of the neglected areas were small towns and rural regions.[xi] According to a 1917 parliamentary inquiry, "not a single municipally maintained public library is to be found in the central Glamorgan block of the coalfield."[xii] Miners' libraries filled that vacuum: they were rarely established where public libraries already existed.[xiii]

Though affluent intellectuals denigrated the "Little Bethels"[8] of the mining regions, collier-intellectuals recognized that they provided an enormous stimulus for debate and literary analysis, not unlike the yeshivas[9] of Eastern Europe. Durham miner Jack Lawson conceded that "there were tendencies to narrowness and hypocrisy" in the chapels, but

> if Britain holds a comparatively advanced position in her social movements to-day [1932] it is largely because the eighteenth-century Methodist Revival[10] saturated the industrial masses with a passion for a better life, personal, moral, mental, and social.... The chapel gave them their first music, their first literature and philosophy to meet the harsh life and cruel impact of the crude materialistic age. Here men first found the language and art to express their antagonism to grim conditions and injustice. Their hymns and sermons may have been of another world, but the first fighters and speakers for unions, Co-op. Societies, political freedom, and improved conditions, were Methodist preachers.

It was at a Methodist society that Lawson first found working people who shared his intellectual passions. One had been well into his thirties before his wife taught him to read: in his old age he was successfully tackling the New Testament in Greek and Nietzsche.[11] Others

---

5 A penny reading was a read performance catering to working-class people due to the low cost of admission (one penny).

6 A college in Oxford founded in 1899 for working-class adult students.

7 The Workers' Educational Association (WEA), founded in 1903 by Albert Mansbridge, worked to promote educational opportunities for working-class people.

8 A bethel is a nonconformist chapel, especially a Baptist or Methodist one.

9 "An Orthodox Jewish college or seminary" (*OED*).

10 An evangelical revival responsible for revitalizing Christianity in Wales. Begun in the 1730s, it ended in the late 1790s with the death of several important church leaders.

11 Friedrich Nietzsche (1844–1900), German philosopher and critic famous for his exclamation "God is dead."

ultimately became teachers, ministers, musicians, social workers, and even professors. Their houses were open to each other and they visited on impulse:

> We talked pit-work, ideals, the Bible, literature, or union business. The piano rattled, the choir was in action, and we sang with more abandon than any gang who has just learned to murder the latest film song.... I was encouraged to express myself; to preach and to speak. I was given their warm, helpful friendship, and the hospitality of their homes. No longer was I "queer" or "alone." My thoughts and dreams were given direction. Even when they did not understand or agree they encouraged, and ignorant and intelligent alike combined to set my feet firmly on the road I had haphazardly been looking for.[xiv]

The parents of D.R. Davies (b. 1889)[12] had no formal education and could not read English until fairly late in life, but his father (a collier) composed Welsh poetry and hymns, as well as a cantata performed by the chapel choir. Their home was often filled with neighbors discussing religion:

> Conversation was invariably about things that mattered, and ideas were the staple of intercourse. Without knowing it, I breathed a strong, stimulating intellectual atmosphere. In later years I realized what a great advantage I had enjoyed. It has been my lot to know at different times wealthy, polished, and educated families amongst whom argument about great ideas was bad form. An entirely different and better start was mine. In my homelife, it was ideas that mattered. By their intellectual intensity my parents created in me a zest for ideas which gave direction to my life.... My home did for me as a boy what the University is supposed to do, according to Newman,[13] for youth—it awoke and encouraged a love of ideas for their own sake. And that advantage outweighed most of the handicaps under which I lived, handicaps neither few nor light.

All the children had music lessons and were singers, one with the Moody Manners Opera Company. "I was constantly listening to Bach, Handel, Mozart, Mendelssohn, and Schubert-oratorios, cantatas and masses," Davies recalled. There was one schoolteacher who, in a class of 60, "create[d] in his pupils an independent passion for knowledge," and inspired Davies to

---

12 David Richard Davies (1889–1958), Welsh religious figure and journalist who rose from the working class to a position of prominence in British intellectual and religious society.

13 John Henry Newman (1801–90), English religious scholar whose 1871 book *The Idea of a University* argued that the purpose of the university should be the diffusion and extension of the liberal arts (as opposed to professional or commercial skills and knowledge).

read Macaulay's *History of England* before his twelfth birthday. Because it was leavened with that spacious enthusiasm for music, literature, history, and theological debate,

> the Welsh Nonconformity in which I was reared did not make for narrowness and fanaticism of mind as so many of the frustrated, embittered critics of my generation have maintained. Today [mid-1950s] we are living upon the capital of those same "tin Bethels," and when that gives out (as it is now doing) the futility and leanness of our contemporary life will become more obvious and disastrous. It is true that our fathers, in Wales, taught us a religion of cast-iron dogma, which, according to all the theories, should have made us obscurantists,[14] inhabiting a very small world. But it did not. In some mysterious way we became freemen of a spacious world. Along beside the narrow dogma went a broad culture. What happened to me demonstrates that fact clearly. Can anything promote a wider interest than history? And history led to politics, which, in turn, opened the door on many intellectual horizons. And music. It fed the spirit as an instrument of perception, as an organ of knowledge. It made for inner refinement. We had few of the graces and polish of manners, characteristic of an affluent society, but music gave us something better. It created in us a fastidiousness of moral as well as literary taste. It gave us a sense of the necessary relation between content and form. I very much doubt whether, fundamentally, Eton or Harrow would have given me a better start, educationally, than the "tin Bethel," the elementary council school, and my home.

Even the perpetual Bible reading, in English and Welsh, stimulated an appetite for secular literature. "I defy any child of ordinary intelligence to read the Bible constantly (in the Authorized Version) without acquiring a genuine literary taste, a sense of style, and at least a feeling for the beauty of words. Before I was 12 I had developed an appreciation of good prose, and the Bible created in me a zest for literature," propelling him directly to Lamb, Hazlitt's essays, and Ruskin's *The Crown of Wild Olive*.[15] Later, after a day of exhausting mine work, he would attend union meetings, chapel meetings, literary and debating societies, lectures, and eisteddfodau, and then do some fairly heavy reading. He joined the library committee of the Miners' Institute in Maesteg, made friends with the librarian, and advised him on acquisitions.

---

14 Those who would deliberately restrict knowledge or prevent the facts or truth of a matter from being known.

15 Charles Lamb (1775–1834), English writer best known for his essays; William Hazlitt (1778–1830), English critic; John Ruskin (1819–1900), English writer, painter, and critic of literature, art, and culture whose 1866 work *The Crown of Wild Olive* was a collection of social satire.

Thus he could read all the books he wanted: Marx, Smith, Ricardo, Mill, Marshall, economic and trade union history, *Fabian Essays*, Thomas Hardy, Meredith, Kipling, and Dickens.[xv] [16]

If it still seems amazing that such a vital cultural life could flourish in the coalfields—that the Ton-yr-efail Workmen's Institute could spend £45 for the *Oxford English Dictionary*—one miner offered a fairly mundane explanation. As he saw it, all British workingmen were legendary hobbyists. Some gardened, played football, or bred dogs; others pursued literature, philosophy, or classical music with the same intensity.

> Every miner has a hobby. Some are useful; some are not. Some miners take up hobbies as amateurs; some study to escape from the pit. I did. Why do we do so many things? It's difficult to say. It may be a reaction from physical strain. The miner works in a dark, strange world. He comes up into light. It is a new world. It is stimulating. He wants to do something. It may be, in good times, pigeon racing, fretwork, whippet racing, carpentry, music, choral singing, or reading. Think what reading means to an active mind that is locked away in the dark for hours every day! Why, in mid-Rhondda there are 40,000 books a month in **circulation** from four libraries....[xvi]

Stephen Walsh[17] (b. 1859), the Lancashire collier and Labour MP, offered another explanation:

> There is no place like a mine for promoting discussion. There is something in the never-absent danger, in being shut away underground, that draws men to each other, that makes them anxious to break the darkness and sense of loneliness by talk on subjects many and various. And so, in our discussions, I found that my book-learning, my ability to introduce fresh topics, gave me a status far beyond my years, and no doubt I caught something of the art of public speaking in delivering little expositions or lectures to my mates on things I had read about.[xvii]

---

16 Karl Marx (1818–83), German political, economic, and social philosopher cited as a founder of socialist thought (also known as Marxism); Adam Smith (1723–90), Scottish political, economic, and social philosopher cited as a founder of free market and capitalist thought; David Ricardo (1772–1823), English economist influenced by Smith's laissez-faire philosophy; John Stuart Mill (1806–73), English economic philosopher linked with utilitarianism; Alfred Marshall (1842–1924), English economist who theorized supply and demand; the *Fabian Essays* were a collection of essays published in 1889 by the socialist Fabian Society; Thomas Hardy (1840–1928), English writer associated with Naturalism; George Meredith (1828–1909), English Victorian writer best known for his novels; Rudyard Kipling (1865–1936), English writer who addressed British imperialism in India; Charles Dickens (1812–70), English novelist who was critical of the working and living conditions of the poor.

17 Stephen Walsh (1859–1929), English miner who rose through the trade unions, eventually becoming a Member of Parliament.

[...]

Welsh miners did not have to consult Matthew Arnold[18] to recognize the liberating power of culture. They experienced it first-hand and saw it in their workmates. In the village of Penrhiwceiber the intellectual lights were Ted, a collier who read 30 books a year, and Jeff, an engine driver who played "The Rustle of Spring" on the piano and invited his friends over to enjoy his impressive library of classical recordings:

> At such times we did not feel we were colliers doing menial and dangerous jobs in the bowels of the earth, but privileged human beings exposed to something extraordinary. Most of us were badly or barely educated, but such young men as Ted and Jeff who, alone and without help and encouragement, educated themselves, and having drunk the wine of knowledge they seemed to glow with pride. The work they were engaged in, lowly as it was, never depressed them. They neither grumbled about the work they did, nor did they envy others in better positions on the surface of the pit. These characteristics I noticed about men such as Ted and Jeff, and from the examples of such men I was able to develop my own pride, my own search for knowledge which eventually enabled me to leave such a dangerous and difficult occupation.... These two characters, their attitudes, their personalities, their cheerfulness, their honesty, and their kindness, I am sure made the rest of us feel that culture had done much to make them better men. They were never crude, never resorted to bouts of bad language and temper, or said mean things about others, although they took a "lot of stick" from many pit workers for being different.[xviii]

[...]

"Apart from religion," recalled a Durham colliery blacksmith (b. 1895), "perhaps the most important influence at work in the village was the colliery institute. It provided some sort of alternative to the chapels, and churches, in that there was a Library."[xix] Percy Wall (b. 1893) described his institute as a "blatantly utilitarian" building with a "square, cemented front" and a "drab and poorly lit" reading room, but it offered a wonderful escape from a dull Welsh village:

> I could view the future through the words of H.G. Wells,[19] participate in the elucidation of mysteries with Sherlock Holmes,[20] ... or penetrate darkest

---

18 Matthew Arnold (1822–88), English writer noted for his cultural analysis.

19 H.G. Wells (1866–1946), English writer noted for his works of science fiction.

20 Sherlock Holmes is a fictional detective who is the most famous creation of Sir Arthur Conan Doyle (1859–1930), a Scottish author.

> Africa with Rider Haggard[21] as my guide. I could laugh at the comic frustrations of coaster seaman or bargee at the call of W.W. Jacobs.[22] What a gloriously rich age it was for the story teller! ... When the stories palled there was always the illustrated weeklies with their pictures of people and conditions remote from my personal experience but opening vistas of a large expanding world of architecture, art, travel, and home life in foreign lands I could never expect to visit. I could laugh with *Punch* or *Truth*, although some of the humour was much too subtle for my limited education. Above all I could study the *Review of Reviews* and learn therein the complexities of foreign affairs.[xx]

All that was fascinating if only because there were few other distractions in most Welsh mining towns. One housewife depended on Women's Co-operative Guild lectures to keep up her morale in a village where the only other recreations were a cinema, a British Legion hall, and some unfinished athletic fields.[xxi] Besides the institutes, the chapels, and the pits, there might be one other center of discussion in a mining town:

> As the Workmen's Institutes were considered the miners' Universities the shoemaker's sheds were considered their Common Room, and therein the young "listened to the wisdom of the ancients." ... These village cobbler's shops, in fact, were often cells of flourishing cultural activity, the boot repairers themselves often being thoughtful and wellread men who played active parts in the cultural, social and religious life of the village, keen Eisteddfodwyr, nonconformists to the core, politically minded, displaying at all times an interest in current affairs generally and the world around them.[xxii]

II. Marx, Jane Eyre, Tarzan

Except for the occasional schoolteacher, shopkeeper, or clergyman, the miners' libraries served a working-class clientele; and miners determined acquisitions. The book selection committee at Tredegar was headed by that stalwart of the Labour Party's[23] left wing, Aneurin Bevan.[24] The borrowing records of these libraries—unlike those of public libraries—can therefore offer a profile of working-class reading preferences uncontaminated by middle-class cultural hegemony. Only three usable registers out of the hundred-odd South Wales miners' libraries have survived,

21 Sir Henry Rider Haggard (1856–1925), English novelist whose most famous work, *King Solomon's Mines* (1885), took place in Africa.

22 William Wymark Jacobs (1863–1943), English writer of short stories.

23 The Labour Party originated in the early twentieth century as a political outlet for the British working class.

24 Aneurin Bevan (1897–1960), a Welsh politician who led a left-wing faction of the Labour Party.

but they are the best source we have to address the question that every study of reader response must begin with: Who read what?

Historians of the Welsh coalfields have offered three possible answers: *Das Kapital*, *Jane Eyre*, or *Tarzan of the Apes*. South Wales was a hotbed of labor militancy where, according to historians of the left, many workers were well-versed in the Marxist classics. Then there is *The Corn is Green* school of novels and memoirs, which describe a thriving autodidact culture in the coalfields, where colliers fervently studied the classics in adult education classes. The third answer was proposed in 1932 by Q.D. Leavis in *Fiction and the Reading Public*. Mrs. Leavis was nostalgic for a pre-lapsarian[25] Elizabethan age, when the masses enjoyed Shakespeare and Marlowe. In the Victorian period, however, the reading public began to divide between high and low literature, and after the First World War the two audiences were irreconcilably divorced. The masses now consumed rubbishy crime fiction and romances, while the great modernists—Lawrence, Joyce, Woolf, Eliot[26]—were read only by small educated **coteries**.

Frankly, Mrs. Leavis's methods of literary sociology were crude. She dismissed out of hand the notion that you might ask people what they were reading and why they were reading it. Instead, she stationed herself in Boot's **Circulating Libraries** with a notebook: since Boot's specialized in light best-sellers, she got the results she was looking for. She also seized on the statistic that three out of every four books borrowed from public libraries were fiction, which she took as *prima facie* evidence of low literary tastes. (It proves more conclusively that Mrs. Leavis retained the Victorian literary prejudice against fiction.)[xxiii]

We can test all these theories against three miners' libraries, beginning with the Tylorstown Workmen's Institute. We have the complete borrowing record for the year 1941, when there was a total of 7,783 loans.[xxiv] Most of them fit Mrs. Leavis's definition of trash literature-books with titles such as *Corpses Never Argue* (13 loans), *Lumberjack Jill* (19), *A Murder of Some Importance* (24), *The Mysterious Chinaman* (18), *Anything But Love* (31), *The Flying Cowboys* (31), and P.G. Wodehouse's deathless *Right-Ho Jeeves* (17). The standard adventure novels also had their fair share of readers—Jack London's *White Fang* (17), Conan Doyle's *His Last Bow* (6) and *The Lost World* (15), Victor Hugo's *The Hunchback of Notre Dame* (12), Alexandre Dumas's *The Man in the Iron Mask* (4) and *The Three Musketeers* (11), John Buchan's *The Thirty-Nine Steps* (5), James Fenimore Cooper's *The Last of the Mohicans* (2), *Robinson Crusoe* (1), and *The Swiss Family Robinson* (5). There was considerable demand for such children's classics as *Little Women* (20), *The Prince and the Pauper* (8), and a remarkable Victorian survival, Hesba Stretton's *Jessica's First Prayer* (13).

On the whole, the greats and near-greats among the Victorians and Edwardians did not fare well. John Galsworthy's *A Modern Comedy* (4) and *The Forsyte Saga* (1), H.G. Wells's *Kipps* (1) and *The Island of Dr. Moreau* (3), Arnold Bennett's *Hilda Lessways* (2) and *Anna of the Five Towns* (2), Charles Reade's *Peg Woffington* (2) and *The Cloister and the Hearth* (1), Wilkie Collins's

25 Originally referencing the pure state of mankind before the fall of Adam and Eve.

26 D.H. Lawrence (1885–1940), James Joyce (1882–1941), Virginia Woolf (1882–1941), and T.S. Eliot (1888–1965) were all writers associated with high, intellectual modernism.

The Woman in White (5), Elizabeth Gaskell's *North and South* (1) and *Mary Barton* (2), and Rudyard Kipling's *Plain Tales from the Hills* (2) were all outpaced by A.J. Cronin's *The Citadel* (6) and Stella Gibbons's spoof *Cold Comfort Farm* (16). Bernard Shaw had a large number of readers, but they were spread thinly across his various works: *Man and Superman* (2), *Heartbreak House* (3), *Misalliance* (1), *Back to Methuselah* (1), *The Doctor's Dilemma* (4), *Androcles and the Lion* (2), *Pygmalion* (1), *John Bull's Other Island* (2), *Major Barbara* (1), *Plays for Puritans* (2), *Plays Pleasant* (4), *Plays Unpleasant* (1), and his novel *Cashel Byron's Profession* (1). Only one classic could compete with the best-sellers: *Pride and Prejudice* was loaned no less than 25 times, but that was in the wake of the 1940 film version starring Greer Garson and Laurence Olivier, and Austen's popularity did not carry over to *Mansfield Park* (2). The only Dickens novel much in demand was *A Tale of Two Cities* (7), followed by *David Copperfield* (3), *Barnaby Rudge* (1), and *Oliver Twist* (1). Shakespeare's plays and a volume on Shakespeare's characters were borrowed a total of six times, *Gulliver's Travels* seven, *Anna Karenina* only three, Bacon's essays once, Longfellow's poems once. It may seem remarkable that Willa Cather's *Death Comes for the Archbishop* was checked out eight times, but a 1930 poll of readers of the *Sunday Dispatch* placed it among the post-war novels most likely to be read a generation hence.[xxv]

Mrs. Leavis bemoaned the indifference of the reading public to modernist literature, and Tylorstown confirms her pessimism. *A Passage to India* was borrowed once, Eugene O'Neill's *Strange Interlude* once, Robert Graves's *Goodbye to All That* twice. It seems extraordinary that all of five readers took out Virginia Woolf's *The Years*; but even including those, the fact remains that literary modernism accounted for barely one in a thousand loans.

Though Tylorstown was in what was supposed to be Britain's Red Belt, there was scarcely more interest in politics. The collection included biographies of Labour Party leaders George Lansbury (2 loans), Keir Hardie (1), and James Maxton (2). There were a few readers of foreign affairs, as represented by John Gunther's *Inside Europe* (5) and Michael Oakeshott's *Social and Political Doctrines of Contemporary Europe* (2). Beyond Reuben Osborn's *Freud and Marx* (2), there was hardly any demand for either these thinkers. Books by or about Lenin were taken out by six readers, Hewlett Johnson's *The Socialist Sixth of the World* by five, but the invasion of Russia on 22 June did not increase interest in the Soviet Union. Politics were more palatable if cast in the form of a dystopian thriller: there were eleven borrowers of Jack London's *The Iron Heel*, a prophecy of fascism that inspired Orwell's *Nineteen Eighty-Four*.

[...]

This neglect of politics was entirely typical. A survey of 19 miners' libraries **catalogues** between 1903 and 1931 found that all the social sciences accounted for only 5.3 per cent of book stock; at only one library did the proportion rise above 10 per cent. There was nothing by Marx on the shelves at Treharris in 1925, Tredegar in 1917, or the Cwmaman Institute in 1911; and only 1.6 per cent of stock at Cwmaman was in the "Politics, Economics and Socialism" section. Granted, many libraries built up their socialist collections over time, especially during the "Red Thirties," but though Tredegar eventually acquired the complete works of Lenin, he remained unread. At Cwmaman, as at other miners' libraries, readers mainly demanded fiction, which rose from 52.6 per cent of loans in 1918 to 81.7 per cent in 1939: politics never accounted for more than 0.5 per cent. At the Senghenydd Institute library in 1925, on the eve of the General Strike, the proportions were 93.4 per cent fiction, 0.4 per cent economics.[xxvi] Any historian of working-class culture in early twentieth-century Britain must deal with this inescapable fact: the readers of Marx and Lenin were infinitesimal compared with the fans of Mrs. Henry Wood.

Very revealing, in this context, is a 1937 survey of 484 unemployed men aged 18 to 25 in Cardiff, Newport, and Pontypridd. Only 3 per cent were involved in any kind of political organization, compared with 16 per cent in religious groups, 11 per cent in sports clubs, and 6 per cent in adult education classes. One might expect these young men to be the shock troops of discontent, but none of them completely rejected Christianity. Though only 8 per cent were active church members, 35 per cent attended church or chapel at least once a month. Only seven of these men were politically active—either Labour, Communist, or Conservative. Fifty-seven per cent identified reading as a major leisure activity, but it was usually the daily paper (if their family took in one), mainly for sports, news headlines, and the horoscope. They read books for escape (Westerns, aviation, crime and detective stories), purchasing cheap paperbacks, then exchanging them among friends, family, and comrades in the Employment Exchange[27] queue. Hardly anyone was aware that such books were available at the public library—only 20 per cent ever visited the libraries, and just 6 per cent were regular borrowers. Another escape was the cinema: nearly everyone went at least once a month, 22 per cent at least twice a week. Only 8 per cent listened to anything on the radio but dance bands and variety: everything else was dismissed as "highbrow."[xxvii]

Where, then, were the Marxist miners of South Wales? The most plausible answer is that the literary and political interests of Welsh working people could vary enormously from town to town. As an adult education bulletin noted in 1929, the Welsh valleys were remarkable for their isolation:

> The miner or his wife may pay a visit to Cardiff once or twice a year, or spend Bank Holiday on Barry Island, but it is quite likely that he has never been into the next valley, while the one beyond that may be entirely *terra incognita* to him. Communications are bad, and the geographical isolation has led to a corresponding mental isolation. This is aggravated by the fact that the whole population of the valley is dependent on the coal industry. There is no variety in industrial life, and there is almost no differentiation into social grades such as may be found in any ordinary town. This makes for an extraordinarily friendly spirit; there is little shyness and much hospitality. But it has tended to make also for a narrowness of outlook. The miner may never have met an agriculturalist, a factory worker, or a docker, nor mixed with any society but that found in his own immediate surroundings. He never sees either the

27 A state-run center for unemployed workers.

> inside or the outside of a really fine building, be it church or office, public building or home. His horizon is formed by the tops of the bare hills which for so long have shut him away from the rest of the world. His middle distance is furnished with the seemingly endless rows of slate-roofed cottages, each as cramped and ugly as the one which he and his family occupy, and his foreground is the tiny kitchen, the untidy street, or the narrow seam of coal at which he expects to spend 47 hours every week between the ages of 14 and 70. Death is an ever-present possibility down the pit; life seems anyhow precarious when the chance of employment is, at the best, dependent on unknown forces and incomprehensible world movements, or, at the worst, dependent on the word of an unpopular manager, himself the tool of some remoter authority distrusted and disliked.

This cultural environment was hospitable to sectarian dogmas of various kinds: Welsh Nonconformity, miners' syndicalism,[28] and the Marxism preached by the National Council of Labour Colleges (itself subsidized by the South Wales Miners' Federation). Steeped in the Welsh tradition of theological debate, miners plunged quite readily into adult classes in philosophy and history, though instructors often found them wedded to a simplistic economic determinism: "Any superstructure of Church or State, institutions or art, was disregarded as being irrelevant." A class that included some non-miners was likely to be receptive to a more complex

view of historical causation.[xxviii] The village of Mardy was a "little Moscow," where in 1933 ninety colliers were studying the proletarian philosopher Joseph Dietzgen [1828–88] at the Miners' Institute,[xxix] but reading tastes were very different in Tylorstown, just a few miles down the valley. Miners in the anthracite[29] region to the west, around Llanelly, Swansea, and Port Talbot, were not so Marxist as those farther east;[xxx] and Aneurin Bevan's Tredegar was a moderate Labour town with hardly any Communists.[xxxi] The intellectual climate could vary dramatically from mineshaft to mineshaft: as one collier explained, "The conveyor face down the Number 2 Pit was a university," where Darwin, Marx, Paine,[30] and modernist theology were debated, while "the surface of Number 1 Pit a den of grossness."[xxxii]

These extreme cultural variations can also be attributed partly to the fact that literary activities in a given community usually depended on the initiative of a few energetic individuals. Whatever their class, whether they patronized miners' institutes or Boot's Circulating Libraries, readers relied heavily on the advice of librarians in choosing books. A miner with a

---

28 "A movement among industrial workers having as its object the transfer of the means of production and distribution from their present owners to unions of workers for the benefit of the workers, the method generally favored for the accomplishment of this being the general strike" (*OED*).

29 A hard, compact variety of coal.

30 Charles Darwin (1809–82), English naturalist and geologist, best known for his contributions to evolutionary theory. For Karl Marx, see p. 318, note 16. Thomas Paine (1737–1809), an English-American political writer and activist who wrote in support of the American and French revolutions.

passion for the English classics was a likely candidate for institute librarian: in that capacity he could acquire the books he wanted to read himself and recommend them to his neighbors. In Penrhiwceiber the collier who supervised the Miners' Library three evenings a week steered a fellow pit worker toward Jack London, Gorky, A.E. Coppard, Chekhov, Maupassant, and Flaubert's *Madame Bovary* and *A Simple Hearth.*[xxxiii] If Marxists were in charge of acquisitions (and they often were) they could do the same for leftist literature.[xxxiv] And if no one in town provided intellectual guidance, there was always *Tarzan of the Apes.*

Library acquisitions policies could shape reading habits, especially in isolated villages where there were few other sources of books. This pattern becomes apparent in the borrowing ledger of our third miners' library, maintained by the Markham Welfare Association. Here at last we find a coal town with classic literary tastes. In the first period covered by the ledger (September 1923 to December 1925), Jane Austen, the Brontës, Dickens, and George Eliot are the most popular authors. In Markham as in Cynon and Duffryn, no one borrowed Marx, but there was a continuing demand for Mrs. Henry Wood. Even in the depressed inter-war years, there were still a few readers of Victorian self-help tracts: Samuel Smiles, James Hogg's *Men Who Have Risen,* and W.M. Thayer's *From Log Cabin to White House.*

Then there is a gap in the ledger. In September 1928 a new Markham Village Institute was opened, paid for mainly by the Miners' Welfare Fund.[xxxv] The record resumes in March 1932, revealing that reading habits had hardly changed at all over nearly a decade. Indeed, judging from the borrowings, it appears that the Markham Library acquired very few if any new volumes. The probable cause was the prolonged and deep depression that crippled the coal industry from the early 1920s. After the boom years of the First World War and the immediate post-war period, demand for coal collapsed. French and German mines resumed full production, more efficient American mines captured markets, oil was becoming an increasingly important energy source. Daily wages, which averaged as much as 21s. 63/4d. in February 1921, were down to 9s. 51/2d. by October 1922. Between 1920 and 1937, 241 pits closed in South Wales, the employed workforce shrank from 271,161 to 126,233, and total annual wages plummeted from £65 million to £14 million.[xxxvi] The Welsh unemployment rate was 13.4 per cent in December 1925, 27.2 per cent in July 1930, and in the Merthyr area as high as 47.5 per cent by June 1935.[xxxvii]

The miners' institutes had been funded by deductions from miners' wages, the Miners' Welfare Fund, and by local governments. Now all these sources dried up. Between 1920 and 1928 the Cwmaman Workmen's Institute and Library saw its income cut from more than £2,500 to just over £450. At the same time, circulation more than doubled, from 14,966 to 31,054. That was a common pattern throughout South Wales, where armies of unemployed miners had plenty of time on their hands and few other distractions. If their libraries did not close down completely, librarians' wages were slashed, central heating was done without, and acquisitions of new books came to a dead stop. (Even in good times the Miners' Welfare Fund rarely subsidized the purchase of books.) The book budget for the Ferndale Workmen's Institute went from more than £315 in 1920 to zero in 1929. Under those conditions, the old stock would be borrowed over and over again until it was reduced to waste paper. By 1929, investigators for the Carnegie Foundation were reporting that, in the typical miners' library,

50 to 100 per cent of the collection was unfit for circulation. By 1937, many libraries had bought no new books in the past decade.

[...]

The lack of new books only encouraged literary conservatism among the miners, who continued to read Victorian bestsellers into the 1930s. Even in prosperous times their libraries had relied partly on purchases and donations of used books, and they always tended to preserve their old stock. Of 1,433 volumes in the Treharris Institute library catalog in 1894, about 900 were still there 31 years later; and all but 30 of the 953 volumes in the 1896 Cymmer Institute catalog were in the 1913 catalog as well.[xxxviii]

Availability, according to Q.D. Leavis, explains why the masses attended Shakespeare in 1600: "Happily they had no choice." Except for bearbaiting and a few **chapbooks**, what else competed for their attention?[xxxix] In the twentieth century, she argued, capitalism produced an ever-increasing flood of trash novels—and by virtue of their sheer volume, these diverted readers from the great books. In an isolated mining village, where there was nothing much to read but some tattered copies of Victorian classics, the corruption of reading tastes might be delayed, but inevitably *The Bowery Murder* and *The Slave Junk* would penetrate the remotest Welsh valleys. As if to confirm Mrs. Leavis, the Markham library acquired, by March 1935, a new batch of books by lowbrow authors: Warwick Deeping, Jeffery Farnol, E. Phillips Oppenheim, Edgar Wallace. The borrowing record up to October 1936 does indeed manifest a literary Gresham's Law, with bad books forcing out the good. In the rush to read *Anna the Adventuress*, *Captain Crash*, *The Sloane Square Mystery*, and *Pretty Sinister*, borrowings of the English classics drop precipitously.

The next phase in the ledger, from April 1937 to March 1940, reveals an even more striking shift in quite another direction, produced by a world in crisis. Ethiopia had been conquered, the Japanese had invaded China, a civil war was raging in Spain, a European war was on the horizon. In Markham, the escapist fiction that was so popular a few years before had dramatically given way to the literature of political commitment: Zola's *Germinal* (18 loans), Henri Barbusse's anti-war novel *Under Fire* (7), Walter Brierley's *Means Test Man* (11), Upton Sinclair's *Oil!* (22), Ralph Bates's *Lean Men* (on the Spanish Revolution of 1931, 13 loans), Mulk-Raj Anand's *The Coolie* (9), and Robert Tressell's bitter proletarian novel *The Ragged Trousered Philanthropists* (20). Markham miners read *Quiet Flows the Don* (10) and the socialist realism of Feodor Gladkov's *Cement* (22). *Salka Valka*, a portrait of Icelandic fishermen by Halldor Laxness, won a large following (18 loans) with its Christian communist message. The same readers still found Marx hard to tackle, but 10 of them borrowed Engels's *The Origin of the Family*. Proletarian intellectuals like T.A. Jackson, Bert Coombes, W.H. Davies, Willie Gallacher, and Joseph Dietzgen had a few borrowers each. But even in this politically conscious phase, readers in all three communities were more interested in conflicts abroad than in issues closer to home. Ellen Wilkinson's polemic on unemployment in Jarrow, *The Town That Was Murdered* had only one borrower. There was more interest in Agnes Smedley's

China Fights Back (7), John Langdon-Davies's *Behind the Spanish Barricades* (3), and *Mein Kampf* (6). Hywel Francis may have exaggerated the proletarian internationalism of the Welsh coalfields, but it certainly existed here, where the banner of the Markham Miners' Lodge proclaimed "The World is Our Country: Mankind are Our Brethren."[xl]

The final section of the register covers July to December 1940—the Battle of Britain—and once again there is a marked change in borrowing habits. Now politics gives way to *Outlaws of Badger Hollow*, *Murder Must Advertise*, Sherlock Holmes, Edgar Wallace, and Marie Corelli. Perhaps the Nazi-Soviet Pact had dampened interest in Russia. The war had created new jobs, but not necessarily in the mines: many former colliers now made long and tiring commutes to munitions factories.[xli] That might explain why the people of Markham now sought relief in easy reading. Only two of them borrowed anything as challenging as *Point Counter Point*—the only appearance of modernist literature in the entire ledger.

III. Decline and Fall

There were, then, intellectuals and Marxists among the Welsh colliers, but they were minorities concentrated in certain places and certain intervals in time. As the prime movers behind the miners' libraries, they represented the last efflorescence of the Victorian ethos of mutual improvement. When they died or moved away (between 1921 and 1931 more than a third of the population aged fifteen to twenty-nine left the Rhondda valleys) there were no successors to carry on the institutes. By 1934 the signs of decline were obvious:

> To-day a number of the Institutes are dormant; housed in dull buildings, painted in sombre browns and deadly terra cotta; cinema and billiards going strong and education going weak; a complete neglect of the needs of women and girls, and more often than not of the younger generation of boys; no cooperation with other Institutes; a very small annual addition of new books; little or nothing being done to help the leisure problem of the unemployed.[xlii]

In 1937 the Blaina Institute had 300 to 400 members (down from 1,000) paying 3d. weekly. (The population of the district had fallen by more than a quarter since 1923.) Books could still be borrowed from the institute library for 1 d. each, and nearly 400 individuals did so, but of those only thirty went in for any kind of serious or leftist literature: the rest only read escapist fiction. Lectures at the Blaina Institute still had a following, but adult education was much less popular and far less available than it had been before the war.[xliii]

Maes yr haf Educational Settlement, established in 1927, found a ready audience among unemployed miners for its courses in philosophy and history, and it succeeded in overcoming the isolation of the mining villages, where even diligent autodidacts knew little of towns in the next valley. Among its students, as one observer noted, it managed "to create a sense of confidence in the outside world, and so to help break through the reluctance and doubt of men trained from childhood with little or no idea of other places or other work beyond that of mining." In so doing, however, *Maes yr haf* encouraged the best minds to leave the coalfields. As early as 1929, it was apparent that

> The keenest people—those who are attracted by the prospect of further education—are also those who have, or who gain, the enterprise to embark on new ventures and a new life far removed from the old. Incidentally, this creates a real difficulty in the maintenance of attendance and standards of work in the classes.... *Maes yr haf is* continually losing some among its most promising students; it would be failing in duty if it did not encourage and help men to leave the stricken locality. It is only by working out to its own destruction continually in this sense, that the Settlement can make its fullest contribution to South Wales.[xliv]

Walter Haydn Davies, a colliery worker turned adult education teacher, recalled that most members of his miners' institute debating society aimed to acquire the intellectual skills necessary for upward mobility. "By the time the late Twenties came most of us had obtained positions in such institutions as the church, in teaching, the police force, the automobile industry, in electricity and chemicals, and in the distributive trades." There was also a singer, a labor relations officer with the National Coal Board, a miners' agent, some colliery officials, and a bookie.[xlv] In 1939 an investigator reported a general awareness among miners that the decline of coal was irreversible. Of fifty colliers' sons in an elementary school, he found only six who wanted to go into the mines, of whom four aspired to be foremen. All the students at a Junior Technical School were aiming at other lines of work, usually clerical, teaching, or skilled mechanical.[xlvi]

"There are marvelous opportunities for educational and cultural development, of which we were deprived in our days," said an old miner-intellectual after the Second World War, "but they are not used." Only the least educated and ambitious remained in the pits, and their reading tastes ran to romances and crime stories.[xlvii] Welfare institutes closed their libraries as the expansion of public library services made them superfluous. One Yorkshire coal town had no public library until 1925, and no full-time librarian until 1942. By 1953 the public library was issuing more than 5,000 books a month in a community of 14,000, and had effectively replaced the reading room at the imposing Miners' Welfare Institute, which was no longer used for that purpose.[xlviii] In Bargoed the miners' institute only issued 2,661 books in 1961, down from 33,021 in 1931. The typical institute had become, said one ex-collier, a "stark waste of froth and strip-tease, surrounded by the slick decor of vinyl-covered easy chairs and formica-covered tables and glistening counters that click to the sound of glass."[xlix] The Tredegar Institute, which spent more than £1,000 a year on books in the late 1940s, was broken up in 1964. Nearly all of its magnificent collection is lost.[l] The last Rhondda colliery (Mardy) closed in 1990. Only two Welsh miners' libraries (at the Cwmaman Institute and Trecynon Hall) survived to the end of the century.[li]

For comparison, one could look to the vast network of libraries maintained by the German Social Democratic Party and trade union movement. The trade unions alone supported at least 547 libraries in 1911. By then they were already reporting patterns of borrowing that would later show up in the Welsh miners' libraries. The Central Workers' Library in Gotha was typical: in 1909 light literature accounted for 1,818 loans, more than two-thirds of the total. There was limited demand for the classics (150 loans), science (162), history (239), and social science (66), and scarcely any interest in party literature (13) or trade unionism (6). A Mittweida library reported that in 1909 its 404 volumes of literature had been checked out 6,288 times, more than 15 loans per volume, whereas 552 volumes on politics and economics were borrowed 1,076 times, just under two loans per volume. There is evidence, moreover, to support Mrs. Leavis's theory that increasing availability of light reading crowded out serious books. Between 1891 and 1911, loans of fiction from the Berlin Woodworkers' Library increased from 14.6 to 70.4 per cent of the total; at the same time, natural science fell from 13.5 to 3.4 per cent, social science from 22.7 to 2.2 per cent, poetry from 12.6 to 4.3 per cent. German workers did read novels with a social conscience, such as *Germinal* and Disraeli's *Sybil*, and they were interested in Utopian literature, particularly August Bebel's *Woman Under Socialism* and Edward Bellamy's *Looking Backward*. But like their counterparts in South Wales, they found Marx difficult to digest. Friedrich Stampfer borrowed Karl Kautsky's popularization of *Das Kapital* and found only the first twenty pages heavily thumbed: the rest was "virgin purity."[lii] By and large, then, Mrs. Leavis was right, but with some qualifications. Though Welsh miners certainly had an enormous appetite for thrillers, Westerns, and tepid sex, they did not entirely ignore Charlotte Brontë. They did ignore the moderns, but in the late 1930s more than a few of them wanted to know more about Germany, Spain, the Soviet Union, and even Iceland. The "mass reading public" was not an undifferentiated mass: even within the circumscribed area of the Welsh coalfields, reading tastes could vary considerably over time and between communities. And after all, these conclusions are based largely on a sample of only three towns: they may well be upset when someone finds a fourth library ledger. Perhaps, across the valley, they were reading *Mrs. Dalloway*.[31]

Notes

i. For an account of the latter, see David Shavit, *Hunger for the Printed Word: Books and Libraries in the Jewish Ghettos of Nazi-Occupied Europe* (Jefferson, NC: McFarland, 1997), ch. 1.

ii. Christopher M. Baggs "The Miners' Libraries of South Wales from the 1860s to 1939" (PhD Diss., U of Wales, Aberystwyth, 1995), 510–11, is the definitive history of the movement. See particularly ch. 8 for the tricky calculations involved in estimating the number of libraries and the size of their collections. See also his "'Well Done, Cymmer Workmen!' The Cymmer Collieries Workmen's Library, 1893–1920," *Llafur* 5.3 (1990): 20–27.

iii. James Hanley, *Grey Children* (London: Methuen, 1937), 32–37.

iv. Peter Stead, "Wales and Film," in *Wales between the Wars*, ed. Trevor Herbert and Gareth Elwyn Jones (Cardiff: U of Wales P, 1988), 166.

v. D.J. Davies, *The Tredegar Workmen's Hall 1861–1951* (n.p., 1952), 80–93.

vi. John Benson, *British Coalminers in the Nineteenth Century* (London: Longman, 1989), 152–54. J. Ginswick, ed., *Labour and the Poor in England and Wales 1849–1851*, 2 (London: Frank Cass, 1983), 57–60.

---

31 *Mrs. Dalloway*, a modernist novel by Virginia Woolf, was originally published in 1925.

vii. Geraint H. Jenkins, *Literature, Religion and Society in Wales, 1660–1730* (Cardiff: U of Wales P, 1978), 24, 129–30, 198–99, 209–10, 254, 288–90, 293–99, 303–04.

viii. Walter Haydn Davies, *The Right Place—The Right Time* (Llandybie: Llyfrau'r, 1972), 206–10.

ix. Richard Lewis, *Leaders and Teachers: Adult Education and the Challenge of Labour in South Wales, 1906–1940* (Cardiff: U of Wales P, 1993), 62.

x. Harold Marks, "Some WEA Statistics: How Efficient Are the Districts?" *Highway* 32 (March 1940): 64.

xi. Alec Ellis, "Rural Library Services in England and Wales before 1919," *Library History* 4 (Spring 1977): 69.

xii. Commission of Enquiry into Industrial Unrest, No. 7 Division, *Report of the Commissioners for Wales, including Monmouthshire*, Parl. Sess. Papers, 1917–18, vol. XV, Cd. 8688, 12, 19, 28, 30.

xiii. Baggs, "Miners' Libraries," 141, 148–50.

xiv. Jack Lawson, *A Man's Life* (London: Hodder & Stoughton, 1932), 109–15.

xv. D.R. Davies, *In Search of Myself* (London: Geoffrey Bles, 1961), 18–19, 27–31, 36, 51–52.

xvi. H.V. Morton, *In Search of Wales* (London: Methuen, 1932), 247–49.

xvii. Stephen Walsh, "How I Got On: Life Stories by the Labour MPs," *Pearson's Weekly* (29 March 1906): 691.

xviii. Robert Morgan, *My Lamp Still Burns* (Llandysul: Gomer, 1981), 90–91.

xix. R.W. Morris, "Autobiography of R.W. Morris," B[runel] U[niversity] L[ibrary], 8.

xx. Percy Wall, "Hour at Eve," BUL, ch. 15.

xxi. Mrs. F.H. Smith, in *Life as We Have Known It*, ed. Margaret Llewelyn Davies (London: Hogarth Press, 1931), 71–72.

xxii. Davies, *Right Place*, 104–05.

xxiii. Q.D. Leavis, *Fiction and the Reading Public* (London: Chatto & Windus, 1932), 4–7, 43.

xxiv. The complete borrowing record for Tylorstown, the neatly complete record for the Markham Welfare Association Library, and a discussion of the methodological problems involved in using such documents, are in Jonathan Rose, "Marx, Jane Eyre, Tarzan: Miners Libraries in South Wales, 1923–52," *Leipziger Jahrbuch zur Buchgeschichte* 4 (1994): 187–207. The borrowing records for all three miners' libraries are held by the library of the University of Wales, Swansea.

xxv. Leavis, *Fiction and the Reading Public*, 36.

xxvi. Baggs, "Miners' Libraries," 386–92, 403, 423–30.

xxvii. A.J. Lush, *The Young Adult* (Cardiff: U of Wales P Board, 1941), 47, 50, 72, 79–82.

xxviii. "Adult Education in the Rhondda Valley," *Bulletin of the World Association for Adult Education* 40 (May 1929): 19–21.

xxix. Hymie Fagan, "An Autobiography," BUL, 93.

xxx. T. Brennan, E.W. Cooney, and H. Pollins, *Social Change in South-West Wales* (London: Watts, 1954), 69–70.

xxxi. Dai Smith, *Aneurin Bevan and the World of South Wales* (Cardiff: U of Wales P, 1993), 209.

xxxii. Davies, *Right Place*, 102–04.

xxxiii. Robert Morgan, *My Lamp Still Burns* (Llandysul: Gomer, 1981), 116.

xxxiv. The activity of Marxists on miners' library committees is charted in Hywel Francis, "The Origins of the South Wales Miners' Library," *History Workshop*, 2 (Autumn 1976): 183–205, esp. Appendix 6.

xxxv. Miners' Welfare Fund, Annual Report, 1929, 38–39.

xxxvi. Hywel Francis and David Smith, *The Fed: A History of the South Wales Miners in the Twentieth Century* (London: Lawrence & Wishart, 1980), 33, 48.

xxxvii. Kenneth O. Morgan, *Rebirth of a Nation: Wales 1880–1980* (New York: Oxford UP, 1981), 211–12.

xxxviii. Baggs, "Miners' Libraries," 167–68, 268–71, 330.

xxxix. Leavis, *Fiction and the Reading Public*, 83–85.

xl. Hywel Francis, *Miners Against Fascism: Wales and the Spanish Civil War* (London: Lawrence & Wishart, 1984), 29–39.

xli. E.D. Lewis, *The Rhondda Valleys* (London: Phoenix House, 1959), 260–61.

xlii. Thomas Jones, "Workmen's Libraries and Institutes," in *Leeks and Daffodils* (Newtown: Welsh Outlook, 1942), 137.

xliii. Philip Massey, "Portrait of a Mining Town," *Fact* 8 (1937): 10, 27, 50.

xliv. "Adult Education in the Rhondda Valley," 22, 27.

xlv. Davies, *Right Place*, 239.

xlvi. G.H. Armbruster, "The Social Determination of Ideologies: Being a Study of a Welsh Mining Community" (PhD Diss., U of London, 1940), 154–57, 161.

xlvii. Ferdynand Zweig, *Men in the Pits* (London: Victor Gollancz, 1949), 90–92, 108–09.

xlviii. Norman Dennis, Fernando Henriques, and Clifford Slaughter, *Coal Is Our Life* (London: Eyre & Spottiswoode, 1956), 127, 167–68.

xlix. Davies, *Right Place*, 226–28; Zweig, *Men in the Pits*, 90–92, 108–09.

l. *South Wales Coalfield Project*, National Register of Archives, 237–39.

li. They were nearly closed in 1998, and were saved only by a last-minute restoration of a subsidy from the Rhondda Cynon Taff County Borough Council. Rob Thompson, "Village Libraries Win a Stay of Execution," *Western Mail* (4 March 1998).

lii. Hans-Josef Steinberg, "Workers' Libraries in Germany before 1914," trans. Nicholas Jacobs, *History Workshop* 1 (Spring 1976): 166–80.

CHAPTER 4

Intermediality

21.

Pierre Bourdieu, "The Field of Cultural Production, or: The Economic World Reversed," ed. Randall Johnson. Cambridge: Polity P, 1993. 29–73

Pierre Bourdieu (1930–2002) was Professor of Sociology at the Collège de France, and he also directed the Centre de Sociologie Européenne (CSE) in Paris from 1968 until his death in 2002. He developed a number of influential theoretical vocabularies and investigative frameworks, the most important of which have been the concepts of cultural, social, and symbolic capital. While it has long been understood that one's command over economic resources affects one's opportunities and successes, Bourdieu asserted that there were other forms of capital that played a similar role: social capital, or resources based on membership in a group or other network of support and influence; cultural capital, or resources derived from knowledge, skill, and education; and finally symbolic capital, or resources based on prestige, honors, or recognition. Relatedly, Bourdieu elaborated on the concept of the habitus, a set of socially acquired skills, habits, and dispositions.

One of his most important essays, and the one most relevant to this Reader, is excerpted below (taken from his book of the same name, first published in 1993). Here Bourdieu describes (and diagrams) his conception of "the field of cultural production" as it existed in nineteenth-century France, one that encompasses a wide range of cultural productions from well-known literary genres such as poetry and the novel to journalism and vaudeville. In order to examine the social conditions under which value is ascribed to cultural products, it is important, according to Bourdieu, to examine the entire social field and the various possible positions within it. According to Bourdieu, one of the chief obstacles to understanding how cultural production comes to be valued is society's belief in the "charismatic ideology of 'creation,'" whereby creators (such as authors) are invested with near-divine status.[1] His work attempts to elaborate a theory of the cultural field by stripping creators of this status and situating artistic works of all kinds within the social conditions of their production, circulation, and consumption.

One way in which Bourdieu attempts to situate cultural production can be seen in the diagram included in this essay (p. 348), where Bourdieu charts the degree of

---

1 Pierre Bourdieu, *The Rules of Art: Genesis and Structure of the Literary Field,* ed. Susan Emanuel (Cambridge: Polity P, 1996), 167.

"consecration," or cultural approval, bestowed upon a given type of artistic production, and the level of audience, or popularity, afforded to these works. For example, vaudeville at once enjoyed a low cultural status and was highly popular, in opposition to avant-garde poetry,[2] which was highly consecrated but had only small readerships. An additional complication is that, for Bourdieu, any such field of cultural production is always shifting and contested: shifting because the boundaries are porous (there being low barriers to entrance into the cultural field, as participation often requires little economic or cultural capital) and contested (as the occupants of different positions in the field are constantly struggling to defend or improve their positions).

Whereas D.F. McKenzie's essay in Chapter 1 (pp. 45–62), and Jerome McGann's essay in Chapter 2 (pp. 113–24), articulate a sociological approach to bibliographical and textual studies, Bourdieu articulates a sociological approach to cultural production in general. Bourdieu's essay is an important launching point for this chapter since he argues that no one form of cultural production (such as literature) can be understood apart from other cultural products (such as visual art), and further that the cultural field itself must be situated within a larger sociological and political frame of reference in order to be understood.

The Field of Cultural Production, or: The Economic World Reversed

336 O Poésie, ô ma mère mourante
Comme tes fils t'aimaient d'un grand amour
Dans ce Paris, en l'an mil huit cent trente:
Pour eux les docks, l'Autrichien, la rente
Les mots de bourse étaient du pur hébreu.
—Théodore de Banville, "Ballade de ses regrets pour l'an 1830"[3]

I. Preliminaries

Few areas more clearly demonstrate the heuristic efficacy of *relational* thinking than that of art and literature. Constructing an object such as the literary field[i] requires and enables us to make a radical break with the substantialist mode of thought[4] (as Ernst Cassirer[5] calls it) which tends to foreground the individual, or the visible interactions between individuals, at the expense of the

2 Original or experimental.

3 "O poetry, O my dying mother, / How your sons loved you with a great love / Here in Paris, in the year 1830: / For them the docks, the Austrian, the private income / The words of the stock exchange were all pure Hebrew." Théodore de Banville, "Ballad of his regrets for 1830."

4 Substantialism is the doctrine that there are substantial realities behind phenomena.

5 Ernst Cassirer (1874–1945) was a German idealist philosopher who united scientific and non-scientific modes of thought.

structural relations—invisible, or visible only through their effects—between social positions that are both occupied and manipulated by social agents which may be isolated individuals, groups, or institutions.[ii] There are in fact very few other areas in which the glorification of "great individuals," unique creators irreducible to any condition or conditioning, is more common or uncontroversial—as one can see, for example, in the fact that most analysts uncritically accept the division of the corpus that is imposed on them by the names of authors ("the work of Racine") or the titles of works (*Phèdre* or *Bérénice*).

To take as one's subject of study the literary or artistic field of a given period and society (the field of Florentine painting in the quattrocento[6] or the field of French literature in the Second Empire[7]) is to set the history of art and literature a task which it never completely performs, because it fails to take it on explicitly, even when it does break out of the routine of **monographs** which, however interminable, are necessarily inadequate (since the essential explanation of each work lies outside each of them, in the objective relations which constitute this field). The task is that of constructing the space of positions and the space of the position-takings [*prises de position*] in which they are expressed. The science of the literary field is a form of *analysis situs*[8] which establishes that each position—e.g., the one which corresponds to a genre such as the novel or, within this, to a sub-category such as the "society novel" [*roman mondain*] or the "popular" novel—is subjectively defined by the system of distinctive properties by which it can be situated relative to other positions; that every position, even the dominant one, depends for its very existence, and for the determinations it imposes on its occupants, on the other positions constituting the field; and that the structure of the field, i.e., of the space of positions, is nothing other than the structure of the distribution of the capital of specific properties which governs success in the field and the winning of the external or specific profits (such as literary prestige) which are at stake in the field.

The *space of literary or artistic position-takings*, i.e., the structured set of the manifestations of the social agents involved in the field—literary or artistic works, of course, but also political acts or pronouncements, manifestos or polemics, etc.—is inseparable from the *space of literary or artistic positions* defined by possession of a determinate quantity of specific capital (recognition) and, at the same time, by occupation of a determinate position in the structure of the distribution of this specific capital. The literary or artistic field is a *field of forces*, but it is also a *field of struggles* tending to transform or conserve this field of forces. The network of objective relations between positions subtends[9] and orients the strategies which the occupants of the different positions implement in their struggles to defend or improve their positions (i.e., their position-takings), strategies which depend for their force and form on the position each agent occupies in the power relations [*rapports de force*].

---

6 The Quattrocento refers to the fifteenth-century cultural Renaissance in Italy.

7 The Second Empire is the regime of Napoleon III from 1852–70.

8 Latin for "picking apart of place."

9 Generally used as a mathematical term, meaning to delimit.

Every position-taking is defined in relation to the *space of possibles* which is objectively realized as a *problematic* in the form of the actual or potential position-takings corresponding to the different positions; and it receives its distinctive *value* from its negative relationship with the coexistent position-takings to which it is objectively related and which determine it by delimiting it. It follows from this, for example, that a position-taking changes, even when the position remains identical, whenever there is change in the universe of options that are simultaneously offered for producers and consumers to choose from. The meaning of a work (artistic, literary, philosophical, etc.) changes automatically with each change in the field within which it is situated for the spectator or reader.

This effect is most immediate in the case of so-called classic works, which change constantly as the universe of coexistent works changes. This is seen clearly when the simple *repetition* of a work from the past in a radically transformed field of compossibles[10] produces an entirely automatic *effect of parody* (in the theater, for example, this effect requires the performers to signal a slight distance from a text impossible to defend as it stands; it can also arise in the presentation of a work corresponding to one extremity of the field before an audience corresponding structurally to the other extremity—e.g., when an avant-garde play is performed to a bourgeois audience, or the contrary, as more often happens). It is significant that breaks with the most orthodox works of the past, i.e., with the belief they impose on the newcomers, often take the form of *parody* (intentional, this time), which presupposes and confirms. In this case, the newcomers "get beyond" ["*dépassent*"] the dominant mode of thought and expression not by

explicitly denouncing it but by repeating and reproducing it in a sociologically non-congruent context, which has the effect of rendering it incongruous or even absurd, simply by making it perceptible as the arbitrary convention it is. This form of heretical break is particularly favored by ex-believers, who use pastiche or parody as the indispensable means of objectifying, and thereby appropriating, the form of thought and expression by which they were formerly possessed.

This explains why writers' efforts to control the reception of their own works are always partially doomed to failure (one thinks of Marx's "I am not a Marxist"[11]); if only because the very effect of their work may transform the conditions of its reception and because they would not have had to write many things they did write and write them as they did—e.g., resorting to rhetorical strategies intended to "twist the stick in the other direction"—if they had been granted from the outset what they are granted retrospectively.

One of the major difficulties of the social history of philosophy, art, or literature is that it has to reconstruct these spaces of original possibles which, because they were part of the self-evident givens of the situation, remained unremarked and are therefore unlikely to be mentioned in contemporary accounts, chronicles, or memoirs. It is difficult to conceive of the vast amount of information which is linked to membership of a field and which all contemporaries immediately invest in their reading of works: information about institutions—e.g., academies, journals, magazines, galleries, **publishers**, etc.—and about persons, their relationships, liaisons, and quarrels,

---

10 A philosophical term, referring to when one thing is compatible or possible in conjunction with another.

11 Apparently said by Marx about his exasperations with his French followers.

information about the ideas and problems which are "in the air" and circulate orally in gossip and rumor. (Some intellectual occupations presuppose a particular mastery of this information.) Ignorance of everything which goes to make up the "mood of the age" produces a derealization[12] of works: stripped of everything which attached them to the most concrete debates of their time (I am thinking in particular of the connotations of words), they are impoverished and transformed in the direction of intellectualism or an empty humanism. This is particularly true in the history of ideas, and especially of philosophy. Here the ordinary effects of derealization and intellectualization are intensified by the representation of philosophical activity as a summit conference between "great philosophers"; in fact, what circulates between contemporary philosophers, or those of different epochs, are not only **canonical** texts, but a whole philosophical doxa[13] carried along by intellectual rumor—labels of schools, truncated quotations, functioning as slogans in celebration or polemics—by academic routine and perhaps above all by school manuals (an unmentionable reference), which perhaps do more than anything else to constitute the "common sense" of an intellectual generation. Reading, and *a fortiori*[14] the reading of books, is only one means among others, even among professional readers, of acquiring the knowledge that is mobilized in reading.

It goes without saying that, in both cases, change in the space of literary or artistic possibles, is the result of change in the power relation that constitutes the space of positions. When a new literary or artistic group makes its presence felt in the field of literary or artistic production, the whole problem is transformed, since its coming into being, i.e., into difference, modifies and displaces the universe of possible options; the previously dominant productions may, for example, be pushed into the status either of outmoded [*déclassé*] or of classic works.

[...]

II. The Field of Cultural Production and the Field of Power

In Fig. 4.1, the literary and artistic field (3) is contained within the field of power (2), while possessing a relative autonomy with respect to it, especially as regards its economic and political principles of hierarchization. It occupies a *dominated position* (at the negative pole) in this field, which is itself situated at the dominant pole of the field of class relations (1). It is thus the site of a double hierarchy: the *heteronomous*[15] principle of hierarchization, which would reign unchallenged if, losing all autonomy, the literary and artistic field were to disappear as such (so that writers and artists became subject to the ordinary laws prevailing in the field of power,

12 To be deprived of a connection with the real.

13 What is taken for granted and unquestioned in any particular society, or, here, amongst a group of thinkers.

14 From the Latin phrase, *argumentum a fortiori*, which denotes "argument 'from [the] stronger [reason].'" The phrase is usually taken to mean "even more likely" or "with even more certainty."

15 Subject to an external law or standard.

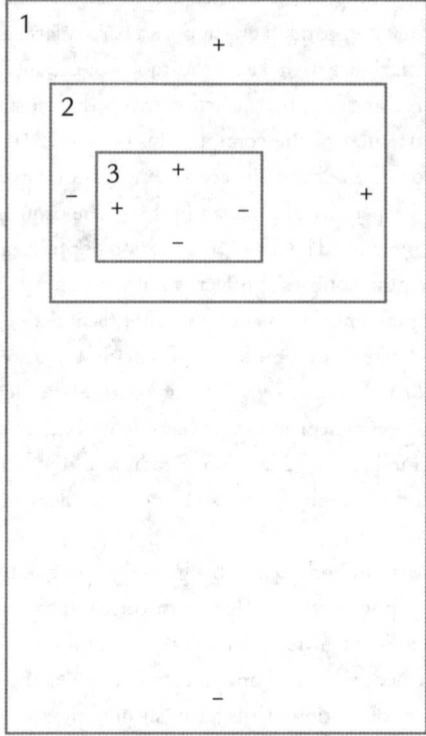

Fig. 4.1: Diagram of the artistic field (3), contained within the field of power (2) which is itself situated within the field of class relations (1). '+' = positive pole, implying a dominant position; '-' = negative pole, implying a dominated position. Reprinted with permission.

and more generally in the economic field), is *success*, as measured by indices such as book sales, number of theatrical performances, etc. or honors, appointments, etc. The *autonomous* principle of hierarchization, which would reign unchallenged if the field of production were to achieve total autonomy with respect to the laws of the market, is *degree specific consecration* (literary or artistic prestige), i.e., the degree of recognition accorded by those who recognize no other criterion of legitimacy than recognition by those whom they recognize. In other words, the specificity of the literary and artistic field is defined by the fact that the more autonomous it is, i.e., the more completely it fulfills its own logic as a field, the more it tends to suspend or reverse the dominant principle of hierarchization; but also that, whatever its degree of independence, it continues to be affected by the laws of the field which encompasses it, those of economic and political profit. The more autonomous the field becomes, the more favorable the symbolic power balance is to the most autonomous producers and the more clear-cut is the division between the field of restricted production, in which the producers produce for other producers, and the field of large-scale production [*la grande production*], which is *symbolically* excluded and discredited (this symbolically dominant definition is the one that the historians of art and literature *unconsciously* adopt when they exclude from their object of study writers and artists who produced for the market and have often fallen into oblivion). Because it is a good measure of the degree of autonomy, and therefore of presumed adherence to the disinterested values which constitute the specific law of the field, the degree of public success is no doubt the main differentiating factor. But lack of success is not in itself a sign and guarantee of election, and *poètes maudits*,[16] like "successful playwrights," must take account of a secondary differentiating factor whereby some *poètes maudits* may also be "failed writers" (even if exclusive reference to the first criterion can help them to avoid realizing it), while some box-office successes may be recognized, at least in some sectors of the field, as genuine art.

Thus, at least in the most perfectly autonomous sector of the field of cultural production, where the only audience aimed at is other producers (as with Symbolist poetry[17]), the economy of practices is based, as in a generalized game of "loser wins," on a systematic inversion of the fundamental principles of all ordinary economies: that of business (it excludes the pursuit of profit and does not guarantee any sort of correspondence between investments and monetary gains), that of power (it condemns honors and temporal greatness), and even that of institutionalized cultural authority (the absence of any academic training or consecration may be considered a virtue).

One would have to analyze in these terms the relations between writers or artists and publishers or gallery directors. The latter are equivocal figures, through whom the logic of the economy is brought to the heart of the sub-field of production-for-fellow-producers; they need to possess, simultaneously, economic dispositions which, in some sectors of the field, are totally alien to the producers and also properties close to those of the producers whose work they valorize and exploit. The logic of the structural homologies[18] between the field of publishers or gallery directors and the field of the corresponding artists or writers does indeed mean that the former present properties close to those of the latter, and this favors the relationship of trust and belief which is the basis of an exploitation presupposing a high degree of misrecognition on each side. These "merchants in the temple"[19] make their living by tricking the artist or writer into taking the consequences of his or her statutory professions of disinterestedness.

This explains the inability of all forms of economism, which seek to grasp this anti-economy in economic terms, to understand this upside down economic world. The literary and artistic world is so ordered that those who enter it have an interest in disinterestedness. And indeed, like

16 In French, "accursed poets," those living outside of or in antagonism to society.

17 A poetic movement launched in France by the publication of *Les Fleurs du Mal* (*The Flowers of Evil*, 1857) by Charles Baudelaire (1821–67).

18 Groups are homologous because they occupy the same position within Bourdieu's model.

19 An allusion to the merchants or money-changers operating in the temple in Jerusalem, whom Jesus ejects from the temple. The story is told in all four of the gospels.

prophecy, especially the prophecy of misfortune, which, according to Weber,[20] demonstrates its authenticity by the fact that it brings in no income, a heretical break with the prevailing artistic traditions proves its claim to authenticity by its disinterestedness.[iii] As we shall see, this does not mean that there is not an economic logic to this charismatic economy based on the social miracle of an act devoid of any determination other than the specifically aesthetic intention. There are economic conditions for the indifference to economy which induces a pursuit of the riskiest positions in the intellectual and artistic avant-garde, and also for the capacity to remain there over a long period without any economic compensation.

i. The Struggle for the Dominant Principle of Hierarchization

The literary or artistic field is at all times the site of a struggle between the two principles of hierarchization: the heteronomous principle, favorable to those who dominate the field economically and politically (e.g., "bourgeois art") and the autonomous principle (e.g., "art for art's sake"), which those of its advocates who are least endowed with specific capital tend to identify with degree of independence from the economy, seeing temporal failure as a sign of election and success as a sign of compromise.[iv] The state of the power relations in this struggle depends on the overall degree of autonomy possessed by the field, that is, the extent to which it manages to impose its own norms and sanctions on the whole set of producers, including those who are closest to the dominant pole of the field of power and therefore most responsive to external demands (i.e., the most heteronomous); this degree of autonomy varies considerably from one period and one national tradition to another, and affects the whole structure of the field. Everything seems to indicate that it depends on the value which the specific capital of writers and artists represents for the dominant fractions, on the one hand in the struggle to conserve the established order and, perhaps especially, in the struggle between the fractions aspiring to domination within the field of power (bourgeoisie and aristocracy, old bourgeoisie and new bourgeoisie, etc.), and on the other hand in the production and reproduction of economic capital (with the aid of experts and cadres).[v] All the evidence suggests that, at a given level of overall autonomy, intellectuals are, other things being equal, proportionately more responsive to the seduction of the powers that be, the less well-endowed they are with specific capital.[vi]

The struggle in the field of cultural production over the imposition of the legitimate mode of cultural production is inseparable from the struggle within the dominant class (with the opposition between "artists" and "bourgeois") to impose the dominant principle of domination (that is to say—ultimately—the definition of human accomplishment). In this struggle, the artists and writers who are richest in specific capital and most concerned for their autonomy are considerably weakened by the fact that some of their competitors identify their interests with the dominant principles of hierarchization and seek to impose them even within the field, with the support of the temporal powers. The most heteronomous cultural producers

20 Max Weber (1864–1920), German sociologist, philosopher, and political economist best known for *The Protestant Ethic and the Spirit of Capitalism* (1905).

(i.e., those with least symbolic capital) can offer the least resistance to external demands, of whatever sort. To defend their own position, they have to produce weapons, which the dominant agents (within the field of power) can immediately turn against the cultural producers most attached to their autonomy. In endeavoring to discredit every attempt to impose an autonomous principle of hierarchization, and thus serving their own interests, they serve the interests of the dominant fractions of the dominant class, who obviously have an interest in there being only one hierarchy. In the struggle to impose the legitimate definition of art and literature, the most autonomous producers naturally tend to exclude "bourgeois" writers and artists, whom they see as "enemy agents." This means, incidentally, that sampling problems cannot be resolved by one of those arbitrary decisions of positivist ignorance which are dignified by the term "operational definition": these amount to blindly arbitrating on debates which are inscribed in reality itself, such as the question as to whether such and such a group ("bourgeois" theater, the "popular" novel, etc.) or such and such an individual claiming the title of writer or artist (or philosopher, or intellectual, etc.) belongs to the population of writers or artists or, more precisely, as to who is legitimately entitled to designate legitimate writers or artists.

The preliminary reflections on the definitions of the object and the boundaries of the population, which studies of writers, artists and, especially, intellectuals, often indulge in so as to give themselves an air of scientificity, ignore the fact, which is more than scientifically attested, that the definition of the writer (or artist, etc.) is an issue at stake in struggles in every literary (or artistic, etc.) field.[vii] In other words, the field of cultural production is the site of struggles in which what is at stake is the power to impose the dominant definition of the writer and therefore to delimit the population of those entitled to take part in the struggle to define the writer. The established definition of the writer may be radically transformed by an enlargement of the set of people who have a legitimate voice in literary matters. It follows from this that every survey aimed at establishing the hierarchy of writers predetermines the hierarchy by determining the population deemed worthy of helping to establish it. In short, the fundamental stake in literary struggles is the monopoly of literary legitimacy, i.e., *inter alia,* the monopoly of the power to say with authority who are authorized to call themselves writers; or, to put it another way, it is the monopoly of the power to consecrate producers or products (we are dealing with a world of belief and the consecrated writer is the one who has the power to consecrate and to win assent when he or she consecrates an author or a work—with a **preface**, a favorable review, a prize, etc.).

While it is true that every literary field is the site of a struggle over the definition of the writer (a universal proposition), the fact remains that scientific analysts, if they are not to make the mistake of universalizing the particular case, need to know that they will only ever encounter historical definitions of the writer, corresponding to a particular state of the struggle to impose the legitimate definition of the writer. There is no other criterion of membership of a field than the objective fact of producing effects within it. One of the difficulties of orthodox defense against heretical transformation of the field by a redefinition of the tacit or explicit terms of entry is the fact that polemics imply a form of recognition; adversaries whom one would prefer to destroy by ignoring them cannot be combated without consecrating them.

The "*Théâtre libre*"[21] effectively entered the sub-field of drama once it came under attack from the accredited advocates of bourgeois theater, who thus helped to produce the recognition they sought to prevent. The "*nouveaux philosophes*"[22] came into existence as active elements in the philosophical field and no longer just that of journalism—as soon as consecrated philosophers felt called upon to take issue with them.

The *boundary* of the field is a stake of struggles, and the social scientist's task is not to draw a dividing line between the agents involved in it by imposing a so-called operational definition, which is most likely to be imposed on him by his own prejudices or presuppositions, but to describe a *state* (long-lasting or temporary) of these struggles and therefore of the frontier delimiting the territory held by the competing agents. One could thus examine the characteristics of this boundary, which may or may not be institutionalized, that is to say, protected by conditions of entry that are tacitly and practically required (such as a certain cultural capital) or explicitly codified and legally guaranteed (e.g., all the forms of entrance examination aimed at ensuring a *numerus clausus*).[23] It would be found that one of the most significant properties of the field of cultural production, explaining its extreme dispersion and the conflicts between rival principles of legitimacy, is the extreme permeability of its frontiers and, consequently, the extreme diversity of the "posts" it offers, which defy any unilinear hierarchization. It is clear from that the field of cultural production demands neither as much inherited economic capital as the economic field nor as much educational capital as the university sub-field or even sectors of the field of power such as the top civil service—or even the field of the "liberal professions."[viii] However, precisely because it represents one of the *indeterminate sites* in the social structure, which offer ill-defined posts, waiting to be made rather than ready made, and therefore extremely elastic and undemanding, and career paths which are themselves full of uncertainty and extremely dispersed (unlike bureaucratic careers, such as those offered by the university system), it attracts agents who differ greatly in their properties and dispositions but the most favored of whom are sufficiently secure to be able to disdain a university career and to take on the risks of an occupation which is not a "job" (since it is almost always combined with a private income or a "bread-and-butter" occupation).

The "profession" of writer or artist is one of the least professionalized there is, despite all the efforts of "writers' associations," "Pen Clubs," etc. This is shown clearly by (*inter alia*) the problems which arise in classifying these agents, who are able to exercise what they regard as their main occupation only on condition that they have a secondary occupation which provides their main income (problems very similar to those encountered in classifying students).

21 A theater company operating from 1887 to 1896 in the Montmartre district of Paris, France, important for its productions of theatrical naturalism. The term literally means "free theater."

22 A loose group of French philosophers who rejected Marxism in the early 1970s, and who used non-traditional forms of media including television and newspapers to make their arguments. The term literally means "new philosophers."

23 Latin: "closed number," i.e., a quota system that limits the number of entrants admissible to an academic institution.

[...]

III. The Structure of the Field

Heteronomy arises from *demand*, which may take the form of personal *commission* (formulated by a "patron" in Haskell's[24] sense of a protector or client) or of the sanction of an autonomous *market*, which may be *anticipated* or *ignored*. Within this logic, the *relationship to the audience* and, more exactly, economic or political interest in the sense of interest in success and in the related economic or political profit, constitute one of the bases for evaluating the producers and their products. Thus, strict application of the autonomous principle of hierarchization means that producers and products will be distinguished according to their degree of success with the audience, which, it tends to be assumed, is evidence of their interest in the economic and political profits secured by success.

The duality of the principles of hierarchization means that there are few fields (other than the field of power itself) in which the antagonism between the occupants of the polar positions is more total (within the limits of the interests linked to membership of the field of power). Perfectly illustrating the distinction between relations of interaction and the structural relations which constitute a field, the polar individuals may never meet, may even ignore each other systematically, to the extent of refusing each other membership of the same class, and yet their practice remains determined by the negative relation which unites them. It could be said that the agents involved in the literary or artistic field may, in extreme cases, have nothing in common except the fact of taking part in a struggle to impose the legitimate definition of literary or artistic production.[ix]

The hierarchy by degree of real or supposed dependence on audience, success, or the economy itself overlaps with another one, which reflects the degree of specific consecration of the audience, i.e., its "cultural" quality and its supposed distance from the center of the specific values. Thus, within the sub-field of production-for-producers, which recognizes only the specific principle of legitimacy, those who are assured of the recognition of a certain fraction of the other producers, a presumed index of posthumous recognition, are opposed to those who, again from the standpoint of the specific criteria, are relegated to an inferior position and who, in accordance with the model of heresy, contest the legitimation principle dominant within the autonomous sub-field, either in the name of a new legitimation principle or in the name of a return to an old one. Likewise, at the other pole of the field, that of the market and of economic profit, authors who manage to secure "high-society" successes and bourgeois consecration are opposed to those who are condemned to so-called "popular" success—the authors of rural novels, music-hall artists, *chansonniers*,[25] etc.

---

24 Francis Haskell is the author of *Patrons and Painters: A Study in the Relations between Italian Art and Society in the Age of the Baroque, Revised and Enlarged Edition* (New Haven, CT: Yale UP, 1980).

25 Singer-songwriters.

i. *The Duality of Literary Hierarchies and Genres*

In the second half of the nineteenth century, the period in which the literary field attained its maximum autonomy, these two hierarchies [of economic/popular success and cultural legitimacy] seem to correspond, in the first place, to the specifically cultural hierarchy of the genres—poetry, the novel, and drama—and secondarily to the hierarchy of ways of using them which, as is seen clearly in the case of the theater and especially the novel, varies with the position of the audiences reached in the specifically cultural hierarchy.

The literary field is itself defined by its position in the hierarchy of the arts, which varies from one period and one country to another. Here one can only allude to the effect of the hierarchy of the arts and in particular to the dominance which poetry, an intellectual art, exerted until the sixteenth century over painting, a manual art,[x] so that, for example, the hierarchy of pictorial genres tended to depend on their distance—as regards the subject and the more or less erudite manner of treating it—from the most elaborate model of poetic discourse. It is well known that throughout the nineteenth century, and perhaps until Duchamp, the stereotype which relegated the painter to a purely manual genre ("stupid as a painter") persisted, despite the increasing exchange of symbolic services (partly, no doubt, because the painters were generally less rich in cultural capital than the writers; we know, for example, that Monet, the son of a Le Havre grocer, and Renoir, the son of a Limoges tailor, were much intimidated in the meetings at the Café Guerbois[26] on account of their lack of education).[27] In the case of

the field of painting, autonomy had to be won from the literary field too, with the emergence of specific criticism and above all the will to break free from the writers and their discourse by producing an intrinsically polysemic[28] work beyond all discourse, and a discourse about the work which declares the essential inadequacy of all discourse. The history of the relations between Odilon Redon[29] and the writers—especially Huysmans[30]—shows in an exemplary way how the painters had to fight for autonomy from the *littérateur* who enhances the illustrator by advancing himself, and to assert the irreducibility of the pictorial work (which the professional critic is more ready to recognize).[xi] The same logic can be used to analyze the relations between the composers and the poets: the concern to use without being used,

26 A café in Paris in which many artists regularly gathered during the late nineteenth century.

27 Marcel Duchamp (1887–1968), French artist commonly associated with Dadaism and Surrealism; Claude Monet (1840–1926), French painter and leader of the Impressionist movement; Pierre-Auguste Renoir (1841–1919), French Impressionist painter.

28 Consisting of multiple, co-existent meanings.

29 Odilon Redon (1840–1916), French painter aligned with Symbolism and sometimes referred to as precursor to Dadaism and Surrealism.

30 Joris-Karl Huysmans, born Charles-Marie-Georges Huysmans (1848–1907), French novelist who was also an art critic closely associated with the Impressionist movement.

to possess without being possessed, led some composers (Debussy,[31] for example) to choose to set mediocre texts which would not eclipse them.

From the economic point of view, the hierarchy is simple and relatively stable, despite cyclical fluctuations related to the fact, for example, that the more economically profitable the various genres, the more strongly and directly they are affected by recession.[xii] At the top of the hierarchy is drama, which, as all observers note, secures big profits provided by an essentially bourgeois, Parisian, and therefore relatively restricted, audience—for a very few producers (because of the small number of theaters). At the bottom is poetry, which, with a few, very rare exceptions (such as a few successes in verse drama), secures virtually zero profit for a small number of producers. Between the two is the novel, which can secure big profits (in the case of some naturalist novels),[32] and sometimes very big profits (some "popular" novels), for a relatively large number of producers, from an audience which may extend far beyond the audience made up of the writers themselves, as in the case of poetry, and beyond the bourgeois audience, as in the case of theater, into the *petite bourgeoisie*[33] or even, especially through municipal **libraries**, into the "labor aristocracy."[34]

From the point of view of the symbolic hierarchies, things are less simple since, as can be seen from Fig. 4.2, the hierarchies according to distance from profits are intersected by hierarchies internal to each of the genres (i.e., according to the degree to which the authors and works conform to the specific demands of the genre), which correspond to the social hierarchy of the audiences. This is seen particularly clearly in the case of the novel, where the hierarchy of specialties corresponds to the hierarchy of the audiences reached and also, fairly strictly, to the hierarchy of the social universes represented.

The complex structure of this space can be explained by means of a simple model taking into account, on the one hand, the properties of the different arts and the different genres considered as economic enterprises (price of the product, size of the audience, and length of the economic cycle) and, on the other hand, the negative relationship which, as the field increasingly imposes its own logic, is established between symbolic profit and economic profit, whereby *discredit* increases as the audience grows and its specific competence declines, together with the value of the recognition implied in the act of consumption. The different kinds of cultural enterprise vary, from an economic standpoint, in terms of the unit price of the product (a painting, a play, a concert, a book, etc.) and the cumulative number of purchasers; but they also vary according to the length of the production cycle, particularly as regards the speed with which profits are obtained (and, secondarily, the length of time during which they are secured). It can be seen that, although the opposition between the short cycle of products which sell rapidly and the long

31 Achille-Claude Debussy (1862–1918), French composer whose music is often compared to the Impressionist and Symbolist movements in art and literature.

32 Naturalism was a literary movement in France, Britain, and America, from the 1880s to the 1940s, that used realism to argue that social conditions, heredity, and environment were inescapable forces in shaping human character.

33 Refers to the lower middle class.

34 Refers to self-educated members of the working classes.

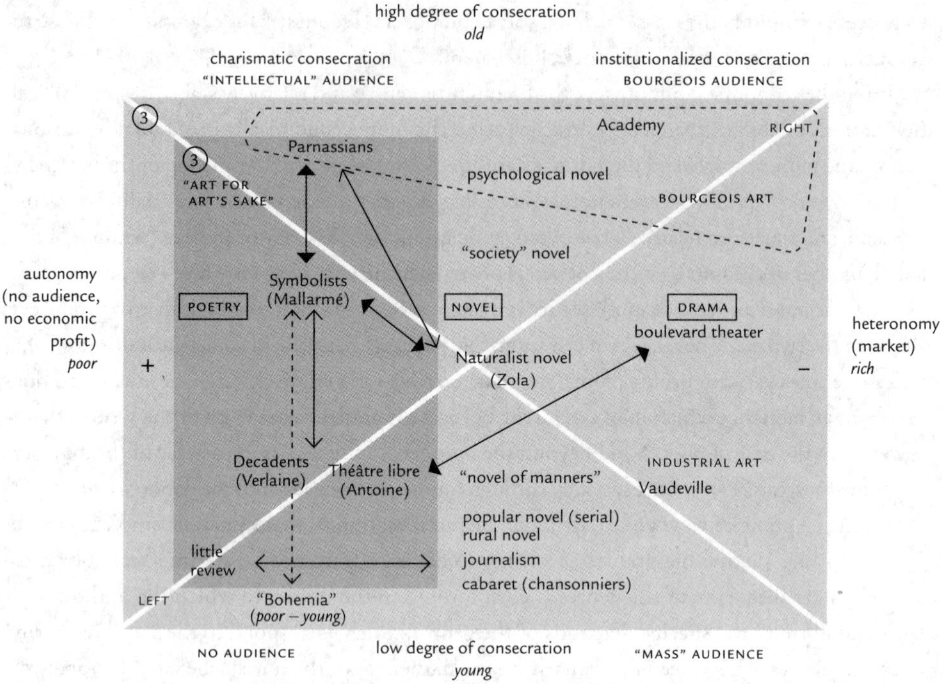

high degree of consecration
old
charismatic consecration
"INTELLECTUAL" AUDIENCE
institutionalized consecration
BOURGEOIS AUDIENCE
3
Academy
RIGHT
Parnassians
3
"ART FOR ART'S SAKE"
psychological novel
BOURGEOIS ART
"society" novel
autonomy (no audience, no economic profit) *poor*
Symbolists (Mallarmé)
POETRY
NOVEL
DRAMA
boulevard theater
heteronomy (market) *rich*
+
Naturalist novel (Zola)
–
Decadents (Verlaine)
Théâtre libre (Antoine)
"novel of manners"
INDUSTRIAL ART
Vaudeville
popular novel (serial)
rural novel
little review
journalism
cabaret (chansonniers)
LEFT
"Bohemia" (*poor – young*)
NO AUDIENCE
low degree of consecration
young
"MASS" AUDIENCE

Fig. 4.2: French literary field in the second half of the nineteenth century; '+' = positive pole, implying a dominant position; '-' = negative pole, implying a dominated position. Reprinted with permission.

cycle of products which sell belatedly or slowly is found in each of the arts, they differ radically in terms of the mode of profit acquisition and therefore, because of the connection that is made between the size of the audience and its *social quality*, in terms of the objective and subjective relationship between the producer and the market.

There is every difference between painters who, even when they set themselves in the avant-garde, can expect to sell to a *small number of connoisseurs* (nowadays including museums) works whose value derives partly from the fact that they are produced in limited numbers, and the writer who has to sell to an audience that is as wide as possible but one which, as it grows, is no doubt less and less composed of connoisseurs. This explains why the writers are, much more than painters, condemned to have an ambivalent attitude towards sales and their audience. They tend to be torn between the internal demands of the field of production, which regard commercial successes as suspect and push them towards a heretical break with the established norms of production and consumption, and the expectations of their vast audience, which are to some degree transfigured into a populist mission (Zola,[35] for example, endeavored to invoke a popular legitimacy to sublimate commercial success by transforming it into popular success). As for the dramatists, they are situated between the two poles. Established playwrights can earn

35 Émile-Édouard-Charles-Antoine Zola (1840–1902), French Naturalist writer.

big profits through repeated performances of the same work; for the others, as for composers, the main difficulty is to get their work performed at all.

Thus, the relationship of mutual exclusion between material gratification and the sole legitimate profit (i.e., recognition by one's peers) is increasingly asserted as the exclusive principle of evaluation as one moves down the hierarchy of economic gratifications. Successful authors will not fail to see this as the logic of resentment, which makes a virtue of necessity; and they are not necessarily wrong, since the absence of audience, and of profit, may be the effect of privation as much as a refusal, or a privation converted into a refusal. The question is even harder to resolve, at least summarily, since the collective bad faith which is the basis of a universe sustained by denial of the economy helps to support the effort of individual bad faith which makes it possible to experience failure in this world as election hereafter, and the incomprehension of the audience as an effect of the prophetic refusal to compromise with the demands of an audience attached to old norms of production. It is no accident that ageing, which dissolves the ambiguities, converting the elective, provisional refusals of adolescent bohemian life into the unrelieved privation of the aged, embittered bohemian, so often takes the form of an emotional crisis, marked by reversals and abjurations which often lead to the meanest tasks of "industrial art,"[36] such as vaudeville or cabaret,[37] and of political pamphleteering. But, at the other end of the scale of economic profits, a homologous[38] opposition is established, through the size of the audience, which is partly responsible for the volume of profit, and its recognized social quality, which determines the value of the consecration it can bestow, between bourgeois art, which has an honored place in society, and industrial art, which is doubly suspect, being both mercantile and "popular."

Thus we find three competing principles of legitimacy. First, there is the specific principle of legitimacy, i.e., the recognition granted by the set of producers who produce for other producers, their competitors, i.e., by the autonomous self-sufficient world of "art for art's sake," meaning art for artists. Secondly, there is the principle of legitimacy corresponding to "bourgeois" taste and to the consecration bestowed by the dominant fractions of the dominant class and by private tribunals, such as *salons*,[39] or public, state-guaranteed ones, such as academies, which sanction the inseparably ethical and aesthetic (and therefore political) taste of the dominant. Finally, there is the principle of legitimacy which its advocates call "popular," i.e., the consecration bestowed by the choice of ordinary consumers, the "mass audience." It can be seen that poetry, by virtue of its restricted audience (often only a few hundred readers), the consequent low profits, which make it the disinterested activity *par excellence*, and also its prestige, linked to the historical tradition initiated by the Romantics, is destined to charismatic legitimation which is given to only a few individuals, sometimes only one per generation and, by the same

---

36 Art that is oriented toward a mass market or that aims to be popular.

37 Vaudeville is a comic performance, often involving songs, popular in the early twentieth century; cabaret is entertainment performed at a nightclub or restaurant, while patrons eat and/or drink.

38 Having the same position.

39 Refers to a gathering of individuals in a private home to converse about cultural matters; popular in France in the seventeenth and eighteenth centuries.

token, to a continuous struggle for the monopoly of poetic legitimacy and a succession of successful or abortive revolutions: Parnassians against Romantics, Symbolists against Parnassians, neoclassicists against the early Symbolists, neo-Symbolists against neoclassicists.[40]

Although the break between poetry and the mass readership has been virtually total since the late nineteenth century (it is one of the sectors in which there are still many books published at the author's expense), poetry continues to represent the ideal model of literature for the least cultured consumers. As is confirmed by analysis of a dictionary of writers (such as the *Annuaire national des lettres*), members of the working and lower middle classes who write have too elevated an idea of literature to write realist novels; and their production does indeed consist essentially of poetry—very conventional in its form—and history.

The theater, which directly experiences the immediate sanction of the bourgeois public, with its values and conformisms, can earn the institutionalized consecration of academies and official honors, as well as money. The novel, occupying a central position in both dimensions of the literary space, is the most dispersed genre in terms of its forms of consecration. It was broadly perceived as typical of the new mercantile literature, linked to the newspaper and journalism by **serialization** and the impact they gave to it, and above all because, unlike the theater, it reached a "popular" audience; with Zola and Naturalism it achieved a wide audience which, although socially inferior, provided profits equivalent to those of the theater, without renouncing the specific demands of the art and without making any of the concessions typical of "industrial" literature; and, with the "society" novel [*roman mondain*], it was even able to win bourgeois consecrations previously reserved for the theater.

[...]

IV. Positions and Dispositions

[...]

i. The Habitus and the Possibles

The propensity to move towards the economically most risky positions, and above all the capacity to persist in them (a condition for all avant-garde undertakings which precede the demands of the market), even when they secure no short-term economic profit, seem to depend to a large extent on possession of substantial economic and social capital. This is, first, because economic capital provides the conditions for freedom from economic necessity, a private income [*la rente*] being one of the best substitutes for sales [*la vente*], as Théophile Gautier said to Feydeau:

40 Different styles of French poetry in the nineteenth century.

"Flaubert[41] was smarter than us ... He had the wit to come into the world with money, something that is indispensable for anyone who wants to get anywhere in art."[xiii]

Those who do manage to stay in the risky positions long enough to receive the symbolic profit they can bring are indeed mainly drawn from the most privileged categories, who have also had the advantage of not having to devote time and energy to secondary, "bread-and-butter" activities. Thus, as Ponton shows,[xiv] some of the Parnassians,[42] all from the petite bourgeoisie, either had to abandon poetry at some stage and turn to better-paid literary activities, such as the "novel of manners," or, from the outset, devoted part of their time to complementary activities such as plays or novels (e.g., François Coppée, Catulle Mendès, Jean Aicard), whereas the wealthier Parnassians could concentrate almost exclusively on their art (and when they did change to another genre, it was only after a long poetic career). We also find that the least well-off writers resign themselves more readily to "industrial literature," in which writing becomes a job like any other.

It is also because economic capital provides the guarantees [*assurances*] which can be the basis of self-assurance, audacity, and indifference to profit—dispositions which, together with the flair associated with possession of a large social capital and the corresponding familiarity with the field, i.e., the art of sensing the new hierarchies and the new structures of the chances of profit, point towards the outposts, the most exposed positions of the avant-garde, and towards the riskiest investments, which are also, however, very often the most profitable symbolically, and in the long run, at least for the earliest investors.

[...]

Notes

i. Or any other kind of field; art and literature being one area among others for application of the method of object-construction designated by the concept of the field.

ii. Since it is not possible to develop here all that is implied in the notion of the field, one can only refer the reader to earlier works which set out the conditions of the application in the social sciences of the relational mode of thought which has become indispensable in the natural sciences (P. Bourdieu, "Structuralism and Theory of Sociological Knowledge," *Social Research*, 35.4 [1968]: 681–706) and the differences between the field as a *structure of objective relations* and the *interactions* studied by Weber's analysis of religious agents or by interactionism (P. Bourdieu, "Une interprétation de la sociologie religieuse de Max Weber," *Archives européennes de sociologie*, 12.1 [1971]: 3–21).

iii. M. Weber, *Ancient Judaism* (Glencoe, IL: Free P, 1952).

iv. The status of "social art" is, in this respect, thoroughly ambiguous. Although it relates artistic or literary production to external functions (which is what the advocates of art for art's sake object to

41 Théophile Gautier (1811–72), French poet, novelist, critic, and journalist; Georges Feydeau (1862–1921), French playwright; Gustave Flaubert (1821–80), French novelist.

42 A group of French poets active in the later nineteenth century and associated with the doctrine of "art for art's sake."

about it), it shares with art for art's sake a radical rejection of the dominant principle of hierarchy and of the "bourgeois" art which recognizes it.

v. The specific, and therefore autonomous, power which writers and artists possess *qua* writers and artists must be distinguished from the alienated, heteronomous power they wield *qua* experts or cadres—a share in domination, but with the status of dominated mandatories, granted to them by the dominant.

vi. Thus, writers and artists who are "second-rank" in terms of the specific criteria may invoke populism and social art to impose their reign on the "leading intellectuals" who, as has happened in China and elsewhere, will protest against the disparity between the revolutionary ideal and the reality, i.e. the reign of functionaries devoted to the Party. See M. Goldman, *Literary Dissent in Communist China* (Cambridge, MA: Harvard UP, 1967).

vii. Throughout this passage, "writer" can be replaced by "artist," "philosopher," "intellectual," etc. The intensity of the struggle, and the degree to which it takes visible, and therefore conscious, forms, no doubt vary according to the genre and according to the rarity of the specific competence each genre requires in different periods, i.e., according to the probability of "unfair competition" or "illegal exercise of the profession." (This no doubt explains why the intellectual field, with the permanent threat of casual essayism, is one of the key areas in which to grasp the logic of the struggles which pervade all fields.)

viii. Only just over a third of the writers in the sample studied by Rémy Ponton had had any higher education, whether or not it led to a degree. See Rémy Ponton, "Le champ littéraire de 1865 à 1905" (Dissertation, Paris: École des Hautes Études en Sciences Sociales, 1977), 43. For the comparison between the literary field and other fields, see C. Charle, "Situation du champ littéraire," *Littérature* 44 (1981): 8–20.

ix. This struggle can be observed as much in the literary field as in the artistic field (with the opposition between "pure" art and "bourgeois" art) and in each genre (with, for example, the opposition between avant-garde theater and "middle brow" boulevard theater).

x. See R.W. Lee, *Ut pictura poesis: The Humanistic Theory of Painting* (New York: W.W. Norton, 1967); F. Bologna, *Dalle arte minori all' industrial design: storia di un' idealogia* (Bari: Laterza, 1972).

xi. See D. Gamboni, "Redon écrivain et épistolier," *Revue d'art* (1980): 68–71, and "Remarques sur la critique d'art, l'histoire de l'art et le champ artistique à propos d'Odilon Redon," *Revue suisse d'art et d'archéologie* 2 (1982): 57–63.

xii. C. Charle, *La crise littéraire à* l'époque du naturalisme (Paris: Presses de l'École Normale Supérieure, 1979), 37.

xiii. Cited by Cassagne, *La Théorie de l'art pour l'art en France chez les derniers romantiques et les premiers réalistes* (Geneva: Slatkine Reprints, 1979), originally published Paris, 1906, 218.

xiv. Ponton, "Le champ littéraire de 1865 à 1905," 69–70.

22.

David Scott Kastan, "From Playhouse to Printing House; or, Making a Good Impression," *Shakespeare and the Book*. Cambridge: Cambridge UP, 2001. 14–49

David Scott Kastan (b. 1946) is George M. Bodman Professor of English at Yale University. He is the author of several books on Shakespeare and Early Modern drama, the editor of plays by Shakespeare and Marlowe, and the Editor in Chief of the *Oxford Encyclopedia of English Literature*. His recent work historicizes the production, transmission, and reception of Early Modern texts. In *Shakespeare and the Book* (2001), Kastan investigates the transformation of Shakespeare's plays from scripts to be performed into printed texts to be read. He also examines how Shakespeare's plays continued to be transformed into other material forms—into popular entertainment in the centuries after Shakespeare's death, and, in our own age, into electronic media. Kastan's work explores the concept of intermediality by foregrounding the connections (and gaps) between print, the theater, and other media.

The chapter excerpted below examines some of the discontinuities between the realm of performance and the publishing practices that brought Shakespeare's plays into print. Here Kastan demonstrates that scholars have historically miscomprehended the migration of Shakespeare's plays "[f]rom playhouse to printing house." In providing a detailed account of the printing of Shakespeare's plays in his lifetime, Kastan overturns many assumptions about authorship and publishing practices to reveal the disconnection between Shakespeare's career as a playwright and the commercial marketing of his plays in print. According to Kastan, dramatists in the Early Modern period often had little control over the publishing of their plays, and Shakespeare himself took no interest whatsoever in overseeing the printing of his plays. Thus, Kastan cautions that we must avoid imposing modern conceptions of authorship on the printed plays. He develops his argument by showing that authorship was itself largely unimportant to the marketing of printed plays, with many of Shakespeare's plays having been published anonymously; as he explains, "the authority of the text was theatrical rather than authorial" (31). Kastan's larger point is that Shakespeare involved himself in the writing and performance of his plays only, and furthermore that printed plays were "the ephemera of an emerging entertainment industry," not "the artifacts of high culture we take them for today." Kastan concludes that "Performance no more animates the text than does the text record the performance. They are dissimilar and discontinuous modes of production" (p. 7).

From Playhouse to Printing House; or, Making a Good Impression

—Who's that?
—No one. The author.
—*Shakespeare in Love*

The joke from the popular film is obvious enough, though it always gets a laugh. The film's invented investor, Fennyman, asks about a person that he has noticed standing on stage, and Henslowe[1] replies that he is "No one," just "the author." What is funny, of course, is not merely that Henslowe thinks of the author as "no one," but that the particular "no one" that Fennyman has pointed to is Shakespeare, who more than any person of that era, has become unmistakably *someone*—and someone precisely because he has preeminently become The Author. Shakespeare was, not surprisingly, "the man of the millennium" in many polls as the zeros of the year 2000 rolled into view. The familiar image of a man with a receding hairline and shiny forehead, a ruff around his neck, and a quill pen in hand serves not only to identify Shakespeare "the author" but increasingly has become an emblem of human creativity itself.

But the film's joke also speaks an often overlooked truth. Within the collaborative economies of the early modern theater, an author—even Shakespeare—was, if not exactly "no one," hardly the cynosure[2] of the cultural world, hardly even "the author," as we have come to know that role, of his plays. It was an actors' theater: Richard Burbage and Edward Alleyn were the celebrities of the age, rather than Shakespeare and Marlowe.[3] Playwrighting was a kind of piece-work, providing the scripts for an emerging entertainment industry, scripts that legally belonged to the theater companies and which were inevitably subjected to the contingencies of performance. Even Shakespeare, a sharer in the company for which he wrote during most of his career, would have had his plays altered as they remained in the repertory—cut, revised, modified for specific playing locations and occasions—alterations that may or may not have originated with him or have even received his approval. Certainly as the plays stayed in the repertory after his retirement from the company around 1612 and death in 1616, hands other than his own determined what was played.

Shakespeare's lack of interest in publishing his plays is tacit acknowledgement of the performative aspect of drama, if not also of the inescapable collaborations of its realization. Perhaps reluctant

1 Philip Henslowe (1550–1616) was a theatrical entrepreneur, involved with some of the theaters where Shakespeare's plays were first staged. His diary is an important source for information about theater in Renaissance London. He was portrayed by the actor Geoffrey Rush in the film *Shakespeare in Love* (1998).

2 Guiding star.

3 Richard Burbage (1567–1619) of the King's Men and Edward Alleyn (1566–1626) of the Admiral's Men were two of the most popular actors of the Elizabethan theater; Christopher Marlowe (1564–93), English poet and playwright often referred to as an early rival of Shakespeare's.

to claim an authority over them that he did not have by seeing them into print, Shakespeare contented himself with their availability in the theater. Their plasticity there may well have seemed to him truer to their nature than the fixity they would achieve on the printed page.[i]

Certainly in the theater, in the various forms in which they have been played, they have had a long and successful run. But if Shakespeare cared little about their publication, it should not be forgotten that their theatrical longevity has been in part enabled because the plays did reach print. Although arguably Shakespeare does not "live" on the page quite as vitally as he does in the theater, at very least we must grant that in print he is *preserved*. It is not an entirely happy metaphor, I admit. Living beings are preferable to mummies, and print, in any case, does not preserve language as firmly as formaldehyde preserves bodies. Nonetheless, without print there is no Shakespeare for all time. It is in the printing house that his scattered "limbs" are collected and cured, as Heminge and Condell[4] say, remembered as a body of work.

Such remembering is of course no more exact than any other act of memory. Psychologists know that memory is never a perfect witness to the event remembered; it represses, displaces, and falsifies; nonetheless it is informative, though less as an objective representation of the event than as the over-determined register of the event's reception and assimilation. Print remembers similarly; it too falsifies even as it recalls and records, incorporating elements separate from that which it would overtly remember. The Shakespeare remembered in the printing house is inevitably something other than Shakespeare—both more and less than his originary presence. His corpus is reconstructed by sets of motivations and practices that leave their marks upon the text, distorting it even as they preserve and set it forth.

This is not to return to the notion of an ideal text independent of the processes of its materialization; it is to recognize that the text, like the past, is never available in unmediated form. This mediation is precisely what marks it as text, exactly as that which marks the past as past is the impossibility of an unmediated engagement with it. We, of course, engage Shakespeare only in mediated form. One could say that this means that we never actually engage Shakespeare, but to the degree that this is true it is merely an uninteresting literalism. Shakespeare is available precisely because "Shakespeare," in any meaningful sense other than the biographical, is—and has always been—a synecdoche[5] for the involved mediations of the playhouse and printing house through which he is produced.

The printed plays that preserve Shakespeare for us are all in various ways deficient, yet, precisely in their distance from the ideal text of editorial desire (and, as that desire projects it, authorial intention), they witness to the complex conditions of authorship that shaped his theatrical career. Shakespeare has become virtually the iconic name for authorship itself, but he wrote in circumstances in which his individual achievement was inevitably dispersed into—if not compromised by—the collaborations necessary for both play and book production.

4 John Heminge (c. 1556–1630) and Henry Condell (d. 1627) were English actors who are perhaps most famous for preparing Shakespeare's First Folio for publication in 1623.

5 A figure of speech in which a part of something represents the whole or the whole of something represents one of its parts.

Nonetheless, Shakespeare's apparent indifference to the publication of his plays, his manifest lack of interest in reasserting his authority over them, suggests how little he had invested in the notions of individuated authorship that, ironically, his name has come so triumphantly to represent. Literally his investment was elsewhere: in the lucrative partnership of the acting company. He worked comfortably within its necessary collaborations, and clearly felt no need to claim his play texts as his own as they began to **circulate** in print and be read.

In this regard, Shakespeare is perhaps somewhat more anomalous than many have supposed. While no doubt the great majority of playwrights "had no mind to be a man in Print," as Robert Davenport[6] says of himself in his **preface** "To the knowing Reader" of *King John and Matilda* (1655), many playwrights did not merely allow but actively sought publication to restore their intentions to the play they had written. Although all playwrights would have anticipated that their plays would be shaped by the demands of performance, their scripts legally being the property of the acting company (and the genre itself, as we are often reminded, existing as a subliterary form perhaps incapable of sustaining the burden of literary ambition), many playwrights consciously turned to print to preserve their creation in its intended form.

Notoriously, Ben Jonson[7] labored to rescue his plays from the theatrical conditions in which they were produced, seeking to make available for readers a play text of which he could be said in some exact sense to be its "author." The 1600 **quarto** of *Every Man Out Of His Humor* insists on its **title page** (Fig. 4.3) that it presents the play "As It Was First Composed by the Author B.I. Containing more than hath been Publickely Spoken or Acted."

Here Jonson asserts the authority of the literary text over the theatrical script, reversing the tendency to offer the play to a reading audience, in the familiar formula, "as it hath bene sundry times playd," as the 1600 quarto of *Henry V* (Fig. 4.4) has it. Even more remarkable is the 1605 quarto of *Sejanus*, to which Jonson contributes a preface in which he again announces that the printed text is "not the same with that which was acted on the publike stage." But in the published quarto, rather than merely restoring theatrical cuts, he has in fact removed and rewritten the work of a collaborator. While admitting that "A second pen had a good share" in what was played, in the printed text Jonson replaces the work of his unnamed co-author with his own words never acted, disingenuously claiming that his motive in inserting his own "weaker (and no doubt lesse pleasing)" language was only a reluctance "to defraud so happy a *Genius* of his right, by my lothed vsurpation" (sig. ¶ 2^{r}).[8]

But if Jonson's aggressive determination to extract his plays from the customary collaborations of the theater is unique, his desire for a printed text that will preserve the dramatist's intended form is not. Other playwrights similarly saw print as the medium in which their intentions could be made visible at least to their readers. In the 1623 quarto of *The Duchess of Malfi*,

6 Robert Davenport (fl. 1624–40), English playwright.

7 Ben Jonson (1572–1637), English playwright, poet, and literary critic noted for his satirical style.

8 I.e., this quotation occurs on the **recto** of the second **leaf** of the gathering signed with the printer's **signature** "¶."

The Comicall Satyre of

EVERY MAN, OVT OF HIS HVMOR.

AS IT WAS FIRST COMPOSED
by the AUTHOR B. I.

Containing more than hath been Publickely Spoken or Acted.

VVith the ſeuerall Character of euery Perſon.

*Non aliena meo preßi pede | * ſi propius ſtes*
*Te capient magis | * & decies repetita placebunt.*

LONDON,
Printed for *William Holme*, and are to be ſold at his Shop
at Sarjeants Inne gate in Fleetſtreet.
1600.

Fig. 4.3: Ben Jonson, *Every Man Out of His Humor* (1600), title page, STC 14767. Reproduced by permission of The Huntington Library, San Marino, California.

Webster[9] adds an anxious **marginal** note next to the italic text of a song sung by the churchmen in Act 3: "The Author disclaimes this Ditty to be his" (sig. H2^{r}). More positive in its use of print is Barnabe Barnes's[10] *The Devil's Charter* (1607), which advertises itself conventionally on the title page that it is presented "as it was plaide before the Kings Maiestie, upon Candlemasse night laste: by his Majesties Servants," and then adds: "But more exactly revewed, corrected, and augmented since by the Author, for the more pleasure and profit of the Reader." A year later, Thomas Heywood[11] insists in his **epistle** "To the Reader" in his *Rape of Lucrece* that it has not been "my custome ... to commit my plaies to the presse"; nonetheless, on account of the copies that have "accidently come into the Printers handes" in "**corrupt** and mangled" form, "This therefore I was the willinger to furnish out in his natiue habit" (sig. A2^{r}). In 1640, Richard Brome[12] adds an epistle to *The Antipodes* in which the "Curteous Reader" is told that this **playbook**, too, contains "more than was presented upon the *Stage*," where "for superfluous length (as some of the *Players* pretended)," cuts were made. Brome says that for this printed **edition** he thought it "good al should be inserted according to the allowed *Original*; and as it was, at first, intended for the *Cock-pit Stage*" (sig. L4^{v}). For Brome, as for Heywood and Barnes, print restores and preserves the play he wrote, and, incidentally, his remarks reveal that it was the uncut, authorial text that was "allowed" by the Master of the Revels.[13]

Shakespeare, however, never asserted any such proprietary right over his scripts or expressed any anxiety about their printed form. His plays, of course, were subjected to theatrical necessities, revised by various hands to allow them to play successfully within the two hours traffic of his

stage, but never did Shakespeare feel obliged to "furnish" the play he wrote in its "natiue habit." Somewhat less than half of his dramatic output ever appeared in print while he lived, and of the plays that were published none is marked by any effort on his part to insure that the printed play accurately reflected what he had written. In their epistle "to the great Variety of Readers" in the 1623 **folio**, Heminge and Condell tell the would-be purchasers of the volume that the collection contains Shakespeare's plays exactly "as he conceiued the[m]," but that extravagant claim is never one Shakespeare felt inspired to make himself about any printed edition of his work.

Only 18 of his 37 plays were published in his lifetime, and none in an edition that Shakespeare avowed as his own. Still, with 10 reprinted one or more times, at least 42 separate editions reached print before he died. (If one counts *The Taming of a Shrew*[14] as Shakespeare's, there are 45 surviving editions of 19 plays.) Clearly Shakespeare's plays were successful not only in the theater but also in the **bookstalls**, where they found a substantial reading audience. The first part

---

9 John Webster (c. 1580–c. 1632), English playwright best known for his tragedies.

10 Barnabe Barnes (bap. 1571–d. 1609), English poet and dramatist.

11 Thomas Heywood (c. 1573–1641), English poet, dramatist, and actor.

12 Richard Brome (c. 1590–1652), English playwright of the Jacobean period.

13 A holder of a position within the Royal household responsible for licensing entertainments at court.

14 Three editions of the play appeared before the printing of Shakespeare's *The Taming of the Shrew* in the First Folio in 1623. The authorship of this play, and its relationship to *The Taming of the Shrew*, are the subject of scholarly dispute.

THE
CRONICLE
Hiſtory of Henry the fift,
With his battell fought at *Agin Court* in
France. Togither with *Auntient*
Piſtoll.

As it hath bene ſundry times playd by the Right honorable
the Lord Chamberlaine his ſeruants.

LONDON
Printed by *Thomas Creede*, for Tho. Milling-
ton, and Iohn Busby. And are to be
ſold at his houſe in Carter Lane, next
the Powle head. 1600.

Fig. 4.4: *Henry V* (1600), title page, STC 22289. Reproduced by permission of The Huntington Library, San Marino, California.

of *Henry IV* appeared in six editions before his death, and a seventh before the folio was published in 1623. *Richard II* was published five times, as was *Richard III*. Several other plays were reprinted three times. At the time of his death, the total number of editions of Shakespeare's plays far exceeded that of any other contemporary playwright, and indeed no single play to that time had sold as well as *1 Henry IV*. (Even if one extends the time frame to 1640, only three plays—the anonymous *Mucedorus*, Kyd's *Spanish Tragedy*, and Marlowe's *Dr. Faustus*—appear in more editions than *1 Henry IV*'s seven, *Mucedorus*, somewhat improbably to modern taste, topping the list with 14 printings between 1598 and 1639.)

While he lived, Shakespeare arguably had some competitors for theatrical preeminence, but what has often been overlooked is that as a published dramatist he had none. In our various measures of Shakespeare's greatness, we have usually ignored the fact that in his own age more editions of his plays circulated than of any other contemporary playwright. Eventually the prolific Beaumont and Fletcher[15] would close the gap, but they never actually surpassed Shakespeare. Ironically, although he never sought his success as in print, he is the period's leading published playwright.

The reason that this has not been observed may be that print has seemed to many an inauthentic calculus of Shakespeare's achievement, but more likely it is simply, that this success literally "goes without saying"; it appears to us inevitable that Shakespeare's plays would reach print and thrive in that medium. In his own time, however, that success was hardly assured. We see the drama as the most compelling cultural manifestation of the age and Shakespeare as its most extraordinary figure, but Shakespeare wrote in an environment in which plays, at least English plays, had not yet emerged as a literary genre; they were much like film scripts in the movie industry today. **Publishers** did not rush to publish new plays, largely because there was not a large and reliable market for them. Although William Prynne,[16] in 1633, disgustedly insisted that playbooks were "now more vendible[17] than the choicest sermons," claiming that "above forty thousand Play-bookes have beene printed and vented within these two years,"[ii] even by his tendentious[18] accounting, plays still represented only a small percentage of the books that were purchased. In the 1630s, **booksellers** sold something like 20 times as many religious books (sermons, catechisms, bibles, and theological works) as they did plays.[iii]

Peter Blayney has usefully reminded us of what is all too easy to forget, given history's judgments on the period's cultural achievement plays, even Shakespeare's plays, were a relatively insignificant piece of the book trade. They were at best a risky publishing venture. "No more than one play in five would have returned the publisher's initial investment inside five years," Blayney tells us, and "not one in twenty would have paid for itself during its first year."[iv] While Shakespeare provided some publishers with considerable profit, 8 of the 18 plays that appeared in his lifetime

15 Francis Beaumont (c. 1585–1616) and John Fletcher (1579–1625) were a prolific playwriting duo in Jacobean England.

16 William Prynne (1600–69), English Puritan religious and political writer and noted anti-theatricalist.

17 Commercially appealing; likely to sell well.

18 Advancing a particular agenda.

did not merit a second edition before he died. And it is worth remembering that *Venus and Adonis*[19] was published in 16 editions by 1636, 7 more than even the most successful of his plays.

In spite of the literary ambitions of some playwrights, printed plays were generally considered **ephemera**, among the "rifferaffes" and "baggage books" that Thomas Bodley[20] would not allow in his **library** lest some "scandal" attach to it by their presence.[v] Publishers did regularly assume the risk of printing plays (though, between 1590 and 1615, on average only about 10 were published a year), but they could not have done so imagining either that they were preserving the nation's cultural heritage or about to make their own fortune.

Plays were published in essence because they could be. In a commercial environment where publishing was largely opportunistic, plays were for a publisher a relatively inexpensive investment. If they did not, as Blayney says, offer a reliable "shortcut to wealth" (p. 389), they did allow a publisher the chance to make some money without great financial exposure. **Manuscripts** became available, probably at a cost to the publisher of no more than two pounds a piece. No record of any payment for a play survives, but evidence like that from the *Second Part of the Return From Parnassus*, where the **printer** John Danter (of whom more later) is imagined offering an author "40 shillings and an odde pottle of wine" for a manuscript, suggests that this was something like the going rate for a small book.[vi] The play text would usually be printed in small pica **type**[21] on nine **sheets** of the cheapest available paper. For an edition of 800, which was probably all a publisher would risk, the total costs of copy, **registration**, and printing would be about eight pounds. With playbooks retailing at around 6d. (viz., the "testerne"[22] the publishers of the 1609 *Troilus and Cressida* hope its readers will think "well bestowd" with the play's purchase) and
wholesaling at 4d., a publisher, especially one who sold his own books, could break even with the sale of about 500 copies and might then begin to turn a modest profit, which would average about a pound a year—certainly not a spectacular windfall but not an insubstantial contribution to the financial health of the **stationer's** business.[vii]

[...]

Of course, many plays never reached print at all. Those that did, almost certainly less than a fifth of the number played, arrived at their publishers from a variety of sources, and in the absence of anything like our modern **copyright** law, the publishers had no obligation to inquire scrupulously into their **provenance**. All that was legally required to establish title was that they not violate another stationer's claim to the text and that they follow the proper channels of authority in securing their right. If there was no prior claim, a publisher was free to print his copy with

---

19 A poem by Shakespeare based on passages from Ovid's *Metamorphoses*.

20 Sir Thomas Bodley (1545–1613), English scholar who founded the Bodleian Library at the University of Oxford.

21 A small typeface that would allow the publisher to maximize the number of characters appearing per page.

22 A colloquial term for six pence (i.e., 6d.).

no regard for its author's rights or interests. As George Wither[23] wrote in 1624: "by the lawes and Orders of their Corporation, they can and do setle vpon the particular members thereof p[e]rpetuall interest in such Bookes as are Registred by them at their Hall ... notwithstanding their first Coppies were purloyned from the true owner, or imprinted without his leaue."

Until the first modern copyright law was passed in 1709, this remained the case. Copyright belonged to the publisher not to the author, and the legal situation, as Wither bitterly noted, served the publisher's interest at the expense of that of both the author and the reading public: "If he gets any written Coppy into his powre, likely to be vendible; whether the Author be willing or no, he will publish it; and it shall be contriued and named alsoe, according to his owne pleasure: which is the reason, so many good Bookes come forth imperfect, and with foolish titles."[viii]

[...]

[...] Wither's main accusation, at least with regard to the drama, is true. Stationers for the most part showed little interest in either the quality or the origin of the dramatic texts they printed; they cared mainly that it be "vendible." Textual scholars, the heirs of Wither's dismay, have often used this fact to motivate their narratives of the transmission of Shakespeare's text. They similarly have stigmatized the stationers, or at least some, as dishonest and incompetent, all too willing to attempt a quick profit by publishing a **pirated** text of a play. But in truth the pirates, as Blayney and Laurie Maguire, among others, have recently reminded us, are largely bogeys of our imagination, functions of an anachronistic understanding of both the playhouse and the printing house.[ix] This is not to say that publishers did inevitably purchase their copy from the author or some other apparently legitimate owner; it is, however, to emphasize that stationers knew that the author's permission was not necessary to publish the work, and knew as well that in the case of drama the very notion of authorship is problematic. In any precise sense, the only pirates, and there were some, were those publishers who undertook to print a book that properly belonged to another stationer.

Unquestionably plays were often published without their authors' consent or even knowledge, and in forms of which no doubt their playwrights would never have approved; but this should not be taken as anything more than evidence of the usual—and fully legal—procedures of the contemporary book trade. A potential publisher would purchase a manuscript of a play, which might in some cases be authorial, though it could as well be a **scribal copy** made for the acting company or for a collector, or a **transcript** made by one or more actors. For the potential publisher it made no difference; no one of these granted the publisher any clearer authority over the text. All he would have been concerned with was that the manuscript not cost too much, that it be reasonably legible, and that no other stationer have a claim to the play.

23 George Wither (1588–1677), English poet and pamphleteer who was also an advocate for authorial copyright protection.

There are some examples of writers objecting to the publication of defective versions of their work, although these inevitably reveal how limited their ability was to oppose unauthorized publication. Usually the most they could do was provide authorized copy to replace the unsanctioned printing. Thus, Samuel Daniel[24] explains the publication of the second edition of his *Vision of the Twelve Goddesses* in his dedication to the Countess of Bedford:

> *Madame*: In respect of the vnmannerly presumption of an indiscreet Printer, who without warrant hath divulged the late shewe at Court ... I thought it not amisse seeing it would otherwise passe abroad to the prejudice both of the Maske and the inuention, to describe the whole forms thereof in all points as it was then performed ...[x]

Similarly, Stephen Egerton,[25] in a preface to the second edition of one of his sermons that had been taken down by a listener in shorthand, says that had it been his own doing originally he would have "beene more carefull in the manner of handling ... And therefore that which I now do, is rather somewhat to qualifie an errour that cannot be recalled, then to publish a worke that may be in any way greatly commodious to other."[xi] Both Daniel and Egerton are frustrated by the deficient texts that were published, but neither assumes that the publication of an unauthorized text is a legal issue. In the face of the publication of texts that neither author either delivered to or saw through the press, both realize that they have little recourse except to provide a better text for a new edition. 363

Regardless of the title page claims, playbooks were often unauthorized, published, that is, in editions that differed not only from the author's intended text but even from the text as it had been reshaped in performance; but these were not *illegal* printings. They do not provide evidence of criminal or dishonest business practices. Indeed this is true even for the so-called "bad quartos" of Shakespeare's plays. While these editions differ substantially from the familiar versions in which we know the play, and are arguably inferior if not corrupt, there is nothing to suggest their publishers knew them so. They operated in these cases very much as they did in all other publishing ventures, purchasing a play text on which they thought they might make a profit by having it printed and sold.

A published play text, we should remember, was not a priceless literary relic but a cheap **pamphlet**; it represented not the immortal words of a great writer but the work of professional actors whose skill involved improvisation as much as recall. The play itself had various lives in different theatrical venues, each of which would enforce changes upon the text. Why then would a publisher ever think in terms of the reliability or authority of the text?

Yet even if however improbably, a publisher did so think, how would he recognize textual corruption? We hear a mangled phrase from a bad quarto, and our familiarity with the received

---

24 Samuel Daniel (1562/63–1619), English poet and historian.

25 Stephen Egerton (1555?–1621?), an English clergyman and leading Puritan preacher who actively sought to reform the Church of England.

text instantly reveals the deficiency. "To be, or not to be, I there's the point." There is no more familiar or compelling evidence of the manifest deficiency of Q1 *Hamlet*[26] (sig. D4^{v}). But if we did not know the more familiar version would we think the line flawed? And indeed the putative corruption "I there's the point"—is of course a perfectly uncorrupt Shakespearean line. It appears in *Othello*, after Othello painfully comes to see that his worst fears about Desdemona's betrayal must be true, revealingly in language that shows how fully he has internalized the pernicious racism that Iago exploits: "And yet how Nature erring from it selfe." Iago instantly interrupts, determined that there should be no retreat from the damning knowledge: "I, there's the point" (3.3.231–32, TLN 1854–55). In *Othello*, the line marks a moment of unmistakably Shakespearean power along the tragic trajectory of the play; in *Hamlet* it marks the corruption of the text.

[...]

I am not saying that Q1 *Hamlet* is as good a play as the *Hamlet* that we usually read (though I would say that it is a better play than has generally been allowed, and certainly not "*Hamlet* by Dogberry,"[27] as Brian Vickers has termed it[xii]) I am saying only that such questions of literary judgment should not be allowed to color our understanding of the textual history. When we see that history backwards, through the filter of a cultural authority not fully achieved until the mid-eighteenth century, inevitably we get it wrong. Shakespeare, one could say, was not exactly Shakespeare during his own lifetime.

An obvious example: when his plays were first published, his name was not what distinguished them in the bookstalls. As is well known, eight of Shakespeare's plays were published over four years before one appeared in print with his name on the title page. Cuthbert Burby first included Shakespeare's name on the quarto of *Love's Labor's Lost* (Fig. 4.5) in 1598, and even then hardly as a ringing affirmation of authorship, the title page asserting only that the play was "Newly corrected and augmented By *W Shakespere*," the name set in small italic type. Previously editions of *Titus Andronicus, 2 and 3 Henry VI, The Taming of the Shrew, Romeo and Juliet, Richard II, Richard III*, and *1 Henry IV*, had all been published with no indication that Shakespeare was the playwright. The plays, with the exception of *2 Henry VI*, all advertise the authority of the text as theatrical rather than authorial, by insisting that it is published "As it was Plaide."

One should, of course, conclude that what this means is that before 1598 the name "Shakespeare" on the title page was not yet seen as sufficient inducement for a potential customer to purchase a play text at a bookstall. Indeed, most published plays advertised their theatrical auspices, emphasizing for us yet again that the drama was still subliterary, its audience, even

26 The First Quarto edition of *Hamlet* was published in 1603; it is much shorter than either the Second Quarto or First Folio editions and has generally been known as the "bad quarto," believed to have less authority than either of the other two editions.

27 Dogberry is a character in Shakespeare's play *Much Ado about Nothing* who has become famous for his comically inept use of language.

A
PLEASANT
Conceited Comedie
CALLED,
Loues labors loſt.

As it vvas preſented before her Highnes
this laſt Chriſtmas.

Newly corrected and augmented
By W. Shakeſpere.

Imprinted at London by *W.W.*
for *Cutbert Burby.*
1598.

Fig. 4.5: *Love's Labor's Lost* (1598), title page, STC 22294. Reprinted with the permission of the Folger Shakespeare Library.

for the published play, understood primarily as theatergoers. The six-penny pamphlets were a relatively cheap way of happily recalling a performance or catching up with one that had unhappily been missed. Richard Hawkins reminds the potential buyers of his edition of *Philaster* (1628) that the play "was affectionately taken, and approoved by the Seeing Auditors, or Hearing Spectators (of which sort I take, or conceive you to be the greatest part)," though he anticipates also that his edition will be "eagerly sought for not onely by those that haue heard & scene it, but by others that haue merely heard therof" (sig. A2[v]).

As excitement about a production waned with time, however, the published play would normally become less marketable: "When they grow stale they must be vented by Termers and Cuntrie chapmen," says Middleton[28] in his preface to *The Family of Love* (1608), distressed that publication of his play had not taken place "when the newnesse of it made it much more desired" (sig. A1v). Printed plays do seem for the most part to be tied to theatrical success, published with the hope, as Brome says in his epistle to *The Antipodes*, that "the publicke view of the world entertayn it with no lesse welcome, then that private one of the stage already has given it" (sig. A2[v]); or, as Heywood writes in his preface to *Greene's Tu Quoque* (1614): "since it hath past the Test of the stage with so generall an applause, pitty it were but it should likewise haue the honour of the Presse" (sig. A2[r]).

The "honour of the Presse" was usually reserved for plays that had succeeded on stage (*Troilus and Cressida* and *The Knight of the Burning Pestle* are the notable exceptions, for each the dramatic failure functioning as a sign of its sophistication[xiii]); and not surprisingly then, title pages usually advertised their plays as the records of performance rather than as the registers of a literary intention. Whatever the actual status of the underlying manuscript, if the market for playbooks was largely playgoers then the strategy makes sense. Within a theatrical economy, display of an author's name on a play text offered no particular commercial advantage. It does seem, however, that, at least in Shakespeare's case, this was in the process of changing. In 1598, reprints of both *Richard II* and *Richard III* were published that did include Shakespeare's name on the title page, and in 1599, a new edition of *1 Henry IV* was reissued with Shakespeare's name added. In the remaining years before Shakespeare died, 29 editions of 18 separate plays were published, only 8 of which appeared without identifying Shakespeare as the playwright.

Most remarkable in this regard is the edition of *King Lear* published by Nathaniel Butter[29] in 1608, with a title page (Fig. 4.6) not merely identifying Shakespeare as the playwright but trumpeting his authorship at the head of the page and in a larger **typeface** than had ever before been used for his name: "M. William Shak-speare: / *HIS* / True Chronicle Historie of the life and / death of King LEAR and his three / Daughters." Here the play is displayed and celebrated as Shakespeare's, but the printed text is no more exclusively "*HIS*" than any of the other published plays that had previously escaped his control. It is a poorly printed play (indeed the first that its printer, Nicholas Okes, had ever undertaken), and Shakespeare did not oversee its publication or concern himself with the imperfect results.

28 Thomas Middleton (1580–1627), English playwright.

29 Nathaniel Butter (bap. 1583–d. 1664), English bookseller.

M. William Shak-ſpeare:

HIS

True Chronicle Hiſtorie of the life and death of King LEAR and his three Daughters.

With the vnfortunate life of Edgar, *ſonne* and heire to the Earle of Gloſter, and his ſullen and aſſumed humor of TOM of Bedlam:

As it was played before the Kings Maieſtie at Whitehall vpon S. Stephans *night in Chriſtmas Hollidayes.*

By his Maieſties ſeruants playing vſually at the Gloabe on the Bancke-ſide.

LONDON,

Printed for *Nathaniel Butter*, and are to be ſold at his ſhop in *Pauls* Church-yard at the ſigne of the Pide Bull neere S[t]. *Auſtins* Gate. 1608

Fig. 4.6: *King Lear* (1608), title page, STC 22292. Reprinted with the permission of the Folger Shakespeare Library.

The play is obviously presented as Shakespeare's, but it literally belongs to Butter, the publisher who owns and controls the text, asserting Shakespeare's authorship as a marketing strategy, both to capitalize on Shakespeare's reputation and to differentiate this play from an anonymous play text of 1605, *The True Chronicle History of King Lear* (Fig. 4.6). Shakespeare's name functions on the 1608 title page perhaps as much to identify the playbook as the playwright. In either role, of course, it serves as a mark of distinction, but Shakespeare is here always the publisher's Shakespeare, not the author himself, a simulacrum[30] invented to protect and promote the publisher's property.[xiv]

The 1608 *Lear* quarto, then, does at least seem to point to Shakespeare's growing literary reputation. Butter, though he is unconcerned to provide a carefully printed text, is eager to offer what he publishes as Shakespeare's play and not merely as the record of performance by the King's men. Here is the earliest incontrovertible evidence of what in 1622 Thomas Walkley would claim in his edition of *Othello* (1622): that "The Authors name is sufficient to vent his work." Certainly Butter believed this true, publishing in 1605 an edition of *The London Prodigall* with a title page claiming that it is "By William Shakespeare." We cannot know whether or not Butter thought the play was in fact by Shakespeare, but obviously he thought Shakespeare's name would help sell the playbook.

[...]

368 But if some publishers were indeed convinced that "Shakespeare" on the title page would help sell books, others seemed less certain about the marketability of the playwright's name. *Titus Andronicus*, for example, was published in 1594 with no indication of its author, only that it had been "Plaide by the Right Honourable the Earle of *Darbie*, Earle of *Pembrooke*, and Earle of *Sussex* their servaunts." The reticence about authorship here was no doubt because in 1594 the theatrical provenance of the play was more impressive than its still little-known author; but the play was reissued two more times after its first printing (once in 1600 and again in 1611), with title pages that carefully updated its theatrical history but each still with no acknowledgment that Shakespeare was its author.

Similarly, in 1599, Cuthbert Burby published the second edition of *Romeo and Juliet*, but that title page gives no indication that the play was by Shakespeare; and, lest this be taken only as evidence that even by 1599 the value of Shakespeare's name was still being negotiated, 10 years later *Romeo and Juliet*, like *Titus*, was published again, still without identifying Shakespeare as the playwright. And indeed about 11 years after that, roughly the time when Thomas Walkley was insisting upon the commercial value of Shakespeare's name, yet another edition of *Romeo and Juliet* (Q4) appeared, which again failed to identify its author—though interestingly a variant title page was issued that does claim the play was "Written by *W. Shakespeare*."[xv] This edition (with its two separate title pages) was published by John Smethwick, who, on the basis of the titles he controlled, apparently was invited in as a minor

---

30 A copy for which no original exists.

partner in the consortium of stationers who combined to publish the first folio. I take it that Smethwick, who had acquired the rights to the play from Nicholas Ling in 1607, had prepared a new edition of *Romeo and Juliet*, a reprint of the 1609 printing, and issued it with a reset version of the earlier title page on which Shakespeare's name does not appear. The variant title page (with Shakespeare's name) seems almost certainly to have been printed later, most likely issued sometime after negotiations for the folio rights revealed to Smethwick the nature of his property. (It is very improbable that the authorial title page was issued first, as there is no obvious commercial reason to remove Shakespeare's name, but there is an obvious one to add it.) But until the issue of the variant title page of *Romeo and Juliet*, Smethwick, just like Edward White, the publisher of the later *Titus* quartos, had published two editions of the play he controlled without identifying either as Shakespeare's; and, though it may seem incredible to us, it is at least possible that Smethwick, like White, did so without knowing that Shakespeare was the author.

How this could be the case is instructive. Both plays were first published by John Danter, *Titus Andronicus* in 1594, the first of Shakespeare's plays to appear in print or at least the earliest surviving publication, and *Romeo and Juliet* in 1597. Danter was an active stationer in London in the 1590s before his death at age 34 in October 1599; in his eight-year career he printed or published 79 editions of 67 separate titles, mainly popular forms, like ballads, pamphlets, and plays. Danter's professional behavior, however, has been consistently denigrated as immoral and inept. E.K. Chambers, for example, identified Danter as "a stationer of the worst reputation," and R.B. McKerrow wrote of the 1597 *Romeo and Juliet* that "like all his work, 369
it was very badly printed."[xvi] W.W. Greg agreed, combining the two judgments into general misgiving: "any dramatic quarto with which [Danter] was concerned is necessarily suspect in the first instance." Danter's career, Greg concludes, "is nothing but a record of piracy and secret printing."[xvii] For D. Allen Carroll, similarly, the whole career is tainted: "Everyone knows of the odor which attaches itself to the name of Danter."[xviii]

But this may be another case where our anachronistic hopes and expectations for Shakespeare's text have infected our historical judgment; "the odor which attaches itself to the name of Danter" may not be the fetid scent of fraudulence or incompetence but only the homely smell of workmanlike activity. Danter did find himself entangled in various difficulties with the **Stationers' Company**, but they were for the most part the sort of disputes that affected almost every member of the guild at one time or other. In 1586, Danter was one of six stationers accused of violating Francis Flower's patent to print *Accidence*, a popular Latin grammar, and with the others he was found guilty of illegal printing and "Dyshabled to prynte, otherwyse then as Iourneymen," as the Stationers' Court decreed; nonetheless in 1589 he was sworn and admitted a freeman of the company.[xix] In 1593 arbitration was ordered for some unnamed conflict that Danter had with Henry Chettle and Cuthbert Burby, a dispute inconsequential enough, however, that the three men on and off continued to work with one another to the end of the decade. More seriously, in 1597, he had his presses and type "defaced and made vnservciable for pryntinge" for printing the *Jesus Psalter*, a work of Catholic devotion, "without aucthoritie."[xx]

Danter's court record marks him as at worst a recusant[31] but hardly a wicked or even particularly unruly stationer. In almost all regards, including the difficulties he gets into with the Company, he behaves very much like other members of the book trade. The animus that attaches to him results mainly from his publication of the "bad quarto" of *Romeo and Juliet* in 1597. It is that offence that is "rank" and "smells to heaven"—or at least to the acute olfactory sense of the **new bibliographers**. Danter is guilty of printing an imperfect text of one of Shakespeare's plays. There is no reason, of course, to think he knew it imperfect, and the printing itself is unremarkable, except that half way through the text the type font changes. Rather typically, the observation of this fact produces more derision: "never was a masterpiece ushered into the world in a worse manner," said Plomer,[xxi] but in truth the change in font reveals only that the printing was shared, probably with Edward Allde. Such shared printing was not uncommon (Dekker's *The Honest Whore* and the three 1604 quartos of *The Malcontent* are examples[xxii]), and **typographically** little marks the **composition** and **presswork** as defective, and indeed it is not in any sense a poorer printing job than Q2, the so-called "good quarto" of *Romeo and Juliet*.[xxiii] The play, however, was not registered by Danter, and the absence of an entry, coupled with a text that seems to have been adapted for performance and perhaps reconstructed by its actors, has led to its vilification, most recently by a scholar as normally judicious as David Bevington, who calls it "a pirated edition issued by an unscrupulous publisher."[xxiv]

Danter's *Romeo and Juliet*, however, was not a "pirated edition," and neither the quality nor the provenance of the text can be used to prove its publisher "unscrupulous." Printing a play that had been abridged for performance or even one recalled and reassembled by its actors did not violate any law or regulation. No stationer had a prior claim to the text of *Romeo and Juliet*, and Danter's avoidance of the expected registration procedures may have been motivated by nothing more nefarious than his desire to save the required fees. His usual habits, it is worth noting, were more conventional. He was involved in the publication of nine plays, three of which he printed for other stationers; of the six he published himself, four were properly registered, including *Titus Andronicus*.

[...]

In any case, *Romeo and Juliet* fared better than its publisher. By 1599 Danter was dead, his family destitute; that same year; Cuthbert Burby reissued the play in a new edition, "Newly Corrected, Augmented, and Amended." Printed by Thomas Creede, this second quarto (which is about 700 lines longer than Q1) seems to have been printed from Shakespeare's papers, which must have been received directly from the acting company. This seems to be another occasion, like those involving Samuel Daniel or Stephen Egerton, where an effort was made to substitute an authorized text for one that was deemed deficient.

But, interestingly, however much the new edition of *Romeo and Juliet* was motivated by the desire to establish an *authorized* text, the effort does not involve the establishment of an *author*.

---

31 A Catholic who would not attend Church of England services.

Q2 may well be, as many bibliographers believe, a "good quarto" deriving from Shakespeare's own papers, but what should not be forgotten is that neither the publisher nor the supplier of the good text thought it useful to say so. The play is once again published by Burby as a performance text, printed "as it hath bene sundry time publiquely acted," though arguably that describes the theatrically abridged text of Q1 more accurately than it does Q2, which, deriving from the playwright's papers, seemingly deserves precisely what it is denied: the acknowledgment that it is by William Shakespeare.[xxv] Such acknowledgment, however, was not forthcoming.

Burby's receipt, in whatever manner, of Shakespeare's papers does not mark his edition as any more regular than Danter's. Indeed Burby's rights to the play most likely derive from some unrecorded negotiation with Danter. They had on occasion worked together. Danter had printed *The Cobbler's Prophecy* for Burby in 1594, and, more revealingly, the previous year Danter had entered the play *Orlando Furioso* and then transferred his title to Burby with the proviso, as the Stationers' Register records it, "(Danter to have the printing)." It is even possible that Burby's publication of *Love's Labor's Lost* similarly derives from a negotiation with Danter, who, it is plausible to think, may have printed the lost quarto that Burby's 1598 edition offers as "Newly corrected and augmented By *W. Shakespere*." In any case, though unregistered, Burby's rights to *Romeo and Juliet* were unquestioned, and in 1607 he transferred his title to Nicholas Ling. Nine months later, Ling transferred the rights to *Romeo and Juliet*, along with 15 other titles, to John Smethwick, who (as we have seen) printed an edition of the play in 1609, again advertising it as "Newly corrected, augmented, and amended"—though in fact the title page, like the text itself is a simple reprint of Q2—and again omitting the name of the playwright, as he did once more in 1622, until he decided to issue the variant title page.

Since its first appearance in 1597, then, the play had belonged to four men, none of whom had felt obligated by either bibliographic scruple or commercial consideration to acknowledge Shakespeare's authorship. As the play became a less familiar element in the repertory of the King's men (and indeed no record survives of any production after 1598), the recurring title page claim that the play was printed "as it hath Beene sundrie times publiquely acted" inevitably became more gestural than descriptive, and as Shakespeare's name had become increasingly "vendible" in the marketplace of print, it is hard to imagine that if he was recognized as the play's author his name would not have been used to help sell the editions (as indeed it is on the variant 1622 title page).

But play texts, we must again remind ourselves, had not yet fully made the transition from the ephemera of an emerging entertainment industry to the artifacts of high culture. They did not yet demand an author, and in some sense they did not deserve one, the text being so fully a record of the collaborative activities of a theatrical company. As publishers transferred titles to such works there is no reason to think the author's name would automatically attach itself and follow along. Today we hear the title *Romeo and Juliet* and instantly supply Shakespeare's name. In 1597, in 1599, in 1609, and even in 1622, the Shakespearean **canon** did not yet firmly exist. The publishers who printed the play were arguably unaware, and certainly unimpressed, that they were printing a play by Shakespeare. In this regard it is worth noting that the Stationers' Register entry that records the transfer of titles from Ling to Smethwick has items like "Master DRAYTONS *Poemes*," "master GREENES *Arcadia*," and "SMYTHS *common Wealth of England*";

the plays, however, are anonymous: "ROMEO and JULETT," "The Taming of A Shrewe," "Loues Labour Lost," and "a booke called Hamlett."

Authorship is important to us, heirs of a romantic conception of writing as individual and originary, and if it was indeed important to some of Shakespeare's contemporaries, it was not particularly important to Shakespeare himself or to the publishers who first brought his plays to the reading public. In setting forth his plays, they did not see their task as the preservation of the work of the nation's greatest writer; they were seeking only some small profit with limited financial vulnerability, as with their six-penny pamphlets they turned Shakespeare into "a man in Print" and made his plays available to desiring readers.

Notes

i. As a number of textual scholars have observed, even this fixity has its limits, not least because of the proof-reading and correction process in the printing house, which would almost always result in every individual copy of a particular print run differing from all others in its arrangement of corrected and uncorrected sheets. Nonetheless, there is little evidence that contemporaries felt this fact, if they recognized it at all, as an unsettling of the printed text. Even when a publisher did call attention to the variant copies that existed, it is with remarkable equanimity, as in William Gouge's *The Whole-Armor of God* (1616), where the publisher's note on Errata says: "If therefore thou meete with any slippe that may make the sence obscure, compare the Boke with some others, and thou maist find it amended" (sig. A10^{v}). Here the fact that copies differed does not disrupt the text's meaning but rather provides a way to secure it.

ii. William Prynne, *Histrio-Mastix: The Players Scourge* (London, 1633), sig. **6^{v}; though, in fact, assuming print runs of 800–1000, his figure may be about right.

iii. See Kari Konkola, "'People of the Book': The Production of Literary Texts in Early Modern England," *Publication of the Bibliographic Society of America* 94 (2000): 5–31, esp. 18, note 26.

iv. Peter W.M. Blayney, "The Publication of Playbooks," in *A New History of Early English Drama*, ed. John D. Cox and David Scott Kastan (New York: Columbia UP, 1997), 389. See also Mark Bland, "The London Book-Trade in 1600," in *A Companion to Shakespeare*, ed. David Scott Kastan (Oxford: Blackwell, 1999), 450–63.

v. *Letters of Thomas Bodley to Thomas James, First Keeper of the Bodleian Library*, ed. G.W. Wheeler (Oxford: Oxford UP, 1926), 219, 222. Two playbooks, however, did in fact find their way into the early collection of the Bodleian; the 1620 Library catalogue lists Robert Daborne's *A Christian Turn'd Turke* (1612) and Thomas Heywood's *The Four Prentices of London* (1615). Bodley had, of course, died in late January 1613, but as there are only these two plays in the collection by 1620 their presence seems more likely to be accidental than to mark a change of Library policy.

vi. *The Three Parnassus Plays*, ed. J.B. Leishman (London: Nicholson and Watson, 1949), 247–48. John Stephens, in his *Cynthia's Revenge* (London, 1613), speaks of authors who "gape after the drunken harvest of forty shillings, and shame the worthy benefactors of *Hellicon*" (sig. A2^{v}); and George Wither, in *The Schollers Purgatory* (London, 1624), similarly notes that stationers "cann hyre for a matter of 40 shillings, some needy IGNORAMUS" (sig. Ii^{v}).

vii. This analysis is obviously heavily indebted to Peter Blayney's extraordinary reconstruction of the economics of playbook publishing in his "The Publication of Playbooks," esp. 405–13.

viii. George Wither, *The Schollers Purgatory* (London, 1624), sigs. B6^{v}-7^{r}, H5^{r}.

ix. Blayney observes that "we have been too busy chasing imaginary pirates" to understand how play texts normally found their way into print ("The Publication of Playbooks," 394). Piracy, as Laurie E. Maguire notes, "relates technically to the circumstances of publication, where it means the infringement of one stationer's rights by another." See her *Shakespearean Suspect Texts: The "Bad" Quartos and Their Contexts* (Cambridge: Cambridge UP, 1996), 16. See also Cyril Bathurst Judge, *Elizabethan Book-Pirates* (Cambridge, MA: Harvard UP, 1934).

x. Samuel Daniel, *The Vision of The Twelve Goddesses* (London, 1604), sig. A3^{r}.

xi. Stephen Egerton, *A Lecture preached by Maister Egerton, at the Blacke-friers 1589* (London, 1603), sig. A4^{r}.

xii. Vickers, "Hamlet by Dogberry: A Perverse Reading of the Bad Quarto," *Times Literary Supplement*, 24 December 1993, 5.

xiii. On this aspect of *Knight of the Burning Pestle*, see Zachary Lesser, "Walter Burre's Knight of the Burning Pestle," *English Literary Renaissance* 29 (1999): 22–43; Troilus, of course, was published in 1609, with two separate title pages, one announcing the play "As it was acted by the Kings Maiesties servants at the Globe," and one, with only the indication that it was "Written by William Shakespeare" and printed with the publisher's advertisement claiming that it was a "new play" that was "neuer clapper-clawd with the palms of the vulgar."

xiv. Some of this material on the *King Lear* title page appears in different form in my *Shakespeare after Theory* (New York: Routledge, 1999), 37 and 81.

xv. George Walton Williams has dated this edition 1622; see his "The Printer and the Date of *Romeo and Juliet* Q4," *Studies in Bibliography* 18 (1965): 253–54.

xvi. E.K. Chambers, *The Elizabethan Stage*, vol. 3 (Oxford: Oxford UP, 1923), 187; and *A Dictionary of Printers and Booksellers … 1557–1640*, gen. ed. R.B. McKerrow (London: Bibliographical Society, 1910), 84.

xvii. W.W. Greg, *Two Elizabethan Stage Abridgements: "The Battle of Alcazar" and "Orlando Furioso": An Essay in Critical Bibliography* (Oxford: Oxford UP, 1923), 130.

xviii. D. Allen Carroll, "Who Wrote Greenes Groatsworth of Witte (1592)?" *Renaissance Papers 1992*, ed. George Walton Williams and Barbara J. Baines (Durham, NC: Southeast Renaissance Conference, 1993), 75.

xix. *Records of the Court of the Stationers' Company, 1576–1602*, ed. W.W. Greg and E. Boswell (London: The Bibliographical Society, 1930), 21 (3 Nov. 1586); and *A Transcript of the Stationers' Registers*, ed. Edward Arber, vol. 2 (London, 1875), 706 (30 Sept. 1589) […].

xx. Greg and Boswell, eds., *Records of the Court of the Stationers' Company*, 46, 56 (5 March 1593; to April 1597).

xxi. Henry R. Plomer, "The Printers of Shakespeare's Plays and Poems," *The Library*, 2nd series, 7 (1906): 153.

xxii. See W. Craig Ferguson, *Valentine Simmes* (Charlottesville: U of Virginia P, 1968), 86–89.

xxiii. Harry Hoppe calculated 0.9 printer's mistakes per page in Q1 and 1.4 in Q2. See his *The Bad Quarto of "Romeo and Juliet": A Bibliographic and Textual Study* (Ithaca, NY: Cornell UP, 1948), 8–9.

xxiv. *The Complete Works of Shakespeare*, ed. David M. Bevington (New York: HarperCollins, 1992), A-14.

xxv. Jill L. Levenson, editor of the new Oxford edition of *Romeo and Juliet*, asserts that Q1 "shows clear signs of connection with performance"; Q2, however, she argues, with its "duplication of several passages," shows the marks of "authorial revision" and therefore must be based on "authorial working papers rather than a manuscript used in the theatre." See her "Editing *Romeo and Juliet*: 'A challenge[,] on my life,'" *New Ways of Looking at Old Texts, II*, ed. W. Speed Hill (Tempe, AZ: Medieval and Renaissance Text Society, 1998), esp. 69.

23.

Margaret J.M. Ezell, "The Social Author: Manuscript Culture, Writers, and Readers," *Social Authorship and the Advent of Print.* Baltimore: Johns Hopkins UP, 1999. 21–44

Margaret J.M. Ezell (b. 1955) is Distinguished Professor of English at Texas A & M University, working in the field of late-seventeenth- and early-eighteenth-century literary culture. She has written extensively on the history of Early Modern women writers and female literary culture generally as well as on theories of authorship, reading, and handwritten culture in particular. In her previous books, *The Patriarch's Wife: Literary Evidence and the History of the Family* (1987) and *Writing Women's Literary History* (1993), Ezell argues that the failure to address women's involvement in literary culture before 1700 stemmed from dismissive and ultimately ahistorical notions of manuscript culture. In *Social Authorship and the Advent of Print* (1999), Ezell argues that scholars have ignored—or at the very least undervalued—evidence of the continuity of manuscript practices into the eighteenth century.

As in the essay by Brenda R. Silver on Virginia Woolf (above, pp. 181–98), Ezell contends that new editorial and book-historical methodologies are required for feminist scholarship. Both Silver and Ezell demand attention to the manuscripts of women writers: Silver because writers such as Woolf may have expressed themselves more freely in manuscript, and Ezell because Early Modern women often circulated their writing in manuscript, and not simply because print was not an available option for them. In the chapter excerpted below, Ezell contends that many scholars continue to treat print, even implicitly, as the superior medium, and that this privileging of print has perpetuated the dismissal of Early Modern women's writing. Instead of conceiving of manuscript as a less desirable form of publication that resulted from a lack of choice over publication venues, Ezell demonstrates that many women and men had good reasons to prefer manuscript over print.

What Ezell provides, through detailed accounts of surviving manuscript records, is a clear sense of the flourishing nature of manuscript culture well into the eighteenth century. Ezell describes manuscript culture as a social activity, involving the composition, exchange, copying, circulation, correction, annotation, and preservation of handwritten literary texts. She also forcefully argues for a more nuanced conception of authorship, one that finds a middle ground between the "private" author, who writes only for herself and perhaps a select few, and a "public" author, who writes for print and hence an indiscriminate readership. Ezell puts forward a model of social authorship in which literary production is embedded in a particular community, with writers and readers regularly exchanging roles in the creation and dissemination of handwritten texts.

The Social Author: Manuscript Culture, Writers, and Readers

> "I absolutely prohibite and discharge any of my Posterity from lending [this manuscript] or dispersing them abroad. They are to remain in the House of Pennicuik."
> —Sir John Clerk, *Memoirs of the Life of Sir John Clerk of Penicuik*

> "The prime lesson one learns from studying these manuscripts in depth is that in [the early seventeenth century], from which so much remains unprinted, one never dares make too confident an assertion about poets, poems or poetry: a new manuscript may turn up tomorrow which radically alters the picture."
> —Mary Hobbs, "Early Seventeenth-Century Verse Miscellanies and Their Value for Textual Editors"

In her studies of **manuscript miscellanies** from the first part of the seventeenth century, Mary Hobbs declares that "the proper use of manuscript miscellanies is, in short, the way to a fuller, more accurate, study of early seventeenth-century poetry."[i] One of the first issues to consider when discussing later-seventeenth-century **manuscript** authorship in comparison with print publication practices in early modern England, Scotland, and Wales is the simple pragmatic matter of getting into print, and whether or not conditions of authorship had universally changed from that suggested by Hobbs's remarks. Was print a more desirable technology for writers, in particular literary authors, living in the latter part of the seventeenth century? At its most elemental level, assuming that the author desired to be in print (which, as we shall see in this essay, cannot automatically be assumed to be the case, even in the early eighteenth century),[ii] the whole issue of the relationship between writers and print technology in early modern Britain comes down to considering the following questions. Suppose an author, living in a small village in the 1650s or even as late as the 1690s, wrote a poem: What were his or her options to secure readers? What are the terms and models we have available to describe the experience of authorship in this period? How have the terms that have been used to narrate the process of authorship and progress of print shaped our perspectives on past experiences and our expectations about early modern literary culture?

Before tackling the pragmatics of print, we must gain a clearer sense of what manuscript authorship entailed, of what the expectations of both its authors and its readers were. At this stage, the latter part of the seventeenth and the first part of the eighteenth century still lack a clear description of the nature of manuscript literary activity, much less a theory of nonprint literary culture, of the sort that critics working with late medieval and Renaissance texts have been constructing.[iii] In this study, I am not dealing with the phenomenon described by Harold Love as "**scribal publication**," whereby professional **scribes** reproduced the appearance of print texts, but instead I am concerned with that group of writers and readers who used script as an alternative or in addition to purchased printed texts.

Love's study, important as it is for understanding the texture of Restoration[1] literary life, demonstrates one of the problems of discussing the culture of authorship during this period. Even though the subject of Love's study is manuscript texts, the focus of the analysis is largely in the context of print and its norms. For example, we see the privileging of print in his choice to analyze the social function of script texts as vehicles "by which ideologically charged texts could be distributed through the governing class, or various interest-groups within that class, without their coming to the knowledge of the governed."[iv] In the same way, in Love's view, women writers chose scribal texts because "the stigma of print bore particularly hard on women writers" (i.e., they would have chosen print if they dared).[v] Love also believes that women's "literary writings circulated in this way were quantitatively of minor significance beside the texts by women writers dealing with the practical conduct of the household, the preparation of food and clothing and the treatment of illness. Personal collections on these subjects were regarded with great pride by their compilers" (58).

Unlike Love, I believe that we have little or no sense of the actual scale of women's literary participation in manuscript culture apart from a few celebrated examples. Until quite recently little effort has been made to catalogue and reconstruct patterns in women's manuscript texts to provide an inclusive overview of literary activities rather than isolated, individual authors.[vi]
Certainly, given our current state of knowledge, we have little or no sense of the pride (or lack thereof) felt by women authors who used manuscript **circulation** for literary materials in comparison to domestic ones.

This perception of the author's motive for choosing manuscript text over print—that it was for political reasons—is also the view of manuscript authorship in the Restoration espoused by Woudhuysen. Looking at the practice over the course of the seventeenth century, Woudhuysen, along with Marotti, sees the trajectory of the practice as follows: "By about 1640 scribal publication seems to have begun to decline.... [It] faltered in the 1640s and the 1650s, but gained new life with the Restoration, playing a leading role in the dissemination of satirical writings."[vii] The point made by Love, and Woudhuysen, about writers using script to circumvent censorship is perfectly correct, but the implication behind the terms of analysis is that we seek to understand the manuscript text by analyzing it for what it is *not*, that is, it is "not print" because of the structures of power. The investigative starting point appears to be "why didn't this author use print?" rather than "what is this author attempting to do?"

As in earlier studies involving manuscripts from this period, such as David Vieth's *Attribution in Restoration Verse*, which attempts to bring editorial order to the chaotic world of Restoration **coterie** verse exchanges, the critical focus also tends to be on the *problems* manuscripts and

---

1 King Charles II returned to England in 1660, marking the return (or "restoration") of monarchy to England after the execution of his father, Charles I in 1649, and the English Civil Wars.

coterie groups create for print editors; part 3 of Love's study is concerned with editing scribally published texts. Who wrote which lines? Which of the multiple manuscript copies is "authentic" and which of the multiple manuscript versions will best serve as the **copy-text** for a print **edition**? All of these legitimate editorial questions divert our attention, however, from the manuscript culture that creates such confusion in its refusal to conform to the linear chronology of the modern print text: a rough draft leads to a final draft or copy-text, which leads to print. Instead of seeking to describe the activities of the author and his or her manuscripts before they are forever fixed in print, current studies of manuscripts from the late seventeenth and early eighteenth centuries have instead focused on their relationship to print culture and how best to convert them to print volumes.

[...]

What has been left out of existing literary histories of the Restoration and early eighteenth century is a sense of authorship and readers that existed independently from the conventions and the restrictions of print and commercial texts. While we are quite content to accept the fact that the quality of John Donne's secular verse or Sir Philip Sidney's was not compromised because they were "amateur" authors writing for a coterie readership, when we study the latter part of the seventeenth century, we seem to impose Samuel Johnson's later-eighteenth-century pronouncement that only blockheads write for anything except money.[2] There exists an imaginative gap in our thinking about writers during this transition period that led traditional histories into awkward and anachronistic configurations in the attempt to see them as prototype "modern" authors.

We see this configuration, for example, in traditional literary histories that tend to be organized around Dryden and Pope,[3] two of the most successful commercial poets of their generations, or around the evolution of particular commercial literary genres. As we shall see in the next essay [in Ezell's book], the treatment of Pope in particular has focused on his commercial writings and his relationship with the paid hack writers of Grub Street.[4] The standard literary histories extol the rise of the novel or commercial fiction during this period; likewise, the late seventeenth and early eighteenth centuries have assumed crucial importance in women's literary histories because of the ability of women to earn money through writing at this time. What has gotten lost in the focus on the professional author and the increasing popularity of commercial genres is any sense of a thriving amateur, social literary culture, such as we have seen explored for the early part of the seventeenth century by Mary Hobbs,

2 John Donne (1572–1631), English metaphysical poet; Sir Philip Sidney (1554–86), English author; Samuel Johnson (1709–84), English writer, biographer, **lexicographer**, and literary critic.

3 John Dryden (1631–1700), immensely popular English writer; Alexander Pope (1688–1744), English author of poetry and critical essays noted for his satire.

4 Derogatory nickname given to a street in London where many lower-class professional writers (called "hacks") worked in the eighteenth century.

Katherine Duncan-Jones, Arthur F. Marotti, and H.R. Woudhuysen. Although we have excellent studies of individual writers' manuscripts and their relationship to print production during this period, we have no sense of the patterns or practices of authorship as part of a group. We certainly have little sense of authorship for those writers residing outside London or the university cities, male or female. Unlike studies of the late sixteenth and early seventeenth centuries, traditional literary histories of the end of the seventeenth and the start of the eighteenth centuries have not yet developed a concept of an author's "public" that does not involve "publication" because of our fascination with the new possibilities for the commercial author and commodity-consuming reader.

I.

To fill in some of the missing gaps in our perception of early modern manuscript authorship, we must begin with some very basic, practical questions. In simple terms of production, obviously, script texts could be produced at home, or even during travel, as long as the author was able to write or dictate to someone else. Several types of manuscript texts were produced, which have traditionally been classified as follows: single **sheets**, often showing folds where they were included as part of a letter; "**common place books**," which Vieth described as showing signs of being compiled over a period of time, with changes of ink, handwriting, and presentation, with heterogeneous contents; and "manuscript miscellanies," which he characterizes as "typically ... a homogeneous collections *[sic]* of poems with perhaps some related prose pieces, likely to reflect careful selection and arrangement" and to have been copied over a short period of time.[viii]

We can see all of these types of literary production in action in the mid seventeenth-century collection called the Tixall Papers, which comprise the papers of the Aston family and include verses exchanged in letters, commonplace books, and several manuscript volumes of verse, compiled and arranged as volumes by members of the family. This collection, which was first edited by a family descendant in 1813, offers a partial presentation of long-past literary lives of men and women for whom reading, writing, and poetry were a passion and lifelong occupation.

The Aston and Thimelby families, along with their friends and relatives, lived relatively near one another in Lincolnshire and Staffordshire, linked by marriage and by their Catholic faith. As their nineteenth-century editor, Arthur Clifford, characterized the group,

> they were individuals of five distinct families, inhabiting a line of country in the very center of England, and none at a very great distance from the others. The Priory at St. Thomas [Constance Aston Fowler's home], is three miles from Tixall [the family home], which is five from Ballamore; and from that to Canwell is fifteen, which places are all in Staffordshire. From Canwell to Irnham [Gertrude Aston and Edward Thimelby's home] in Lincolnshire is about five and thirty miles.[ix]

In the **preface** to *Tixall Poetry*, Clifford describes how, on a search for documents relating to Sir Ralph Sadler,[5] the housekeeper at Tixall gave him a "great trunk" filled with papers, so many that he declares it took him 10 days to sort through them. "It was a bumper, brimful, and overflowing," he recalls; "the enormous mass appeared to consist of papers of every sort, and size: the surface of which was most respectably defended, by a deep and venerable layer of literary dust."[x]

After separating out what he considered to be the "literary" manuscripts, Clifford divided the materials into four groups, which forms the organization for his edition. The first section consists of the contents of a small **quarto** volume, with no cover but with "Her. Aston, 1658," on the outer **leaf**; the second section is from another small quarto, with no cover, whose first poem is "Mrs. Thimelby on the Death of her only child"; the third section of Clifford's volume is from a **folio** covered in **parchment** with "William Turner his booke 1662" inscribed on the outside and on the inside cover, "Catherin Gages booke," which Clifford decided were poems collected by Catherine Gage, Lady Aston; and the fourth section was composed of "a large quantity of loose scraps of paper, sheets, half-sheets, backs of letters, and the like, scribbled over with verses."[xi]

The first three texts, the volumes Clifford lists as being by Herbert Aston, Gertrude Thimelby, and Catherine Gage, have not been recovered, but two other manuscript volumes apparently not described here by him have been found, one by Herbert Aston and the other by Constance Aston Fowler.[xii] Between the two existing manuscript volumes and Clifford's nineteenth-century edition of the missing ones and the family correspondence, we have

an extended example of the dynamics of manuscript authors and readers, in addition to information about how manuscript texts were produced, disseminated, and preserved in provincial areas.

The fourth section of *Tixall Poetry* was assembled from single-sheet texts, poems found on what Clifford describes as "backs of letters, or other scraps of paper."[xiii] In addition to poems by members of the Aston family—Sir Walter Aston, the head of the family; his third son, Herbert Aston, and his wife, Katherine Thimelby; his daughter Gertrude Aston Thimelby and her husband, Edward Thimelby; and his youngest child, Constance Aston Fowler—these "scraps" and letters record poems by Sir Richard Fanshawe, Sidney Godolphin, Edmund Waller, and John Dryden, which Clifford believed he was publishing for the first time.[xiv] The "backs" of the letters not only served as scratch paper, as Clifford suggests, but clearly also were a means of transmission and of preservation of these single pieces. Clearly, too, the network of families not only exchanged their own verses in letters but also transmitted single copies of poems they read by others in manuscript form.

From such scraps of paper, several manuscript volumes were created. While her brother Herbert was serving with his father and with Sir Richard Fanshawe on a diplomatic mission in Spain, Constance Aston Fowler repeatedly wrote to him to send her some verses—"I want some good ones to put in my booke."[xv] Constance Aston Fowler constructed her own private **anthology**, in which she mingled the poems of her family with ones by Ben Jonson,

5 Sir Ralph Sadler (1507–87), English diplomat.

Henry King, and John Donne.[6] It is important to note of this text that Fowler was not simply collecting edifying sayings or transcriptions from printed sources; rather, she was compiling her "book" through selecting "good" verses.[xvi] It is also of interest that in addition to her father's and her brother's poetic contributions, her sister Gertrude was a contributor, too, as was their friend Lady Dorothy Shirley; thus both men and women actively participated in this literary compilation.

At a later date, Herbert Aston's wife created another volume of her husband's verse. Concerning the construction of this volume, Herbert Aston wrote to his sister, "My Mrs. havinge nothinge else to doe this winter, hath made a slight collection of all my workes. Wherefore you must make an inquiry into all your papers, and if you find any of mine that beginn not as in this note, you must send them her by the first opportunity."[xvii] He then includes a list of first lines of the poems his wife has already assembled. This example raises several interesting general points concerning manuscript authorship and readership. It is clear that manuscript verse existed in several formats: the initial one, obviously, transmitted through letter and forming part of a collection of loose papers or "scraps." The recipient of such script texts then frequently contributed a verse reply to the originating text, also on a loose sheet. It is the collection and arrangement of these loose materials that form the sequences in the later manuscript volume.

It is also interesting to note that Herbert Aston is not certain who has which of his texts. He requests his sister to go through her collected papers to see if she can find any poems with first lines not on the list he sends her, that is, poems of which he, the author, has no copies. Neither of these manuscript volumes was compiled with the intent to secure a **printer**; both were literary compilations, however, involving the talents and editorial skills of several individuals, using a range of manuscript texts in various forms compiled into a "book."

As we continue looking at examples from later on in the century, from the 1650s and 1660s, we find similar patterns for compilation volumes involving the labors either of family members or of nearby friends and community. Around 1651, Patrick Cary, the brother of the Cavalier hero Lucius Cary,[7] created a small manuscript volume, which was eventually published as *Poems from a manuscript written in the Time of Oliver Cromwell* (1771) and then edited and reduced by Sir Walter Scott[8] (who also encouraged Arthur Clifford's efforts) in 1819. His modern editor, Sister Veronica Delany, describes the creation of this manuscript volume of 30 poems as a compilation of social verses and religious meditations written while the young Patrick Cary was staying in a small Hampshire village, Wickham, with his sister, Lady Victoria Uvedale. The manuscript, in Cary's hand in a small notebook with a black leather cover, is divided into two

6 Ben Jonson (1572–1637), English playwright and poet; Henry King (1592–1669), English poet and religious figure.

7 Lucius Cary (1610–43), English soldier who fought on the side of King Charles I against the Parliamentarians during the English Civil War and was killed in battle.

8 Sir Walter Scott (1771–1832), Scottish poet and novelist who enjoyed tremendous popular and critical success in the early nineteenth century.

sections; Delany notes that the pages containing songs show evidence of candle grease and wine stains, suggesting that the volume enjoyed an extended, if messy, literary life with generations of readers.

The first section is entitled "Triviall Ballades" and dated "1651 August 20th," with the declaration that the pieces are "writt here in obedience to Mrs Tomkins commands"; the second section, composed of religious and meditative verse, has on its opening page an inscription, "I will sing unto the lord (Ps xiii.6)," with a coat of arms, a Tudor rose, and "Warneford, 1651."[xviii] This section also features an interesting set of carefully drawn **emblems**. The result is a volume demonstrating not only the range of the young author's literary tastes but also that of his readership:

> A varied flow of verse now came from the young man's pen. Political satires pelted Cromwell[9] with high-spirited abuse; pastoral poems reflected the pleasures of the exile returned; love poetry paid debonair tribute to the ladies of the Uvedale circle, an appreciative audience, while witty occasional verse captured the atmosphere of Wickham and the friendly maisons of the neighborhood.[xix]

Cary's sister Victoria had been a maid of honor at the court of Henrietta Maria[10] and had appeared in Walter Montagu's[11] *The Shepheards Paradise* and Davenant's masques *The Temple of Love* and *Salamacida Spolia* in the mid and late 1630s; in 1640, she married Sir William Uvedale, the treasurer of the Chamber.[xx] In the autumn of 1650, she welcomed her younger brother to Wickham after his "brief inglorious effort" at becoming a monk at the Benedictine cloister of St. Gregory's Priory, Douai.[xxi] Back in England, he clearly enjoyed a social community of like-minded Royalist[12] readers, whom he portrayed along with their servants and children in his occasional verse.[xxii] [13]The manuscript text he created not only was read by family members and friends residing nearby during the author's lifetime but eventually found its way into print a century after his death.

[...]

In another compilation volume, whose contents appear to have been composed between 1670 and 1690, we can see traces of this process whereby the provincial manuscript writer participated

9 Oliver Cromwell (1599–1658) was an English military and political leader who became Lord Protector of the Commonwealth of England, Scotland, and Ireland during the English Civil War.

10 Henrietta Maria (1609–69), Frenchwoman married to King Charles I of England.

11 Walter Montagu (1604/5–77), English playwright, courtier, and religious figure.

12 Refers to supporters of King Charles I and the monarchy during the English Civil War.

13 Verse written to celebrate or commemorate a given occasion, whether private or public, such as a birthday or a coronation.

in a network of verse exchange, collected his own works, and finally compiled them into a volume in order to revise and edit it. John Chatwin matriculated at Emmanuel College, Cambridge, in 1682, apparently when he was only fifteen.[xxiii] Chatwin, who also appears on the college books as "Chattins," was a contemporary of Matthew Prior's,[14] who matriculated at St. John's College, Cambridge, the same year. Chatwin took a BA degree in 1685 and simply vanished from record. During his years at Cambridge, he produced quite a sizeable manuscript text of 280 pages of verse—complete with the **title page** "poems" and "a table" of titles at the end of the volume; Chatwin left the last 80 **pages** blank, providing an opportunity for him to continue adding pieces.[xxiv] From these references to particular events and people, it would appear that the pieces were composed when the poet was between 16 and 18 years of age: as Peter Giles, the only other commentator on his text, observed in 1897, the young poet had "no mean command of the rhyming couplet"; Giles added, "They are certainly as good as the effusions of Prior which can be traced to his undergraduate days, and Prior was considerably older when he entered College."[xxv]

In this volume, believed by Giles to be a compilation volume arranged by the author rather than a chronological accumulation, there are poems referring to his time as a student at Emmanuel College, Cambridge ("To His Tutor, who punish'd Him for going to the Tavern"), some pieces that are strictly occasional, and some that commemorate national political and literary events. In addition to several poems on drinking and gout (the latter of which seems contrived for so young a poet), Chatwin preserved his poem "Made in the Tunns on a chamber-pot," referring to the "Three Tunns" inn on Castle Hill in Cambridge, which has the memorable opening "Hail serviceable Utensil!"[xxvi] Other poems are concerned with more public social events and are addressed to friends who lived in Leicestershire, such as his godfather, William Cole, of Lutterworth, a justice of the peace; Chatwin wrote an elegy for Cole's first wife, Barbara, who died in the early 1680s, and an epithalamium[15] for his second marriage to "Emm," the daughter of "Major Warner."[xxvii] The Leicestershire origins of the volume are reinforced by other poems specifically concerned with a group of friends in the area: Chatwin laments the death of John Burroughs, rector of Stoneby, and includes a poem apparently composed in a friend's garden at the nearby village of Ashby Magna, "A Coppy of Verses made under the Yew Tree in the Honourable Mr. Finch's Orchard in Ashby Magna."[xxviii]

In addition to his poems addressing family and local Leicestershire occasions, Chatwin was engaged by national events. The volume includes a poem on the anniversary of the death of Charles I, an elegy on the death of Charles II, and an epithalamium for the marriage of Princess Ann to Prince George of Denmark (1683).[16] The last was Chatwin's only printed poem, appearing in the Cambridge University collection celebrating the marriage, *Hymenaus Cantabrigiensis*,

14 Matthew Prior (1664–1721), English poet.

15 An occasional poem written in celebration of a marriage.

16 Charles I (1600–49), King of Great Britain and Ireland from 1625–49, was executed in 1649 after being convicted of treason; Charles II (1630–85) became King of Great Britain and Ireland in 1660 after returning from exile in France; Prince George of Denmark (1653–1708), married to Queen Anne of Great Britain and Ireland (1665–1714), Queen from 1702–14.

published by John Hayes (1683), whose other contributors included William Fleetwood (future bishop of Ely), Charles Montagu (Trinity; afterwards earl of Halifax), and Matthew Prior.[17] The poem on the death of Charles II is immediately followed in the manuscript volume by "Congratulations" to James II;[18] he also wrote on the death of Buckingham, the duke of Ormond.

Chatwin's volume demonstrates his precocious skill in creating suitable verses not only for national occasions but also for events of note in the literary world. His poem "To the Pious Memory of Mrs. Ann Killigrew" demonstrates his enthusiasm both for her verse (which has him declaring, "Till she appear'd all Poetry lay dead / O'recharg'd and stifled in Its Infant-bed") and for Dryden's famous ode on the same occasion.[xxix] He also writes on the death of Nell Gwynn,[19] which suggests that even a young man raised in Leicester and in a strongly Puritan college in Cambridge could follow the royal scandals and London theater life. It is also worth noting that several of his poems are written in response to reading the poetry of others. In addition to the commemorative verse on Anne Killigrew's writings, Chatwin addresses one poem "To Astrea on her Poems,"[xxx] which, given the reference to her praise of "Daphnis" (Creech), is clearly Aphra Behn.[20]

It is not clear where or in what format Chatwin read Killigrew or Behn, but it is obvious from the contents of his volume that he was reading the manuscripts of other provincial poets. One such trace of Chatwin's reading found in his own manuscript verse is "On Mr. Wanley's most ingenious Poem the Witch of Endor."[xxxi] Born in 1634 in Leicester, Nathaniel Wanley was the rector of Trinity Church in Coventry, having received his BA degree from Trinity College, Cambridge, in 1653 and his MA degree in 1657. In 1658, he was the minister at "Beeby" in Leicester; he married Ellen Bunton and had five children, one of whom was Humphrey Wanley, the future librarian for Harley. The poem praised by Chatwin, Wanley's "The Witch of Endor," exists in two manuscripts but was not printed until L.C. Martin "recovered" Wanley's verse in 1925.[xxxii]

As with the anonymous young man in Hampshire, Chatwin (or a later reader, perhaps Rawlinson) also went through and x-ed through several poems, although, in the same manner as the previous volume, none of the strikeouts actually hinders the poem from being read. Like the strike-throughs marking the verse of the young man from Wickham, these poems tended to be his more erotic fantasies, such as "Lying on the Bed with Her," which concludes, "For the soft Raptures wee so well did prove, / I'de scorn, nay hate the petty joyes above,"[xxxiii] and "The Fatigue," which opens, "When in my Armes charming Sylvia lay."[xxxiv] Chatwin published only one of the poems in this volume, although several are of very good style and polish. As this volume documents, he did circulate his manuscript verse, using it to respond to what he read and to comment on the significant public events of his day, both locally and nationally.

17 John Hayes (d. 1705), Cambridge University printer from 1658–1705; William Fleetwood (1656–1723), English bishop and political figure; Charles Montagu (1661–1715), English politician and poet.

18 James II (1633–1701), King of England, Scotland, and Ireland from 1685–88; overthrown in 1688 in the Glorious Revolution.

19 Eleanor Gwyn (1651?–87), English actress and mistress of King Charles II.

20 Anne Killigrew (1660–85), English poet; Aphra Behn (1640?–89), English writer notable for being the first professional female writer and for her role in the early development of the novel form.

Chatwin did save his texts, revise them, and finally, too, create a volume with a title page, whose contents he also continued to revise and edit, and quite clearly he and his readers considered his activity to be that of an "author" even though publication was never a feature.

A more elusive example can be found in the manuscript volume of John Hooper, a small **vellum**-bound paper volume whose contents appear to have been composed in the 1660s and perhaps early 1670s.[xxxv] There are two possible candidates among Oxford students at this time for the poet, the most likely being John Hooper, the son of "Hieron" of Hatherly, Devon; he was admitted to Exeter College as a "Pauper Puer,"[21] matriculating 29 November 1667 at age 19.[xxxvi] It has a title page with "Verses" on it, and the author identifies himself at the end of a poem "uppon ye deathes of my Father and Brother who dyed in the yeare 1665." The title page also states the location to be "Devon," and in "To my Mother / Mis Mary Hooper" there is a notation in the side margin "A New Yeares Gift" (4r, 3r). On the **verso** side of this last poem is "Abraham Ivory" in a different hand. In addition to the poems about or to family members, the little volume contains meditations on Luke and Hosea and poems celebrating significant events in his friends' lives: "Epithilamium In celebration of the happie Nuptual of the much honord Master Hine and [?] endeared consort." Hooper also responds to the poetry of others, as seen in "A poem of Mr: Gosnalls who made it uppon the death of Miss Sarah Hawes." This volume appears to fall within the realm of Vieth's manuscript miscellanies, giving the appearance of having been a compilation of the author's works made during a comparatively short period of time; the titles of the poems suggest that Hooper had been a practicing poet in Devon, as well as a reader of the manuscript verse of others, for some years before the volume was assembled.

Another example of a family literary collection from the opposite end of the social scale is found in the texts of Dudley, 4th Lord North (1602–77). Like Patrick Cary's verses, some of Lord North's writings were printed after his death, but only after they had enjoyed several decades of literary life in script form. His verse and prose works, of which at least three compilation copies were made, were created over 1666 and 1667 by North's wife, Ann, with his knowledge and approval. North's twentieth-century editor, Dale Randall, dates one version, the Perkins manuscripts, as being made in the 1670s, just prior to the author's death in 1677; a shorter version had been sent to his son John early in 1667—on the volume's arrival, John wrote to thank his mother and to express the hope that his father would do likewise with his prose writings.[xxxvii] The last dated poem in the Perkins manuscripts is 1663, the last prose piece 1666. As Randall notes, it is a substantial volume of work with 148 pages of writing (all on the **rectos** of the leaves); the other volume, which was sent to son John, is calculated by Randall to consist of 118 recto and verso leaves of text.

Like Herbert Aston's wife, Lady North was responsible for turning her husband's scattered literary productions into long compilation volumes. Her son Roger said of her, "She not only wrote over whatever her lord had for the entertainment of his solitude composed into books, but kept strict accounts of all the household affairs and dealings whatsoever."[xxxviii] In the opening declaration, North thanks his wife and offers a context for the pieces that follow in the volume.

---

21 A student of limited means who supports himself by working in the university.

"Since freely of your selfe you have taken a resolution, to coppy out these imperfect essays of myne in the way of poetry, and soe to give them a fayrer character, than otherwise they can deserve," North begins,

> it now becomes fitt that I should give you some accompt of theyr condition, least those few besydes your selfe (for they were never designed to bee made publike) whoe shall come to have a view of them should to the reading bring an expectation too much to theyr disadvantage.... The truth is that a rapsody, or masse of things, soe different in nature, and composed at tymes of lyfe, and coniunctures soe abhorrent one from the other, can very hardly appeare good, and the rather because theyre Author, as hee was noe wayes by nature designed to Appollo his lawrell,[22] soe hee never affected the honor to attayne it; and where there is noe ambition, there can hardly arise perfection.[xxxix]

In describing his literary career, North notes that some of the early poems really should not survive to see the light of day without correction by some "lesse partiall penn then myne, if not to bee quite obliterated." Other more serious poems, written later in his life, were "born" upon some "sadd occasion, or else upon a burden of perplexed thoughts, the very being delivered (a terme well known to you Ladyes) could not but bring with it, much ease and satisfaction to mee

the Parent." Still other poems, "light and slight enough for recreation," explore imaginary "obiects of Love," while some of them are "not without a reall obiect, nor were it iniurious to any, if you should assume it to your selfe, to bee the person intended."

[...]

Although North states that the poems were not "designed" to be made public, the three volumes became public objects. Randall speculates that one of the volumes, the Perkins manuscripts, served as the base text for the posthumous publication of North's essay *Light in the Way to Paradise* (1682), the verse sections of the volume being sealed closed by strips of paper and sealing wax and the prose sections being soiled and marked by black printer's ink (103–04). North's oldest son, Charles, to whom two of the volumes are addressed (the Rougham Hall and Perkins manuscripts), published some of his father's prose pieces (as North had done for his father); Charles's brother Roger recorded in a manuscript preface to his *Life* that their father wrote

> divers slight Essays, and some verses, wch he tituled Light in the way to Paradise. These 2 last, his eldest son caused to be published with his

22 Highly regarded poets were said to have received the laurel of Apollo, the Greek god of poetry among many other things.

> name to it, viz. Dudley the 2d (misprinted for the 2d Dudley) Lord North. These were at first designed to remain with his family in **MSS**, and not to be published, but there is no harm done.[xl]

It is interesting to speculate, first, how he could know the intention of the author that the multiple manuscripts remain in the family, especially given the family history of posthumous publications, and, second, what "harm" he envisioned might arise from family literature being made public property.

These issues—of whether a text was "designed" to be "Publicke" and what "harm" could be anticipated by a script author appearing in print are only a few of the challenges facing the literary historian attempting to understand literary culture in the later seventeenth century. When confronted by assertions such as North's concerning his lack of intention to make his text "publicke," we have traditionally felt that (1) such statements are classic examples of private or closet writing, "aristocratic," dilettante[23] literature, insignificant in terms of literary history because the texts formed no school, or (2) by preserving his manuscripts and by permitting several compilations of them, North had already imagined a more general readership, even if it is not, as in Habermas's model of a public sphere,[24] where access is guaranteed to all citizens.

If we accept the first interpretation, we must then dismiss the literary activities and contributions of most of the writers of the early and mid-seventeenth century. We would have to reconfigure our perceptions of **canonical** authors including Cowley, Waller, Suckling, and Lovelace, all of whom participated in this type of manuscript literary culture before printing their texts.[25] We would likewise have to rethink where we place in our notion of authorship writers such as Anne Bradstreet and Katherine Philips, whose texts appeared without their authorization, or Thomas Traherne and Anne Killigrew, whose texts were published after their death.[26]

Although the 1620s and 1630s may be described by several critics as the "golden age of MS verse compilation," the practice obviously by no means vanished in the 1650s and well up through the early 1700s, even for authors not engaged in exchanging satires and lampoons.[xli] As Marotti observes, the Restoration significantly changed the sociopolitical context of manuscript transmission and compilation,[xlii] and, indeed, parts of the Cary manuscript volume compiled in the 1650s with its anti-Cromwell satires might have had a more difficult time being printed at that time; however, if its author had sought a printer, we do find anti-Cromwell pieces making their way from manuscript volumes into print during that same period, so politics may not have been

23 Someone displaying only surface-level knowledge of a particular subject.

24 Jürgen Habermas (b. 1929), German philosopher whose concept of the bourgeois public sphere, in which private citizens come together in order to create social meaning, is still extremely influential in critical theory.

25 Abraham Cowley (1618–67), Edmund Waller (1606–87), Sir John Suckling (1609–42), and Richard Lovelace (1618–57) were all English poets.

26 Anne Bradstreet (c. 1612–72), American poet; Katherine Philips (1632–64), English poet; Thomas Treherne (1637–74), English poet.

the only factor influencing the mode of transmission.[xliii] On the other hand, there are a host of practical advantages for the provincial writer of using script rather than print to circulate his or her writings, whether the topic was controversial or banal.

[...]

One obvious conclusion that can be drawn from even these limited examples of scribal authorship and the manuscript text in its social context is that our definitions of "public" and "private" sit awkwardly with the particulars of the readership of manuscript texts. We traditionally have used "public" in the sense of meaning "published" and "private" in the sense of "personal." Here, we have texts whose readership was controlled through physical access to them rather than **censorship** imposed from an external agency and which was limited by the author's design, no matter (as we shall see in the discussion of literary **piracy**) how imperfect the control mechanisms actually were. On the other hand, they were not "private" in the sense that their readership was restricted only to God and the author, or even to the author's immediate family. What we tend to see is a "private" mode that, by its very nature, is permeated by "public" moments of readership, when the text is circulated and copied. The text, although not universally available to any purchasing reader, nevertheless engages in a "social" function.

An example of the intertwined nature of the private/public/social spheres can be seen in a manuscript volume compiled by Elizabeth Brackley and Jane Cavendish, the daughters of William Cavendish, the duke of Newcastle, by his first wife.[xliv] I have previously used that text to interrogate the then popular critical terms to describe women's writings as *closet texts*, which were viewed as "entirely private forms of writing not destined for publication and dealing with what limited experience might come within the circumference of a lady's life."[xlv] What the contents of this so-called closet manuscript volume demonstrated, however, was that the text was clearly a "social" one: a collaborative production, designed to please a reasonably extensive audience. Instead of being a defiant or subversive act, these pieces serve as a formal effort to confirm threatened social values and relationships.

By collapsing "public" into "publication," we seriously misconstrue the literary practices of such women and overlook the importance of the social function of literature for women as well as men writing in the so-called Cavalier tradition. In Earl Miner's analysis of male verse written in the Civil War years, in particular the poetry of friendship, poetry "sustains and continues the little society of the good few, and it demonstrates as well powers of mind and feeling"; this is also the model of social verse found in this "closet" volume.[xlvi] Although Miner does not in his discussion consider either the practice of circulating verse in manuscript or the participation of women other than as subjects of such verse, his analysis of the choice of subject and genre underlines the central importance of being an author and of being a "good" reader during the mid-seventeenth century. This type of social function goes far beyond what Love calls "bonding" through the formation of a literary clique through exclusion[xlvii] and looks instead at the extent to which intellectual and literary life, as well as politics, was created, invigorated, and sustained through the writing and reading of script texts.

Kathryn R. King has more recently used this concept of the "social text" to analyze Jane Barker's *Poetical Recreations* (1688) and to reconstruct the young woman's circle of readers.[xlviii] [27] King finds that "far from being alienated, eccentric, tormented, or—in another version of the romantic narrative—a lonely voice from the periphery, Barker was engaged in literary exchange with a number of fellow poets, including at least three Cambridge students and (probably) a London **bookseller**" before the poems were published without her consent in 1687.[xlix] King concludes that for Barker, a "youngish unmarried woman," writing poetry and exchanging it "was a social as well as an intellectual act, an opportunity to exercise the mind, talents, and personality in acts of textual sociability."[l] The cases of Burghope,[28] Cavendish, Brackley, and Barker, from quite different social backgrounds and under quite different circumstances of composition, show a similar pattern: the manuscript text operates as a medium of social exchange, often between the sexes, neither private nor public in the conventional sense of the terms, and a site at which women could and did comment on public issues concerning social and political matters.

It is important to note here (in contrast to Love's suggestion) that manuscript culture was not the province of women, in opposition to print culture as being the domain of men. In the examples of the university student John Chatwin and the almost monk Patrick Cary, and from Lord North to Mr. Hooper of Devon, it becomes clear that this type of authorship was equally attractive to both sexes and to a range of social classes. The dynamic network of writer and reader that in my view characterizes manuscript literary culture and social authorship is created by the process of being an author rather than by the production of a single text, in Eisenstein's terms,[29] one capable of being fixed, attributed, and **catalogued**. Likewise, a reader in a manuscript culture, with a fluid text constantly subject to change, is responsible for participating in literary production as well as consumption; it is interesting to note here, too, how often the role of the reader of manuscript text becomes conflated with the roles of editing, correcting, or copying the text and extending its circulation of readers.

This is a type of authorship quite far removed from the characterization of it given by Kernan as aristocratic and authoritarian. Indeed, script authorship permitted a middle-class woman living in a small village, such as Marie Burghope, to have a cultivated audience, allowed Jane Barker to have literary connections with Cambridge and London, and created a means through which the teenage student John Chatwin was in literary exchange with the older, established author Nathaniel Wanley. One reason we associate manuscript author practices with "aristocrats" is because there was, pragmatically, a higher chance of these texts surviving for several generations and thus of being recovered. Manuscript texts have a much better chance of being preserved and passed down if their authors had established family homes or residences.[li]

---

27 Jane Barker (bap. 1652–d. 1732), English writer.

28 Marie Burghope, late-seventeenth-century English poet whose manuscript poetry circulated among literary groups.

29 A reference to Elizabeth Eisenstein's conceptions of print authorship. See Eisenstein's essay in Chapter 3, pp. 215–30, above.

[...]

In conclusion, these examples suggest several adjustments we must make in our understanding of literary culture at large in the latter part of the seventeenth century. First, we must reconsider our assumptions about who participated in manuscript writing and reading: manuscript circulation was not confined to "aristocrats" and courtiers, although obviously practiced by them, and it was not identified as being primarily female activity, either, even at the end of the seventeenth century after the increased availability of cheap print and **publishers**. As we have seen in the examples of the Aston, Cary, and North families, male authors participated with enthusiasm in the creation of social texts for their circles of family and friends. Nor, indeed, was manuscript literary circulation restricted to poetry or short pieces. In this essay, we saw the posthumous publication of Dudley North's essays by his son, and in the following essay [in Ezell's book], we will find similar patterns of authorship in the example of Ralph Thoresby, for whom, for most of his life, manuscript transmission was the preferred mode of transmittal for a variety of scientific, antiquarian, and political treatises.

One of the problems with our existing literary histories is that our current modes of analyzing authorship do not deal with this type of author who had no desire to publish or to "go public," except to form theories to explain the motivation behind what *we* see as authorial self-destruction. In our existing formulas for talking about the author, such an individual who wrote but did not intend to publish must have either been prevented from considering publish-

ing by various social powers (whether national politics or domestic), as in J.W. Sanders's thesis concerning male Tudor courtier poets,[30] or was so unskilled that no printer could be found to meet the author's unfulfilled need.

Even more telling, despite the excellent studies of the practice in the earlier seventeenth century and the recognition of the continued existence of the practice in the latter part of it, we still evaluate whole generations of early modern authors on the basis of their publication records. Students are introduced to the early seventeenth century with a description of literary activity and authorship that is clearly based on print as the marker of evaluation. One standard textbook depicts the literary climate for seventeenth-century women as bleak: "not even fine ladies were always sure of their spelling and punctuation," and except for letters and diaries, women writers' "contributions to **belles-lettres** were not many."[lii] Here, examples such as Margaret Cavendish,[31] who because of her "great wealth and social privilege" was "less inhibited from writing and publishing," are immediately contrasted by "Lady Mary Wroth, [who,] after one rash act of publication, was silenced for the rest of her life." The final observation before a student finally encounters the poems is that "though women struggled (and with only partial success) to find voices of their own, the age to come would speak more assuredly because of them."[liii]

---

30 The argument that there was a stigma against print, based on social convention, within certain aristocratic groups: see J.W. Sanders, "The Stigma of Print: A Note on the Social Bases of Tudor Poetry," *Essays in Criticism* 1 (1951): 139–64.

31 Margaret Cavendish (1623?–73), English writer.

In this 1993 example of literary history's treatment of gender and authorship, several important points should be noted. First, there is no indication in the account that fine gentlemen also had problems with spelling and punctuation according to modern standards because there was no standardized scheme of either spelling or punctuation. There is no indication that men who were contemporaries of the women cited also did not publish all of their texts. Finally, having a "voice" is equated with being in print, with the obvious implication that "work" is equated with print texts and anything else, manuscript copy in particular, is only "silence." The sole criterion of the success of these generations of women writers is the amount they *published*, with no mention of the amount they actually *wrote*. Intentionally or not, we thus train our students to classify literary activity with print as the superior mode and to employ false gender dichotomies when interpreting early modern texts.

As suggested by the examples of the Aston, Cary, and North families, along with the studies of individuals such as Mollineux[32] and Burghope, manuscript authorship was still a flourishing feature of literary life in the later seventeenth century and well into the early eighteenth. In these examples, we can find suggestions for further investigation; although the odds of a manuscript text's or volume's survival increased if it became part of a significant family's **library**, prefaces and printer's notes found in posthumous editions also indicate texts with more humble social origins. Suffice it to say, at this preliminary stage of the process of description, that literary life in late-seventeenth-century Britain included for both readers and writers the presence of scribal copies in competition with printed texts, texts their authors had no desire to have printed and for which we as critics have yet to create an accurate vocabulary, much less a complete description. What the literary history of the so-called Restoration and early Augustan[33] periods still needs is an investigation of the ways in which earlier modes of literary transmission still shaped authors' practices and readers' perceptions and a more flexible definition of the nature of "public," "private," and "social" modes of authorship.

Notes

i. Mary Hobbs, "Early Seventeenth-Century Verse Miscellanies and Their Value for Textual Editors," *English Manuscript Studies, 1100–1700* 1 (1989): 182–210. Like most commentators, Hobbs notes that "the peak period of manuscript verse miscellanies seems, for some reason, to have been the 1630s," but in contrast to editorial tradition, she offers a strong argument for the use of manuscript miscellanies rather than relying solely on printed texts in creating scholarly editions (200).

ii. For views on authors who did not desire to be published, see Margaret J.M. Ezell, *The Patriarch's Wife: Literary Evidence and the History of the Family* (Chapel Hill: U of North Carolina P, 1987), chap. 3. For earlier periods, the classic study is J.W. Sanders, "The Stigma of Print: A Note on the Social Bases of Tudor Poetry," *Essays in Criticism* 1 (1951): 139–64. This original theory of the social importance of avoiding print for the group Sanders identifies as the "Courtier" poets has been challenged by Steven W. May, "Tudor Aristocrats and the Mythical 'Stigma of Print,'" *Renaissance Papers* 10 (1980): 11–18, who finds that the theory of the supposed "social code" obliging aristocrats to shun the press, "handy and time-honored as it

32 Mary Mollineux (1651–96), English Quaker writer.

33 A style of writing associated with the early eighteenth century in England.

has become, does not square with the evidence" (11). May further explores the role of poetry in Elizabeth's court in his most recent study, *The Elizabethan Courtier Poets: The Poems and Their Contexts* (Columbia: U of Missouri P, 1991).

iii. As note ii suggests, the latter part of the sixteenth and the earlier seventeenth centuries have had much more scholarly attention directed to the phenomenon of scribal verse circulation; any editor of John Donne or Sir Philip Sidney, for example, must deal with the complexities posed by the circulation of his work in manuscript. For discussions of manuscript authorship during this period, see Arthur F. Marotti, *Manuscript, Print, and the English Renaissance Lyric* (Ithaca, NY: Cornell UP, 1995), in which he observes that while the 1620s and 1630s have been called "the golden age of MS verse compilation" by critics, "many large collections, in fact, were assembled though the 1640s, 1650s, and into the Restoration period," although he believes that "the re-establishment of the monarchy significantly changed the sociopolitical context of manuscript transmission and compilation and the number of such collections dropped markedly" (68–69). See also Wendy Wall, *The Imprint of Gender. Authorship and Publication in the English Renaissance* (Ithaca, NY: Cornell UP, 1993), which is specifically interested in the development of a concept of authorship as masculine, which emerged through social controversies over print and the "specific genres, strategies, and gestures through which that gendering occurred" (3–4). For studies focused on a particular author's literary experiences, see Richard B. Wollman, "The 'Press and the Fire': Print and MSS Culture in Donne's Circle," *Studies in English Literature, 1599–1900* 33 (1993): 85–97; Alan MacColl, "The Circulation of Donne's Poems in Manuscript" in *John Donne: Essays in Celebration*, ed. A.J. Smith (London: Methuen: 1972), 28–46; Katherine Duncan-Jones's detailed study of Sidney, *Sir Philip Sidney: Life, Death, and Legend* (Oxford: Clarendon P, 1986), and, more recently, *Sir Philip Sidney: Courtier Poet* (New Haven, CT: Yale UP, 1991), along with H.R. Woudhuysen's excellent study of Sir Philip Sidney's participation in manuscript circulation and of the professional scribes who created the manuscript copies in *Sir Philip Sidney and the Circulation of Manuscripts, 1558–1640* (Oxford: Clarendon P, 1996). As this essay shows, I am indebted to both Marotti and Woudhuysen but disagree on the nature of manuscript circulation and on its seeming rate of decline.

iv. Harold Love, *Scribal Publication in Seventeenth Century England* (London: Oxford UP, 1993), 177.

v. Ibid., 54.

vi. In 1997, the Perdita Project was established by Nottingham Trent University; its goal is to compile a database, to be published on the Internet, of early modern women's manuscript texts.

vii. H.R. Woudhuysen, *Sir Philip Sidney and the Circulation of Manuscripts, 1558–1640*, 391.

viii. David Vieth, *Attribution in Restoration Poetry* (New Haven, CT: Yale UP, 1963), 23–24. The definition of terms found in the first volume of the *Index of English Literary Manuscripts*, ed. Peter Beal (New York: Bowker, 1980), is also useful for making the distinction between manuscript miscellanies and commonplace books. See also Peter Beal's comments in "Notations in Garrison: The Seventeenth-Century Commonplace Book," in *New Ways of Looking at Old Texts*, ed. W. Speed Hill (Binghamton, NY: Renaissance Text Society, 1993): 131–47.

ix. Arthur Clifford, ed., *Tixall Poetry* (Edinburgh, 1813), xxvii. For a detailed analysis of the family connections, see Victoria Elizabeth Burke, "Women and Seventeenth-Century Manuscript Culture: Miscellanies, Commonplace Books, and Song Books Compiled by English and Scottish Women, 1600–1660" (PhD Diss., Oxford U, 1996), and Jenijoy LaBelle, "The Huntington Aston Manuscript," *Book Collector* 29 (1980): 542–67, and "A True Love's Knot: The Letters of Constance Fowler and the Poems of Herbert Aston," *Journal of English and Germanic Philology* 79 (1980): 13–31.

x. Clifford, *Tixall Poetry*, viii.

xi. Ibid., x.

xii. Beinicke Library, Yale University, Osborne MS b.4; Huntington Library, HM 904.

xiii. Ibid., xiii.ch.

xiv. Ibid., xiii.ch.

xv. Arthur Clifford, ed., *Tixall Letters*, 2 vols., 2 (Edinburgh, 1815), 133.

xvi. See also Victoria Burke, "Women and Early Seventeenth-Century Manuscript Culture: Four Miscellanies," *Seventeenth Century* 12 (1997): 135–50, for discussion of Fowler's labors.

xvii. Clifford, *Tixall Poetry*, xxii.

xviii. *The Poems of Patrick Cary*, ed. Sister Veronica Delany, 4 (Oxford: Clarendon P, 1978), 41.

xix. Ibid., liii.

xx. Ibid., l-li.

xxi. Ibid., xlv-xlvii.

xxii. This same type of Royalist audience for literary manuscript materials during the Interregnum is also demonstrated in the manuscript volume compiled by the daughters of the duke of Newcastle, Lady Elizabeth Brackley and Jane Cavendish, which I discuss in "'To Be Your Daughter in Your Pen': The Social Functions of Literature in the Writings of Lady Elizabeth Brackley and Lady Jane Cavendish," *Huntington Library Quarterly* 51 (1988): 281–96.

xxiii. Peter Giles, "An Unknown Emmanuel Poet," *Emmanuel College Magazine* 9 (1897): 2.

xxiv. Bodleian Library, MS Rawl.poet.94.

xxv. Giles, "An Unknown Emmanuel Poet," 12, 22.

xxvi. Bodleian Library, MS Rawl.poet.94, 116.

xxvii. Cole was a staunch Royalist, who was proposed for one of Charles II's new orders of knighthood, the "Knights of the Royal Oak," an honor that Chatwin celebrates in a poem in the volume. For further details concerning Cole, see John Nichols, *The History and Antiquities of the County of Leicester*, 2nd ed., 4 (London, 1813), 272.

xxviii. This was Heneage Finch, the second son of the earl of Nottingham and himself the future earl of Aylesford. For information about Burroughs, see Giles, "Unknown Emmanuel Poet," 2–4; for information about Finch, see Nichols, *History and Antiquities*, 2, 17.

xxix. Bodleian Library, MS Rawl.poet.94, 149–50.

xxx. Ibid., 50.

xxxi. Ibid., 115.

xxxii. Wanley's poem is found in British Library MSS Harleian 6646 and 6922. L.C. Martin, "A Forgotten Poet of the Seventeenth Century," *Essays and Studies* 11 (1925): 5–31; see also Martin's 1928 Oxford edition of Wanley's verse.

xxxiii. Bodleian Library, MS Rawl.poet.94, 48.

xxxiv. Ibid., 108.

xxxv. Bodleian Library, MS Rawl.poet.208.

xxxvi. Joseph Foster, *Alumni Oxonienses: The Members of the University of Oxford, 1500–1714*, 2 (1891; reprint, Nendeln, Liechtenstein: Kraus Reprint, 1968), 742. The other possibility among Oxford students would be Joseph Hooper, also of Devon, admitted to Wadham College, 23 May 1667, age seventeen.

xxxvii. Dale B.J. Randall, *Gentle Flame: The Life and Verse of Dudley, Fourth Lord North (1602–1677)* (Durham, NC: Duke UP, 1983), 100–01.

xxxviii. Ibid., 165.

xxxix. Ibid., 128.

xl. St. John's College, MS bb, James 613, vol. 1, [41]; quoted in Randall, *Gentle Flame*, 106.

xli. Marotti, *Manuscript, Print, and the English Renaissance Lyric*, 68–69; Woudhuysen, *Sir Philip Sidney*, 391.

xlii. Ibid., 69.

xliii. Cary's anti-Crowmell verses were in fact mild compared with those of Thomas Weaver, who compiled a manuscript volume of verse (Bodleian Library, MS Rawl.poet.211), which among other pieces contained dated "Carols" for Christmas attacking the government. Some of the contents of this manuscript text were published in 1654 as *Songs and Poems of Love and Drollery*, by "T.W."
xliv. For a more extended discussion of this, see Ezell, "'To Be Your Daughter in Your Pen'"; for a later example, see Katherine King's analysis of Jane Barker's texts in "Jane Barker, *Poetical Recreations*, and the Sociable Text," *ELH* 61 (1994): 551–70. [Elizabeth Brackley (1626–63), Jane Cavendish (1620/21–69), and William Cavendish (bap. 1593–d. 1676) were all English poets.]
xlv. Angeline Goreau, *Reconstructing Aphra: A Social Biography of Aphra Behn* (Oxford: Clarendon P, 1980), 153–54.
xlvi. Earl Miner, *The Cavalier Modes from Jonson to Cotton* (Princeton, NJ: Princeton UP, 1971), 275.
xlvii. Harold Love, *Scribal Publication*, 180.
xlviii. King, "Jane Barker, *Poetical Recreations*, and the Sociable Text," *ELH* 61 (1994): 551–70. See also Kathryn R. King and Jeslyn Medoff's recent bio-bibliographical study of Barker for further information concerning the author's practices in exile in France in "Jane Barker and Her Life (1652–1732): The Documentary Record," *Eighteenth-Century Life* 21 (1997): 16–38.
xlix. King, "Jane Barker," 563.
l. Ibid.
li. Marie Burghope's text, for example, survived because it was part of the Huntington family library and was bought as part of a collection of that family's papers.
lii. "The Early Seventeenth Century," in *The Norton Anthology of English Literature*, 6th ed., 1 (New York: Norton, 1993), 1079.
liii. Ibid.

24.

Paula McDowell, "Towards a Genealogy of 'Print Culture' and 'Oral Tradition,'" *This Is Enlightenment*. Ed. Clifford Siskin and William Warner. U of Chicago P, 2010. 229–46

Paula McDowell is Associate Professor of English at New York University. She specializes in Restoration and eighteenth-century literature and print culture. She is the author of *The Women of Grub Street: Press, Politics and Gender in the London Literary Marketplace, 1678–1730* (Oxford, 1998), an important reconstruction of the prominent roles women in the middle and working classes played in writing, publishing, and distributing publications. McDowell's groundbreaking recovery of women's involvement in the book trades is also characterized by attentiveness to the oral and print practices in which women were involved; specifically, she uncovers multiple examples of women's involvement in political, commercial, and religious speech as balladeers, hawkers, and preachers, and their involvement in the printing, publishing, and distribution of printed texts. In this chapter as well, McDowell suggests that historical printed writing that attempts to collect or theorize oral culture must be examined alongside actual oral practices, including recitation, preaching, singing, and speechifying.

Whereas in an earlier essay (see above, pp. 353–74), Kastan explores how (for Shakespeare in particular) the world of the stage (in which his plays were performed) and the world of the print marketplace (in which his plays were marketed and sold) were essentially discontinuous, in this essay McDowell argues for a closer relationship between print and oral cultures, although one that is difficult to disentangle given that the concept of "oral culture" was in fact created retrospectively. The following essay offers an overview of the development of the use of terms such as "orality" and "print culture": the former is a product of the eighteenth century, whereby "the spread of print commerce triggers heightened reflection on oral communication," and the latter is a product of twentieth-century scholars attempting to theorize oral culture. Thus, McDowell recovers an eighteenth-century discourse about oral culture that was itself a product of the rising dominance—and commercialism—of print (and nostalgia for a putatively uncommercialized form of literary exchange). Her essay also locates the origins of an "'antagonistic' model of oral and literate communication" in the very print productions that sought to re-present, or remediate, oral culture. That is, McDowell identifies in mid- to later-eighteenth-century written discourse the construction of an evolutionary model of media shift, one in which older forms of technology are seen as giving way to newer ones—a model which, she points out, scholars are still attempting to debunk.

Towards a Genealogy of "Print Culture" and "Oral Tradition"

I. Origins of the "Oral-Literate Equation"

In a 1987 conference paper titled "The Oral-Literate Equation: A Formula for the Modern Mind," Eric A. Havelock looked back over his career and tried to pinpoint a moment when this formula first began to make sense to scholars. He mused, "[G]oing back twenty years, or even less, I do not think that the program of a colloquium of distinguished scholars from five countries would have carried the title '**Orality** and **Literacy**.' To be sure, phrases like 'oral formula' and 'oral composition' in connection with Homer[1] had come into currency at Harvard ... after the Second World War ... because of the close connection of Milman Parry and Albert Lord with that university." But even then, "the application of these terms was still met with strong resistance from conservative scholars."[i] In Milman Parry's published doctoral thesis, "L'Épithète traditionnelle dans Homère" (1928), the "founding document of the modern Homeric oralist theory of composition," was gaining notice in the United States, and in 1951, "the oral-literate question (as it was later to become) received impetus from a very unexpected

quarter when Harold Innis published *The Bias of Communication*."[ii] In 1958, Walter Ong published *Ramus: Method and the Decay of Dialogue*, "a preliminary exposure of a problem that was to bear directly upon the oral-literate equation but coming this time from the study and practice of rhetoric." Then, in 1962–63, there appeared to be a "breakthrough":

> Within the space of less than twelve months there appeared four publications that, in retrospect, can be said to have made a joint announcement: that orality (or oralism) had to be put on the map.... These works were *The Gutenberg Galaxy* by McLuhan (1962), *La pensée sauvage* by Lévi-Strauss (1962), an article by Jack Goody and Ian Watt entitled "The Consequences of Literacy" (1963), and finally *Preface to Plato* by myself (1963).... *Was this grouping as it occurred a pure accident or did it reflect a common and widespread response, even if an unconscious one, in France, England, the United States, and Canada, to a shared experience of a technological revolution in the means of human communication?* Radio, not to mention its immediate predecessor, the telephone, and its successor, television, was transforming the reach of the spoken, that is, of the oral, word.[iii]

---

1 Greek poet from around the eighth or ninth century BCE and supposed author of the *Odyssey* and the *Iliad*; also commonly cited as the greatest epic poet in Western history.

In 1967, a few years after this "breakthrough," Ong himself remarked the way that a relatively sudden awareness of media shift in one generation seemed to trigger groundbreaking insights into parallel historical moments:

> Awareness of the succession of media stages and wonder about the meaning of this succession are themselves the product of the succession.... [O]nly as we have entered the electronic stage has man become aware of the profundity of differences, some of which have been before his eyes for thousands of years ... between the old oral culture and the culture initiated with writing and matured with alphabetic type.... As late as the 1930s ... the differences between speech and writing were still impossibly occluded for even the most astute scholars.[iv]

In both Havelock's and Ong's accounts of the twentieth-century emergence of the concept of oralism and the heuristic of "orality and literacy," scholarly efforts to come to terms with the technological revolution of "electronic culture" led to a breakthrough in thinking about "orality" and "oral culture." Today, Havelock concludes, "the nouns *orality* and *oralism* are on a different footing, symbolizing conceptions that have extended far beyond Homer and the Greeks."[v]

II. "Print Culture": Origins of the Term

397

The same years that Havelock and Ong retrospectively identified as witnessing a "breakthrough" in studies of "orality" and "oral culture," Marshall McLuhan employed the term "print culture" as one among many similar terms ("**typographic** era," "**Gutenberg** era," "mechanical era," "electric age," and so forth) in *The Gutenberg Galaxy: The Making of Typographic Man* (1962). Particularly striking is the way that McLuhan's use of "print culture" was a self-conscious extension of earlier work on orality by Parry and Lord. He begins *The Gutenberg Galaxy* with the statement:

> The present volume is in many respects complementary to *The Singer of Tales* by Albert B. Lord. Professor Lord has continued the work of Milman Parry, whose Homeric studies had led him to consider how oral and written poetry naturally followed diverse patterns and functions.

He states that he will extend this focus on difference, contrasting the "Gutenberg era" with oral, written, and electronic societies: "[T]he enterprise which Milman Parry undertook with reference to the contrasted *forms* of oral and written poetry is here extended to the *forms* of thought and the organization of experience in society and politics."[vi] As the subtitle of his book, "The Making of Typographic Man," makes clear, McLuhan held that the introduction and spread of printing had profound implications not only for society but also for the human psyche. Five years later, in 1967, McLuhan's student, Ong, would employ the term "typographic culture" as part of an explicitly developed evolutionary model of media shift whose distinct phases include "oral culture," "**scribal culture**," "typographic culture," and the "electronic stage." Significantly, though, Ong's evolutionary model initially consisted of only three "stages": "in terms of communications media, cultures can be divided ... into three successive stages: (1) oral or oral-aural (2) script, which reaches critical breakthroughs with the invention first of the alphabet and then later of alphabetic moveable type, and (3) electronic."[vii] Writing and print were modeled as one "stage." As late as 1971, Ong was still using the phrase "writing-and-print culture," suggesting that he did not yet see print as a distinct phase but rather as an outgrowth or extension of writing.[viii]

In 1979, Elizabeth L. Eisenstein's *The Printing Press as an Agent of Change: Communications and Cultural Transformations in Early-Modern Europe* launched the term "print culture" into common parlance.[2] Today, thirty years later, it seems remarkable that Eisenstein's explanation of her use of this specific term in her eight-hundred-page work consists of a brief remark in the **preface** and two footnotes in the opening chapter. In the preface, she references McLuhan's work on "print culture," then states that her own subject is not the consequences of printing in general but "how printing altered *written communications within the Commonwealth of Learning*.... the term 'print culture' is used throughout this book in a special parochial Western sense: to refer to post-Gutenberg developments in the West."[ix] In the two footnotes in the main body of the text, she references work by Havelock, Goody, Watt, and Ong on "the distinction between oral and literate cultures." But she emphasizes that her book focuses on another kind of difference: "despite passing reference to the work

of McLuhan and Ong in Goody's introduction, the difference between scribal culture and print culture tends to be blurred by arguments which contrast alphabetic with ideographic writing[3] and oral with written transmission but not script with print."[x] In a recent exchange with Adrian Johns, Eisenstein reiterates the original intellectual context of *The Printing Press as an Agent of Change*, again referencing the work of Walter Ong. Responding to a reviewer's charge that her use of "print culture" in *Printing Press* is "curiously metaphysical," she writes, "I had used the term quite specifically to contrast diverse procedures employed by **scribes** and **manuscript** dealers with those employed by **printers**—substituting 'scribal culture' and 'print culture' for the more recondite[4] terms '**chirographic** culture' and 'typographic culture,' used by Walter Ong."[xi]

Despite immediate and ongoing critique of Eisenstein's thesis, the term and concept of "print culture" are today evoked more than ever by Book Historians, literary scholars, and media theorists. In a review of *The Printing Press as an Agent of Change* that appeared almost as soon as the book was published, William Bouwsma acknowledged Eisenstein's work as a major contribution to early modern history yet accused her of taking "the printing press itself entirely out of history. For Eisenstein, print seems to be an independent force in human affairs, a cause but never a result of historical processes. She refuses to see it as a tool, brought into

---

2 See the selection from Eisenstein's book in Chapter 3, pp. 215–30, above.

3 A system of writing wherein concepts are represented by symbols instead of words.

4 Obscure.

existence and exploited by forces outside itself."[xii] In his 1990 study of the "cultural meaning of printedness" in colonial America, Michael Warner similarly critiques what he labels the "Whig-McLuhanite model of print history"—especially the assumption that "technology has an ontological[5] status prior to culture." In the work of McLuhan, Eisenstein, and others, he observes, "Print technology is seen as having a logic internal to itself, a logic which then exerts causative force in human affairs."[xiii] Most recently, Adrian Johns has mounted a full-scale critique of Eisenstein's notion of print culture.[6] In his view, Eisenstein's print culture "is characterized primarily in terms of certain traits that print is taken to endow on texts" (especially fixity). But at least until the nineteenth century, "Eisenstein's print culture does not exist." "Print culture" does not emerge directly from the press; instead, "the very identity of print itself has had to be *made*."[xiv] Today, Eisenstein herself laments that the term print culture is "in danger of becoming a meaningless cliché." In particular, she warns, "'Eighteenth-Century Print Culture' is used as an umbrella title to cover miscellaneous topics."[xv] Nonetheless, despite three decades of critique and refinement of the term and concept of print culture, the proliferation of projects and institutions under the rubric of "print culture studies" seems if anything to have intensified. Witness, for instance, the title of a recent valuable collection of essays, *Agent of Change: Print Culture Studies after Elizabeth L. Eisenstein* (2007), in a series titled Studies in Print Culture and the History of the Book.[xvi]

III. If Print Culture Had to Be Made, Who Made It? The Eighteenth Century as Turning Point 399

Print culture, then, did not just appear with the invention of printing. In Britain, there was a time lag of about three centuries between the introduction of printing technology and the crystallization of anything we can without major qualifications label a "print society." To make matters still more complicated, the phrase "print culture" is anachronistic for the eighteenth century. No eighteenth-century author employed this phrase (or the corollary "oral culture") for, as Raymond Williams and others have shown, the word "culture" was not used as a noun signifying "a particular way of life" until the nineteenth century: "Culture as an independent noun, an abstract process or the product of such a process, is not important before lC18 and is not common before mC19."[xvii] [7] At the turn of the nineteenth century, "culture" took on new and important meanings, but until then, it typically meant "the 'tending of natural growth,' and then, by analogy, a process of human training."[xviii] Many early eighteenth-century authors wrote extensively about the spread of print, and especially, what they took to be the alarming expansion of the press after the lapse of the **Licensing Act** in 1695. But authors such as

5 Related to being itself, inherent.

6 See the selection from Johns's book, *The Nature of the Book: Print and Knowledge in the Making*, in Chapter 3, pp. 267–88, above.

7 Williams uses a system of abbreviations in *Keywords*: lC18 means late eighteenth century; mC19 means mid-nineteenth century.

Jonathan Swift and Alexander Pope[8] represent the spread of print commerce as contributing to a decline of culture in the sense of cultivation. In the judgment of Martinus Scriblerus, Pope's fictional "learned commentator" on his mock-epic poem *The Dunciad*, "Providence ... permitted the invention of Printing as a *scourge* for the sins of the learned"—not as a superior vehicle of learning or tool for the advancement of judgment, morals, or taste.[xix] Nonetheless, while these authors do not employ the term "print culture," they do gesture—satirically—toward this concept. Literary texts are a valuable—if notoriously tricky—register of contemporary awareness of media shift, and Pope, Swift, and other members of the satiric "Scriblerus Club" exhibit an intense awareness of dramatic contemporary changes happening around them having to do with printing. It is no accident that McLuhan held up *The Dunciad* as one of the "four massive myths of the Gutenberg transformation of society." "It is to *The Dunciad*" he pronounced, "that we must turn for the epic of the printed word.... For here is the explicit study of plunging of the human mind into the sludge of an unconscious engendered by the book."[xx]

The early eighteenth century was a decisive transitional period in the history of the British book trade. In 1695, the Printing or Licensing Act of 1662 was allowed to lapse for good, ending pre-publication censorship and government and **Stationers' Company** restrictions on the number of presses, printers, and apprentices. The decades immediately following were a time of anarchic expansion: while the Printing Act had tried to limit the number of master printers in all of England to 24, by 1705 there were between 65 and 70 printing houses in London alone.[xxi] Despite the efforts of the Stationers' Company to regain control of the trade—including a decade of failed attempts to renew the Licensing Act and so protect ancient guild privileges—an older, guild-based model of control was being displaced by a more openly competitive commercial model. This shift is often represented as the demise of a more "gentlemanly" culture of printing, but for the vocal printer-author Elinor James it signaled a decline in the "Art and Mistery" of an ancient craft authorized by the Crown. As James urged in one of her many **broadside** petitions to Parliament urging renewal of the Licensing Act, "Printing is not a Trade as other Trades are, but it is an Art and Mistery that ought ... not to be made so common, as that it should be slighted and trampled under Foot."[xxii] For most of James's lifetime (c. 1645–1719), the London book trade was small and closely knit, but by the mid-eighteenth century, the print trade had penetrated into the provinces, and "by 1800, print issued from hundreds of presses operating in London and almost every small town in the country."[xxiii] There is no question that printing deeply affected English life between 1450 and 1695, but in the eighteenth century, "printing began to affect the structure of social life at every level." Most important, for the eighteenth-century literary authors I will consider all too briefly next, print was "restructuring rather than merely modifying" the world of letters.[xxiv]

8 Jonathan Swift (1667–1745), Irish poet, essayist, and early novelist noted for his satirical work; Alexander Pope (1688–1744), English author of poetry and critical essays likewise noted for his satire.

IV. Pope, Swift, and Print: *The Dunciad* and *A Tale of a Tub*

For twenty-five years after the lapse of the Licensing Act, Elinor James lamented the transformation of the ancient "Art and Mistery" of printing to a mere commercial "Trade." The early eighteenth century also saw the development of a powerful satiric construct of commercial print society. Authors such as Swift and Pope lived through a time of significant, *specific* economic and political reconfigurations of the press, and their perceptions of change are powerfully registered in texts such as *A Tale of a Tub* (partly drafted in 1696–97; pub. 1704) and *The Dunciad* (1728–43). While these texts are commonly read as indictments of "print culture," such readings overstate their case.[xxv] Neither Swift nor Pope was anti-print. Instead, what James McLaverty has observed of Pope might also be said of Swift: we need to acknowledge both "the Pope who loved print and the Pope who hated it."[xxvi] It was not print technology, the spread of printing, or print per se that was making these authors feel like an epochal shift had occurred. Rather, there was a sense that what we would call a "technology" was on the brink of being *used* in profoundly new ways. The distinctive self-consciousness of these authors about print and its users makes them (and the other "Scriblerians") powerful commentators on what we might call media shift. With the collapse of pre-publication licensing and Stationers' Company control, there was in these authors' view "no public punishment left, but what a good Writer inflicts."[xxvii] Printing and letters were being reduced to mere market-oriented trades without adequate moral, legal, and economic safeguards. One of Swift's key concerns in *A Tale of a Tub* is the religious and political threat of uncontrolled print: "[N]ew levies of wits, all appointed (as there is reason to fear) with pen, ink, and paper, which may at an hour's warning be drawn out into **pamphlets** and other offensive weapons" to attack church and state.[xxviii] Swift also satirizes modern methods for coping with the vast overproduction of knowledge—especially **indexes**, digests, and other tools for navigating and sorting printed books. In "A Digression in Praise of Digressions," he observes that the would-be wits "of this age have discovered a shorter and more prudent method to become *scholars* and *wits*, without the fatigue of *reading* or of thinking.... the profounder, and politer method, [is] to get a thorough insight into the *index*, by which the whole book is governed and turned, *like fishes* by the *tail*."[xxix] In *The Dunciad*, Pope similarly satirizes "shameless, mercenary **booksellers**," ill-judging **patrons**, and the fickle, undiscerning public, but he emphasizes that Dulness affects all sectors of society. McLuhan was not unjustified in describing *The Dunciad* as a "myth ... of the Gutenberg transformation of society,"[xxx] for the way that the poem represents the reach and influence of print, especially in book 4, does come close to our modern sense of a culture as a "whole network of social relations" or "total way of life."

In later versions of Pope's poem, certain broad social changes seem to start happening almost as if by themselves. The spread of printing produces something unexpected—though not necessarily inherent in the technology. Print—or rather, new *uses* of print—are contributing to a total, hegemonic takeover of religious, political, educational, and other institutions. But it is not only human agency but also a *lack* of human action due to unawareness or indifference that is triggering these effects. For Pope, the willingness of literate gentlemen to allow themselves to be caught up in the fog of Dulness is at least as much of a problem as too many bad writers.

In his reading of the *Dunciad,* Alvin Kernan ascribes to Pope the view of Marshall McLuhan that print ushers in dramatic cognitive, as well as social, shifts: "[T]he kind of mental confusion that McLuhan refers to was, in fact, Pope's central satiric subject."[xxxi] But Augustan poets, I suggest, are not working with abstract concepts like "print logic" or "typographic man." Pope would never have dreamed of separating the technology of printing from its users. (In fact, his satire was criticized for being too personal.) He used the word "print" chiefly as a verb, not a noun—to indicate a process, not a product.[xxxii] It is not print per se but specific human uses of and responses to print that are the problem. Furthermore, while Pope does associate the spread of print with massive (and possibly even cognitive) shifts, it is not a direct causal relationship, nor is it an inevitable one. Pope was not a **technological determinist.** *The Dunciad* is at once a topical poem *and* a prophecy of a future that need not necessarily happen. It is up to humane intellectuals to scrutinize and shape the directions of a communications technology; to make what Paul Starr calls "constitutive choices."[xxxiii]

V. The Spread of Print Commerce Triggers Heightened Reflection on Oral Communication

In the twentieth century, attempts by Parry, Lord, Ong, and others to understand oral poetry and "oral culture" led to the coining of the term "print culture." In the eighteenth century, by way of contrast, attempts to theorize the implications of print triggered a distinctly new degree of self-conscious reflection on oral communication and its actual and potential threatening intersections with an unrestrained press. Augustan authors made sense of what seemed to them the new world of print commerce by linking it to familiar "vulgar" or popular oral practices. In *The Dunciad,* Pope states as the subject of his poem in brief the movement of the "Smithfield Muses"[9] to the "ear of Kings."[xxxiv] Pope's great "epic of the printed word"[xxxv] is filled with ears, mouths, and tongues—dangerous bodily organs of sense. In book 2, Queen Dulness commands the dunces to learn "the wond'rous pow'r of Noise." The mock heroic games held to celebrate the new King of Dulness include a noise-making contest wherein a "thousand tongues are heard in one loud din."[xxxvi] Similarly, in *A Tale of a Tub,* Swift constructs his satire in opposition not only to the degradations of the literary marketplace (and the threat of uncontrolled print) but also particular oral practices. Throughout the eighteenth century, for instance, dissenting[10] preachers' oral appeal to the masses was an enormous concern. Anglican authors expressed alarm that the populace was being seduced by "enthusiasts"—especially Quakers and Methodists—more cunning in the use of intonation and gesture in public speaking. As a freshly ordained clergyman, Swift knew that at this time of widespread illiteracy, tongues and ears were the chief organs of mass manipulation. In his satire of "corruptions in Religion and Learning," he foregrounds tongues and ears, as much as books and pamphlets, as powerful organs of sedition

9 Smithfield was the site of the annual Bartholemew Fair; the "Smithfield Muses" suggest the fairground entertainments that now amuse the high as well as low.

10 Those who did not belong to the Church of England were called Nonconformists or Dissenters.

and dissent.[xxxvii] Indeed, he depicts so broad a range of human vocal activities—from belching to humming to preaching to droning—that for once the impossibly broad category of "orality" seems to fit, as these practices can't easily be subsumed under any narrower label such as "speech." Swift's satire reminds us that oral communication is more than a verbal (or even vocal) phenomenon. In his satire of "the learned Aeolists," who "maintain the original cause of all things to be *wind*" he depicts a dissenting preacher swollen with inspiration:

> In this posture he disembogues[11] whole tempests upon his auditory, as the spirit from beneath gives him utterance, which issuing *ex adytis* and *penetralibus*,[12] is not performed without much pain and gripings. And the wind in breaking forth deals with his face as it does with that of the sea, first *blackening*, then *wrinkling*, and at last *bursting it into a foam*.[xxxviii]

Similarly, in *The Dunciad*, Pope satirizes both dissenting preachers and Grub Street authors as braying asses. In the aforementioned noise-making contest, he compares the competitors ("Authors, Stationers") to "long-ear'd" asses, then compares the asses' music to the "Sound" made by the "lab'ring lungs" of "Enthusiast" preachers—most notably Methodist leader George Whitefield,[13] who was known for his field preaching to enormous crowds.[xxxix] Augustan authors do not satirize "print culture" and "orality." Nevertheless, in works such as *The Dunciad* and *A Tale of a Tub*, Pope and Swift reflect on and register threatening oral practices as part of their extended meditation upon the problems and possibilities of print. 403

VI. The Theological Notion of Oral Tradition

In *A Tale of a Tub* Swift satirizes not only "low" oral practices but also the high theological notion of oral tradition. In his allegory of the three brothers, pointedly named Peter, Martin, and Jack, he vehemently rejects the idea of reliable oral tradition as a dangerous Papist hoax. The 1680s saw the intensification of longstanding debates between Protestants and Catholics concerning Scripture versus tradition as a rule of faith. For Anglican authors faced with the prospect of a Catholic king, this was a question of urgent national political importance, "a major war in the history of ideas, in which big guns on both sides were employed."[xl] The official position of the Catholic church was that truth was to be found in *both* Scripture and unwritten tradition, but in the tense political context of the 1680s (and the heated environment of polemical debate generally) Catholic polemicists such as English priest John Gother[14] intensified their arguments for the stability and reliability of oral tradition as preserved in the Church versus the uncertainty

11 Usually the place where a river flows out of its mouth and into the ocean; used figuratively here.

12 Meaning out of the innermost shrines and holy places, a Latin phrase adapted from Virgil's *Aeneid*.

13 George Whitfield (1714–70), English Protestant religious figure famous for his evangelistic sermons delivered in England and in the English colonies in North America.

14 John Gother (d. 1704), English Catholic priest and writer.

of textual transmission and interpretation. As one anonymous polemicist remarked in 1685, "of late ... *Oral Tradition* has quite carried away *the Credit*."[xli]

Throughout the eighteenth century, Anglicans remained deeply suspicious of the proposition that any unwritten tradition preserved by the Church might be considered of equal authority to the Bible. Swift depicts the father of Peter, Martin, and Jack handing his sons his *written* will, providing each brother with an immortal coat (implicitly, the doctrine of Christianity). The will contains "full Instructions" concerning the care of these coats, and the sons observe these instructions, until one day they realize that their coats are out of style: "[T]hey went immediately to consult their father's Will, read it over and over, but not a word of the *shoulder-knot*" (a fashion trend they wish to follow). "What should they do?"[xlii] When they can't find passages authorizing shoulder-knots, brother Peter sets his siblings to searching the will for constituent letters (a, b, c, and so on!) that can be reshuffled into passages authorizing any new fashion he wishes to implement. At this point in the text, a footnote by Anglican William Wotton[15] scoffs, "When the Papists cannot find anything which they want in Scripture they go to *Oral Tradition*."[xliii] Later, another footnote (this time likely by Swift himself) also scorns the Catholic doctrine of oral tradition: "By this is meant *tradition*, allowed to have equal authority with the scripture, or rather greater."[xliv] Later in life, Swift would revisit the question of oral tradition in *Gulliver's Travels* (1726). Book 4 depicts a society of virtuous horses, the Houhynhynms, who pass down valuable customs, learning, and letters via tradition because they have no books. But Swift never seriously entertained the possibility that any complex, valuable body of knowledge could be passed down entirely without writing, and in this way he was typical of his era. His purpose in *Gulliver's Travels* is "satiric rather than ethnographic"[xlv] (these are horses, after all!) and crucially, the Houhynhynms are not Christians—and so could never be mistaken for Catholics.

VII. The Crystallization of an Ethnographic Concept of Oral Tradition

Throughout the eighteenth century, the dominant understanding of "oral tradition" remained theological. Around 1730, however, one increasingly sees this phrase used in an ethnographic context. In 1724, two years before *Gulliver's Travels*, Jesuit missionary Joseph François Lafitau's *Moeurs des sauvages amériquains* advanced the enlightened idea that "savages" without writing might nonetheless have a highly developed system of laws, customs, and arts preserved through oral tradition. Lafitau lived among the Iroquois near Montreal from 1712 to 1717, and his modern editors credit him with having founded comparative ethnology.[xlvi] While he never advanced a systematic argument for "oral tradition," his grounding in Catholic theological notions of tradition may have helped him to move beyond the widespread assumption of European intellectuals that cultures without writing were lawless and barbaric. In the 1730s, classical scholars began cautiously advancing arguments for the possibility of sophisticated oral societies. The eighteenth century would see a major re-evaluation of Homeric poetry: a shift from a neoclassical approach, emphasizing what was universal and timeless, to a new interest in the specific

15 William Wotton (1666–1727), English Protestant religious figure also interested in linguistics.

historical circumstances affecting the production of works of art. Increasingly, there was a sense that Homer's poetry belonged to a particular period of social development and that its most puzzling characteristics (such as the repetition of epithets[16]) might be explained if the poetry was understood in its original social, political, and geographical contexts. Primitivists[17] were developing the idea of the relativity of human societies, and in 1735, Edinburgh scholar Thomas Blackwell's[18] *Enquiry into the Life and Writings of Homer* linked Homer's art to his "rude society" and its particular stage of development with respect to manners, language, and political and social organization. Blackwell never suggested that Homer could not read or write (this would have been a shocking proposition), but he argued that Homer owed the vigorousness of his language to his "primitive" environment. In 1769, the traveler and antiquarian Robert Wood[19] in his *Essay on the Original Genius and Writings of Homer* (1775) explicitly suggested that Homer could not read or write.[xlvii] His proposal was greeted with scorn by many contemporaries, but it was taken seriously by the German classicist F.A. Wolf,[20] whose own *Prolegomena ad Homerum* (1795) would greatly influence Homeric scholarship. Eighteenth-century debates concerning Homer and oral tradition were foundational to modern oral-formulaic theory and to Milman Parry's discovery of the workings of oral-formulaic epithets in Yugoslavian epic poetry. In eighteenth-century Britain, few scholars valorized Homer's "rude and unlettered state of society" to the extent that Jean-Jacques Rousseau[21] did in his unpublished *Essay on the Origin of Languages* (c. 1762–63). As Rousseau famously declared, "other poets had written; Homer alone had sung. And people have always listened in rapture to these songs, even when Europe has been overrun by barbarians who try to judge what they are incapable of experiencing."[xlviii] Nonetheless, clas- 405
sical scholars and other learned gentlemen increasingly exercised nostalgia for "rude societies" before the invention of letters. They especially lamented the decline of what Edinburgh moral philosopher Dugald Stewart[22] would later call "the culture of memory."[xlix] As Wood mused, "in a rude and unlettered state of society the memory is loaded with nothing that is either useless or unintelligible; whereas modern education employs us chiefly in getting by heart, while we are young, what we forget before we are old."[l]

After about 1760, the number of British (especially Scottish) texts advancing arguments for sophisticated oral societies rose dramatically. That year, Highlander James Macpherson[23] began

16 A characteristic of Homeric poetry is the use of epithets, in which adjectives or adjectival phrases are consistently linked with a noun, such as "rosy-fingered dawn." The belief was that this repetition was useful to bards who were reciting poetry from memory.

17 Primitivism refers to a philosophical perspective holding that primitive societies were more natural and enlightened than contemporary society.

18 Thomas Blackwell (1701–57), Scottish scholar of classical history and literature.

19 Robert Wood (1716/17–71), traveling classical scholar.

20 Friedrich August Wolf (1759–1824), German classical scholar interested in **philology**.

21 Jean-Jacques Rousseau (1712–78), Enlightenment philosopher, born in Geneva, perhaps most famous for his concept of the social contract.

22 Dugald Stewart (1753–1828), Scottish philosopher.

23 James Macpherson (1736–96), Scottish poet and literary collector.

publishing his phenomenally popular Ossianic poetry, claiming to have translated fragments of ancient oral poetry passed down from a third-century Highland bard chiefly by word of mouth. Macpherson was a student at Aberdeen College where Thomas Blackwell was principal; he also came under the influence of rhetorician Hugh Blair,[24] who suggested that pre-literate cultures were fertile ground for the growth of impassioned, "epic" language. Macpherson's scandalous claims for a sophisticated bardic tradition of oral poetry were notoriously debated even among his fellow Scots, but they also triggered extensive scholarly research into Celtic cultures, and the Ossian phenomenon raised the question of sophisticated oral societies to the level of a "popular" debate. By the end of the eighteenth century, we see an epochal shift in attitudes toward "oral tradition," and the crystallization of the modern secularized version of this concept.

VIII. "Rescuing" the Oral, 1: The Elocution Movement

In their own era of print and perceived rising literacy, eighteenth-century poets, rhetoricians, antiquarians, and others began to rethink and valorize the legacy and power of the human voice (sometimes even "vulgar" voices) in new ways and to model themselves as heroic "rescuers" of valuable oral traditions they depicted as on the brink of being lost. The 1730s onward also saw the flowering of the elocution[25] movement, as a wide variety of entrepreneurs sought to restore ancient eloquence for distinctly modern purposes. Elocutionists such as John "Orator" Henley[26] (d. 1756) or the Irish actor-turned-elocutionist Thomas Sheridan[27] (the father of playwright and renowned parliamentary orator Richard Brinsley Sheridan) made a new commercial opportunity out of what used to be one branch of classical rhetoric. Between 1726 and 1756, Henley operated an oratory above a meat market in the heart of working London where he lectured on elocution to socially diverse audiences. Later in the century, Sheridan lectured at a more polite level to audiences in major urban centers throughout England, Ireland, and Scotland. In their oral/physical performances, Henley, Sheridan, and other elocutionists at once touted and embodied those elements of spoken communication that cannot be fully reproduced in written language (tone, pitch, cadence, and especially, gesture). Sheridan argued that the propagation of writing, print, and even literacy had undermined public speaking skills. In his *Lectures on Elocution* (1762), he proposed that "some of our greatest men have been trying to do that with the pen, which can only be performed by the tongue."[li] Echoing Sheridan, Hugh Blair held that "though Writing may answer the purposes of mere instruction, yet all the great and high efforts of eloquence must be made, by means of spoken, not of written, Language."[lii] The eighteenth century saw a renewed fascination with the human body as a powerful (and potentially universal) communications medium: a neglected tool that might beneficially be exploited in a variety of arenas. Elocutionists especially lamented the "decline of pulpit oratory": the cold restraint of

24 Hugh Blair (1718–1800), Scottish religious figure and literary critic.

25 The ability to speak clearly and expressively, especially with distinct pronunciation and articulation.

26 John Henley (1692–1756), English unorthodox religious figure famous for his expressive preaching style.

27 Thomas Sheridan (1719–88), Irish actor and **lexicographer**.

Anglican preachers, and accordingly, the missed opportunities to engage the populace through an impassioned, physical style of preaching. At the same time, though, later eighteenth-century elocutionists such as Sheridan worked hard to distinguish their own genteel oral endeavors from the practices of groups such as the Quakers or the Methodists who were already making powerful use of the same insights. The elocutionists' arguments for the superior expressive power of oral communication might appear to challenge widespread European assumptions about the superiority of writing, but re-read in the context of their own media moment, it becomes clear that Sheridan and his contemporaries, like Pope and Swift earlier in the century, were theorizing oral communication chiefly as a means of grappling with the changing institutional contexts of *print.* "The cheapness of books," Sheridan observed in 1762 with considerable ambivalence, "has made the art of ... reading familiar to the lowest people."[liii] Eloquence was a new tool of distinction in an increasingly literate age.

IX. "Rescuing" the Oral, 2: The Polite Ballad Revival and Ballad Scholarship

The eighteenth century also saw the emergence of a substantial print discourse about ballads.[28] In commentaries in periodicals, in prefaces to collections of ballads, in essays printed in these collections, and elsewhere, a wide variety of authors commented positively and negatively upon balladry as a hybrid oral and textual practice. In Britain, ballads were closely linked to commercial printing; they were also commonly represented as associated with the "lower sort." But over the course of the century, the polite ballad revival and especially the rise of ballad scholarship 407
would forge significantly new ways of conceptualizing ballads. In compiling his phenomenally successful **anthology** *Reliques of Ancient English Poetry* (1765), clergyman Thomas Percy[29] collected his ballads from print and manuscript sources (including broadsides). But in his ambitious "Essay on the Ancient Minstrels in England," appended to the *Reliques*, he represented the "Old Heroic Ballads" in his collection as the "select remains of our ancient English bards and minstrels": "oral itinerant poet[s]" who "probably never committed [their rhymes] to writing." The descendants of these noble old bards, he speculated, were tragically displaced by "an inferior sort" of "ballad-*writers* ... for the press."[liv] By the 1780s, one detects the crystallization of a new *confrontational* model of balladry, whereby an earlier, more "authentic" tradition of "minstrel song" is seen as having been displaced by commercial print.[lv] In 1781, 23-year-old John Pinkerton[30] left his native Edinburgh for London to publish his own collection, *Scottish Tragic Ballads*. Energized by his readings of Percy and Macpherson and indebted to Blair's argument for the virtues of "oral tradition" in his "Critical Dissertation Upon the Poems of Ossian" (1763), Pinkerton prefaced his collection with a "Dissertation on the Oral Tradition of Poetry" in which he aspired to give an "account of the utility of the Oral Tradition of Poetry, in that barbarous state of society which *necessarily* precedes the invention of letters."[lvi] Whereas Percy had only gestured toward an

---

28 A song that tells a story.

29 Thomas Percy (1729–1811), English writer, antiquarian scholar, and clergyman.

30 John Pinkerton (1758–1826), Scottish poet and historical scholar.

evolutionary model of media shift (the idea of a shift "from" oral "to" literate society), Pinkerton explicitly modeled an inevitable development whereby one stage "necessarily" follows on (and displaces) another. The eighteenth century saw the origins of modern evolutionary models of media shift. In Pinkerton's "Dissertation," this model could not be more starkly confrontational: "In proportion as Literature advanced in the world Oral Tradition disappeared."[lvii]

Percy's idealized narrative of "oral itinerant poet[s]" contributed to later ballad editors' conviction that certain *living* practices of ballad singing were surviving traces of feudal oral traditions. Glasgow editor William Motherwell[31] opened his own collection *Minstrelsy, Ancient and Modern* with a bold claim: "This interesting body of popular poetry, part of which, in point of antiquity, may be fairly esteemed equal, if not superior, to the most ancient of our written monuments, has owed its preservation principally to oral tradition."[lviii] By comparing early eighteenth-century discussions of balladry—such as Joseph Addison's[32] in the *Spectator*,[lix] where ballads are assumed to be at once oral *and* printed—to later eighteenth- and nineteenth-century scholarly (re)constructions of "authentic" ballads, we see the eighteenth-century emergence of confrontational models of print and oral tradition. Over the course of the century, I suggest, heightened reflection on the spread of *print* contributed to a new conceptualizing of valuable ballad traditions as innately *oral*. Eighteenth-century ballad scholars forged a sharp *conceptual* (not actual) separation between "oral" and "printed" ballads. In so doing, they contributed to the later binary of "orality and literacy" that many ballad scholars are still working to undo today.[lx]

At the same time, though, one cannot emphasize strongly enough that this was a highly *selected* form of "oral tradition" that was being re-valued by later eighteenth- and nineteenth-century scholars. In a larger book project, I am interested in the polite "re-discovery" of oral tradition *in relation to contemporary oral* practices—especially, those "vulgar" or popular oral practices that learned gentlemen routinely condemned (for instance, lay preaching, "Billingsgate rhetoric,"[33] urban political activism, or "old wives' tales," to name only a few). In order to exercise their nostalgia for an era before print commerce, ballad collectors such as Percy had to associate "valuable" ballads with a distant past and an oral tradition that was imagined as separable from print commerce. These scholars strategically avoid any consideration of contemporary broadside ballad singing (especially topical, political, or bawdy ballads), for this still-vibrant aspect of what we might now call "popular oral culture," tainted by the marketplace and associated with social and political unrest, was not the legacy that genteel or professional scholars wished to preserve.

---

31 William Motherwell (1797–1835), Scottish poet and editor best known for his work on ballads.

32 Joseph Addison (1672–1719), English author most famous for his work with Richard Steele on two periodicals, *The Spectator* and *The Tatler*.

33 Billingsgate was a London fish market that became known for the rude and scolding language of the fishwives who worked there.

X. Origins of Evolutionary Models of Media Shift: Conjecturing Oral Societies

In her account of "the printing press as an agent of change," Eisenstein links the spread of printing and the development of "a new and distinctly modern historical consciousness."[lxi] With the introduction of printing, she suggests, "less effort was required to preserve and pass on what was known.... Successive generations began to pride themselves on knowing more than had their forebears.... Human history itself acquired the character of an indefinitely extended unfolding sequence."[lxii] In the late eighteenth century, we begin to see the idea of communications technologies as part of an inevitable, unfolding sequence of human history. In sketching out developmental models of mankind, later eighteenth-century Scottish moral philosophers, especially those whom Dugald Stewart would later label conjectural historians, gestured toward modern evolutionary models of media shift. In their efforts to trace the origins of commercial society, authors such as Adam Smith in his *Lectures on Rhetoric and Belles Lettres,* Adam Ferguson in his *Essay on the History of Civil Society,* William Robertson in *A View of the Progress of Society* and *History of the Discovery and Settlement of America,* and Henry Home, Lord Kames in his *Sketches of the History of Man* confronted and coped with a paucity of records for the earliest stages of mankind.[34] Accordingly, they worked backward from what was known, employing assumptions about Providence and human nature and developing a series of working abstractions such as "society," "the economy," and "progress."[lxiii] Scottish intellectuals saw their nation being rapidly transformed, and they contrasted the modern commercial towns of Glasgow and Edinburgh with what seemed to be the contemporaneous survival of older forms of social organization in the Highlands.[lxiv] Seeking to account for these differences and organize them into an explanatory framework that could be used as a tool for further investigation, they developed a new model of history, the "four-stages" theory. Stadial theory held that society naturally progressed over time through a series of phases, each corresponding to a different mode of subsistence (hunter-gatherer, pasturage, agriculture, and commerce) and each with its own characteristic institutions, economy, manners, and social arrangements. These phases were linked not only to different forms of economic organization and social and artistic development[lxv] but also, in some instances, to developments in the history of communications (such as the invention of letters, alphabetic writing, and especially, printing). At such moments, we come close to the idea that individual societies move inexorably forward through a succession of communications stages beginning with the development of speech. Ronald L. Meek suggests that we should see four-stages theory as "the first great theoretical embodiment" of "the notion of techno-economic determinism, and the principal of cultural evolutionism."[lxvi] While this succession of communications "stages" was most often viewed as "progress," one also sees elite nostalgia for the supposed benefits of "rude societies"

34 Adam Smith (1723–90), Scottish philosopher most famous for his pioneering of a free market capitalist ideology; Adam Ferguson (1723–1816), Scottish philosopher; William Robertson (1721–93), Scottish religious figure and historian; Henry Home, Lord Kames (1696–1782), Scottish jurist and philosophical writer.

without complex communications technologies. In *The Origin and Progress of Language* (6 vols., 1773–92), James Burnett, Lord Monboddo[35] questioned whether the invention of writing had on the whole contributed to the advancement of human knowledge.[lxvii] Ironically, highly literate authors such as Monboddo deployed the posited virtues of an unlettered, distant "past" to critique their own "inauthentic" historical moment of writing and print.

Across the English Channel, the fugitive Marquis de Condorcet[36] was hurriedly drafting his *Sketch for a Historical Picture of the Progress of the Human Mind* (pub. posthumously in 1795). Like British conjectural historians, Condorcet aspired to trace the development of the human mind "as it manifests itself ... from generation to generation.... Such a picture is historical, since it ... is based on the observation of human societies throughout the different stages of their development."[lxviii] He divided up history into ten ages rather than four, but he too modeled the history of mankind as a continuous chain: "All peoples whose history is recorded fall somewhere between our present degree of civilization and that which we still see amongst savage tribes.... so welding an uninterrupted chain between the beginning of historical time and the century in which we live."[lxix] He also systematically linked various stages of human social development to developments in the technology of communications. In a move that surely anticipates what Ruth Finnegan and others have critiqued as the "Great Divide" model of orality and literacy, he represents the "before" and "after" of alphabetic writing as "two great eras of the human race."[lxx] With the development of the alphabet, he enthused, "all that was necessary was to know how to recognize and reproduce these very few signs, and this final step assured the progress of the human race forever."[lxxi] But Condorcet's most triumphant stage is the period "from the invention of printing to the time when philosophy and the sciences shook off the yoke of authority."[lxxii] For him, as for Luther, the invention of printing was an epochal event, inaugurating a new age of human history that would end priestly oppression. Condorcet self-consciously worked backward from his own historical moment, noting that he had to "conjecture the stages" due to the "scarcity of records."[lxxiii] Meanwhile, Dugald Stewart was also explicitly measuring human progress in terms of various communications developments (especially the spread of printing): "[T]he means of communication afforded by the press, have, in the course of two centuries, accelerated the progress of the human mind, far beyond what the most sanguine hopes of our predecessors could have imagined."[lxxiv] Mary Poovey has suggested that one effect of the conjectural historians' "efforts to generate systematic knowledge was the production of a set of abstractions, which rapidly became the objects of these sciences."[lxxv] Was one such abstraction "oral society," eventually leading to the coinage of an even more influential abstraction, "oral culture"? Stewart came close to conjecturing an oral "stage" of society in terms anticipating our modern concept of oral culture when, in an ambiguous usage in which "culture" could be read either as a verb or a noun, he writes of the "culture of memory" and "the principles on which the culture of memory depends."[lxxvi]

35 James Burnett, Lord Monboddo (bap. 1714–d. 1799), Scottish judge and scholar of early anthropology.

36 Marie-Jean-Antoine-Nicolas de Caritat, marquis de Condorcet (1743–94), French philosopher and political thinker whose ideas are representative of the Enlightenment.

The eighteenth century saw the emergence of a sustained discourse questioning the effects of different media forms. The dramatic proliferation of print and the specter of future mass literacy generated widespread consideration of the nature and implications of media shift. In this essay I have contributed toward a genealogy of the ideas of "print culture" and "oral tradition." I have sketched the eighteenth-century emergence of an originally negative, but increasingly positive idea of oral tradition and suggested that literate groups' ideas about oral forms and practices developed in an especially close dialectical[37] relationship with ideas about *print* (especially print commerce). Today, a valuable and growing body of work on "oral culture" in early modern Britain by scholars such as Keith Thomas, Daniel Woolf, Adam Fox, and Alexandra Walsham routinely stresses that "literacy" did not displace "orality." Rather—in the terms of this scholarship—"literacy and orality co-existed ... in a mutually enriching equilibrium."[lxxvii] But where, we must ask, did this model of a division into "literacy and orality" come from in the first place? It is to the mid- and later eighteenth century, I have suggested, that we can trace the development of an "antagonistic" model of oral and literate communication, and the related development of "evolutionary" models of media shift (the idea that one media "stage" succeeds and/or displaces another).[lxxviii] "Orality," "print culture," and so on are not so much *things* as abstract concepts with interwoven histories. They are aspects of a heuristic that we employ, rather as our eighteenth-century predecessors did, in an attempt to organize and understand complex phenomena.

Notes

i. Eric A. Havelock, "The Oral-Literate Equation: A Formula for the Modern Mind," in *Literacy and Orality*, ed. David R. Olson and Nancy Torance (Cambridge: Cambridge UP, 1991), 13–27, 11. 411

ii. See Milman Parry, "L'Épithète traditionnelle dans Homère," *The Making of Homeric Verse: The Collected Papers of Milman Parry*, ed. Adam Parry (Oxford: Oxford UP, 1971, 1928), 1–190.

iii. Ibid., 12–15. Emphasis added.

iv. Walter J. Ong, *The Presence of the Word: Some Prolegomena for Cultural and Religious History*, Terry Lectures (New Haven, CT: Yale UP, 1967), 17–18.

v. Havelock, 11. Havelock and other theorists of what Ong calls "primary oral cultures (cultures with no knowledge at all of writing)" employ the concept of "orality" in a specific sense that needs to be distinguished from the vague usage in common parlance today. Nonetheless, it should be noted that the term "orality" is not a modern coinage but dates back to at least 1666, where it was used in a theological context as part of a vigorous ongoing debate concerning scripture versus "oral tradition" as the rule of faith (discussed below).

vi. Marshall McLuhan, *The Gutenberg Galaxy: The Making of Typographic Man* (Toronto: U of Toronto P, 1962), 1. Emphasis in original.

vii. Ong, *The Presence of the Word*, 17.

viii. Walter Ong, *Ramus, Method, and the Decay of Dialogue: From the Art of Discourse to the Art of Reason* (Chicago: U of Chicago P, 2004), 91.

ix. Elizabeth L. Eisenstein, *The Printing Press as an Agent of Change: Communications and Cultural Transformations in Early-Modern Europe* (Cambridge: Cambridge UP, 1979), xiv.

x. Ibid., 9, note 16. See also 9 note 18.

---

37 Relating to an intellectual dialogue.

xi. Elizabeth L. Eisenstein, "An Unacknowledged Revolution Revisited," *American Historical Review* 107.1 (2002): 87–105, 88.

xii. William Bouwsma, "Review of Eisenstein, *The Printing Press as an Agent of Change*," *American Historical Review* 84 (1979): 1356–57, 1357.

xiii. Michael Warner, *The Letters of the Republic: Publication and the Public Sphere in Eighteenth-Century America* (Cambridge, MA: Harvard UP, 1990), xi, 5, 7, 5.

xiv. Adrian Johns, *The Nature of the Book: Print and Knowledge in the Making* (Chicago: U of Chicago P, 1998), 10, 19, 2. For a more recent commentary, see Johns, "How to acknowledge a revolution," *American Historical Review* 107 (2002): 106–25.

xv. Eisenstein, "An Unacknowledged Revolution Revisited," 88, note 9.

xvi. Sabrina Alcorn Baron, Eric N. Lindquist, and Eleanor F. Shevlin (eds.), *Agent of Change: Print Culture Studies after Elizabeth L. Eisenstein*, Studies in Print Culture and the History of the Book (Amherst: U of Massachusetts P, 2007; in association with The Center for the Book, Library of Congress). This volume contains essays by Ann Blair, Roger Chartier, Peter Stallybrass, and myself, among others.

xvii. Raymond Williams, *Keywords: A Vocabulary of Culture and Society* (New York: Oxford UP, 1985), 90, 88. See also Williams, *Culture and Society, 1780–1950* (New York: Harper & Row, 1966); A.L. Kroeber and Clyde Kluckhohn, *Culture: A Critical Review of Concepts and Definitions* (New York: Vintage Books, 1952); and Clifford Siskin, *The Work of Writing: Literature and Social Change in Britain, 1700–1830* (Baltimore: Johns Hopkins UP, 1998), 72–74.

xviii. Williams 1966, xiv.

xix. Alexander Pope, *The Dunciad in Four Books* [1743], ed. Valerie Rumbold, Longman Annotated Texts (New York: Longman/Pearson Education, 1999), 70. Emphasis added.

xx. McLuhan, *The Gutenberg Galaxy: The Making of Typographic Man*, 147, 255.

xxi. Michael Treadwell, "London Printers and Printing Houses in 1705," *Publishing History* 7 (1980): 5–44, 6. I explore some of the implications of the lapse of the Licensing Act in Paula McDowell, *The Women of Grub Street: Press, Politics, and Gender in the London Literary Marketplace, 1678–1730* (Oxford: Clarendon P, 1998). See also John Feather, *A History of British Publishing* (London: Routledge, 1988), and Raymond Asbury, "The Renewal of the Licensing Act in 1693 and Its Lapse in 1965," *Library*, 5th ser., 33 (1978): 296–322.

xxii. James, *To the Honourable House of Commons. Gentlemen, Since You have been pleased to lay such a heavy Tax upon Paper*, n.d. (c. 1696–98), reprinted in Elinor James, *Elinor James: Essential Works*, ed. Paula McDowell, The Early Modern Englishwoman, series 2: Printed Writings, 1641–1700; part 2, vol. 11. (Aldershot: Ashgate, 2005), 96–97. James was the grandmother of Jacob Hive [...].

xxiii. James Raven, "The Book Trades," in *Books and Their Readers in Eighteenth-Century England: New Essays*, ed. Isabel Rivers (London: Leicester UP, 2001), 1–34, 1.

xxiv. Alvin B. Kernan, *Samuel Johnson and the Impact of Print* (Princeton, NJ: Princeton UP, 1989), 48, 9.

xxv. See, for instance, Kernan's reading of Pope through the lens of McLuhan in Alvin B. Kernan, *Samuel Johnson and the Impact of Print* (Princeton, NJ: Princeton UP, 1989), 8–16.

xxvi. J. McLaverty, *Pope, Print, and Meaning* (Oxford: Oxford UP, 2001), 1. See also David F. Foxon, *Pope and the Early Eighteenth-Century Book Trade*, Lyell Lectures, 1975–1976, rev. and ed. James McLaverty (Oxford: Clarendon P, 1991).

xxvii. Pope, *The Dunciad in Four Books*, 34.

xxviii. Jonathan Swift, *A Tale of a Tub and Other Works*, eds. Angus Ross and David Woolley (Oxford: Oxford UP, 1999), 18.

xxix. Ibid., 70. [...].

xxx. McLuhan, *The Gutenberg Galaxy*, 147.

xxxi. Kernan, *Samuel Johnson and the Impact of Print*, 15.
xxxii. See, for instance, *An Epistle from Mr. Pope, to Dr. Arbuthnot* (London, 1734), in which Pope repeatedly uses the word "print," but only as a verb.
xxxiii. Paul Starr, *The Creation of the Media: The Political Origins of Modern Communications* (New York: Basic Books, 2004), 1–7 and passim.
xxxiv. Pope, *The Dunciad in Four Books*, 97, 1:2.
xxxv. McLuhan, *The Gutenberg Galaxy*, 255.
xxxvi. Pope, *The Dunciad in Four Books*, 2: 221–268.
xxxvii. Swift, *A Tale of a Tub*, 2.
xxxviii. Ibid., 75. Emphasis in original.
xxxix. Pope, *The Dunciad in Four Books*, 2: 31; 247–58.
xl. Marcus Walsh, "Text, 'Text,' and Swift's A Tale of a Tub," *The Modern Language Review* 85.2 (1990): 290–303, 291.
xli. Anon., *An Enquiry: Whether Oral Tradition or the Sacred Writings, Be the Safest Conservatory and Conveyance of Divine Truths, Down from Their Original Delivery, through All Succeeding Ages in Two Parts* (London: Printed for Robert Clavel, 1685), A4r.
xlii. Swift, *A Tale of a Tub*, 38.
xliii. Ibid., 39 n.
xliv. Ibid., 40 n.
xlv. Nicholas Hudson, "'Oral Tradition': The Evolution of an Eighteenth-Century Concept," *Tradition in Transaction: Women Writers, Marginal Texts, and the Eighteenth-Century Canon*, ed. Alvaro Ribeiro, S.J., and James G. Basker (Oxford: Clarendon P, 1996), 161–76, 165. I have also benefited here from Hudson's "O *Divinum Scripturae Beneficium*!"
xlvi. Joseph-François Lafitau, *Customs of the American Indians Compared with the Customs of Primitive Times* [1724], ed. and trans. William N. Fenton and Elizabeth L. Moore. 2 vols. (Toronto: Champlain Society, 1974–77), 1: lxxxvi. Lafitau's work was originally published as *Moeurs des sauvages amériquains, comparées aux moeurs des premiers temps*.
xlvii. Significantly, Wood's essay was first published privately in 1767 and 1769 as *An Essay on the Original Genius of Homer* [no place of publication given on title page]. Only after his death in 1771 was the title changed to *An Essay on the Original Genius and Writings of Homer* (London, 1775).
xlviii. Jean-Jacques Rousseau, *Essay on the Origin of Languages* [c. 1762–63], reprinted in Jean-Jacques Rousseau and Gottfried Herder, *Two Essays on the Origin of Language*, ed. and trans. John H. Moran and Alexander Gode (Chicago: U of Chicago P, 1966), 24. Rousseau also briefly speculates that Homer might have been unable to write.
xlix. Stewart, *Elements of the Philosophy of the Human Mind*, Part 1 [1792], reprinted in Dugald Stewart, *The Collected Works of Dugald Stewart*, ed. William Hamilton. 11 vols. (Edinburgh: T. Constable and Co., 1854–60), 2: 391.
l. Robert Wood, *An Essay on the Original Genius and Writings of Homer* (London: Printed by H. Hughs for T. Payne and P. Elmsly, 1775), 260.
li. Thomas Sheridan, *A Course of Lectures on Elocution* [1762] (New York: B. Blom, 1968), xii.
lii. Hugh Blair, *Lectures on Rhetoric and Belles Lettres* [rev. ed., 1785], ed. Linda Ferreira-Buckley and S. Michael Halloran (Carbondale: Southern Illinois UP, 2005), 74.
liii. Sheridan, *A Course of Lectures on Elocution*, 247.
liv. Thomas Percy (ed.), *Reliques of Ancient Poetry, Consisting of Old Heroic Ballads, Songs, and Other Pieces of Our Earlier Poets, Together with Some Few of Later Date* [3 vols., 1765], ed. Henry B. Wheatley (New York: Dover, 1886; reprint, 1966), preface 1: 7; appendix 1: 348, 380.

lv. I argue this in detail in "'The Art of Printing Was Fatal'" (Paula McDowell, "'The Art of Printing Was Fatal': Print Culture and the Idea of Oral Tradition in Eighteenth-Century Ballad Discourse," *British Ballads and Broadsides, 1550–1800*, ed. Patricia Fumerton and Anita Guerrini [Aldershot: Ashgate P, 2010]) and "'The Manufacture and Lingua-facture of *Ballad-Making*" (Paula McDowell, "'The Manufacture and Lingua-facture of *Ballad-Making*': Broadside Ballads in Long Eighteenth-Century Ballad Discourse," *Eighteenth Century: Theory and Interpretation* 47.2–3 [2006]: 151–78). See also Maureen McLane's essay in this volume [i.e., *This Is Enlightenment*, where this essay originally appeared] ("Dating Orality, Thinking Balladry: Of Milkmaids and Minstrels in 1771," *Eighteenth Century: Theory and Interpretation*, 47.2–3 [2006]: 131–34.)

lvi. John Pinkerton, *Scottish Tragic Ballads* (London: J. Nichols, 1781), ix-xxvii, x. Emphasis added.

lvii. Ibid., xv.

lviii. William Motherwell, *Minstrelsy, Ancient and Modern* [1827], 2 vols. (Boston: W.D. Ticknor & Co., 1846), 1:3.

lix. See Joseph Addison and Richard Steele, *The Spectator*, 5 vols., ed. Donald Frederic Bond (Oxford: Clarendon P, 1965), 70 (21 May 1711), 74 (25 May 1711), and 85 (7 June 1711).

lx. For recent attempts to undo this binary, see Fumerton and Guerrini, *Ballads and Broadsides 1500–1800* (Burlington, VT: Ashgate, 2010); Ruth Perry (ed.), "Ballads and Songs in the Eighteenth Century," Spec. issue, *Eighteenth Century: Theory and Interpretation* 47.2–3 (2006); [McLane, "Dating Orality"]; and McDowell, "The Manufacture."

lxi. Eisenstein, *The Printing Press as an Agent of Change*, 184.

lxii. Elizabeth Eisenstein, *Print Culture and Enlightenment Thought*, Hanes Lecture. Hanes Foundation, Rare Book Collection/University Library (Chapel Hill: U of North Carolina, 1986), 6.

lxiii. See Mary Poovey, *A History of the Modern Fact: Problems of Knowledge in the Sciences of Wealth and Society* (Chicago: U of Chicago P, 1998), especially 15.

lxiv. Johannes Fabian suggests that the "denial of coevalness" of actually coexisting peoples is a "constitutive phenomenon" of the modern discipline of anthropology, a discipline whose origins he traces to this period (Matti Bunzl, foreword to Johannes Fabian, *Time and the Other: How Anthropology Makes Its Object* [New York: Columbia UP, 2003], x-xi).

lxv. See, for instance, Blair's "Critical Dissertation on the Poems of Ossian," where he explicitly links the characteristics of Ossian's oral poetry to his "very remote aera": "there are four great stages through which men successively pass in the progress of society. The first and earliest is the life of hunters; pasturage succeeds to this, as the ideas of property begin to take root; next agriculture; and lastly, commerce. Throughout Ossian's poems, we plainly find ourselves in the first of these periods of society" (reprinted in James Macpherson, *The Poems of Ossian and Related Works*, ed. Howard Gaskill [Edinburgh: Edinburgh UP, 1996], 345–408; 353).

lxvi. Ronald L. Meek, *Social Science and the Ignoble Savage* (Cambridge: Cambridge UP, 1976), 242. See also McLane, "Dating Orality," which shows how James Beattie's poem "The Minstrel; or, The Progress of Genius" adapts stadial theory to theorize the evolution of poetry since "rude ages."

lxvii. James Burnett Monboddo, *Origin and Progress of Language*, 6 vols., 2 (Edinburgh: Printed for J. Balfour and T. Cadell, 1773–92), 24–25.

lxviii. Antoine-Nicolas de Condorcet, [1795; orig. French 1793], *Sketch for a Historical Picture of the Progress of the Human Mind*, trans. June Barraclough, with intro. by Stuart Hampshire (London: Weidenfeld and Nicolson, 1955), 4.

lxix. Ibid., 8.

lxx. Ibid., 9.

lxxi. Ibid., 7.

lxxii. Ibid., 99.

lxxiii. Ibid., 8, 171.

lxxiv. Stewart, *Life ... of Adam Smith* [1793], reprinted in Hamlton, ed., *Works* (1854–60), 10: 54.

lxxv. Mary Poovey, *A History of the Modern Fact: Problems of Knowledge in the Sciences of Wealth and Society* (Chicago: U of Chicago P, 1998), 15.

lxxvi. Stewart, *Elements of the Philosophy of the Human Mind*, Part 1 [1792], reprinted in Hamilton, ed., *Works* (1854–60), 2: 391.

lxxvii. Alexandra Walsham, "Reformed Folklore? Cautionary Tales and Oral Tradition in Early Modern England," *The Spoken Word: Oral Culture in Britain, 1500–1850*, ed. Adam Fox and D.R. Woolf (Manchester: Manchester UP, 2002), 173–95, 173.

lxxviii. For a concise critique of the "stages" model of media shift, see Harold Love, "Early Modern Print Culture: Assessing the Models," *Paregon: Journal of the Australian and New Zealand Association for Medieval and Early Modern Studies* 20.1 (2003): 45–64.

25.
Matt Cohen,
"Native Audiences,"
The Networked Wilderness: Communicating in Early New England. Minneapolis: U of Minnesota P, 2010. 29–64

Matt Cohen (b. 1970) is an Associate Professor in the Department of English at the University of Texas, Austin, where he works in the fields of early American literature, digital humanities, and the history of the book. In *The Networked Wilderness* (2010), he examines the complex communication systems that prevailed in the early settlement of New England. Like Paula McDowell (pp. 395–415), Cohen is interested in the relation between oral and print cultures, and, like her, he doesn't see print culture as simply superseding or absorbing oral culture. Indeed, one of his principal aims is to re-think the narrative that interprets settler and native clashes as a struggle between print and oral culture (with the former dominating the latter). On the one hand, within settler communities "eloquence and rumor were as much a source of power as writing" (p. 1); on the other hand, indigenous communication was not entirely oral, as "totemic symbols, wampum,[1] and other physical forms carried messages, even over long distances" (p. 2). He asks how our scholarly methods would change if we conceived of "Natives and English [as] both oral and inscribing peoples," suggesting a model of "multimedia literacy" as "a better characterization of American communication norms" (p. 2).

Cohen's methodology is potentially far-reaching for the discipline of book history, insofar as he shows that book-historical methods can be used to examine not merely written texts and even oral exchanges, but also other media of communication, such as "traps, paths, wampum, monuments, medical rituals, and other messaging systems," all of which are sites of meaning that can be interpreted and decoded (p. 4). The subject of the chapter excerpted below, titled "Native Audiences," is Thomas Morton's Maypole festival. Here Cohen argues that Morton's Maypole functioned as a "publishing venue," that it was at once an invitation to trade and "a tool for distributing information publicly" both orally and in writing (in the form of oral pronouncements and handwritten notices attached to the pole). According to Cohen, Morton's Maypole opened up a new public space that challenged the Pilgrim leaders' efforts to control communication. Cohen proceeds to examine the reception of this Maypole performance by the multiple audiences who witnessed it in person as well as those in New England, England, and Holland who read his account of it in *New English Canaan* (1637).

---

1 Wampum are traditional sacred beads of the Eastern woodland tribes of northeastern North America. They were often used by colonists as currency to trade with Native Americans.

Native Audiences

Thomas Morton's Maypole,[2] at the plantation he called Ma-re Mount, once served as an axis of revelry and outrage. First Natives and ambitious fur traders danced around it, and then angry Puritans circled it, closing in to destroy it. Once it took narrative form in Morton's *New English Canaan* (1637), it began a career as an axis not in space but in time for at least two ongoing stories and their successive tellers. For students of Native American culture, Morton's work is considered one of the most reliable accounts of contact-era northeastern woodlands societies. In this historical ethnography, the Maypole ceremony stands as an unspoken ideal of ethnic harmony and non-violent, cross-cultural curiosity. For American literary history, Morton's story has been a powerful one, drawn on by writers from Washington Irving to Robert Lowell,[3] Morton's persecution and complaint seeming to voice the struggle of an imaginative writer against a politicized, unironic publishing regime. Morton's invocation as part of a story that authors have told about themselves, fashioning themselves for the literary marketplace, has helped bolster teleological[4] critical readings of the development of American literature. The inevitable theme of American imaginative writing, such readings imply, is an ongoing confrontation between carnivalesque democratic liberalism and prudish aristocratic conservatism.

Morton's appeal changes when it is re-situated in the context of the production and reception of *New English Canaan* by three audiences: in England, in the Native American eastern woodlands, and in the Dutch printing world of fugitive English writers.[i] In form, this chapter will join

the Maypole dance, taking hold of the ribbons of evidence about each of these three audiences in turn, joining and then backing away from the interpretive carnival Morton's work has generated. Bringing the history of the book to bear on Morton's text, those who teach texts by Morton and his nemesis William Bradford[5] can begin to move beyond Hawthornian[6] comedy-versus-prudery readings of American cultural production. As a result, a different, more sophisticated sense of what colonists felt was at stake when they wrote about themselves and America emerges. Morton's Maypole and his *New English Canaan*, both of which explicitly raised issues of public communication and **literacy** in the northern settlements, can be used instead to sketch out a conflict over information cultures and social power in early New England.

The tension between Thomas Morton and both the Pilgrims (at Plymouth) and the Puritans (at Massachusetts Bay) has been an enduring, productively controversial episode for cultural historians of New England. What made these religious dissenters pursue Morton

---

2 Thomas Morton (c. 1579–1647), anti-Puritanical early American colonist; a Maypole is the centerpiece of the May Day celebrations, including a dance involving decorative ribbons.

3 Washington Irving (1783–1859), early American writer; Robert Lowell (1917–77), American confessional poet.

4 An interpretation that sees a process as developing toward a purposeful end.

5 William Bradford (1590–1657), English Puritan leader who became the governor of the Plymouth Colony in New England.

6 Nathaniel Hawthorne (1804–64), American writer noted for his stark, moralistic stories and novels.

so violently? Scholars have pointed to Morton's paganism as a psychological threat and his fur-trading with Natives as an economic one. Yet the dent he made in Plymouth's economic interests was minor, and the psychic problems Morton's merrymaking posed to a supposedly blunt, humorless Pilgrim leadership provoked one of the longest and wittiest sections in William Bradford's *Of Plymouth Plantation*.[ii]

This chapter argues that while Morton's poems were important, it was more particularly his mode of presenting them that constituted the core of his challenge to the Pilgrims. Religious leaders tried to exert a stern censorship over communication in all forms in New England, and this conditioned early colonial culture in profound ways.[iii] Publishing something in the seventeenth century, we have come to understand, had a meaning broader than its print-bound connotations today—it included posting or proclaiming documents in a public place. This was the method Morton first chose to publicize his densely allusive poetry.

For Bradford and the Puritan settlers' other leaders, a centralized communications structure was the foundation of a sustainable community, but technologies of communication in early New England were diverse. They included posted **manuscript** messages, letters, oral proclamations (usually from the pulpit), printed texts (usually from Europe), song, and word of mouth (often during commercial transactions). Diaries and journals that might be considered private today were often shared, family Bibles were used to record lineage, and it was not uncommon for worshippers to memorize and transcribe sermons. Settlers invented and adapted a host of methods for communicating with American Indians, from using translators to drawing pictograms or consulting language guides.[iv] 419

Religious leaders among the settlers, as eager to escape the censorship of England as to establish a community of saintly worship, constantly struggled to keep these technologies under their control. They seldom succeeded thoroughly.[v] Morton's liberties—both in form and content—struck at the heart of this mechanism of social power. What the settlers described as Morton's rebellious immorality was in fact one expression of his self-inscription in international intellectual currents, a priority that would become clear in *New English Canaan*.[vi] This account extended the challenge that the Maypole poems began and, within a transatlantic print sphere, dramatized the episode at Morton's Ma-re Mount as a collision of ideas about communication. As my analytical dance around the Maypole hopes to show, the book served as a stage for a contest over communication and colonization that involved at least three systems—English, Native American, and Dutch.

I. "Their Postures That So Much Bewitch"

The historical outline of Morton's involvement with the Pilgrims and the Puritans is an essential starting ground.[vii] Thomas Morton came to New England in 1625 with a man named Captain Wollaston as one of the partners in a private colonizing venture. Morton was a lawyer and no spring chicken; by best estimates he was over forty years old when he first came to America. (Morton's subsequent revels may sound like an early modern version of a fraternity party at first reading, but they were not the product of mere youthful irreverence in a new land.)[viii] Not long after establishing their plantation, Wollaston left for Virginia with most of the plantation's men, whose terms of service he sold once they arrived. Together with the remaining men, Morton expelled the lieutenant who had been left to keep order, took over the plantation himself, and renamed it Ma-re Mount.[ix] In the course of developing fur trade connections and exploring his land, Morton began carousing with the Native Americans in the vicinity. He revived old English holidays, beginning with the May Day festival.[7] As one historian has observed, this act implicitly associated his plantation with contemporary English state-sponsored strategies of "conservative cultural revival" that attempted to direct nostalgia for the Elizabethan age into popular opposition to the Puritans.[x] Morton, too, was competitive in the fur trade, boldly outmaneuvering the Pilgrims for furs on the Kennebec River.

Arrested by Plymouth authorities in the spring of 1628, Morton was deported to England, under the official charge of selling guns to the natives. He came back about a year later (since the English officials insisted on demonstrable evidence of his crimes, and there was none) and was soon arrested again by the new Massachusetts Bay colony. Once more banished to England, during the next few years Morton wrote and published *New English Canaan*, an account of his travails, the customs of the Natives, and the natural world of New England. The publication of the book was, in part, a political ploy to support another of his activities during this time—an attempt in 1634 to get the royal Privy Council[8] to revoke the patent for the Massachusetts Bay colony by way of a quo warranto[9] suit against the settlers. Morton served both as a witness and as a solicitor in the suit. After more than a decade, spurred to emigrate by the success of the Puritan revolution, he returned to North America. He was taken prisoner yet again after being denounced by John Winthrop and died shortly after his release from jail.[xi]

The colonists used extensive legal acrobatics to get Morton repeatedly into custody; "the very savagery of his treatment at the hands of the Pilgrim fathers and the Puritan magistracy," Michael Zuckerman observes, "suggests that they knew all too well that in his freedom there was something extraordinary at stake."[xii] The consensus among historians has been that the extraordinary something was Morton's interference with Plymouth's fur trade. Karen Kupperman points out, "Plymouth could not pay off its debts to its English backers without control of the New England fur trade."[xiii] This explanation has become the dominant one; even literary critics have assumed the underlying economic rationalism of the Puritans, in part because it seems evident that differences over lifestyle choices could not have been severe enough to warrant the exertions required to deport Morton in Plymouth's difficult early days.

Yet this does not explain why Morton continued to appear to be a threat into his dotage (he was about 69 years old when he was released from jail after Winthrop's accusations). Nor does it explain why in at least one document justifying Plymouth's action Bradford does not emphasize the gun trafficking charge as a factor. Economically, Morton was a small competitor among many

7 Holiday celebration that began in medieval Europe; the Puritans considered it to be a pagan holiday.

8 A committee of the monarch's closest advisors who gave advice on affairs of state.

9 A writ requiring the person to whom it is directed to show by what authority they act.

others and never came close to making a fortune in the New England trade. But when Morton's Maypole and his narrative about the colony are read in the context of the history of European colonial and indigenous American communications networks and their importance to social power, his incursions loom larger. They emerge as a threat more to delicate and experimental political structures than to the momentary economic competitiveness of Plymouth. Morton's opposition defined itself explicitly by its use of print, literacy, and publication to challenge authority structures built on control over those modes of communication.

Let us think of the Maypole as a publishing venue. Morton himself refers to it as a kind of beacon for traders, but if we see it as a sophisticated communications tool, with poems tacked on for communal reading in a public place, it assumes a different significance. Fourteen years before the first printing press was established in Cambridge, Massachusetts Bay, Morton built a tool for distributing information publicly—and for creating a space of authority for oral proclamations as well—that competed with the Pilgrim leaders' control over local oral and written exchanges. It is significant that Morton deliberately includes the detail that the Maypole was erected with the help of Natives, for they emerge as his touchstone in the claim against Puritan authority: "And upon May-day they brought the Maypole to the place appointed ... and there erected it with the help of Salvages, that came thether of purpose to see the manner of our Revels."[xiv] In this and the following two sections, I will move through the different performance environments compressed into this comment about the witnessing of "the manner of our Revels" to map how the audiences of English colonials dealing with Morton, his Algonquian trade partners, and the producers and consumers of *New English Canaan* in the Netherlands might have read this scene.

The most renowned content of the Maypole was a series of allegorical poems, presented as riddles or ciphers. It is unfortunate that more is not known about the way these controversial poems were circulated, beyond their posting on the Maypole. We can assume at least that they were in manuscript until transcribed (or recomposed) in *New English Canaan*. English observers on both sides of the incident point to the presence of the poems on the pole during the May Day ceremony and to the Maypole itself as the locus of Morton's power. John Endicott even took extra trouble at a dangerous time of year to cut the pole down before his settlement party made camp at Salem for the winter.[xv] From the standpoint of communications technologies, the life cycle of Morton's poems looks something like this: he first published them in manuscript in (and to help create) a makeshift, negotiated public sphere; in all likelihood he established their validity with an oral performance; and finally, after encountering resistance, he upped the ante by releasing them in an established print sphere—Europe.[xvi]

Past readings of these poems have focused on their content—certainly the dense intermingling, unprioritized and untypological,[10] of classical and biblical references must have infuriated the plain-speaking, iconoclastic Pilgrim leaders.[xvii] In composing them, Morton used both an ironic narrative voice and a knowledge of his neighbors' rhetoric to attack their authority. As Hall has emphasized, Puritan preachers at this time increasingly borrowed from popular cultural

---

10 Biblical typology occurs when events in the Old Testament are read as foreshadowing events depicted in the New Testament or when figures from classical mythology are read as foreshadowing Biblical ones.

forms, including sensational poetry and stories, to boost the appeal and the accessibility of their spiritual message. Morton's use of poetry reversed this tactic, creating a poetry that was more difficult to understand, favoring the ludic,[11] nimble reading skips of participants in the revels against those of the not-understanding Puritan leaders.[xviii] By calling attention to the deliberate construction of this comprehension gap, Morton positioned both the form and the content of his poems as being constitutively at odds with Puritan reading practices.

But he implies an even more radical potential for his poetry as published on the Maypole. David Shields observes of riddle-poems, "Because riddles spoke to a wide audience, all who regarded themselves something more than witless, they invoked a general public. They could be considered the citizenship exam for membership in the republic of letters."[xix] This understanding of the relationship between form and audience is evocative for Morton's situation: the riddle could be used simultaneously to set boundaries on wit and on citizenship in his ideal plantation. Significantly, in this case those within the boundaries included a good number of Native Americans. Morton takes pains to point out that the residents of his plantation all knew what the poem meant. In making such a claim, Morton moves from a local reading community to an international one, implicitly relating the development of literacy to both university learning and the ideal of civil participation:

> And this the whole company of the Revellers at Ma-re Mount, knew to be the true sence and exposition of the riddle: that was fixed to the Maypole, which the Seperatists were at defiance with? some of them affirmed, that the first institution thereof, was in memory of a whore; not knowing that it was a Trophe erected at first, in honor of Maja, the Lady of learning which they despise; vilifying the two universities with uncivile termes; accounting what is there obtained by studdy is but unnecessary learning; not considering that learninge does inable mens mindes to converse with climents of a higher nature then is to be found within the habitation of the Mole.[xx]

Morton's publishing tactic restricts proper interpretation to a specific, deviant sector of New England's settlements—anathema to the Pilgrim leaders' sense of community structure and the flow of information controlled by religious leaders. Control of literacy, and by extension the parameters of interpretation ("the true sence and exposition"), was seen as essential to the survival of a dissenting religious group. Whatever the Natives' actual participation in Morton's community, Morton's positioning of the Native Americans against the Pilgrims in the field of English ideas about literacy is a radical juxtaposition.[xxi]

New English Canaan makes a complex argument for a plural, literate culture of intellectual exchange, and it makes this argument in part by representing Indians as protoliterate by English standards of the time—as already involved in Morton's world of information **circulation**. By contrast, the Pilgrim leaders are depicted as manipulating a half-literate set of followers,

---

11 Spontaneously playful.

reinforcing their power by restricting interpretation and making, as one of Morton's **marginal** notes declares, "*Booke learning despised.*"[xxii] This argument begins early in Morton's book. Performing a linguistic analysis on chosen Algonquian words in comparison to Latin and Greek terms, Morton asserts a common theory of the time: that the "originall of the Natives of New England may be well conjectured to be from the scattered Trojans, after such time as Brutus departed from Latium."[xxiii] Evidence from language and speech performances is significant for Morton, who points out that the dynamics of encounter tend to produce creolization:[12] "this is commonly seene where 2. Nations traffique together, the one indevouring to understand the others meaning makes them both many times speak a mixed language, as is approoved by the Natives of New England, through the covetous desire they have, to commerce with our nation, and wee with them."[xxiv] Sandra Gustafson reminds us of the intellectual context in which Morton was reading and recording his experience with American languages:

> Speech, too, has its technologies, as Renaissance students of rhetoric knew well. Humanists who sought to recuperate the ancient world developed a shared understanding of "the central role of rhetorical skill and achievement in human affairs." ... To Europeans in the age of humanistic eloquence, oratory was the most recognizable native speech genre as well as the one most crucial for them to interpret.[xxv]

Morton also claims that "it seemes originally, [they] have had some litterature amongst them, 423
which time hath Cancelled and worne out of use."[xxvi] "Literature" in this context can only mean an oral tradition, but Morton's explanation of its disappearance is phrased elliptically. "Worne out" evokes a sense of physical decay, as of a manuscript, while "use" implies instead a gradual decline in the social need, consistent with the phases of oral transmission. It is as if Morton were uncomfortable with the idea of speech technologies powerful enough to sustain a tradition almost from the time of Ilium,[13] as he proposes.

An often-cited incident, in which Morton teaches a Native how to read, initiates a more direct undermining of non-conformist Protestant concepts of literacy. Morton structures this attack by building a contrast between the Native capacity for, desire for, and participation in Morton's linguistic sphere and the dissenters' irresponsible use of theirs—both with the Americans and with their own worshippers. The key in this argument is his use of the *Book of Common Prayer*, which the Separatists[14] rejected. As Morton tells the story, he uses the pronoun "we" to reify what he considers the responsible approach to colonizing "them," the Americans—a binary logic that thus shuts out the Separatists entirely:

---

12 The mixing of cultures that can produce new languages and cultural identities.

13 Ancient city in present-day Turkey; more commonly known as Troy, centerpiece of the Trojan War, most famously described in Homer's *Iliad*.

14 The Puritans were separatists who left England in order to separate themselves from the state-backed Anglican Church (or the Church of England).

> And that wee that use the booke of Common prayer, doo it to declare to them, that cannot reade, what Kytan has commaunded us, and that wee doe pray to him with the helpe of that booke; and doe make so much accompt of it, that a Salvage (who had lived in my howse before hee had taken a wife, by whome hee had children) made this request to mee.... That I would let his sonne be brought up in my howse, that hee might be taught to reade in that booke: which request of his I granted; and hee was a very joyfull man to thinke, that his sonne should thereby (as hee said) become an Englishman.[xxvii]

This is a fascinating passage in many ways, from Morton's dramatization of the religious lesson (substituting the Algonquian term "Kytan" for God) to his ventriloquization[15] of an Indian in the act of offering that powerful evidence of successful, beneficent English colonization: demonstration of the belief that language acquisition creates a kind of citizenship. In the context of his larger argument, this passage performs the work of showing Native capacity to learn while simultaneously claiming that Morton's paternalistic, text-based method is one that produces Native desire for Englishness.

Morton spins the tangled political web initiated by Native literacy by deprecating the usual apical[16] stage of mastery, writing proficiency. Instead, his narrative valorizes indigenous skills in oral presentation and readiness to learn English as being potentially as powerful as writing—

and as racial qualities that must be properly nurtured.[xxviii] However lackadaisical they may have been about it in practice, in theory the settlers did not resist teaching Natives to read and speak English. But the methods Morton chose, and the rewards of literacy he offered, upset the social hierarchies Protestant English literacy was designed to create.

New English Canaan is a text that demands acrobatic reading practices capable of interpreting the topography of the page together with dense allusive content. At one point, Morton uses a bibliographical metaphor, the textual gloss (interpretive marginal commentary printed or written alongside an interlocutor's text), to make his literacy case in a slightly different way. A merchant comes ashore to find his plantation burned; the Pilgrims did it, but they blame it on Indians, "deploring the disaster of his Plantation and glozing upon the text, alledging the mischeivous intent of the Salvages there."[xxix] Morton himself is the victim of the next "glosse upon their malice," when he is arrested in chapter 15.[xxx] This metaphor makes fun of the Separatists' method of interpreting Scripture but becomes, as it recurs throughout the narrative, a more fundamental accusation that English non-conformists are using the technology of the textual gloss irresponsibly. As we will later see, the interpenetration of visual and textual elements on which Morton's text relies does not stop with the use of such metaphors.

---

15 The act of speaking for someone else.

16 Of or belonging to the apex; in other words, writing is conceived as a more sophisticated accomplishment than reading.

To complete his literacy argument, Morton removes himself from the picture momentarily and contrasts the Puritans and the Americans on the grounds of oral expression. In his discussion of the Americans in "Of Theire Subtilety," Morton praises their politics, tactics, and rhetoric (part 1, chapter 14). The centerpiece of "Of a Battle fought at the Massachussets, betweene the English and the Indians" is an example of powerful Native eloquence, quoted as the words of the sachem[17] of the Passonagessit territories, Chickatawbut, following the defacing of the grave of Chickatawbut's mother by the English (part 3, chapter 3). This speech projects a Native communications culture with an inextricable interplay of visual and verbal inscription. It ascribes to Indian political rhetoric a reliance on the diachronic[18] power of monuments that, reassuringly for his European audience, preserves familiar class distinctions:

> [A] spirit cried aloude (behold my sonne) whom I have cherisht, see the papps that gave thee suck, the hands that lappd thee warme and fed thee oft, canst thou forget to take revenge of those uild people, that hath my monument defaced in despitefull manner, disdaining our ancient antiquities, and honourable Customes: See now the Sachems grave lies like unto the common people, of ignoble race defaced: thy mother doth complaine, implores thy aide against this theevish people, new come hether.[xxxi]

This appeal to public memory is underwritten and authorized by a self-deprecatory distancing of the speaker. The first part of Chickatawbut's speech is reported as a message from this female "spirit," while the significance of the declaration is left open to communal designation, "to have your Councell, and your aide likewise."[xxxii] As such, the speech evidences a responsible use of power reminiscent, for European readers, of models from classical antiquity. Morton also points out that in the development and differentiation of vocabulary Americans are meticulous: "the Salvages are significant in their denomination of any thing."[xxxiii] Building on these assertions of linguistic and rhetorical competence, Morton finds it telling that the local Native word for Englishmen (which he claims originates in interactions with the Plymouth settlers) is "*Wotawquenange*, which in their language signifieth stabbers or Cutthroates."[xxxiv]

By contrast, when the colonial leaders speak, Morton argues, they fail to convince without appealing to fear and uncertainty. He insists that the Plymouth settlers—and by extension, non-conformist worshipers elsewhere—are being manipulated by speakers who, to an educated person, are not convincing:

> Socrates sayes, *loquere ut te videam.*[19] If a man observe these people in the exercise of their gifts, hee may thereby discerne the tincture of their proper calling, the asses eares will peepe through the lyons hide.... I will deale

17 A leader of a Native American tribe.

18 I.e., enduring.

19 Latin: Speak that I may know thee.

> fairely with them; for I will draw their pictures cap a pe,[20] that you may discerne them plainely from head to foote in their postures that so much bewitch ... these illiterate people to be so fantasticall, to take Ionas taske[21] upon them without sufficient warrant.[xxxv]

Here Morton offers remediation, in which his writing translates a deceptive **orality**: he will "draw" for us readers in the correct "tincture" what is obscured by the oral projections of Separatist orators. (He even uncharacteristically re-phrases his own foreign phrases in this section, exemplifying the openness he claims the non-conformists lack.) This argument is crucial to Morton's claims that preaching—the chief power mechanism of the Puritan and Separatist leaders—misleads the illiterate, as compared to the text and community-based experience of literacy seen in the examples of the Maypole and the American boy he claims to have taught to read.

[...]

While the tiny circulation of *New English Canaan* prevented any studied response among the settlers to Morton's claims about Native literacy, the Puritan leaders' reactions to the Maypole and the poems show an awareness of its potential as an alternative publishing space. In a private letter to Sir Ferdinando Gorges justifying their arrest of Morton, for example, Bradford did not stress the official charge of gun trading:

> That which further presseth us to send this party, is the fear we have of the growing of him and his consorts to that strength and height, by the access of loose persons, his house be a receptacle for such, as we should not be able to restrain his inordinariness when we would, they living without all fear of God or common honesty, some of them abusing the Indian women most filthily, as it is notorious.[xxxvi]

Bradford's diction here is in some ways deliberately deceptive. The pronoun "we," as it did in Morton's narrative, establishes a communal norm that is threatened. But Morton ("his") increases to "they" when "loose persons" are added, performing grammatically the population growth Bradford fears at Ma-re Mount. "Loose" here signifies settlers unassociated with any particular plantation and possibly Americans as well, but could also have implied immorality, wantonness.[xxxvii] Bradford thus allows the mission to take on moral and political importance without saying so explicitly until the issue of the presence of indigenous women at the plantation is raised. Accusations of interracial sexuality and the presumption that Plymouth should be able to "restrain" Morton ("to restrain his inordinariness when we would") run together in the same sentence. That the activities of Ma-re Mount could be "notorious" was fundamental

20 Head to foot.

21 Jonas (the Greek and Latin name is Ionas) from the Old Testament was sent to Nineveh to preach.

to the problem. Morton's publishing tactics were working to produce a rumored "inordinariness," the exact nature of which had to be left vague, as a potential, in order to justify taking him by force.

Of Plymouth Plantation, while more witty, exhibits the same semantic struggles to re-shape Morton's challenge in moral terms. In his famous description of the Maypole, Bradford moves from drinking to dancing to interracial "frisking," then adds a sentence fragment in an attempt to get at the delusionary quality of this carnival:

> They also set up a maypole, drinking and dancing about it many days together, inviting the Indian women for their consorts, dancing and frisking together like so many fairies, or furies, rather; and worse practices. As if they had anew revived and celebrated the feasts of the Roman goddess Flora, or the beastly practices of the mad Bacchanalians.[xxxviii] [22]

Bradford here parries the implied ironic hysteria of the scene he is describing with his own accusatory pun—"fairies" becoming "furies"—but loses control of his pronouns, allowing the Indians to become in readers' imaginations part of the "they" that "had anew revived" heathen celebrations. While Bradford's text parries Morton's accusations both of Pilgrim dullness and ignorance of classical tradition, it dangerously (by its own standards) permits Native Americans to participate in Englishness (however reprehensible) and borders on prurience[23] in its obsession with "riotous prodigality and profuse excess."[xxxix] The threat of Morton's publishing venue called forth a risky response as leaders like Bradford tried to make themselves appear to be more responsible administrators of American systems.

II. American Audiences

But how much were American Indians participating in Englishness in Morton's revels? And perhaps more important, what would it mean to consider not just the "native" audience of Englishmen to which Morton was writing, but the Native Americans he and the Pilgrims depended on for both food and financial gain as an audience for his Maypole writings? One of the paradoxes of the study of print culture in early New England is that not many people at the time read the texts that have become central to the study of the northeastern contact zone. Morton's work, which was printed in Amsterdam, was not read widely because many copies of the book were confiscated at the docks as a result of English strictures on foreign-printed books in English. Certainly few copies made it to America.[xl] It is possible that Morton's American audience for the Maypole festival was larger than the audience in his native England for *New English Canaan*. A consideration of these questions adds another layer to the implications of the Maypole episode and accounts of it, prompting a methodological shift in my argument.

---

22 Flora is the Roman goddess of flowers and spring; Bacchus is the Roman god of wine and intoxication.

23 Excessive fascination or curiosity about sexual matters.

On one level, Morton's inclusion of Natives was at least as much a rhetorical device as it was a recording of a fact, when it came to English literacy. There is unfortunately no known evidence other than Morton's account and panicked reactions from the Pilgrims to suggest the specific ways in which Natives were involved in Morton's literary circle. Morton, according to recent scholars, appears to have had an admirable command of the language of the Algonquians he encountered.[xli] It is entirely possible, as he suggests in New English Canaan, that Morton delivered orally some version of the poems during the May Day festivities. By his own account quoted above, at one point he shepherded a Native to literacy in English, at least to speaking and reading. (Certainly later it was not uncommon for Native youths to be raised as servants in white households partly for this purpose.) And Jack Dempsey has pointed out that Morton's poems hail a Native audience by including American events such as the devastating sickness brought on by European contact in 1616–19.[xlii] But as Kupperman observes in *Indians and English*, New World narratives from the exploration and settlement era made a series of conventional arguments that had to balance claims that American Indians were allies and assets with legitimate accounts of the problems they posed. The colonists knew that if they made the Americans out to be completely savage, it "would imply a devastating comment on the American environment and its capability of sustaining complex cultures ... The American natives in these early works were ready to be taught, and ripe for study."[xliii]

[...]

428 In the case of the Maypole, the notion of the homograph can serve as a way of beginning to address the question of the links between English and Native American audiences. Literally, a "homograph" is a "word of the same written form as another but of a different origin and meaning," such as "red," which indicates a color in English but a net in Spanish.[xliv] In what follows, the sense of what "word" means in this definition is broadened but still applies to either a material object (such as a Maypole) or an aggregation of gestures that require such a material context (the Maypole ritual, the ceremonial reading of poems from a sheet of paper). Such objects or gestures must also be recognized as the center of temporary apparent agreement about "meaning," regardless of the actual diversity of interpretations among observers. "Homograph," because it is a term grounded in the materiality of gesture or inscription, is more precise than "homolog," which could still suggest unanswerable metaphysical questions, leaving the problematic critical desire for understanding in place. Homo*graph* insists on the coincidence of inscribed or performed structures (which could conceivably be extended to homo*aurality*, difficult to recover though that would be), against the presumed logical or intellectual isomorphism[24] of the homolog. This concept has potential for structuring the analysis of moments in colonial situations in which communication was clearly happening independent of the assumption of understanding. The homograph as a communicative possibility haunts the belief that a common humanness or, even at its most equivocal, a meaningful connection of some kind that makes rationality imaginable necessarily underwrites communication.[xlv]

---

24 A one-to-one correspondence.

What might Morton's Native audience have been? It was presumably a group of Massachusett people, but possibly included travelers, traders, or wanderers from other eastern woodlands societies—and probably women as well as men. Several scholars have suggested that the Maypole ceremony might have made a certain kind of sense to the Native Americans who Morton claims helped him and his men put up the Maypole. What is hazarded here is based on linguistic, anthropological, and historical work on southeastern New England societies of the early seventeenth century (work that is examined in more depth in chapter 3 [of Cohen's book]). An obvious initial condition is the recognition that Morton was a comparatively astute European observer of Native culture; it is therefore entirely possible that he was using the May Day event to do purposeful culture brokering. Having told us about Native ceremonies that he had witnessed earlier in *New English Canaan*, Morton opens the possibility that, deliberately or not, with the Maypole and other more performative parts of the Maypole ceremony he created the kind of visual and aural affinity that might be called an intercultural homograph. The village-central poles that appear in many east coast Native archaeological sites and in some other European reports form the most obvious homograph with the Maypole (see Fig. 4.7 and Fig. 4.8).

These poles had military, gaming, and other uses associated with assembly, always intertwined with spiritual implications. Their specific symbolic capital is difficult to re-construct, but Kathleen Bragdon points out:

> Many Algonquian-speaking people believe that the Cosmic Axis, located at the center of the world, serves as a pathway through the openings in the layers of the universe. The Axis, like the World Cedar Tree, which emerges through this same pathway, connects the levels of the cosmos. In many recorded rituals, circular pits, lodges, or other ceremonial structures, placed at the point of intersection between earth and sky, and earth and underworld, represent a symbolic entrance to both worlds.

Morton's ceremony, anchored by a pole and occurring on a prominence, may have borne enough similarities to eastern Native social rituals to present itself as this kind of liminal or connecting ritual space.[xlvi]

The buck horns that Morton reports were placed at the top of the Maypole might have evoked Manitou, the Algonquian concept of spirit-power, by way of totemic signification, a system that associated animal names, and sometimes complete transformation into such animals, with particular kinship or social groups within a society. This affinity would have been sophisticated, involving a number of possible metonymies.[25] In terms of gender and sexuality, the buck horns, when combined with the Maypole, form a phenomenological common ground. The specific totem, the buck, would have carried both sexual or reproductive connotations and gender-role denotations based on food-gathering and maturity ritual patterns. Morton, whose plantation was engaged in fur trading, not agriculture, might have been read as attempting to signal his ability to

25 Metonymy is a figure of speech that stands in to substitute for or as a symbol of something else.

Fig. 4.7: Theodore DeBry's engraving of a Roanoke village depicts ritual posts (B and C). Note the specially shaped listening hut in cornfield (F), designed both to shelter a guard and to gather and focus (or project) sounds. The John Carter Brown Library at Brown University, Providence, Rhode Island.

Fig. 4.8: Diorama of Cofitachequi, Wateree Valley, as it might have appeared in 1540, featuring village-central poles. The South Carolina State Museum, Columbia, South Carolina. Photograph by Susan Dugan.

provide for his companions within the bounds of a culture that identified hunting and trapping with masculinity at all levels of the social hierarchy. Archaeological evidence from a Mohegan site in Connecticut "suggests that deer provided close to 90 per cent of the edible mammal meat in early contact times" in southern New England.[xlvii] Totemic signification here might have been functioning alongside, rather than overwriting, an economic or material meaning.

[...]

How the Maypole ceremony was enacted, then, would have been significant to American Indian observers. Morton's former life at the Inns of Court,[26] the surviving contemporary accounts of his character, and his use of elements from English performance culture in *New English Canaan* suggest that he had a flair for the dramatic. As a sachem figure, Morton would have been expected to lead the ceremonies, to hail his audience, and to solicit its responses as well.[xlviii] Perhaps Morton's holding forth, with a mixture of levity and gravity, looked familiar; and in particular, his inclusion of everyone—the specific mentioning of Natives at various points in his poems and songs—might have persuaded a Native audience that Morton respected the rhetorical norms of Indian country.

26 The group of official institutions for legal education and accreditation in England consisting of Inner Temple, Middle Temple, Lincoln's Inn, and Gray's Inn.

Lest this sound too utopian, too much like the culture-crossing hybrid manqué[27] of Morton's story popular from US fiction, it is useful to underscore that in this interpretation, Morton's homographesis was in the service of asymmetries of power. He advertised a domination-based relationship with the Natives that would be affected by learning, mastering, and putting to English use the extant communications techniques and material culture of the Natives. He would not have wanted the authority of either the *pawwaw*[28] or the warrior (unlike, perhaps, Edward Winslow or John Underhill, as we will see in later chapters [of Cohen's book]), but that of a sachem. This inverts our received interpretation of Morton's May Day event: the quality of misrule that *New English Canaan* attributes, tongue in cheek, to the festival may in fact have been only a print performance for the native English audience. For Morton's American audience, far from misrule, the manipulation of material and performative elements of public ritual, totemic signification, and sachemship would have constituted a claim to the establishment of order.

Finally, there is the question of what the presumably handwritten poems would have stood for, from the standpoint of Native American audiences. Germaine Warkentin, along with Peter Wogan, claims, against James Axtell and others, that "the importance of literacy to the ideology of European culture ... has obscured for us evidence suggesting that Native peoples took writing in their stride."[xlix] Warkentin's work on the ritual place of wampum as a sign-carrying mechanism—one that necessitated an accompanying performance in order to be decoded—suggests parallels with Morton's use of poetry and the Maypole. If the account in *New English Canaan* is roughly accurate, the poems were probably read out loud, oralized along with the songs Morton mentions, and then tacked in written form to the ceremonial post. Morton's public performance of the text, combined with its symbolic display on the pole and with the presumed generosity of the May Day feast, would have marked Morton as someone trying to command authority. Deliberately, accidentally, or something in between, Morton may have exploited "what Native signification systems seem to exploit with real cultural flair," in Warkentin's estimation, "the performative element that establishes a narrator, orator, or shaman[29] as a privileged reader charged with communicating the textual artifact's meaning."[l]

Still, it seems that Morton did not garner enough authority with the region's Natives to earn him powerful allies against Plymouth. As we will see in the next chapter [of Cohen's book], he was, for one thing, competing with savvy Separatist negotiators. He was also not collaborating with the powerful Narragansetts[30] or the rising star Massasoit of the Wampanoag.[31] But Native polities, too, might have had as many fears as Plymouth did about Morton's attempts to become a communications node in the area. For very different reasons, those fears might

---

27 I.e., failed or of unfulfilled potential.

28 "Among North American Indians: a priest, shaman, or healer" (*OED*).

29 A Native American religious healer.

30 A Native American tribe from present-day Rhode Island.

31 Massasoit (c. 1590–1661), chief of the Wampanoag tribe, an American tribe from present-day Massachusetts and Rhode Island.

equally have been rooted in the uses of the Maypole. But before returning to the question of Morton's fate and the communications system that brought him to his end under the power of John Winthrop, I consider a final set of performances connected to the publication event of the Maypole. Here Morton's agency as an author, as the principal performer of the event, is less important than the book itself—the physical embodiment, *New English Canaan*. As printed, published, distributed, and possibly read, this book was another space of performance, one with different but structurally similar homographs, gestures, and relationships among author, audience, and material medium when read in the transatlantic print world. It was here that the potential audiences for the Maypole converged, with what were for some readers troubling implications.

[...]

From a twenty-first-century perspective, New English Canaan can seem progressive, given its focus on indigenous language and culture. But it also helped forge foundational imperial technologies—the hierarchies of literacy over orality and of English as center and Native as subordinate periphery. What Bradford saw as the dangerous hybridity enabled by the Maypole, its "frisking" interracial bodies and its communicational "inordinariness," seems to position Morton as a cultural critic able to see the connections among sexuality, communications technology, and social power in English colonization. But Morton's use of hybridity sought to bring Native Americans under English "cultivation" and political rule, not to establish a conscious program of negotiated cultural exchange that might preserve indigenous self-determination.

Still, Morton's famous Maypole was more than a pagan symbol or beacon for degenerate fur smugglers. It exemplifies the interpenetration of media in the communications networks that shaped power in the northern colonies. The poems written at Morton's tiny plantation served a local purpose. When published on the Maypole, however, they offered a more general challenge to the representational hegemony of the Pilgrim leaders. Back in England, Morton took his argument to another level, portraying the Puritan leaders as naive pedagogues exploiting illiterates—showing to advantage his own high ironic style but always taking into account the power of literacy to organize culture and create access to that culture for individuals. Morton, years before the Antinomian controversy,[32] critiqued the nascent Puritan matrix of communication and authority, proposing an alternative public sphere. In this argument, perhaps his own intellectual touchstone, but certainly his rhetorical fulcrum, was the relationship of Native Americans to the different mechanisms of communication they encountered. They reveled and traded openly with Morton, while inventing new words for untrustworthiness as

32 Antinomianism was a Christian philosophy—later labeled heretical—that rejected the necessity of following Biblical laws due to the belief that grace alone was necessary for salvation. The Antinomian controversy occurred in 1636 in Massachusetts Bay Colony between magistrate John Winthrop and the "Antinomians" or "Free Grace Advocates," the most prominent of whom was Anne Hutchinson.

a result of interacting with the Pilgrims. His complaint that the Pilgrims were taking advantage of illiterates should be seen as a basic statement about power in society. The Maypole was an attempt to act on that episteme,[33] bringing a different brand of public communication to New England.

Notes

i. See also Bruce Daniels, *Puritans at Play: Leisure and Recreation in Colonial New England* (New York: St. Martin's, 1996). On the literary legacy of Morton and the Maypole, see John McWilliams, *New England's Crises and Cultural Memory: Literature, Politics, History, Religion, 1620–1860* (New York: Cambridge UP, 2004), especially 44–73.

ii. "Thomas Morton of Merrymount," from chapter 19 of William Bradford, *Of Plymouth Plantation, 1620–1647*, ed. Samuel Eliot Morison (New York: Modern Library, 1967), 204–10. On Morton's comparatively light impact on Plymouth's economics, see Neal Salisbury, *Manitou and Providence: Indians, Europeans, and the Making of New England, 1500–1643* (New York: Oxford UP, 1982). [Bradford wrote *Of Plymouth Plantation* to describe the story of the Puritan pilgrims as they fled England, eventually founding Plymouth Colony.]

iii. The literature in this area is voluminous, but among the influential books that take information circulation as a central concern are Perry Miller, *The New England Mind: The Seventeenth Century* (Cambridge, MA: Harvard UP, 1939); Richard Brown, *Knowledge Is Power: The Diffusion of Information in Early America, 1700–1865* (New York: Oxford UP, 1991); David D. Hall, *Worlds of Wonder, Days of Judgment: Popular Religious Belief in Early New England* (Cambridge, MA: Harvard UP, 1990); and Kenneth A. Lockridge, *A New England Town: The First Hundred Years, Dedlham, Massachusetts, 1636–1736* (New York: Norton, 1970). For examinations of the place of literacy and textuality in Native American cultures, see Brian Swann and Arnold Krupat, eds., *Recovering the Word: Essays on Native American Literature* (Berkeley: U of California P, 1987); Jennifer E. Monaghan, *Learning to Read and Write in Colonial America* (Amherst: U of Massachusetts P, 2005); Lisa Brooks, *The Common Pot: The Recovery of Native Space in the Northeast* (Minneapolis: U of Minnesota P, 2008); Hilary Wyss, *Writing Indians: Literacy, Christianity, and Native Community in Early America* (Amherst: U of Massachusetts P, 2000); Robert Allen Warrior, *The People and the World: Reading Native Nonfiction* (Minneapolis: U of Minnesota P, 2005).

iv. Another dissenter (and lawyer), Thomas Lechford, returned to Europe to publish his critique of the Separatists in 1642. See Thomas Lechford, *Plain-Dealing, or News from New-England* (Boston: Wiggin & Lunt, 1867). Child wrote *New England's Jonas Cast Up in London* to support advocates of religious freedom in New England who distributed petitions written by hand—for potential signers, the inability to get such a petition printed in New England would have resonated with the argument for religious toleration. See also the discussion of Samuel Gorton's radical challenge to the government of Massachusetts Bay in Philip Gura, *A Glimpse of Sion's Glory: Puritan Radicalism in New England, 1620–1660* (Middletown, CT: Wesleyan UP, 1984).

v. Grantland Rice writes that up until 1662 there was a "flowering of a unique exchange of transatlantic civic criticism," in large part because of "the New England theocracy's effectiveness in suppressing printed commentary within the colonies, an activity which ... reemphasized the political nature of public writing, and the concurrent lapse of censorship enforcement in England" (Rice, *Transformation of Authorship in America* [Chicago: U of Chicago P, 1997], 24–25). Morton opted for the more liberal

33 A system of knowledge.

presses of Amsterdam. On censorship in London, see Annabel Patterson, *Censorship and Interpretation: The Conditions of Writing and Reading in Early Modern New England* (Madison: U of Wisconsin P, 1984); and Jean-Christophe Agnew, *Worlds Apart: The Market and Theatre in Anglo-American Thought, 1550–1750* (New York: Cambridge UP, 1986).

vi. Morton's text is reprinted in Dempsey's edition of *New English Canaan*, ed. Jack Dempsey (Scituate, MA: Digital Scanning, 2000) and in facsimile in Peter Force, *Tracts and Other Papers Relating Principally to the Origin, Settlement, and Progress of the Colonies in North America: From the Discovery of the Country to the Year 1776*, vol. 2 (Washington, DC: Peter Force, 1838). Quotations from *New English Canaan* in this chapter are taken from the Amsterdam edition of 1637 (Thomas Morton, *New English Canaan, or New Canaan, containing an Abstract of New England* [Amsterdam: J.F. Stam, 1637]) held by the Henry E. Huntington Library.

vii. I draw heavily here on the summary in Michael Zuckerman, "Pilgrims in the Wilderness: Community, Modernity, and the maypole and Merry Mount," *New England Quarterly* 50.2 (1977): 255–77. Dempsey's biography in *New English Canaan* gives a good sense of the scholarship on Morton. See also Minor Wallace Major, "William Bradford versus Thomas Morton," *Early American Literature* 5.2 (1970): 1–13, and "Thomas Morton and His *New English Canaan*" (PhD Diss., U of Colorado, 1957).

viii. For the story of Morton's unfortunate marital career prior to emigrating, see Dempsey's edition of *New English Canaan*, part 2, 73–81; and Philip Ranlet, "The Lord of Misrule: Thomas Morton of Merry Mount," *New England Historical and Genealogical Register* 134 (October 1980): 282–90.

ix. Ma-re Mount had five names within about a year: Passonagessit, Mount Wollaston, Ma-re Mount, Merry-Mount (Bradford's influential modification), and Mount Dagon (Endicott's designation after cutting down the Maypole). The constant renaming suggests the ideological power of space in a land with small, interdependent settlements. I use Morton's original, punning name, which he claimed meant "mount-by-the-sea" but which also implied the aural interpretation Bradford orthographically cements as "merry." See also Arthur J. Krim, "Acculturation of the New England Landscape: Native and English Toponymy of Eastern Massachusetts," *New England Prospect: Maps, Place Names, and the Historical Landscape*, ed. Peter Benes (Boston: Boston UP, 1980), 69–88.

x. Thomas Cartelli, "Transplanting Disorder: The Construction of Misrule in Morton's *New English Canaan* and Bradford's *Of Plymouth Plantation*," *English Literary Renaissance* 27.2 (1997): 260.

xi. Zuckerman, "Pilgrims in the Wilderness," 256; Donald F. Connors, *Thomas Morton* (New York: Twayne, 1969).

xii. Zuckerman, "Pilgrims in the Wilderness," 257.

xiii. Karen Ordahl Kupperman, "Thomas Morton, Historian," *New England Quarterly* 50.4 (1977): 661; see also John Demos, "The Maypole of Merry Mount," *American Heritage* 37.6 (October-November 1986): 82–87.

xiv. *New English Canaan*, 132.

xv. See Zuckerman, "Pilgrims in the Wilderness," 257. Puritan leaders continued for some time to enact this brand of poetic justice directed at the medium; Israel Stoughton in 1635 and Roger Williams at around the same time, for example, had to destroy their own manuscripts as punishment for sedition against the Bay Colony. See Louise A. Breen, *Transgressing the Bounds: Subversive Enterprises among the Puritan Elite in Massachusetts, 1630–1692* (New York: Oxford UP, 2001), 21–22.

xvi. For evidence about the relative literacy of Morton's servants, see Dempsey's edition of *New English Canaan*, 83–219.

xvii. For a history of the relationship of Puritanism to learning, see John Morgan, *Godly Learning: Puritan Attitudes towards Reason, Learning, and Education, 1560–1640* (Cambridge: Cambridge UP, 1986). Readings of the poems include Jack Dempsey, "Reading the Revels: The Riddle of May Day in *New English Canaan*," *Early American Literature* 34.3 (1999): 282–312; and Edith Murphy, "'A Rich Widow, Now to Be

Tane Up or Laid Downe': Solving the Riddle of Thomas Morton's 'Rise Oedipeus,'" *William and Mary Quarterly* 53.4 (October 1996): 755–68.

xviii. David D. Hall, *Cultures of Print: Essays in the History of the Book* (Amherst: U of Massachusetts P, 1996), 52.

xix. David Shields, *Civil Tongues and Polite Letters in British America* (Chapel Hill: U of North Carolina P, 1997), 162.

xx. *New English Canaan*, 137.

xxi. For a discussion of sixteenth-century theories of Native American language, see Stephen Greenblatt, *Learning to Curse: Essays in Early Modern Culture* (New York: Routledge, 1990), 16–39. Morton's account and use of Native literacy departs from the binary model outlined by Greenblatt, evidence of an evolution in the politics of colonial linguistics. On settler English literacy education as rooted in religious concepts and discourse, see Monaghan, *Learning to Read and Write in Colonial America*, especially 19–45.

xxii. *New English Canaan*, 116.

xxiii. Ibid., 22.

xxiv. Ibid., 20.

xxv. Sandra M. Gustafson, *Eloquence Is Power: Oratory and Performance in Early America* (Chapel Hill: U of North Carolina P, 2000), 5.

xxvi. *New English Canaan*, 19.

xxvii. Ibid., 50.

xxviii. See Stephen Greenblatt's "Racial Memory and Literary History," *PMLA* 116.1 (January 2001): 48–63, for a rumination on what this might have meant in the early modern era. While Morton draws on a philological tradition arguing that culture is embedded in language, his treatment makes clear the contextual powers that shape language and understanding. As Kupperman has noted, this kind of ideological contradiction was often forced by the attempt to textualize evidence from encounters (Karen Ordahl Kupperman, *Indians and English: Facing off in Early America* [Ithaca, NY: Cornell UP, 2000]).

xxix. *New English Canaan*, 113.

xxx. Ibid., 138.

xxxi. Ibid., 107.

xxxii. Ibid., 107.

xxxiii. Ibid., 82.

xxxiv. Ibid., 112.

xxxv. Ibid., 175. "Cap a pe": *cap-a-pied*. On the historical role of posture and gesture in public speaking, see Gustafson, *Eloquence Is Power*; Jay Fliegelman, *Declaring Independence: Jefferson, Natural Language, and the Culture of Performance* (Stanford, CA: Stanford UP, 1994). Morton's use of the term "postures" here also suggests a parody of the Puritan iconoclasm discussed in the Introduction.

xxxvi. Bradford quoted in Major, "William Bradford versus Thomas Morton," 6.

xxxvii. The *Oxford English Dictionary* lists a host of early modern meanings for the term "loose," including a connotation having to do with freedom from indenture that may well be resonant in Bradford's comment, given Morton's appropriation of his partner's bonded men. The more enduring meaning related to digestion may also be active in Bradford's characterization [...].

xxxviii. Bradford, *Of Plymouth Plantation*, 205–06.

xxxix. Ibid., 206.

xl. Paul R. Sternberg, "The Publication of Thomas Morton's *New English Canaan* Reconsidered," *Papers of the Bibliographical Society of America* 80.3 (1986): 372; see also Dempsey's edition of Morton, *New English Canaan*, xxix.

xli. See Kupperman, *Indians and English*; and Dempsey's edition of Morton, *New English Canaan*.

xlii. Morton, *New English Canaan*, ed. Dempsey, 229–30.

xliii. Kupperman, *Indians and English*, 2. At times, this line of reasoning runs the risk of arguing for the Natives as companions to colonization, rather than as "the colonized"; Morton backs down quickly from several of these arguments, which Kupperman examines in detail.

xliv. Lee Edelman, *Homographesis: Essays in Gay Literacy and Cultural Theory* (New York: Routledge, 1994), 12.

xlv. Edelman's use of this term is based in psychoanalytic criticism and a historical account of the politics of homosexuality. Edelman theorizes a queer practice out of the possibilities of the homograph, what he calls homographesis, "a mode of strategic or analytic resistance to the logic of regulatory identity" (13). My use of the term attempts to elaborate on the communicative dynamics engaged by Richard White's notion of the middle ground, in which linguistic and cultural misunderstanding is a historical driver no less potent than negotiation or violence (White, *Middle Ground: Indians, Empires, and Republics in the Great Lakes Region, 1650–1815* [New York: Cambridge UP, 1991]).

xlvi. Kathleen J. Bragdon, *Native People of Southern New England*, 185. See also Timothy R. Pauketat, *The Ascent of Chiefs: Cahokia and Mississippian Politics in Native North America* (Tuscaloosa: U of Alabama P, 1994), especially 185; on the use of poles in Delaware Big House ceremonies, see Elisabeth Tooker, ed., *Native North American Spirituality of the Eastern Woodlands: Sacred Myths, Dreams, Visions, Speeches, Healing Formulas, Rituals and Ceremonials* (Mahwah, NJ: Paulist P, 1979), 104; Lynne P. Sullivan, "Mississippian Households and Community Organization in Eastern Tennessee," *Mississippian Communities and Households*, ed. J. Daniel Rogers and Bruce D. Smith (Tuscaloosa: U of Alabama P), 99–123; and in the same volume, Mark W. Mehrer and James M. Collins, "Household Archaeology at Cahokia and Its Hinterlands." Ma-re Mount was at Mount Wollaston, now Quincy, Massachusetts.

xlvii. William C. Sturtevant, ed., *Handbook of the North American Indians*, Vol. 15 (Washington, DC: Smithsonian Institution, 1978), 160. On totems, see Kathleen J. Bragdon, *Native People of Southern New England, 1500–1650* (Norman: U of Oklahoma P, 1996), 185.

xlviii. Bragdon, *Native People of Southern New England*, 143.

xlix. Germaine Warkentin, "In Search of 'The Word of the Other': Aboriginal Sign Systems and the History of the Book in Canada," *Book History* 2 (1999): 12; Peter Wogan, "Perceptions of European Literacy in Early Contact Situations," *Ethnohistory* 41.3 (Summer 1994): 407–29.

l. Warkentin, "In Search of 'The Word of the Other,'" 17. Patricia Fumerton's recent work on homosociality and broadside posting in Renaissance England's alehouses suggests the possibility that Morton might also have been using the aesthetics of public posting to generate camaraderie among his servant-class men of both Native and English origin. Reconciling these two groups would not have been easy, but the social panic it induced suggests that Morton was better than most at the task (Fumerton, "Not Home: Alehouses, Ballads, and the Vagrant Husband in Early Modern England," *Journal of Medieval and Early Modern Studies* 32.3 [Fall 2002]: 493–518).

26.

Meredith McGill, "Circulating Media: Charles Dickens, Reprinting, and Dislocation of American Culture," *American Literature and the Culture of Reprinting, 1834–1853*. Philadelphia: U of Pennsylvania P, 2003. 109–40

Meredith McGill (b. 1961) is Associate Professor of English and Director of the Center for Cultural Analysis at Rutgers University. Her research examines a variety of topics in American book and cultural history. The following excerpt is from *American Literature and the Culture of Reprinting, 1834–1853* (2003), in which she examines American resistance to tightening control over intellectual property in the mid-nineteenth century. McGill's focus is on the lack of international copyright, a condition that allowed widespread re-printing of foreign books in America at very low prices. She also documents the decentralized market for print in America during this period, which provided a sharp contrast with the more centralized publishing that prevailed in Britain and Europe.

With chapters on the legal battles over intellectual property and the writing careers of major authors on both sides of the Atlantic, including Charles Dickens, Edgar Allan Poe, and Nathaniel Hawthorne, McGill argues that "the proliferation of cheap, reprinted texts and the reliance of the book trade on periodical publishing realigned relations between author, publisher, editor, and reader, upended the hierarchy of genres, and troubled the boundaries of the text-as-object" (p. 2). By combining economic, publishing, and copyright history, McGill persuasively attributes the emergence of a national literature in America at least in part to a vibrant, unregulated market in transatlantic literature. In this regard, McGill employs book-historical methods similar to those undertaken in previous essays by Raven (pp. 289–312) and Rose (pp. 313–33), specifically to excavate the material origins of a national literary culture.

The chapter included here further explores the interplay between oral and print cultures in McGill's examination of Charles Dickens's 1842 tour of the United States (in which he read from his novels to public gatherings) and the narratives he published about it. She also, like Matt Cohen (pp. 417–37), examines the multimedia landscape of America, which was not dominated by any single media form (such as the printed book) but rather continued to be shaped by oral culture and print journalism. For McGill, the decentralized literary marketplace of nineteenth-century America was a function both of the unregulated flow of foreign and domestic print, and of the intermingling of multiple forms of print, performative, and oral cultures.

Circulating Media: Charles Dickens, Reprinting, and Dislocation of American Culture

The history of American resistance to international **copyright** illustrates the power of the figure of the author to simplify and distort the politics of print. As I have argued, what from the perspective of an author-centered literary culture looks like an unconscionable violation of authors' rights was understood in the antebellum period[1] as a struggle between competing visions of a rapidly expanding marketplace. Although an international copyright law was repeatedly invoked as indispensable to the development of a national culture, the production and **circulation** of printed texts flourished in the absence of such a law; what was at stake was not the existence but the definition of national culture. The argument that a universal application of the principle of authors' rights would stabilize the volatile trade in books was decisively turned back by **publishers** and tradesmen who were less concerned with regulation than with the need to preserve decentralization across the market for printed goods.

Literary critics have generally assumed that the expansion of print culture coincided with and reinforced the emergence of commercial nationalism, but debates over literary property suggest instead that the market for print in the 1830s and 1840s was shaped by the Jacksonian resistance to centralized development. Andrew Jackson[2] was swept into office on a wave of populist suspicion of the elite abuse of political power and the widespread perception that northern capitalists reaped disproportionate benefits from the extension of market culture. His controversial refusal to re-charter the national bank and his commitment to the restraint of credit were a direct assault on the policies of John Quincy Adams and Henry Clay,[3] who promoted integrated plans of national development that relied on centralized finance and oversight. Encouraging economic growth while preventing the consolidation of capital was an explicit aim of Jacksonian democrats, but a long-standing skepticism about the pursuit of development on a national scale is suggested by the refusal of presidents from Madison to Polk[4] to provide federal funding for a national transportation system. The rapid growth of market culture raised intractable questions about the terms of Union and about the nature and legitimacy of federal authority. Antebellum debates over print culture, like those concerning internal improvements and the national bank, were driven by the need for means and modes of circulation that could resist being co-opted by a central power.

1 Refers to the period between the American War of Independence in the 1770s and the outbreak of the Civil War in 1861.

2 Andrew Jackson (1767–1845), the seventh president of the United States of America.

3 John Quincy Adams (1767–1848), sixth president of the United States of America and also a diplomat, serving as Secretary of State under President James Monroe before his own presidency and as a Congressman afterwards; Henry Clay (1777–1852), American politician who served as a US congressman and as a US senator.

4 James Madison (1751–1836), fourth president of the United States; James Knox Polk (1795–1841), eleventh president of the United States.

In this chapter, I will examine Charles Dickens's 1842 tour of the United States and the narratives he published in its wake in order to trace some of the contours and consequences of the decentralized literary marketplace. Dickens's visit not only brought the popular author into close contact with his far-flung American readers, it also brought into sharp relief critical differences between English and American systems of publishing. The culture of re-printing was so alien to Dickens that he had difficulty comprehending why his vocal support for international copyright posed a serious threat to his literary reception. Nevertheless, as I will argue, the shape of Dickens's incomprehension speaks eloquently about what he and we, who are equally estranged from this culture, can neither value nor perceive.

If Dickens's accounts of his travels bear witness to the problematic decentralization of American culture chiefly in the form of violated expectations, American re-prints of Dickens's texts will enable us to trace some of the ways in which debates over national credit, internal improvements, and literary property are reciprocally imagined and cross-referred. These re-prints will also enable us to mark the imbrication[5] of a decentralized print culture with the protection of slavery. Long before the question of the legitimacy of national law was crystallized by the problematic legal status of the fugitive slave,[6] the debate over slavery was cast as a question of circulation. Not only was the national distribution of texts that discussed slavery regarded by slaveholding communities as a significant threat to their safety, the southern interdiction of abolitionist **pamphlets** was countenanced and reinforced by a Jacksonian understanding of the limits of federal power.[i] Both the opposition to international copyright and the defense of slavery relied on a weak central government's deference to local authority. In his American narratives, 441
Dickens explicitly links a depraved indifference to slavery to the licentiousness of the American press. The history of the unauthorized re-printing of Dickens's texts will enable us to weigh his insights into the dangers of uncontrolled circulation against American fears about centralized power and against re-print publishers' confidence in the meliorative[7] effect of common property[8] in Dickens.

I. Property in Dickens: The 1842 Tour

In September 1841, exhausted from the pressures of **serial publication**, Charles Dickens signed a contract with his publishers that gave him 14 months' respite from writing in exchange for agreeing to commence a new work in monthly numbers in November of the following year. In the interim he would receive a monthly stipend as an advance on royalties for the novel he

5 Overlapping.

6 Slaves who fled across state boundaries were subject to federal laws that required their return to their masters.

7 Improving.

8 In the absence of an international copyright agreement, Dickens's texts were considered "common property" insofar as they were available for reprinting to all publishers without the payment to the author (or owner of the copyright).

had promised and a substantial loan drawn against the profits of a book he would write on his American travels. Logically speaking, then, Dickens's travel narrative precedes and sponsors his American tour. Despite his repeated and no doubt genuine assertion that he traveled to the United States to see "the Republic of [his] imagination,"[ii] Dickens is throughout this tour an author, delightedly exclaiming in a letter to John Forster soon after he arrived: "I have a book, already."[iii] The problem of the form, format, and mode of distribution of popular literature is with Dickens from the very beginning of his American tour.[iv]

Dickens comes to North America as an observer of character and customs, but soon discovers that he is "the observed of all observers."[v] While he initially finds this position thrilling—in a typical moment of grandiosity and expansion, he writes to Forster: "I wish you could have seen the crowds cheering the Inimitable in the streets"[vi]—he is quickly discomfited by his extreme lack of privacy. Dickens becomes a traveling spectacle, a mobile figure of authorship. Crowds throng the streets wherever he goes; he is overwhelmed with invitations to public and private functions in his honor. His American secretary records that within days of his arrival, Dickens could be found eating breakfast while dictating replies to an already voluminous correspondence even as a sculptor modeled his bust, running back and forth to measure his head with calipers. While Dickens is still in Boston, the papers are full of plans for a "Boz Ball"[9] and public dinner in New York complete with lavish decorations, fulsome speeches by statesmen and literati, and tableaux vivants[10] illustrating familiar passages from his works.[vii]

Some hint of what will go wrong for Dickens is evident from the first official welcome dinner in Boston where his presumptive role as an observer of the new world is met by a series of speeches that invoke the breadth of his books' circulation, Dickens's *already* thorough penetration of American culture and consciousness. Josiah Quincy[11] waxes typically eloquent:

> In the empty schoolroom, the boy at his evening task has dropped his grammar, that he may roam with Oliver or Nell. The traveller has forgotten the fumes of the crowded steamboat, and is far off with our guest, among the green valleys and hoary[12] hills of old England. The trapper beyond the Rocky Mountains has left his lonely tent, and is unroofing the houses in London with the more than Mephistopheles[13] at my elbow.[viii]

---

9 "Boz" was one of Dickens's middle names and pen name used by him for his first collection, *Sketches by Boz* (1836), though his readers continued to call him Boz throughout his career. On 14 February 1842, a "Boz Ball" was held in his honor at the Park Theater in New York, with 3,000 guests in attendance.

10 A form of entertainment, in which people pose silently to represent a motionless scene.

11 Josiah Quincy, Jr. (1802–82) was mayor of Boston at the time of Dickens's visit and delivered the welcome address, quoted below.

12 Ancient or venerable.

13 Mephistopheles is the name of a devil. The "more than Mephistopheles" is Asmodeus, another devil. He appears in a popular novel by Alain-René Lesage called *le Diable boiteux* (1707), where he lifts the roofs off houses to reveal the wickedness of the inhabitants.

Quincy suggests that Dickens will discover not a society waiting for his appraisal, but a complex reciprocal gaze, a people prepossessed by Dickens to the extent that they no longer seem to inhabit the landscape.

The real trouble comes—and with it, an intensification of negative publicity that makes Dickens extremely uncomfortable—after the public dinner in Hartford at which, for the second time, he speaks up in favor of international copyright. It is clear from his letters that Dickens thought he was speaking nobly and disinterestedly on behalf of British and American authors, speaking as the momentarily empowered representative of a group with common interests. Americans, however, had heralded Dickens's arrival as proof of the power and honor of popular affection. "The occasion that calls us together is almost unprecedented in the annals of literature," Quincy opined, "A young man has crossed the ocean with no hereditary title, no military laurels, no princely fortune, and yet his approach is hailed with pleasure by every age and condition and on his arrival he is welcomed as a long-known and trusted friend."[ix] In appealing for payments to foreign authors, Dickens appeared to discount the value of his American reception, in the words of one reviewer, "urging upon those assembled to do honor to *his genius*, to look after *his purse* also."[x] He also threatened rhetorically to exclude the very readers whose enthusiasm had justified these ostentatious (and frequently exclusive) celebrations. As Quincy took care to note, Dickens had captivated Americans across differences of "age and condition." He had not simply included the "humble and oppressed" in his novels as objects of sympathy; cheap re-prints of his serialized fiction had enabled them to be drawn into the orbit of literary culture as actual or potential readers. A more savvy Dickens might have been warned off his course by a toast directly following his Hartford speech, a toast that one reporter ridiculed, but made a point of marking as untutored speech: "[Mr. Miles] commenced with the angels, approximated to the patriarchs, floundered through Republican resolutions, and ended in 'pop'lar literature,' which ... could not be 'monopolated' by any aristocracy."[xi] But Dickens seems not to have understood that his popularity in America was in part a function of the lack of international copyright, the system of re-printing he continued publicly to attack.[xii]

Dickens's importance to antebellum American thinking about literary property is clear from how quickly the subject of debate—the question of the need for international copyright—gets transformed into the question of what Dickens was doing in speaking about it. Dickens can't simply voice an opinion, he exemplifies the problem of which he speaks. Dickens characteristically responds to negative newspaper publicity by insisting that he had not *intended* to speak on international copyright, thereby delivering himself from the charge of self-interest.[xiii] The American press, however, reads Dickens's assertions that he spoke only out of solidarity with other gentleman authors as proof that he was both mercenary and plotting—that he came not voluntarily, to be celebrated by his readers, but as a national emissary on behalf of British trade. This theory gains considerable momentum as Dickens's trip wends south toward Washington, where the last of Henry Clay's international copyright bills is under consideration.[xiv]

Extremely troubled by "assertions that [he] was no gentleman, but a mercenary scoundrel"[xv] Dickens tries to stage his disinterestedness, placing supportive letters and a pro-copyright petition signed by British authors in American newspapers and magazines, and going out of his way to give the impression that these testimonials have been volunteered and not solicited.[xvi] Dickens hoped that a display of solidarity from other gentleman authors would insulate him from allegations of unworthy motives, but his efforts to exonerate himself only exacerbate the situation. The publication of these letters looks to many Americans like collusion, further proof that Dickens is the hired agent of British authors and publishers.[xvii] The newspaper controversy repeatedly grounds to a halt at this impasse of mutual suspicion: Dickens's aristocratic use of gentlemanly anonymity to conceal networks of trade is met by a democratic notion of authorship as subjection to circulation—the American press's insistence that authors are and should be a kind of common property.

The pressure that such a model of authorship places on an author's singular, if circulating, body is apparent from Dickens's often comical letters to friends describing American attempts to parcel him out for distribution: landing from a steamboat in New York, he is greeted by "some twenty or thirty people, screwing small dabs of fur out of the back of [his] costly great coat";[xviii] he becomes afraid to get his hair cut "lest the barber (bribed by admirers) should clip it all off for presents."[xix] As his tour progresses, however, Dickens becomes increasingly concerned by his inability to control his public appearances, both in person and in print. Despite the fact that after his New York experience, he had firmly declined all invitations to public dinners and receptions, Dickens is manipulated into holding a "levee"[14] by a group of Philadelphia tradesmen who feared that "the *soi disant*[15] magnates" of the city would "monopolize" his visit. Complaining that access to Dickens had become the "*exclusive property* of a self-delegated clique," they forced him to hold a reception in his hotel room by publishing an announcement in the newspaper, transforming a private courtesy into a public invitation.[xx] Dickens's awareness of his vulnerability to a mass-public, one whose relation to him and his writing is mediated chiefly or only by the press, causes a shift in his critique of the culture of re-printing. Moving beyond his outrage at the injustice of payments never made, Dickens expresses astonishment and revulsion at the violence done to his texts, and by extension, to himself, when his writing is circulated in newspapers. In a letter to Henry Brougham,[16] he complains that a foreign writer "not only gets nothing for his labors, though they are diffused all over this enormous Continent, but cannot even choose his company. Any wretched halfpenny newspaper can print him at its pleasure—place him side by side with productions which disgust his common sense."[xxi] Writing to his brother-in-law while awaiting response to the British authors' published letters of support, Dickens is a good deal more explicit about the way in which newspaper re-printing disrupts his sense of social order:

> Is it not a horrible thing that scoundrel-**booksellers** should grow rich here from publishing books, the authors of which do not reap one farthing[17]

14 A public assembly of the Sovereign at court, or a reception in honor of a specific individual.

15 Self-proclaimed.

16 Henry Brougham (1778–1868), founder and influential contributor to the *Edinburgh Review*; he became an MP and later Lord Chancellor (a member of cabinet and responsible for the judicial system).

17 A quarter of a penny, under the old British monetary system.

> from their issue, by scores of thousands? And that every vile, blackguard,[18] and detestable newspaper,—so filthy and so bestial that no honest man would admit one into his house, for a water-closet door-mat—should be able to publish those same writings, side by side, cheek by jowl, with the coarsest and most obscene companions, with which they *must* become connected in course of time, in people's minds? Is it tolerable that besides being robbed and rifled, an author should *be forced* to appear in any form—in any vulgar dress—in any atrocious company—that he should have no choice of his audience—no controul over his own distorted text?[xxii]

To be subject to re-printing is to be forced into such proximity with the coarse and the obscene that one could easily be mistaken for them ("*forced* to appear" in such "vulgar dress"). Dickens is appalled at a print culture that fails to enforce reliable genre and class distinctions, and at the collapse of the structures of mediation that hold authors at a safe remove from the distribution and reception of their work. Rather than relieving him of agency, Dickens's lack of control over his texts makes him feel personally accountable for their mode of circulation.

In oscillating between scatology[19] and self-righteousness, expressing disgust at and assuming excessive responsibility for the newspaper circulation of his texts, Dickens's letter exemplifies the crisis of agency brought about by unauthorized reprinting. Unable to find his own authority reflected in and buttressed by a hierarchically organized publishing industry, Dickens exaggerates the wealth and power of the "scoundrel-booksellers" and retrospectively projects greater command over his English readers than he actually possesses: does Chapman & Hall's[20] proprietary control over the price and issue of his **editions** actually give him "choice" over his audience in England? If the figure of the author-as-proprietor provides a useful fiction behind which publishers can consolidate power, it also shields writers from their subjection to the market by exaggerating their sense of agency. The spectacle of Dickens's lack of control over the circulation of his texts in America causes him to fantasize about a mode of relation to his writing and his readers that was never wholly within his grasp.[xxiii] During his travels, Dickens is repeatedly disarmed by his unmediated exposure to the means by which his fiction is popularly distributed. Thus, while he is happy to accept decorous praise at a formal reception from a representative group of his working-class readers,[xxiv] he is shocked at the temerity of an itinerant bookseller who visits him in his rooms and tries to bully him into offering financial assistance on the grounds that he was the first to sell Dickens's books in New York and thus had materially contributed to his renown.[xxv] A similar astonishment at authors' intimate subjection to the means of distribution is apparent in Dickens's account of his initial landing in Boston when what he takes to be newsboys, leaping on board the boat in an attempt to sell him a paper, turn out to be editors competing to introduce themselves and to circulate news of his arrival.[xxvi]

---

18 Unscrupulous.

19 Writing concerned with excrement and excretory functions.

20 Dickens's publishers in Britain.

One index of the stubbornness of the stalemate between the figure of the author as wholly removed from or wholly absorbed by trade is that Dickens's account of his trip in his travel narrative, *American Notes for General Circulation* (1842), deletes all reference to his literary reception—indeed, nearly all reference to the literary itself. A hostile *Blackwood's*[21] reviewer tellingly derided the book as "the play of Hamlet with the character of Hamlet omitted," arguing that Dickens's literary fame had shielded him from "the men and manners of America." Had Dickens desired to be the observer instead of the observed, the reviewer argued, he needed to have traveled incognito; *American Notes* is ultimately little more than the story of a "perpetual and very unpleasant locomotion."[xxvii]

Indeed, one might read the narrative itself as structured by a series of complex displacements: the displacement of the subject of international copyright from its pages; the elimination of the literary itself from *American Notes*, as if Dickens had actually traveled as the anonymous observer that *Blackwood's* chided him for not having been; the elimination of the chapter "Introductory and Necessary to be Read," which explains and attempts to justify this omission;[xxviii] the displacement of the treatment of slavery and the licentiousness of the press—the "peculiar institutions" that Dickens represents as causes of and analogues for his sense of dispossession—from the narrative proper so that they appear as objects of critique outside the framework of the voyage; and, finally, the obsessive repetition/displacement *of American Notes* into the serialized novel *Martin Chuzzlewit*.[22]

[...]

II. Circulation and Slavery

At the end of his narrative, Dickens tries valiantly to turn this culture of disseminated repetition against itself. In a highly polemical, topical chapter narrated from the vantage point of a successful "Passage Home," Dickens bitterly attacks both the brutality of slave-owners and the hypocrisy of the "false republic"[xxix] that sustains them through indifference, trusting in the weak supervision of public opinion to protect the slave from cruelty. Dickens strongly condemned slavery within the body of his narrative as his trip took him south as far as Richmond, but while he is traveling, slavery actually offers Dickens a strange kind of reassurance. His moral certainty of its depravity helps to stabilize his narrative perspective, enabling him to read the landscape allegorically. For example, passing through Virginia farmland, Dickens observes that it "was once productive; but the soil has been exhausted by the system of employing a great amount of slave labor in forcing crops, without strengthening the land." Here the slave-owners' use of force is self-condemned; the barrenness of the land testifies to the injustice of the system. For Dickens, the southern countryside offers an ideal coincidence of transgression and retribution:

---

21 *Blackwood's Edinburgh Magazine*, founded in 1817, was an influential nineteenth-century literary magazine.

22 Novel by Charles Dickens published serially between 1743–44 in which the main character, Martin Chuzzlewit, travels to America; for this fictionalized account, Dickens drew on his own 1842 tour.

> Dreary and uninteresting as its aspect is, I was glad to the heart to find anything on which one of the curses of his horrible institution has fallen; and had greater pleasure in contemplating the withered ground than the richest and most thriving cultivation in the same place could have afforded me. In this district, as in all others where slavery sits brooding ... there is an air of ruin and decay abroad, which is inseparable from the system.[xxx]

Slavery makes legible a reciprocity between land and culture that eludes Dickens elsewhere in his narrative. The confidence with which he interprets vistas, buildings, and customs as "tokens" of "things below the surface,"[xxxi] and the pleasure he takes in affixing moral judgment to a particular location differentiate the south from the many "dreary and uninteresting," blighted scenes to follow.

Dickens's separate chapter on slavery, however, inaugurates a radical change in both tone and mode. With this chapter, Dickens finally stops circulating, shifting from recounting his disconnected, serial experiences to addressing the nation as a whole from the vantage point of his return to England. From this perspective, the institution of slavery seems maddeningly to elude the "curses" that so decisively settle on the landscape. In order to counter slaveholders' ostensible control over the representation of slavery—their ability to manipulate public opinion so that it protects rather than censures them—Dickens adopts the familiar abolitionist strategy of turning the testimony of slave-owners against themselves. Quoting a series of newspaper advertisements for the identification and return of runaway slaves, Dickens holds Americans publicly accountable for the violence and degradation of slavery, indicting the institution and the print culture that supports it by capturing ephemeral and scattered newspaper notices on the single plane of his page:

> "Ran away, the negro Manuel. Much marked by irons."
> "Ran away, the negress Fanny. Had on an iron band about her neck."
> "Ran away, a negro boy about twelve years old. Had round his neck a chain dog collar with 'De Lampert' engraved on it."
> "Ran away, the negro Hown. Has a ring of iron on his left foot. Also, Grise, his wife, having a ring and chain on the left leg."
> "Ran away, a negro boy named James. Said boy was ironed when he left me."
> "Committed to jail, a man who calls his name John. He has a clog of iron on his right foot which will weigh four or five pounds."
> "Detained at the police jail, the negro wench, Myra. Has several marks of lashing and has irons on her feet."
> "Ran away, a negro woman and two children. A few days before she went off, I burnt her with a hot iron, on the left side of her face. I tried to make the letter M."[xxxii]

Dickens's passionate experiment in undermining slavery from within is complicated by his unacknowledged and unresolved struggle with the politics of print. As M. Giulia Fabi has noted, Dickens's juxtaposition of advertisements that detail slave-owners' inscriptions on the bodies of their problematically mobile property not only serves to condemn human bondage, it also recalls the repressed context of the debate over literary property.[xxxiii] Dickens focuses attention on the excruciating and ineradicable marks on the bodies of slaves as a way of forcing Americans to own up to horrors that are too easily ignored. And yet his use of this brutal writing to ascribe agency and assign responsibility covers for two failures of inscription. As scholars long have known, Dickens's list of newspaper advertisements is itself an unacknowledged borrowing from abolitionist Theodore Weld's pamphlet *American Slavery As It Is: Testimony of a Thousand Witnesses* (1839).[xxxiv] Moreover, it is an act of unauthorized re-printing that hides the traces of its theft by suppressing the sources of the slave-notices themselves. Weld had authenticated his documentary account of "the *condition* of American slaves" by indicating the particular issues of the local and regional newspapers in which these notices appeared and, where possible, providing the "names and residences" of their authors "as vouchers for the truth of their statements."[xxxv] Dickens, in turn, chooses from among the horrors Weld lists in chapters on "Tortures, By Iron Collars, Chains, Fetters, Handcuffs, &c." and "Brandings, Maimings, Gun-Shot Wounds, &c," erasing local contexts as a way of making a general point about the ordinariness of these atrocities as they are mediated by the press. But this is a documentary claim that obscures its documentation, one that explicitly disavows "partial evidence from abolitionists"[xxxvi] and dislocates torture from its source. The inscriptive violence Dickens records, then, is very much his own signature, reflecting not only slave-owners' attempts to mark and to control the bodies of their slaves, but also Dickens's attempt to exercise his own authority over a disturbingly elusive subject, his struggle to establish national responsibility for slavery from a proliferation of local instances.

Unlike Weld, Dickens doesn't intend for his moral condemnation to redound upon individuals and communities. Dickens's list of atrocities is an intervention in national culture that depends as much on erasure as inscription. Just as his claim to impartiality is leveraged by the suppression of his politically volatile source, so his attempt to place accountability for slavery on a national footing is necessarily detached from the localities in which these atrocities occur, dislocated from reference because the nation as such cannot be reduced to particular places. Desiring to annex the authoritative public voice of the press to his first-person, impressionistic narrative while at the same time holding his own text aloof from the newspapers he deplores, Dickens recirculates fragments of American newspaper culture shorn of its characteristic locality, summoning the sense of simultaneity crucial to imagining the nation by sheer force of parallelism and juxtaposition.

And yet, Dickens's attempt to approximate the authority of the "public prints"[xxxvii] while countering their centrifugal tendencies is hopelessly compromised by his reliance on the medium he condemns. Dickens is unable to establish a moral position external to print culture. He can only describe the nation as a whole by recapitulating and denouncing the extraordinary stories that circulate in print. Despite his attempt to rise above partisan politics and to claim the authority of a firsthand witness—"I shall not write one word," he claims, "for which I have not had ample proof and warrant"[xxxviii]—Dickens's critique of slavery devolves into to an attack on the representation of slavery, an attack that re-circulates horrific descriptions even as it claims that degradation invariably attends their consumption.[xxxix] Detached from Weld's apparatus of authentication, Dickens's catalogue of "liveries of mutilation"[xl] threatens to float free of reference, slipping from moral condemnation into voyeurism, representing not "the condition of American slaves" but the condition of national description, the violence of Dickens's desire to produce a stable referent for the nation. Dickens's self-defeating attempt to transform his text into a site for the redemptive re-deployment of a heterogeneous and dispersed newspaper culture suggests one of the exasperating strengths of a strategically weak central government—its ability to dodge accountability by rendering itself too dispersed to be targeted for critique.

Dickens attempts to produce in and through his text some sense of the governing authority that American society lacks, but he repeatedly gets caught between reference and demonstration, trying to point to something his text is performing. For instance, he represents the nation as defined by the omnipresence of its "licentious Press,"[xli] but his attribution of centralized powers of corruption to this personified figure is belied by his own efforts to assemble scattered evidence of social depravity from newspapers in remote locations. Dickens evokes a world of unremitting and contagious violence by reproducing newspaper reports of brutal acts from settlements in outlying territories, inferring that the cause of this violence
is exposure to slavery in person or in print.[xlii] Here, Dickens's own text stands as a proxy for 449
the central authority he cannot locate, the extravagance of his tone attesting to his frustration with the attenuation of his evidence. For Dickens, only a singular "Press," to which he attributes universal reach and comprehensive political and social power, could possibly be responsible for such degeneration:

> while that Press has its evil eye in every house, and its black hand in every appointment in the state, from a president to a postman; while, with ribald slander for its only stock in trade, it is the standard literature of an enormous class, who must find their reading in a newspaper, or they will not read at all; so long must its odium be upon the country's head, and so long must the evil it works, be plainly visible in the republic.[xliii]

In excoriating the press, Dickens grants it the same self-confirming status as both cause and evidence of national corruption that he had ascribed to slavery while traveling though the south. And yet his own rhetorical strategies attest to the maddening fragmentation of American newspaper culture; ironically, only "standard literature" such as *American Notes* and other texts subject to unauthorized reprinting could achieve anything like the kind of circulation Dickens describes.

[…]

Fig. 4.9: "Charles Dickens as He Appears When Reading," *Harper's Weekly* (1867). American Antiquarian Society.

III. *Martin Chuzzlewit*, the Social Order, and the Medium of Print

[...]

On his final tour of the United States in the winter of 1867–68, Dickens did much to short-circuit the unauthorized distribution of his work and to close the gap between author and reader that the re-printers had exploited. Rather than allowing his audience to receive him on their own terms, Dickens traveled through the northeast and mid-west performing his authorship, reading selections from his repertoire to sold-out audiences. In these readings, Dickens gave voice to a handful of his most popular characters using a minimalist mode of self-presentation, standing alone on the stage behind a small desk "against a dark background in a frame of gas-light, which [threw] out his face and figure to the best advantage" (Fig. 4.9).[xliv] In subordinating his authorial persona to the impersonation of his characters—"It was not Dickens, but the creations of his genius, that seemed to live and talk and act before the spectators"[xlv]—Dickens steers audiences away from a definition of the author as an external guarantor of the nature or quality of a printed book, toward a model of authorship as immanent and evanescent presence, a mode of authentication that is bound up with the notion of authorial voice and that ideally passes through the author's scarce and vulnerable body. This work of redefinition is richly registered in the newspaper coverage of Dickens's second tour as editors divide between cynically calculating the unprecedentedly large sums of money he was earning from his readings, and expressing concern for the author's manifest physical frailty.[xlvi]

Fig. 4.10: "The Black Driver," *American Notes for General Circulation* (1868). American Antiquarian Society.

During this tour, Dickens tries one final time to recast and redeem the most persistently problematic text of his oeuvre, *American Notes for General Circulation*. In one of the few public events he agrees to attend on the tour, Dickens gives a short after-dinner speech to "two hundred representatives of the Press" offering "honest testimony to the national generosity" in the matter of his reception, and expressing astonishment at the many signs of national improvement he has witnessed: "changes in the amount of land subdued and peopled, changes in the rise of vast new cities, changes in the growth of older cities almost out of recognition, changes in the graces and amenities of life, changes in the Press."[xlvii] As proof of his sincerity, Dickens promises both to publish this tribute "in [his] own Journal" when he returns to England, and to insist that a record of his gratitude and approval be attached to all subsequent editions of *American Notes* and *Martin Chuzzlewit*: "This testimony, so long as I live, and so long as my descendants have any legal right in my books, I shall cause to be republished, as an appendix to every copy of those two books of mine in which I have referred to America."[xlviii]

Dickens's promise to "cause" his speech "to be republished" as an appendix to his texts is a strange concession. It is both an exercise of and an attempt to augment his authority over his widely circulated, wayward texts. His request that his final words on America "be fairly read as inseparable from" his earlier "experiences and impressions" concedes the method but not the victory to his American re-publishers.[xlix] And yet even as Dickens speaks, he is far from controlling the troubling resonances produced by his attempt to tighten authorial control over literary property. Dickens's 1867–68 reading tour was financially guaranteed by the Boston publishing firm Ticknor & Fields, which entered into an agreement with Dickens in 1866 to produce a set of authorized editions of his work.[l] As the "only authorized representatives in America of the whole series of [Dickens's] books,"[li] Ticknor & Fields stood to take advantage of the publicity that would be generated from the famous author's visit, and timed the release of their edition of *American Notes* to coincide with news of his imminent arrival. The illustration selected for the **frontispiece** to this volume, however, jarringly recalls the highly fraught pre-war connection between literary property and national development (Fig. 4.10). Striking the keynote of this authorized edition is "The Black Driver," a thinly drawn minstrel[23] figure from Dickens's brief sojourn in the south, a Cockney in blackface whom Dickens tellingly describes as "a kind of insane imitation of an English coachman."[lii] It is difficult, finally, to know which edition of *American Notes* should represent Dickens's "general circulation" in America. Is Dickens the inadvertent narrator of the disconnected Jacksonian infrastructure, the provocateur who stimulates a defense of decentralization in finance, government, and print, and who traces the disturbing connection between the proliferation of print cultures and the protection of the system of slavery? Or is he the tool of a publishing firm that consolidates its authority by deploying the image of a former slave armed with a whip, a harbinger of northern forces who will subjugate the south in part through the imposition of federally funded internal improvements? Dickens himself couldn't possibly tell.

Notes

i. For Postmaster General and Jackson appointee Amos Kendall's "implicit rejection of the superiority of federal law" (271) when it came to postal employees' obligations to their communities, see Richard John, *Spreading the News: The American Postal System from Franklin to Morse* (Cambridge, MA: Harvard UP, 1995), 257–80.

ii. Letter to W.C. Macready, March 22, 1842, Charles Dickens, *The Letters of Charles Dickens*, ed. Madeline House and Graham Storey, vol. 3 (Oxford: Clarendon P, 1974), 156.

iii. February 4, 1842, Dickens, *Letters*, vol. 3, 50.

iv. For an account of Dickens's precarious financial state—"mortgaged on all sides and possessing scarcely any copyrights of present value" (126)—and for an astute reading of the boldness of Dickens's and his publishers' gamble on the long term benefits of the interruption of serialization, the year of respite, and the success of the travel narrative, see Robert Patten, *Charles Dickens and His Publishers* (New York: Oxford UP, 1978), 119–38.

v. Dickens, quoting *Hamlet* in, i, 154, in a letter to John Forster, January 21, 1842, Dickens, *Letters*, vol. 3, 15.

vi. January 21, 1842, Dickens, *Letters*, vol. 3, 15.

---

23 Popular before the Civil War, minstrel shows were performed by troupes of white entertainers wearing black makeup (black-face); they performed skits, songs, and dance routines, and tended (especially in the lead up to the Civil War) to be racist and pro-slavery.

vii. For a detailed account of Dickens's American reception, see William Glyde Wilkins, *Charles Dickens in America*, 1911, reprint (New York: Haskell House, 1970).

viii. Wilkins, *Charles Dickens in America*, 32.

ix. Wilkins, *Charles Dickens in America*, 23–24. William Cullen Bryant [American poet and journalist, (1794–1878)] echoed this language in an editorial in the *New York Evening Post* the day of the New York dinner, claiming that Dickens's reception had articulated new, democratic criteria for excellence and honor: "a young man, without birth, wealth, title, or a sword, whose only claims to distinction are his intellect and heart, is received with a feeling that was formerly rendered only to emperors and kings." See Sidney Moss, *Charles Dickens' Quarrel with America* (Troy, NY: Whitson, 1984), 2.

x. Moss, *Charles Dickens' Quarrel*, 3.

xi. New Haven *Commercial Herald*, quoted in Wilkins, *Charles Dickens in America*, 95.

xii. An editorial in the *New World* on February 12, 1842, put it bluntly: "Has Mr. Dickens yet to learn that to the very absence of such a law as he advocates, he is mainly indebted for his widespread popularity in this country? To that class of his readers—the dwellers in log cabins, in our back settlements—whose good opinion, he says is dearer to him than gold, his name would hardly have been known had an international copyright law been in existence." Even the pro-copyright press drew the connection. Arguing that "the evil of which he complains should be remedied," the New York *Morning Courier* nevertheless regretted Dickens's "ill-timed" comments, noting that his "reputation in the United States arises from the fact, that his writings have been placed within the reach of every reader by reason of their [sic] being no restriction upon the copyright" (quoted in Paul Davis, "Dickens and the American Press, 1842," *Dickens Annual* 4 [1968]: 67).

xiii. In his New York speech, Dickens claimed a right to speak on copyright, "a question of universal literary interest," on the grounds that there had not been "the faintest unworthy reference to self in any word" he had addressed to his American audience (K.J. Fielding, *The Speeches of Charles Dickens* [New York: Oxford UP, 1960], 28). His published preface to a series of letters from British authors supporting international copyright similarly claims that "the sentiments that I have expressed on all public occasions...are not merely my individual sentiments, but are ... the opinions of the great body of British authors" (Wilkins, *Charles Dickens in America*, 250; Dickens, *Letters*, vol. 3, 213). Dickens's most ferocious attempt to deliver himself from the charge of self-interest came after his return to England when the *Edinburgh Review* alleged that he had gone to America "as a kind of missionary in the cause of International Copyright." Dickens vehemently replied in a letter to the *Times* that "It occurred to me to speak (as other English travelers connected with literature have done before me) ... when I found myself in America" (Wilkins, *Charles Dickens in America*, 239–40). For analysis of the excessive and self-indicting nature of Dickens's protestations, see Moss, *Charles Dickens' Quarrel*, 60–66 and Alexander Welsh, *From Copyright to Copperfield: The Identity of Dickens* (Cambridge, MA: Harvard UP, 1987), 38.

xiv. The American press was unaware that Dickens carried in his "portmanteau a petition for an international copyright law, signed by all the best American writers, with Washington Irving at their head" (Letter to John Forster, February 27, 1842, Dickens, *Letters*, vol. 3, 92), although the *New World* suspected that "his *business* in visiting the United States at this season of the year—a season not usually chosen by travelers for pleasure" was "to procure, or to assist in procuring, the passage, by Congress, of an International Copyright Law" (quoted in Dickens, *Letters*, vol. 3, 83). For Dickens's presentation of this petition to Henry Clay, see Frederick Saunders, "A Reminiscence in Copyright History," *Publishers' Weekly* 33 (June 30, 1888): 988.

xv. Letter to John Forster, February 24, 1842, Dickens, *Letters*, vol. 3, 83.

xvi. For Dickens's prefatory letter, see Dickens, *Letters*, vol. 3, 213; for the appended letters and memorial, see Dickens, *Letters*, vol. 3, 621–24.

xvii. See for example the response of *the Boston Courier*, quoted in Dickens, *Letters*, vol. 3, 215.

xviii. Letter to Daniel Maclise, March 22, 1842, Dickens, *Letters*, vol. 3, 154.

xix. Letter to Frederick Dickens, March 22, 1842, Dickens, *Letters*, vol. 3, 149. See also the newspaper report quoted in a footnote, which details one barber's use of Dickens's locks, Dickens, *Letters*, vol. 3, 80.

xx. See Dickens, *Letters*, vol. 3, 74–75, and Wilkins, 152–60.

xxi. March 22, 1842, Dickens, *Letters*, vol. 3, 145.

xxii. Letter to Henry Austin, May 1, 1842, Dickens, *Letters*, vol. 3, 230.

xxiii. The difficulty of thinking about authorial agency under conditions of unauthorized reprinting is not simply Dickens's problem; it is richly reflected in the criticism, which tends to overestimate the coordination of the American newspaper press as a way of assigning blame for the failure of Dickens's tour. Jerome Meckier's account of "The Newspaper Conspiracy of 1842" (Jerome Meckier, *Innocent Abroad: Charles Dickens's American Engagements* [Lexington: UP of Kentucky, 1990]) both reflects and reflects on the problem when he describes Dickens as "the victim of an informal conspiracy" (41): how much design, how much responsibility can one attach to an act of unauthorized reprinting? The experience of the editors of the Worcester *Aegis* with the circulation of an intimate personal description of Dickens is pertinent here. Chagrined that their attempt to represent their "first impression" of Dickens had "travelled further" than they "could have anticipated," and had "found its way into papers where it will be likely to meet the eye of Mr. Dickens," the editors apologized for the effect their comments might have when read out of context (quoted in Davis, "American Press," 64). While Dickens might indeed have suspected collusion, encountering this oddly detailed description of his physical characteristics in local papers in many of the places he visited, the offense is attributable to a decentralized and copy-hungry press, not an organized conspiracy. Dickens demonstrates his awareness of how authorial agency could be both exerted and effaced through this medium when he suggests that Cornelius Felton send copies of the British authors' letters of support to four carefully chosen newspapers; see his "Letter to C.C. Felton," April 29, 1842, Dickens, *Letters*, vol. 3, 214–15. Literary critics have been less resourceful than Dickens was in responding to the challenges to authorial and editorial agency posed by the system of reprinting. Despite their impressive mastery of the texts, the chain of events, and the social conditions that structured Dickens's tour, the need to blame and to exonerate individuals frequently locks Meckier and the chief defender of the American press, Sidney Moss, into recapitulating nineteenth-century charges of newspaper conspiracy and gentlemanly collusion rather than moving beyond them.

xxiv. See his reference to the "Carmen of Hertford [sic], who presented themselves in a body in their blue frocks, among a crowd of well-dressed ladies and gentlemen, and bade me welcome through their spokesmen. They had all read my books, and all perfectly understood them" (letter to W.C. Macready, March 22, 1842, Dickens, *Letters*, vol. 3, 158–59).

xxv. See Dickens's letters to John S. Bartlett and John Forster, February 24, 1842, Dickens, *Letters*, vol. 3, 79, 85.

xxvi. For Dickens's epistolary account of this episode, see his letter to John Forster, January 29, 1842, Dickens, *Letters*, vol. 3, 33; for its incorporation into his travel narrative, see Charles Dickens, *American Notes for General Circulation*, Arnold Goldman and John Witley, eds. (New York: Penguin Books, 1985), 74. Dickens dissolves this ambiguity and erases his own vulnerability in Charles Dickens, *Martin Chuzzlewit*, ed. P.N. Furbank (New York: Penguin Books, 1995), where these figures become newsboys hawking sensationalist and exploitative penny dailies (317–18).

xxvii. "Dickens's American Notes for General Circulation," by Q.Q.Q. [Samuel Warren], *Blackwood's Edinburgh Magazine* 52 (December 1842): 783–801; 787.

xxviii. Although appearing in many twentieth-century editions, this chapter was first printed posthumously in Forster's biography. See John Forster, *The Life of Charles Dickens*, vol. 1 (London: Chapman and Hall, 1872), 304–07.

xxix. *American Notes*, 271.

xxx. Ibid., 180.
xxxi. Ibid., 183.
xxxii. Ibid., 274.
xxxiii. See M. Giulia Fabi, "Representing Slavery in Nineteenth-Century Britain: The Anxiety of Non/Fictional Authorship in Charles Dickens *American Notes* and William Brown's *Clotel*," *Images of America: Through the European Looking Glass*, ed. William L. Chewin (Brussels: VUB UP, 1997), 125–40. Noting the "literary inversion of Dickens's real-life priorities," Fabi argues that in Dickens's narrative, slavery becomes "the very visible, but nevertheless coded, literary signifier of that discontent with the United States which had initially coalesced around the (literarily invisible) issue of copyright" (132). I would alter her formula to emphasize the instrumentality of slavery, not the substitution of one issue for the other. Slavery does not stand in for copyright so much as serve as an opportunity for Dickens to intervene in the culture of reprinting.
xxxiv. See Louise H. Johnson, "The Source of the Chapter on Slavery in Dickens's *American Notes*," *American Literature* 14.4 (January 1943): 427–30.
xxxv. Theodore Weld, *American Slavery as It Is: Testimony of a Thousand Witnesses* (New York: Arno P, 1968), [iv], [iii].
xxxvi. *American Notes*, 277.
xxxvii. Ibid., 283.
xxxviii. Ibid., 269.
xxxix. Dickens's attempt to establish a firm relationship between frontier violence and the institution of slavery continues to drift back to scenes of reading: "Do we not know that the worst deformity and ugliness of slavery are at once the cause and the effect of the reckless license taken by these freeborn outlaws? Do we not know that the man who has been born and bred among its wrongs; who has seen in his childhood husbands obliged at the word of command to flog their wives; women, indecently compelled to hold up their own garments that men might lay the heavier stripes upon their legs, driven and harried by brutal overseers in their time of travail, and becoming mothers on the field of toil, under the very lash itself; *who has read in youth and seen his virgin sisters read*, descriptions of runaway men and women, and their disfigured persons, which could not be published elsewhere, of so much stock upon a farm, or at a show of beasts:—do we not know that that man, whenever his wrath is kindled up, will be a brutal savage?" (*American Notes*, 283; emphasis mine). The violent American in this passage is above all a voyeur, an "overseer" both of the degradation of slave women and of his sisters' access to forbidden knowledge, a man made savage by seeing and reading.
xl. *American Notes*, 284.
xli. Ibid., 287.
xlii. This is a loose enough chain of cause and effect to implicate violence in England: "When knives are dawn by Englishmen in conflict let it be said and known: 'We owe this change to Republican Slavery'" (*American Notes*, 284).
xliii. *American Notes*, 288.
xliv. Kate Field, *Pen Photographs of Charles Dickens's Readings: Taken from Life*, ed. Carolyn J. Moss (Troy, NY: Whitston, 1998), 12. For a "Schedule of Dickens's Readings in America," see 96–99.
xlv. *Boston Daily Journal*, December 5, 1867, quoted in Moss, *Charles Dickens's Quarrel*, 271–72.
xlvi. For a detailed account of the American press response to Dickens's 1868 tour, see Moss, *Charles Dickens's Quarrel*, 232–324.
xlvii. *American Notes*, 295.
xlviii. Ibid., 296.
xlix. Ibid., 296.

l. For this arrangement, in which Ticknor & Fields promised to pay Dickens a royalty for each volume sold and to import and sell Chapman and Hall's "Illustrated Library Edition," see Moss, *Charles Dickens's Quarrel*, 213–15. Moss usefully documents the angry reaction of T.B. Peterson & Brothers to this arrangement. T.B. Peterson had been paying the Harper Brothers for access to advance sheets that the Harpers obtained by sending regular payments to Dickens. Notwithstanding Dickens's pride in the honorable nature of his agreement with Ticknor & Fields, one newspaper likened the arrangement to "selling that which was already sold" (217).

li. Advertisement, inside cover, *American Notes for General Circulation* (Boston: Ticknor & Fields, 1867).

lii. Ibid., 178.

CHAPTER 5

Remediating

27.

Jerome J. McGann, "The Rationale of Hypertext," *Radiant Textuality: Literature after the World Wide Web.* Basingstoke and New York: Palgrave, 2001. 53–74

Jerome McGann (b. 1937) is an important textual editor and editorial theorist, but he is also at the forefront of efforts to develop digital tools for scholarship. In this essay, McGann brings these two aspects of his work together to reflect on the potential of digital tools such as hypertext to transform our understanding of the work of scholarly editors. His essay "The Rationale of Hypertext" is a self-conscious attempt to revisit and update W.W. Greg's seminal essay "The Rationale of Copy-text" (included in this volume, p. 125–38). In his original essay, Greg laid out the reasons why an editor might choose one early text of a work as the basis of a new edition of the work. The editor would then emend this "copy-text" to reflect the author's later revisions, as well as correcting errors that had crept into it in the process of printing. McGann, having previously taken issue with some of Greg's conclusions in his book *A Critique of Modern Textual Criticism* (1983), argues in this essay that digital technologies make the whole concept of a copy-text obsolete, and allow traditional editions to be replaced (or at least supplemented) by online archives of texts that will permit new kinds of reading and study.

McGann asserts that traditional scholarly editions are powerful technologies for studying how works have been transmitted over time, and how textual variants have been introduced in the process. But, in his view, they have one major drawback: they are books. Editors make a new book in order to study books from the past, which means there is a whole category of information about the physical appearance of those past books that it is very difficult for editors to represent in their new books (which, of course, have their own physical appearance). Traditionally, editors have had to choose one of two routes. They can create a facsimile of an earlier text, which includes a lot of information about the physical appearance of that text, but little or no information about how it varies from other texts. Or they can create an "eclectic" edition, which includes a lot of information about how different texts of the work vary from each other, but little or no information about the physical appearance of any of them. In preparing the edition, the editor collects a lot of information about both these things, but it is difficult to present all this information in the final edition.

Digital archives, McGann claims, can present all this information at once, and can therefore combine the benefits of a facsimile with those of an eclectic edition. Rather than offering an edition in the traditional sense, these digital projects place an archive of material online, which may include page-images of manuscripts or early editions, transcripts, and records of textual variants, along with an interface that allows users to search and collate the materials to facilitate further study. These kinds of online archive can include material in media that cannot easily or economically appear in a printed book, such as performances of songs or scenes from plays, and high-quality color images. They are therefore especially suited to the works of artists who produced work in more than one medium, such as Robert Burns, who wrote poems to be read and songs to be sung, Dante Gabriel Rossetti, who produced both poems and paintings (often tackling the same subject in two media), or William Blake, who created composite artworks that combine textual and visual elements. The interfaces of digital archives also allow the material to be searched and manipulated in ways that are either impossible or prohibitively time-consuming when using a physical book. McGann himself founded the Rossetti Archive, which puts into practice some of the ideas he advances here, and the Networked Infrastructure for Nineteenth-Century Electronic Scholarship (NINES), which aims to assess and federate a number of archives of this kind, providing a single portal that allows users to access several of them at once. This essay, then, offers a vision of how new technologies are transforming how literary critics and scholars relate to the poems, plays, and novels that they study.

The Rationale of Hypertext

> To see a world in a grain of sand
> And a heaven in a wild flower,
> Hold infinity in the palm of your hand
> And eternity in an hour.
> —William Blake, "Auguries of Innocence"[1]

> Or if it indeed be so, that this other Space is really Thoughtland, then take me to that blessed region where I in Thought shall see the insides of all solid things.... In that blessed region of Four Dimensions, shall we linger on the threshold of the Fifth, and not enter therein? Ah, no! Let us rather resolve that our ambition shall soar with our corporal ascent.
> —E.A. Abbott, *Flatland. A Romance of Many Dimensions*[2]

Lofty reflections on the cultural significance of information technology are commonplace now. Tedious as they can be, they serve an important social function. Some distribute general

---

1 William Blake (1757–1827), "Auguries of Innocence" (c. 1804), 1–4. Blake was an English poet and printmaker whose works often combine text and visual imagery.

2 Edwin Abbott (1838–1926), *Flatland* (1884).

knowledge to society at large, some send it to particular groups whose professional history makes information about information an important and perhaps problematic issue.[i]

Literary scholars comprise just this kind of group. If certain features of the new information technologies have overtaken us—for instance, the recent and massive turn to word processing—more advanced developments generate suspicion. When one speaks to colleagues about the emergence of the electronic **library**, information networks, or about the need and usefulness of making scholarly journals electronic, brows grow dark and troubled. And yet it is clear to anyone who has looked carefully at our postmodern condition that no real resistance to such developments is possible, even if it were desirable.

In this chapter I focus primarily on a particular feature of literary works—their physical character, whether audial[3] or visible. I shall be pointing out why these features are important in a literary point of view and also sketching certain practical means for elucidating these textual features. This last matter is also the most difficult. The methodology I shall be discussing requires the scholar to learn to use a new set of scholarly tools.

One final introductory comment. My remarks here apply only to textual works that are instruments of scientific knowledge. The poet's view of text is necessarily very different. To the imagination the materialities of text (oral, written, printed, electronic) are incarnational, not vehicular, forms. But for the scientist and scholar, the media of expression are primarily conceptual utilities, means rather than ends. Scholars often seek to evade or supersede an expressive form to the extent that it hinders the conceptual goal (whether it be theoretical or practical). But good poets do not quarrel with their tools in this way, even when they are developing technical innovations. As William Morris famously observed, "You can't have art without resistance in the materials."[4]

Here I shall work entirely within the terms of this distinction between a scholarly/scientific and an artistic/aesthetic point of view. Establishing the usefulness of the distinction is important, of course, for the purposes of this chapter's argument. But the same move will prove equally important in the later chapters of the book, in which I shall be working to explore the fault lines in this same distinction. As we shall see, efforts toward "rethinking textuality"—traditional as well as digital—are impeded by the uncritical assumption of the authority of this same distinction. We will come at a later point to see how this distinction functions and under what circumstances one might want either to assume it or to set it aside.

I. The Book as a Machine of Knowledge

Let us begin with the question "why": *Why* take up these new digital tools or seek new editing methods, especially when both tasks make such demands upon us? At this point most scholars know about the increased speed and analytic power that computerization gives and about the

3 Related to or perceived by the sense of hearing.

4 William Morris (1834–96) was a socialist writer and textile artist associated with the Pre-Raphaelite movement.

"information highway" and its scholarly possibilities. Major changes in the forms of knowledge and information are taking place. From a literary person's point of view, however, the relevance of these changes can appear to be purely marginal: for whatever happens in the future, whatever new electronic poetry or fiction gets produced, the literature we inherit (to this date) is and will always be bookish.

Which is true—although that truth underscores what is crucial in all these events from the *scholar's* point of view: We no longer have to use books to analyze and study other books or texts. That simple fact carries immense, even catastrophic, significance. Until now the book or **codex** form has been one of our most powerful tools for developing, storing, and disseminating information. In literary studies, the book has evolved (over many centuries) a set of scientific engines—specific kinds of books and discursive genres—of great power and complexity. Critical and other scholarly **editions** of our cultural inheritance are among the most distinguished achievements of our profession.

When we use books to study books, or hard copy-texts to analyze other hard copy-texts, the scale of the tools seriously limits the possible results. In studying the physical world, for example, it makes a great difference if the level of the analysis is experiential (direct) or mathematical (abstract). In a similar way, electronic tools in literary studies don't simply provide a new point of view on the materials, they lift one's general level of attention to a higher order. The difference between the codex and the electronic *Oxford English Dictionary* provides a simple but eloquent illustration of this. The electronic *OED* is a metabook, that is, it has

consumed everything that the codex *OED* provides and reorganized it at a higher level. It is a research tool with greater powers of consciousness. As a result, the electronic *OED* can be read as a book or it can be used electronically. In the latter case it will generate readerly views of its information that cannot be had in the codex *OED* without unacceptable expenditures of time and labor.

Scholarly editions comprise the most fundamental tools in literary studies. Their development came in response to the complexity of literary works, especially those that had evolved through a long historical process (as one sees in the Bible, Homer, the plays of Shakespeare). To deal with these works, scholars invented an array of ingenious tools: **facsimile** editions, critical editions, editions with elaborate notes and contextual materials for clarifying a work's meaning. The limits of the book determined the development of the structural forms of these different mechanisms; those limits also necessitated the periodic recreation of new editions as relevant materials appeared or disappeared, or as new interests arose.

So far as editing and textual studies are concerned, codex tools present serious difficulties. To make a new edition one has to duplicate the entire productive process and then add to or modify the work as necessary. Furthermore, the historical process of documentary descent generates an increasingly complex textual network (the word "text" derives from a word that means "weaving"). Critical editions were developed to deal with exactly these situations. A magnificent array of textual machinery evolved over many centuries.

Brilliantly conceived, these works are nonetheless infamously difficult to read and use. Their problems arise because they deploy a book form to study another book form. This symmetry between the tool and its subject forces the scholar to invent analytic mechanisms that must be displayed and engaged at the primary reading level—for example, apparatus structures, descriptive **bibliographies**, calculi of variants, shorthand reference forms, and so forth. The critical edition's apparatus, for example, exists only because no single book or manageable set of books can incorporate for analysis all of the relevant documents. In standard critical editions, the primary materials come before the reader in abbreviated and coded forms.

The problems grow more acute when readers want or need something beyond the semantic content of the primary textual materials—when one wants to hear the performance of a song or ballad, see a play, or look at the physical features of texts. Facsimile editions answer to some of these requirements, but once again the book form proves a stumbling block in many cases. Because the facsimile edition stands in a one-to-one relation to its original, it has minimal analytic power—in sharp contrast to the critical edition. Facsimile editions are most useful not as analytic engines, but as tools for increasing access to rare works.

Editing in codex forms generates an **archive** of books and related materials. This archive then develops its own meta-structures—**indexing** and other study mechanisms—to facilitate navigation and analysis of the archive. Because the entire system develops through the codex form, however, duplicate, near-duplicate, or differential archives appear in different places. The crucial problem here is simple: The logical structures of the "critical edition" function at the same level as the material being analyzed. As a result, the full power of the logical structures is checked and constrained by being compelled to operate in a bookish format. If the coming of the book vastly increased the spread of knowledge and information, history has slowly revealed the formal limits of all hardcopy's informational and critical powers. The archives are sinking in a white sea of paper.

Computerization allows us to read "hardcopy" documents in a non-real or, as we now say, a "virtual" space-time environment. This consequence follows whether the hardcopy is being marked up for electronic search and analysis, or whether it is being organized hypertextually. When a book is translated into electronic form, the book's (heretofore distributed) semantic and visual features can be made simultaneously present to each other. A book thus translated need not be read within the time-and-space frames established by the material characteristics of the book. If the hardcopy to be translated comprises a large set of books and documents, the power of the translational work appears even more dramatically, since all those separate books and documents can also be made simultaneously present to each other, as well as all the parts of the documents.

Of course, the electronic text will be "read" in normal space-time, even by its programmers: the mind that made (or that uses) both codex and computer is "embodied." This means that, from the user's point of view, computerization organizes (as it were) sequential engagements with non-sequential forms of knowledge and experience—immediate encounters with abstract or complexly mediated forms. If the limits of experience remain thus untranscended through computerization's virtual enginery, however, the new tools offer a much clearer and more capacious view of one particular class or "order of things"—in this case, the order of those things we call texts, books, documents.

II. Hyperediting and Hypermedia

The electronic environment of hyperediting frees one to a considerable extent from these codex-based limits. Indeed, computerization for the first time releases the logical categories of traditional critical editing to function at more optimal levels. But "editing" text through word processors is not, in the view being taken here, "hyperediting" because word processing engines are structured only for expressive purposes. On the other hand, the deployment of "**hypertext**" software should not be judged a necessity of hyperediting. The electronic *OED* does not use hypertext but it is certainly a hyperediting project. So too is the work initiated by Peter Robinson and the COLLATE program[5] he has developed. To function in a "hyper" mode, an editing project must use computerization as a means to secure freedom from the analytic limits of hardcopy-text.[ii]

Nonetheless, hypertext programs provide the clearest model for hyperediting. Hypertexts allow one to navigate through large masses of documents and to connect these documents, or parts of the documents, in complex ways. The relationships can be predefined (as in George Landow's various "webs," like *The Dickens Web*) or they can be developed and pursued "on the fly" (through the relationships created in the SGML mark-up of a work[6]). They are called hypermedia programs when they have the power to include audial and/or visual documents in the system. These documentary networks may or may not be interactively organized (for input by the reader/user). They can be distributed in self-contained forms (for example, on CD-ROM disks, like *The Perseus Project*[7]) or they can be structured for transmission through the network. In this last case, the basic hypertext structure is raised to a higher power (but not to a higher level): a networked structure (say, W3) of local hypertexts opens out into a network of networks.

I rehearse these matters, which are familiar enough to increasing numbers of scholars, to remind us that the different purposes of different scholars determine the choice of an actual hyperediting procedure. The range of options also indicates that hyperediting should be seen as a nested series of operational possibilities (and problems). In my own view, for example, a fully networked hypermedia archive would be an optimal goal. Because such an archive of archives is not yet a practical achievement, however, one must make present design decisions in a future perfect tense. What that means in practice is the following: (1) that the hyperediting design for a specific project be imagined in terms of the largest and most ambitious goals of the project

---

5 COLLATE text editing software was developed in the 1990s to aid with the collation and analysis of works preserved in multiple sources. One notable application was its use in the Canterbury Tales Project, headed by Peter Robinson, where it was used for comparative studies of multiple manuscript versions.

6 Mark-up refers to the system of annotations that governs how software displays digital text. SGML refers to a category of mark-up languages including HTML and XML.

7 The Perseus Project originated in 1987 to offer collections of digital resources for the study of Ancient Greece. After publishing two CD-ROMs, it launched a digital library site and it has now expanded to include resources for other periods, such as the Italian Renaissance.

(rather than in terms of immediate hardware or software options); and (2) that the design be structured in the most modular and flexible way, so that inevitable and fast-breaking changes in hardware and software will have a minimal effect on the work as it is being built. In practice, then, one would not lock into a front-end hypertext system pre-maturely or choose computer platforms or hardware because of current accessibility. Similarly, one wants to store data in the most complete forms possible (both as logically marked-up e-text and as high-resolution digitized images).

Obviously this paper cannot deal with all these matters in any extended way. One topic will be paramount: the importance, as I see it, of organizing a hyperediting project in hypermedia form. Hypereditions built of electronic text alone are easier to construct, of course, but they can only manipulate the semantic level of the original work. Hypermedia editions that incorporate audial and/or visual elements are preferable since literary works are themselves always more or less elaborate multimedia forms. When Pound spoke of the three expressive functions of poetry—phanopoeia, melopoeia, and logopoeia[8]—he defined the optimal expressive levels that all textual works possess by their nature as texts. Texts are language visible, auditional, and intellectual (gesture and [type]script, voice and instrumentation, syntax and usage).

III. The Necessity of Hypermedia

The most direct way to show this need is through a set of examples. In these illustrations I shall move from a straightforward presentation of the elementary material demands raised by texts, to the more complex interpretive issues that those demands create.

[...] [In a short section omitted here, McGann discusses songs and ballads by Robert Burns, which reference melodies and traditions of recitation or performance that cannot be accommodated in the traditional printed edition.]

When I was asked to edit the *New Oxford Book of Romantic Period Verse* I wanted to print texts that stayed as close to the original ones as possible. I also wanted to print a good deal of the most characteristic and popular work of the period, as well as work (for example, Blake's) that only came into prominence at a much later time.

So I wanted color facsimiles of Blake and color facsimiles of a poem like William Roscoe's "The Butterfly's Ball and the Grasshopper's Feast." And I wanted to print one of the most popular and important satires of the day, William Hone's "The Political House that Jack Built," with the

8 Ezra Pound (1885–1972), American Modernist poet, coined the term logopoeia to express how poetic language draws on the context and conventional usage patterns of words in order to generate meaning. He contrasts this with phanopoeia, the evocation of visuality, and melopoeia, the evocation of musical and rhythmic qualities.

original (and closely integrated) Cruikshank[9] illustrations. And I had other similar ideas. As it turned out, various commercial and institutional circumstances shot down most of these plans. All that remains of them is a facsimile of the wonderful Hone/Cruikshank satire.

The *New Oxford Book* is a reader's edition, not a critical edition. Nonetheless, it is a reader's edition sieved through a scholarly conscience. To give adequate reading texts of Blake, then, it ought to have given us color facsimiles. The edition doesn't do that, and it is less than I had hoped as a result. Of course the edition does many other things, and does them (I hope) well. Its unusual organization is something not every press would have permitted, especially in such a well-established series. But in the matter of visual materials, the edition's limits are clear.

I give this example partly to foreground the technical, commercial, and institutional realities that determine what scholars can do in book forms. [...] The present example reminds us how poetical texts frequently use the visual features of their media as part of their imaginative field. Just as Burns's[10] poetry almost always exploits the language's auditional forms and materials, Blake's almost always exploits the print medium for expressive effects. A text of Blake's *Songs*, for example—whether critical or otherwise—that does not at a minimum give us a color facsimile, is simply an inadequate text.

These two examples may stand as paradigms for a whole range of textual materials that scholarly editing to this point in time has not dealt with very well. We have had many fine editions of ballads and songs since the late eighteenth century, but none has been able to accommodate, except in minimal ways, the auditional features of the texts. Similarly, expressive **typography** and other visually significant features of book design have been handled to date in facsimile editions, which rarely—and never adequately—incorporate critical and scholarly apparatuses into their structure. The failure to meet the latter needs is especially apparent in the work produced during the periods I have been most involved with. The renaissance of printing that took place in the late nineteenth century utterly transformed the way poetry was conceived and written. In England, William Morris and D.G. Rossetti stand at the beginning of a poetical history that to this day shows no signs of abatement.[11] The evolution of the modernist movement could (and at some point should) be written as a history of book production and text design.

These developments in England and America trace themselves back to William Blake, whose work was put into **circulation** and made historically significant largely through the efforts of the pre-Raphaelites, especially Rossetti. Blake's work thus forecasts the massive opening of the textual field that took place in the nineteenth century, when image and word began to discover new

9 William Roscoe (1753–1831), English historian, abolitionist, though he is now best known for his children's book, "The Butterfly Ball"; George Cruikshank (1792–1878) was a noted English caricaturist and book illustrator, famous for his works of political satire; William Hone (1780–1842), English writer, satirist, and bookseller.

10 Robert Burns (1759–96) was a Scottish poet who often incorporated Scots dialect into his English poetry.

11 D.G. Rossetti (1828–82), English poet, illustrator, painter, and founder of the Pre-Raphaelites.

and significant bibliographical relations. Technological breakthroughs like **lithography** and steel **engraving** are more than causes accelerating these events. They are the signs of a culture-wide effort for the technical means to raise the expressive power of the book through visual design.

An adequate critical representation of such work has to this point been seriously hampered by the limits of the book as a critical tool. To date, for example, it has been impossible to produce a true critical edition of the works of Blake. Because Blake's texts operate simultaneously in two media, an adequate critical edition would have to marry a complete facsimile edition of all copies of Blake within the structure of a critical edition. One needs in such a case not a critical edition of Blake's work but a critical archive. This archive, moreover, must be able to accommodate the **collation** of pictures and the parts of pictures with each other as well as with all kinds of purely textual materials. Hypermedia structures for the first time make this kind of archive possible; indeed, work toward the development of such a Blake archive is now underway.[12]

The problem of editing Blake's work in a thoroughly critical way is not peculiar to Blake's idiosyncratic genius, however; it is symptomatic and widespread. To show how and why this is the case I offer three further examples, all from the nineteenth century. The first and third involve authors as famous as Blake, Emily Dickinson, and William Wordsworth.[13] The second will also be brought forward under an authorial sign, the once-celebrated poet Laetitia Elizabeth Landon.[14] The examples of Dickinson and Landon will show the structure and extent of the editing problems already glimpsed through the example of Blake's work. We conclude with a discussion of the historical significance of the most recent critical editions of Wordsworth.

[...]

It has taken 100 years for scholars to realize that a typographical edition of Dickinson's writings—whether of her poetry or even her letters—fundamentally misrepresents her literary work. A wholesale editorial revaluation of Dickinson is now well under way. A particularly telling example appeared recently in an article by Jeanne Holland on the Dickinson poem "Alone and in a Circumstance." Holland's facsimile reprint of the poem shows a work structured in a close, even a dialectical, relation to its physical materials.[iii]

Dickinson set up a kind of gravitational field for her writing when she fixed an uncanceled[15] three-cent stamp (with a locomotive design) to a sheet of paper and then wrote her poem in the space she had thus imaginatively created. Whatever this poem "means," the meaning has been visually designed—more in the manner of a painter or a graphic artist than in the manner of writers who are thinking of their language in semantic or—more generously—linguistic terms.

---

12 This archive, at <www.blakearchive.org>, is now well advanced. It aims to include not only every work produced by William Blake, but every copy of every work, encoded for online viewing and searching.

13 Emily Dickinson, American poet (1830–86); William Wordsworth, English poet and writer (1770–1850).

14 Laetitia Elizabeth Landon (1802–38), English poet.

15 Stamps that have passed through the postal system are marked, or "canceled" to prevent them being re-used.

One could easily multiply instances of this kind of text construction in Dickinson's work. As we know, she refused what she called "the auction" of print publication. All of her poetry—including those few things put into print during her lifetime without her permission—was produced as handicraft work. This means that her textual medium is treated in the writing process as an end in itself—ultimately, as part of the aesthetic field of the writing. Again and again in Dickinson's work we observe her using the physique of the page and her scripts as expressive vehicles of art. In an age of print publication, **manuscripts** of writers tend to stand *in medias res*, for they anticipate a final translation into that "better world" conceived as the printed word. In Dickinson's case, however, the genres that determine the aspirations of her work are scriptural rather than bibliographical: **commonplace book** writing, on one hand, and letter writing, on the other.

To edit her work adequately, then, one needs to integrate the mechanisms of critical editing into a facsimile edition—which is precisely the kind of thing that codex-based editing finds exceedingly difficult to do.

[...]

In this case I ask you to recall the Cornell Wordsworth, in particular the three volumes devoted to *The Prelude*: Stephen Parrish's edition of the "Two Book" Prelude (1977), W.J.B. Owen's edition of the "Fourteen Book" *Prelude* (1985), and Mark Reed's edition of the "Thirteen Book" *Prelude* (1993). All three are models of their kind, meticulous and thorough. Nonetheless, in their heroic efforts to represent that original complex and unstable scene of writing, these editions—*coming at just the historical moment that they do*—have put a period to codex-based scholarly editing.

Here is a true story that may help to explain my meaning. Several years ago I wrote to Mark Reed to ask who was going to edit the "Five Book" *Prelude*. He wrote back and said there would be no such edition since (a) that particular form of the work only attained a fleeting existence,[16] and (b) the *Prelude* project was already dauntingly large and, from the **publisher's** point of view, textually repetitive. Instead, his edition would provide a narrative description and textual history of the "Five Book" *Prelude*. He sent me a copy of this narrative, which eventually appeared as part of his edition.

Mark Reed narrativized the "Five Book" *Prelude* for one reason only: The book format (including the commercial factors governing that format) did not lend itself to printing yet another *Prelude* volume in the Cornell series. Too much of the material was viewable in the other volumes. Indeed, the limits of the codex imposed all kinds of constraints on the editors of Wordsworth's great uncompleted work, so that one will find it difficult to use: on one hand full of scholar's codes, on the other cumbersome when one wishes to compare different documents and texts.

---

16 Having previously completed a version in two "books," Wordsworth worked on, and nearly completed, a five-book version of his autobiographical poem *The Prelude* between January and March 1804, but by the end of March had decided to expand the project. The poem grew to 13 books, and later to 14.

As I have already pointed out, these problems inhere in the codex form itself, which constrains the user of the critical edition to manipulate difficult systems of abbreviation and to read texts that have (typically) transformed the original documents in radical ways. In an electronic edition, however, both of these hindrances can be removed. Precisely because an electronic edition is not itself a book, it is able to establish itself in a theoretical position that supervenes the (textual and bookish) materials it wishes to study. The operations carried out by the traditional book-based abbreviation systems continue to be performed in the electronic edition, of course, for they are central to the whole idea of the scholar's critical edition. In the computerized edition, however, the reader does not have to learn or even encounter the codes in order to execute critical operations (e.g., moving back and forth across different parts of books or separate volumes, carrying out analytic searches and comparisons). These operations are performed on command but out of sight. In addition, of course, the computerized structure allows the reader to undertake searches and analyses of the material that would have been impossible, even unimaginable, in a codex environment.

IV. Conclusion: The Rossetti Hypermedia Archive

Hyperediting is what scholars will be doing for a long time. Many difficult problems will have to be dealt with, of course, including major problems hardly touched on here: questions of **copyright**, for instance, or the whole array of problems posed by the emergence of the vast electronic information network that is even now coming into being. In the immediate context, multimedia hyperediting poses its own special difficulties.

For instance, hypermedia projects (like *The Perseus Project*, for instance) are notably constrained by a structural feature of the digitized images they employ. When these images are introduced into a hypermedia structure, they have had to serve as simple illustrations; for the (bitmapped) information in the digitized image cannot be searched and analyzed as electronic texts can be.

How to incorporate digitized images into the computational field is not simply a problem that hyperediting must *solve*; it is a problem created by the very arrival of the possibilities of hyperediting. In my own case, the Rossetti hypermedia archive was begun exactly because the project forced an engagement with this problem. Those of us who were involved with *The Rossetti Archive* from the beginning spent virtually the entire first year working at this problem. In the end we arrived at a double approach: first, to design a structure of SGML markup tags for the physical features of all the types of documents contained in *The Rossetti Archive* (textual as well as pictorial); and second, to develop an image tool that permits one to attach anchors[17] to specific features of digitized images. Both of these tools effectively open visual (and potentially audial) materials to the full computational power of the hyperediting environment.

---

17 An anchor is a piece of text that marks the beginning and/or end of a hypertext link. Here McGann refers to a protocol for attaching anchors to parts of an image, which has since been used extensively in both the Blake Archive and the Rossetti Archive.

At this writing the DTDs (Document Type Definitions) for all textual materials, including digitized materials, are fully operational. The image tool is currently in its first release.

It is important to realize that the Rossetti project is an archive rather than an edition. When a book is produced it literally closes its covers on itself. If its work is continued, a new edition, or other related books, have to be (similarly) produced. A work like the Rossetti hypermedia archive has escaped that bibliographical limitation. It has been built so that its contents and its webwork of relations (both internal and external) can be indefinitely expanded and developed.

The "hyper" organization has also permitted the archive to escape another bookish horizon that has profoundly affected editorial theory and textual scholarship. A major aspect of this scholarship has been the investigation of ancient texts—in particular, the scholarly reconstruction of such works from textual remains that have been seriously broken over time. Such work encouraged scholars to focus on a single text, the ideal goal of their reconstructive operations.

In more modern periods, however, the textual remains are often very numerous. The history of the texts of Wordsworth and Blake and Dickinson is not seriously fractured. Indeed, the scholarly problem in such cases is how to sort out the relations of the documents and put all those relationships on display. However, the goals of classical scholarship and the material formalities of the book encouraged scholars to imagine and produce single-focus works—editions that organized themselves around what used to be called a "definitive" text, the source and end and test of all the others.

Whatever the virtues of this kind of focus—there are many—one would like to be free to choose it or not, as one needs. In most cases scholars confront a vast, even a bewildering, array of documents. Determining a single focus can be analytically useful, even imperative for certain purposes. On the other hand, one can easily imagine situations where a single determining focus hinders critical study. Besides, in many other cases one would like the possibility to make *ad hoc* or provisional choices among the full array of textual alternatives—to shift the point of focus at will and need. One cannot perform such operations within the horizon of the book. A hypermedia project like *The Rossetti Archive* offers just these kinds of possibilities, for the data in the archive is not organized hierarchically. It resembles more that fabulous circle whose center is everywhere and whose circumference is nowhere.

The change from paper-based text to electronic text is one of those elementary shifts—like the change from manuscript to print—that is so revolutionary we can only glimpse at this point what it entails. Nonetheless, certain essential things are clear even now. The computerized edition can store vastly greater quantities of documentary materials, and it can be built to organize, access, and analyze those materials not only more quickly and easily, but at depths no paper-based edition could hope to achieve. At the moment these works cannot be made as cheaply or as easily as books. But very soon, I am talking about a few years, these electronic tools will not only be far cheaper, they will also be commonplace. Already scholars are creating electronic editions in many fields and languages and are thereby establishing the conventions for the practice of hyperediting. *The Rossetti Archive* is one project of this kind.

V. Coda. A Note on the Decentered Text

Editors and textual theorists interested in computerized texts appear to differ on a significant point: whether or not hyperediting requires (even if it be at some deep and invisible level) a central "text" for organizing the hypertext of documents. My judgment is that it doesn't.

The question here can and often does get quite muddled. Enthusiasts for hypertext sometimes make extravagant philosophical claims, and skeptics are then drawn toward sardonic reactions. Hypertext is no more a sign of the Last Days than was **moveable type** five centuries ago.

To say that a hypertext is not centrally organized does not mean—at least does not mean to me—that the hypertext structure has no governing order(s), even at a theoretical level. Clearly such a structure has many ordered parts and sections, and the entirety of the structure is organized for directed searches and analytic operations. In these respects the hypertext is always structured according to some initial set of design plans that are keyed to the specific materials in the hypertext and to the imagined needs of the users of those materials.

Two matters are crucial to remember here, however. First, the specific material design of a hypertext is theoretically open to alterations of its contents and its organizational elements at all points and at any time. Unlike a traditional book or set of books, the hypertext need never be "complete"—though of course one could choose to shut the structure down if one wanted, close its covers as it were. But the hypertextual order contains an inertia that moves against such a shutdown. So, for example, if one were to create a hypertext of (say) *King Lear*, the "edition" *as it is a hypertext* can pass forward in time indefinitely. Someone will have to manage it, but if it remains hypertextual it will incorporate and then go beyond its initial design and management. It will evolve and change over time, it will gather new bodies of material, and its organizational substructures will get modified, perhaps quite drastically.

The second point goes to the matter of the conceptual form of hypertext as such (as opposed to the specific implementation of that form for certain materials and purposes). Unlike a traditional edition, a hypertext is not organized to focus attention on one particular text or set of texts. It is ordered to disperse attention as broadly as possible. Of course it is true that every *particular* hypertext at any particular point in time will have established preferred sets of arrangements and orderings, and these could be less, or more, decentralized. The point is that the hypertext, unlike the book, encourages greater decentralization of design. Hypertext provides the means for establishing an indefinite number of "centers" and for expanding their number as well as altering their relationships. One is encouraged not so much to find as to make order—and then to make it again and again, as established orderings expose their limits.

An important historical fact might be usefully recalled: that the Internet, which is an archive of archives, was originally designed precisely as a decentered, nonhierarchical structure. The point was to have an information network that could be destroyed or cut at any point, at any number of points, and still remain intact as a structured informational network. The theory of hypertext flows directly from this way of imagining a non-centralized structure of complex relationships. With hypertext, as with the Net, the separate parts of the ensemble (nodes on the Net, files in a hypertext) are independently structured units. That kind of organization ensures that relationships and connections can be established and developed in arbitrary and stochastic[18] patterns.

This kind of organizational, form resembles our oldest extant hypertextual structure, the library, which is also an archive (or in many cases an archive of archives). As with the Internet and hypertext, a library is organized for indefinite expansion. Its logical organization (for example, the Library of Congress [LC] system) can be accommodated to any kind of physical environment, and it is neutral with respect to user demands and navigation. Moreover, the library is logically "complete" no matter how many volumes it contains—no matter how many are lost or added.

[...] [In a brief section omitted here, McGann compares this decentralized organizational structure to the experience of browsing in a library.]

In a hypertext, each document (or part of a document) can therefore be connected to every other document (or document part) in any way one chooses to define a connection. Relationships do not have to be organized in terms of a measure or standard (though subgroups of organization can be arbitrarily defined as non-arbitrary forms). From a scholarly editor's point of view, this structure means that every text or even every portion of a text (i.e., every logical unit in the hypertext) has an absolute value within the structure as a whole unless its absolute character is specifically modified.

The Rossetti Archive imagines an organization of its texts, pictures, and other documents in this kind of non-centralized form. So when one goes to read a poetical work, no documentary state of the work is privileged over the others. All options are presented for the reader's choice. Among those options are arbitrary constraints that can be placed on the choices available. These constraints, which can be defined at any level of the organization, can be invoked or revoked at will. The point is that the structure preserves the independence of every document because the organization, like the Net, is "divided into packets, [with] each packet separately addressed." Since each of these packets has "its own authority to originate, pass, and receive messages," each is free to "wind its way through the [archive] on an individual basis."[iv] Of course that is a metaphoric way of putting the matter: Files in a hypertext, like documents in a library, are not active agents. It is the user who moves through the hypertext. Nevertheless, the ordering of the hypertext materials is, by default, arbitrary and discrete. If the archive contains any more centralized or hierarchical structures, these have to be (arbitrarily) introduced. Furthermore, if they are introduced, the extent of their authority over the user has to be (arbitrarily) defined as well.

The problem here returns us once again to the fundamental issue of the relation of (hard copy) text to (electronic) hypertext. The decentralized forms of hypertextual archives clearly possess logical structure. That structure is designed to facilitate navigation through the archived materials irrespective of the purposes of the navigation.[v] When the hypertext is used to manage study of and navigation through complex bodies of (hardcopy) documentary materials—the kinds that

18 Following random probability patterns, so that outcomes may be analyzed but not precisely forecast.

traditional scholarly editors deal with—a special type of "decentralism" appears. The exigencies of the book form forced editorial scholars to develop fixed points of relation—the "definitive text," "**copy-text**," "ideal text," "Ur text," "standard text," and so forth—in order to conduct a book-bound navigation (by coded forms) through large bodies of documentary materials. Such fixed points no longer have to govern the ordering of the documents. As with the nodes on the Internet, every documentary moment in the hypertext is absolute with respect to the archive as a whole, or with respect to any subarchive that may have been (arbitrarily) defined within the archive. In this sense, computerized environments have established the new "rationale of hyper-text."[vi]

But we have to add one word more on this matter because this discussion of the decentered text has left out of account the actual implementation of the theoretical design. It has left out of the account the user interface that organizes and delivers the logical design of the archive to specific persons. The interface one encounters in the actual Rossetti archive is, in fact, anything but decentered. In this respect it is quite like every other scholarly and educational hypertext work known to me—The Perseus Project, say, or any of George Landow's "webs." All are quite "centered" and even quite non-dynamical in their presentational structure. We want to be aware of this since a major part of our future work with these new electronic environments will be the search for ways to implement, at the interface level, the full dynamic—and decentering—capabilities of these new tools.

Notes

i. An earlier publication of this chapter, in *The Electronic Text: Investigations in the Method and Theory of Computerized Textuality*, ed. Marilyn Deegan and Kathryn Sutherland (Oxford: Oxford UP, 1997), 19–46 contained a series of graphical illustrations of *The Rossetti Archive*. 473

ii. The simplest definition of hypertext is Theodore Nelson's "non-sequential writing" (*Literary Machines* [Sausalito, CA: Mindful, 1990], sec. 5, 2). Nelson's book is a classic introduction to hypertext. For other introductory information about hypertext and hypermedia, and about the projects mentioned in this and the next paragraphs, see *Hypertext/Hypermedia Handbook*, ed. Emily Berk and Joseph Devlin (New York: Internet Publications, McGraw Hill, 1991); *The Digital Word. Text-Based Computing in the Humanities*, ed. George P. Landow and Paul Delany (Cambridge, MA: The MIT P, 1993); *Hypertext: The Convergence of Contemporary Critical Theory and Technology* (Baltimore: Johns Hopkins UP, 1992); *Hypermedia and Literary Studies*, ed. George P. Landow and Paul Delany (Cambridge, MA: MIT P, 1991); Jay David Bolter, *Writing Space: The Computer, Hypertext, and the History of Writing* (Hillsdale, NJ: Lawrence Erlbaum, 1991).

iii. This revaluation of Dickinson studies was sparked by the great facsimile edition of the poet's original fascicles, edited by R.W. Franklin, *The Manuscript Books of Emily Dickinson*. Since then the work of Susan Howe and her students has been only slightly less significant, especially the edition of Dickinson's fragments edited by Marta Werner (Ann Arbor: U of Michigan P, 2000) and the essay by Jeanne Holland, "Scraps, Stamps, and Cutouts." Howe's seminal essay is indispensable: "These Flames and the Generosities of the Heart." See also Paula Bennett, "By a Mouth that Cannot Speak: Spectral Presence in Emily Dickinson's Letters," *The Emily Dickinson Journal* 1 (1992): 76–99 and my own "Emily Dickinson's Visible Language," *The Emily Dickinson Journal* 2 (1993): 40–57. Martha Nell Smith is currently the head of the Emily Dickinson Editorial Collective, a group of scholars committed to seeing Dickinson's work re-edited so as to expose its "sumptuary values," i.e., the scripts and visible designs that are such an important feature of the writing.

iv. Quoted from Bruce Sterling, "Internet," *The Magazine of Fantasy and Science Fiction*, Science Column no. 5 (February 1993). I quote here from the text of the column that was made available through a network mailing list.

v. For discussion of the structure of hypertext (and a critique of rather loose representations of its decentralized form) see Ross Atkinson, "Networks, Hypertext, and Academic Information Services: Some Longer Range Implications," *College & Research Libraries* 54.3 (May 1993): 199–215.

vi. Textual scholars will understand that this chapter stands in a consciously revisionist relation to W.W. Greg's great essay "The Rationale of Copy-Text."

28.

Ray Siemens, Meagan Timney, Cara Leitch, Corina Koolen, and Alex Garnett, "Toward Modeling the Social Edition: An Approach to Understanding the Electronic Scholarly Edition in the Context of New and Emerging Social Media," *Literary and Linguistic Computing* 27.4 (December 2012): 445–61

The mere fact that there are five named authors for this essay, as well as three research groups, suggests the collaborative nature of work that characterizes much of the digital humanities. Ray Siemens (b. 1966) is Canada Research Chair in Humanities Computing and Distinguished Professor in the Faculty of Humanities at the University of Victoria, in English with cross appointment in Computer Science; Meagan Timney, Cara Leitch, Corina Koolen, and Alex Garnett, are former or current graduate students working at the University of Victoria. Siemens and his Electronic Textual Cultures Lab (ETCL) have been at the forefront of both theorizing and implementing new forms of digital textual studies, specifically in relation to two early Tudor manuscript miscellanies: the *Henry VIII Manuscript* (BL Add Ms 31922), and the *Devonshire Manuscript* (BL Add Ms 17492). This essay asks how the conception of the scholarly edition is being transformed "in the context of new and emerging social media." This essay therefore reflects back on the issues addressed in Chapter 2 of this Reader—exploring the new opportunities for textual scholarship afforded by digital media. The essay posits a basic typology of electronic scholarly editions: dynamic text, hypertextual edition, dynamic edition, and finally, the social edition (all described in detail in the essay). These different models reflect both differences in the use of new technologies and different conceptions of what is relevant and appropriate to an edition. The essay makes a strong case for the development of a social edition, which can allow us to see "the scholarly text as a process rather than a product, and the initial, primary editor as a facilitator, rather than progenitor, of textual knowledge creation." As the authors point out, one must articulate a model of a scholarly edition before it is designed and implemented: a dynamic edition and a social edition can be imagined, though they do not yet exist in practice.[1]

1 The release of the wiki-edition of the Devonshire manuscript, developed by this group of authors (amongst others), means that a social edition arguably does now, in fact, exist: see <http://en.wikibooks.org/wiki/The_Devonshire_Manuscript>.

Toward Modeling the Social Edition: An Approach to Understanding the Electronic Scholarly Edition in the Context of New and Emerging Social Media[i]

I. Introduction: Extending Electronic Editorial Traditions

In the very early days of the world wide web, but well into a period in which our community understood the positive and transformative impact that computational technique has had on scholarly editing, Fortier reminded us that literary studies is and always has been focused on the engagement of texts regardless of interpretive theoretical predisposition.[ii] In digital literary studies, that textual focus manifests in a number of theories about the nature of the text in general and the electronic scholarly **edition** in particular, and has developed such that we can begin to construct, in relatively straightforward manner, a basic typology of electronic scholarly editions via the approach each type takes in handling and engaging its textual materials: from edited electronic text plus analytical tools for its readers (dynamic text), to text plus a static set of additional supporting materials in digital form for reader navigation and subsequent analysis (**hypertextual** edition), to text augmented by both dynamic analytical means and hypertextually-linked access to fixed resources plus automated means of discovering and interrelating external resources (dynamic edition). Such a typology, reductive as it may be, allows us to look forward—as Robinson, Shillingsburg, Bryant, McGann, Gabler and many others (as well as those mentioned, beyond specific citation) have encouraged us to do variously—to what lies ahead in our treatment of the text, and the textual editions, that lie at the core of our contemplation in literary studies and similar disciplines.[iii]

Well into what is often called the age of Web 2.0—becoming immersed as we are in a generation of online tools facilitating collaboration, information sharing, and interoperability ... immersed as we are by social media interaction on the web—it is worth noting that the types of electronic scholarly editions we see prominently today were largely developed before the ubiquity of the web that we now enjoy and do not accurately reflect the full range of useful possibilities present for academic engagement and interaction around the textual materials that are our focus. While the electronic medium is most certainly a productive space in which to present and analyze editions, it is increasingly more difficult to ignore the influence of new and emerging possibilities for the electronic scholarly edition in the current phase in the social formation of the web. As such, our understanding of the electronic scholarly edition in its current form requires reconsideration in light of the collaborative potential of already extant and newly-emerging digital technologies; put another way, we need to extend our understanding of the scholarly edition in light of new models of edition production that embrace social networking and its commensurate tools. Toward understanding the scholarly edition in the context of new and emerging social media, this paper and its appendices[2] offer an early engagement of pertinent

---

2 The appendices have been removed: they may be viewed here: <web.uvic.ca/~siemens/pub/2011-SocialEdition.pdf>.

issues and, ultimately, a utility-based consideration in an academic context of the toolkit that allows us to consider the *social* edition as an extension of the traditions in which it is situated and which it has the potential to inform productively.

II. A Rough Typology of the Scholarly Electronic Edition

Historically, the scholarly edition relied on the print medium and the expertise of a single authority or editor at its helm—something almost immediately challenged by the provision of text in electronic, readily malleable, and ultimately re-combinable and redistributable form. One of the first models of the movement from the print to the electronic edition is typically referred to as the *dynamic text.* Its principles articulated most fully in the late 1980s, the dynamic text emphasizes extant textual and linguistic relationships; its historical roots are in word-based scholarly activities such as **concordance** creation and **indexing**, **collation**, collocation and distribution, attribution and dating, rhyme and content analysis, while allowing the reader to engage with the text *dynamically.*[iv] In practical terms, this model of the electronic edition is the combination of a properly encoded electronic text with text-retrieval and analysis software.[v] What makes this type of edition *dynamic* is the way in which the computer facilitates a non-linear interaction with the text. In essence, the dynamic edition structures and treats the text as a database. This database structure allows the reader to draw a good deal of text-based information that is not as easily accessible to the reader of the same work in print. In addition to its disseminative and editorial flexibility, a chief benefit of this sort 477
of edition is that it combines text with tools, speeding academic reading-related tasks. The dynamic text automates reading-related functions that would likely not be carried out without the assistance of the computer because of the expense in time involved. A *computer-assisted analysis* of the text and a linear *reading* of it are acts that become closely affiliated and, potentially, equivalent.

Following quickly, with the rise of hypertext, the *hypertextual edition*[vi] exploits the ability of hypertextual organization to facilitate a reader's interaction with the apparatus (textual, critical, and otherwise) that traditionally accompanies scholarly editions, and with relevant external textual and graphical resources, critical materials, and so forth,[vii] and is seen by some as a technological manifestation of social theories of editing that were transformative near the end of the last century. As with the dynamic text, all of the interactions facilitated by a hypertextual edition could be carried out, hypothetically, with a print edition; here, however, that edition would have to be supplemented by the resources (paper-based, audio, video) of an excellent **library** and considerable leg-work. What is hypothetically available to the reader in a research library, or group of libraries, is here made immediately available, encouraging use of the resources by the reader in a seamless fashion; as such, the hypertextual edition, like the dynamic text, also makes accessible dimensions of the text not normally or conveniently available to readers, but does so by providing immediate access to a different sort of material than that handled by the dynamic text. Moreover, as with the dynamic text, the hypertextual edition affords a type of intertextuality[3] that produces a critical reader with a potentially more powerful grasp of that which is being read than one employing print resources alone. Lastly, because of the broad range of materials that can be incorporated therein, both because of the economy of data storage in the electronic medium and the benefits of hypertextual navigation, the hypertextual edition can quite comfortably accommodate many 'types' of editions: documentary, genealogical, **copy-text**, multiple version, socially-based, eclectic, **variorum**, and so forth.

[...]

Moving forward, the argument toward the *dynamic edition* is founded, first, in the observation that the two perspectives on the electronic scholarly edition, dynamic and hypertextual, should be united in practice as they are, seemingly, in theory so that the reader can take advantage of both dynamic interaction with the text *and* its related materials, and also reap the benefits of the fixed hypertextual links that typify the standard relation of materials we find in a scholarly edition. It is then augmented by the notion that even these types of editions, like their print counterparts in many ways, are objects that attempt to represent or fix at a single moment in time the work of an unfixed, ever-evolving—and thus dynamic—scholarly community engaged in the process of stockpiling scholarship, as Frye might note.[viii] As the argument goes: electronic editions that live up to the potential of the medium, especially in terms of the inclusivity that it allows, must also be *dynamic*; they must be able to navigate the contents of the edition in familiar ways, and also able to reflect and draw upon the growing, evolving, and unfixed stockpile of scholarship that relates to the matter of the edition.[ix] The dynamic edition, of which there is not yet a exemplifying touchstone, is predicated on the possibility that the level of interaction one can enjoy with an electronic edition itself, if facilitated in the style of the dynamic text, can replace much of the interaction that one typically has with a text's accompanying materials via explicit hypertextual links in a hypertextual edition. The principles of computationally-facilitated interaction allowed by the dynamic text, which indexes and concords itself, are transferrable to the realm of textual apparatus and commentary as typically modeled in the hypertextual edition, and well beyond into all materials in the medium that relate to the matter of any edition. Such an edition has the ability, in effect, to annotate itself and provide its own apparatus, employing sophisticated software to automate the process of formalizing the associations we take for granted in current editions.

In this, we capitalize on a growing ability to manage, and to navigate, what is available in relation to our electronic scholarly editions in a dynamic manner.[x] The premise for this navigation is found in humanistic assumptions of the relations that exist within and among texts; it rises out of an accepted understanding of intertextuality, explicitly manifest. A hypertext, which in its best definition is a "multisequentially read text,"[xi] embraces such an understanding, and implementations of hypertextual structures rely on the fact that one instance of textual material has association with other instances; in short, such structures

3 Overlaps, similarities, and/or cross-referencing between different texts.

rely on the fact that intertextuality exists, and their advancement, further, can be managed by varied means, including algorithmic. At base, we might see in this a connection to the founding functional premises of socially-facilitated interaction on the web—a useful point of derivation to consider.

III. Some Pertinent Activities of the Humanist, in the Context of the Commons

Just as the textual core of the literary-based scholar's activity has remained fairly stable over time—even as the ways in which the scholar may access and interact with that core have changed considerably—the core of activities traditionally involved in humanities scholarship have altered very little since the professionalization of academic study during the nineteenth century. Recent work toward articulating them and even modeling them computationally, as independent basic activities or in clusters of related activities, has been a valuable occupation of the digital humanities community, especially among those who build computational tools for humanistic use;[xii] much of this work is situated around key activities of humanities scholars as described by Unsworth among the seven scholarly primitives essential to humanistic work: discovering, annotating, comparing, referring, sampling, illustrating, and representing.[xiii]

Not surprisingly, digital scholarly editions have aspects of their functional interaction modeled to facilitate these activities, since the earliest dynamic texts integrating digital tools with electronic text, and typically in the context of what might best be described as a humanistic 479
workflow that is modeled computationally.

[...]

... [T]wo evolving concepts are central to this: the social dimension of McGann's model of multi-dimensional textuality and the idea of the community of practice, broadly construed. In "Marking Texts of Many Dimensions," McGann outlines a key dimension of textuality as *social*, which is production- and reception-oriented[xiv]—an area in which digital textual modeling and mediation is noted to have, at the time, been least successful. Here, we see the social dimension of reading and analysis identified implicitly for broadening via computational facilitation, a notion extended further, and in broader context, when McGann notes in the context of humanistic labor and engagement that "There are crowds of us yet to be sourced."[xv]

These crowds exist in large part in communities of practice situated around humanistic methods and materials. The term 'community of practice' refers to a group that forms around a particular interest, where individual members participate in collaborative activities of various kinds. Active involvement in the group is key; through this involvement, group members "develop a shared repertoire of resources: experiences, stories, tools, ways of addressing recurring problems—in short a shared practice."[xvi] Knowledge-building communities as a particular kind of community of practice take "as an explicit goal the development of individual and collective understanding."[xvii] In academe, we have noted communities of practice via varied names, and have described such large and now well-established initiatives as the Text Encoding Initiative—and even humanities computing and the digital humanities, earlier—in these terms; indeed, the digital humanities readily understand such collaborative formations.[xviii] With the facilitation of social media, there is a growing movement in humanities knowledge-building communities to expand the scope of community membership beyond academics, and into the interested and engaged general public, to those practicing what has come to be termed citizen scholarship. Greenberg identifies three modes of citizen scholarship—contributory, collaborative, and cocreated—in each, the traditional scholarly community of practice is extended to include public expertise while still valuing the experience, resources, and tools already in place; based on experience with humanities projects that have had extra-academic appeal and active engagement, many in our community have highlighted ways in which digital scholarship can welcome the contributions of participants from outside academia, via means of control and regulation that are not wholly foreign to processes used by humanists traditionally.[xix] The key to success in this instance is being very clear in our understanding of what it is we do, how we do it, and how we evaluate the results of what we've done across our pertinent activities,[xx] regardless of how we articulate, group, and model those activities.

IV. The General Scope of Social Software Applicable to the Scholarly Edition

Within this framework, then, it is worth considering what is of most use to the scholarly edition from among the abundance of interactive digital tools with which scholars may choose to engage, and that might augment and enable communities of practice as they may exist around the texts that lie at the core of our consideration—tools, both scholarly and non-scholarly, that facilitate the sharing of and interaction with data in various ways, and offer new possibilities for community-driven scholarship. The majority of these tools fall into the broad category of 'social software', which is, notes Boyd, "based on supporting the desire of individuals to affiliate, their desire to be pulled into groups to achieve their personal goals."[xxi] At core, social software comes in many kinds, often grouped based on the nature of their interaction with (and with others interacting with) digital objects: knowledge creation and sharing, media sharing, blogs, **bibliographic** and bookmarking tools, aggregators, collaborative (scholarly) editing, massively multi-player online games (MMOGs), peer to peer social networks, project management software, and wide-scope content management systems, among others.

While useful to consider social software within these many and broad divisions, it is most productive in the context of this paper to focus more specifically, with scope limited to those most readily applicable to the pursuit of the next steps of the scholarly edition.... Their most functional organization here is via their use in relation to the *social* edition, emphasizing the crucial features of these tools and the ways in which they engender new modes of engagement with digital objects, such as (1) collaborative annotation, (2) user-derived content, (3) folksonomy tagging, (4) community bibliography, and (5) shared text analysis. What follows is an overview of some of the current possibilities in each category:

1. COLLABORATIVE ANNOTATION: A chief scholarly primitive, annotation is crucial to scholarly editorial activities. While older models privilege the annotations of a single editor, social tools such as BioNotate (<http://bionotate.sourceforge.net>), Google Wave (<http://wave.google.com>), digress.it (<http://digress.it>; formerly CommentPress), Reframe it (<http://reframeit.com>), and Diigo (<http://www.diigo.com>) allow for community knowledge creation. These collaborative systems usually require the installation of a toolbar that allows for annotation layering to promote "the incremental growth of information as users review others' thoughts on a resource before adding their own."[xxii] Diigo, which markets itself as a "group knowledge repository," serves as a prime example here, as it comprises the key features of annotation: highlighting and markup (known as sticky notes), as well as searchable tags and bookmarks.[xxiii]

2. USER-DERIVED CONTENT: Some online repositories allow for the creation of user-derived content, or the collection and management of fully-searchable exhibits comprising multiple digital objects. The opportunity for collaborative knowledge building is most prevalent in sites that already contain large-scale collections, as the exhibits are by necessity limited by the scope of the material available. Some prime examples include the Library of Congress's Flickr Stream (<http://www.flickr.com/photos/ 481
library_of_congress/>), Indexhibit (<http://www.indexhibit.org/>), and the *Networked Infrastructure for Nineteenth-Century Electronic Scholarship* (NINES) Collex (<http://www.nines.org>).[xxiv]

3. FOLKSONOMY TAGGING: Collaborative or social tagging is "the process by which many users add metadata in the form of keywords to shared content."[xxv] The term now most often used to describe this type of user-generated cataloguing is *folksonomy*, which is defined as "the result of personal free tagging of information and objects [...] for one's own retrieval. The tagging is done in a social environment (usually shared and open to others). Folksonomy is created from the act of tagging by the person consuming the information."[xxvi] The English **Broadside** Ballad Archive (http://emc.english.ucsb.edu/ballad_project) uses a type of "user-generated metadata"[xxvii] to manage and catalogue images. Other applications that manage knowledge using folksonomy include many media sharing sites such as Flickr (<http://flickr.com>), Twitter (<http://twitter.com>), bookmarking sites such as Del.icio.us, as well as Diigo (above).[xxviii]

4. COMMUNITY BIBLIOGRAPHY: Social Bibliographies relate closely to collaborative tagging and also participate in knowledge creation. These tools

allow users to collect and catalogue references and resources using academic citations, folksonomy tagging, and link sharing. Some of the most popular community bibliography tools include Zotero (<http://www.zotero.org>; see also Cohen,[xxix] Digg (<http://digg.com>), reddit (<http://www.reddit.com>), StumbleUpon (<http://www.stumbleupon.com>), Connotea (<http://www.connotea.org>), CiteULike (<http://www.citeulike.org>), and BibSonomy (<http://www.bibsonomy.org>). BibSonomy, for example, is a 'social bookmark and publication sharing system.' Twitter (<http://www.twitter.com>) has also allowed groups of users to share links and resources, especially within the digital humanities community (see Priem and Costello and Ross for other academic uses).[xxx]

5. TEXT-ANALYSIS: Digital humanities textual analysis "involves the application of algorithmically facilitated search, retrieval, and critical processes that, originating in humanities-based work, have been demonstrated to have application far beyond."[xxxi] Examples include Voyeur's embedded widgets (<http://voyeur.hermeneuti.ca>), and Ivanhoe (<http://patacriticism.org/ivanhoe>), which allows for community analysis of literary texts. While many text analysis applications exist, the exploration of the social potential of these tools is still only in its nascent stages.

[...]

Pertinent characteristics shared by these tools, and the interactions and augmentations they facilitate, is that they are user-rather than creator-driven, evolving rather than fixed, collective rather than individual, expansive rather than inclusive, and open source rather than proprietary and closed.[xxxii]

V. A Toolkit, Toward Modeling the Social Edition

What sits at the intersection of social media and the scholarly edition in electronic form is founded, at its core, via these tools that offer us new ways to work together, for our editions to work together, and for us to work with others. Despite Stephen Nichols's call to "dismantle the silo model of digital scholarship,"[xxxiii] many electronic scholarly editions, like print editions, continue to exist as self-contained units that do not encourage interaction with other resources, and they do not yet actively encourage or facilitate interaction among the communities of practice they serve or even among those who have the most knowledge to bring to bear. These tools, and others like them, can help remedy this. The *social* edition grows from the spirit of Greg Crane's exhortation, and others like it, that "[w]e need to shift from lone editorials and monumental editions to editors ... who coordinate contributions from many sources and oversee living editions."[xxxiv] And, indeed, documented movement in this direction is already well underway with projects such as EEBO interactions, "a social networking resource for *Early English Books Online*," George Mason University's "Crowdsourcing Documentary Transcription: An Open Source Tool," *Transcribe Bentham*, and more.[xxxv] These projects, and others like them, point to a growing need in the scholarly community to expand our knowledge communities using the social technologies at our disposal. Building on existing, expanding, and newly-emerging communities of practice in combination with the model of Web 2.0, we can appropriately harness the power of specifically social tools, the majority of which move in some way towards combining digital social interaction with scholarly activities.

This has a destabilizing effect; such tools facilitate a model of textual interaction and intervention that encourage us to see the scholarly text as a process rather than a product, and the initial, primary editor as a facilitator, rather than progenitor, of textual knowledge creation. The most conservative electronic scholarly editions or **archives** have used computation chiefly to "describe and express print-, visual-, and audio-based material in tagged and searchable electronic form,"[xxxvi] in many ways mimicking interactive structures more suitable to possibilities of the print medium rather than the digital one; this teleological, **codex**-based model sees the editor as a single authority, a mediator between the text and the reader, where the editorial entity determines and shapes what is important to the reader, focuses the editorial and analytical lens, and ultimately exerts immense control over what the reader can engage. While it is nothing new to interrogate the "single authoritative text,"[xxxvii] and to consider the change in the structure of authority offered by the digital edition especially in relation to the dynamic nature of a digital text,[xxxviii] the integration of social tools into the electronic scholarly edition pushes the boundar- 483
ies of authority further, shifting power from a single editor, who shapes the reading of any given text, to a group of readers comprising a community whose interpretations themselves form a new method of making meaning out of the material.[xxxix] In a *social* edition, textual interpretation and interrelation are almost wholly created and managed by a community of users participating in collective and collaborative knowledge building using Web 2.0 technologies. Further, in expanding the community of practice—beyond a single editorial entity, to an academic group, and even beyond that group into citizen scholars—we cannot avoid challenging current notions of personal and institutional authority, and the systems in which they are perpetuated;[xl] the *social* edition privileges a new kind of scholarly discourse network that eschews traditional institutionally-reinforced hierarchical structures and relies, instead, upon those that are community-generated.[xli] Taken together, in this the social edition appears to represent welcome extension of recent accepted and understood movements in editorial theory.

In brief, with the tools of social media at its center, the *social* edition is process-driven, privileging interpretative changes based on the input of many readers; text is fluid, agency is collective, and many readers/editors, rather than single editor, shape what is important and, thus, broaden the editorial lens as well as the breadth, depth, and scope of any edition produced in this way. A definitively *social* edition employs web 2.0 tools for activities such as transcription, user bookmarking and bibliography-building, flagging and tagging, commenting and annotating,[xlii] linking to contextual material (especially for names and integration of bibliographic information), glossary and other analytical functions, and all other pertinent activities that sit at the evolving intersection of social media and the electronic scholarly edition. Relying on dynamic knowledge building and privileging process over end result, this expansive structure offers new scholarly workflows and hermeneutical[4] method that build, well, on what we already do.

This all said, the *social* edition is not something—at least not *yet* something—that we can clearly describe and typologize as readily as we now can the dynamic text, the hypertextual edition, and the dynamic edition; but the same could be said of the dynamic text, the hypertextual edition, and the dynamic edition at the times our community was busy experimenting with their precepts and building blocks, through theoretical engagement and prototypical experimentation. Regardless, the basic tenets of such a scholarly electronic edition are beyond first discernment, and indeed are becoming more readily visible almost daily through the evolution and adoption in our community of social media methods and its practices that we are increasingly and more regularly bringing to the electronic editions we produce.

Whatever it is that sits at the intersection of social media and the scholarly edition in electronic form—whatever the *social* edition manifests itself as—as our community has known through our conjoint development of the dynamic text, the hypertextual edition, and the dynamic edition, the *social* edition is something that we will articulate and define, through theory and functional prototyping, together.

Notes

i. Earlier versions of this work were presented by Leitch, Timney, and Siemens, variously, in 2010 and 2011 to groups at gatherings of the Modern Language Association (Los Angeles), Digital Humanities (Stanford University), the Institute for English Studies (London), the Renaissance Society of America (Montreal), Archives and the Profession (University Texas Austin), Congress of the Humanities and Social Science Federation of Canada (Concordia University), Huygens Institute (The Hague), University of Victoria, and elsewhere.... In addition to benefiting greatly from discussion with those via these forums, and from comments of *LLC*'s anonymous reviewers, at its core this article results from the combined consideration and work of a number of researchers across several research groups—including members of the ETCL, the Implementing New Knowledge Environments (INKE) project, and the Public Knowledge Project (PKP), with writing up to the earlier-circulated draft (as above) coordinated chiefly by Timney. The phrase "social edition" was, to our knowledge, coined by Leitch, describing aspects of the phenomena reflected on in this paper our group was discussing in 2009. Final coordination, writing, and revision of this paper were carried out by Siemens, with the assistance of Garnett, Koolen, and others from the research groups credited.

The authors wish to express their gratitude for the support and feedback on the paper received by those in these forums, and from *LLC*'s reviewers. In response to comments from the reviewers and the community about the nature of the material presented in this paper, it is accompanied by two integral appendices [not reprinted here], the first addressing pertinent issues to online reading and interaction (Koolen, Garnett), and the second an unpublished white paper on social networking drawn upon by several researchers in the area (Leitch).

ii. P.A. Fortier, "Theory, Methods and Applications: Some Examples in French Literature," *Literary and Linguistic Computing* 6.3 (1991): 192–96.

4 Related to issues of interpretation.

iii. Peter L. Robinson, "Electronic Editions for Everyone," *Text and Genre in Reconstruction. Effects of Digitization on Ideas, Behaviours, Products and Institutions*, ed. Willard McCarty (Cambridge: Open Book Publishers, 2010), 145–63; Peter Shillingsburg, *From Gutenberg to Google: Electronic Representations of Literary Texts* (Cambridge: Cambridge UP, 2006); John Bryant, *The Fluid Text. A Theory of Revision and Editing for Book and Screen* (Ann Arbor: U of Michigan P, 2002); Jerome McGann, *Radiant Textuality: Literature after the World Wide Web* (New York: Palgrave Macmillan, 2001); Hans W. Gabler, "Theorizing the digital scholarly edition," *Literature Compass* 7.2 (2010): 43–56.

iv. Ray Siemens, "Text Analysis and the 'Dynamic' Edition? A Working Paper, Briefly Articulating Some Concerns with an Algorithmic Approach to the Electronic Scholarly Edition." *CHWP* A.37/65 (2005).

v. D. Ian Lancashire, "Working with Texts," Paper delivered at the *IBM Academic Computing Conference* (Anaheim, 1989).

vi. See also Peter Robinson and Hans Walter Gabler (eds), "Introduction. Making Texts for the Next Century" spec. issue of *Literary and Linguistic Computing*, 15.1 (2000); and Peter Robinson, "The One Text and the Many Texts," *Literary and Linguistic Computing*, 15 (2000): 5–14.

vii. Charles B. Faulhaber, "Textual Criticism in the 21st Century," *Romance Philology* 45 (1991): 123–48.

viii. Northrop Frye, "Literary and Mechanical Models," *Research in Humanities Computing 1: Select Papers from the ALLC/ACH Conference*, ed. Ian Lancashire (Oxford: Clarendon P, 1991), 3–13.

ix. See also Jerome McGann, "The Rationale of HyperText," *Electronic Text. Investigations in Method and Theory*, ed. Kathryn Sutherland (Oxford: Clarendon P, 1997), 19–46 [see also above, pp. 459–74]; Charles L. Ross, "The Electronic Text and the Death of the Critical Edition," *The Literary Text in the Digital Age*, ed. Richard J. Finneran (Ann Arbor: U of Michigan P, 1996), 225–32; and George P. Landow, "Footnotes, Endnotes, and the Experience of Reading Hypertext."

x. Such an edition embraces an electronic context and notion of inclusivity that Vannevar Bush
("As We May Think," *Atlantic Monthly* 176 (1945): 101–08), Northrop Frye ("Literary and Mechanical 485
Models"), William Winder ("Texpert Systems," *Scholarly Discourse and Computing Technology: Perspectives on Pedagogy, Research, and Dissemination in the Humanities*, ed. Ray Siemens and William Winder, spec. issue of *Text Technology* 6.3 (1996): 159–66. Reported in *Computing in the Humanities Working Papers* (1997)), and Ted Nelson ("A New Home for the Mind?" Datamation [PlugIn] 41.1 (1995)) have articulated; such an edition also requires that a significant amount of related scholarly material is available in electronic form.

xi. Landow, "Footnotes."

xii. See, for brief example and earlier state of the field, John Bradley, "Text Tools," *A Companion to Digital Humanities*, ed. Susan Schreibman, Ray Siemens, and John Unsworth (Oxford: Blackwell, 2004).

xiii. John Unsworth, "Scholarly Primitives: What Methods Do Humanities Researchers Have in Common, and How Might Our Tools Reflect This?" (2000).

xiv. Jerome McGann, "Marking Texts of Many Dimensions," *Companion to Digital Humanities*, ed. Susan Schreibman, Ray Siemens, and John Unsworth (Oxford: Blackwell, 2004), 198–217, 214. From McGann we adopt the following critical and theoretical points: (1) the recognition that scholars read what Barthes calls the "plural text" by reading across dimensions and (2) a concern that "digitization ... situates the critical agent outside the field to be mapped and re-displayed" (206). McGann identifies a text's dimensions as *linguistic* (semantic and grammatical markers), *graphical/auditional* (textual materiality), *documentary* (descriptors tied to specific object: bibliography, paleography, provenance), *rhetorical* (categorization, ordering, arrangement), *semiotic* ("patterned relationships throughout the textual system" (214), and *social* (production and reception history) (213–15). These codes and dimensions are neither prescriptive nor exhaustive but provide opportunities to read a text from different perspectives.

Of the six dimensions, digital texts to date have been most successful in mediating the first four but have had more limited success with the semiotic and social dimensions. This is not to say that current edition models do not address the semiotic dimension, which McGann describes as the "patterned relationships throughout the textual system" (214) or include information about a text's production and reception history. In current models of digital editions, the problem is that we are not capturing the fluid state of a text's production and reception as it is remediated online. Where we see an opportunity to intervene is in extending these dimensions to include an ongoing interrogation of the social and semiotic life of the text. McGann's delineation of "N-dimensions" offers a promising shift in paradigm, a shift, we would suggest, that points us directly to the construction of a specifically *social* edition that takes this fluidity into account. McGann writes that,

> Traditional textual conditions facilitate textual study at an inner standing point because all the activities can be carried out—can be represented—in the same field space, typically, in a bibliographical field. Subject and object meet and interact in the same dimensional space—a situation that gets reified for us when we read books or write about them. Digital operations, however, introduce a new and more abstract space of relations into the study-field of textuality. This abstract space brings the possibility of new and in certain respects greater analytic power to the study of traditional texts. (205)

His proposed model affords a broadening of our conceptual understanding of the layers of reading; or, reading across dimensions.

xv. Jerome McGann, "Introduction," *Online Humanities Scholarship: The Shape of Things to Come*, ed. Jerome McGann, with Andrew Stauffer, Dana Wheeles, and Michael Pickard (Houston: Rice UP, 2010).

xvi. Etienne Wenger, "Communities of Practice"; see also Etienne Wenger, "Communities of Practice: Learning as a Social System," *Systems Thinker* 9.5 (1998): 1–10; Daniel J. Cohen, "Engaging and Creating Virtual Communities," *Proceedings of the Cultural Heritage Online Conference* (Florence, Italy, 2009), 28–32; and Darren Cambridge, Soren Kaplan, and Vicki Suter, "Community of Practice Design Guide: A Step-by-Step Guide for Designing & Cultivating Communities of Practice in Higher Education" (Educause, 2005).

xvii. Christopher M. Hoadley and Peter G. Kilner, "Using Technology to Transform Communities of Practice into Knowledge-Building Communities," *SIGGROUP Bulletin* 25.1 (2005): 31–40, 33.

xviii. James A. Inman, Cheryle Reed, and Peter Sands, *Electronic Collaboration in the Humanities* (Mahwah, NJ: Lawrence Erlbaum, 2004).

xix. Josh Greenberg, "The Institution and the Crowd," Presentation (2010). Specific instances of this have become almost too numerous to list. For one example, see Greg Crane, "Give Us Editors! Re-inventing the Edition and Re-thinking the Humanities," *The Shape of Things to Come* (Charlottesville, VA: March 2010). For more general discussion of this, see Avi Santo and Christopher Lucas. "Engaging Academic and Nonacademic Communities Through Online Scholarly Work," *Cinema Journal* 48.2 (2009): 129–38, and, on the very closely related topic of social media's role in expanding the work of academe into its larger public context, see John Seely Brown and Richard P. Adler, "Minds on Fire: Open Education, the Long Tail, and Learning 2.0," *Educause Review* 43.1 (2008): 16–20, 22, 24, 26, 28, 30, 32; Roumen Nikolov, "Towards University 2.0: A Space Where Academic Education Meets Corporate Training" (Arnhem, The Netherlands: IPROF-09: ICT Professionalism: a Global Challenge, 2009); John Unsworth, "University 2.0," *The Tower and The Cloud. Higher Education in the Age of Cloud Computing* (EDUCAUSE, 2008), 227–37; and Amy Mollet, "Taking a Leaf Out of Poliakoff's Book: Embracing New Online Platforms Is Necessary for the Positive Survival of Academic Impact and Debate," *Impact of Social Sciences* (9 June 2011). For background and expansion, see "Background and History" in Leitch's overview and bibliography in the second appendix.

xx. For some, this might raise concerns related to qualitative assurance; in this vein, see among many others, Kathleen Fizpatrick, "Peer-to-Peer Review and the Future of Scholarly Authority,"

Cinema Journal 48.2 (2009): 124–29. At the moment, the most useful discussions are taking place at conferences and in the blogosphere.

xxi. Stowe Boyd, "Are You Ready for Social Software?" */message*. (2006, n.p.).

xxii. "7 Things You Should Know About Collaborative Annotation," *Educause* (2009, n.p).

xxiii. In this context, see also, among others: Ilia A. Ovsiannikov, Michael A. Arbib, and Thomas H. Mcneill, "Annotation Technology," *International Journal of Human-Computer Studies* 50.4 (1999): 329–62; Catherine C. Marshall, "Annotation: From Paper Books to the Digital Library," *Proceedings of the Second ACM International Conference on Digital Libraries* (Philadelphia: ACM, 1997), 131–40; Joanna Wolfe, "Annotation Technologies: A Software and Research Review," *Computers and Composition* 19.4 (2002): 471–97; Jane Hunter et al. "The Open Annotation Collaboration: A Data Model to Support Sharing and Interoperability of Scholarly Annotations," *Digital Humanities 2010: Conference Abstracts* (London: Office for Humanities Communication; Centre for Computing in the Humanities, 2010), 175–78; Audrey Watters, "Long Live Marginalia! ReadSocial Brings Annotations to Digital Literature" (*ReadWriteWeb*, 24 March 2011); Frederic Lardinois, "Reframe It Brings Facebook, Twitter, & Web Luminaries to Its Annotation Tool" (*ReadWriteWeb*, 30 March 2009); J.J. Cadiz, A. Gupta, and J. Grudin, "Using Web Annotations for Asynchronous Collaboration Around Documents," *Proceedings of the ACM Conference on Computer Supported Cooperative Work* (ACM: New York, 2000); and Stephen J.A. Yang et al., "A Collaborative Multimedia Annotation Tool for Enhancing Knowledge Sharing in CSCL," *Interactive Learning Environments* (2011).

xxiv. In this context, see also, among many others: Jennifer Howard, "Social Media Lure Academics Frustrated by Traditional Publishing," *The Chronicle of Higher Education* 57.25 (2011): n.p.; Kathleen Fitzpatrick, "CommentPress: New (Social) Structures for New (Networked) Texts," *Journal of Electronic Publishing* 10.3 (2007); Sara Kjellberg, "I Am a Blogging Researcher: Motivations for Blogging in a Scholarly Context," *First Monday* 15.8 (2010): n.p.; Janice W. Fernheimer, Lisa Litterio, and James Hendler, "Transdisciplinary ITexts and the Future of Web-Scale Collaboration," *Journal of Business and Technical Communication* 25.3 (2011): 322–37; Curt Hopkins, "Mendeley Throws Open the Doors to Academic Data," *ReadWriteWeb*, 29 April 2010.

xxv. Scott A. Golder and Bernardo A. Huberman, "The Structure of Collaborative Tagging Systems," *Journal of Information Science* 32.2 (2006): 198–208.

xxvi. Thomas Vanderwall, "Folksonomy" (2007): n.p.

xxvii. Adam Mathes, "Folksonomies—Cooperative Classification and Communication through Shared Metadata" (2004).

xxviii. See also Marieke Guy and Emma Tonkin, "Folksonomies: Tidying up Tags?" *D-Lib Magazine* 12.1 (2006): n.p.

xxix. Daniel J. Cohen, "Creating Scholarly Tools and Resources for the Digital Ecosystem: Building Connections in the Zotero Project," *First Monday* 13.8 (2008): n.p.

xxx. Jason Priem and Kaitlin Light Costello, "How and Why Scholars Cite on Twitter," *Proceedings of the ASIS&T Annual Meeting* (Pittsburgh, PA, 2010); Claire Ross et al., "Enabled Backchannel: Conference Twitter Use by Digital Humanists," *Journal of Documentation* 67.2 (2011): 214–37. See also: David G. Hendry, J.R. Jenkins, and Joseph F. McCarthy, "Collaborative Bibliography," *Information Processing and Management* 42.3 (2006): 805–25; and, for social bookmarking, Enrique Estelles, Esther del Moral, and Fernando González, "Social Bookmarking Tools as Facilitators of Learning and Research Collaborative Processes: The Diigo Case," *Interdisciplinary Journal of E-Learning and Learning Objects* 6 (2010): 175–91; Tony Hammond et al., "Social Bookmarking Tools (I): A General Review," *D-Lib Magazine* 11.4 (2005): n.p.; and Ben Lund et al., "Social Bookmarking Tools (II): A Case Study—Connotea," *D-Lib Magazine*, 11.4: n.p.

xxxi. Susan Schreibman, Ray Siemens, and John Unsworth, "The Digital Humanities and Humanities Computing: An Introduction," *A Companion to Digital Humanities*, ed. Susan Schreibman, Ray Siemens, and John Unsworth (Oxford: Blackwell, 2004), vii.
xxxii. For a more detailed discussion of Web 2.0, see Tim O'Reilly, "What Is Web 2.0?" (2005), and Tim O'Reilly and John Battelle, "Web Squared: Web 2.0 Five Years On," *Web Summit* (San Francisco, CA, 2009).
xxxiii. Stephen Nichols, "Time to Change Our Thinking: Dismantling the Silo Model of Digital Scholarship" (2009).
xxxiv. Crane, "Give Us Editors!"
xxxv. See Melissa Terras's excellent list of collaborative projects ("Crowdsourcing Manuscript Material," (2009)). The George Mason project is described as "an open source tool that would allow scholars to contribute document transcriptions and research notes to digital archival projects, using the Papers of the War Department as a test case."
xxxvi. Susan Schreibman, Ray Siemens, and John Unsworth. "The Digital Humanities and Humanities Computing: An Introduction," *A Companion to Digital Humanities*, ed. Susan Schreibman, Ray Siemens, and John Unsworth (Oxford: Blackwell, 2004), vi.
xxxvii. See, among others, Peter L. Shillingsburg, *Scholarly Editing in the Computer Age* (Athens: U of Georgia P, 1986), 16.
xxxviii. See Peter L. Shillingsburg, *From Gutenberg to Google: Electronic Representations of Literary Texts* (Cambridge: Cambridge UP, 2006); Peter L. Shillingsburg, *Resisting Texts: Authority and Submission in Constructions of Meaning* (Ann Arbor: U of Michigan P, 1998), and Mats Dahlström, "How Reproductive Is a Scholarly Edition?" *Literary and Linguistic Computing* 19.1 (2004): 17–33. Dahlström writes, "the web edition turns into a large resource archive and editorial laboratory, and even more often into a more or less temporary interface to a changing, dynamic digital archive" (18).

xxxix. In doing so, we do not question authority in terms of the multiple variants of a manuscript, for example, but more broadly ask how readers have collective power to make meaning from multiple texts. With an understanding that an edition performs "the considered act of reproducing or altering texts" (G.T. Tanselle, "The Varieties of Scholarly Editing," *Scholarly Editing*, ed. D.C. Greetham [New York: MLA, 1995], 9–32, 10), the socialized text moves us towards a broader understanding of the text itself as an authorial and social entity; however, the traditional scholarly edition (whether in a print or digital medium) nonetheless follows a "top-down" model that, in its interpretative and representational aspects, is static once published. Digital humanists have already questioned the genre of the database (Lev Manovich, "Cultural Analytics: Analysis and Visualization of Large Cultural Data Sets," *Manovich.net* (30 September 2001)), and spoken to the importance of providing both digital facsimiles and encoded source-texts (Epson S. Ore, "Monkey Business, or What Is an Edition?" *Literary and Linguistic Computing* 19.1 (2004): 35–44, 35). The discussion that follows on the social *edition* naturally extends to the construction of a social "archive" (Dean Irvine, "Editing Archives/Archiving Editions," *Journal of Canadian Studies* 40.2 (2006): 183–211, 184). Irvine has offered a productive way of understanding the socialized text:

> Instead of superseding current critical editions—whether in print or online—or privileging one version or editorial practice over others, these digital archives could potentially enfold any number of critical and non-critical editions into an indexed network in which each edition is experienced as a socialized text—that is, social objects embedded in an apparatus that bears witness to the history of the edition's production, transmission, and reception. (202–03)

To construct a social edition we must rely on earlier theories of editorial practice and disciplinary conventions to determine our source text and ultimately the digital representation of that text (Shillingsburg,

Scholarly Editing, Tanselle, "The Varieties," McGann [various]). But as a further step in socialization, the paratext, rather than the text, becomes the focal point.

xl. The single-authored monograph has become both the gold ring and bête noire for those seeking tenure in the humanities, and has seen much (re)consideration in recent times. More to the point: with its lack of a single, authoritative editor, the social edition may seem to some to be a freewheeling invitation to early-career stasis. It is important that while we are imagining the form the social edition will take that we also imagine how it will be received by our institutions. Work in discussion by the Modern Language Association's Committee on Information Technology is heartening. Currently, their "Short Guide to Evaluation of Digital Work" includes a section on best practices in "enrichment" that reads "[i]n some cases enrichment can take the form of significant new scholarship organized as interpretative commentary or essay trajectories through the material.... Such interpretative curation is itself scholarly work that can be evaluated as a form of exhibit or essay" (Geoffrey Rockwell, "Short Guide to Evaluation of Digital Work," [2009]). The work of the editor of the social edition is to make this kind of curation possible for members of the community of practice to undertake. By acting as a facilitator for community enrichment, the scholar or scholars heading up a social edition project must demonstrate considerable editorial skill in identifying possible avenues for interpretation and technological sensitivity in finding ways to make this kind of editing work.

xli. See Fitzpatrick, "CommentPress":

> Scholars operate in a range of conversations, from classroom conversations with students to conference conversations with colleagues; scholars need to have available to them not simply the library model of texts circulating amongst individual readers but also the coffee house model of public reading and debate. This interconnection of individual nodes into a collective fabric is, of course, the strength of the network, which not only physically binds individual machines but also has the ability to bring together the users of those machines, at their separate workstations, into one communal whole.

xlii. Collaborative annotation offers a particularly rich toolkit for the humanities scholar, and seems a prudent place to begin to envision the interactivity inherent within the social edition.

29. N. Katherine Hayles, "How We Read: Close, Hyper, Machine," *ADE* Bulletin No. 150, 2010: 62–79

Katherine Hayles (b. 1943) is Professor and Director of Graduate Studies at Duke University. She holds advanced degrees in both literature and chemistry, and has been at the forefront of efforts to describe and theorize electronic literature, the history of technology, information and media, and digital humanities. Her book, *How We Became Posthuman: Virtual Bodies in Cybernetics, Literature and Informatics* (1999), won the Rene Wellek Prize for the Best Book in Literary Theory for 1998–99, and *Writing Machines* (2002) won the Suzanne Langer Award for Outstanding Scholarship. Both books as well as her other work explore the co-evolution of humans and machines, and, in particular, the effects of machines on narrative, reading, and cognition. The following essay examines how reading and cognition are being impacted by the shift from print to digital based sources. According to Hayles, although "Reading has always been constituted through complex and diverse practices," the emergence of new technologies compels us "to re-think what reading is" (p. 508). Hayles theorizes a transition from close-reading methodologies, associated with print, towards hyperreading and machine reading, qualitatively different processes available to us with digital-based media. Hayles, however, is sensitive to empirical studies that suggest that linear reading enabled by print may possess certain advantages over web-based reading. She proposes a flexible and overlapping model of reading styles that would not leave one mode of reading behind, but would embrace some of the potentiality afforded by new forms of digital reading.

How We Read: Close, Hyper, Machine

The evidence is mounting: people in general, and young people in particular, are doing more screen reading of digital materials than ever before. Meanwhile, the reading of print books and of literary genres (novels, plays, and poems) has been declining over the last twenty years. Worse, reading skills (as measured by the ability to identify themes, draw inferences, etc.) have been declining in junior high, high school, college, and even graduate schools for the same period. Two flagship reports from the National Endowment for the Arts,[1] *Reading at Risk*, reporting the results of their own surveys, and *To Read or Not to Read*, drawing together other large-scale

1 The National Endowment for the Arts (NEA), established in 1965 by an act of Congress, is an independent federal agency in charge of awarding grants that support various individual and community artistic endeavors.

surveys, show that over a wide range of data-gathering instruments the results are consistent: people read less print, and they read print less well. The leads the NEA chairman, Dana Gioia, to suggest that the *correlation* between decreased literary reading and poorer reading ability is indeed a *causal* connection.[2] The NEA argues (and I of course agree) that literary reading is a good in itself, insofar as it opens the portals of a rich literary heritage (see Griswold, McDonnell, and Wright for the continued high cultural value placed on reading).[i] When decreased print reading, already a cultural concern, is linked with reading problems, it carries a double whammy.

Fortunately, the news is not all bad. A newer NEA report, *Reading on the Rise*, shows for the first time in more than two decades an uptick in novel reading (but not plays or poems), including among the digitally native young adult cohort (ages 18–24). The uptick may be a result of the Big Read initiative[3] by the NEA and similar programs by other organizations; whatever the reason, it shows that print can still be an alluring medium. At the same time, reading scores among fourth and eighth graders remain flat, despite the No Child Left Behind initiative.[4] Notwithstanding the complexities of the national picture, it seems clear that a critical nexus occurs in the juncture of digital reading (exponentially increasing among all but the oldest cohort) and print reading (downward trending with a slight uptick recently). The crucial questions are these: how to convert the increased digital reading into increased reading ability and how to make effective bridges between digital reading and the **literacy** traditionally associated with print.

Mark Bauerlein (a consultant on the *Reading at Risk* report), in the offensively titled *The Dumbest Generation: How the Digital Age Stupefies Young Americans and Jeopardizes Our Future*, makes no apology for linking the decline of reading skills directly to a decrease in print reading, issuing a stinging indictment to teachers, professors, and other mentors who think digital reading might encourage skills of its own. Not only is there no transfer between digital reading and print reading skills in his view, but digital reading does not even lead to strong *digital* reading skills.[ii] I found *The Dumbest Generation* intriguing and infuriating in equal measure. The book is valuable for its synthesis of a great deal of empirical evidence, going well beyond the 2009 NEA report in this regard; it is infuriating in its tendentious refusal to admit any salutary effects from digital reading. As Bauerlein moves from the solid longitudinal data on the decline in print reading to the digital realm, the evidence becomes scantier and the anecdotes more frequent, with examples obviously weighted toward showing the inanity of online chats, blogs, and Facebook entries. It would, of course, be equally possible to harvest examples showing the depth, profundity, and brilliance of online discourse, so Bauerlein's argument here fails to persuade. The

2 A relationship of cause and effect; in other words, the decrease in reading skills is the result of less literary reading.

3 The Big Read is an NEA program wherein individual communities hold a month-long initiative to encourage the reading and discussion of a particular group of books throughout diverse sections of the community.

4 The No Child Left Behind Act of 2001 is a standards-based initiative proposed by President George W. Bush that was aimed at raising educational achievement nationwide.

two earlier NEA reports[iii] suffer from their own problems; their data do not clearly distinguish between print and digital reading, and they fail to measure how much digital reading is going on or its effects on reading abilities.[iv] Nevertheless, despite these limitations and distortions, few readers are likely to come away unconvinced that there is something like a national crisis in reading and that it is especially acute with teen and young adult readers.

At this point, scholars in literary studies should be jumping on their desks and waving their hands in the air, saying "Hey! Look at us! We know how to read *really* well, and we know how to teach students to read. There's a national crisis in reading? We can help." Yet there is little evidence that the profession of literary studies has made a significant difference in the national picture, including on the college level, where reading abilities continue to decline even into graduate school. This is strange. The inability to address the crisis successfully no doubt has multiple causes, but one in particular strikes me as vitally important. While literary studies continues to teach close reading to students, it does less well in exploiting the trend toward the digital. Students read incessantly in digital media and write in it as well, but only infrequently are they encouraged to do so in literature classes or in environments that encourage the transfer of print reading abilities to digital and vice versa. The two tracks, print and digital, run side by side, but messages from either track do not leap across to the other side.

I. Close Reading and Disciplinary Identity

To explore why this should be so and open possibilities for synergistic[5] interactions, I begin
by revisiting that sacred icon of literary studies, close reading. When literary studies expanded its purview in the 1970s and 1980s, it turned to reading many different kinds of "texts," from Donald Duck to fashion clothing, television programs to prison architecture.[v] This expansion into diverse textual realms meant that literature was no longer the de facto center of the field. Faced with the loss of this traditional center, literary scholars found a replacement in close reading, the one thing virtually all literary scholars know how to do well and agree is important. Close reading then assumed a preeminent role as the essence of the disciplinary identity.

Jane Gallop undoubtedly speaks for many when she writes, "I would argue that the most valuable thing English ever had to offer was the very thing that made us a discipline, that transformed us from cultured gentlemen into a profession [i.e., close reading].... Close reading—learned through practice with literary texts, learned in literature classes—is a widely applicable skill, of real value to students as well as to scholars in other disciplines."[vi] Barbara Johnson, in her well-known essay "Teaching Deconstructively," goes further: "This [close reading] is the only teaching that can properly be called literary; anything else is history of ideas, biography, psychology, ethics, or bad philosophy."[vii] For Gallop, Johnson, and many others, close reading not only assures the professionalism of the profession but also makes literary studies an important asset

5 A connection between two processes, fields, etc. wherein both work to improve or strengthen the other. Here Hayles means that combining the teaching of different media (print and digital) can improve students' overall understanding of the text being read.

to the culture. As such, close reading justifies the discipline's continued existence in the academy, including the monies spent to support literature faculty and departments. More broadly, close reading in this view constitutes the major part of the cultural capital[6] that literary studies relies on to prove its worth to society.

Literary scholars generally think they know what is meant by *close reading*, but, looked at more closely, it proves not so easy to define or exemplify. Jonathan Culler, quoting Peter Middleton, observes that "close reading is our contemporary term for a heterogeneous and largely unorganized set of practices and assumptions."[viii] John Guillory is more specific when he historicizes close reading, arguing that "close reading is a modern academic practice with an inaugural moment, a period of development, and now perhaps a period of decline."[ix] He locates its prologue in the work of I.A. Richards, noting that Richards contrasted close reading with the media explosion of his day, television. If that McLuhanesque[7] view of media is prologue, then digital technologies, Guillory suggests, may be launching the epilogue. Citing my work on hyperattention[8] (more on that shortly), Guillory sets up a dichotomy between the close reading recognizable to most literary scholars—detailed and precise attention to rhetoric, style, language choice, and so forth through a word-by-word examination of a text's linguistic techniques—to the digital world of fast reading and sporadic sampling. In this he anticipates the close versus digital reading flagrantly on display in Bauerlein's book.

Amid the heterogeneity of close reading techniques, perhaps the dominant one in recent years has been what Stephen Best and Sharon Marcus call "symptomatic reading." In a special issue of *Representations*, Best and Marcus launch a frontal assault on symptomatic reading as it was inaugurated by Fredric Jameson's immensely influential *The Political Unconscious*. For Jameson, with his motto "Always historicize," the text is an alibi for ideological formations that are subtextual. The heroic task of the critic is to wrench a text's ideology into the light, "massy and dripping," as Jameson puts it,[x] so that it can be unveiled and resisted.[xi] The trace of symptomatic reading may be detected in Johnson: listing textual features that merit special attention for close reading, she includes such constructions as "ambiguous words," "undecidable syntax," and "incompatibilities between what a text says and what it does."[xii] Most if not all these foci are exactly the places where scholars doing symptomatic reading would look for evidence of a text's subsurface ideology.

After more than two decades of symptomatic reading, however, many literary scholars are not finding it a productive practice, perhaps because (like many deconstructive readings) its results have begun to seem formulaic, leading to predictable conclusions rather than compelling insights.

---

6 Theorized by Pierre Bourdieu (1930–2002), cultural capital refers to the value of intellectual assets specifically instead of economic assets. Bourdieu's essay, "The Field of Cultural Production," can be found above, p. 335–52.

7 Referring to Marshall McLuhan (1911–80), Canadian scholar of communications and media theory.

8 See Hayles's essay "Hyper and Deep Attention: The Generational Divide in Cognitive Modes," wherein she describes hyperattention as "characterized by switching focus rapidly among different tasks, preferring multiple information streams, seeking a high level of stimulation, and having a low tolerance for boredom" (187); see p. 509, note xxxvii below.

In a paraphrase of Gilles Deleuze and Félix Guattari's famous remark, "We are tired of trees," the *Representations* special issue declared, "We are tired of symptomatic reading." The issue's contributors are not the only ones who feel this way. In panel after panel at the conference sponsored by the National Humanities Center in spring 2010, entitled "The State and Stakes of Literary Studies," presenters expressed similar views and urged a variety of other reading modes, including "surface reading," in which the text is examined not for hidden clues but its overt messages; reading aimed at appreciation and articulation of the text's aesthetic value; and a variety of other reading strategies focusing on affect, pleasure, and cultural value.

II. Digital and Print Literacies

If one chapter of close reading is drawing to an end, what new possibilities are arising? Given the increase in digital reading, obvious sites for new kinds of reading techniques, pedagogical strategies, and initiatives are the interactions between digital and print literacies. Literary studies has been slow to address these possibilities, however, because it continues to view close reading of print texts as the field's essence. As long as this belief holds sway, digital reading will at best be seen as peripheral to our concerns, pushed to the margins as not "really" reading or at least not compelling or interesting reading. Young people, who vote with their feet in college, are marching in another direction—the digital direction. No doubt those who already read well will take classes based on close reading and benefit from them, but what about others whose print-reading skills are not as highly developed? To reach them, we must start close
to where they are, rather than where we imagine or hope they might be. As David Laurence observes, "good teachers deliberately focus on what the reader can do, make sure that both teacher and student recognize and acknowledge it, and use it as a platform of success from which to build."[xiii]

This principle was codified by the Belarusian psychologist L.S. Vygotsky in the 1930s as the "zone of proximal development." In *Mind in Society: The Development of Higher Psychological Processes*, he defined this zone as "[t]he distance between the actual developmental level as determined by independent problem solving and the level of potential development as determined through problem solving under adult guidance, or in collaboration with more capable peers."[xiv] The concept implies that if the distance is too great between what one wants someone else to learn and where instruction begins, the teaching will not be effective. Imagine, for example, trying to explain *Hamlet* to a three-year-old (an endless string of "Why?" would no doubt result, the all-purpose response of young children to the mysterious workings of the adult world). More recent work on "scaffolding"[xv] and Ron Tinsley and Kimberly Lebak on the "zone of reflective capacity"[xvi] extends the idea and amplifies it with specific learning strategies. These authors agree that for learning to occur, the distance between instruction and available skills must be capable of being bridged, either through direct instruction or, as Vygotsky notes, through working with "more capable" peers. Bauerlein instances many responses from young people as they encounter difficult print texts to the effect the works are "boring" or not worth the trouble. How can we convey to such students the deep engagement we feel with challenging literary texts? I argue that we cannot do this effectively if our teaching does not take place in the zone of proximal development, that is, if we are focused exclusively on print close reading. Before opinion solidifies behind new versions of close reading, I want to argue for a disciplinary shift to a broader sense of reading strategies and their interrelation.

In 1999, James Sosnoski presciently introduced the concept of hyperreading, which he defined as "reader-directed, screen-based, computer-assisted reading."[xvii] Examples include search queries (as in a Google search), filtering by keywords, skimming, hyperlinking, "pecking" (pulling out a few items from a longer text), and fragmenting.[xviii] Updating his model, we may add juxtaposing, as when several open windows allow one to read across several texts, and scanning, as when one reads rapidly through a blog to identify items of interest. There is considerable evidence that hyperreading differs significantly from typical print reading, and moreover that hyperreading stimulates different brain functions than print reading.

For example, Jakob Nielsen's consulting team, which advises companies and others on effective web design, does usability research by asking test subjects to deliver running verbal commentaries as they encounter web pages. Their reactions are recorded by a (human) tester; at the same time, eye-tracking equipment records their eye movements. The research shows that web pages are typically read in an F pattern.[xix] A person reads the first two or three lines across the page, but as the eye travels down the screen, the scanned length gets smaller, and, by the time the bottom of the page is reached, the eye is traveling in a vertical line aligned with the left margin. (Therefore the worst location for important information on a web page is on the bottom right corner.) In Bauerlein's view, this research confirms that digital reading is sloppy in the extreme; Bauerlein would no doubt appreciate Woody Allen's quip, "I took a speed reading course and was able to read *War and Peace* in twenty minutes. It involves Russia."[xx] Nevertheless, other research not cited by Bauerlein indicates that this and similar strategies work well to identify pages of interest and to distinguish them from pages with little or no relevance to the topic at hand.[xxi]

As a strategic response to an information-intensive environment, hyperreading is not without precedent. John Guillory, in "How Scholars Read," notes that "[t]he fact of quantity is an intractable empirical given that must be managed by a determined method if analysis or interpretation is to be undertaken."[xxii] He is not talking here about digital reading but about **archival** research that requires a scholar to move through a great deal of material quickly to find the relevant texts or passages. He identifies two techniques in particular, scanning (looking for a particular keyword, image, or other textual feature) and skimming (trying to get the gist quickly). He also mentions the book wheel, a physical device invented in the Renaissance to cope with the information explosion when the number of books increased exponentially with the advent of print. Resembling a five-foot-high Ferris wheel, the book wheel held several books on different shelves and could be spun around to make different texts accessible, in a pre-digital print version of hyperreading.

In contemporary digital environments, the information explosion of the Web has again made an exponentially greater number of texts available, dwarfing the previous amount of print materials by several orders of magnitude. In digital environments, hyperreading has become a necessity. It enables a reader quickly to construct landscapes of associated research fields and subfields;

it shows ranges of possibilities; it identifies texts and passages most relevant to a given query; and it easily juxtaposes many different texts and passages. Google searches and keyword filters are now as much part of the scholar's tool kit as hyperreading itself. Yet hyperreading may not sit easily alongside close reading. Recent studies indicate that hyperreading not only requires different reading strategies than close reading but also may be involved with changes in brain architecture that makes close reading more difficult to achieve.

Much of this evidence is summarized by Nicholas Carr in *The Shallows: What the Internet Is Doing to Our Brains.*[xxiii] More judicious than Bauerlein, he readily admits that web reading has enormously increased the scope of information available, from global politics to scholarly debates. He worries, however, that hyperreading leads to changes in brain function that make sustained concentration more difficult, leaving us in a constant state of distraction in which no problem can be explored for very long before our need for continuous stimulation kicks in and we check email, scan blogs, message someone, or check our RSS feeds.[9] The situation is reminiscent of Kurt Vonnegut's[10] satirical short story "Harrison Bergeron,"[xxiv] in which the pursuit of equality has led to a society that imposes handicaps on anyone with exceptional talents. The handsome, intelligent eponymous protagonist must among other handicaps wear eyeglasses that give him headaches; other brainiacs have radio transmitters implanted in their ears, which emit shrieking sounds two or three times every minute, interrupting their thoughts and preventing sustained concentration. The final satirical punch comes in framing the story from the perspective of Bergeron's parents, Hazel and George, who see their son on TV when he proclaims his anti-handicap manifesto (with fatal results for him), but, hampered by their own handicaps, they cannot concentrate enough to remember it.

The story's publication in 1961 should give us a clue that a media-induced state of distraction is not a new phenomenon. Walter Benjamin,[11] in "The Work of Art in the Age of Mechanical Reproduction," wrote about the ability of mass entertainment forms such as cinema to make distracted viewing into a habit (as opposed to the contemplative viewing of a single work of art). Even though distraction, as Jonathan Crary has shown, has been a social concern since the late 1800s, there are some new features of web reading that make it a powerful practice for re-wiring the brain.[xxv] Among these are hyperlinks that draw attention away from the linear flow of an article, very short forms such as tweets that encourage distracted forms of reading, small habitual actions such as clicking and navigating that increase the cognitive load, and, most pervasively, the enormous amount of material to be read, leading to the desire to skim everything because there is way too much material to pay close attention to anything for very long.

---

9 RSS (*Rich Site Summary*) are web feed formats used to publish frequently updated works (such as blogs or news sites) in a standardized form.

10 Kurt Vonnegut (1922–2007), American writer associated with humanism and known for his distinct mix of science fiction, humor, and cultural criticism.

11 Walter Benjamin (1892–1940), Jewish German critic of art, science, culture, and literature who helped recognize and theorize the emergence of the modern age.

III. Reading on the Web

What evidence indicates that these web-specific effects are making distraction a contemporary cultural condition? Several studies have shown that, contrary to the claims of early **hypertext** enthusiasts such as George Landow, hyperlinks tend to degrade comprehension rather than enhance it. The following studies, cited by Carr in *The Shallows*, demonstrate the trend. Erping Zhu, coordinator of instructional development at the Center for Research on Learning and Teaching at the University of Michigan, had test subjects read the same online passage but varied the number of links. As the number of links increased, comprehension declined, as measured by writing a summary and completing a multiple-choice test. Similar results were found by two Canadian scholars, David S. Miall and Teresa Dobson, who asked 70 people to read Elizabeth Bowen's[12] short story "The Demon Lover." One group read it in a linear version, and a second group with links. The first group outperformed the second on comprehension and grasp of the story's plot; it also reported liking the story more than the second group. We may object that a print story would of course be best understood in a print-like linear mode; other evidence, however, indicates that a similar pattern obtains for digital-born material. D.S. Niederhauser, R.E. Reynolds, D.J. Salmen, and P. Skolmoski had test subjects read two online articles, one arguing that "knowledge is objective," and the other that "knowledge is relative." Each article had links allowing readers to click between them. The researchers found that those who used the links, far from gaining a richer sense of the merits and limitations of the two positions, understood them less well than readers who chose to read the two in linear fashion.[xxvi] Comparable evidence was found in a review of 38 experiments on hypertext reading by Diana DeStefano and Jo-Anne LeFevre, psychologists with the Centre for Applied Cognitive Research at Canada's Carleton University.[xxvii] Carr summarizes their results, explaining that in general the evidence did not support the claim that hypertext led to "an enriched experience of the text."[xxviii] One of their conclusions was that "increased demands of decision-making and visual processing in hypertext impaired reading performance," especially in relation to "traditional print presentation."[xxix]

Why should hypertext and web reading in general lead to poorer comprehension? The answer, Carr believes, lies in the relation of working memory (i.e., the contents of consciousness) to long-term memory. Material is held in working memory for only a few minutes, and the capacity of working memory is severely limited. For a simple example, I think of the cell-phone directory function that allows me to get phone numbers, which are given orally (there is an option to have a text message sent of the number, but for this the company charges an additional fee, and being of a frugal disposition, I don't go for that option). I find that if I repeat the numbers out loud several times so they occupy working memory to the exclusion of other things, I can retain them long enough to punch the number. For retention of more complex matters, the contents of working memory must be transferred to long-term memory, preferably with repetitions to facilitate the integration of the new material with existing

12 Elizabeth Bowen (1899–1973), Anglo-Irish writer of novels and short stories.

knowledge schemas. The small distractions involved with hypertext and web reading—clicking on links, navigating a page, scrolling down or up, and so on—increase the cognitive load on working memory and thereby reduce the amount of new material it can hold. With linear reading, by contrast, the cognitive load is at a minimum, precisely because eye movements are more routine and fewer decisions need to be made about how to read the material and in what order. Hence the transfer to long-term memory happens more efficiently, especially when readers re-read passages and pause to reflect on them as they go along.

Supplementing this research are other studies showing that small habitual actions, repeated over and over, are extraordinarily effective in creating new neural pathways. Carr recounts the story told by Norman Doidge in *The Brain That Changes Itself* of an accident victim, Michael Bernstein, who had a stroke that damaged his brain's right side, rendering his left hand and leg crippled.[xxx] He entered an experimental therapy program that had him performing routine tasks with his left arm and leg over and over, such as washing a window and tracing alphabet letters. "The repeated actions," Carr reports, "were a means of coaxing his neurons and synapses to form new circuits that would take over the functions once carried out by the circuits in the damaged area in his brain."[xxxi] Eventually, Bernstein was able to regain most of the functionality of his unresponsive limbs. We may remember in *The Karate Kid* film (1984) when Daniel LaRusso (Ralph Macchio) is made to do the same repetitive tasks over and over again by his kung fu teacher, Mr. Miagi (Pat Morita). In contemporary neurological terms, Mr. Miagi is retraining the young man's neural circuits so he can master the essentials of kung fu movements.

These results are consistent with a large body of research on the impact of (print) reading on brain function. In a study cited by the French neurophysiologist Stanislas Dehaene, a world-renowned expert in this area, researchers sought out siblings from poor Portuguese families that had followed the traditional custom of having an elder sister stay home and watch the infant children while her younger sister went to school.[xxxii] Raised in the same family, the sisters could be assumed to have grown up in very similar environments, thus serving as a way to control other variables. Using as test subjects six pairs of illiterate-literate sisters, researchers found that literacy had strengthened the ability to understand the phonemic structure of language. Functional magnetic resonance (fMRI)[13] scans showed pronounced differences in the anterior insula, adjacent to Broca's area (a part of the brain associated with language use). "The literate brain," Dehaene summarizes, "obviously engages many more left hemispheric resources than the illiterate brain, even when we only *listen* to speech.... The macroscopic finding implies a massive increase in the exchange of information across the two hemispheres."[xxxiii]

Equally intriguing is Dehaene's "neural recycling" hypothesis, which suggests that reading re-purposes existing brain circuits that evolved independently of reading (because literacy is a mere eye blink in our evolutionary history, it did not play a role in shaping the genetics of our

13 Functional Magnetic Resonance Imaging (fMRI) technology analyzes brain function by measuring blood flow through the brain.

Pleistocene brains[14] but rather affects us epigenetically[15] through environmental factors). Crucial in this regard is an area he calls the brain's "letterbox," located in the left occipito-temporal region[16] at the back of the brain. This area, fMRI data show, is responsible for letter and phonemic recognition, transmitting its results to other distant areas through fiber bundles. He further argues that brain architecture imposes significant constraints on the physical shapes that will be easily legible to us. He draws on research demonstrating that 115 of the world's diverse writing systems (alphabetical and ideographic[17]) use visual symbols consisting mostly of three strokes (plus or minus one). Moreover, the geometry of these strokes mirrors in their distribution the geometry of shapes in the natural environment. The idea, then, is that our writing systems evolved in the context of our ability to recognize natural shapes and that scribal experimentation used this correspondence to craft writing systems that would most effectively re-purpose existing neural circuitry. Dehaene thus envisions "a massive selection process: over time, **scribes** developed increasingly efficient notations that fitted the organization of our brains. In brief, our cortex did not specifically evolve for writing. Rather, writing evolved to fit the cortex."[xxxiv]

Current evidence suggests that we are now in a new phase of the dance between epigenetic changes in brain function and the evolution of new reading and writing modalities on the web. Think, for example, of the F pattern of web reading that the Nielsen research revealed. Canny web designers use this information to craft web pages, and reading such pages further intensifies this mode of reading. How quickly neural circuits may be re-purposed by digital reading is suggested by Gary Small's experiments at the University of California, Los Angeles, on the effects of web reading on brain functionality. Small and his colleagues were looking for digitally naive subjects; they recruited three volunteers in their fifties and sixties who had never performed Google searches.[xxxv] This group was first tested with fMRI brain scans, wearing goggles onto which were projected web pages. Their scans differed significantly from another group of comparable age and background who were web savvy. Then the naive group was asked to search the Internet for an hour a day for five days. When re-tested, their brain scans showed measurable differences in some brain areas, which the experimenters attributed to new neural pathways catalyzed by web searching. Citing this study among others, Carr concludes that "[k]nowing what we know today, if you were to set out to invent a medium that would rewire our mental circuits as quickly and thoroughly as possible, you would probably end up designing something that looks and works a lot like the Internet."[xxxvi]

14 Refers to the accelerated evolution of human brain function during a period in the Earth's history that stretches from 2,588,000 years ago to 11,700 years ago.

15 Relating to "the theory of that the germ is brought into existence (by successive accretions), and not merely developed, in the process of reproduction" (*OED*).

16 The part of the brain adjacent to the occipital and temporal bones of the skull, at the lower back portion of the cortex.

17 Pertaining to a communication system that uses ideograms (graphic symbols that convey an idea or concept).

[...]

IV. The Importance of Anecdotal Evidence

Faced with these complexities, what is a humanist to do? Obviously, few scholars in the humanities have the time—or the expertise—to backtrack through cited studies and evaluate them for correctness and replicability. In my view, these studies may be suggestive indicators but should be subject to the same kind of careful scrutiny we train our students to use with web research (reliability of sources, consensus among many different researchers, etc.). Perhaps our most valuable yardstick for evaluating these results, however, is our own experience. We know how we react to intensive web reading, and we know through repeated interactions with our students how they are likely to read, write, and think as they grapple with print and web materials. As teachers (and parents), we make daily observations that either confirm or disconfirm what we read in the scientific literature. The scientific research is valuable and should not be ignored, but our experiences are also valuable and can tell us a great deal about the advantages and disadvantages of hyperreading compared with close reading, as well as the long-term effects of engaging in either or both of these reading strategies.

Anecdotal evidence hooked me on this topic five years ago, when I was a Phi Beta Scholar for a year and in that capacity visited many different types of colleges and universities. Everywhere I went, I heard teachers reporting similar stories: "I can't get my students to read long novels anymore, so I've taken to assigning short stories"; "My students won't read long books, so now I assign chapters and excerpts." I hypothesized then that a shift in cognitive modes is taking place, from the deep attention characteristic of humanistic inquiry to the hyperattention characteristic of someone scanning web pages.[xxxvii] I further argued that the shift in cognitive modes is more pronounced the younger the age cohort. Drawing from anecdotal evidence as well as such surveys as the Kaiser Foundation's *Gen M* report,[xxxviii] I suggested that the shift toward hyperattention is now noticeable with college students. Since then, the trend has become even more apparent, and the flood of surveys, books, and articles on the topic of distraction is now so pervasive as to be, well, distracting.

For me, the topic is much more than the latest research fad, because it hits me where I live: the college classroom. As a literary scholar, I deeply believe in the importance of writing and reading, so any large-scale change in how young people read and write is bound to capture my attention. In my work on hyperattention (published just when the topic was beginning to appear on the national radar), I argued that deep and hyperattention each have distinctive advantages. Deep attention is essential for coping with complex phenomena such as mathematical theorems, challenging literary works, and complex musical compositions; hyperattention is useful for its flexibility in switching between different information streams, its quick grasp of the gist of material, and its ability to move rapidly among and between different kinds of texts.[xxxix] As contemporary environments become more information intensive, it is no surprise that hyperattention (and its associated reading strategy, hyperreading) is growing and that deep attention (and its correlated reading strategy, close reading) is diminishing, particularly among young adults and teens. The problem, as I see it, lies not in hyperattention/hyperreading as such, but rather in the challenges the situation presents for parents and educators to ensure that deep attention and close reading continue to be vibrant components of our reading cultures and interact synergistically with the kind of web and hyperreading in which our young people are increasingly immersed.

Yet hyper and close reading are not the whole story. I earlier referred to Sosnoski's definition of hyperreading as "computer-assisted."[xl] More precisely, it is computer-assisted human reading. The formulation alerts us to a third component of contemporary reading practices: human-assisted computer reading, that is, computer algorithms used to analyze patterns in large textual corpora[18] where size makes human reading of the entirety impossible. Machine reading ranges from algorithms for word-frequency counts to more sophisticated programs that find and compare phrases, identify topic clusters, and are capable of learning. Given the scope, pervasiveness, and sophistication of contemporary programs used to parse[19] texts, it seems to me quite reasonable to say that machines can read. One could, of course, restrict "read" to human beings, arguing that reading implies comprehension and that machines calculate but do not comprehend. However, some human readers (beginners, for example) may also read with minimum or no comprehension. Moreover, the line between (human) interpretation and (machine) pattern recognition is a porous boundary, with each interacting with the other. Hypotheses about meaning help shape the design of computer algorithms, and the results of algorithmic analyses refine, extend, and occasionally challenge intuitions about meaning that formed the starting point for algorithmic

design. Putting human reading in a leak-proof container and isolating machine reading in another makes it difficult to see these interactions and understand their complex synergies. Given these considerations, saying computers cannot read is from my point of view merely species chauvinism.

In a field like literary studies, misunderstandings of the efficacy and importance of machine reading are commonplace. Even such a perceptive critic as Culler falls back on caricature when, in writing about close reading, he suggests, "It may be especially important to reflect on the varieties of close reading and even to propose explicit models, in an age where electronic resources make it possible to do literary research without reading at all: find all the instances of the words *beg* and *beggar* in novels by two different authors and write up your conclusions."[xli] In other words, close reading is the garlic that will ward off the vampire of machine reading. The anxiety here is palpable, nowhere more so than in his final phrase ("write up your conclusions"), which implies that drawing conclusions from machine analysis is a mechanical exercise devoid of creativity, insight, or literary value. Even Guillory, a brilliant theorist and close reader, while acknowledging that machine reading is a useful "prosthesis for the cognitive skill of scanning," concludes that "the gap in cognitive level between the keyword search and interpretation is for the present immeasurable."[xlii] There are two misapprehensions here: that keyword searches exhaust the repertoire of machine reading and that the gap between analysis and interpretation yawns so wide as to form an unbridgeable chasm rather than a dynamic interaction.

---

18 Literally, bodies or groups; specifically, in this case, collections of text stored by computer.

19 To break into parts so as to better explain the whole.

Given these misconceptions, explicit recapitulation of the value of machine reading is useful. Although it may be used with a single text and reveal interesting patterns, its more customary use is in analyzing large corpora too vast to be read by a single person. Preeminent in this regard is the work of Franco Moretti, who uses the term "distant reading," an obvious counterpoise to close reading.[xliii] Careful reading of his work reveals that this construction lumps together human and machine reading; both count as "distant" if the scale is large. I think it is useful to distinguish between human and machine reading because the two situations (one done by a human assisted by machines, the other done by computer algorithms assisted by humans) have different functionalities, limitations, and possibilities. Hyperreading may not be useful for large corpora, and machine algorithms have limited interpretive capabilities.

If we look carefully at Moretti's methodology, we see how firmly it refutes the misunderstandings referred to above. His algorithmic analysis is usually employed to pose questions. Why are the lifetimes of many different genres limited to about 30 years?[xliv] Why do British novels in the mid-eighteenth century use many words in a title and then, within a few decades, change so that titles are no more than three or four words long?[xlv] How to explain changes in narrative conventions such as free indirect discourse when the novel moves from Britain to British colonies?[xlvi] I find Moretti's work intriguing for the patterns he uncovers, but I am flat out delighted by the ingenious explanations he devises to account for them. So far beyond the mechanical exercises Culler imagines are these explanations that I would not hesitate to call many of them brilliant. When the explanations fail to persuade (as Moretti candidly confesses is sometimes the case even for him), the patterns nevertheless stand revealed as entry points for interpretations advanced by other scholars who find them interesting.

I now turn to explore the interrelations between the components of an expanded repertoire of reading strategies that includes close, hyper, and machine reading. The overlaps between them are as revealing as the differences. Close and hyperreading operate synergistically when hyperreading is used to identify passages or to home in on a few texts of interest, whereupon close reading takes over. As Guillory observed, skimming and scanning here alternate with in-depth reading and interpretation.[xlvii] Hyperreading overlaps with machine reading in identifying patterns. This might be done in the context of a Google keyword search, for example when one notices that most of the work on a given topic has been done by X, or it might be done when machine analysis confirms a pattern already detected by hyper (or close) reading. Indeed, skimming, scanning, and pattern identification are likely to occur with all three reading strategies; their prevalence in one or another is a matter of scale and emphasis rather than clear-cut boundary.

Since patterns have now entered the discussion, we may wonder what a pattern is. This is not a trivial question, largely because of the various ways in which patterns become manifest. Patterns in large data sets may be so subtle that only sophisticated statistical analysis can reveal them; complex patterns may nevertheless be apprehended quickly and easily when columns of numbers are translated into visual forms, as with fMRI scans. Verbal patterns may be discerned through the close reading of a single textual passage or grasped through hyperreading of an entire text or many texts. An anecdote may be useful in clarifying the nature of pattern. I once took a pottery class, and the instructor asked each participant to make several objects that would constitute a series. The series might, for example, consist of vases with the same shapes but different sizes, or it might be vases of the same size in which the shapes underwent a consistent set of deformations. The example shows that differences are as important as similarities, for they keep a pattern from being merely a series of identical items. I therefore propose the following definition: a pattern consists of regularities that appear through a series of related differences and similarities.

Related to the idea of pattern is the question of meaning. Since entire books have been written on the subject, I will not attempt to define meaning but merely observe that wherever and however it occurs, meaning is sensitively dependent on context. The same sentence, uttered in two different contexts, may mean something entirely different in one compared with the other. Close reading typically occurs in a monolocal context (that is, with a single text). Here the context is quite rich, including the entire text and other texts connected with it through networks of allusions, citations, and iterative quotations. Hyperreading, by contrast, typically occurs in a multilocal context. Because many textual fragments are juxtaposed, context is truncated, often consisting of a single phrase or sentence, as in a Google search. In machine reading, the context may be limited to a few words or eliminated altogether, as in a word-frequency list. Relatively context-poor, machine reading is enriched by context-rich close reading when close reading provides guidance for the construction of algorithms; Margaret Cohen points to this synergy when she observes that for computer programs to be designed, "the patterns still need to be observed [by close reading]."[xlviii] On the other hand, machine reading may reveal patterns overlooked in close reading, a point Willard McCarty[xlix] makes in relation to his work on personification in Ovid's *Metamorphoses*.[20] The more the emphasis falls on pattern (as in machine reading), the more likely it is that context must be supplied from outside (by a human interpreter) to connect pattern with meaning; the more the emphasis falls on meaning (as in close reading), the more pattern assumes a subordinate role. In general, the different distributions between pattern, meaning, and context provide a way to think about interrelations between close, hyper, and machine reading.

The larger point is that close, hyper, and machine reading each have distinctive advantages and limitations; nevertheless, they also overlap and can be made to interact synergistically with one another. Maryanne Wolfe reaches a similar conclusion when, at the end of *Proust and the Squid*, she writes,

> We must teach our children to be bitextual or multitextual, able to read and analyze texts flexibly in different ways, with more deliberate instruction at every stage of development on the inferential, demanding aspects of any text. Teaching children to uncover the invisible world that resides in written words needs to be both explicit and part of a dialogue between learner and teacher, if we are to promote the processes that lead to fully formed expert reading in our citizenry.[l]

I agree wholeheartedly with the goal: the question is how, precisely, to accomplish it?

---

20 Ovid (43 BCE–17/18 CE), whose full name was Publius Ovidius Naso, was a Roman poet best known for *Ars amatoria* and *Metamorphoses*, a book of myths written in hexameter.

V. Synergies between Close, Hyper, and Machine Reading

Starting from a traditional humanistic basis in literature, Alan Liu in the English department at the University of California, Santa Barbara, has been teaching undergraduate and graduate courses that he calls Literature+, which adopt as a pedagogical method the interdisciplinarity facilitated by digital media. He asks students "to choose a literary work and treat it according to one or more of the research paradigms prevalent in other fields of study," including visualization, storyboarding, simulation, and game design. Starting with close reading, he encourages students to compare it with methodologies in other fields, including the sciences and engineering. He also has constructed a "tool kit" on his web site that includes links to software packages enabling students with little or no programming experience to create different modes of representation of literary texts, including tools for text analysis, visualization, mapping, and social-network diagramming. The approach is threefold: it offers students traditional literary training; it expands their sense of how they can use digital media to analyze literary texts; and it encourages them to connect literary methodologies with those of other fields they may be entering. It offers close reading not as an unquestioned good but as one methodology among several, with distinctive capabilities and limitations. Moreover, because decisions about how to encode and analyze texts using software programs require precise thinking about priorities, goals, and methodologies, it clarifies the assumptions that undergird close reading by translating them into algorithmic analysis.

An example of how the "Literature+" approach works in practice is the project entitled "*Romeo and Juliet*: A Facebook Tragedy."[li] Three students working collaboratively adapted Shakespeare's play to the Facebook model, creating maps of social networks using the Friend Wheel (naturally, the Montagues are all "friends" to each other, and so are the Capulets), filling out profiles for the characters (Romeo is interpreted as a depressive personality who has an obsessive attachment to his love object and who has corresponding preferences for music, films, and other cultural artifacts that express this sensibility), and having a fight break out on the message-board forum using a Group called The Streets of Verona. The Wall feature was used to incorporate dialogue in which characters speak directly to one another, and the Photos section allowed one character to comment on the attributes of another. The masque at which Romeo and Juliet meet became an Event, to which Capulet invited friends in his Friend Wheel. From a pedagogical point of view, the students were encouraged to use software with which they were familiar in unfamiliar ways, thus increasing their awareness of its implications. The exercise also required them to make interpretive judgments about which features of the play were most essential (since not everything could be included) and to be precise about interactions between relationships, events, and characters. Linking traditional literary reading skills with digital encoding and analysis, the "Literature+" approach strengthens the ability to understand complex literature at the same time it encourages students to think reflectively on digital capabilities. Here digital and print literacies mutually reinforce and extend each other.

Lev Manovich's "Cultural Analytics" is a series of projects that starts from the premise that algorithmic analyses of large data sets (up to several terabytes[21] in size), originally developed

21 A measure of computer information composed of one trillion bytes.

for work in the sciences and social sciences, should be applied to cultural objects, including the analysis of real-time data flows.[lii] In many academic institutions, high-end computational facilities have programs that invite faculty members and graduate students in the arts and humanities to use them. For example, at the University of California, San Diego, where Manovich teaches, the Supercomputer Center sponsored a summer workshop in 2006, Cyberinfrastructure for the Humanities, Arts, and Social Sciences. At Duke University, where I teach, the Renaissance Computing Institute (RENCI) offers accounts to faculty members and students in the arts and humanities that allow them to use computationally intense analysis. In my experience, researchers at these kinds of facilities are delighted when humanists come to them with projects. Because their mission is to encourage widespread use across and among campuses and to foster collaborations among academic, government, corporate, and community stakeholders, they see humanistic inquiry and artistic creation as missing parts of the picture that enrich the mix. This opens the door to analysis of large cultural data sets such as visual images, media content, and geospatial mapping combined with various historical and cultural overlays.

An example is Manovich's analysis of *Time* magazine covers from 1923–89. As Manovich observes, ideal sites for cultural analytics are large data sets that are well structured and include metadata about date, publication venue, and so forth. The visualization tools that he uses allow the *Time* covers to be analyzed according to subject (for example, portraits versus other types of covers), color gradients, black-and-white gradients, amount of white space, and in other ways. One feature is particularly useful for building bridges between close reading and machine analysis: the visualization tool allows the user both to see large-scale patterns and to zoom in to see a particular cover in detail, thus enabling analyses across multiple scale levels. Other examples include Manovich's analysis of one million manga[22] pages using the Modrian software, sorted according to gray-scale values; another project analyzes scene lengths and gray scale values in classic black-and-white films. While large-scale data analyses are not new, their applications in the humanities and arts are still in their infancy, making cultural analytics a frontier of knowledge construction.

Of course, not everyone has access to computation-intensive facilities, including most parents and teachers at smaller colleges and universities. A small-scale example that anyone could implement will be helpful. In teaching an honors writing class, I juxtaposed Mary Shelley's *Frankenstein*[23] with Shelley Jackson's *Patchwork Girl*,[24] an electronic hypertext fiction written in proprietary *Storyspace* software. Since these were honors students, many of them had already

---

22 "A Japanese genre of cartoons and comic books ... typically having a science-fiction or fantasy theme" (*OED*).

23 Mary Wollstonecraft Shelley (1797–1851), English novelist most famous for writing *Frankenstein*, a gothic novel published in 1818; married to the English Romantic poet Percy Bysshe Shelley.

24 Shelley Jackson (born 1963), writer born in the Philippines known for experimentation with textual forms, including such works as *Patchwork Girl* (1995), a hypertext rewriting of *Frankenstein*, and *Skin*, a story written in tattoos on the bodies of participants.

read *Frankenstein* and were, moreover, practiced in close reading and literary analysis. When it came to digital reading, however, they were accustomed to the scanning and fast skimming typical of hyperreading; they therefore expected that it might take them, oh, half an hour to go through Jackson's text. They were shocked when I told them a reasonable time to spend with Jackson's text was about the time it would take them to read *Frankenstein*, say, ten hours or so. I divided them into teams and assigned a section of Jackson's text to each team, telling them that I wanted them to discover *all* the lexias (i.e., blocks of digital text) in their section and warning them that the *Storyspace* software allows certain lexias to be hidden until others are read. Finally, I asked them to diagram interrelations between lexias, drawing on all three views that the *Storyspace* software enables.

As a consequence, the students were not only required to read closely but also to analyze the narrative strategies Jackson uses to construct her text. Jackson focuses some of her textual sections on a narrator modeled on the female creature depicted in *Frankenstein*, when Victor, at the male creature's request, begins to assemble a female body as a companion to his first creation.[liii] As Victor works, he begins to think about the two creatures mating and creating a race of such creatures. Stricken with sexual nausea, he tears up the female body while the male creature watches, howling, from the window; throws the pieces into a basket; and rows out onto a lake, where he dumps them. In her text Jackson re-assembles and re-animates the female creature, playing with the idea of fragmentation as an inescapable condition not only for her narrator but for all human beings. The idea is reinforced by the visual form of the narrative, which (in the *Storyspace* map view) is visualized as a series of titled text blocks connected by webs of lines. Juxtaposing this text with *Frankenstein* encouraged discussions about narrative framing, transitions, strategies, and characterization. By the end the students, who already admired *Frankenstein* and were enthralled by Mary Shelley's narrative, were able to see that electronic literature might be comparably complex and would also repay close attention to its strategies, structure, form, rhetoric, and themes. Here already-existing print literacies were enlisted to promote and extend **digital literacy**.

These examples merely scratch the surface of what can be done to create productive interactions between close, hyper, and machine reading. Close and hyperreading are already part of a literary scholar's tool kit (although hyperreading may not be recognized or valued as such). Many good programs are now available for machine reading, such as *Wordle*, which creates word clouds to display word-frequency analysis, the advanced version of the *Hermetic Word Frequency Counter*, which has the ability to count words in multiple files and to count phrases as well as words, and other text-analysis tools available through the TAPoR text-analysis portal (<http://digitalresearchtools.pbworks.com/Text+Analysis+Tools>). Most of these programs are not difficult to use and provide the basis for wide-ranging experimentation by students and teachers alike. As Manovich says about cultural analytics and Moretti proclaims about distant reading, machine analysis opens the door to new kinds of discoveries that were not possible before and that can surprise and intrigue scholars accustomed to the delights of close reading.

What transformed disciplinary coherence might literary studies embrace? Here is a suggestion: literary studies teaches literacies across a range of media forms, including print and digital, and focuses on interpretation and analysis of patterns, meaning, and context through close, hyper, and machine reading practices. Reading has always been constituted through complex and diverse practices. Now it is time to re-think what reading is and how it works in the rich mixtures of words and images, sounds and animations, graphics and letters that constitute the environments of twenty-first-century literacies.

Notes

i. Wendy Griswold, Terry McDonnell, and Nathan Wright, "Reading and the Reading Class in the Twenty-First Century," *Annual Review of Sociology* 31 (2005): 127–41.

ii. Mark Bauerlein, *The Dumbest Generation: How the Digital Age Stupefies Young Americans and Jeopardizes Our Future* (New York: Penguin, 2009), 93–111.

iii. *Reading at Risk: A Survey of Literary Reading in America* (NEA, June 2004), Web, Accessed 1 September 2010; and *To Read or Not to Read: A Question of National Consequence* (NEA, November 2007), Web, Accessed 27 August 2010.

iv. Matthew G. Kirschenbaum, "Reading at Risk: A Response," *Learning Technologies* (U of Maryland, 21 July 2004), Web, Accessed 1 September 2010.

v. See Robert Scholes, *The Rise and Fall of English: Reconstructing English as a Discipline* (New Haven, CT: Yale UP, 1999).

vi. Jane Gallop, "Close Reading in 2009," *ADE Bulletin* 149 (2010): 15–19, 15.

vii. Barbara Johnson, "Teaching Deconstructively," *Writing and Reading Differently: Deconstruction and the Teaching of Composition and Literature*, ed. G. Douglas Atkins and Michael L. Johnson (Lawrence: UP of Kansas, 1985), 140–48, 140.

viii. Jonathan Culler, "The Closeness of Close Reading," *ADE Bulletin* 149 (2010): 20–25, 20.

ix. Gallop, "Close Reading," 8.

x. Fredric Jameson, *The Political Unconscious: Narrative as a Socially Symbolic Act* (Ithaca, NY: Cornell UP, 1981). Quoted in Mary Thomas Crane, "Surface, Depth, and the Spatial Imaginary: A Cognitive Reading of *The Political Unconscious*," Spec. issue of *Representations* 108 (2009): 76–97, 92.

xi. See Crane, "Surface," for a close analysis of Jameson's metaphors.

xii. Jameson, *The Political Unconscious*, 141–42.

xiii. David Laurence, "Learning to Read," *ADE Bulletin* 145 (2008): 3–7, 4.

xiv. L.S. Vygotsky, *Mind in Society: The Development of Higher Psychological Processes*, ed. Michael Cole, Vera John-Steiner, Sylvia Scribner, and Ellen Souberman, 14th ed. (Cambridge, MA: Harvard UP, 1978), 86.

xv. See Margaret Robertson, Andrew Fluck, and Ivan Webb, *Children, On-line Learning and Authentic Teaching Skills in Primary Education*. University of Tasmania (U of Tasmania, n.d.), Web, Accessed 13 December 2010.

xvi. See Ron Tinsley and Kimberly Lebak, "Expanding the Zone of Reflective Capacity: Taking Separate Journeys Together," *Networks* 11.2 (2009): 1–11, Web, Accessed 1 September 2010.

xvii. James Sosnoski, "Hyper-Readers and Their Reading Engines," *Passions, Pedagogies, and Twenty-First Century Technologies*, ed. Gail E. Hawisher and Cynthia L. Selfe (Logan: Utah State UP; Urbana, IL: National Council of Teachers of English, 1999), 161–77, 167.

xviii. Ibid., 163–72.

xix. Jakob Nielsen, "F-Shaped Pattern for Reading Web Content," *Alertbox* (2006): n.p., Web, Accessed 1 September 2010.

xx. Quoted in Stanislas Dehaene, *Reading in the Brain: The Science and Evolution of a Human Invention* (New York: Viking, 2009), 18.

xxi. See E. Sillence, P. Briggs, P.R. Harris, and L. Fishwick, "How Do Patients Evaluate and Make Use of Online Health Information?" *Social Science and Medicine* 64 (2007): 1853–62.
xxii. John Guillory, "Close Reading: Prologue and Epilogue," *ADE Bulletin* 149 (2010): 8–14, 13.
xxiii. Nicholas Carr, *The Shallows: What the Internet Is Doing to Our Brains* (New York: Norton, 2010).
xxiv. Kurt Vonnegut, "Harrison Bergeron," *Welcome to the Monkey House* (1961; New York: Dell, 1998), 7–14.
xxv. Jonathan Crary, *Suspensions of Perception: Attention, Spectacle, and Modern Culture* (Cambridge, MA: MIT P, 2000). For summary, see Patricia M. Greenfield, "Technology and Informal Education: What Is Taught, What Is Learned," *Science* 323.5910 (2009): 69–71.
xxvi. D.S. Niederhauser, R.E. Reynolds, D.J. Salmen, and P. Skolmoski, "The Influence of Cognitive Load on Learning from Hypertext," *Journal of Educational Computing Research* 23.3 (2000): 237–55.
xxvii. Diana DeStefano and Jo-Anne LeFevre, "Cognitive Load in Hypertext Reading: A Review," *Computers in Human Behavior* 23.3 (2007): 1616–41.
xxviii. Quoted in Carr, *The Shallows*, 129.
xxix. Ibid.
xxx. Ibid., 30–31.
xxxi. Ibid., 30.
xxxii. Dehaene, *Reading in the Brain*.
xxxiii. Ibid., 209.
xxxiv. Ibid., 171.
xxxv. Gary Small and Gigi Vorgan, *iBrain: Surviving the Technological Alteration of the Modern Mind* (New York: Harper, 2008), 15–17.
xxxvi. Carr, *The Shallows*, 116.
xxxvii. N. Katherine Hayles, "Hyper and Deep Attention: The Generational Divide in Cognitive Modes," *Profession* (2007): 187–99.

xxxviii. D.F. Roberts, U.G. Foehr, and V. Rideout, *Generation M: Media in the Lives of 8–18 Year Olds: A Kaiser Family Foundation Study* (Kaiser Family Foundation, March 2005), Web, Accessed 1 September 2010.
xxxix. Researchers in the field of attention studies identify three major types of attention: controlled attention, capable of being focused through conscious effort; stimulus-driven attention, a mode of attentiveness involuntarily attracted by environmental events, such as a loud noise; and arousal, a general level of alertness (see Torkel Klingberg, *The Overflowing Brain: Information Overload and the Limits of Working Memory* [Oxford: Oxford UP, 2009], 21 for a summary). In these terms, deep attention is a subset of controlled attention, and hyperattention bridges controlled and stimulus-driven attention.
xl. Sosnoski, "Hyper-Readers."
xli. Culler, "The Closeness," 24.
xlii. John Guillory, "How Scholars Read," *ADE Bulletin* 146 (2008): 8–17, 13.
xliii. Franco Moretti, *Graphs, Maps, Trees: Abstract Models for a Literary History* (London: Verso, 2005).
xliv. Ibid.
xlv. Franco Moretti, "Style, Inc.: Reflections on Seven Thousand Titles (British Novels, 1740–1850)," *Critical Inquiry* 36.1 (Autumn 2009): 134–58. [See Moretti's article below, p. 525.]
xlvi. Moretti, *Graphs*.
xlvii. John Guillory, "How Scholars Read."
xlviii. Margaret Cohen, "Narratology in the Archive of Literature," Spec. issue of *Representations* 108 (2009): 51–75, 59.
xlix. Willard McCarty, *Humanities Computing* (London: Palgrave, 2005), 53–72.

l. Maryanne Wolf, *Proust and the Squid: The Story and Science of the Reading Brain* (New York: Harper, 2007), 226.

li. Helen Skura, Katia Nierle, and Gregory Gin, "*Romeo and Juliet*: A Facebook Tragedy," *Literature and Cross-Disciplinary Models of Literary Interpretation* (PBWorks, 2008), Web, Accessed 1 September 2010.

lii. Manovich, "Cultural Analytics."

liii. N. Katherine Hayles, "The Invention of Copyright and the Birth of Monsters: Flickering Connectivities in Shelley Jackson's *Patchwork Girl*," *Journal of Postmodern Culture* 10.2 (2001): n.p., Web, Accessed 1 September 2010.

30.
Andrew Piper,
"Turning the Page (Roaming, Zooming, Streaming),"
Book Was There: Reading in Electronic Times.
Chicago: Chicago UP, 2012. 45–61

Andrew Piper (b. 1973) is Associate Professor in the Department of Languages, Literatures, and Cultures at McGill University. A scholar of German literature and a book historian, his first book, *Dreaming in Books: The Making of the Bibliographic Imagination in the Romantic Age* (2009), explored the material and imaginative investments made in books at the turn of the nineteenth century in Europe and North America. In *Book Was There*, he also considers reading from a historical and material perspective—but does so by carefully considering the physical nature of the book, asking how it has shaped our relation to reading, and the transformative nature of the transition to digital media (and the different devices we now use to read). Piper is particularly interested in investigating the embodied nature of reading: chapters in *Book Was There* consider the various senses employed in reading a physical book (touch, vision) and the material practices we undertake while reading a physical printed or handwritten object (turning pages, annotation). For Piper, new digital forms present opportunities, but also inevitable losses as we move away from an intimate physical relationship we have had with our reading material for centuries.

In the chapter excerpted here, Piper examines the page as the basic unit of the codex, providing some analytical analogies for understanding the operation of page and our interactions with it (pages, he claims, can be conceptualized as windows, frames, individuations, mirrors, and folds). Piper also suggests that thus far designers of digital books have failed to depart from the paradigm of the page (the ubiquity of the pdf is a good example of a digital form that merely mimics a printed one). Offering a few examples of more innovative attempts to reimagine the page for the screen, Piper suggests that the digital page may be differently conceived in terms of what it allows us to do with it (roam, zoom, stream). Only then will digital reading have the potential to enhance the experience of reading beyond what is already possible with the physical page.

Turning the Page (Roaming, Zooming, Streaming)

Pages so many, paper so much!
—Walter Scott[1] [*Waverley*]

All is leaf!
—J.W. Goethe[2]

The **page** is the atom of the book, its most basic building block (and like atoms it too consists of smaller elements: soot, gum, hide, linen, pulp, thread, so many **bibliographic** quarks). But the page is also a frame, that which marks a boundary. For almost two millennia the page has been the primary way that we have accessed reading. The page is where words assume order, and it is that order that has helped shape the meaning of words for us.

Until now, digital texts have largely not departed from the page view (even if, in an interesting case of double remediation they have incorporated the logic of the **scroll** into the page). Websites are stacked piles of pages, browsers are static "windows," and e-books aren't simulations of books at all, but single pages. In Goethe's words, all is still very much **leaf** or page. Or better yet: today, all is **recto**.

Much of the current debate about the future of reading turns on the crowdedness of the digital page versus its bookish predecessor. There is just too much stuff on the screen now. The webcam portrait is the new face of text. We are breeding generations of distracted readers, people who simply cannot pay attention long enough to finish a book.

This is undoubtedly true, but only to a point. We have of course been here before. "Read much, not many," said Pliny the Younger[3] in the first century AD, initiating a standard refrain about reading through the ages.[i] We have always worried about how to instill careful reading, no matter what the object. Keats[4] said to read one page of poetry per day.[ii] Erasmus[5] suggested to read the Gospels by "bit[ing] off some of this medicine constantly ... chew it assiduously and pass it down into our spiritual stomachs [and] do not cast it up again."[iii] Alongside the slow food movement we now have (once again) appeals for slow reading (and of course anti-regurgitation).[iv]

But we have also been here before in terms of page design. The medieval page reveled in its cacophony (Fig. 5.1). So did the great printed critical **editions** of the sixteenth- and seventeenth-century humanists, like Joseph Scaliger or Daniel Heinsius.[v] As much as I like the

1 Walter Scott (1771–1832), Scottish poet and novelist, best known for his historical novels about Scotland.

2 Johann Wolfgang von Goethe (1749–1832), German writer, artist, and politician, of great celebrity across Europe.

3 Pliny the Younger (61–c. 112 CE) was a Roman lawyer and magistrate.

4 John Keats (1795–1821), English poet of the Romantic period.

5 Desiderius Erasmus Roterodamus (1466–1536), Dutch scholar and theologian.

geometric asceticism that printed pages can take (from early sixteenth-century Aldine editions[6] to Romantic promoters of the wide margins in the nineteenth century), I am also drawn to the full page of the book. The **scribal** and scholarly commitment to textual abundance suggests an exuberance about reading that I hope we will never forget. Our notebooks still often look like this. They are reminders of the spillage of human thought.

Of course there is something markedly different about the digital page. Medieval or Renaissance **marginalia** don't blink. (Is there anything more offensive to the eye than blinking lights, which have always been meant as warning signals?) If e-books today are serene imitators of the modern printed page, "enhanced" e-books, every **publisher's** dream, will soon consist of vast amounts of animation (sound tracks, pop-up windows, and moving images). If I were designing a reader today in our age of enhancement, I would call it The Pygmalion.[7]

It may be that we should no longer even call this reading. Listening to music, watching movies, pointing, and clicking—these have nothing to do with reading. But we should also remember that reading has very often had this "multimedia" quality about it, even if not in such an over-populated sense. Reading has traditionally been imbedded in aural practices of reading aloud (whether in school, church, at the dinner table, before bed, or for the visually impaired), just as, as I tried to show in the last chapter [of Piper's book], it has so often been codefined by the act of looking (ceremonial books, travel books, and coffee-table books to name a few). In my own house as a child, reading was definitely loud. Family members were constantly reading their favorite passages aloud or shouting, "Look at this!" (like a parental pop-up window). Digital texts may be different in degree—in the way they are able to amplify our historical relations to
the page (more crowded, more multimedial)—but they are not truly different in kind. They still do not, as yet, depart from the traditional atomic structure of the book: the page view.

And this is where I think we need to shift the terms of the debate. What matters is not the ability to add links or visual or audio content. This strikes me as just a departure from, not an enhancement of, reading. Rather, what should be at stake is how we may or may not re-conceptualize the *formal structure* of reading. That is why reflecting on the nature of the page, rather than just the technology, is so important. It is the text's architecture, its structural details, that plays as much a role in shaping our reading experiences as the underlying material profile of the book or screen. Only when we re-conceptualize the page as the basic unit of reading are we truly entering into new conceptual terrain.

If our relationship to holding texts and looking at texts will be two of the features that will change most dramatically in the years to come as reading moves from pages to screens, our relationship to the "page" as the fundamental interface of text is also on the verge of potentially undergoing a categorical shift. It bears reflecting on what pages have done and what we would do without them.

---

6 "Aldine edition" is a term used to describe the editions of sixteenth-century Venetian printer Aldus Manutius, who was one of the first to print in **octavo** format, books small enough that they could fit into a pocket.

7 A reference to Ovid's *Metamorphoses*, in which a sculptor's creation, with whom he has fallen in love, is brought to life.

Fig. 5.1: Three versions of Psalm 118 based on St. Jerome's edition. The left column is the Gallican text with Latin interlinear gloss from the church fathers. The middle column is the Roman text with an Anglo-Saxon interlinear translation. And the right column is the Hebrew text with French interlinear translation. From *The Canterbury Psalter* (1147), MS R.17.1 fol. 219v. The Master and Fellows of Trinity College, Cambridge.

First, pages.

Pages are windows. Pages allow us to look through, to transport ourselves into an imaginative space off the page. The use of marginal illustrations (Fig. 5.2), the width of blank margins, the degree of whiteness of the page (which is never truly white), the shape of **typefaces**, and the distances between letters and words—all play a role in facilitating fenestration. But so does the text. Scenes of sleeping, dreaming, meandering, tinkering, and distant viewing (hilltops or cityscapes) are all descriptive techniques of having us see through something. When Virginia Woolf writes of Mrs. Ramsay in *To the Lighthouse*, "And she waited a little, knitting, wondering, and slowly those words they had said at dinner, 'the China rose is all abloom and buzzing with the honey bee,' began washing from side to side of her mind rhythmically,"[vi] I know to let my mind wander, too, to see through the page before me, to enter into the world of Mrs. Ramsay's drifting mind as I then drift back to my own.

Pages are frames. Pages not only allow us to look through, but also at, to see something that has been distilled. Pages are like microscopes, only in reverse. They reduce the world to something comprehensible. Unlike cinema screens, pages are smaller than the world they represent. When the twentieth-century Swiss writer Robert Walser began writing short stories in microscript while residing in a sanitarium, he was trying to find a way to capture this smallness of writing. Pages are an attempt to grasp that which is around us, to bring it down to size, to order it, and finally to save it. As Susan Orlean wrote about her orchid thief, so too of the page: "There are too many ideas and things and people. Too many directions to go. I was starting to believe the reason it matters to care passionately about something, is that it whittles the world down 515
to a more manageable size."[vii] Pages are signs of passion. They whittle, like sculptures with the excess marble chipped away.

We have developed many ways of framing reading over the ages: columns, headpieces,[8] **illuminated** letters, footnotes, and of course punctuation are all ways of bringing words into focus. The introduction of spacing between words in the seventh century, the gradual standardization of punctuation and spelling in the seventeenth century (the great age of dictionaries), or even the vogue in the nineteenth century for presenting classics in double columns (the book as the new pantheon)—these are so many ways of arguing for the orderliness of reading amid the cacophony of texts.[viii] So too is the age-old technique of ekphrasis,[9] of focusing on a single object through the act of description. Description, which is a problem for narratologists (what *happens* when we describe something?), is a way of focusing our attention. It is a verbal form of punctuation. When Balzac[10] writes of a Parisian gambling house, "The various salons are teeming with spectators and players; indigent old men who shuffle along in search of warmth; tormented faces belonging to those whose orgies began in wine and will end up in the Seine,"[ix] this is a world I can know all at once. He has made Paris graspable for me two centuries later and an ocean away.

8 A headpiece is an illustration or ornamental motif that is printed at the head of a chapter in a book.

9 A verbal description of a work of art.

10 Honoré de Balzac (1799–1850), French novelist and playwright.

Fig. 5.2: The Prayer Book of Kaiser Maximilian I (1513) was one of the most important illustrated books of the early sixteenth century and included marginal illustrations by artists such as Albrecht Dürer [1471–1528], Lucas Cranach the Elder [1472–1553], and Albrecht Altdorfer [1480–1538], among others.

Pages are individuations. No matter how large or small, pages are finite. Unlike scrolls, pages are material arguments of individualization. We cannot read the recto and **verso** sides of the page at the same time (although we can intimate that more is to come when the ink bleeds through). As in Augustine's *Confessions*,[11] pages allow us to access the world at random, out of sequence, as a piece.[x] Chapter headings (but not running headers), page numbers (but not gathering **signatures**), stanzas, paragraph breaks, and the numbering of verses are all forms of individuation. So too are rhetorical devices like synecdoche, where the part stands for the whole, and narrative devices like direct speech, which carves the world into different voices. Quotation marks, which came into use in the sixteenth century in France and the seventeenth century in England, are to the page as the page is to the book. As Marjorie Garber has written in her study of quotation marks, the duplication of quotation also implies a duplicity, a taking out of context—quotation marks are the grammatical seams of any text.[xi]

Pages are mirrors. Although we may not be able to read recto and verso of the same page together, we can read them across opposing pages. Like books, pages are always double. As Garret Stewart has reminded us, "Every book is a diptych."[xii] [12] Pages face each other; they comment, reflect, illustrate, or confound one another. The scroll is constitutionally singular, one long **sheet**. Like the filmstrip or the tape spool, it may be comprised of parts sewn together, but the act of splicing is designed to cover over these differences, not highlight them. There is a seamlessness to the scroll that is not true of the book, whose spine is both anatomically and visually prominent. The page is always part of a "gathering," the book the sum of smaller versions of itself. The page argues for a logic of iterability, of sameness with a difference. It is this ability to mirror, 517
to be like, that was behind the long-standing idea of the "book of nature," that the book could be a faithful reflection of nature and that nature was like a book. But also ourselves. In one of the most cherished Romantic novels written in German, *Heinrich von Ofterdingen* (1802),[13] we see how the hero discovers a book in a cave that tells the story of his own life. Deep in the caverns of the book, *Heinrich von Ofterdingen* wants us to know, we see ourselves.

Pages are folds. The page is not just a part, but always a part of. It is a *folded* sheet, or else it would be a **broadside**, poster, or playbill. The essence of the page is the turn. With books reading is experienced as a gradual unfolding. The "foldout"[14] is one of the most popular devices in the history of the book. Whether as a map, a table, a **facsimile** of a handwritten letter, or a pop-up world in a children's book, pages are imagined to unfold in our hands (Fig. 5.3). They convey a sense of the development of readerly thought. However much we like to remind ourselves that books are the first random access machines, there is still a remarkable degree of sequentiality to the technology of the page. In this, pages mirror the growth of nature around us (not to

---

11 *Confessions* is an autobiographical work by St. Augustine of Hippo, written between 397 and 398 CE.

12 A diptych is any object with two flat plates, or tablets, attached with a hinge.

13 An unfinished novel written by the German writer Novalis (pen name for Georg Philipp Friedrich Freiherr von Hardenberg; 1772–1801).

14 A page in a book or magazine that is larger than the format of the book/magazine, and is designed to be folded out to view and folded back into place.

Fig. 5.3: Lothar Meggendorfer [1847–1925] was one of the great innovators in children's book design at the end of the nineteenth century. Here we see a facsimile of one of his most popular works, *Internationaler Circus* (1887). Rare Books and Special Collections, McGill University Library. Reprinted with permission.

mention language). As Goethe remarked, "Nature can only achieve all that it can in a series. She does not make leaps."[xiii] This is one of the reasons that we have spoken of leaves and pages so interchangeably.

Taken all together, then, the book is an amalgam of the arbitrary, the simultaneous, and the sequential. Proust[15] might be said to be its ultimate theorist. He takes the scattered associations of thought and puts them in order, an order that is always bursting at the seams. To lose a sense of sequence, no matter how complex, is ultimately to lose sense. That is why Proust's novel of soporific associations, a work that can only truly be understood at night, begins with the pathway, but also the parallel—the choice to go Swann's way or the Guermantes's way.[16] As the anthropologist Andre Leroi-Gourhan has reminded us, the evolution of the human species was intimately tied to increasing degrees of sequential sophistication in tool cutting.[xiv] No matter how much we are drawn today to the horizontality (and democracy) of distributed cognition, we will always need sequence. Pathways allow us to do things over again; they are technologies of recurrence, perfectibility, and survival. Books, stories, re-counting are primordial defenses against extinction.

---

15 Marcel Proust (1871–1922), French novelist, and author of *À la recherche du temps perdu* (*In Search of Lost Time*), published in seven parts between 1913 and 1927.

16 Different parts of *À la recherche du temps perdu*.

Fig. 5.4: Craig Mod, "Books in the Age of the iPad" (2011). Courtesy of the artist. Reprinted with the permission of Craig Mod.

The digital page, by contrast, is a fake, a simulation called up from distributed data.[xv] It is not really there. The digital page could always be otherwise. It is this ludic aspect of the digital that was one of its most attractive features for early proponents. But what interests me is how the page might itself be otherwise. How might the plane of digital presentation move out of the realm of fakery and embrace its inner self, if it has one?

Roaming. If one of the crucial features of the page is its finitude—that it stops—then one of the first ways to think beyond the page is to transgress its horizontal limits. As an innovative new voice in text design, "Craig Mod," has suggested, we can begin to imagine texts not as stacked pages but as potentially infinite planes (Fig. 5.4).[xvi] Text no longer draws its inspiration from its etymological origins of weaving, but instead from the shape of the "pad" (Apple, as always, helping us see the shape of technology). According to this model, the reading device would remain a lens, much like the page, but now the textual surface is roamable rather than turnable. One of the pleasures of reading the printed page has historically been the way the eye can wander across the page, the way we can take in different parts of the text according to our own plan. Roamable text expands this principle to ever greater dimensions, as reading devices become tools of mobilization rather than iteration. Reading becomes nomadic rather than domestic. Where we "curl up" with a book, we "roam" across a plane. Unlike the branching pathways of links whose routes are difficult to visualize (who has not gotten lost clicking through the web?), the plane seems more navigable to me. It insists on the knowledge of adjacency. There can be no jumping across the plane, as in a book or a **hypertext**; one must pass through something on the way to something else. Reading assumes a topological structure, one that was latent in the printed page (or even hypertext), but that becomes even more central in understanding the reading "plane." In learning

Fig. 5.5: Aya Karpinska, *Shadows Never Sleep* (2009). Courtesy of the artist. Reprinted with the permission of Aya Karpinska.

how to roam, we are initiated more consciously, perhaps more critically, into the nature of our interconnected textual universe.

Zooming. Of all the technologies that have changed how we see our world, the satellite is surely one of the most important.[xvii] Google Earth is the popularized version of the satellite view. For all of its reputation as a search engine, I think one of Google's most significant contributions is the way it has changed how we visualize information, the way zooming has been irreversibly integrated into our understanding of both space and text. If roaming expands the horizontal edges of the page, zooming bursts through the page's two-dimensionality.[xviii] It returns us to the realm of microscopy, but perhaps also to the foldout or pop-up. Rather than release us into another space—the traditional dreamscape of the book-zooming suggests a constant quest for the beneath. Like Facebook, there is a preformationist logic at work here, as though everything is contained within everything else. It is only a matter of following the path downward, which is also a path backward to the beginning. Zoomtext has a genetic quality about it.

Aya Karpinska's *Shadows Never Sleep* (2009), a recent enchanting example of what she calls "a zoom narrative" (Fig. 5.5), is a telling example of the way such digital drilling down is indebted to the association of reading and interiority that emerged out of the eighteenth century and whose most poignant symbol, as we saw in the last chapter [of Piper's book], was the silhouette. Karpinska's whimsical text boxes of cutout images show us the way sentences have become pixilated, divorced from their normal grammar in the same way that the digital page is no longer connected to the spine of the book. But her choice of words is also a reminder of how this new art of discovery is tied to a sense of the anxiety that belonged to childhood. In a world of zooming we are always peering "in corners," "under the bed," "beneath the pillow." As with young children, there is a beneath or behind to all things. In Karpinska's evocative terms, we "stretch and shudder, whip and creep." When Walter Benjamin[17] wrote his brief memoir of growing up in Berlin, he spoke of how children have a special knowledge of a home's corners (not for nothing was a popular German folk hero called "Faithful Eckhart," *Ecke* being the German word for corner). Like the little paper cutout dolls in Karpinska's *Shadows Never Sleep*, zoomtext returns us to a state of such childlike knowledge of the recess. It is a world filled with curiosity and wonder, but also disorientation, nervousness, and superstition. It suggests the way life online lends itself toward feelings of conspiracy and heteronomy—of being acted upon, the inverse of the book's imagined autonomy.

Streaming. One of the most important aspects of the page is its stability. When I turn it, it doesn't disappear (unless it rips and we all know how traumatic that is). But much writing today takes the form of what David Gelernter has called "lifestreams" (blogs, feeds, tweets, etc.), similar to the "Prayer Companion" used by the nuns in York, England, that streams statements gathered from the web that begin with the words, "I feel."[xix] This kind of digital writing is by definition *en route*; it both comes and goes. Just as the page argues for its structural iterability—you can have as many as you like in one book (up to a point)—it also argues for the same principle at the level of experience. You can keep reading the same page over and over again (again, up to a point). Indeed the institutional study of literature, which for many is anathema to the pleasure of reading, is premised on this idea of re-reading. Streams, on the other hand, are defined by their ephemerality. You can never step in the same one twice.

Writers for millennia have dreamed of writing as a stream. It is a means of imagining our way past the discrete nature of the book or the letters of the alphabet. In place of the isolated character there would be nothing but flow, what the poet Friedrich Hölderlin called "the streaming word."[18] Or, as Emily Dickinson[19] wrote:

> Tell all the Truth, but tell it slant—
> Success in Circuit lies.[xx]

---

17 Walter Benjamin (1892–1940), German literary critic and philosopher.

18 Friedrich Hölderlin (1770–1843), major German poet.

19 Emily Dickinson (1830–86), American poet.

The book, in all its finiteness, could never accommodate such dreams of fluidity. We still lack a satisfactory interface that would allow us to engage, pass on, and then let go of the new information streams. We have spent so much time worrying about the transience of digital texts—that unlike books they seem so impermanent—we have forgotten to install techniques of forgetting them, too. The point of Twitter is not to store it, as the Library of Congress has recently begun to do, but to create efficient means of letting it go, to embrace a kind of writing (and reading) that is expirable. What would be the best way to visualize writing as a stream and not as a plane or page?

This past week my son was home sick from school. Like most parents, I let him go on the computer so I could get a few things done. When I went down to see what he was doing, I found him "reading" Lego building instructions. There are much worse things he could have discovered, and again like most parents we've learned the hard way not to allow any unchaperoned time online anymore. He's five and although he cannot read yet, there he was meticulously making his way through "page" after "page" of a PDF file he had downloaded (how he had learned this I have no idea) of some extremely lethal flying machine. One by one he studied the pages upon which shapes were coming together to produce more complex shapes, overseen by the large bold numbers in the upper right hand corner of each page.

As we learned in the last chapter [of Piper's book] about the visual nature of reading, the building instructions that so fascinated my son mirror in many ways how we construct letters

from more elementary shapes. Alphabet and architecture are closely related domains. It is no coincidence that his interest in these booklets corresponds to the very year in which he is beginning to learn to make the shape of letters himself (a process that is difficult for him and that I will return to in the next chapter [of Piper's book]). But equally important is the sequentiality of it all, the way number and letter coalesce in a constructive process. Much recent research suggests that counting, a number sense, precedes language, rather than the other way around as was previously thought.[xxi] A notion of order, magnitude, and succession may underlay our ability to use language, the cognitive pre-condition of that famed idea of universal grammar. My son's love of building instructions tells us something important about the intimate relationship between sequence and knowledge, whether it be literate or arithmetic.

As we think about designing new reading interfaces in the future, I hope we can begin to move past the boundaries of the page, to stop faking it so to speak. Nothing seems more misguided than creating websites that are meant to look like books or books that are meant to look like websites. If one day, in the words of Walter Scott's fictional publisher, there are simply too many pages and paper costs too much to continue to make books, then we might want to impersonate the book online. Until then, I hope we continue to think beyond the page.

But on a deeper level, reviewing the list of digital alternatives above reveals the way these new forms of reading preserve, albeit in altered form, a basic aspect of seriality that belonged to the printed page, and of course the scroll before it. The logic of the page was that of the fold and the turn; it was both unique and serially adjacent to what followed, which was also structurally similar. In each of the cases above, whether roaming, zooming, or streaming, we continue to move serially, only in new ways—we zoom through, roam past, or stream by. As Nietzsche[20] said of man, "Regardless of where he lives, the desert and the cave are always with him," and presumably, so too is the stream.[xxii]

The successful reading interfaces of the future, whether handwritten, print, or digital, will ideally continue to preserve this sense of the "pathway." It is one of the oldest forms of human understanding, where mental thought mirrors how we make our way physically through the world. Unlike the so-called information superhighway, on the pathway (or even the road) I am aware of where I am, of moving through space. The truth of this sentiment is reflected not only in the deep anthropological record of tool-making or the more recent cognitive experiments from the psych lab. It is also there in the way it forms the core of one of our most recurringly popular genres of storytelling, the road narrative. From the picaresque wanderings of Encolpius in the first century *Satyricon* to Lazarillo de Tormes in the sixteenth century, to the accidental urgency of Jack Kerouac in the twentieth, to the cinematically inspired digital work of Young-Hae Chang's *Dakota* at the opening of the twenty-first century, passing through space mirrors our passage through time and, ultimately, through thought.[21] I want my children to learn how to learn one thing after another, to accept that there is a before and an after in life. I think reading books is still one of the best ways we have of reminding us of this fact. As Goethe once remarked, "It would be a lowly art that allowed itself to be understood all at once."[xxiii]

Notes

i. Pliny the Younger, *Letters*, vol. 2, Trans. William Melmoth (Cambridge, MA: Harvard UP, 1961), 27.

ii. John Keats, *Letters*, 4th ed., ed. Maurice Buxton Forman (London: Oxford UP, 1952), 101.

iii. Erasmus, *Collected Works*, vol. 10, Trans. R.A.B. Mynors and Alexander Dalzell (Toronto: U of Toronto P, 1992), 74. Erasmus was echoing the well-known biblical trope of eating God's word in Ezekiel 2:9–10.

iv. John Miedema, *Slow Reading* (Duluth, MN: Litwin Books, 2009).

v. Evelyn B. Tribble, *Margins and Marginality: The Printed Page in Early Modern England* (Charlottesville: U of Virginia P, 1993).

vi. Virginia Woolf, *To the Lighthouse*, ed. Stella McNichol (London: Penguin, 2000), 129.

vii. Susan Orlean, *The Orchid Thief* (New York: Ballantine, 2000), 109.

viii. Paul Saenger, *Space between Words: The Origins of Silent Reading* (Stanford, CA: Stanford UP, 1997).

ix. Honoré de Balzac, *The Wild Ass's Skin*, trans. Herbert J. Hunt (London: Penguin, 1977), 22.

x. For the argument that the codex is fundamentally about a non-linear access to reading, see Peter Stallybrass, "Books and Scrolls: Navigating the Bible," *Books and Readers in Early Modern England*, ed. Jennifer Andersen and Elizabeth Sauer (Philadelphia: U of Pennsylvania P, 2002), 42–79.

xi. Marjorie Garber, "" (Quotation Marks)," *Critical Inquiry* 25.4 (1999): 653–79.

---

20 Friedrich Wilhelm Nietzsche (1844–1900), German philosopher and poet.

21 *Satyricon*, a Roman novel of the first century CE, believed to have been written by Petronius (c. 27–66 CE); *The Life of Lazarillo de Tormes and of His Fortunes and Adversities*, published by an anonymous Spanish novelists in 1554; Jack Kerouac (1922–69), American novelist and poet best known for his novel *On the Road* (1957); Young-Hae Chang Heavy Industries is a Korean-based web artist group. All works referenced are narratives of the road.

xii. Garrett Stewart, *The Look of Reading* (Chicago: U of Chicago P, 2006), 131.

xiii. J.W. Goethe, *Begegnungen und Gespräche*, ed. Renate Grumach (Berlin: de Gruyter, 1999), 2414.

xiv. Andre Leroi-Gourhan, *Gesture and Speech*, trans. Anna Bostock Berger (Cambridge, MA: MIT P, 1993).

xv. As Lev Manovich writes, "Regardless of whether new media objects present themselves as linear narratives, interactive narratives, databases, or something else, underneath, on the level of material organization, they are all databases." Lev Manovich, *Language of New Media* (Cambridge, MA: MIT P, 2001), 228. For this reason Alan Liu calls the digital interface a "data pour," the result of a "query" of structured language that resides elsewhere. Alan Liu, "Transcendental Data: Toward a Cultural History and Aesthetics of the New Encoded Discourse," *Critical Inquiry* 31.1 (2004): 49–84. N. Katherine Hayles employed early on the productive notion of the "flickering signifier" to describe the impermanence of digital text. See *How We Became Posthuman: Virtual Bodies in Cybernetics, Literature and Informatics* (Chicago: U of Chicago P, 1999), 25–49.

xvi. Craig Mod, "Books in the Age of the iPad," March 2010. Every age needs its French philosophers, and the work of Gilles Deleuze and Felix Guattari, especially their work on the "plateau," seems to have become a new point of reference for our contemporary moment. For a primer, see Gilles Deleuze and Felix Guattari, *A Thousand Plateaus*, trans. Brian Massumi (Minneapolis: U of Minnesota P, 1987).

xvii. For an introduction to satellite culture, see Lisa Parks, *Cultures in Orbit: Satellites and the Televisual* (Durham, NC: Duke UP, 2005).

xviii. For John Cayley, this new three-dimensionality of writing owes much of its origins to the mobilization of writing *in time* through the medium of the film credit sequence. Cayley's insight is interesting for how it draws attention to the way other media like film are important, and often overlooked, influences on the development of reading. John Cayley, "Writing on Complex Surfaces," *Dichtung Digital* 35 (2005).

xix. "The iPad in the Eyes of the Digerati," *New York Times*, April 6, 2010.

xx. Emily Dickinson, *The Complete Poems*, ed. Thomas H. Johnson (New York: Little Brown, 1961), 506.

xxi. See in particular the work of Sara Cordes and Rachel Gelman, "The Young Numerical Mind: When Does It Count?," *Handbook of Mathematical Cognition*, ed. Jamie I.D. Campbell (New York: Psychology P, 2005), 128–42, and Stanislas Dehaene, *The Number Sense: How the Mind Creates Mathematics* (Oxford: Oxford UP, 2011).

xxii. Friedrich Nietzsche, *Unfashionable Observations*, trans. Richard T. Gray (Stanford, CA: Stanford UP, 1995), 192.

xxiii. J.W. Goethe, *The Man of Fifty*, trans. Andrew Piper (London: Hesperus P, 2004), 23.

31.

Franco Moretti, "Style, Inc. Reflections on Seven Thousand Titles (British Novels, 1740–1850)," *Distant Reading*. London and New York: Verso, 2013. 179–210

Franco Moretti (b. 1950) is Professor of English and Comparative Literature at Stanford University. He founded the Center for the Study of the Novel and, with Matt Jockers, the Literary Lab at Stanford. Among other books, he has written *Atlas of the European Novel 1800–1900* (1998), *Graphs, Maps, Trees* (2005), and *Distant Reading* (2013); he is also the editor of *The Novel* (2006). His work addresses the history of the novel as "the first truly planetary form" (*The Novel* I:ix). In order to write these kinds of histories, which involve huge numbers of texts, Moretti claims we need to abandon "close reading" (at least temporarily) in favor of what he terms "distant reading." Using quantitative methods drawn from the social sciences, as well as other methodologies for visualizing large amounts of data (such as maps, graphs, and trees), Moretti has influentially charted a new course for literary analysis. In the following essay, Moretti asks what can be learned by examining the 7,000 titles of novels published in Britain between 1740 and 1850. For Moretti, the focus on titles allows us to "catch a glimpse of the literary field as a whole" (p. 526), and "to see a larger literary field" (p. 530), and thus to engage in distant reading. While it would be nearly impossible to read and analyze 7,000 novels, it becomes somewhat more manageable if one focuses on the titles of those 7,000 novels. Here Moretti can reach some definite, quantifiable conclusions: that the length of titles shortened considerably over the period in question, for example. Moretti doesn't stop here, but asks: why was it that as the market for novels expanded, the number of words used to introduce them to the public shrank so significantly? According to Moretti, quantitative analysis can present us with numbers and patterns, but the data requires analysis; as he says, "any new approach—quantitative, digital, evolutionary, whatever—must ... prove that it can do formal analysis, better than we already do" (p. 534).

Style, Inc. Reflections on Seven Thousand Titles (British Novels, 1740–1850)[1]

[...]

The British novel, from 1740 to 1850. Peripheral, often despised at the beginning of the period, by its end the novel has moved very close to the core of the national culture. So, this is an important century, for this literary form. But, truth be told, the historical framework of this study has been largely dictated by an extrinsic reason: unlike earlier and later periods, from 1740 to 1850 we have very good **bibliographies**. Which is to say, good lists of titles; in a few years, we will have a digital **archive** with the full texts of (almost) all novels ever published; but for now, titles are still the best way to go beyond the 1 per cent of novels that make up the **canon**, and catch a glimpse of the literary field as a whole. And then, titles are not just a good research tool: they are important in themselves—Walter Scott's first word as a novelist, literally, was 'title' ("The title of this work has not been chosen without the grave and solid deliberation ...')[2]—and they are important because, as Claude Duchet has put it, they are 'a coded message—in a market situation.'[ii] A code, in the market: half sign,[3] half ad, the title is where the novel as language meets the novel as commodity, and their encounter can be extremely illuminating. In what follows, I focus on three moments of this history: first, I describe a major metamorphosis of eighteenth-century titles, and try to explain its causes; next, I suggest how a new type of title that emerged around 1800 may have changed what readers expected of novels; and finally, I make a little attempt at quantitative stylistics,[4] examining some strategies by which titles point to specific genres. Three sections; three pieces in the large puzzle of the literary field.

I

The major metamorphosis of eighteenth-century titles is simple: in the space of two generations, they become much, much shorter. In Fig. 5.6, where their length is measured in the number of words, the median oscillates between ten and twenty words for the first twenty-five years; it drops quickly to ten, around 1770; then to six, by 1790; and it remains there (with minor ups and downs) until the mid nineteenth century. From fifteen or twenty words, to six. And titles don't just become shorter, in the course of these 110 years, they also become much more similar to each other: in Fig. 2 [not reproduced here], the steep drop of the standard deviation (which measures the degree of variation within a system) indicates precisely how rapidly the range

---

1 In the interest of space, we have cut many of Moretti's graphs. We urge readers interested in learning more to consult the full essay from *Distant Reading*.

2 The full sentence is: "The title of this work has not been chosen without the grave and solid deliberation which matters of importance demand from the prudent."

3 The combination of the signifier and the signified, often the combination of a word and its meaning.

4 Methodologies that seek to apply "quantitative" methods to "style" as it is manifest in written language.

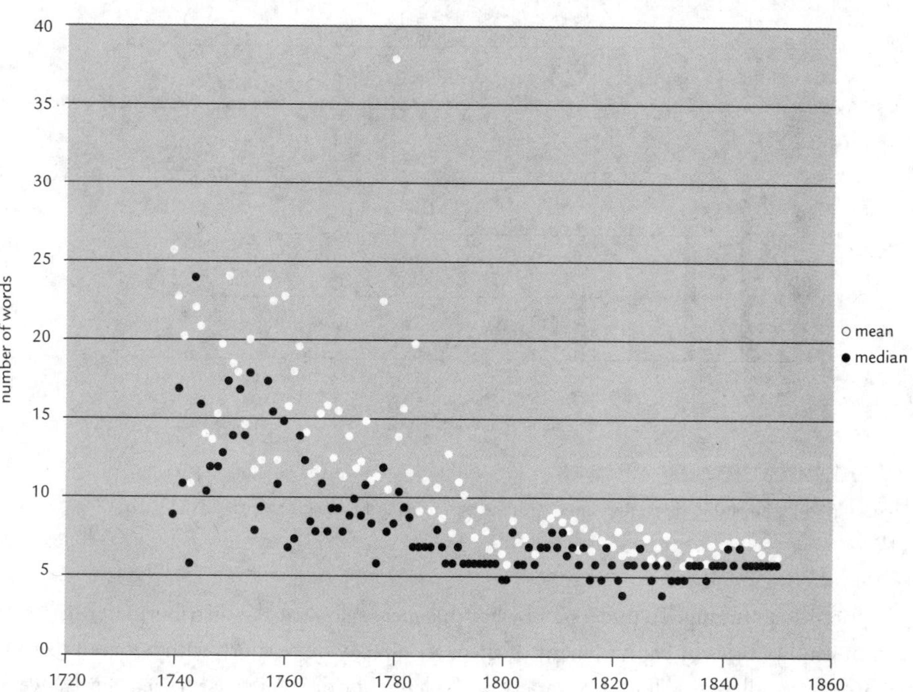

Fig. 5.6: Length of titles.

The chart follows both mean and median length in order to offer a more complete picture of how titles vary: the mean (or average) provides information about the often extravagant length of some titles—while the median draws attention to the "central" length of each given year (that is to say, that which has an equal number of results above and below it). The difference between the two forms of measurement becomes particularly clear in years such as 1780 (with the 346-word-long *History of Miss Harriot Fairfax*) or 1784 (with the 273 words of *The Maid of the Farm; Or memoirs of Susannah James*): in these two instances, the mean balloons to 37.9 and 19.7 respectively, while the median (8.5 and 7) is hardly affected.

Unless otherwise indicated, the sources of all figures are the following: 1740–49: Jerry C. Beasley, *Novels of the 1740s* (Athens, GA, 1982); 1750–69: *British Fiction, 1750–1770: A Chronological Check-List of Prose Fiction Printed in Britain and Ireland*, ed. James Raven (Newark, DE, 1987); 1770–1829: Peter Garside et al., *The English Novel, 1770–1829: A Bibliographical Survey of Prose Fiction Published in the British Isles*, 2 vols. (Oxford, 2000); 1830–36: "The British Novel 1830–36: A Bibliographical Survey of Fiction Published in the British Isles," ed. Garside et al., <www.cardiff.ac.uk/encap/journals/corvey/1830s/index.html>; 1837–50: Andrew Block, *The English Novel, 1740–1850: A Catalogue Including Prose Romances, Short Stories, and Translations of Foreign Fiction*, 2nd ed. (London, 1961). Reprinted with the permission of Franco Moretti.

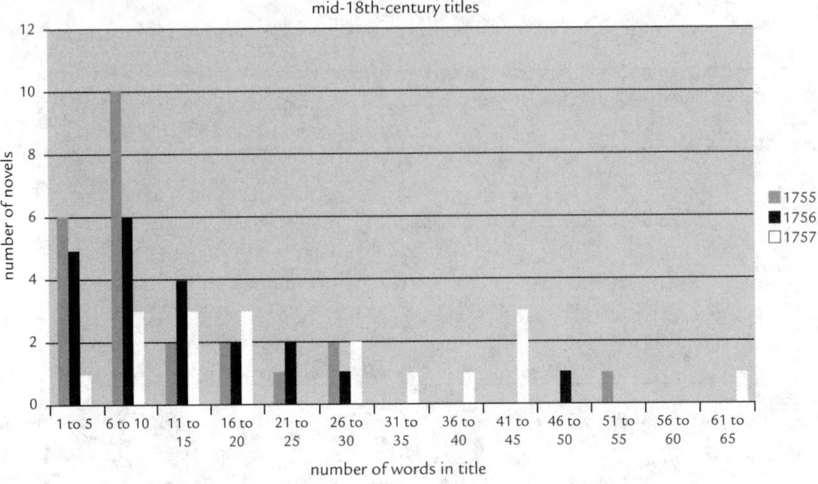

Fig. 5.7: Mid-18th-century titles. Reprinted with the permission of Franco Moretti.

of options is shrinking. To understand what this means, look at the distribution of mid-eighteenth-century titles in Fig. 5.7: many of them are already quite short, with between one and ten words, but there is still a lot of variety, with plenty of titles which use fifteen words, twenty, twenty-five, thirty, forty, or more. A hundred years later this 'tail' is gone, and long titles have virtually vanished.[iii] It's not just that all titles are becoming shorter, in other words; it's also that a certain type of title disappears altogether. How long is 'long' is of course an open question, but if we set the limit at fifteen or twenty words—which is quite long, for a title—then long titles were between 40 and 60 per cent of the total in the mid eighteenth century; by 1800 their number had already dropped to 5 to 10 per cent; eventually, they just disappeared. Why?[iv]

And, before coming to that, what were they like, those long titles—what did they do, with all those words? Usually, they provided a summary of the novel: *A letter from H—g—g, Esq; One of the Gentlemen of the Bedchamber to the Young Chevalier, And the Only Person of his Retinue that attended him from Avignon, in his late Journey through Germany, and elsewhere; Containing Many remarkable and Affecting Occurrences which happened to the P— during the course of his mysterious Progress. To a Particular Friend*. Today, this sounds odd; but actually, a summary at the beginning of a novel makes sense: a novel is a narrative, and the title—the **title-***page*, here one sees why books needed a whole page for their title—the title-as-summary was a *shorter* narrative: it presented the main events of the story, the characters, the setting, the ending. It made sense.

But the cultural ecosystem was changing in a way that was incompatible with it: in the course of the eighteenth century, the publication of novels in Britain grew dramatically, from a few books a year in the early decades, to twenty-five or so in mid-century, seventy to eighty around 1800, and about a hundred a year in early Victorian times. And as more novels circulated, two things happened. In the third, and even more so in the fourth quarter of the eighteenth century,

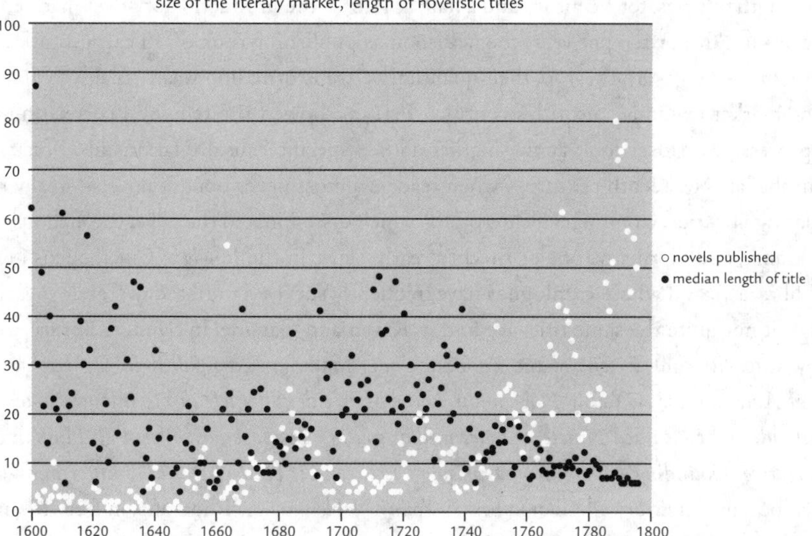

Fig. 5.8: Size of the literary market; length of novelistic titles.

Additional source: 1600-1700, Charles C. Mish, ed., *English Prose Fiction, 1600-1700: A Chronological Checklist*, Charlottesville, VA 1967.

As long as only a few novels per year are published, the median length of titles keeps oscillating between 10 and 40–50 words; after the first 'rise' of the 1720s and '30s, however, it drops below 20, and below 10 during the late-eighteenth century take-off first noticed by Clifford Siskin. Earlier on, more ephemeral publishing spurts (1655–60; the 1680s) had also coincided with a marked drop in the length of titles. Reprinted with the permission of Franco Moretti.

the *Monthly*[5] and other magazines started to publish reviews of many new novels, making title-page summaries somewhat superfluous: as the literary system grew, in other words, some of its functions became more specialized, 'freeing' titles from having to provide a detailed description. And then, as the number of new novels kept increasing, each of them had inevitably a much smaller 'window' of visibility on the market, and it became vital for a title to catch quickly and effectively the eye of the public. Summaries were not good at that. They were good at describing a book in isolation: but when it came to standing out in a crowded marketplace, short titles were better—much easier to remember, to begin with (but not only). That's why long titles disappeared: because between the size of the market, and the length of titles, a strong negative correlation emerged: as the one expanded, the other contracted. Nothing much had changed,

5 *The Monthly Review*, a London-based periodical that was first published in June 1749 and was edited by Ralph Griffiths until his death in 1803 (the publication continued until 1845). The *Monthly* published an extensive number of novel reviews.

in the length of titles, for a century and a half, as long as the production of novels had remained stable around five or ten per year; then, as soon as publishing took off in earnest, titles immediately shrank (Fig. 5.8). By 1790, their 'quantitative' transformation was virtually complete.[v]

The market expands, and titles contract. Fig. 5.8 showed the temporal correlation of the two processes; a closer look at the market adds a specific causal relationship. Because 'market,' in the late eighteenth century—when readers almost never bought novels—really means: **circulating libraries.** Commercial enterprises, which disseminated the novel throughout Britain (and France, and Germany: one of Brecht's[6] early plays, In the *Jungle of Cities*, opens in one of these libraries), and whose **catalogues** have frequently survived until today. Catalogues: lists of titles. But not quite the same titles we find in Raven and Garside. In Sander's **library**, in 1780s Derby, *Capacity and Extent of the Human Understanding; Exemplified in the Extraordinary Case of Automathes: A Young Nobleman; who was Accidentally left in his Infancy, upon a desolate Island, and continued Nineteen Years in that solitary State, separate from all Human Society. A Narrative abounding with many surprising Occurrences, both Useful and Entertaining to the Reader*, becomes: *History of Automathes, A Young Nobleman*. At Phorson's, in Berwick, in 1790, *Unfortunate Sensibility; or, the Life of Mrs L*****. Written by Herself. In a Series of Sentimental Letters. Dedicated to Mr. Yorick, in the Elysian Fields* becomes *Unfortunate Sensibility*. At Sael's, in the Strand, in 1793, *Emmeline, the Orphan of the Castle* becomes *Emmeline*.[7] And so on.

A coded message, in a market situation. And the key institution of the market takes the code, and *compresses* it: typically, to a proper name. Libraries couldn't waste space on a catalogue page; they didn't want any confusion between this novel and that; the spine of the book had only room for a few words anyway; and then, readers were getting used to novels, and needed less 'guidance' from titles.[vi]

So, the average length decreased, long titles disappeared, and, at the opposite end of the spectrum, titles with only one, two, or three words multiplied rapidly: they were 5 per cent in the 1740s and '50s, but by 1800 they were already around 20 to 30 per cent, and had completely traded places with the long titles which had been their predecessors. It's the same thing that happened in advertising a hundred years later, when the detailed descriptions of the nineteenth century were replaced by the evocative oblique brevity of today's ads; *literally* the same thing: title-pages with long summaries of novels were often used as flyers, and pasted around to advertise a book. But short titles, as we will see, were not just better titles—they were better ads, too.

Titles allow us to see a larger literary field, I said at the beginning of this study; and the first thing we see in this larger field, at this moment in history, is the force of the market: how its growth creates a major constraint on the presentation of novels. This of course doesn't mean that all titles gave the same answer to the pressure of the market; but it does mean that they all had to face the same question: How could one shorten a message—without losing information?

6 Bertolt Brecht (1898–1956), a German playwright well-known for his practice of epic theater.

7 John Sanders was a bookseller in Derby; William Phorson was a publisher in Berwick; George Sael was a bookseller in the Strand, in London, an active hub for publishing and bookselling activity in the eighteenth and nineteenth centuries.

There was a lot of information in summaries: what happened to it? Was it—gone? reformulated? replaced by something else? I will return to this in a moment; now let me close this first section by acknowledging a limit of this investigation: I began by showing the average length of titles, but I then shifted to very long and very short titles—and I did so, because these trends are much more dramatic than the slow decline of the average, and thus also much easier to talk about. Which is not exactly *wrong* (after all, those trends are real!), but, even aside from a question of completeness—of the 7,000 titles in the study, around 900 are 'long,' 1,600 'short,' and 4,500 somewhere in between—the focus on extremes misses a decisive aspect of quantitative work: what really counts, here, are not a few major and rapid changes, but many small and slow ones.

But the trouble is, we literary historians don't really know how to think about what is frequent and small and slow; that's what makes it so hard to study the literary field as a whole: we must learn to find meaning in small changes and slow processes—and it's difficult. Especially so, in the case of titles: which are by definition the most public part of a book, hence the most subject to censorship: what we find in titles reflects the 'legitimate irradiation'[8] of existing ideas, wrote Jean-Louis Flandrin, and it's true, titles are so 'respectable'; and again, how do you make respectable messages interesting ...?[vii]

II

Very short titles: one, two, or three words. Where the question that interests me is, How can a couple of words stand in for hundreds of pages? What does it mean, that they should do so? For summaries, it's clear: they are scaled-down versions of the whole story. Two words? So, I started looking at these short titles, and found three main clusters within the group: proper names (*Octavia*; *George Barnwell*), which make up around one-third of the total; the article-noun (*The Steam-Boat*; *The Smuggler*) and article-adjective-noun combinations (*The Tuscan Vase*; *The Invisible Gentleman*) just below 30 per cent; and conceptual abstractions (*Fatality*; *Enthusiasm not Religion*) around 10 per cent. 'A large change in size inevitably carries with it a change of form,' wrote J.B.S. Haldane,[9] and here one sees how right he was: a title with twenty words and one with two are not the same creature, one larger and one smaller; they are different animals altogether. Different *styles*. There is a 'less is more' elegance to short titles—*Persuasion*; *Emma*; *Mansfield Park*—that was unthinkable in summaries; there, the aim was to squeeze as many things as possible into the front page—more is more, as it were—and if the title turned out to be a mess, so be it: *Robinson Crusoe*'s mentioned an episode that doesn't even appear in the novel (*An Account how he was at last as strangely deliver'd by* PYRATES: pyrates? what pyrates?)—it didn't really matter. But a short title is a delicate structure, sensitive to every small change. Consider the article-noun, and article-adjective-noun combinations: similar forms, similar semantic horizon—*The Monk*, 1796; *The New Monk*, 1798—and so at first I assumed that

8 Illumination of understanding.

9 J.B.S. Haldane (1892–1964), British-born scientist.

the adjective wouldn't change much: the monk and the new monk: big deal; the adjective would specify the noun, as adjectives do, but no more than that.

And instead, it turns out that the adjective does not specify the semantic field; it transforms it. In the article-noun combination, half of the titles describing a social type evoke an exotic-transgressive field—*The Fakeer, The Vampyre, The Fire-Eater, The Pirate, The Sabbath-Breaker, The Spectre, The Rebel, The Epicurean, The Mussulman, The Libertine, The Parricide* ...—and only a small minority evokes the idea of the 'familiar' (wife, brother, father, daughter, etc.). But when an adjective is added to the title, the ratio is exactly reversed: fakeers and libertines drop from 50 to 20 per cent, while wives and daughters rise from 16 to 40 per cent: *The Unfashionable Wife, The Discarded Daughter, The Infidel Father, The Rival Brothers, The Posthumous Daughter, The False Friend, The Maniac Father* ... Without adjectives, we are in a world of adventures; with adjectives, in a destabilized domesticity. The adjective is the only change, but it changes everything. And of course, once you think about it, it makes sense: if all that is in the title is a noun, then that noun must guarantee an interesting story all by itself, and vampires and parricides are a very good choice; but if an adjective is present, then even the most familiar figures can be estranged into infidel fathers and posthumous daughters. The adjective relocates narrative from substance to accident, as it were. And again, it makes sense: the adjective introduces *predication*[10] within the title, and predication is the germ of storytelling. 'The wife' is a stable quantity; the *unfashionable* wife is a question mark: why is she unfashionable? what does her husband think? her daughters? This is why short titles are so interesting: they are on the border: between two and three words lies the invisible barrier that separates storytelling from—something else, which we'll see in a minute.

Common nouns are frequent, in short titles, but proper names are even more frequent, especially at the turn of the century, when one title in twelve (1786–90), then one in ten (1791–95), then almost one in seven (1796–1800), consists of a proper name, and nothing else: *Emily*; *Henry*; *Georgina*. The growth of the market forced titles to become shorter, and, as we saw in circulating libraries' catalogues, proper names were a great way to do so: one word, and a novel was immediately singled out from the rest.[viii] Singled out, by pointing to its protagonist; a choice which was not inevitable—of the 'six masterpieces' of the Chinese canon, for instance, none was ever shortened to a proper name, because none had a name in the title to begin with—but which has been typical of European narrative since Greek and medieval times (probably, because in our tradition the central character has always played a greater role). And of course, in the late eighteenth century, protagonist mostly means female protagonist: a woman's name, and often just a *first* name: *Lucy, Caroline, Belinda, Emma* ... Heroines who lack a last name: a very simple, very crude hint, typical of the British marriage plot[11] (which reaches its apex in these decades): they lack a husband. But the wider field also shows how quickly the gender asymmetry was reversed in the 1820s and '30s, and how frequent the heroine's *last* name could actually be.[ix] In both cases, the main changes were almost certainly caused by shifts in the system of genres:

10 A condition that requires further explanation.

11 A common trope in the early novel wherein a female character proceeds through trials and is rewarded by marriage at the end of the novel.

the historical novel's rise to prominence after 1815, for instance, with its mostly male heroes;[x] or the marriage plot becoming embedded within genres like the *Bildungsroman*[12] and the industrial novel,[13] where the heroine acquired a public life, which was promptly mirrored in titles like *Jane Eyre* or *Mary Barton*. Again, see how much can be done with how little, in short titles: one word, and the image of the heroine rotates 180 degrees: from private, to public. Short titles were a constraint imposed by the market, yes, but the constraint could also be a fantastic opportunity for the literary imagination: the art of allusion, of condensation: the title as trope, ultimately. Odd twist: the market promoting—style.

The market expanded, titles contracted; by 1790, as we have seen, the issue of length had been settled, and didn't really change for at least sixty years. But something else did change, between 1790 and 1850, and the last type of title I will discuss in this section—abstractions—will help us to understand what. Abstractions were usually a single word (*Generosity, Indiscretion, Independence, Delusion*), or a conceptual pair (*Liberality and Prejudice, Jesuitism and Methodism*), and although they were never very frequent, in the first quarter of the century, and especially in the 1820s, they were not insignificant, thanks largely to the tireless Barbara Hofland, who in the five years from 1823 to 1827 published, one after the other, *Integrity, Decision, Patience, Moderation, Reflection,* and *Self-Denial*. And as you read these titles you realize that abstractions here really means—ethics. Nineteenth-century ethics; previously, abstractions had often emphasized moral violations (*Disobedience, Indiscretion, Fatality, Retribution, False Gratitude, The Relapse, Conscious Duplicity* ...), but after 1800 it is the *construction* of the ethical that is highlighted: *Self-Control, Conduct, Discipline, Correction, Decision, Reformation*. Morality not as purity, but as work: one takes one's own self and transforms it, in a process that is both spiritual and pragmatic. Hofland's *Moderation*, wrote the *Monthly Review* in 1825, is 'fabricated ... to ... strongly enforce a precept in morals of great practical utility'—and that moral precept fabricated for practical utility is really the dawn of Victorianism.

When titles were summaries, they of course used verbs (*The misfortunes in which this young woman has been cruelly involved* etc. etc.); but once summaries disappear, so do verbs (aside from the occasional *Says She to Her Neighbour, What?*), and titles like *Patience* or *Moderation* are the logical endpoint of the process: titles that sound more and more like nominal sentences. A grammatical form that 'places the utterance beyond all temporal or modal localization, and beyond the subjectivity of the speaker,' wrote Benveniste in his classic analysis of this type of sentence: beyond subjectivity, beyond temporal localization ... the telos[14] of nominal sentences is the *abolition of contingency*: 'they don't describe a situation,' Benveniste again, 'they posit an absolute.'[xi] *Self-Control; Patience; Integrity*: they don't describe a situation, not even in the minimal way of maniac fathers and unfashionable wives; they don't allude to what happens in the novel, or to where and when it takes place; they posit an absolute, and that absolute is of course

12 A novel characterized by the protagonist's coming-of-age journey.

13 A genre of the early Victorian literature, these novels depict the difficult lives of the working classes as manufacturing was being mechanized and industrialized.

14 The final end or purpose of something.

the meaning of the novel. This was the great historical achievement of abstractions: they made titles meaning-ful: nothing *but* meaning, as if the essence of the novel had been distilled and purified of all narrative contingency. And readers, faced with this type of title, have to change their expectations: the first thing they are told about the novel asks them to imagine, not so much a story, but *the point* of the story: the point of the story as a single, unifying concept. And this is important. That titles became short is interesting, yes, but in the end, So what? That by becoming short they adopted a signifying strategy that made readers look for a unity in the narrative structure—this is a perceptual shift which has persisted for 200 years. And mediocre conservative writers did more to make it happen than anyone else.[xii]

I have discussed abstractions next to proper names, because they both make for very short titles; but, clearly, their relationship to plot is completely different: proper names are a part of the story, whereas abstractions are an *interpretation* of it. It would be tempting to say that names have a metonymic[15] relationship to the novel, and abstractions a metaphoric one; but if characters' names (and the—rarer—place names like *Minerva Castle* or *Mansfield Park*) are indeed metonymies of the plot, abstractions are not quite metaphors,[xiii] and in fact it is curious how *few* metaphors are there, in these 7,000 titles.[xiv] By the end of the century they are everywhere (*The Belly of Paris, The Doll, Ghosts, The Octopus, Heart of Darkness, The Beast in the Jungle*), so they must have taken root sometime in the third quarter of the nineteenth century, and the glimpses one gets suggest a lot of hesitation on the part of writers: Gaskell[16] shifting at the last minute from *Margaret Hale* to *North and South* (proper name to metaphor); Dickens doing the opposite, from *Nobody's Fault* to *Little Dorrit*. Announcing a story with a metaphor must have seemed strange—and it is strange: if abstractions are removed from the plot, then metaphors are twice removed: interpretations that *require an interpretation*, as it were. But it is precisely this 'difficulty' of metaphors that holds the secret of the title-as-ad. Eighteenth-century summaries told readers a lot of things about the novel, yes; but they never really engaged their intelligence. And instead, by puzzling and challenging readers, metaphors induced them to take an active interest in the novel from the very first word. If you are trying to sell a product, that's exactly what you want.

Summaries, adjectives, proper names, nominal sentences, metonymies, metaphors ... In a minute I will turn to articles (and am thinking of sections on conjunctions and participles). This is a quantitative study: but its units are linguistic and rhetorical. And the reason is simple: for me, formal analysis is the great accomplishment of literary study, and is therefore also what any new approach—quantitative, digital, evolutionary, whatever—must prove itself against: prove that it can do formal analysis, better than we already do. Or at least: equally well, in a different key. Otherwise, what is the point?

15 A metonymy is a figure of language wherein a part of something stands in for its whole, in this case the title of the book represents its whole meaning.

16 Elizabeth Cleghorn Gaskell (1810–65), British writer of novels and short stories.

III

As the market expands, titles contract; as they do that, they learn to compress meaning; and as they do that, they develop special 'signals' to place books in the right market niche. 'Had I, for example, announced in my **frontispiece,** "Waverley, a Tale of other Days," must not every novel-reader have anticipated a castle scarce less than that of Udolpho[17] ... a "Sentimental Tale" would ... have been a sufficient presage of a heroine with a profusion of auburn hair ... "a Tale of the Times" [of] a dashing sketch of the fashionable world' ... *Tale of other Days, Sentimental Tale, Tale of the Times*: that these words would make readers think of specific genres is of course true—and trivial: it's obvious. The code may be in the market, but it remains transparent. And instead, the interesting cases are the opaque ones: where the signal works, and we somehow know what kind of a novel we have in our hands, but we don't know why we know it, because it is all conveyed by traits that escape our attention; 'subliminal,' as we used to say.

Let me illustrate this point with two genres—the so-called anti-jacobin[18] and 'new woman'[19] novels—that are separated by a hundred years:[xv] two explicitly ideological genres, which rely heavily on contemporary politics, and whose titles have thus a lot in common—except for one detail. Among anti-jacobin titles, 36 per cent begin with the definite article (*The Banished Man, The Medallion, The Parisian, The Democrat*) and 3 per cent with the indefinite; a result which is perfectly aligned with the rest of the field, since at the time the overall frequencies are 38 and 2 per cent.[xvi] New woman titles, no; the definite article is obviously still present, in 24 per cent of the cases, but the use of the indefinite leaps from 2, or 3, to 30 per cent of the cases. Now, this is odd, not only because it is completely out of scale with anything else I have found, but because in many other ways the conventions of the two genres are quite similar. *The* democrat; *A* blue-stocking:[20] two well-known figures of the contemporary political scene; why is the article different? *The* infidel father; *A* hard woman; the same grammar, the same dissonance between adjective and noun; why is the article different? What do the articles do, that they need to be different? An essay by Harald Weinrich offers an answer; for Weinrich, the starting point to understand linguistic categories is always the text, and, since all texts are linear, 'there are always two main directions in which the attention of the reader may be directed': backwards, or forwards: backwards, towards what we already know from the text, and forwards, towards what we don't.[xvii] And the simplest way to alert the reader's attention is—articles: the definite article announcing a noun as something that we already know (thus directing our attention backwards); and the indefinite suggesting the opposite: Take heed, here comes something that you haven't

17 *The Mysteries of Udolpho*, a gothic novel published by Ann Radcliffe in 1794.

18 The name given to those in Britain who opposed the supporters of the French Revolution (the Jacobins were one of the French revolutionary parties). Here Moretti refers to the genre of the anti-Jacobin novel.

19 The New Woman was a feminist ideal that arose in the late nineteenth century to describe an independent, career-oriented woman. Again, Moretti refers to a genre of novels that represented, or in some way engaged with, the ideal of the New Woman.

20 A highly educated, intellectual woman.

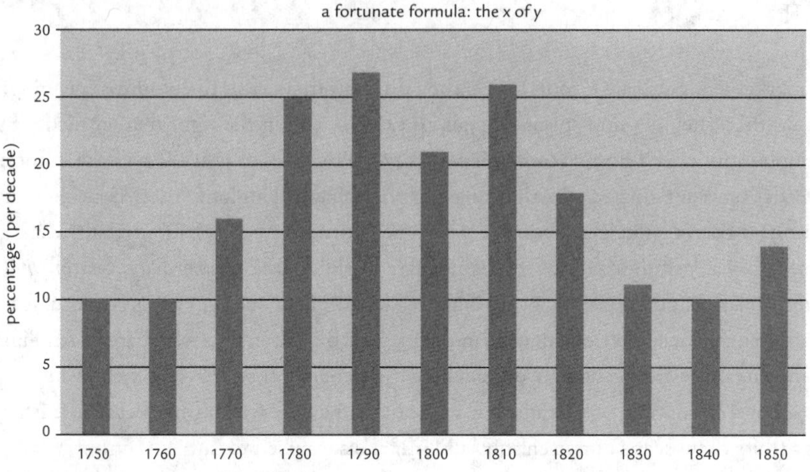

Fig. 5.9: A fortunate formula: the 'x of y.' Reprinted with the permission of Franco Moretti.

encountered yet. The first time the wolf appears in *Little Red Riding Hood* it is 'a' wolf; afterwards, 'the' wolf, forever. So: *A Girton Girl, A Hard Woman, A Mummer's Wife, A Domestic Experiment, A Daughter of Today, A Semi-detached Marriage*: what the article 'says' is that we are encountering all these figures *for the first time*; we think we know what daughters and wives are, but we actually don't, and must understand them afresh. The article announces the novel as a challenge to received knowledge. And instead, 'the' democrat, 'the' parisian, 'the' infidel father ... we know these people! Anti-jacobin titles don't want to change received ideas, they want to *use* them: the French Revolution has multiplied your enemies—beware.

Here is a modest example of what quantitative stylistics could do: take those units of language that are so frequent we hardly notice them and show how powerfully they contribute to the construction of meaning.[xviii] Which is also the point of my last example: a formula that, at first sight, looks as flat and uninspiring as could be: *The Duchess of York, The Novice of Corpus Domini, The Heir of Montgomery Castle*: let's call it 'the x of y.' As Figure 5.9 shows, the formula has always been quite frequent in titles, never dropping below 10 per cent of the total; but around 1800 its frequency increases, and if we look more closely at those decades, we find that the surge does not occur evenly everywhere, but is almost entirely concentrated in a single genre, which is the gothic.[21] There, 'the x of y' appears three times more often than in the rest of the corpus (Figure 5.10), which is too big a difference to be the product of chance, especially since something very similar also occurs within the gothic itself: we all know that the word 'castle' was

21 The gothic novel is "a genre of fiction characterized by suspenseful, sensational plots involving supernatural or macabre elements and often ... having a medieval theme or setting" (*OED*).

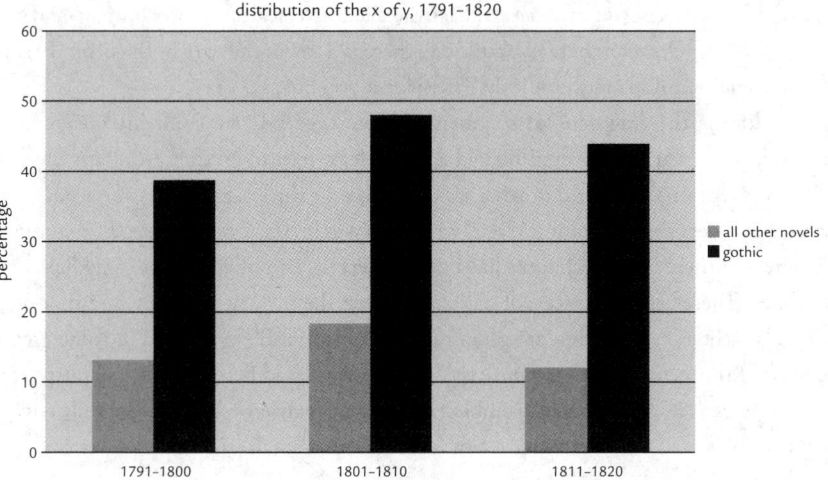

Fig. 5.10: Distribution of the x of y, 1791–1820. Reprinted with the permission of Franco Moretti.

the shibboleth[22] of the genre's imagination, from *The Castle of Otranto* onwards; well, in gothic titles 'the x of y' occurs three times more often than 'castle'.

But why? Castles in gothic titles, it makes sense. The x of y? Here semantics helps; if we look at the 'x' in the formula, we find that 'romance' appears in 7 per cent of the cases (*The Romance of the Pyrenees*), a cluster of genre indicators like mysteries, horrors, secrets, adventures in 13 per cent (*The Horrors of Oakendale Abbey*), personal nouns in 34 per cent (*Emmeline, or the Orphan of the Castle*), and space nouns in 41 per cent of the total: from *The Castle of Otranto* in 1764 to *The Mines of Wielitzka* and *The Rock of Glotzden* a half century later. So, in three-quarters of the cases 'the x of y' specifies an 'x' which is either a person or a space. And when we move from the subject of the formula to its predicate—from the x to the y—what we find is so striking that I don't even need a graph to point it out: *The Romance of the Pyrenees, The Horrors of Oakendale Abbey, The Orphan of the Castle, The Castle of Otranto, The Mines of Wielitzka, The Rock of Glotzden* … in 82 per cent of the cases, the 'y' is a space: a person defined by a space, or, most frequent of all, a space defined by another space. *The Castle of Otranto*: a spatial noun specified by a place name.

There are many intriguing traits to gothic titles—this is the genre that discovers that readers like villains, for instance, and shamelessly parades them in titles—but space is really the cornerstone of the convention: place names are much more frequent than human proper names; spatial nouns like castle, abbey, forest, cave, etc., show up in 50 per cent of the cases; and there are even other kinds of geographical signals, like *A Sicilian Romance* or *The Danish Massacre*. Nothing is as typical of gothic titles as this fixation with space; and of course this is true not just of titles, but of gothic novels: where space is dark, labyrinthine, cold; it imprisons, it terrifies, it kills …

22 A common feature of the genre, used so frequently as to be almost devoid of meaning.

'The x of y' takes this power of space, and activates it at two scales at once: human, and geographical. *The Castle of Otranto*: there is a building; there is a town; they are both gothic. Escape from the castle, you're still in southern Italy. There is no way out.

'Literature is the fragment of fragments,' wrote Goethe[23] in Wilhelm Meister's *Years of Wandering*, the great sad novel of his old age: 'the least part of all that ever happened and was spoken was written down, and of what was written only the least part has survived ...'. 'Of this history we possess the last volume alone,' wrote Darwin in *The Origin of Species*:[24] 'of this volume, only here and there a short chapter has been preserved, and of each page, only here and there a few lines.' There are differences, of course, between the history of nature and that of culture: the 'fossils' of literary evolution are often not lost, but carefully preserved in some great library, like most of those 7,000 novels whose titles I have discussed here; but for the purposes of our knowledge, it's as if they too had crumbled into dust, because we have never really tried to read the entire volume of the literary past. Studying titles is a small step in that direction.

Notes

i. This article has been greatly improved by exchanges with Sam Bowles, David Brewer, Bob Folkenflik, Matthew Jockers, David Krakauer, and Michael Silverstein: to all of them, my thanks. A further, more abstract study (co-authored with Matthew Jockers and David Krakauer) should soon extend and refine the argument that follows.

ii. Claude Duchet, "'La Fille abandonnée' et 'La Bête humaine': Éléments de titrologie romanesque," *Littérature* 12 (December 1973): 50.

iii. The thirty novels in the *New York Times* best-seller list in November 2006 used between one and six words; the forty in November 2008, between one and seven. In both cases, the mean was around 2.7 words—slightly higher than Austen's 2.0.

iv. Counting the number of words in a title ... But what exactly is a title? Among the novels for the year 1802, Peter Garside's masterful bibliography lists *Delaval. A Novel. In three Volumes*. But are expressions that point so explicitly to extra-textual realities like '*in three Volumes*' (or 'dedicated to Her Royal Highness The Dutchess of York,' 'from the French of M. Victor Hugo,' and so on) really part of the title? In my opinion, no; and so, useful as such information is in other respects, I have removed it from the database, leaving the title in question as *Delaval. A Novel*. But what about 'A Novel' ('A Romance,' 'A Tale,' 'In a Series of Letters')? Here, the reference is not so much extra-, as meta-textual: all these markers designate a *class*, rather than a specific book: invaluable for the analysis of novelistic sub-genres, they have little or nothing to say about individual cases. As a consequence, I have preserved them the first few times they appear in a title (when they are presumably indicating something new and specific about the given book), and deleted them thereafter; making an exception for those bizarre cases where the wider class is evoked only in order to estrange it: 'A Rhapsodical Romance,' 'A Dramatic Novel,' 'A Neapolitan Tale'—and also, sure enough, '*A Novel Without a Hero*.'

This said, since my choices may strike some readers as not merely subjective but perverse, Fig. 6 [not reproduced] charts the length of titles as they appear in the bibliographical sources, without any intervention on my part. As a comparison with Fig. 5.6 shows, the general trend does not change much:

---

23 Johann Wolfgang von Goethe (1749–1832), famous German writer and statesman.

24 Charles Darwin (1809–82), English naturalist best known for his development of evolutionary theory.

the decline in length is slightly less dramatic (the median being significantly higher for the first forty years, and then stabilizing around seven or eight words rather than six), but equally evident.

v. The other type of title that disappeared in the late eighteenth century was the 'title-compilation,' like the 1772 *The Egg, Or the Memoirs of Gregory Giddy, Esq: With the Lucubrations of Messrs. Francis Flimsy, Frederick Florid, and Ben Bombast. To which are Added Private Opinions of Patty Pout, Lucy Lucious, and Priscilla Positive.* Also the *Memoirs of a Right Honourable Puppy. Or Bon Ton Display'd: Together with Anecdotes of a Right Honourable Scoundrel. Conceived by a Celebrated Hen, and Laid Before the Public by a Famous Cock-feeder.* Just as summaries drew the reader's attention to the multiplicity of episodes along the diachronic axis, compilations foregrounded a 'horizontal' proliferation of perspectives, characters, and locations—a naive, picaresque-like poetics of 'variety' (to use a keyword of the age), at the very moment when novelistic structure was becoming tighter and more homogeneous. Out of step with the times, summaries and compilations became even more unimaginable in the nineteenth century.

vi. If everything was really pushing towards shorter titles—observed Sam Bowles during a discussion of this paper—shouldn't these be 'rewarded' by the cultural ecosystem, and be on average more successful than other types? Yes, they should; and since James Raven had already identified which of the 1,400 novels published between 1770 and 1799 had been reprinted at least five times by 1829 (see his 'Historical Introduction: The Novel Comes of Age,' in T*he English Novel 1770–1829: A Bibliographical Survey of Prose Fiction Published in the British Isles*, vol. I, Oxford 2000, p. 40), I compared the lengths of these sixty-five titles to the median for their years—fully expecting them to be significantly shorter. That, however, turned out not to be the case: thirty-two of the titles were indeed shorter than the median, but twenty-nine were longer (at times, much longer), and four were exactly the same length.

vii. Jean-Louis Flandrin, 'Sentiments et civilisation. Sondage au niveau des titres d'ouvrages,' *Annales*, September-October 1965, p. 939. Later I hope to study the 'average title' of these 110 years, taking as a starting point the formula in 'or' (*Pamela, or Virtue Rewarded; Vensenshon; or, Love's Mazes; Manfrone; or, The One-Handed Monk*). There are over 2,000 such titles in the database, most of which use between three and fifteen words, thus occupying exactly the middle of the field. To get a sense of the morbid diffusion of 'or' in eighteenth-century titles, let me just say that it is the fourth-most-frequent word of the database, following 'the,' 'of,' and 'a' (and preceding 'and'!); by contrast, in Gaskell's *North and South*, 'or' is the forty-fourth-most-frequent word; in *Our Mutual Friend*, the fifty-fifth.

viii. Needless to say, different names—Evelina, Mary and Moll; Edward, Tom and Dick—evoked very different semantic associations: a great topic for further study.

ix. That female protagonists are more often indicated by their full name than by their first name is one of the surprises of this study. In the century under investigation, the old aristocratic (and often French) form of the proper name—Rosa de Montmorien, Eloise de Montblanc—found a newer, 'bourgeois' (and British) incarnation in Alice Lemington, or Margaret Graham; the golden age of the marriage plot, and of titles mentioning first names only, falls in between these two alternative typologies.

x. If one looks at the entire period in question, men's names outnumber women's by about 10 per cent, probably because many novelistic subgenres—most travel narratives, nautical tales, later 'Irish' novels, war stories, Newgate novels—were quite unlikely to have female protagonists. That the 'Emma' type of title should immediately come to mind when thinking of proper names in titles, is a sign of its exceptional power of allusion, and of the centrality of the marriage plot in the modern English novel.

xi. 'The Nominal Sentence,' in *Problems in General Linguistics*, 1966, Miami 1971, pp. 138, 142.

xii. Why them? Perhaps, because there was much in common between the conservative reaction to the French Revolution (for which basic social values had to be preserved from historical transformation), and the type of titles I am discussing here (for which fundamental ethical absolutes had to be freed from narrative relativization).

xiii. Nor are they allegories or personifications: Hofland's *Moderation* is not meant to come alive and be part of a story like its homonym in the 1669 *History of Moderation; or, The Life, Death and Resurrection of Moderation: together with her Nativity, Country, Pedigree, Kindred, Character, Friends, and also her Enemies.*
xiv. It's only at the very end of the period that they begin to appear: *Loss and Gain* (1848), *Rough and Smooth* (1849), *Shadows and Sunshine, Flies in Amber*, and *The Swan's Egg* (1850). In general, if the years between 1790 and 1830 see the establishment of metonymies and abstractions, no further novelties seem to emerge between 1830 and 1850: instead of looking for new forms of brevity, writers seem to devote their best energies to the second title, as if that were the key to the problem: *Helen Halsey. A Tale of the Borders. A Romance of Deep Interest; The Slave Captain; A Legend of Liverpool; Goals and Guerdons: Or, The chronicles of a life. By a very old lady; Rebecca and Rowena. A Romance Upon Romance.*
xv. See the bibliographies included in M.O. Grenby, *The Anti-Jacobin Novel*, Cambridge 2001, and Ann Ardis, *New Women, New Novels*, New Brunswick 1990.
xvi. In the *New York Times* best-seller list of November 2008, 38 per cent of the titles began with the definite article, and 6 per cent with the indefinite: not that different from two centuries earlier.
xvii. Harald Weinrich, 'The Textual Function of the French Article,' in Seymour Chatman, ed., *Literary Style: A Symposium*, Oxford 1971, p. 226.
xviii. The model here remains John Burrows's analysis of Austen's characters' styles in *Computation into Criticism*; that he did it twenty years ago, without the help of today's technology, puts us all to shame.

32. Ted Striphas, "E-Books and the Digital Future," *The Late Age of Print: Everyday Book Culture from Consumerism to Control.* New York: Columbia UP, 2009. 19–46

Ted Striphas is an Associate Professor in the Department of Communication and Culture at Indiana University. In his book *The Late Age of Print* and the blog he maintains at <www.thelateageofprint.org> he argues that rather than saying that digital technologies have caused the death of print, we should think of ourselves as living in the late age of print. Like the "late capitalism" theorized by Frederick Jameson in his important book *Postmodernism, Or, The Cultural Logic of Late Capitalism* (1991), the "late age of print" involves, on one hand, the logical development of aspects inherent to print culture, and, on the other, a significantly new phase in our relationship with print.

Examining such recent cultural phenomena as Oprah Winfrey's book club and the massive success of the Harry Potter books, Striphas shows how the late age of print can still include massive sales for at least some printed books. But at the same time as some printed books reach very large markets, e-books and digital downloads reduce the market share of printed books and threaten print's place as the primary medium through which we experience written texts. Rather than eagerly anticipating the end of the printed book or nostalgically mourning its passing, then, Striphas insists that we should try to understand how recent commercial, legal, and technological changes have altered how printed matter functions in the lives of individual readers and in society as a whole.

In the extract reprinted here, Striphas considers how the printed book and the e-book function differently as commodities in the world of "late capitalism." In some respects, printed books do not function like other commodities. Most commodities don't have the same kind of secondary, often non-monetized, circulation as printed books, for example. Few other commodities are borrowed, lent, shared, and re-sold as often as books. And, through public libraries, local governments use public money to buy books and make them available to the public for free, which doesn't happen to other commodities.

Striphas points out that in some respects e-books make books more like other commodities. E-books limit these kinds of secondary circulation: you can't lend them, sell them second hand, or—for the most part—borrow them from libraries. In this way, e-books function more like other commodities than printed books do. On the other hand, Striphas says, e-books call into question some ideas that have been basic to capitalism, such as the idea that the seller loses all rights over the commodity at the point of sale, and that the buyer acquires the right to dispose of the commodity as she sees fit.

E-books therefore have a complex relationship with capitalism. In some ways, they allow capitalist practices and assumptions to penetrate into areas of production and consumption and work and pleasure that it was previously difficult for them to reach. In other ways, they force us to re-think the nature of such building-blocks of capitalism as the commodity and the transaction. Striphas published *The Late Age of Print* in 2009, when e-books were still a new innovation, but his analysis continues to offer a helpful way of thinking about the economics of e-books and their relationship to the print trade.

E-Books and the Digital Future

At exactly 12:01 a.m. on March 14, 2000, Simon & Schuster began an experiment: the **publisher** released best-selling author Stephen King's first digital electronic book, or e-book, the 67 page novella *Riding the Bullet,* on the Internet. By 11:59 p.m. on the fifteenth, an estimated half million people had downloaded King's story, prompting Jack Romanos, Simon & Schuster's president, to declare the experiment a resounding success: "We believe the e-book revolution will have an impact on the book industry as great as the paperback revolution of the 60s."[i] Later that year, the soon-to-be notorious accounting firm of Arthur Andersen joined the celebration of e-books. In a dubious feat of actuarial prowess, Andersen's consultants predicted that by 2005 no less than 10 per cent of all books sold in the United States would be in electronic form.[ii] It appeared that the dusty old era of printed books was finally poised to give way to a sublime digital future.

Several years and a healthy dose of cynicism later, it seems clear that these heady claims about e-books were suffused with the same millennial hopes and dreams that had helped fuel the late 1990s dot-com boom and its accompanying faith in a resplendent techno-future. Despite the efforts of Stephen King, Simon & Schuster, and Arthur Andersen to locate themselves within the vanguard of an e-book revolution, the latter hasn't quite reached the fevered pitch that book industry insiders had anticipated. The turning point seems to have occurred around 2001 when, in the words of *Publishers Weekly,* the book industry trade magazine, e-book denizens faced a "reality check." Sluggish sales and the economic downturn following the 9/11 terrorist attacks in the United States led many hardware manufacturers and e-book publishers to divest themselves of their interest in e-books. Their doing so followed on the heels of Stephen King's decision, in December 2000, to discontinue writing his second e-book, *The Plant,* after the number of those who had downloaded installments from his website without paying had grown too high by his estimation.[iii]

Still, interest in and sales of e-books have rebounded of late. A 2003 report by the Open E-book Forum found that close to a million e-books had been sold in 2002, generating nearly $8 million in revenue; the first half of 2003 saw healthy, double-digit increases in units of sale over the preceding year. A second report, compiled by the Association of American Publishers, showed more modest gains of nearly $3 million in e-book sales among the top eight trade publishers. Of course, these reports don't account for the innumerable e-books that people acquire for free from sites such as the University of Virginia Library's EText Center (now the Scholars' Lab). In 2001 alone the **library** recorded over three million e-book downloads of works that had passed into the public domain. Moreover, major academic textbook publishers such as McGraw-Hill and Thomson Learning continue to pursue e-books in earnest, with the former reporting per month revenue from e-publishing in 2002 in the hundreds of thousands of dollars.[iv]

Two other higher-profile e-book ventures not only have helped to renew public interest in the technology but have also prompted some to begin imagining a world in which the content of books—perhaps of *all* books now in existence—would be little more than a click away. Since 2004, search engine giant Google has been busy digitizing part or all of the printed book collections of 29 (and counting) major research libraries. The company's self-described "moon shot," also known as Book Search, promises to make content from millions of books freely available to those with Internet access, and perhaps one day even to realize the promise of a massively cross-referenced universal library accessible to all.[v] On November 19, 2007, online retailer Amazon.com released Kindle, a portable electronic reading device whose express purpose, according to CEO Jeff Bezos, would be to bring books—"the last bastion of analog"—into the digital realm.[vi] Onboard mobile phone technology probably makes Kindle the first portable electronic reading device to provide for ubiquitous two-way communication between bookseller and consumer (available only in North America at the time of this writing). According to Bezos, "Our vision is that you should be able to read any book in any language that's ever been printed, whether it's in print or out of print, and you should be able to buy and get that book downloaded to your Kindle in less than 60 seconds."[vii]

Despite all this think-big entrepreneurial optimism, many continue to doubt the worth of 543
e-book technologies. Take a cartoon published in a 2005 edition of the *Chronicle of Higher Education*, whose caption reads: "The problem with e-books is that they are e-books." If this tautological statement makes us laugh, we do so most likely because we share a highly specific, normative vision of books and book reading. This vision, which has been propounded for decades by journalists, literary humanists, educators, and academic theorists, places printed books and solitary, immersive acts of reading center stage in the bibliographic mise-en-scène. The joke works because for many people it's intuitive to see e-books as crude copies of vaunted originals—that is, of printed books—and, in turn, to imagine the reading of electronic content as intellectually or experientially impoverished.[viii]

Amusing though they may be, jokes like these are anything but innocent. They're defensive assertions fueled by even more fundamental assumptions about the relationship between electronic and printed books. Just as "video killed the radio star,"[1] many partisans of print believe that e-books threaten to kill off their paper-based counterparts. Their fears may not be altogether unfounded. Some book-scanning projects have resulted in the destruction and discarding of countless printed books because of the method by which the **codex** volumes are prepared for flatbed scanning, namely, the "guillotining" of their spines.[ix] (Google's method is the exception here.)

1 The song "Video Killed the Radio Star" was recorded by The Buggles in 1979, lamenting the decline of radio as a mass medium. In 1981 the music video for the song was the first video aired on the newly debuted MTV network.

However, it's not just the physical form of printed books that seems to be imperiled in the so-called digital age. Critics worry that their content could be jeopardized as well. The lack of standardization of e-books, combined with the penchant among hardware and software developers for "upgrading" file formats out of existence, would appear to render the digital existence of book content tenuous at best.[x] E-books thus appear to some as harbingers of loss—of knowledge, authority, history, artistry, and meaning.

How could it be that e-books seem to offer equal parts promise and peril? It's not enough simply to say they're complex and contradictory cultural artifacts. Most—perhaps all—such objects are. What's crucial to explore, rather, is the intricate web of social, economic, legal, technological, and philosophical determinations that collectively have produced them as such. The aim of this chapter is to map the conditions leading to the emergence of e-books in the late age of print and to investigate what's at stake politically in current debates about their worth. Instead of trying to champion or condemn e-books, I'm more interested in considering their embeddedness within the broader history of consumer capitalism and property relations. Beyond their ability (or lack thereof) to store and retrieve information, what's most intriguing to me about e-books is their capacity to *manage* it and, by extension, the actions of those who purchase or otherwise consume e-book content. I argue that e-books are an emergent technological form by which problems pertaining to the ownership and **circulation** of printed books are simultaneously posed and resolved.

The first section of this chapter represents a ground clearing of sorts. Because so much of the debate surrounding e-books has tended to hinge on the degree to which they reproduce the

form and function of their printed counterparts, I want to spend some time sifting through this particular line of argument. My aim is to challenge the assumptions about originality, presence, and authenticity by which the debate gets framed so as to open up a different line of conversation about the history and social function of e-books. The next two sections explore some of the key conditions of emergence of e-books. I begin by investigating how, in the second quarter of the twentieth century, a host of cultural intermediaries promoted printed book ownership as a means to consolidate the budding consumer capitalism. Next I trace how concerns about the ownership, circulation, and reproduction of printed books helped fuel a fear that the latter had become troublesome with respect to expanding capitalist relations of production in the final quarter of the twentieth century. The final section explores how some contemporary e-book technologies embody and attempt to resolve this perceived problem, especially through the implementation of digital rights management schemes.

I suppose this chapter is about the disappearance of information, though not exactly in the sense the partisans of print would take it. Though I may share their concerns about the well-being of the historical record in the late age of print, ultimately that is of lesser importance to me. More significant is the growing power of holders of intellectual property (IP) rights[2] to make information appear and disappear whenever they see fit—often for a fee.

---

2 A legal concept under which individuals are granted legal rights governing intangible objects, often of an intellectual or creative nature, such as works of art, literature, and music, inventions, patents, phrases, designs, and symbols.

I. A Book by Any Other Name

With characteristic fanfare for all things technologically sublime, in July 1998 Steve Silberman of *Wired* magazine reported on the impending release of "Book 2.0"—a host of new, portable e-book readers set to be unveiled in American consumer markets. In referring to this generation of e-books as such, Silberman framed the devices as the latest iteration of an extant technology. Their purpose, therefore, was not only to repeat but also to improve upon the most familiar qualities of printed books. A certain sense of loss nevertheless pervades his account of reading Kakuzo Okakura's *Book of Tea*[3] on a Rocket e-book. "I won't be returning this *Book of Tea* to its little slipcase on my shelf," he observed. "I miss the way the printed book's type, with its tiny irregularities, is a Western equivalent of the wayward bristles that make a brush stroke more living than a line. But through the text—the bits—alone, Okakura's mind speaks."[xi]

Silberman could read *The Book of Tea* on screen, but he seemed to do so despite, not because of, the intervening technology. Boredom loomed, and the traces of what he took to be Okakura's presence are all that sustained his interest. Even they, purportedly, had been diminished, given how the e-book reader Silberman was using seemed to atomize the author's soulful prose into innumerable electronic impulses and then to reassemble them into lifeless, uniform digital text. Silberman claimed that e-books fail because, although they repeat, they don't repeat well enough. That is, they fail to duplicate the serendipitous flaws and minor variations that he believes imbue industrially manufactured printed books with warmth, difference, and depth—a personality akin to the aura Walter Benjamin[4] said had *declined* because 545
of mass reproduction.[xii]

Essayist Sven Birkerts's[5] popular *Gutenberg Elegies: The Fate of Reading in an Electronic Age* offers a similarly dour account of the relationship between printed and digital text. Birkerts recognizes that screens and digits increasingly complement both written and printed artifacts in patterning communication and social interaction, facilitating the circulation of people and things and, more abstractly, conditioning our relations to space-time. He goes further, however, in questioning the larger social and epistemological consequences that allegedly flow from what he describes as the "triumph of the screen and the digital program":[xiii]

> Nearly weightless though it is, the word printed on a page is a thing.
> The configuration of impulses on a screen is not—it is a manifestation,

---

3 *The Book of Tea* (1906) is an extended essay by Japanese scholar and art critic Kakuzo Okakura (1862–1913). It explores the influence of tea rituals on Japanese philosophy and aesthetics, highlighting the value of simplicity.

4 Walter Benjamin (1892–1940) was a philosopher and cultural critic. In his 1936 essay "The Work of Art in An Age of Mechanical Reproduction," he explores the idea of a work of art's "aura" as a condition of originality and authenticity possible only in the direct presence of that work, and therefore lost when that object is reproduced.

5 Sven Birkerts (b. 1951), American essayist and critic.

> an indeterminate entity both particle and wave, an ectoplasmic arrival and departure. The former occupies a position in space—on a page, in a book, and is verifiably there. The latter, once dematerialized, digitized back into storage, into memory, cannot be said to exist in quite the same way. It has potential, not actual, locus.... The same word, when it appears on the screen, must be received with a sense of its weightlessness—the weightlessness of its presentation. The same sign, but not the same.[xiv]

The electronic word may repeat its printed counterpart as pure sign, but the word's transformation into abstract electronic impulses evidently leaves it listless, impalpable, diffuse—the same but different, deficient. Birkerts goes on to contend that this apparent dematerialization of the word results in the toppling of a whole tradition of textual authority. This coup d'état is epitomized by claims about the author's death, an insistence on readers' power, and a belief that writing occurs under conditions of erasure.[xv]

Clearly Birkerts believes that our choices of reading and writing media are deeply consequential—even political—acts. Given his commitment to a quite traditional model of textual authority, it should come as no surprise that he eschews technologies that reduce the splendor of writing and reading to the vulgar processing of words. He writes: "I type these words on an IBM Selectric [typewriter] and feel positively antediluvian: My editors let me know that my quaint Luddite habits are gumming up the works, slowing things down for them."[xvi] Birkerts nevertheless delights in having opted to write with a typewriter rather than a computer. His editors' frustrations confirm for him that his choice constitutes more than a mere preference for one technology over another. He sees his decision as an act of defiance against a hostile insurgency, a social order in which speed, ephemerality, and relativism apparently rule the day.

Yet it is precisely here—in the confidence Birkerts feels in slowly, methodically, t-y-p-i-n-g o-u-t w-o-r-d-s on his IBM Selectric—that his claims about presence, social power, and media begin to get all jammed up. Langdon Winner[6] once famously quipped that "technology is license to forget."[xvii] Indeed, only a profound act of forgetting could sustain Birkerts's claims about the transparency of typewriting. His typewriter, after all, is not only mechanical but electrical (hence, *Selectric*), and as such it's a technology engaged in an abstract process of rendering. The mechanical energy Birkerts exerts in his keystrokes doesn't directly result in the words he sees and reveres on the printed page. These words aren't signs that would index his "hand" in any straightforward way. Rather, they result from the machine's transduction of his keystrokes into electrical impulses, which then induce corresponding movements in the typewriter's mechanism. Like it or not, an electrical charge infuses all of Birkerts's writing, a charge produced by the very machine IBM touted in a 1962 advertising campaign as a device not for slowing you down but for making you "faster ... more productive."[xviii]

6 Langdon Winner (b. 1944), American political theorist; his work focuses mainly on the social and political context of contemporary technological development.

Perhaps, then, the electricity flowing through the machine's intervening circuitry is the culprit. Would a purely mechanical typewriter more fully manifest Birkerts's presence in, and thus his authority over, the words he produces? We cannot know for sure because an answer by anything other than inference would require us to detect and quantify traces of latent "spirit" energy—a pursuit more in keeping with the field of parapsychology.[xix] Nevertheless Martin Heidegger's[7] lectures between 1942 and 1943 on the philosopher Parmenides[8] offer a useful point of historical comparison. Here is what he says about the mechanical typewriter's prospects for conveying personality and authority: "Mechanical writing deprives the hand of its rank in the realm of the written word and degrades the word to a means of communication. In addition, mechanical writing provides this 'advantage,' that it conceals the handwriting and thereby the character. The typewriter makes everyone look the same."[xx] It is, in other words, a technology of abstraction, one that seems to flatten the depths of difference into a bland uniformity.

How can a **typescript** evidence mechanism, homogeneity, and loss for Heidegger, while the very same document embodies personality, difference, and plenitude for Birkerts? Complicating matters even further, in the *Phaedrus*[9] Plato (speaking through the figure of Socrates) impugned the hand for its apparent incapacity to manifest the authenticity of speech in writing—the same hand whose rank or authenticity Heidegger would exalt more than two millennia later.[xxi]

Given these conflicting accounts, the problem with e-books may have less to do with boredom, habit, or the authority of authors and their words than with their grounding in a logic of representation. The intellectual history of reading and writing technologies consists, as it were, of a recursive series of laments about the apparent incapacity of these technologies to represent or manifest fully—the word, presence, personality, meaning, intention, and beyond. It is, moreover, a history so densely laden with contradictions and role reversals that a time when something besides loss and alienation ruled the day seems almost unimaginable. Thus, we shouldn't presume to know that the point of e-books is to represent the formal or experiential qualities many people attribute to the reading of printed books, even if commentary, advertising, and common sense may be telling us otherwise. That's a historically produced and learned relation, not an inherent one.[xxii]

That said, it would be imprudent to suggest that printed and electronic books necessarily share no relation—or at best only an imaginary one. The latter are called e-books, after all, and the name should count for something. Yet if the history and politics of e-books cannot be reduced to the formal qualities they may or may not share with printed books, then we're confronted with two specific challenges: to explore a more diverse set of connections e-books share with both printed books and a host of other technologies; and to account for the embeddedness of e-books in a broader context of social, legal, and political-economic relations. [...]

---

7 Martin Heidegger (1889–1976), German philosopher; his writings are primarily concerned with questions of ontology, or the study of being.

8 Parmenides, ancient Greek philosopher (early 5th century BCE).

9 Platonic dialogue composed around 370 BCE. It uses the frame of discussions of love to debate the proper use of rhetoric.

II. Disappearing Digits

William Gibson [b. 1948] is probably best known as the author of numerous cyber-punk novels, most notably *Neuromancer*. Gibson also authored a lesser-known, limited-edition work called *Agrippa (A Book of the Dead)* [...] which bore an uncanny resemblance to the book of the future. Released in 1992, it was "an electronic book designed to disappear as soon as it [was] read."[xxiii] More accurately, *Agrippa* was a hybrid work consisting of digital/electronic text encoded on a three-and-a-half-inch computer disk and a collection of printed materials, all contained within a high-tech package designed to degenerate upon exposure to air and visible light. The disk contained not only the story of *Agrippa*, "a poetic effusion about [Gibson's] father, who died when he was very young,"[xxiv] but encryption algorithms designed to ensure that the digital text would disappear as the text scrolled down the computer screen for the first and only time.[xxv]

Agrippa was a perfectly logical endeavor in light of the legislative initiatives, litigation, and technologies of reproduction that collectively challenged the cultural and economic values ascribed to mass-produced commodities in the first half of the twentieth century. Once accessed, it was improbable that *Agrippa* would circulate in the pass-along book trade. Like the book of the future, embedded technology undermined the possibility of the text's persistence and thus forestalled its circulation. Similarly, *Agrippa*'s electronic text sidestepped the question of lending rights since it would vanish before libraries could catalog it, much less lend the book to more than one borrower.[xxvi] Finally, *Agrippa* posed a novel solution to the related issue of reproduc-

ibility since its built-in encryption algorithms prevented duplication of the text.[xxvii]

Agrippa admittedly is somewhat of an extreme case in that it's the only electronic book of which I'm aware that disappears after a single use. Yet in other ways it was prophetic, given the book industry's renewed concerns about the passing along of printed books and its high hopes about e-books and digital rights management schemes mitigating at least some aspects of the perceived problem. For instance, in a 2001 article on electronic publishing, e-book publisher Matt Moynahan commented on how the lending of library books "add[s] up to approximately 1.7 billion royalty-free reads each year." He went on to estimate that as many as a billion more "royalty-free reads" resulted yearly from the pass-along and used-book trades.[xxviii] Little wonder, then, that algorithms akin to those the programmers used to encrypt *Agrippa* have become fairly common among commercial software and hardware developers anxious to regulate the dissemination of digital e-book content.

In July 2000 LockStream Corporation released a media delivery and rights management system intended for use with e-books and other forms of digital content. The company promised that copies of any files encrypted by their system would automatically degrade upon being made, thus rendering copied content inoperative or inaccessible.[xxix] Similarly, in 2001 e-book publisher RosettaBooks announced its release of a special edition of mystery novelist Agatha Christie's *And Then There Were None*. What distinguished this edition was a "time-limit license" that granted users a total of 10 hours of access to the e-book for the meager sum of a dollar. Rights management software kicked in thereafter to render the text unreadable unless the user opted to renew the license for an additional dollar or purchase the title outright for five dollars.[xxx]

In 2004 textbook publishing giant McGraw-Hill began releasing e-books whose embedded rights management software locks them to the specific computers onto which they're downloaded, thereby forestalling any possibility of their duplication or circulation. The company's other main e-book format, which is online only, registers the total number of paying-customer page views and typically restricts them to four views per each edition's total number of pages. A company spokesperson provided this (depressing) rationale for limiting customers' page views to such a low number: "We arrived at that figure after talking with professors.... They said, read it once, study for the midterm, study for a final, and read it one more time. Four ought to be ample."[xxxi] Collectively these e-books and their digital rights management schemes compel users to cede to e-book publishers, software developers, and other interested parties much of their ability to circulate, dispose of, and reproduce whatever titles they've purchased.

The problem of circulating and reproducing printed books is not only embedded in technological artifacts. Federal legislation also embodies this concern. In 1998 Congress unanimously approved the Digital Millennium Copyright Act (DMCA), a sweeping piece of legislation that, among numerous other provisions, prohibits end users of **copyrighted** material from bypassing encryption systems or distributing information that might permit others to do so. One of the first tests of the DMCA occurred in July 2001, when the Federal Bureau of Investigation (FBI) arrested Russian computer programmer Dmitry Sklyarov, who had come to the United States to attend a computer hackers' convention. The FBI alleged that he had written Advanced e-book Processor for his employer, ElcomSoft, a program that permits users of Adobe's e-book software to circumvent the program's safeguards against copying electronic books. Sklyarov was released five months later 549
after agreeing to testify against his employer in exchange for immunity from prosecution.[xxxii]

Sklyarov's arrest and ElcomSoft's subsequent prosecution underscore what a year earlier the *New York Times* had called the book industry's "ultimate nightmare." Peer-to-peer (P2P) music file sharing had recently entered the popular imagination thanks to the launch and immediate notoriety of Napster in 1999. The ease with which the service allowed music lovers to trade MP3 files directly with one another online, and thereby to circumvent the music industry, left many cultural producers fearing for the effects of P2P. The book industry was no exception, given its fascination at the time with the prospects of digital publishing. Hence the fear that "digital books will go the way of digital music: circulating for free over the Internet, at the mercy of pirates and hackers."[xxxiii] However, even after the court-ordered shutdown of Napster in 2001 and the company's subsequent reorganization into a paid service, the book industry still found itself in P2P's long shadow. In 2008 *Newsweek* reported on BookSnap, a new scanning device, or "book ripper," that would allow ordinary consumers to digitize their personal libraries. The story opened with the question, "Could the publishing industry get Napsterized?," which actually referred to the next generation of file-sharing and social networking sites that had grown up in Napster's wake.[xxxiv] Although *Newsweek* raised doubts about the user-friendliness of BookSnap, the implication behind the question it raised about home book scanning was clear enough: given the ease with which anyone with a few hundred dollars and an Internet connection can reproduce and redistribute book content, the long-term survival of the book industry was increasingly dependent on its ability to lock that content down.

As anyone knows who has scanned or photocopied a chapter from a printed book, the trouble with—or perhaps the best part about—intellectual property (IP) law is that while multiple parties maintain a controlling legal interest over the disposal of a specific intellectual property, that interest isn't always practical or enforceable.[xxxv] While IP law unquestionably carries a significant degree of prohibitive force, it provides a legal remedy only after acts of duplication have occurred. It doesn't perforce forestall acts of duplication. Put another way, IP law doesn't so much protect against the process of duplicating copyrighted materials as redress the result of their duplication.[xxxvi] Digital encryption, on the other hand, prohibits the duplication and circulation of e-books before acts of duplication can occur—in extreme cases by erasing e-books after only a single use. Digital encryption thus allows authors, publishers, and others to monitor and regulate the disposition of e-books in ways that exceed the scope of existing intellectual property laws by circumventing such exceptions as fair use and the first-sale doctrine.[xxxvii] The technology does so by empowering interested parties to establish and maintain unprecedented levels of practical control over the social life of e-books and other forms of digital information even after the transfer of ownership (i.e., purchase) has occurred.

III. A Different Story to Tell

At the outset of this chapter I mentioned Google's book-scanning project, Book Search. By way of conclusion, I want to spend some time reflecting on it. Beyond the prospect of compiling a voluminous, cross-referenced digital library, what's striking about Google's initiative is the bizarre ambivalence surrounding it. Under the auspices of the Association of American Publishers, five presses—McGraw-Hill, Pearson Education, Penguin USA, Simon & Schuster, and John Wiley & Sons—filed a federal lawsuit against Google in October 2005 alleging copyright infringement. What makes the case so strange, however, is that the presses that brought the suit also happen to be partners in Google Book Search. How can one explain this apparent contradiction?

The simple answer is: the publishers who've partnered with and who are now suing Google object to the company's scanning of any books other than those they've specifically authorized. Their issue isn't with Book Search but rather with Google Library, the book-scanning operation whose aim is to digitize part or all of the printed book collections of major research libraries. Although Google Library is a facet of Book Search, it operates independently of the partnership agreements drawn up with a host of book publishers who want to promote their titles online. In the words of Pat Schroeder, former congresswoman and now president and CEO of the Association of American Publishers: "While authors and publishers know how useful Google's search engine can be and think the Print Library could be an excellent resource, the bottom line is that under its current plan Google is seeking to make millions of dollars by freeloading on the talent and property of authors and publishers."[xxxviii]

The answer may be more complex when considered in light of the preceding discussion of printed and electronic books. Because it's clear that the publishers who are suing Google want it both ways, one might be tempted to describe their actions as hypocritical.

They're not. Instead, their actions are a function of the peculiar—even ambivalent—status of books-as-commodities in the late age of print. On the one hand, the publishers are trying to promote printed books (and, presumably, printed book ownership) by using one of the most salient publicity vehicles of our time, the Internet, and, more specifically, Google, its most widely used search engine. In this way their actions are in keeping with the logic of consumer capitalism, whose influence has been felt in the book industry at least since the second quarter of the twentieth century, if not earlier. On the other hand, the lawsuit expresses a not altogether consonant impulse, a concern about how to control the reproduction and circulation of book content following a given volume's initial sale. Again, the issue here is ownership and its thorny status in the late age of print.

Both the controversy surrounding Book Search and the topics discussed in this chapter suggest that the social relations of commodity ownership characteristic of the first three quarters of the twentieth century continue to dominate today's market economy. By the same token, they also show that these relations have been troubled relentlessly since Bernays's book sneak campaign in the 1930s all the way up to *Agrippa*, the DMCA, and beyond. Given that many of today's most popular, commercially available e-book technologies allow cultural producers to micromanage the persistence, use, and circulation of content, these technologies are symptomatic of—indeed, further—the tense and uneven process of transforming three core principles of consumer capitalism: the belief that the widespread private ownership and accumulation of mass-produced consumer goods is desirable from the standpoint of capitalist production; the assumption that the sale of a certain item implies the more or less complete transfer of 551
ownership rights to that item; and the principle that commodity ownership consists, in part, in the right to make use of the goods you've purchased with minimal—and, ideally no—outside interference by the party from whom you've purchased them.

E-books clearly have an important story to tell beyond their ability to reproduce the form and function of printed books. Theirs is a story about the logic of capitalist accumulation and how it has been shifting over the last century. Today's e-book technologies constitute the end result of more than 50 years' worth of effort to render problematic people's accumulation and circulation of printed books, as well as those of other mass-produced goods. As such, e-books both express and embody a practical critique of consumer capitalism. This is no cause for celebration, however. Whatever critique of capitalism they offer ultimately advances a more intensive mode of capitalist accumulation, one significantly premised on the management of commodities and hence the ways in which consumers interact with them. E-books don't suggest a waning of consumer capitalism. On the contrary, they point to its intensification or, rather, to the emergence of new practices of *controlled consumption*, a theme I will pursue in subsequent chapters [of Striphas's book].

Though I've examined the changing conditions whereby people have incorporated books into their everyday lives, on balance I've perhaps focused more on the efforts of cultural producers to re-shape specific book technologies—and book culture more broadly—to suit their own ends. In the next chapter [of Striphas's book] I demonstrate how specific social classes and communities have turned to large-scale retail bookstores as a means of challenging patterns of inequality at the level of the everyday.

Notes

i. Quoted in David D. Kirkpatrick, "Forecasts of an E-book Era Were, It Seems, Premature," *New York Times*, August 28, 2001, A1. King's novella was encrypted to prevent its being printed, duplicated, or e-mailed.

ii. Ibid.

iii. Jim Milliot and Calvin Reid, "Reality Check," *Publishers Weekly*, January 7, 2002, 36–38; Kirkpatrick, "Forecasts of an E-book Era Were Premature"; Calvin Reid, "Stephen King Happy About 'The Plant,'" *Publishers Weekly*, August 7, 2000, 57; Calvin Reid, "King to Take Hiatus from 'The Plant,'" *Publishers Weekly*, December 4, 2000, 10; M.J. Rose, "E-Books Live on After Mighty Fall," *Wired*, December 18, 2001.

iv. Milliot and Reid, "Reality Check," 37; Calvin Reid, "Selling E-books to Academic, Trade Markets," *Publishers Weekly*, March 25, 2002, 13; Calvin Reid, "E-book Sales Up 30% in First Half of '03," *Publishers Weekly*, September 22, 2003, 12; and Rose, "E-Books Live on."

v. Jeffrey Toobin, "Google's Moon Shot," *New Yorker*, February 5, 2007, 30–35; Kevin Kelly, "Scan This Book!" *New York Times Magazine*, May 14, 2006. See also Siva Vaidhyanathan, "The Googlization of Everything and the Future of Copyright," *UC Davis Law Review* 40.3 (2007).

vi. Quoted in Steven Levy, "The Future of Reading," *Newsweek*, November 26, 2007, 57.

vii. Jeff Bezos, interview by Charlie Rose, *Charlie Rose Show*, PBS, November 19, 2007.

viii. According to Pat Schroeder, president and CEO of the Association of American Publishers, "We've been ready to sell e-books for 20 years ... [but] everybody still likes physical books." Quoted in Steven Levy, "Rip This Book? Not Yet," *Newsweek*, February 18, 2008, 24.

ix. Nicholas A. Basbanes, *Patience and Fortitude: A Roving Chronicle of Book People, Book Places, and Book Culture* (New York: HarperCollins, 2001), 503. See also Nicholson Baker, *Double Fold: Libraries and the Assault on Paper* (New York: Random House, 2001), 65–72.

x. Basbanes, *Patience and Fortitude*, 499; Rober Coover, "The End of Books," *New York Times Book Review*, June 21, 1992.

xi. Steve Silberman, "Ex Libris: The Joys of Curling Up with a Good Digital Reading Device," *Wired*, July 1998.

xii. Walter Benjamin, "The Work of Art in the Age of Mechanical Reproduction," in *Illuminations: Essays and Reflections*, ed. Hannah Arendt, trans. Harry Zohn (New York: Shocken Book, 1968), 217–51.

xiii. Sven Birkerts, *The Gutenberg Elegies: The Fate of Reading in an Electronic Age* (New York: Fawcett Columbine, 1994), 188.

xiv. Ibid., 154–55.

xv. Ibid., 163, 188. See also Roland Barthes, "The Death of the Author," in *Image, Music, Text*, trans. Stephen Heath (New York: Hill and Wang, 1977), 142–48; Michel Foucault, "What Is an Author?," in *Language, Counter-Memory, Practice: Selected Essays and Interviews*, ed. Donald F. Bouchard, trans. Donald F. Bouchard and Sherry Simon (Ithaca, NY: Cornell UP, 1977), 113–38; and Jacques Derrida, *Of Grammatology*, rev. ed., trans. Gayatri Chakravorty Spivak (Baltimore: Johns Hopkins UP, 1997).

xvi. Birkerts, *The Gutenberg Elegies*, 28. Note that in the 2006 edition Birkerts admits to having succumbed to using a computer. He does, however, continue to write out his screeds longhand before finalizing them on his laptop. Sven Birkerts, *The Gutenberg Elegies: The Fate of Reading in an Electronic Age*, 2nd ed. (New York: Faber and Faber, 2006), xi, 231–33.

xvii. Langdon Winner, *Autonomous Technology: Technics-Out-of-Control as a Theme in Political Thought* (Cambridge, MA: MIT P, 1978), 315.

xviii. "The IBM Selectric Typewriter Was Introduced on July 31, 1961," <http://www.etypewriters.com/se-thumb.htm>.

xix. For engaging critiques of the spiritual idea in the history of media as well as in media studies, see John Durham Peters, *Speaking Into the Air: A History of the Idea of Communication* (Chicago: U of Chicago P, 1999), 63–108; and Jeffrey Sconce, *Haunted Media: Electronic Presence from Telegraphy to Television* (Durham, NC: Duke UP, 2000).

xx. Martin Heidegger, *Parmenides*, trans. André Schuwer and Richard Rojcewicz (Bloomington: Indiana UP, 1992), 81. For a perceptive discussion of the typewriter, its relationship to communicative practice, and to changing conceptions of human being, see Friedrich A. Kittler, *Gramophone, Film, Typewriter*, trans. Geoffrey Winthrop-Young and Michael Wutz (Stanford, CA: Stanford UP, 1999), 183–263.

xxi. Plato, *The Phaedrus: Compiled with an Introduction and Commentary by R. Hackforth* (Cambridge: Cambridge UP, 1972), 156–64. Of course, Plato goes on to say that human speech itself is a degraded copy of the divine Word, and as such it suffers—and we suffer—for its finitude.

xxii. For an astute discussion of the problem in relation to the history of sound reproduction, see Jonathan Sterne, *The Audible Past: Cultural Origins of Sound Reproduction* (Durham, NC: Duke UP, 2003), 215–86.

xxiii. John F. Baker, "Electronic Art Book ... for One Read Only," *Publishers Weekly*, June 29, 1992, 28.

xxiv. Ibid.

xxv. Since its initial release in 1992, the text has become widely available on the Internet, apparently as a result of both illegal hacking and its official release to a series of online bulletin boards in the mid-1990s.

xxvi. An article in *Details* magazine reported: "[Dennis] Ashbaugh [the artist who collaborated with Gibson on *Agrippa*] is gleeful about the dilemma [*Agrippa*] will pose to librarians. To register the book's copyright, he must send two copies to the Library of Congress. To classify it, they must read it, and to read it, they must destroy it." Gavin Edwards, "Cyber Lit," *Details*, June 1992, <http://www.textfiles.com/sf/cyberlit.txt>.

xxvii. However, there was still the possibility that someone might possess sufficient technical knowledge and expertise to crack the code illegally, which apparently did happen. See note xxv.

xxviii. Paul Hilts, "BookTech Looks at E-Publishing," *Publishers Weekly*, March 5, 2001, 46. Interestingly, Moynahan sees the passing along of books as an untapped marketing opportunity rather than lost revenue. This is a suggestive insight, one the book industry would do well to heed. I would add that the traditional higher cost of hardbound library editions partly offsets "lost revenue."

xxix. Paul Hilts, "Locking with LockStream," *Publishers Weekly*, July 3, 2000, 27.

xxx. "RosettaBooks to Publish 'Time Limit' Ebook," *Publishers Weekly*, August 13, 2001, 157.

xxxi. Quoted in Scott Carlson, "Online Textbooks Fail to Make the Grade: Students Prefer Handling Pages the Old-Fashioned Way," *Chronicle of Higher Education*, February 11, 2005, A36. For more on digital "locking," see Andrea L. Foster, "In a Pilot Program, 10 College Bookstores Begin Selling Digital Textbooks," *Publishers Weekly*, September 2, 2005, 45.

xxxii. Jennifer Lee, "US Arrests Russian Cryptographer as Copyright Violator," *New York Times*, July 18, 2001, C8; idem, "In Digital Copyright Case, Programmer Can Go Home," *New York Times*, December 14, 2001, C4; Steven Levy, "Busted by the Copyright Cops: How a Controversial Intellectual Property Law Got a Russian Programmer Thrown in Jail," *Newsweek*, August 20, 2001, 54. In a stunning decision ElcomSoft was acquitted in December 2002 of having violated the DMCA. Although the jury found the Advanced eBook Processor Program indeed violated the statute, it nevertheless determined that ElcomSoft's violation of the law was not willful.

xxxiii. David D. Kirkpatrick, "With Plot Still Sketchy, Characters Vie for Roles: The Struggles Over E-Books Abound, Though Readership Remains Elusive," *New York Times*, November 27, 2000, C1.

xxxiv. Levy, "Rip This Book?," 24.

xxxv. "Intellectual property law" refers to a juridical framework consisting of copyright statutes, patent laws, publicity rights, trademark laws, and attendant case law. Outside the United States one would need to include the moral rights of authors.

xxxvi. Laurie Stearns, "Copy Wrong: Plagiarism, Process, Property, and the Law," in *Perspectives on Plagiarism and Intellectual Property in a Postmodern World*, ed. Lise Buranen and Alice M. Roy (Albany: SUNY P, 1999), 9. Stearns's discussion specifically addresses the relationship between plagiarism and copyright and, as such, I've adapted her argument. See also Tarleton Gillespie, *Wired Shut: Copyright and the Shape of Digital Culture* (Cambridge, MA: MIT P, 2007), 256.

xxxvii. According to Lawrence Lessig, "Protection by technology can often reach far beyond the protection of the law." *The Future of Ideas: The Fate of the Commons in a Connected World* (New York: Random House, 2001), 256. Peter Jaszi has termed this new set of legal-cum-practical controls "paracopyright." See "Intellectual Property Legislative Update: Copyright, Paracopyright, and Pseudo-Copyright," paper presented at the Association of Research Libraries Membership Meeting, May 1998, 3, <http://www.arl.org/arl/proceedings/132/luncheon/jaszi.html>. See also Yochai Benkler, *The Wealth of Networks: How Social Production Transforms Markets and Freedom* (New Haven, CT: Yale UP, 2006), 415. Fair use refers to a key exception in copyright law protecting the appropriation of copyrighted material for the purpose of parody, criticism, and education, under specific conditions. The first-sale doctrine stipulates that the purchaser of a copyrighted work, not the copyright holder, possesses the right to sell it or give it away once the purchaser has legally acquired it. Both provisions were codified in the US Copyright Act of 1976 (17 U.S.C., sec. 107 and 109, resp.).

xxxviii. "Publishers Sue Google Over Plans to Digitize books," press release, *Association of America Publishers*, October 19, 2005, <http://www.publishers.org/press/releases.cfm?PressReleaseArticleID=292>. See also, Toobin, "Google's Moon Shot"; Kelly, "Scan This Book!"; and Vaidhyanathan, "The Googlization of Everything and the Future of Copyright."

33.

Anthony Grafton, "Codex in Crisis: The Book Dematerializes," *Worlds Made by Words: Scholarship and Community in the Modern West*. Cambridge, MA: Harvard UP, 2009. 288–326

Anthony Grafton (b. 1950) is the current Henry Putnam University Professor at Princeton, where he has taught since 1975. He is a specialist in the history of ideas, and in particular the classical scholarship of the early modern period. In this field, he has published a number of studies about the history of scholarship, including a major two-volume study of Joseph Scalinger, one of the great scholars of the Renaissance, and *Defenders of the Text: The Traditions of Scholarship in the Age of Science, 1450–1800*. Grafton's interests, however, extend well beyond his particular areas of expertise. He has been president of the American Historical Association and is an editor of the *Journal of the History of Ideas*. He has written on a wide variety of topics for magazines such as *The New Republic*, *The American Scholar*, *The New Yorker*, and *The New York Review of Books*, to which he has contributed a number of essays on current topics such as the future of universities and the impact of digital technologies on scholarship and education.

The essay re-printed here started life as a *New Yorker* article, which was then published in an extended form as a hand-stitched pamphlet issued by a small craft publisher in New York called The Crumpled Press. It was then incorporated as the final chapter in Grafton's book *Worlds Made by Words: Scholarship and Community in the Modern West* (it is re-printed here, in an edited form, from the book). In *Worlds Made by Words*, Grafton traces the ways in which scholars from the Renaissance to the present have used printed books and the libraries and universities in which they are gathered, curated, catalogued, and stored, as the basis of communities of knowledge. In this final chapter, he considers what it means for such communities when the material objects and institutions that bound them together move into the virtual world.

Grafton situates the Google Books digitization project in the context of the long-standing dream of a universal library, and suggests some of the reasons why it will not realize that dream. He examines the extent of Google's ambitions, and some of the problems that beset its digitization project in its current form. One problem is that Google ignores certain classes of books, for example early printed books. Another is that the "metadata"—the indexed information about each book—is often unreliable as a result of the automated ways in which Google collects it. A final problem—and an insurmountable one—is that certain kinds of study require access to the original document in its physical form. If a document needs to be authenticated, for example, the quality of the paper, the watermarks, and the chemical makeup of the ink may all need to be examined. Grafton therefore concludes that, at least for the foreseeable future, readers and scholars will need to be familiar with both the electronic interfaces of online libraries such as Google Books and the traditional institutions such as libraries that amass and catalogue physical books and archives.

Codex in Crisis: The Book Dematerializes

Alfred Kazin[1] began work in 1938 on his first book, *On Native Grounds*. The child of poor and diffident Jewish immigrants in Brooklyn, he studied at City College. While uninspired professors processed large classes and Stalinists and Trotskyites turned the cafeteria into a battleground, Kazin somehow developed a passion for literature and began to write reviews. He had little money or backing, yet he managed to put together an extraordinary, comprehensive book, to tell the story of the great American intellectual and literary movements from the late nineteenth century to his own time and to set them in a richly evoked historical context. One institution made his work possible: the New York Public Library at Fifth Avenue and Forty-Second Street, where he spent almost five years. As Kazin later recalled:

> Anything I had heard of and wanted to see, the blessed place owned: first **editions** of American novels out of those germinal decades after the Civil War that led to my theme of the "modern"; old **catalogues** from long-departed Chicago **publishers** who had been young men in the 1890s trying to support a little realism; yellowing, crumbling, but intact sets of the old *Masses* (1911–18), which was to the Stalinist *New Masses*[2] what St. Francis is to the Inquisition.[3]

The **library's** holdings taught him "what hope, élan, intellectual freshness came with those pioneer realists out of the Middle West who said there was no American literature but the one

1 Alfred Kazin (1915–98), American writer, literary critic, and man of letters. He published *On Native Grounds: An Interpretation of Modern American Prose Literature* in 1942.

2 *Masses* was an American political and artistic magazine published monthly and edited by Max Eastman, with art editor John Sloan. It became known both for its socialist political position and its publication of work by a number of urban realist artists who became known as the "Ashcan School." *The Masses* ceased publication in 1918 but was revived as *The New Masses* in 1926, which took an increasingly doctrinaire Communist editorial line.

3 St. Francis of Assisi (1181–1226), a Roman Catholic saint who founded the Franciscan monastic order, is here invoked as a paragon of virtue, simplicity, and tranquility, in opposition to the Inquisition, the twelfth-century attempt to suppress heresy in the Roman Catholic Church, which is invoked as a by-word for violent excess and intolerance of any departure from orthodox views.

they were rushing to create." Without leaving Manhattan, Kazin read his way into "lonely small towns, prairie villages, isolated colleges, dusty law offices, national magazines, and provincial 'academies' where no one suspected that the obedient-looking young reporters, law clerks, librarians, teachers would turn out to be Willa Cather, Robert Frost, Sinclair Lewis, Wallace Stevens, Marianne Moore."[i] [4]

Kazin and his close friend Richard Hofstadter,[5] with whom he shared quick lunches at the Automat, fast games of ping-pong, and an occasional afternoon of newsreels, were only two of the countless writers, readers, and critics who over the centuries have found themselves and their subjects in libraries. It is an old story, quiet and reassuring: bookish boy or girl enters the cool, dark library and discovers loneliness and freedom. For the last ten years or so, however, the cities of the book have been anything but quiet. The computer and the Internet have transformed reading more dramatically than anything since the printing press. In great libraries from Stanford to Oxford, pages turn, scanners hum, databases grow—and the world of books, of **copyrighted** information and repositories of individual copies, trembles.

Scenarios for the apocalypse have often involved books: Revelation mentions letters, describes a book with seven seals, and uses the closing of a book as a vivid metaphor for the end of the physical world: "And the heaven departed as a **scroll** when it is rolled together" (6:14). But at the beginning of the twenty-first century, the rhetorical situation has reversed itself. Great information projects, mounted by Google and rival companies, have elicited millenarian prophecies about texts as we know them: claims that the printed book, magazine, and newspaper are as dead as the trees their paper comes from, and predictions that digital repositories of human knowledge will not only replace but will also improve on them. In 2006, Kevin Kelly, the self-styled "chief Maverick" of *Wired*,[6] published one of the more influential of these in the *New York Times*. In a thoughtful review of the intricate legal issues associated with digitizing books in copyright, Kelly vividly describes the virtual library that Google and its rivals and partners are creating. In the near future, Kelly believes, "all the books in the world" will "become a single liquid fabric of interconnected words and ideas." The user of the electronic library will be able to bring together "all texts—past and present, multilingual—on a particular subject," and by doing so gain "a clearer sense of what we as a civilization, a species, do know and don't know. The white spaces of our collective ignorance are highlighted, while the golden peaks of our knowledge are drawn with completeness."[ii] Others have evoked even more millennial prospects: a universal **archive** that will contain not only all books and articles but also all documents everywhere: the basis for a total history of the human race.

---

4 Willa Cather (1873–1947), Robert Frost (1874–1963), Sinclair Lewis (1885–1951), Wallace Stevens (1879–1955), and Marianne Moore (1887–1972) are all early- to mid-twentieth-century American writers.

5 Richard Hofstadter (1916–70) was an American historian and Professor of American History at Columbia University in New York. He was twice awarded the Pulitzer Prize: in 1956 for *The Age of Reform* and in 1964 for *Anti-intellectualism in American Life*.

6 Kevin Kelly (b. 1952) is the founding executive editor of *Wired* magazine, which is devoted to technology and digital culture.

Librarians, publishers, professors, **printers**—all of us are fascinated by the prospect that such prophets conjure up: a future in which readers in search of information always turn to screens rather than books, and, as e-books improve, even readers in search of pleasure begin to do the same. This prospect infuriates some acolytes of the book: for example, Jean-Noel Jeanneney, historian and former director of the Bibliothèque Nationale de France, who in 2005 published a sad little volume in which he denounced Google Books as a typical American plot, at once imperialist and boorish, rather like the war in Iraq. Google, he argued, will first fill the Web with books in English and then profit by distorting the world of learning and literature. Only energetic countermeasures—preferably sponsored by national governments rather than corporations—can save European literature and scholarship.[iii]

Instinct and experience predispose me to find some substance in critiques of the new textual world. I am a lover of old libraries—the libraries of the 1960s and 1970s, in which I became a scholar. As a student in those years, I lived in what felt like a bibliomaniac's paradise and in retrospect still seems to have been an idyll. Books and journals were cheap, and library budgets were healthy. Even in the United States, the stacks of good libraries from Connecticut to California were loaded with sixteenth- and seventeenth-century tomes that no one had yet declared rare,[7] as well as reprints of anything the library did not possess in its original form. I prowled the vast open-stack collections at the University of Chicago, where I studied, and Cornell and Princeton, where I taught, pulling books off the shelves by dozens, as fascinated by what they could tell me about nineteenth- and twentieth-century scholars and students as by what they revealed about the more distant past I studied.

[...]

But it would be absurd to join Jeanneney's crusade. Enter a word or phrase in any European language in the Google Books search field and you learn immediately that the system already contains thousands of texts in languages other than English. As to the French government, its last great gift to the world of books was the library that Jeanneney directed, a building that looks like the set from some forgotten dystopian sci-fi film of the 1970s—think *Logan's Run*[8]—and is about as much fun to work in. As a liberal, in the current Anglo-American sense, I believe that competent governments do many things better than markets can, but I am not at all sure that France's statist way of providing books for readers is a case in point. The Bibliothèque Nationale deserves credit for its own database, Gallica, which offers a **canon** of carefully selected texts, well digitized, and for its provision of up-to-date foreign books. But it has yet to show that it can, or wants to, mobilize and make accessible to the world a vast, disorderly mass of texts, canonical and non-canonical, for readers to use freely. Many American

---

7 Books that have been "declared rare" by librarians are typically stored in controlled conditions, where readers can request to consult them, and are not available on the open shelves of the library (the "stacks").

8 *Logan's Run* is a 1976 science-fiction film directed by Michael Anderson, set in a dystopian vision of earth in the twenty-third century, in which most residents live in a sealed, domed city.

and British librarians are exuberant about the prospect of bringing the books in their custody to new publics, through new media, and anyone can see why. After all, one thing that Google Books makes clearer every day is that you can study many aspects of French thought and literature as deeply in New York as in Paris, and a lot more efficiently.

I. The Universal Library

The problem is how to understand what is happening right now, as we all try to remain standing against the tidal waves of traditional books and new media that are breaking over us. One vital point, and an easy one to miss, is that the Internet will not in fact bring us a universal library—much less an encyclopedic record of all human experience. None of the firms now engaged in digitization projects claims that it will create anything of the kind. The hype and rhetoric that reverberate around the Web make it hard to grasp what Google and their partner libraries are actually doing, what readers will and will not have access to in the next ten or twenty years. We have clearly reached something of a watershed, a new era in the history of text production and consumption. On many fronts, traditional periodicals and books are making way for blogs, computer databases, and other electronic formats. But magazines and books still sell a lot of copies. The current drive to digitize the written record is one of a number of critical projects in the long saga of our drive to accumulate, store, and retrieve information efficiently. It will result not in the infotopia that the prophets conjure up, but in one more in a series of new information ecologies, all of them challenging, in which readers, writers, and producers of text have learned to survive and flourish.

For centuries—for millennia—the **scribes** and scholars who produced books often were also the ones who organized them in collections and devised ways of helping readers find and master what they needed. As early as the third millennium BCE, Mesopotamian scribes began to catalogue the tablets in their collections. For ease of reference, they appended content descriptions to the edges of tablets, and they adopted systematic shelving for quick identification of related texts. The greatest of ancient collections, the Library of Alexandria, had, in its ambition and its methods, a good deal in common with Google's efforts. It was founded around 300 BCE by Ptolemy I, who had inherited Alexandria, a brand-new city, from Alexander the Great.[9] A historian with a taste for poetry, Ptolemy decided to amass a comprehensive collection of Greek literature, philosophy, and science. Like Google, the library developed an efficient procedure for capturing and reproducing texts. When ships docked in Alexandria, any scrolls found on them were confiscated and taken to the library. The staff made copies for the owners and stored the originals

9 Ptolemy I Soter I, also known as Ptolemy Lagides (c. 367–c. 283 BCE, not to be confused with the astronomer Ptolemy) was a general in the armies of Alexander the Great (Alexander III of Macedon, 356–323 BCE). He ruled Egypt from 323 BCE until his death, and founded the Library of Alexandria.

in heaps until they could be catalogued—a fact that gives some idea of the scale of the operation. Copies of Homer[10] obtained this way were designated "those from ships."

At the collection's height, it contained more than half a million scrolls, a welter of information that forced librarians to develop new organizational methods. For the first time, texts were shelved alphabetically. Faced with this daunting mass, the poet and scholar Callimachus[11] drew up comprehensive **bibliographies**. Enterprising forgers had run up so many fake texts to satisfy the library's appetite that he had to distinguish systematically between the genuine works of the great poets and the spurious ones that the library also possessed. Gradually, the library became a center of focused scholarship, where a series of librarians—Zenodotus of Ephesus, Aristophanes of Byzantium, and Aristarchus of Samothrace—corrected and commented on classic texts. Many details of their work, only partially preserved after the destruction of the library, remain controversial. Yet it seems clear that they not only devised new **philological** methods but also standardized the text of Homer that circulated in Egypt during the Hellenistic and Roman periods—a major achievement in an age when every text was copied by hand.[iv]

Six hundred years after Callimachus, Eusebius, a historian and bishop of the seacoast city of Caesarea in Palestine, assembled and corrected Christian sources in the local library. There he also devised a complex network of cross-references, known as "canon tables," which enabled readers to find parallel passages in the four Gospels—a system that the distinguished modern scholar James O'Donnell recently described as the world's first set of hot links.

II. Google's Empire

The current era of digitalization unquestionably outstrips that of microfilm, in ambition and in achievement. Few individuals ever owned microfilm or microfiche readers, after all, whereas most serious readers in developed countries now have direct access to personal computers or laptops and an Internet connection. The changes wrought by all this are obvious. Even the most traditionally minded of scholars, faced with the need to look up a date, a fact, or a text, generally begins not by going to a library reference room crammed with encyclopedias and handbooks, but by consulting a search engine. "Conservatively," a cheerful editor from Cambridge University Press told me, "95 per cent of all scholarly inquiries start at Google." And that makes sense: Google, the nerdiest of corporations, has roots in the world of books. According to oral tradition, Google's founders started out with a plan to create an electronic database of the books at Stanford and turned to the Web only because it offered, at that time, a smaller sample size. Google's famous search algorithm, moreover, emulates the principle of scholarly citation. By counting up and evaluating earlier links, Google steers users to the sources that others have already found helpful. In a sense, the hypermodern search engine resembles nothing more than a teeming mass of old-fashioned footnotes. Just as footnotes tell

---

10 Homer (eighth century BCE) is a Greek epic poet, traditionally held to be the author of the *Iliad* and the *Odyssey*.

11 Callimachus (310/305–240 BCE) was a poet, critic, and scholar at the Library of Alexandria. He produced the *Pinakes*, a list of books in the library that is usually considered to be the first library catalogue.

you where an author went to dig up his or her facts and quotations, so Google tells you where most people have gone before you in order to learn what you want to know.

For the last few years, Google and its competitors have been at work on staggeringly ambitious projects, designed to transform the way in which all readers go about finding books. Even the scale of this enterprise is hard to fathom. A conservative estimate of the number of books published throughout history is 32 million: currently, though, Google believes that that there could be as many as 100 million. The company collaborates with publishers—there are currently some 10,000 of these so-called Google partners around the world—to provide information about books currently in print, including text samples, to all users of the Web. So do a number of rival companies. As Google, Amazon, and Barnes & Noble compete, the Web has become a vast and vivid online bookstore. Anyone with a laptop can scan dust jackets, read blurbs, and peek between the covers of the limited group of books that can still be bought. Cambridge University Press, which became a partner in 2004, receives 500,000 page views a month from searchers who began at Google or Google Books. In other words, around two-thirds of all the potential customers for the books of the world's oldest publisher start at Google rather than the press's own Web site.

A second, even larger enterprise—the Google Library Project—has brought the company into collaboration with great libraries around the world. Drawing on the vast collections of Stanford, Harvard, Michigan, the New York Public Library, and many others, Google is digitizing as many out-of-print books as possible. It is an extraordinary effort that Google itself describes as designed to "build a comprehensive **index** of all the books in the world." This index, moreover, will enable readers to search all the books it contains and to see full texts of all those not covered by copyright.

It is hard to exaggerate how much material is becoming accessible month by month and what will become accessible in the next few years, for those who study the distant past or the Third World as well as those primarily concerned with the present. Google is flanked by other big efforts. Some are largely philanthropic, like the old standby Project Gutenberg,[12] which provides hand-keyboarded texts of English and American classics, plain in appearance and easy to use, and the distinctive Million Book Project, founded by Raj Reddy at Carnegie Mellon University. Reddy works with partners around world to provide, among other things, online texts in many languages for which character-recognition software is not yet available.

Add in the hundreds of smaller efforts in specialized fields. Perseus, for example, an incredibly useful site based at Tufts, began with Greek and Latin texts and now embraces works from the English Renaissance. Readers can make direct online use of dictionaries, grammars, and commentaries as they struggle through the originals. There are also new commercial enterprises like Alexander Street, which offers libraries beautifully produced electronic collections of everything from "Harper's Weekly" to the letters and diaries of American immigrants. Even the biggest

12 Project Gutenberg, founded in 1971, is a large collection of e-books, free at the point of access and supplied in a variety of text formats. Its texts of out-of-copyright books have been entered by hand to produce accessible text files with limited formatting.

libraries are expanding faster and more vertiginously than Borges[13] could have dreamt, thanks to the electronic resources listed, at length, on their Web pages.

Many librarians view these developments with warm approval. Kristian Jensen is a dapper, hyperarticulate curator of early printed books at the British Library, who worked with Microsoft on a project, now abandoned, to digitize the library's immense holdings in nineteenth-century literature. His usual style is extremely precise and sober, but when he talks about the prospects of digital libraries, he lights up. "You can't help being enthusiastic," he says, at the thought of all this material becoming available to teachers and students at universities and schools all over the world. One way to see what he means is to visit the web site of the Online Computer Library Center[14] and look at their WorldMap. This imaginative application plots numbers of books in public and academic systems around the world, country by country. Ask the WorldMap to show you how many public library books the world's nations boast: you will see the relation of the Northern to the Southern Hemisphere, and of Western nations to their former colonies, all laid out in stark color. Sixty million Britons have 116 million public library books at their disposal, while the more than 1.1 billion Indians have 36 million.[v]

World poverty, in other words, is embodied in lack of print as well as lack of food—it means that citizens of many nations do not have access to their own literature and history, much less to information about other countries. The Internet, as constituted in its short past, has not yet done much to redress this imbalance. In 2005, when I sat in a tin-roofed, incandescently hot West African Internet cafe and tried to answer questions from my students in America, I could find little high-end material on the screen, and neither, by the look of things, could my Beninese fellow users. By now it would be possible to find far more, and better, digital resources, even on a slow PC in Naititingou. As the capillary spread of electrification reaches smaller and smaller cities, as Internet cafes sprout in small Asian, African, and Latin American towns, and as Google and its rivals fill the Web with solid texts, the map of knowledge will undergo a metamorphosis. Capitalism, of all things, is democratizing access to books at an unprecedented pace.

Kazin loved the New York Public Library because it admitted everyone. Even Kazin's democratic imagination could not have envisaged the Web's new world of information and its hordes of actual and potential users. The Internet cannot feed millions of people or protect them from AIDS or flooding. But it could feed an unlimited number of hungry minds with Paine, Gandhi, Voltaire, and Wollstonecraft[15]—as well as the classics of other cultures, and the manuals of

13 Jorge Louis Borges (1899–1986) was an Argentinian short-story writer, essayist, poet, librarian, and translator. His short story "The Library of Babel" imagined a universe that took the form of a vast, infinite library.

14 The Online Computer Library Center is "a non-profit, world-wide, *computer library* service and research organization." See <www.oclc.org>.

15 Thomas Paine (1737–1809), Mahatma Gandhi (1869–1948), Voltaire (1694–1778), and Mary Wollstonecraft (1759–97) were all rights activists.

sciences and trades, in dozens of languages. The consequences may be seismic, bigger and louder and deeper than we can hope to predict.

Some powerful figures in the realm of books, as we have seen, fear that these projects will simply reinforce the world hegemony of English. Google did begin relatively close to home, working with English-language publishers and British and American collections. But the great American and British libraries that first partnered with Google are stuffed with books in all the languages of the world. Paul Leclerc, director of the New York Public Library (NYPL) and an enthusiastic original partner in the Google Books Project, notes that just under half of the millions of books in NYPL are in languages other than English, many of them Asian, Slavic, and African. Richard Ovenden, who works with Google at the Bodleian Library in Oxford, points out that the millions of books that will be digitized are in some forty languages. Meanwhile, libraries on the Continent and elsewhere are signing Google partnership agreements of their own. The mass of old and new texts on the Web will not be an English-only zone.

For all its virtues, the Google Library Project, in its present, working form, has received mixed reviews, and that is understandable. Google shows the reader a scanned version of the page. These are generally accurate and readable—though individual pages can be blurry or obscured, and scanner operators occasionally miss pages or scan them out of order. Sometimes the copy used is imperfect. In the spirit of the movie *Office Space*,[16] at least one scholarly acquaintance has spotted a body part, scanned with the text. Other problems are more serious. Google uses optical character recognition to produce a second version, for use by its search engine, and this process has some quirks.[17] In a **scriptorium** lit by the sun, a scribe could mistakenly transcribe a "u" as an "n," or vice versa.[18] Curiously, the computer makes the same mistakes. If you enter "qualitas"—an important term in medieval philosophy—in Google Book Search, you will find almost 2,000 appearances. But if you enter "qnalitas," a nonword, you will be rewarded with more than 600 references to "qualitas" that you would not have found using the correct term. That is a lot of "qnalitas." If you want to get a sense of the full magnitude of the problem, call up the Google version of a German book printed in the old spiky type, *Fraktur*, and ask to "view plain text"—the text used for search. In many cases, the system will show you page after page of gobbledygook. It seems significant that the German word for both science and scholarship, "Wissenschaft," often appears as "Wiffenschaft" in these random text zones. It is hard to see how errors on this scale will ever be eliminated—any more than the thousands of errors made when the catalogues of the great university and public libraries were converted into databases will ever be corrected as a whole.

16 *Office Space* is a 1999 American comedy directed by Mike Judge about the dissatisfied employees of a software company.

17 Optical character recognition, usually abbreviated to OCR, is the mechanical or electronic conversion of scanned images typewritten or printed text into machine-encoded text.

18 A scriptorium is "a room set apart for writing, especially one in a monastery where manuscripts were copied" (*OED*).

Serious problems also affect the "metadata," or data about data, that Google offers its users. The cataloguing information that identifies any given item is often incomplete or confusing. Multivolume works can be very hard to use, since Google originally treated them as single items (this policy seems to have changed, perhaps in response to users' complaints: the hive mind at work). And the key terms that Google provides in order to characterize individual books are sometimes unintentionally comic. It is not all that helpful, when you are thinking about how to use an old Baedeker guide to Paris, to be told randomly that one of its central concepts is "fauteuil."[19] The possibilities for glitches, and the pretexts for grumbling, are endless. Scholars, whose interests are minutely precise and philological, inclined by disposition and experience to look on the dark side, often concentrate on these blemishes.[vi]

An analogy may help to highlight Google's accomplishments and limitations. In the 1910s and 1920s, Archibald Cary Coolidge[20] supervised the construction and organization of Harvard University's Widener Library, the world's greatest collection of scholarly books. Like the creators of Google, he worked on a grand scale, deliberately building collections not only of rare and famous works but also of "writings which are neither great nor fashionable," since these were essential for "background and filling in." Like them, too, he emphasized the need to make books as accessible as possible, both by creating a library large enough to hold millions of them and by cataloguing them as rapidly as possible. But Coolidge, as William Bentinck-Smith recorded, "led a life of books. He was seldom without them. In his younger days he traveled across Asia with a little trunk load of them," and in later years he read as he walked in the

country.[vii] Accordingly, when Coolidge set out to create a universal library, he did not simply start buying books by the ton. Instead, he searched the world for integral collections that would add new fields to Widener's holdings, systematically building resources for both present and future research. His directing intelligence, and those of the helpers and donors he inspired, played a vital role in making the Widener a uniquely efficient machine for scholarly work; its catalogues were as accurate as its holdings were comprehensive. The Google Library project aims to be genuinely universal, as no material library can, even the Widener. But it lacks the governing vision of a Coolidge, and accordingly operates less as a vast, coherent ordering mechanism than as a gigantic fire hose dousing the world's readers with texts untouched by human hands or minds. Google could do much more for the world's readers if it invited Coolidge's modern counterparts—masters of both the virtual world of information and the sensuous, material world of real books—to plan and shape its virtual library. At present, though, no evidence suggests that Google sees the future of its enterprise in these terms.

At every turn, technical and economic problems confront Google and its rivals and limit their freedom of action. One of the most frequently discussed difficulties is that of copyright. Google estimates, very roughly, that between 5 and 10 per cent of known books are currently in print. Twenty per cent more—those produced between the beginning of print

---

19 "Armchair" (French).

20 Archibald Cary Coolidge (1866–1928) was a Professor of History (1908–28) at Harvard College and the first Director of the Harvard University Library (1910–28).

in the fifteenth century and 1923—are out of copyright. The remainder—perhaps 75 per cent of all books ever printed—are "orphans," still covered by the very long copyright protections currently in force in Europe and North America, but out of print and pretty much out of mind. Rather as the Alexandrian library confiscated scrolls from ships, Google simply scans as many of these as it can, though it lacks legal permission to do so. But this part of the firm's project remains highly controversial. A number of the publishers who use Google to market their new books have sued to prevent Google from scanning books in copyright without obtaining formal permission—a daunting prospect. For the moment, accordingly, Google is not making these works fully available, and a recent legal settlement only makes it possible to show larger portions of such books to Google users.

Then, too, Google has no immediate plans to scan books from the first couple of centuries of printing. When asked why, computer people sometimes explain that the books' fragile condition makes them hard to scan. That is ridiculous: most early books are far less fragile, thanks to the fine rag paper on which they were printed and the glorious craft skills of their makers, than the nineteenth-century novels—mass-produced on wood pulp paper and now dried out and brittle—that Google's scanners are capturing by the hundreds. The real reason is commercial. Rare books require expensive special conditions for copying, and most of those likely to generate a lot of use have already been made available by companies like Chadwyck-Healey and Gale.[21] These descendants of the microfilm houses sell massive collections to libraries and universities, for substantial fees. Early English Books Online (EEBO) offers 100,000 titles printed between 1475 and 1700, 25,000 of them searchable. Eighteenth Century Collections Online provides searchable full texts of around 150,000 books—33 million pages' worth. Massive tomes in Latin and the little **pamphlets** that poured off the presses during the Puritan revolution,[22] schoolbooks, Jacobean tragedies with prompters' notes, and political pamphlets by wild-eyed Diggers[23] are all available in their original form to any main library user in New York or London, Syracuse or Sydney. Google will not directly explore this territory.

Other vast and vital sectors of the world's book production are neither catalogued nor accessible on site, much less available for digitization. Materials from the poorest societies exert little attraction on companies that rely on subscriptions or advertising. Countries where even big city merchants do not take credit cards will not provide online advertisers with orders, or Google with cash flow. One possible outcome of the current race to digitize, then, is a new version of the existing imbalances between north and south, former metropoles and former colonies. The book-deprived inhabitants of sub-Saharan Africa and much of India may be able to read

21 Chadwyck-Healey is the humanities publishing imprint of ProQuest, an online information database. Gale is an American educational publishing company. Both have produced a number of large full-text databases of early printed matter.

22 Refers to the English Civil War (1642–51) between Parliamentarians and Royalists.

23 Members of "a group of radical dissenters formed in England in 1649 as an offshoot of the Levellers, believing in a form of agrarian communism in which common land would be made available to the poor" (*OED*).

Western works of every kind on screen. It is far less certain that they will be able to find and read texts in their own languages.

Whatever happens on screen, the great libraries of the Northern Hemisphere will remain irreplaceable for a long time. One of the best things computerization will do for everyone is simply to pinpoint the location of the books people need. Astonishingly, for all the hundreds of millions of books in American college and university libraries, there are normally no more than five copies of any given book in a language other than English. Google has always described itself as a company that shows users the way to find the information they need, not as the primary provider of that information. In the carefully chosen words of Jim Gerber, director of Content Partnerships, "We want to make sure readers can find books." The company does this job very well—and we would be foolish to expect its managers to take on further tasks for no extra compensation.

The supposed universal library, then, and its companion universal archive, will not be a seamless mass of books, easily linked and studied together, but a patchwork of different interfaces and databases, some open to anyone with a computer and Wi-Fi, others closed to those who lack access or money. The real challenge now is how to chart the tectonic plates of information that are crashing into one another and then to learn to navigate the new landscapes they are creating. Neither Google nor anyone else will fuse the proprietary collections of early books and the local systems created by individual archives into a single accessible mass of information. Though the distant past will also be more accessible than ever before, in a technical sense, once it is captured and preserved as a vast, disjointed mosaic, it may actually recede ever more rapidly from our collective attention.

We will still need our material libraries and archives. In some ways, we have come to understand better than ever before in the last twenty years or so just what makes old-fashioned, bricks-and-mortar collections essential and distinctive. Historians, literary scholars, and librarians have realized, in the words of John Seely Brown and Paul Duguid, that information leads a "social life" of its own.[24] The form in which you encounter a text can have a huge impact on how you use it. Take the simplest case: If you want to make people believe that a given official document—say, a letter from the commanding officer of a young Texan in the Air National Guard—is genuine, you cannot just give people its wording. You have to show that it is on the right sort of paper, entered in the standard form, and typed on the proper Selectric.[25] The only way to know that for certain is to see the original and compare it to others, and in most cases, you can do that only in an archive where they are reliably stored. As scanning technology improves, **watermarks** and

---

24 John Seely Brown is the Independent Co-Chairman of the Deloitte's Center for the Edge and a visiting scholar and advisor to the Provost at the University of Southern California. Paul Duguid is an adjunct professor at the School of Information at the University of California, Berkeley. Together they published *The Social Life of Information* in 2000.

25 Refers to a Selectric Typewriter. Introduced by IBM in 1961, it was the first typewriter to use a golf ball-like type element that moved across the paper, rather than moving the paper carriage across the print mechanism.

other vital signs are becoming more accessible to remote users. But scholarly or even forensic exactitude still requires direct consultation of original documents.

Original documents and books reward us for taking the trouble to find them by telling us things no image can. Duguid describes watching a fellow historian systematically sniff 250-year-old letters in an archive. By detecting the smell of vinegar—which had been sprinkled on letters from towns struck by cholera in the eighteenth century, in the hope of disinfecting them—he could trace the history of disease outbreaks.[viii] Historians of the book, a new and growing tribe, read books as scouts read trails. **Bindings**—custom made, for the most part, in the early centuries of printing—can tell you who owned them and what level of society they belonged to. **Marginal** annotations—which abounded in the centuries when readers habitually went through books pen in hand—identify the often surprising messages that individuals have found as they read. Many original writers and thinkers—Martin Luther, Hester Thrale Piozzi, John Adams, and Samuel Taylor Coleridge[26]—filled their books with notes that are indispensable to understanding their thought. Thousands of forgotten men and women covered Bibles and prayer books, recipe collections and political pamphlets with pointing hands, underlining, and notes that give deep insight into what their books meant to them—and how they cooked their meals, treated their illnesses, and said their prayers.

If you want to capture how a given book was packaged and what it has meant to the readers who have unwrapped it, as many scholars now do, you have to look not just at all the editions but also at all the copies you can find, from original **manuscripts** to cheap reprints. The databases include multiple copies of some titles, but they will never provide all the copies of, say, Adam Smith's *The Wealth of Nations* and the early responses it provoked.[27] Sometimes, too, the processes that have turned material books into electronic texts have stripped them of the rich evidence that their original form could provide. The texts available on EEBO, for example, were not scanned from the originals, but from microfilms. Their bindings are not reproduced, and it is hard to be sure of their original sizes—two densely material sets of clues that scholars constantly use when working out who read, or was expected to read, a given book. To hear books speak, you have to interview them in their original habitat.

III. Publishing without Paper?

It is not just the conditions of research that are changing, but the whole traditional system of writing and publishing—though here, too, the situation is not easy to read. Books, magazines, daily newspapers, and scholarly journals continue to appear. R.R. Bowker, a company

26 Martin Luther (1483–1546), German monk and theologian and leader of the Protestant Reformation; Hester Thrale Piozzi (1741–1821), English writer; John Adams (1735–1826), American president and founding father; Samuel Taylor Coleridge (1772–1834), English poet and critic.

27 Adam Smith (1723–90) was a Scottish philosopher and political economist, believed to be the founder of modern economics. *The Wealth of Nations* (1776) is his *magnum opus* and a foundational text of modern economic theory.

based in New Providence, New Jersey, compiles what was once a book and is now a database, *Books in Print*. According to Bowker, "publishers in the United States, United Kingdom, Canada, Australia, and New Zealand released 375,000 new titles and editions in 2004 ... Including imported editions available in multiple markets, the total number of new English language books available for sale in the English-speaking world in 2004 was a staggering 450,000."[ix] Go to any branch of Borders or Barnes & Noble or their British counterparts, Blackwell's and Waterstone's, and torrents of brightly jacketed new books on every subject confront you—not to mention stacks of periodicals.

[...]

Revolutions, historians know, are often caused not by oppression and disaster, but by rising expectations. More and more, scholars and scientists expect to find everything they need on the Web. Teachers report that even advanced students refuse to trek to the library: articles available only on paper go unread, even if they are classics. Meanwhile, political authorities complain, with justice, that for-profit journals guard the gates to the kingdom of scientific research paid for by public funds, and earn massive profits by doing so. Many argue that all scholarly and scientific journals—and all university presses—should provide free full-text access to their materials to all. In the case of medical research, Congress has mandated that all 80,000 papers produced every year under the sponsorship of the National Institutes of Health be placed on an open federal database, PubMed, once a year has passed from the date of publication.

The Harvard Faculty of Arts and Sciences has gone even further. It has decided that all members of the faculty should post all of their work on an open Harvard Web page. Editors who hope to publish the work of Harvard professors will simply have to accept that a version of the piece in question is already available to the whole world, or allow the professor to post a PDF file of the work as edited and typeset for their journal. [...]

Critics and true believers converge in emphasizing one feature of Web publication above all: its new form. The traditional book and periodical place a single story, told by a master narrator, in the foreground. Even the most aggressive reader has to accommodate him or herself to the given form of the text. And even the most extensive and aggressive handwritten comments wind themselves around the monumental printed text like ivy growing up a pillar.

Web sites, by contrast, place as much emphasis on images as on words and make lateral movement easier than straightforward progress. Votaries[28] urge the reader to give up the crutches of traditional plot and argument in favor of the self-plotted curves and swoops of this new form of reading. They emphasize that the protean text of the Web, which may change hour by hour as a political crisis unrolls or a hurricane is tracked, fits the conditions of modern life, with its lack of stable beliefs and even of stable human selves. Similarly, they argue that Web sites—which can be dipped into freely for one article or image, and which encourage back talk from their readers—fit the dispersed nature of modern life better than stable print media. Others note that this new

28 "A devoted follower, adherent, or advocate of someone or something" (*OED*).

form of reading is not only dynamic but also interactive. Writers can count the number of hits an article receives on a Web page; readers can use an author's name, laid out in **hypertext**, to send an e-mail response. Discussion strings make it possible for all involved to carry on elaborate debates about a provocative column or review. At their most intense, these discussions metamorphosize into a new kind of reading and writing community—all of whose members exert pressure on the choice and treatment of topics, making the Web site itself interactive.

Critics, by contrast, heap obloquy on many features of these new texts—from the fact that some of them overemphasize design, while their words are often transcribed from out-of-copyright sources or compiled by out-of-work "content providers," to the ubiquitous presence of bright marginal strips of advertising. They insist that the prevalence of such fragmented, labile[29] texts may compromise—even undermine—the print-based ability to grasp complex arguments and reason about them that seems critical to preserving a vital liberal democracy. And they argue that the growth of multiple tiny communities based on the Web will undermine the larger social community in which we all live.

Votaries and critics alike exaggerate the novelty of the changes the Web has wrought. The new media of the decades around 1900 transformed the presentation of texts just as radically as the Web has. Newspapers appeared regularly in multiple editions, rapidly bringing headline stories up to date. In Berlin, by the end of the nineteenth century, one of the major papers could be printed, packed, and on its way to distribution within eighteen minutes after news reached the central office. The existence of several editions each day meant that the newspaper could follow a breaking story—like the hunt for an escaped murderer—stage by stage. Sometimes, of course, editors themselves promoted, or even created, stories of this kind. The *Berliner Zeitung* sent a reporter through the city, for example, while urging readers to try to catch him—an effective way to galvanize readers' interest and commitment, brilliantly evoked by Graham Greene in *Brighton Rock*.[30] Kiosks, pillars, and cafes made each new edition available to readers. The city itself spoke, as Peter Fritzsche has shown, spewing an endless stream of stories and sense impressions over its inhabitants.[x]

The newspapers and magazines of the early years of the century did not have the near-total flexibility of the modern web site, and their readers could not skip from one hot link to the next. But their mixture of commerce and culture, their juxtapositions of serious and trivial contents, and their ability to confront readers with the shock of the new were as widely noticed—and sometimes as forcefully deplored—by contemporaries as the similar features of the Web. Like the Web, too, the new magazines and newspapers invited their readers to see themselves as members of a single community. The evidence suggests that they often succeeded. Readership surveys collected information about audience response; readers' letters identified particular stories and articles as controversial or rewarding; and readers of

29 "Liable to change; easily altered" (*OED*).

30 Published in 1938, *Brighton Rock* is a murder thriller set in 1930s Brighton, by English writer Graham Greene (1904–91). At the beginning of the novel, one of the characters comes to Brighton to distribute cards relating to a newspaper stunt similar to the one Grafton describes here.

magazines as diverse as the *Saturday Evening Post* and the *New Yorker* professed that they kept their subscriptions because—as readers wrote to the latter—it says "what I think and feel"; "It has to be good sense, because we agree with everything you say." Those who sent in such messages, as a study of the *New Yorker* by Mary Corey has established, included a bird curator at a museum, a UN official, an editor, doctors, enlisted men, a British war bride and a former chorus boy—about as diverse a group as have ever shared any serious interest.[xi] In some ways, the world of writing has not so much been transformed as restored to a ghostly, faster-moving simulacrum of the media world of half a century ago.

By contrast, the world of serious reading does seem to be changing, in two related ways. As readers gain private, off-site access to treasures once confined to the British and New York Public Libraries, they may stay home in their pajamas rather than schlepping in, like the hard-pressed content providers in George Gissing's *New Grub Street*,[31] to the Valley of the Shadow of the Book.[32] Even in the great years of the nineteenth- and twentieth-century metropolitan library, after all, the greatest scholars—the historian Leopold von Ranke, for example, or the social scientist Werner Sombart—did most of their work in their own enormous collections.[33] In Berlin, where great professors were public figures, richly paid, these might contain as many as 30,000 books. It is hard to feel anything but pleasure at the thought that Google may enable impoverished graduate students to emulate the mandarins[34] of yesterday, and work where they like.

Yet great city and university libraries have long been America's symbolic centers of culture—the nurseries of Kazins and Hofstadters. Traditionally, they have occupied the grandest of public

buildings—material, public testimony to the powers of the book. Pursuing one's studies in an environment like this was a way of learning an artisanal craft. Librarians, older scholars, and graduate students passed on informal advice. The library's own ways of collecting information—like the magnificent subject cards in the old New York Public Library catalogue—directed the reader to extraordinary finds. And a sighting of a celebrity like Frank Manuel or Barbara Tuchman could leave a young student vibrating for weeks with the sense that hard work might lift one from the Valley of the Shadow to Parnassus.[35]

A number of great American cities have recently built big central libraries. They range in style from neo-Beaux-Arts celebrations of the traditional culture of the book to bright, glassy, open civic centers. And as Witold Rybczynski pointed out in a recent "slide-show essay" in *Slate*, the heavy facades and elegant, sterile reading rooms of the libraries in Chicago and San Francisco

---

31 A novel, published in 1891, about a struggling community of writers in London at the end of the nineteenth century, by English writer George Gissing (1857–1903).

32 Grafton plays on the phrase "the Valley of the Shadow of Death," from Psalm 23:4.

33 Leopold von Ranke (1795–1886) was a leading nineteenth-century German historian. Werner Sombart (1863–1941) was a German historical economist.

34 Powerful officials or senior bureaucrats, occupying positions of privilege.

35 Frank Manuel (1910–2003) and Barbara Tuchman (1912–89) were both American historians. Parnassus is a mountain in central Greece associated with Apollo and the Muses and generally regarded as a symbol of poetry.

seem to be crying out "Books still matter! Conan the Librarian[36] is still in charge!" to a public that shows little interest. By contrast, the newer libraries in Seattle and Kansas City are hip, appealing structures that deliberately depart from tradition. Rem Koolhaas did not even equip his ziggurat in Seattle with a reading room.[37] These buildings pull in crowds composed of everyone, from graduate students to tourists to homeless people.[xii]

The lesson Rybczynski draws is simple. Books have probably passed their sell-by date, as some prophets claim. Libraries, as such, are dinosaurs, doomed to extinction. But build a really attractive building and call it a central library—a mall with natural light, interesting spaces, and a comic book shop, like the new library in Salt Lake City—and the punters will come. Not for the books, but for the excitement and the human connections that only a great public space can generate. Libraries, in other words, can survive. But if they insist on their original mission, they will turn into enormous, handsome ghost ships, sailing along with all lights on and no passengers. On the other hand, if administrators decide that they can save libraries by sweeping all their dusty, old-fashioned books into off-site storage and filling their cavernous, loft-like spaces with the cafes and fast computers that might woo the crowds back, these treasure houses will degenerate into bigger versions of Starbucks or Barnes & Noble: splendid public spaces that people frequent to use electronic sources, most of which they could find anywhere. Neither fate seems desirable: and neither will restore the old function of the library as a training center for the crafts of scholarship.

As the books head for off-site warehouses, moreover, reading itself seems to be under threat. The newspapers and magazines of the years around 1900 co-existed with more stable forms of writing—above all the serious book—and presupposed the superiority of engaged, informed study of texts even when they did not promote it. By contrast, the hot link and the search engine seem to symbolize a particular postmodern way of approaching texts: rapid, superficial, appropriative, and individualistic. Readers do not need to master catalogues, to walk stacks, to use bibliographies—much less to work through stacks of books. All they need to do is enter a word or two into Google and compile the results. Some fear that the old-fashioned scholar's memory, stored with texts not only read, but digested and turned into marrow and bone, and the old-fashioned reader's deep play with novels and poetry studied for years, have given way to endless bricolage, mosaics assembled by students and writers who know only the bits of texts they pull from the screen.

A report recently commissioned by the British Library and the Joint Information Systems Committee details the reading practices of contemporary university students, using data drawn from actual search strings. Most students begin their searches for information at Google, rather than a library Web page that lists more refined search engines. Those who consult e-book sites stay on them for an average of four minutes. True, students who consult e-journals stay longer:

36 Reference to Conan the Barbarian, a fictional sword and sorcery hero created by Robert E. Howard.

37 The Seattle Central library, a hypermodern building designed by the architect Rem Koolhaas (b. 1944) and opened in 2004. A ziggurat is a rectangular stepped tower, but the term here is used loosely to describe this angular, asymmetrical, eleven-storey building.

eight minutes, on average. But around 60 per cent of them look at no more than three pages of the article in question, and the majority never return to the site. The reading that most students do on the Web takes the form of "dipping," "cross-checking," and "power skimming"—just as the traditionalists croak.

IV. Future Reading

For now and for the foreseeable future, any serious reader will have to know how to travel down two very different roads simultaneously. No one should avoid the broad, smooth, and open road that leads through the screen into an electronic paradise of texts and images. But if you want to know what one of Coleridge's annotated books or an early "Spiderman" comic really looks and feels like, or if you just want to read one of those millions of books that are being digitized but cannot as yet be opened and read—you still have to do it the old way, and you will have to for decades to come. At Kazin's beloved New York Public Library, the staff loves electronic media. The library has made hundreds of thousands of images from its collections accessible on the Web, and Google is digitizing more than a million books from the stacks. Still, the library has done all this in the knowledge that its collections comprise 53 million items. To ensure that as many of these as possible find users, it must keep bums on pews and books and documents in front of readers.

Sit in your local coffee shop and your laptop can tell you a lot, especially if you wield your search terms adeptly. But if you want deeper, more local knowledge, you will still have to take the narrower path that leads between the lions and up the stone stairs.[38] There—as in great libraries around the world—you will use all the new sources, all the time. You will check musicians' names and dates at Grove Music Online,[39] read Marlowe's Doctor Faustus on Google Books or EEBO, or savor the idiosyncrasies of British justice as exhibited in the online proceedings of the Old Bailey.[40] But these streams of data, rich as they are, will illuminate rather than eliminate the unique books and prints and manuscripts that only the library can put in front of you. For now, and for the foreseeable future, if you want to piece together the richest possible mosaic of documents and texts and images, you will have to do it in those crowded public rooms where sunlight gleams on varnished tables, as it has for more than a century, and knowledge is still embodied in millions of dusty, crumbling, smelly, irreplaceable manuscripts and books.

Notes

i. Alfred Kazin, *New York Jew* (New York: Knopf, 1978), 5–7.

---

38 Reference to the marble lions (named "Patience" and "Fortitude"), sculpted by Edward Clark Potter (1857–1923), which stand outside of the New York Public Library.

39 An online resource for music research created by Oxford University Press, based on the multi-volume print work *Grove Dictionary of Music and Musicians*.

40 The Central Criminal Court of England and Wales; details of cases from its history can now be searched online.

ii. Kevin Kelly, "Scan This Book!," *New York Times*, 14 May 2006.

iii. Jean-Noël Jeanneney, *Quand Google défie L'Europe: Plaidoyer pour un sursaut* (Paris: Mille et une nuits, 2005).

iv. Lionel Casson, *Libraries in the Ancient World* (New Haven, CT: Yale UP, 2001).

v. For the OCLC WorldMap, see <http://www.oclc.org/research/projects/worldmap/default.htm>.

vi. See further Robert Townsend, "Google Books: What's Not to Like?" *AHA Today*, 29 April 2007, <http://blog.historians.org/articles/204/google-books-whats-not-to-like>, and discussion thread.

vii. William Bentinck-Smith, *Building a Great Library: The Coolidge Years at Harvard* (Cambridge, MA: Harvard University Library, 1976).

viii. John Seely Brown and Paul Duguid, *The Social Life of Information* (Boston: Harvard Business School P, 2000), 173–74.

ix. See <http://findarticles.com/p/articles/mi_m0EIN/is_2005_Oct_12/ai_n15686131> (accessed 13 August 2008).

x. Peter Fritzsche, *Reading Berlin 1900* (Cambridge, MA: Harvard UP, 1996).

xi. Mary Corey, *The World Through a Monocle: The New Yorker at Midcentury* (Cambridge, MA: Harvard UP, 1999), 15.

xii. Witold Rybczynski, "How Do You Build a Public Library in the Age of Google?" *Slate*, 27 February 2008.

Glossary

This glossary is designed to help you understand specialist terms used in this Reader, but it is by no means a comprehensive guide to terminology used in bibliography, printing history, or textual scholarship. For fuller information, please consult the following reference works:

- John Carter and Nicolas Barker, *ABC for Book Collectors*, 8th ed. (New Castle, DE: Oak Knoll P, 2004).
- Geoffrey Ashall Glaister, *Encyclopedia of the Book*, 2nd ed. (New Castle, DE: Oak Knoll P, 2001).
- *OED* Online (Oxford University Press).
- Philip Gaskell, *A New Introduction to Bibliography* (New Castle, DE: Oak Knoll P, 2000).
- Elizabeth H. Thompson, *A.L.A. Glossary of Library Terms* (Chicago: American Library Association, 1943).

Almanac

A yearly calendar accompanied by statistics, such as astronomical data, tide times, dates for planting certain crops, weather data, or other information. Originally intended for farmers and fishermen, they were popular among uneducated readers by the seventeenth century in England, and by the eighteenth century also in France and America, where the term was used for other annual publications aimed either at a laboring-class or a bourgeois audience, including fashion almanacs.

Analytical bibliography (see Bibliography)

Anthology

A published collection of writings (which may be excerpts, or short works in their entirety) by multiple authors.

Archive

A collection of historical or public documents, or the building in which these are housed; also used as a term for scientific or academic periodicals from the early eighteenth century.

Belles lettres

A category of writings that encompasses forms of non-fiction prose including literary criticism, essays, and correspondence. French for "beautiful literary works."

Bibliography

Broadly, the study of books as material objects. *Descriptive bibliography* is primarily concerned with discerning and recording in detail the material properties of a document, including its size, format, collation (the arrangement of leaves that make up the book), and the presence or absence of title pages, errata slips, advertisement leaves, and other paratexts. Bibliographers record these details using a system of symbols and abbreviations. *Analytical (or critical) bibliography* uses this study, combined with knowledge of the history of printing, to establish the order in which editions were printed, the order in which pages within a book were printed, and the number of compositors and pressmen who worked on it. This information helps to resolve textual cruces, where editors need to decide which of two variant readings is more likely to reflect the author's intentions. The use of bibliographical procedures to address textual or editorial problems is sometimes called "*New Bibliography*" to distinguish it from the older tradition of treating bibliography primarily as something of interest to collectors of rare books. (See also Paleography.)

Bibliothèque bleue

A collection of small, cheaply produced and illustrated books produced for the semi-literate rural market in France by the Oudot firm of printers and publishers based in Troyes and sold by peddlers in the seventeenth to mid-nineteenth centuries. The majority of these books retold medieval romances, but they also included almanacs with farming advice and weather predictions, biographies of infamous criminals, condensed versions of novels, and devotionals. French for "blue library."

Binder; Bindery; Binding (see Bookbinding)

Blackletter

The group of scripts that emerged in Europe in the twelfth century and formed the design for early printing types. (See also Typography.)

Bookbinding

The process through which printed or manuscript sheets are fastened together and enclosed in a cover, which may be made of materials such as leather, board, or cloth. A process distinct from printing, binding was undertaken by binders (their workshops being known as binderies), although some early printers either were also binders or worked systematically with specific binders. In England from about the sixteenth to the late eighteenth century, arranging for binding seems to have become the purview of booksellers who received works in sheets and then often offered both bound and unbound versions to customers; individualized and often decorative bindings could be a way for book purchasers to customize their books, and they may have purchased works in sheets and then worked with a preferred binder, especially in order to assure the uniformity of a collection. Different bindings could significantly affect the total cost of a book. Only from the nineteenth century on were books routinely sold in their bindings.

Bookseller (as opposed to publisher and printer)

The individual responsible for selling books to the public through a retail bookshop; some booksellers also sold books wholesale to other booksellers. Until roughly the eighteenth century in England the roles of printer, publisher, and bookseller were not always clearly differentiated.

Bookstall

A stall where books are sold; bookstalls became enormously important in England with the advent of the railway. The first train station bookstall was established in 1848, and by 1860 almost all train stations had vendors selling newspapers and cheap books to railway passengers.

Broadside

A document printed on one side only of a single sheet of paper. Originally associated with political proclamations, they also became a mode of transmission for poetry and ballads, and can also be known as *broadsheets, street or stall ballads*, or *blackletter ballads* (due to the predominant use of blackletter type).

Calligraphy

Beautiful handwriting or penmanship.

Cancel (n.)

A part of a book that is substituted for an original part with the aim of modification. Cancels can range in size from a square containing a single letter to several sheets; perhaps most common is the leaf inserted where another leaf containing errors has been cut out. Motivations for inserting a cancel may include the rectification of printer's errors as well as last-minute changes, additions, and deletions.

Canon (adj. canonical)

A body of texts agreed, by general consensus, to have merit and to be worthy of regard and respect; also sometimes used to mean a group of texts firmly attributed to one author. In its non-literary implications, the term may also refer to ecclesiastical authority (for example, canon law, which is the category of rules and regulations governing Christian churches).

Catalogue

A listing (either digital or physical) of books available for a given purpose; in the case of a library's catalogue, this purpose will be consultation and possibly circulation via lending, whereas in the case of a publisher's catalogue, the purpose will be sales.

Catchword

A word printed at the foot of the page, which is the same as the first word on the next page. Catchwords often appear in early printed books, and were used to assist the binder in arranging the sheets in the correct order.

Censorship

Censorship is the suppression of work that is deemed to be objectionable on political, religious, moral, or other grounds, or on the grounds that its publication would compromise national security or endanger the safety of individuals. It may take the form of pre-publication censorship, in regimes that require works to be submitted for review before permitting their publication, or post-publication censorship, where authorities may require published works deemed objectionable to be withdrawn from circulation. Authors and publishers may also engage in self-censorship, moderating or changing their works to avoid adverse reactions.

Chapbook

Small, cheap, paperbound pamphlet or book containing a popular tale, legend, poem, ballad, often of moral or educational character, usually illustrated with a woodcut and distributed by hawkers or chapmen, not booksellers. Since about 1830, the term has been used as a conscious anachronism.

Chirography

The study of handwriting and penmanship.

Circulating library

Established in the latter part of the seventeenth century and most likely originating with booksellers in London, circulating libraries were privately owned, commercial libraries; readers paid a subscription, and in some cases also a small fee, for each book borrowed. Circulating libraries carried a variety of works but were especially important in the circulation of three-volume novels. In the nineteenth century, Mudie's circulating library routinely purchased a large proportion of the total print run of new novels. (See also Library.)

Circulation

Describes the process by which manuscript, print, or oral texts are disseminated. Circulation can take place in more or less conventional ways; it can be narrow or broad; and it can take place across media (e.g., an orally recited poem might be remembered, and then hand-copied and distributed; a printed work could be read aloud; a manuscript could be printed; etc.). All forms of circulation involve the passing of texts between individuals.

Codex (pl. codices)

A document, either printed or in manuscript, in which multiple sheets are stacked, bound along a spine, and generally enclosed by a cover; i.e., the format of most modern books, as opposed to scrolls.

Collation

The physical makeup of a book, or a description of it for the purposes of comparison with other books. The description may be more or less detailed, but will typically contain information about the end-papers, title page(s), and the sheets from which the book is made, including how they are folded and stitched together to make the book. Collation also refers to the comparison and classification of the variant forms of a given text (these may be print or manuscript versions, or a combination of the two). The aim is to identify differences between the texts in which the work appears so as to clarify problems of interpretation, authentication, and textual history.

Colophon

Frequently used in early printed works, a colophon is a statement at the end of the main text giving particulars such as the title, subject of the work, the author, the publisher, the printer, and the date and place of publication. Sometimes found with the device, or imprint, of the printer or publisher and information about the typeface. Since the sixteenth century in England the colophon has been replaced by the title page; however, during the transition period the colophon and the title page were both in use, sometimes in contradiction with one another, when, for instance, a new title page was printed with an out-of-date colophon. The colophon is occasionally used in the present day, mostly in fine-press printing.

Commonplace book

A handwritten collection of extracts, usually compiled in a small notebook, chosen at the discretion of an individual, either as an aid to study or primarily on the basis of personal interest and pleasure, and transcribed by that same individual; may also include original compositions or other material.

Composition

The setting up of type. A compositor takes individual pieces of type from a type case and arranges them in a composing stick to form words and lines of text. The type is then transferred from the composing stick to a metal tray, where the lines of type form a page. Several pages are arranged ("imposed") and assembled into a type forme ready for printing on the handpress. (See also Compositor.)

Compositor

Craftsman who set up type by hand or machine, corrected machine-set compositions, made up and imposed pages, and assembled the type forme. (See also Composition.)

Concordance

An alphabetical index of the principal words in a work or group of works, showing their location in the text, usually giving context, and sometimes supplying a definition.

Copper engraving (see Engraving)

Copyright

Copyright is a legal right to reproduce in some form (print, performance, film, or record) a written, artistic, or musical work, within a defined geographical area. The first copyright law was the Statute of Anne, enacted in England in 1710. The first *international copyright* agreement, the Berne Convention, was passed in 1886; it protected the rights of creators in all countries who had signed the convention. Copyright initially rests with the creator of the work, but it can be transferred to a third party such as a publisher. Subsidiary rights, such as the right to publish translations or to adapt the work for film or television, may be governed by other legal agreements.

Copy-text (see Edition)

Corruption

The introduction of errors into the text in the process of transmission, for example when a scribe copies a word incorrectly, or when a compositor misreads a manuscript when setting it in type.

Coterie

A small, select group of individuals, usually organized with social and/or intellectual aims. Coterie members often wrote texts for, and exchanged them with, other members of the group.

Digital Literacy

The ability to find, navigate, evaluate, use, share, and create content using a range of digital technologies.

Duodecimo

A book printed on sheets folded to make twelve leaves or twenty-four pages. Commonly called a *twelvemo* (12mo, 12o). The size of the book will depend on the size of the sheets, but the large number of folds means that most duodecimos are small books, easily carried in a pocket. For this reason, duodecimo is a common format for prayer books. (See also Format.)

Edition

1) all the copies of a book printed from a single setting of type. In handpress printing, the type is set to produce a book and then broken up and returned to the typecase for use in the next printing job. If the type is reset to print more copies (usually at a later date), then

those copies form a new edition of the work. The number of copies of each edition printed is known as that edition's print run. The title page often includes the number of the edition, or words such as "a new edition." These indicators, however, are not always reliable, since booksellers, printers or publishers sometimes added a new title page to an existing edition, or deliberately misnumbered editions to give the impression that a work was selling very well.

2) a later printing, usually of a canonical work or historical document, prepared by an editor. These editions may be of several kinds. Most editions begin by identifying a text of the work to use as the *copy-text* for the new edition. The editor may then choose to produce a *facsimile reprint* or *diplomatic transcription* of a copy-text, an *eclectic edition* that emends the copy-text to include variant readings found in other texts, a *variorum edition* that includes details of readings from all significant texts of the work, a *parallel text edition* that allows readers to compare two versions on facing pages, or another kind of edition. These choices will depend on the editor's understanding of editorial theory, the textual history of the work under consideration, and the intended audience of the edition.

Editor/Editing

Editing divides into pre- and post-publication editing. An *editor* is anyone who undertakes the editing of a text. The editor's role could be formal or informal; she might be a friend, relative, teacher, colleague, or a professional editor. Pre-publication *editing* involves making suggestions to the author for additions, excisions, revisions, and corrections. This can be done in any medium; for example, an editor might revise a text in manuscript; an author or editor might correct print proofs of a text prior to it being published; a compositor might make further corrections when setting type; and an author or reader might further revise a text after it is published, by adding revisions in handwriting to a copy of a printed text and/or issuing a new edition. Post-publication editing involves emending a text for a new edition of the work. The aim of such editing is usually (but not always) to reflect the author's intentions more precisely than earlier texts of the work have done.

Emblem (adj. emblematic)

A pictorial image that depicts a concept or idea.

Engraving

Engraving is one of several techniques for producing printed images (and the chief reproductive method before the introduction of photography in the second half of the nineteenth century). The engraver scrapes lines into a copper plate with a sharp instrument called a burin, and then spreads ink over the plate and wipes the plate clean. Some ink remains in the grooves made by the burin. A sheet of paper is then laid on the plate and the whole thing is passed through a rotary press, which applies pressure and squeezes some of the ink out of the grooves and onto the paper. This process was used in Europe at least as early as the fourteenth century, and possibly even earlier, for playing cards and religious pictures. It produces high-quality images, but there are three limitations associated with it. First, the printing process is different from that used for letterpress text, which makes it difficult to combine text and image on a single page. Using woodcuts, where the image is cut into the end of a block of wood, allows images to be reproduced alongside text, as woodcuts and letterpress are both printed on the same kind of press. Second, the effort required to work the plate with the burin is considerable, and only the most highly accomplished engravers can produce a wide range of effects, such as shading. *Etching* reduces the effort involved in producing the plate and allows a wider range of effects: in etching, the plate is covered with wax or a similar material, and this wax is scraped away to reveal some areas of the surface of the plate. The plate is then immersed in acid, which eats into the exposed areas. It is then cleaned, inked, and printed in the same way as an engraving. Thirdly, since copper is fairly soft, the plate becomes damaged in the process of printing, which means that only a limited number of images can be produced from each plate. The use of steel plates in place of copper from the mid-nineteenth century onwards allowed larger numbers of impressions from each plate. In some discussions of printed images, "engraving" is used as an umbrella term for all these techniques, as well as a specific term for one of them.

Ephemera

Printed material of a transitory kind, not intended for preservation. Examples include tickets, labels, posters, and playbills.

Epistle

1) a letter from an apostle, for example St Paul, forming part of the New Testament.

2) letters regarded as literary works because of their elegant composition, sometimes written in poetry; collections of letters were made into manuals in the Middle Ages and had become a popular branch of rhetoric by the tenth century.

Errata

A list of typographical errors occurring in a book, along with corrections, also called corrigenda. If the prelims have not yet been completed, the errata are sometimes added to a spare page; otherwise they are printed on a slip or extra leaf and tipped in. When multi-volume books are published at intervals, later volumes sometimes contain lists of errata for the earlier. When errors are not detected until after publishing, only later copies may contain an errata slip or leaf, but since errata slips are prone to accidental detachment or omission, this makes it difficult to verify and poses a problem for collectors. In most cases the book is considered complete with an errata slip if the majority of copies have an errata slip, and vice versa.

Etching

The application of chemicals to a surface so as to either dissolve part of the material, creating a design (the other parts having been previously treated so as to be protected), or create different properties on that surface. (See also Engraving.)

Extensive/Intensive reading

Whereas extensive reading involves reading widely among a larger body of texts with less sustained attention to any given one, intensive reading confines itself to a smaller body of texts that are the subject of careful study and repeated attention. Some historians of reading postulate a shift from intensive to extensive reading as books became cheaper and more widely available.

Facsimile

A copy or reproduction of a manuscript, printed book, map, etc. that attempts to replicate the original as closely as possible.

Fair Copy

A clear or legible manuscript copy, often one that incorporates revisions made on a previous copy.

Folio

A book printed on full-size sheets folded medially once, making two leaves or four pages. (See also Format.)

Format

The way in which printed sheets are folded and gathered together to form the leaves of a book.
In a folio (Fo, 1o) each sheet has been folded once, making two leaves (four pages), where the leaf is half of the original sheet. In a quarto (Qto, 4to, 4o) each sheet is folded twice, making four leaves (eight pages), where the leaves are a quarter of the original sheet. In an octavo (oct., 8vo, 8o) the sheets have been folded to make eight leaves (sixteen pages). In a duodecimo (12mo) each sheet is folded to make twelve leaves (twenty-four pages). Smaller formats are possible and are usually designated 16mo, etc., but these are uncommon.

If the folded sheets are simply stacked on top of each other for sewing, then the format is indicated by a single term. If the sheets are nestled inside each other to form gatherings, the format of the completed book is expressed as, e.g., quarto in eights. The exact size of books in different formats depends on the size of the sheets, which varies according to the manufacturer. For this reason, leaf measurements are normally used when more precision is necessary.

Forme

Body of type that has been arranged into pages and prepared for printing; the frame containing this type.

Frontispiece

An illustration preceding the title page of the book, normally printed on the verso of the front free endpaper facing the title page. A volume is considered to have multiple frontispieces if two or more such leaves precede the title page. It is important to note, as well, that when plates are numbered in an illustrated book, the frontispiece is rarely included in this numbered sequence.

Galleys

Galleys is short for galley proofs, which are preliminary printed copies of a work that the printer sends to the author (or his/her designate), editor, or proofreader for corrections. Galley proofs are named for the galleys, or metal trays, in which a printer (in the days of the handpress) laid and tightened type into place. Galley proofs represent an earlier stage of print production than page proofs, and extensive editing was often expected at the galley stage. Page proofs represent a later part of the prepublication process, when most of the corrections and edits are expected to have already been done. Making corrections at the page-proof stage is generally discouraged as it involves more expense.

Gathering

A number of sheets folded together for binding. (See also Format.)

Gloss

Explanations inserted into a manuscript or printed text for the sake of clarification, either in the case of foreign phrases or difficult meaning. May appear either in the margin or directly in the text, often as footnotes or endnotes.

Gutenberg

Johannes Gutenberg (1398–1468) was a German printer and publisher who used previous technologies in addition to his own inventions to create moveable type and the handpress around 1440.

Half-title (see Title page)

Handpress

A printing press powered by hand, invented around 1440 by Johannes Gutenberg and based on existing presses used for making wine or olive oil. The handpress, along with moveable type, made it possible to produce books much more quickly, reliably, and cheaply than copying by hand. It was replaced by steam-powered rotary presses in the nineteenth century.

Holograph

A manuscript written entirely in the hand of the author.

Hypertext

Digital text that is displayed on the screens of computers or other digital devices and that offers access, commonly through a mouse click, key sequence, or, in the case of touch screens, pressure, at designated points (hyperlinks) to additional text, as well as images and other graphics. Its most familiar application is the World Wide Web.

Illuminated manuscripts

Manuscripts that contain hand-painted decorations, often adorning initial letters, single words, or first lines, but also included in the margins or as full-page illustrations. Illuminations may feature gold, silver, or colored designs.

Imprint

Written formula that specifies the individuals responsible for the production of a book, generally including a name, place of publication, and date; may refer to either a printer's imprint or the publisher's imprint, or to a combination of the two. Most commonly located either on the title page or at the end of the book.

Incipit

Meaning "here begins" in Latin, the incipit was the opening word of a medieval manuscript or early printed work, or of one of its divisions. Sometimes referred to as the title caption if it occurs at the beginning of the book, where it may introduce the author's name and title of the work.

Incunabulum (pl. incunabula)

Derived from the Latin term meaning "thing in the cradle." While more generally it refers to the earliest stages of development in anything, in bibliographic terms it refers to books that were printed from moveable type before 1501.

Index

A list of the predominant topics discussed in a (generally non-fiction) text, arranged alphabetically, that directs readers to the relevant pages on which those topics are discussed. It is generally located at the end of a work.

Intaglio printing

A form of printing where the ink sits in incised areas of the printing surface and is then squeezed out as the printing surface passes through the press. Its most common application in the production of books is to produce engravings or etchings using the rotary press. (See also Engraving; Planographic printing; Relief printing.)

Intensive reading (see Extensive/Intensive reading)

Jobbing work

Printing, usually commercial, that produces documents not catalogued as books, periodicals, or newspapers; examples may include menus, invitation cards, and posters. Most printing houses took on jobbing work, which was done in between printing books and represented a significant portion of the press's income.

Leaf

A leaf is one of the units into which the original sheet is folded to make a book. Each leaf consists of two pages, one on its front side (recto, obverse) and one on its back (verso, reverse). Leaf, leaves are abbreviated as l., ll., or f., ff. (See also Format.)

Lexicography

The practice of writing and compiling dictionaries, and the subsequent study of these practices.

Library

A collection of resources (which may include printed or handwritten texts, as well as digital resources). The collection may be made available to a community of individuals for consultation and/or borrowing. Criteria for belonging to the community of users varies and may include relationships (*family library*, which refers to the collection of books owned by a particular family and thus available to its members and other individuals to whom it chooses to grant access), geography (many *public libraries* are funded through the taxation of the population of a given area), membership in a larger institution that funds the collection

(*university libraries*), or paid subscription (*circulating libraries*). Libraries may vary widely in size and degree of specialization and often evolve complex systems of organization and categorization so as to render their resources available. Increasingly, libraries may offer digital, rather than physical, access to resources (e.g., online journals, e-texts).

Licensing Act

A British Act of Parliament in effect between 1662 and 1695. It granted significant authority to the Stationers' Company, allowing for the imposition of restrictions on the number of printers and presses, and enabling works to be censored prior to publication. Under the Act, a member of the Company could register a given book and then have the exclusive right to print, copy, and publish it. The Act was controversial, and when it was allowed to lapse permanently in 1695 there followed a long series of unsuccessful attempts to introduce replacement legislation.

Linotype

Linotype is a process developed in the late nineteenth century by German-American Ottmar Mergenthaler (1854–99) to facilitate typesetting and casting: after an operator enters text with a keyboard, the machine assembles the matrices (that is, the molds from which type is produced) and casts an entire line of type at once, rather than on a letter-by-letter basis, therefore greatly increasing the speed of typesetting and facilitating, in particular, the publication of newspapers and journals. (See also Typography.)

Literacy

Generally, the ability to read and write (as well as the extent of this ability in a given time period or geographic location), though it may also be used more generally to refer to competence in a given field (for example, *digital literacy*). Historically, the ability to read and write did not always go together, since the two skills were taught separately.

Lithography

A planographic printing process developed at the end of the eighteenth century in Germany that relies on the use of a flat plate (neither incised nor raised) that may be either metal or stone: the image is marked on the plate with an oily substance and the remaining area is treated to render it water-attracting: thus, when inked, the ink is attracted only to the image to be impressed. Widely used in cartography, commercial stationery, and other non-book printed matter, it greatly facilitated the production of color illustrations.

Manuscript

A work written by hand, abbreviated as ms/MS or pluralized as mss/MSS.

Manuscript miscellanies

A term closely associated with *commonplace books*, and sometimes used interchangeably, manuscript miscellanies denote hand-written collections of excerpts, anecdotes, epigrams, and sometimes original writings, generally contained in a notebook or other small, portable format, and intended for private use. Manuscript miscellanies tend to be compiled in a fairly short period of time, and the principle of selection is generally personal pleasure or edification.

Marginalia (adj. marginal)

Material, separate from the main content of a document, which is either written or printed into the margins, often by readers. May include notes, comments, and illustrations, and often (but not always) relates or responds to the main content.

Monograph

A systematic treatise on a particular subject.

Moveable type

Single-letter pieces of type, which are arranged to make words for printing. Once printed, they can be reused to make new words. (See also Compositor.)

MS/MSS (see Manuscript)

New Bibliographers (see Bibliography)

Octavo

A book made by folding the printed sheet to form eight leaves (sixteen pages). Octavos were one of the most common formats in the eighteenth and nineteenth centuries. (See also Format.)

Orality/Oralism

Transmission of information through vocal mechanisms (primarily speech and song) rather than written symbols. *Oral culture* refers to this being the predominant mode of transmission amongst a given group, or in a given time or historical period. *Oral works* are those shared by oral means, sometimes through formalized recitations; as such, they often possess features to aid with memorization and recitation.

Page

One side of a leaf. (See also Format.)

Page proofs (see Galleys)

Paleography

The study of manuscripts, including early forms of handwriting, illumination (illustration of initial letters, margins etc.), rubrication (use of red letters for headings), and the production and circulation of manuscripts.

Palimpsest

Literally a piece of vellum that has been written on, scraped clean, and reused, where erased layers of writing remain visible on close analysis beneath new layers added on top of them. The term is also applied more generally to any piece of writing created, literally or metaphorically, from several layers, drafts, or revisions, where erased or rejected words can still be recovered.

Pamphlet

A short complete work, usually polemical in nature, printed unbound, and making use of either staples or sewn pages instead, occasionally utilizing paper wrappers, and designed for wide circulation.

Papyrus

Writing material made from a large variety of rushes by the ancient Egyptians. In use in Egypt in the eleventh century BCE and in Greece and Rome by the fourth century BCE.

Paratext (adj. paratextual)

Any of the textual elements that surround the main body of a printed book, including but not limited to title pages, half-titles, advertisement leaves, prefaces, errata slips, blurbs, dedications, epigraphs, annotations, appendices, and indices.

Parchment

Used primarily as a writing surface (although sometimes also for binding), parchment is formed from the untanned, split portion of an animal's skin, usually a sheep or goat. It is prepared through a process of stretching and scraping so as to produce an even writing surface.

Patronage

The practice of a wealthy patron, such as a member of the upper class or nobility, who provides support to authors, thereby allowing them to write. Sometimes authors would write works dedicated to or commissioned by a patron.

Philology (adj. philological)

The study of language in written historical sources.

Piracy

Publishing an edition of a work without the permission of the copyright owner. (See also Copyright.)

Plagiarism

Literary theft; the action or practice of taking the work of someone else and presenting it as one's own.

Planographic printing

A family of printing techniques (*lithography* being one example) in which designs are created using a level surface rather than one in which designs are raised (*relief*), or incised (*intaglio*). The surface is prepared so that the design accepts ink (in the case of lithography, through the application of an oil-based substance) and the remainder of the surface is prepared so as to repel it. Thus, when ink is applied, it deposits only on the design, and the rest of the surface appears as white space on the printed page. (See also Relief printing; Intaglio printing.)

Playbook

A printed version of the text of a theatrical drama made commercially available; playbooks could be intended for use by actors in the process of staging the play, or for reading as literary material. Playbooks could originate from a number of manuscript sources: a manuscript written by the playwright himself; a transcribed manuscript offered by, or solicited from, a players' company; a manuscript made available by unauthorized means; or from manuscript versions of performance texts.

Preface

A note preceding the main body of text of a book, which may state the origin, purpose, and scope of the work as well as acknowledgments of assistance. It is distinguished from the introduction, which deals more with the subject of the book.

Prelims/Preliminaries

The pages of a book that precede the actual text, usually given separate pagination with lower-case roman numerals. Can include the title page, frontispiece, preface, introduction, etc.

Pressmark

A mark, sometimes a letter or number and sometimes found in the bottom margin of a printed book, thought to indicate which employee of the printing house typeset or printed certain sheets. Such marks are difficult to decipher, but they were probably used to calculate the wages of pressmen. (See also Signature.)

Presswork

The work undertaken to print a text of images using the printing press, and the arrangement of this work in the printing house. More especially, the work of operating the press, as distinct from pre-press work of composition and imposition, and post-press work of folding, collating, and stitching.

Printer

The individual or company responsible for the physical manufacture of a book through the process of setting text and producing impressions of ink; a given printer would own type and a press and would use these to print the texts brought to him, but would generally have no responsibility for obtaining texts for printing or for ensuring sales of the printed book.

Proofs

Printed versions of an unpublished document made available, to the author and/or other individuals, for the sake of corrections or changes. May include a number of stages (first proofs, revised proofs, final proofs). *Proofing*: the activity of examining and correcting proofs. (See also Galleys.)

Provenance

The source of a book or manuscript and the history of its transmission or ownership, which may be indicated by the owner's name, arms, bookplate, or other evidence within the book; it is less clearly indicated by pressmarks, or it may have to be deduced through auction records or booksellers' catalogues.

Publisher

The individual or company who makes a financial investment in the publication of a given work. Publishers acquired the rights to texts, financed their printing, and stood to gain or lose a profit based on how well the text sold. In some cases, publishers shared the financial risks of publication either with other publishers, or with the author, through a variety of arrangements. Before the eighteenth century, the role of publisher was not always clearly distinguished from that of printer or bookseller.

Quarto

A book made by folding the printed sheet twice, producing four leaves (eight pages). In the sixteenth and seventeenth centuries, this format was commonly used; many of Shakespeare's plays, for example, appeared in quarto format. In the eighteenth and nineteenth centuries, this format tended to be reserved for more expensive books. (See also Format.)

Recto

The front side of a leaf (also known as the obverse). In an open codex, it appears as the right hand page. (See also Verso.)

Registration

The process by which the claim to the right to print a given work was entered into the Official Register of the Stationers' Company. In theory, this meant that only the registered individual (who had to be a member of the Company) could print the text, but this was difficult to enforce, and legislation around registration was irregular. The importance of registration was at its highest while the Licensing Act was in effect between 1662 and 1695. (See also Licensing Act.)

Relief printing

Family of printing techniques (including woodcut, metalcut, and relief etching) in which portions of a surface (which may be wood or metal) are cut away, leaving a design that remains at the original height of the surface (and is then said to be in relief). When ink is applied to the surface, it deposits only on these raised portions, which then appear as the inked portions of the design, while the portions of lower height do not receive ink and appear as the white portions of the design. Along with *intaglio* and *planographic* techniques, relief forms one of the three main groupings of printing techniques. Since printing from moveable type is technically a form of relief printing, other forms of relief printing are relatively easy to incorporate alongside it and this has contributed to their widespread use. (See also Intaglio printing; Planographic printing.)

Roll (see Scroll)

Run (see Edition)

Scribal culture

A culture in which writing with the hand constitutes the dominant mode of communication. Scribal culture refers principally to the period between the invention of writing and the invention of printing. Literacy was largely confined to small groups of individuals (scribes, though the term denotes more specifically individuals responsible for transcribing texts, either from dictation or from another written source) who therefore mediated most forms of written communication. Scribal culture was not destroyed by the invention of printing, but continued in modified forms.

Scribal publication

A term developed by Harold Love to describe a mode of circulating texts (primarily in the seventeenth and eighteenth centuries in England) that relies on private and commercial manuscript production for circulating texts, rather than making them available in print. Importantly, Love has shown that commercial (or paid) scribes continued to prepare copies of manuscripts long after the advent of printing. (See also Scribal culture.)

Scribe (see Scribal culture)

Scriptorium (pl. scriptoria)

The room in a monastery or other religious house devoted to the copying of manuscripts.

Scroll

An early form of book that was written on a strip of papyrus or other material and rolled on one or more rods, also called a rolled book or roll. Papyrus sheets were overlapped and pasted together to form a roll, normally no more than twenty sheets long, or about fifteen feet. The inside of the roll was written on and the outside of the roll was usually left blank. Book rolls, or volumen, could be as long or as short as needed, but were usually about thirty to thirty-five feet. Scrolls were read by unrolling with the right hand, while rewinding the read portion with the left hand. Papyrus rolls generally had eight- to ten-inch columns, containing twenty-five to forty-five lines each, with half inch margins and larger margins at the top and bottom.

Serial publication/Serial production/Serialization

Any literary composition, especially a novel, issued in successive numbers of a periodical. This practice dates from the early eighteenth century in England, but it was not until the nineteenth century that the practice became widespread. An estimated one-third to one-half of popular novelists writing from 1825 were first published in serial form.

Sheets

Pieces of paper that, after printing, may be folded into two, four, or eight pages to generate respectively a folio, quarto, or octavo volume. (See also Format.)

Signature

A small capital letter or numeral usually put in by the compositor in the bottom margin of the first page of each gathering in a book, to assist the binder to put the sheets in the correct order. (See also Pressmark.)

Stamping

A form of embellishing the outside of a book's cover by applying heated metal blocks (or stamps) to the leather cover so as to leave the impression of a design in the leather (as opposed to decoration created by engraving the leather with a sharp tool).

Stationer

A bookseller, printer, or bookbinder.

Stationers' Company

Composed of booksellers, printers, and bookbinders based in London, the Company was formed by Royal Charter in 1557 with the aim of regulating and organizing printing and the book trade. It issued strict rules controlling most aspects of the book trade and also established a Register intended to record the books that a given printer had the right to print.

Stereotype

A printing plate fashioned by using a moldable substance (such as plaster of Paris or papier mâché) to make an impression of set-up type (or another plate), and then filling that impression with liquid metal. Stereotypes allowed for type to be freed up for other projects, and were particularly useful in the case of frequently reprinted works.

Subscription

A method of publication, particularly prevalent in eighteenth-century England, where the printing of a text was financed by contributions from individuals who offered advance payment for their copies. Subscribers were often wealthy and influential; in return for their contributions, texts often included lists acknowledging their subscribers.

Technological determinism

A theory that locates the advent of new technologies as the driving force for social changes and the evolution of cultural values. It posits technology as largely separate from other realms of human activity, and in fact directing the course of those activities, rather than as part of a larger cultural ecology.

Title page

A page at the beginning of a book or work, bearing its full title, and often the author's name, as well as the editor's, etc., and the imprint. The leaf that includes the title page is commonly called the title page, though technically it is the title leaf. The half-title is the title of a book printed on the leaf before the title page.

Transcript

A handwritten or typed copy of an original that attempts to reproduce the original; a *diplomatic transcription* attempts to reproduce the original exactly.

Typeface/Type

A set of characters for printing that share a common appearance; also known as a *font family*. Typefaces in common use today include Times New Roman and Helvetica. In non-specialist use, "typeface" is often used interchangeably with "font"; however, a font is in fact a specific subset of a typeface. Thus Times New Roman is a typeface, while Times New Roman ten point italic is a font.

Typescript

A typed copy of a text.

Typography

The design and process of producing type, as well as the study of this process. Aspects of typography include choice of *typeface* (the design of how characters will appear), size, line length, and questions of spacing between lines (*leading*), words (*justification*), and individual characters (*kerning*).

Variorum (see Edition)

Vellum

Used first as a writing surface for manuscripts, and later as binding and covering, vellum is made from untanned animal skin (usually calf, but sometimes lamb, goat, or deer) stretched so as to generate an even surface. Unlike parchment, which is generally formed from split skin, vellum is usually made using the whole skin. Vellum may also indicate finer quality of parchment. (See also Parchment.)

Vernacular

In literary terms, "vernacular" often refers to the native language of a particular people or country, as opposed to a classical or learned language such as Latin or Greek. The vernacular can also be a form of the native language in common usage, as opposed to the forms used for more formal or official purposes.

Verso

The backside (or reverse side) of a leaf; in an open codex it appears as the left hand page. (See also Recto.)

Volumen (see Scroll)

Watermark

A distinguishing mark or device contained within the wire mesh of the tray in which the pulp settles in the process of papermaking. The subsequent watermark, also called a *paper-mark*, can be seen when the finished product is held against the light. Since watermarks are often dated, they can help to date books, by providing the earliest date the paper could have been in use. Watermarks also provide evidence for the makeup of the book, because their location in the book will be determined by the number of times the sheet has been folded. They can therefore help to determine format when this is difficult to determine by examining the binding or by other means. Some sheets also included a *countermark*, a smaller unit introduced in the seventeenth century that was usually placed on the opposite half of the sheet to the watermark.

Woodcut

An illustration generated by the impression of an inked piece of wood into which a design has been cut (specifically, the non-design portions are cut away, leaving the image in relief). Woodcuts represent the earliest form of printed illustration, appearing in Europe in the fifteenth century, though more ancient examples of the technology are available from Asia.

Further Reading

Adams, Thomas R., and Nicolas Barker, "A New Model for the Study of the Book." *A Potencie of Life: Books in Society*, ed. N. Barker. London: British Library, 1993. 5–43.

Allen, James Smith. *In the Public Eye: A History of Reading in Modern France, 1800–1940*. Princeton, NJ: Princeton UP, 1991.

Anderson, Benedict. *Imagined Communities: Reflections on the Origins and Spread of Nationalism*. London: Verso, 1983.

Anderson, Patricia. *The Printed Image and the Transformation of Popular Culture, 1790–1860*. Oxford: Oxford UP, 1991.

Appadurai, Arjun. *The Social Life of Things*. Cambridge: Cambridge UP, 1986.

Augst, Thomas, and Kenneth E. Carpenter. *Institutions of Reading: The Social Life of Libraries in the United States*. Amherst: U of Massachusetts P, 2007.

Ayers, David. "Materialism and the Book." *Poetics Today* 24.4 (2003): 759–80.

Barchas, Janine. *Graphic Design, Print Culture, and the Eighteenth-Century Novel*. Cambridge: Cambridge UP, 2003.

Barker, Nicolas. *Form and Meaning in the History of the Book: Selected Essays*. London: British Library, 2003.

Bell, Bill, Jonquil Bevan, and Philip Bennet, eds. *Across Boundaries: The Book in Culture & Commerce*. New Castle, DE: Oak Knoll P, 2000.

Bell, Maureen, et al., eds. *Re-constructing the Book: Literary Texts in Transmission*. Aldershot: Ashgate, 2001.

Benedict, Barbara M. *Making the Modern Reader: Cultural Mediation in Early Modern Literary Anthologies*. Princeton, NJ: Princeton UP, 1996.

Black, Fiona A., Bertrum H. MacDonald, and J. Malcolm W. Black. "Geographic Information Systems: A New Research Method for Book History." *Book History* 1 (1998): 11–31.

Bolter, J. David. *Writing Space: Computers, Hypertext, and the Remediation of Print*. 2nd ed. London: Routledge, 2001.

———, and Richard A. Grusin. *Remediation: Understanding New Media*. Cambridge, MA: MIT P, 1999.

Bornstein, George, ed. *Representing Modernist Texts: Editing as Interpretation*. Ann Arbor: U of Michigan P, 1991.

Bowers, Fredson. *Principles of Bibliographical Description*. New Castle, DE: Oak Knoll P, 1994.

Bourdieu, Pierre. *The Field of Cultural Production*. Ed. Randall Johnson. Cambridge: Polity Press, 1993.

Brake, Laurel, et al., eds. *Nineteenth-Century Media and the Construction of Identities*. Basingstoke: Palgrave, 2000.

Bray, Joe, Miriam Handley, and Anne C. Henry. *Ma(r)king the Text: The Presentation of Meaning on the Literary Page*. Aldershot: Ashgate, 2000.

Brown, Matthew P. "Book History, Sexy Knowledge, and the Challenge of the New Boredom." *American Literary History* 16.4 (2004): 688–706.

Cameron, Fiona, and Sarah Kenderdine. *Theorizing Digital Cultural Heritage: A Critical Discourse*. Media in Transition. Cambridge, MA: MIT P, 2007.

Casper, Scott, ed. *Perspectives on American Book History: Artifacts and Commentary*. Amherst: U of Massachusetts P, 2002.

Chappell, Warren. *A Short History of the Printed Word*. New York: Knopf, 1970.
Chartier, Roger, ed. *The Culture of Print: Power and the Uses of Print in Early Modern Europe*. Trans. Lydia G. Cochrane. Cambridge: Polity P, 1989.
———. *Inscription and Erasure: Literature and Written Culture from the Eleventh to the Eighteenth Century*. Philadelphia: U of Pennsylvania P, 2007.
———. *The Order of Books*. Trans. Lydia Cochrane. Stanford, CA: Stanford UP, 1994.
Clapperton, Robert Henderson. *The Paper-Making Machine*. New York: Pergamon, 1967.
Clark, William. *Academic Charisma and the Origins of the Research University*. Chicago: Chicago UP, 2006.
Clayton, Timothy. *The English Print 1688–1802*. New Haven, CT: Yale UP, 1997.
Cohen, Matt. *The Networked Wilderness: Communicating in Early New England*. Minneapolis: U of Minnesota P, 2010.
Dane, Joseph A. *The Myth of Print Culture: Essays on Evidence, Textuality and Bibliographical Method*. Studies in Book and Print Culture. Toronto: U of Toronto P, 2003.
Darnton, Robert. T*he Business of Enlightenment: A Publishing History of the Encyclopédie, 1775–1800*. Cambridge, MA: Belknap P, 1979.
———. *The Case for Books: Past, Present, and Future*. New York: PublicAffairs, 2009.
———. *The Devil in the Holy Water or the Art of Slander from Louis XIV to Napoleon*. Philadelphia: U of Pennsylvania P, 2010.
———. *The Kiss of Lamourette: Reflections in Cultural History*. New York: Norton, 1990.
———. *Revolution in Print*. Berkeley: U of California P, 1989.
———. "What Is the History of Books?" *Books and Society in History*. Ed. Kenneth E. Carpenter. New York: RR Bowker, 1983.

Echard, Siân, and Stephen Partridge. *The Book Unbound: Editing and Reading Medieval Manuscripts and Texts*. Toronto: U of Toronto P, 2004.
Eisenstein, Elizabeth L. *The Printing Press as an Agent of Change: Communications and Cultural Transformations in Early Modern Europe*. Cambridge: Cambridge UP, 1979.
Eliot, Simon, and Jonathan Rose, eds. *A Companion to the History of the Book*. Malden, MA: Blackwell, 2007.
Ezell, Margaret J.M. *Social Authorship and the Advent of Print*. Baltimore: Johns Hopkins UP, 1999.
Feather, John. *A History of British Publishing*. London: Routledge, 1988.
Febvre, Lucien, and Henri-Jean Martin. *The Coming of the Book. The Impact of Printing 1450–1800*. London: Verso, 1976.
Gaskell, Philip. *A New Introduction to Bibliography*. New Castle, DE: Oak Knoll P, 1995.
Gavin, Michael. "Writing Print Cultures Past: Literary Criticism and Book History." *Book History* 15 (2012): 26–47.
Gitelman, Lisa. *Always Already New. Media, History and the Data of Culture*. Cambridge, MA: MIT P, 2006.
———, and Geoffrey B. Pingree, eds. *New Media, 1740–1915*. Cambridge, MA: MIT P, 2003.
Glaister, Geoffrey Ashall, ed. *Encyclopedia of the Book*. New Castle, DE: Oak Knoll P, 1996.
Goldstein, Philip. *Modern American Reading Practices: Between Aesthetics and History*. Basingstoke: Palgrave Macmillan, 2009.
Goodman, Dena. *The Republic of Letters: A Cultural History of the French Enlightenment*. Ithaca, NY: Cornell UP, 1994.
Grafton, Anthony. *Worlds Made by Words: Scholarship and Community in the Modern West*. Cambridge, MA: Harvard UP, 2009.

Greg, W.W. *Collected Papers*. Ed. J.C. Maxwell. Oxford: Clarendon, 1966.

Gutjahr, Paul C., and Megan Benton. *Illuminating Letters: Typography and Literary Interpretation*. Amherst: U of Massachusetts P, 2001.

Habermas, Jürgen. *The Structural Transformation of the Public Sphere: An Inquiry into a Category of Bourgeois Society*. Trans. Thomas Burger with the assistance of Frederick Lawrence. Cambridge: Polity P, 1989.

Hall, David. *Cultures of Print: Essays in the History of the Book*. Amherst: U of Massachusetts P, 1996.

Hayles, N. Katherine. "How We Read: Close, Hyper, Machine." *ADE Bulletin* 150 (2010): 62–79.

Heesen, Anke te. *The World in a Box: The Story of an Eighteenth-Century Picture Encyclopedia*. Chicago: U of Chicago P, 2002.

Howsam, Leslie. *Old Books and New Histories: An Orientation to Studies in Book and Print Culture*. Toronto: U of Toronto P, 2006.

Jajdelska, Elspeth. *Silent Reading and the Birth of the Narrator*. Toronto: U of Toronto P, 2007.

Jenkins, Henry. *Convergence Culture: Where Old and New Media Collide*. New York: New York UP, 2006.

Johns, Adrian. *The Nature of the Book: Print and Knowledge in the Making*. Chicago: U of Chicago P, 1998.

Johnson, William A. *Bookrolls and Scribes in Oxyrhynchus*. Toronto: U of Toronto P, 2004.

Kastan, David Scott. *Shakespeare and the Book*. Cambridge: Cambridge UP, 2001.

Kernan, Alvin B. *Samuel Johnson and the Impact of Print*. Princeton, NJ: Princeton UP, 1989.

Kittler, Friedrich A. *Discourse Networks 1800/1900*. Stanford, CA: Stanford UP, 1990.

Lang, Anouk. *From Codex to Hypertext: Reading at the Turn of the Twenty-First Century*. Amherst: U of Massachusetts P, 2012.

Lerer, Seth. "Epilogue: Falling Asleep Over the History of the Book." *PMLA* 121.1 (2006): 229–34.

Lyons, James, and John Plunkett. *Multimedia Histories: From the Magic Lantern to the Internet*. Exeter: U of Exeter P, 2007.

Lyons, Martyn. *Books: A Living History*. London: Thames & Hudson, 2011.

———. *A History of Reading and Writing in the Western World*. Basingstoke: Palgrave Macmillan, 2010.

Mader, Rodney. "Print Culture Studies and Technological Determinism." *College Literature* 36.2 (2009): 131–40.

Malik, Rachel. "Horizons of the Publishable: Publishing in/as Literary Studies." *English Literary History (ELH)* 75.3 (2008): 707–35.

Martin, Henri-Jean. *The History and Power of Writing*. Chicago: U of Chicago P, 1994.

McCleery, Alistair. "The 1969 Edition of *Ulysses*: The Making of a Penguin Classic." *James Joyce Quarterly* 46.1 (2008): 55–73.

McCoy, Beth A. "Race and the (Para)Textual Condition." *PMLA* 121:1 (2006): 156–69.

McDowell, Paula. "Towards a Genealogy of 'Print Culture' and 'Oral Tradition.'" *This Is Enlightenment*. Ed. Clifford Siskin and William Warner. Chicago: U of Chicago P, 2010.

———. *The Women of Grub Street: Press, Politics, and Gender in the London Literary Marketplace, 1678–1730*. Oxford: Oxford UP, 1998.

McGann, Jerome J. *The Beauty of Inflections: Literary Investigations in Historical Method and Theory*. Oxford: Clarendon, 1985.

———. "The Monks and the Giants: Textual and Bibliographical Studies and the Interpretation of Literary Works." *Textual Criticism and Literary Interpretation*, ed. J. McGann. Chicago: U of Chicago P, 1985. 180–99.

———. *Radiant Textuality: Literature after the World Wide Web*. Basingstoke and New York: Palgrave, 2001.

McGill, Meredith. *American Literature and the Culture of Reprinting, 1834–1853*. Philadelphia: U of Pennsylvania P, 2003.

McKenzie, D.F. *Bibliography and the Sociology of Texts*. London: British Library, 1986.

———. "Typography and Meaning: The Case of William Congreve." *Making Meaning: "Printers of the Mind" and Other Essays*. Amherst: U of Massachusetts P, 2002. 198–236.

McKitterick, David. *Old Books, New Technologies: The Representation, Conservation and Transformation of Books since 1700*. Cambridge: Cambridge UP, 2013.

Miall, David S. "Empirical Approaches to Studying Literary Readers: The State of the Discipline." *Book History* 9 (2006): 291–311.

Moran, James. *Printing Presses: History and Development from the Fifteenth Century to Modern Times*. Berkeley: U of California P, 1973.

Moretti, Franco. *Distant Reading*. London and New York: Verso, 2013.

———. *Graphs, Maps, Trees: Abstract Models for a Literary History*. New York: Verso, 2005.

Myers, Robin, and Michael Harris, eds. *A Millennium of the Book: Production, Design & Illustration in Manuscript & Print, 900–1900*. Winchester: St. Paul's Bibliographies, 1994.

Nash, Paul. "The Abandoning of the Long s in Britain in 1800." *Journal of the Printing Historical Society*, n.s. 3 (2001): 3–19.

Ogborn, Miles, and Charles W. J. Withers. *Geographies of the Book*. Farnham, England: Ashgate, 2010.

Ong, Walter. *Orality and Literacy: The Technologizing of the Word*. London: Methuen, 1982.

Parrish, S.M. "The Whig Interpretation of Literature." *Text: Transactions of the Society for Textual Scholarship* 4 (1988): 343–51.

Pearson, David. *Books as History: The Importance of Books beyond Their Texts*. New Castle, DE: Oak Knoll P, 2012.

Pettegree, Andrew. *The Book in the Renaissance*. New Haven, CT: Yale UP, 2010.

Piper, Andrew. *Book Was There: Reading in Electronic Times*. Chicago: U of Chicago P, 2012.

———. *Dreaming in Books: The Making of the Bibliographic Imagination in the Romantic Age*. Chicago: U of Chicago P, 2009.

Price, Leah. *The Anthology and the Rise of the Novel*. Cambridge: Cambridge UP, 2003.

———. *How to Do Things with Books in Victorian Britain*. Princeton, NJ: Princeton UP, 2013.

———. "Introduction: Reading Matter." *PMLA* 121.1 (2006): 9–15.

———. "Reading: The State of the Discipline." *Book History* 7 (2004): 307–30.

Raven, James. *The Business of Books: Booksellers and the English Book Trade, 1450- 1850*. New Haven, CT: Yale UP, 2007.

Robertson, Frances. *Print Culture: From Steam Press to Ebook*. New York: Routledge, 2013.

Rose, Jonathan. "How to Do Things with Book History." *Victorian Studies* 37.3 (1994): 461–71.

———. *The Intellectual Life of the British Working Classes*. New Haven, CT: Yale UP, 2001.

Rose, Mark. *Authors and Owners: The Invention of Copyright*. Cambridge, MA: Harvard UP, 1993.

Rubin, Joan Shelley, "What Is the History of the History of Books?" *Journal of American History* 90 (September 2003): 555–75.

Shep, Sydney J. "Imagining Post-National Book History." *Papers of the Bibliographical Society of America* 104 (2010): 253–68.

Sher, Richard B. *The Enlightenment and the Book: Scottish Authors and Their Publishers in Eighteenth-Century Britain, Ireland, and America*. Chicago: U of Chicago P, 2006.

Shevlin, Eleanor F. "'To Reconcile Book and Title, and Make 'em Kin to One Another': The Evolution of the Title's Contractual Functions." *Book History* 2 (1999): 42–77.

Siemens, Ray, et al. "Toward Modeling the Social Edition: An Approach to Understanding the Electronic Scholarly Edition in the Context of New and Emerging Social Media." *Literary and Linguistic Computing* 27.4 (2012): 445–61.

Silver, Brenda R. "Textual Criticism as Feminist Practice: Or, Who's Afraid of Virginia Woolf Part II." *Representing Modernist Texts: Editing as Interpretation*. Ed. George Bornstein. Ann Arbor: U of Michigan P, 1991.

Siskin, Clifford, and William Warner, eds. *This Is Enlightenment*. Chicago: U of Chicago P, 2010.

Son, Suyoung. "Publishing as a Coterie Enterprise: Zhang Chao and the Making of Printed Texts in Early Qing China." *Late Imperial China* 31.1 (2010): 98–136.

St. Clair, William. *The Reading Nation in the Romantic Period*. Cambridge: Cambridge UP, 2004.

Stillinger, Jack. *Coleridge and Textual Instability: The Multiple Versions of the Major Poems*. Oxford: Oxford UP, 1994.

Striphas, Theodore G. *The Late Age of Print: Everyday Book Culture from Consumerism to Control*. New York: Columbia UP, 2009.

Suarez, Michael Felix. "Historiographical Problems and Possibilities in Book History and National Histories of the Book." *Studies in Bibliography* 56 (2003–2004): 140–70.

———, and H.R. Woudhuysen. *The Oxford Companion to the Book*. Oxford: Oxford UP, 2010.

Tanselle, G. Thomas. *Textual Criticism and Scholarly Editing*. Charlottesville: U of Virginia P, 1900.

Twyman, Michael. *Breaking the Mould: The First Hundred Years of Lithography*. London: British Library, 2001.

———. *The British Library Guide to Printing*. London: British Library, 1998.

Vander Meulen, David L. "How to Read Book History." *Studies in Bibliography* 56 (2003–2004): 171–93.

Woodmansee, Martha. *The Author, Art and the Market: Rereading the History of Aesthetics*. New York: Columbia UP, 1994.

———. "The Genius and the Copyright: Economic and Legal Conditions of the Emergence of the 'Author.'" *Eighteenth-Century Studies* 17.4 (1984): 425–48.

Permissions Acknowledgments

Pierre Bourdieu. "The Field of Cultural Production, or: The Economic World Reversed." Part I, Chapter 1 of *The Field of Cultural Production*, edited by Randall Johnson. Cambridge: Polity Press, 1993. Reprinted with permission from Elsevier.

Roger Chartier. "Communities of Readers." Chapter 1 of *The Order of Books: Readers, Authors, and Libraries in Europe between the Fourteenth and Eighteenth Centuries*, by Roger Chartier; translated by Lydia G. Cochrane. Copyright © 1994, Polity Press. All rights reserved. Used with the permission of Stanford University Press and Roger Chartier.

Roger Chartier. "The Press and Fonts: Don Quixote in the Print Shop." *Inscription and Erasure: Literature and Written Culture from the Eleventh to the Eighteenth Century*, translated by Arthur Goldhammer. Philadelphia: University of Pennsylvania Press, 2007. Reprinted with permission of the University of Pennsylvania Press.

Matt Cohen. "Native Audiences." *The Networked Wilderness: Communicating in Early New England.* Minneapolis: University of Minnesota Press. Copyright © 2010 by the Regents of the University of Minnesota. Reprinted with the permission of the University of Minnesota Press.

Robert Darnton. "Bibliography and Iconography." *The Devil in the Holy Water or The Art of Slander from Louis XIV to Napoleon.* Philadelphia: University of Pennsylvania Press, 2010. Reprinted by permission of the University of Pennsylvania Press.

Robert Darnton. "What Is the History of Books?" *The Kiss of Lamourette: Reflections in Cultural History.* Copyright © 1990 by Robert Darnton. Used by permission of W.W. Norton & Company, Inc. and Faber and Faber Ltd.

Elizabeth L. Eisenstein. "The Unacknowledged Revolution." *The Printing Press as an Agent of Change.* Cambridge: Cambridge University Press, 1979. Reprinted with the permission of Cambridge University Press.

Margaret J.M. Ezell. "The Social Author: Manuscript Culture, Writers, and Readers." *Social Authorship and the Advent of Print*, pp. 21–44. Copyright © 1999 The Johns Hopkins University Press. Reprinted with permission of Johns Hopkins University Press.

Lucien Febvre and Henri-Jean Martin. *The Coming of the Book: The Impact of Printing, 1450–1800*, translated by David Gerard; edited by Geoffrey Nowell-Smith and David Wooton. London: Verso, 1976. Reprinted with permission.

Anthony Grafton. "Codex in Crisis: The Book Dematerializes," from *Worlds Made by Words: Scholarship and Community in the Modern West*. Cambridge, MA: Harvard University Press, 2009. Originally published in *Codex in Crisis*, The Crumpled Press, October 2008. Reprinted with the permission of Anthony Grafton.

W.W. Greg. "The Rationale of Copy-Text." Excerpted from *Collected Papers* (pp. 374–92). Reprinted by permission of Oxford University Press.

W.W. Greg. "What Is Bibliography?" Excerpted from *Collected Papers* (pp. 75–88). Reprinted by permission of Oxford University Press.

Paul C. Gutjahr and Megan L. Benton. "Reading the Invisible." *Illuminating Letters: Typography and Literary Interpretation*, copyright © 2001 by the University of Massachusetts Press. Reprinted with permission.

N. Katherine Hayles. "How We Read: Close, Hyper, Machine." *ADE Bulletin* No. 150, 2010: 62–79. Reprinted with the permission of the author and the Modern Language Association of America.

Adrian Johns. "Introduction: The Book of Nature and the Nature of the Book." *The Nature of the Book: Print Knowledge in the Making*. Copyright © 1998 by the University of Chicago. Reprinted with permission.

David Scott Kastan. "From Playhouse to Printing House; or, Making a Good Impression." *Shakespeare and the Book*. Cambridge: Cambridge University Press, 2001. Reprinted with the permission of Cambridge University Press.

Beth A. McCoy. Excerpt from "Race and the (Para)Textual Condition." *PMLA* 121:1 (January 2006): 156–69. Reprinted by permission of the copyright owner, the Modern Language Association of America.

Paula McDowell. "Mediating Media Past and Present: Toward a Genealogy of 'Print Culture' and 'Oral Tradition.'" *This Is Enlightenment*, edited by Clifford Siskin and William Warner. Copyright © 2010 by the University of Chicago. Reprinted with permission.

Jerome J. McGann. "The Rationale of Hypertext." *Radiant Textuality: Literature after the World Wide Web*. Palgrave, 2001. Reproduced with the permission of Palgrave Macmillan.

Jerome J. McGann. "Shall These Bones Live?" *The Beauty of Inflections: Literary Investigations in Historical Method and Theory*. Oxford: Clarendon, 1985. Reprinted by permission of Oxford University Press.

Meredith McGill. "Circulating Media: Charles Dickens, Reprinting, and Dislocation of American Culture." *American Literature and the Culture of Reprinting, 1834–1853*. Philadelphia: University of Pennsylvania Press, 2003. Reprinted with permission of the University of Pennsylvania Press.

D.F. McKenzie. "The Dialectics of Bibliography Now." *Bibliography and the Sociology of Texts*. Cambridge: Cambridge University Press, 1999. Reprinted with the permission of Cambridge University Press.

Franco Moretti. "Style, Inc. Reflections on Seven Thousand Titles (British Novels, 1740–1850)," from *Distant Reading* by Franco Moretti. London: Verso Books, 2013. Reprinted by permission of Franco Moretti.

S.M. Parrish. "The Whig Interpretation of Literature." *Text: Transactions of the Society for Textual Scholarship* 4, edited by D.C. Greetham and W. Speed Hill. New York: AMS Press, 1988. Reprinted with the permission of AMS Press.

Andrew Piper. "Turning the Page (Roaming, Zooming, Streaming)." Chapter 3 of *Book Was There: Reading in Electronic Times*. Copyright © 2012 by The University of Chicago. Reprinted with permission.

James Raven. "Markets and Martyrs: Early Modern Commerce." *The Business of Books: Booksellers and the English Book Trade 1450–1850*. London and New Haven: Yale University Press. Copyright © 2007 by James Raven. Reprinted with the permission of Yale University Press.

Jonathan Rose. "The Welsh Miners' Libraries." Chapter 7 of *The Intellectual Life of the British Working Classes*. London and New Haven: Yale University Press. Copyright © 2001 by Jonathan Rose. Reprinted with the permission of Yale University Press.

Ray Siemens, Meagan Timney, Cara Leitch, Corina Koolen, and Alex Garnett. "Toward Modeling the Social Edition: An Approach to Understanding the Electronic Scholarly Edition in the Context of New and Emerging Social Media." *Literary and Linguistic Computing* (2012) 27 (4): 445–461. Reprinted by permission of Oxford University Press.

Brenda R. Silver. "Textual Criticism as Feminist Practice: Or, Who's Afraid of Virginia Woolf Part II." *Representing Modernist Texts: Editing as Interpretation*, edited by George Bornstein. Copyright © 1991 University of Michigan Press. Reprinted with permission.

Index

almanacs, 20, 236, 282, 293
The Ancient Mariner (Coleridge), 165–67, 169–71, 173, 177
"Annales School," 251
anthology, x, 170, 177, 205, 208, 303, 380, 407
archives, 34, 50, 207, 463, 483, 496
  digital, 460, 526
  film archive, 57–58
  notarial archives, 240
  online archives of texts, 459–60
  Welsh miners' libraries, xiv
artists, 94–109
author, xv-xvi, 81, 94–109, 232, 346, 348–49, 354
  in communications circuit, 242
  relationship with printers, publishers, 119, 439
  rights of, 440 (*See also* copyright; pirated editions)
authorial intention, 47, 66, 75, 119, 139–41, 143–45, 147, 165–66, 175, 183–84, 256
  basis for editorial choice, 152
  final, xii, 55, 152, 157–59, 174
  self-censorship, 192
author's revisions, 125, 130, 140, 148
  continual revision throughout career, 151
  horizontal revision and vertical revision, 139, 149
authorship, 353, 355–56, 375
  democratic notion of, 444
  script, 389
  social authorship, 376, 389

banned books. *See* censorship; forbidden books
belles lettres, 224, 390
Benton, Megan L., xi, 63–64
bibliographical approaches to film, television, and other media, 45–46, 57
bibliographies, 525, 560
bibliography, xi, 5, 7, 46, 223, 252
  critical, 3, 5, 8–10, 50, 114–16, 119
  descriptive, 3–6, 8, 50, 52, 56, 117, 208, 463
  "hermetic" or "enumerative," 202, 208
  science of, 3–4, 45
  Vie secrète de Pierre Manuel, 94
"Bibliography and Iconography" (Darnton), 94–109
bibliothèque bleue, 67, 232, 256, 258–59
black authors, editors, 204
blackletter, 17–18, 20, 70–71
Bolter, Jay David, xvii
"The Book: Its Visual Appearance" (Febvre), 15–35
book tariff (1771), 241
Book Was There (Piper), 511
bookbinding, 7, 24, 32–37, 292, 296, 567
bookplates, 7, 295
booksellers, xi, xv, 17, 74–75, 80–82, 221, 232, 279, 290–91, 296, 389
  big squeezing out small, 237
  bookseller-printers, 255
  bookseller-publishers, 258
  choice of suppliers, 238
  Church and State sanctions, 297, 301, 307
  in communications circuit, 244–45
  heretical works, 297
  marketing stratagems, 296–97
  Pope's satirization of, 401
  prosecution, 304
  Rigaud, Isaac-Pierre of Montpellier, 235–41
  risk-taking, 294
  royal sanctions, 301
  sales methods, 293
  scoundrel-booksellers, 444–45
  Shakespeare's plays, 360
bookstalls, 358, 364
Bourdieu, Pierre, xvi
  "The Field of Cultural Production," 335–51
broadsides, 95, 224, 232, 262, 400, 481, 517
Business of Books (Raven), 289
The Business of Enlightenment (Darnton), 231
Butterfield, Herbert, 157
Byron, George Gordon, Lord, 114
  "On This Day I Complete My Thirty-Sixth Year," 120–21

The Calculus of Variants (Greg), 132
calligraphy, 16, 26, 71
cancel, 9, 95
canon, xii, 50, 130, 232, 252, 272, 339, 558
  of criticism, 9
  English poets, 170
  Shakespearean, 370
canonical authors, 387
canonical problem, 177
canonical status, 52–53
catalogues, 6, 57, 235, 258, 294, 389, 482
  of circulating libraries, 530
  of incunabula, 28
  miners' libraries, 322
  publishers, 556
catchword, 9
censorship, xii, 58, 75, 221, 224, 241, 387. *See also* forbidden books
  Citizen Kane (Welles), 53
  freedom of the press, xv
  self-censorship, 189–90, 192–93
Cervantes, Miguel de
  Don Quixote, xi, 73–88
chapbooks, 237, 255, 262, 293, 326
Chartier, Roger, xi, xiv, 15
  "Communities of Readers," 73, 251–63
  The Order of Books, 251
  "The Press and Fonts," 73–88
chirography, 398
circulating libraries, 530
"Circulating Media" (McGill), 439–52
circulation, xi, 94, 121, 253, 440
  Dickens's lack of control over, 445
  e-books, 541
  government controls, 289, 296–97
  manuscript circulation, 88, 377
  Shakespeare's play texts, 356
  slavery and, 446–50
  Welsh miners' libraries, 318
  William Blake, 466
Citizen Kane (film), 45, 52–54, 56
close reading. *See* extensive/intensive reading
codex, x, 261, 462, 543
codex-based editing, 463, 468
"Codex in Crisis" (Grafton), 94, 555–72
Cohen, Matt, xvi, 439
  "Native Audiences," 417–34
  The Networked Wilderness, 417
Coleridge, S.T., 176
  The Ancient Mariner, 165–67, 169–71, 173, 177
  The Eolian Harp, 166
Coleridge and Textual Instability (Stillinger), 165
collaborative annotations, 581
collation, xix, 128, 218, 477
collation of pictures, 467
colophon, 21–22, 64, 292, 295–96
common place books, 379
communications circuit, xiv, 234, 240–42, 251
"Communities of Readers" (Chartier), 73
composition, 11, 48, 69, 75, 161, 293, 370
compositors, 38, 43, 75–76, 88, 133, 127
compositor's errors, 150
computer technology, 57
computerization, 463–64
concordance, 477
copper engraving. *See* engraving
copy-text. *See under* edition
copyright, 12, 50, 57, 294, 439, 557, 565. *See also* intellectual property (IP) law
  belonged to the publisher, 362
  Dickens (no international agreement), xvi, 440–41
  e-books, 94, 549–50
  films, 58
  hyperediting and, 469
  privilèges, 232
copyright law, 361
copyright signs, 204
corruption, 10, 218, 272, 358, 364
coteries, 321, 377–78
critical bibliography. *See* bibliography, critical
critical edition. *See under* edition
A Critique of Modern Textual Criticism (McGann), 459

Darnton, Robert, xiv-xv, 93, 251
  "Bibliography and Iconography," 94–109
  The Business of Enlightenment, 231
  "What Is the History of Books?," xiii, 231–47

descriptive bibliography. *See under* bibliography
"The Dialectics of Bibliography Now" (McKenzie), 45–61
Dickens, Charles, xvi, 444–45
digital age, 43
digital archives, 460, 526
digital encryption, 550
digital libraries, 562
digital literacy, 495, 506
digital media, xvii, xix, 220, 491, 505
digital reading, 492–93, 506, 511
digital text, 483, 522
digital textual analysis, 482
distant reading, xviii, 503, 507, 525
Don Quixote (Cervantes), xi, xiv, 73–88, 256
Dreaming in Books (Piper), 511
Drucker, Johanna, 63, 67
Duguid, Paul, xv
duodecimos, 26

e-books, xvii, xix-xx, 513, 541–51, 558
  copyright, 549–50
  libraries, 461, 543 (*See also* digital libraries)
"E-Books and the Digital Future" (Striphas), 541–51
editing, xi-xii, 161–62, 461. *See also* textual criticism
  earliest-text theory, 167–68
  editorial ethics, 161
  editorial policy, 49, 147
  hypertext, xviii
  new editing methods, 461
  post-publication, xii
  pre-publication editing (by publishers' editors), xii
  substantives, 125, 127–30, 132, 140
edition, 106, 118, 358
  authoritative, xiii, 126–27, 167–68, 218
  copy-text, xii, 56–57, 78, 121, 125–32, 135, 140–41, 152, 167, 378, 459, 473
  critical edition, 130, 133, 140, 152, 462–63, 512
  dynamic edition, 478
  "eclectic" edition, 459
  electronic scholarly edition, 476, 483–84
  fair copy, 55, 140, 142, 160–61
  fallacy of best text, 129
  fine editions, 232
  first edition, 77, 128, 556
  Garland edition of *Ulysses*, 48
  hypertext, 165, 476–78, 484
  limited editions, 31
  print run, 40, 80, 236, 293
  revised, 141, 149–50
  scholarly, xii, 140, 476, 483–84
  undated editions, 9
  variant versions, 159
  variants (textual variants), 113, 140
  variorum editions, xii, 478
edition notations, 204, 268
editor, xiii, 9, 114–16, 119, 125, 127, 129, 152
  black editors, 204–05
  feminist editors, 186–88, 190, 192
  judgment, 130, 132–34, 141–42, 144–45, 157–58
  publisher's, 145–47, 150
  scholarly, 140, 148
"The Editorial Problem of Final Authorial Intention" (Tanselle), 125, 139–54
Eisenstein, Elizabeth, xiv, 15, 231, 267, 272, 274, 276, 398–99, 409
  The Printing Press as an Agent of Change, xiii
  "The Unacknowledged Revolution," 215–26
emblems, 21, 295, 382
engravers, 31, 43, 94–109
engraving, 23, 29–31, 38, 95, 98, 101, 105, 108, 256, 262, 297, 467
  books of engravings, 30
Enlightenment, 221, 225, 238, 240
The Eolian Harp (Coleridge), 166
ephemera, 44, 101, 361
epigraphs, 199
epistle, 358
Epistles of Paul, 46, 257
errata, 133
etching, 106, 297
extensive/intensive reading, xviii, 199, 246, 261, 491, 493–95, 501, 503–06, 525
Ezell, Margaret, xv, xix
  "The Social Author," 375–91
  Social Authorship and the Advent of Print, 375

facsimile, 147, 173, 459, 462, 466, 468, 517
factotums, 296
Febvre, Lucien, 15–16, 65, 251
  "The Book: Its Visual Appearance," 15–35
feminist editors, 186–88, 190, 192
feminist "versioning," 190–92
"The Field of Cultural Production" (Bourdieu), 335–51
film and video, 51–52, 54
fleurons, 35
folio, xii, 25–26, 94, 105, 135, 282
  framed title page, 23
  Shakespeare, 12, 79, 282, 358, 369
  Tixall Poetry, 380
forbidden books, xv, 235, 237, 241, 297, 304. *See also* censorship
format, 6, 24–25, 94, 113, 169
forme, 27, 75–76
Foucault, Michel, xvi
Friedman, Susan Stanford, 181, 189, 193
"From Playhouse to Printing House" (Kastan), 353–72
frontispiece, 23, 207, 296, 535
  American Notes, 452
  in *Vie secrète de Pierre Manuel*, 94–95, 107–08

galleys, 191
Garnett, Alex, xix, 475
gathering, 21
gloss, 170, 204
glossary, 201
Google, 543, 551, 557, 563, 570–72
Google Books, xvii-xviii, xx, 33, 94, 231, 555–56, 558, 561
Google Earth, 520
Google Library, 550
gothic. *See* blackletter
Grafton, Anthony, xx
  "Codex in Crisis," 94, 555–72
Greg, W.W., xi, 45, 157–58, 181, 369
  The Calculus of Variants, 132
  "The Rationale of Copy-text," xii, 125–36, 140, 459
  "What Is Bibliography?," 3–12, 125
Grusin, Richard, xvii
Gutenberg, Johann, 38, 40, 70, 216, 220, 224–25, 232
Gutenberg Bible, 16
Gutjahr, Paul C., xi
  "Reading the Invisible," 63–71

half-title. *See* title page
handpress, xi, 32, 221, 243
Hayles, N. Katherine, xviii
  "How We Read," 491–508
heretical works, 297
Hobbes, Thomas, *Leviathan*, 51
holograph, 133, 172, 175, 183, 188, 191
"How We Read" (Hayles), 491–508
humanism, 21, 24, 29, 479
hyperediting, 464, 469
hyperlinks, 498
hyperreading, xviii, 491, 496, 501, 503–04, 506
hypertext, 177, 463–65, 471, 473, 498–99, 519, 569

iconography, 94
illuminated letters, 515
illuminated manuscripts, 26
illumination, 16–17
illustration, 26–32, 95, 105, 169–70
imprints, 12, 64, 292, 296
incipit. *See* colophon
incunabula, xvii, 16, 219, 222, 226
index, 204, 401, 463, 477, 561
information highway, 462
information technology, 460
intaglio printing, 38–39, 297
The Intellectual Life of the British Working Classes (Rose), 313
intellectual property (IP) law, 550. *See also* copyright
intellectual property (IP) rights, 544
intensive reading. *See* extensive/intensive reading
Internet, xix, 471–73, 500, 559, 562

James, Henry, 149
jobbing work, 290, 292
Johns, Adrian, xiv, xix, 215, 398
  "Introduction: The Book of Nature and the Nature of the Book," 267–84

Joyce, James, xi, 45–46, 48
  Ulysses, 193

Kastan, David Scott, xvi, 395
  "From Playhouse to Printing House," 353–72
  Shakespeare and the Book, 353
Koolen, Corina, xix, 475

The Late Age of Print (Striphas), xix, 541
leaf, 9, 21, 24, 380, 512
Leaves of Grass (Whitman), 151
Leitch, Cara, xix
Leviathan (Hobbes), 51
lexicography, 223
libel, 108–09
library, xx, 25–26, 44, 50, 56, 58, 60, 184, 268, 347, 530, 556, 558, 566
  Boot's Circulating Libraries, 321
  digital libraries, 543, 562
  Library of Alexandria, 218, 559
  off-site access, 568, 570
  personal libraries, 57, 390
  private libraries, 232, 254, 295
  Thomas Bodley, 361
  as training center for the crafts of scholarship, 571
  Welsh miners', 314
Licensing Act (1695), 399–400
licensing laws, 305–06
linotype, 243
literacy, 41, 57, 217, 226, 253, 396–97, 406, 411, 417–18, 425, 428, 492, 495–97, 499. *See also* digital literacy
lithography, 38–39, 43, 101, 467
Locke, John, xi, 45–46, 257

machine reading, 491, 502–04, 506
manuscript, xv, 5–7, 11, 48, 75, 140, 167, 270, 386–87, 468, 567
  authorship and readership, 376, 381
  best or most authoritative, 127
  binding, 32
  as copy-text, 126
  decorated with miniatures, 26
  fair copy, 142
  imitated by early printers, 16–17
  plays, 361–62
manuscript circulation, 121, 306, 390
manuscript codex, 295
manuscript culture, xvi, 69, 375, 377–79, 389
manuscript dealers, 398
manuscript miscellanies, 376, 379
manuscript not intended for publication, 152
manuscript unpublished at death, 160
manuscript versions of Woolf's novels, 184–85
manuscript volume of John Hooper, 385
manuscripts of women writers, 184–85, 375
mapmaking, 30
marginalia, 358, 423, 513, 567
"Markets and Martyrs: Early Modern Commerce" (Raven), 289–307
Martin, Henri-Jean, 15–16, 66
McCoy, Beth A., xiii
  "Race and the (Para)Textual Condition," 199–208
McDowell, Paula, xvi, 417
  "Towards a Genealogy of 'Print Culture' and 'Oral Tradition,'" 395–411
  The Women of Grub Street, 395
McGann, Jerome, xii, 113, 199, 336
  A Critique of Modern Textual Criticism, 459
  "The Rationale of Hypertext," xix, 166, 459–73
  "Shall These Bones Live?," 114–23
McGill, Meredith, xvi
  "Circulating Media," 439–52
McKenzie, D.F., xi, 15, 45, 207, 254, 257, 305, 336
  "The Dialectics of Bibliography Now," 45–61
monographs, 224, 242, 337
Monopoly of Printing, 307
Moretti, Franco, xviii
  "Style, Inc. Reflections on Seven Thousand Titles," 525–38
movable type, 75, 216, 225, 232, 471
multimedia literacy, 417

"Native Audiences" (Cohen), 417–34
Networked Infrastructure for Nineteenth-Century Electronic Scholarship (NINES), 460
The Networked Wilderness (Cohen), 417

new bibliographers. *See* bibliography

octavos, 25–26, 94–95, 235, 257
"On This Day I Complete My Thirty-Sixth Year" (Byron), 120–22
oral culture, 57, 79, 217, 253, 256, 260, 395–96, 398, 406, 408, 410, 417, 425, 439
    product of print culture, xvi
    reading aloud, 262
    women's involvement in, 395
oral traditions, 247, 402, 404, 407, 411
orality, 395, 397, 403, 411, 426
The Order of Books (Chartier), 251

page, 6, 21, 75, 167, 220, 468, 515, 517, 521
    as basic unit of codex, 511–12
    in digital realm, xx, 519
    visual elements on, 64
page layout, 257
page numbers, 204
pagination, 24
paleographer, 7
palimpsests, 160, 187–91, 193, 195
pamphlets, 107, 290, 303, 306, 369, 401, 565
    abolitionist, 441
    format, 25
    play, 362, 366, 372
papyrus, x
paratexts, 199–203, 205, 208
    role in racialized struggle, 204, 207–08
parchment, x, 77, 380
Parrish, Stephen, xii, 140, 167–68, 181
    "The Whig Interpretation of Literature," 157–63
patronage, 223–24, 237, 275, 278, 280, 295, 314, 401
periodical publishing, 439
philologists, 78, 114–16, 119, 122
philology, 6, 115, 117, 127–28, 560
Piper, Andrew, xx
    Book Was There, 511
    Dreaming in Books, 511
    "Turning the Page," 511–23
piracy, 270, 275, 279, 281, 283–84, 294, 387
pirated editions, 235, 237–38, 241, 267, 362, 370
Pizer, Donald, 189
plagiarism, 28, 85–86, 274, 281
planographic printing, 38–39
playbook, 358, 361, 368
"A Practical Theory of Versions" (Stillinger), 165–78
preface, 97, 199, 205, 343, 356
    in Eisenstein's book, 398
    in slave narratives, 201
    to *Tixall Poetry*, 380
preliminaries, 95
The Prelude (Wordsworth), xii, 157
"The Press and Fonts" (Chartier), 73–88
presswork, 221, 293, 370
print culture, 268–69, 271–72, 276–77, 395, 397, 399–400, 402, 411, 417, 439–40, 445
print era, xiii
print run. *See under* edition
print technology, 376
printer, x, 6, 12, 20, 43, 48, 67, 75, 80, 84, 119, 133, 226, 232, 270, 290, 293, 398, 558
    in communications circuit, 243–44
    ecclesiastical licensing, 304
    entrepreneurs, 222–23, 291
    imitation of manuscript, 16–17, 19
    jobbing work, 292
    John Danter, 361
    master printer in the Imprimerie de Franklin, 108
    printer's workshop, 215
    regulations and sanctions, 297, 301, 303–05
printing, 15, 19, 37–44, 292, 410
    block-printing, 27–28
    effect on bookbinding, 33
    electronic production, 37
    industrialization of, 221
    printing house, 273, 355
    printshop, 74, 78, 80, 88, 223
    technological shifts, 37
    tripartite model of, 39
    women's involvement in, 395
printing press, xiii-xv, 17, 41, 222. *See also* movable type
    as agent of change, xiv, 409–10
The Printing Press as an Agent of Change (Eisenstein), xiii

prohibited books. *See* forbidden books
proofing, 282
proofreader, 76, 88
proofs, 34, 48, 74, 76, 135, 145, 172, 191, 216
Protestant Reformation, xiv, 215, 225, 272
provenance, 96, 361, 370
publisher, x, xii, 12, 21–22, 31, 67, 94–109, 172, 221, 232, 257, 260, 269, 297, 338, 440, 468, 558, 568
  Alfred A. Knopf, 64
  businessmen and classical scholars, 222–23
  catalogues, 556
  commercial opportunities from the new technology, 289
  in communications circuit, 242–43
  copyright belonged to, 362
  of *Don Quixote*, 82
  e-books, 513, 542
  increased availability of cheap print and, 390
  plays, 361
  pre-publication approvals, 301, 303
  relationships with authors, printers, 119
  Shakespeare's plays, 360
  state sanctions, 297
  suit against Google, 550
  of the *Vie Secrète*, 93
publishing, women's involvement in, 395
publishing booksellers, 293

quartos, xii, 26, 79, 94, 135, 246, 257
  Every Man Out of His Humor, 356
  Lear, 368
  Tixall Poetry, 380
Questions sur l'Encyclopédie (Voltaire), 235–41

"Race and the (Para)Textual Condition" (McCoy), 199–208
"The Rationale of Copy-Text" (Greg), xii, 125–36, 140, 459
"The Rationale of Hypertext" (McGann), xix, 166
Raven, James, xv
  The Business of Books, 289
  "Markets and Martyrs: Early Modern Commerce," 289–307
readers, 66, 116–17, 119, 232, 255, 260, 262
  in communications circuit, 240, 245–47
  communities of, 251
reading, xiii-xiv, xviii, xx, 252, 256
  digital, xvii-xviii, xx, 492–93, 506, 511
  embodied nature of, 253, 256, 511
  extensive/intensive reading, 246, 261
  history of, 251, 254
  scanning, 496, 503
  skimming, 496, 503
  web reading, 491, 498–500
reading aloud, 513
reading both ways, 189, 193
"Reading the Invisible" (Gutjahr), 63–71
recto, 21, 170, 385, 512
registration, 24, 361–62
relief printing, 38–39, 41
Renaissance, xiv, 272
Restoration, 378
roaming, 519
roll. *See* scroll
Rose, Jonathan, xiv
  The Intellectual Life of the British Working Classes, 313
  "The Welsh Miners' Libraries," 313–29
Rosetti Archive, 460, 469–70
roulette, 34–35

Scientific Revolution, xiv, 215, 272
screen reading, xvii-xviii, xx. *See also* digital reading
scribal copies, 119, 270, 362. *See also* manuscript
scribal copyists, 304
scribal culture, 215, 217–18, 224, 261, 272, 398
scribal letterforms, 70
scribal publication, 377
scribes, 17, 133, 226, 256, 377, 398, 500, 513, 559
  mistakes by, 10, 127
scriptorium, 218, 563
scroll, x, 216, 222, 261, 512, 557
serial playbooks, 307
serial publication, 33
  Charles Dickens, 441
serialization, 350
Shakespeare and the Book (Kastan), 353
"Shall These Bones Live?" (McGann), 114–23
sheets, 6, 24, 41, 75, 94, 135, 290, 361, 517

manuscript texts as single sheets, 379
printer's sheet, 80
sheets of papyrus, x
Siemens, Ray, xix
"Toward Modeling the Social Edition," 475–84
signature, 24, 94–95, 261, 517
Silver, Brenda R., xiii, 140, 375
"Textual Criticism as Feminist Practice," 181–95
social authorship, xix, 376, 389
Social Authorship and the Advent of Print (Ezell), 375
social edition, 482–84
St. Clair, William, 289
stamping, 34, 296
stationer, 222, 290, 292–93, 296, 361–62, 369
Stationers' Company, 290, 294, 301, 303–07, 369
policing services, 304, 400
Stillinger, Jack, xiii, xix, 140, 181
Coleridge and Textual Instability, 165
"A Practical Theory of Versions," 165–78
Striphas, Ted
"E-Books and the Digital Future," 541–51
"Late Age of Print," xix
The Late Age of Print, 541
"Style, Inc. Reflections on Seven Thousand Titles" (Moretti), 525–38
subscription lists, 243

Tanselle, G. Thomas, xii, 181
"The Editorial Problem of Final Authorial Intention," 125, 139–54
technological determinism, 276, 402
Text (journal), 114
"text-mining" applications, xviii
textual criticism, 10, 114–15, 119–20, 126–28, 252. *See also* editing
aesthetics of, 178
intersection of feminist practice, 182, 185–86, 189, 195
"Textual Criticism as Feminist Practice" (Silver), 181–95
textual pluralism, xiii, 166–67, 169, 177
Timney, Meagan, xix, 475
title page, xi, 21–23, 79, 95, 295–96, 528
Chatwin manuscript, 382
Every Man Out of His Humor, 356
Shakespeare's name on, 364, 366, 368
"Toward Modeling the Social Edition" (Siemens et al.), 475–84
transcript, 121, 128, 152, 175–76, 362
translation, 80–81
Twyman, Michael, xi
"What Is Printing?," 37–44
type design, 223
typeface/type, 17–20, 63, 65, 68–70, 83, 205, 282, 361, 366, 515
typescript, 145, 191, 547
typographic culture, 398
typographic era, 397
typography, x-xi, 7, 46, 64, 169, 219–20, 225, 246, 253, 281, 370, 466
Greek typography, 34
in literary interpretation, 63, 65–68
technology factor in history of, 70
in *Vie secrète de Pierre Manuel*, 95

Ulysses (Joyce), 49–50, 193
"The Unacknowledged Revolution" (Eisenstein), 215–26
universal archive, 557, 566
universal library, 555, 559, 566

vellum, 7, 10, 17, 58
vellum binding, 35, 385
vernacular, 17–18, 28, 307
verso, 21, 170, 385, 517
Vie secrète de Pierre Manuel, 93–96
virtual library, 564
Voltaire, *Questions sur l'Encyclopédie*, 235

watermarks, xviii, 7, 566
The Waves (Woolf), 184, 192
holograph drafts of, 183
manuscripts of, 184
web reading, 491, 498–500
"The Welsh Miners' Libraries" (Rose), 313–29
"What Is Bibliography?" (Greg), 3–12, 125
"What Is Printing?" (Twyman), 37–44

"What Is the History of Books?" (Darnton), xiii, 231–47
"The Whig Interpretation of Literature" (Parrish), 157–63
Whitman, Walt, *Leaves of Grass*, 151
The Women of Grub Street (McDowell), 395–411
woodcut, 21–22, 27, 29–30, 43, 258, 296–97
Woolf, Virginia, 182–84, 187
  self-censorship in her revisions, 189–90, 192
  The Waves, 183–84, 192
  The Years, 191
Wordsworth, William, 168–69, 175
  compulsive revisions to his poems, 157, 159
  The Prelude, xii, 157
  unpublished manuscripts, 160–61

xylography, 27–28

The Years (Woolf), 191

The interior of this book is printed on 30% recycled paper.